HAWKS RISING

The Eighty-Five Year
History of
No.25 (Fighter) Squadron
Royal Air Force

FRANCIS K MASON

AN AIR-BRITAIN PUBLICATION

The Royal Air Force's solo aerobatic Tornado F.3 demonstrator for 1991, ZE167, being flown by Flt Lt Archie Neill and Flt Lt Jim Brown of No.25 (Fighter) Squadron. The aeroplane is liveried in a stylised adaptation of the Squadron's black and silver colours to commemorate the 75th Anniversary of its formation in September 1915. In 1992 No.25 Squadron was formally adopted by the town of Folkestone in Kent, thereby recalling the long period between the World Wars when it was based at nearby Hawkinge.

(Photo: courtesy of No.25 (Fighter) Squadron)

HAWKS RISING

The Eighty-Five Year
History of

No. 25 (Fighter) Squadron
Royal Air Force

FRANCIS K MASON

AN AIR-BRITAIN PUBLICATION

Published in the United Kingdom by:

Air-Britain (Historians) Ltd,
12 Lonsdale Gardens,
Tunbridge Wells, Kent TN1 1PA

Sales Dept:

41 Penshurst Road, Leigh,
Tonbridge, Kent TN11 8HL

Correspondence to the editor of this book:

R.C.Sturtivant, 26 Monks Horton Way,
St.Albans, Herts, AL1 4HA
and not to the Tunbridge Wells address

ISBN 0 85130 307 2

Typesetting and Origination by:

Stephen Partington.

Printed in the United Kingdom by:

Ebenezer Bayliss, The Trinity Press,
London Road, Worcester WR5 2JH

The rear cover drawing is by David Howley:
Javelin XH880 of No.25 (Fighter) Squadron in 1960/2.

LIST OF CONTENTS

INTRODUCTION

IT IS OFTEN SUGGESTED that, from the day some warships are first commissioned, they acquire a personality – surely more the product of sentiment than any logic. Yet crews come, and crews go, and still the belief persists. Some ships are said to acquire a reputation for good luck, reliability, battle prowess, contentment throughout the crew, and so on. Others seem to be fated for less commendable attributes. Yet these beliefs persist until the day the ships are paid off for the scrapyards, decades later.

In the Royal Air Force I am sure the same sort of analogy exists and, just as the warships' crews are the 'cutting edge' of the Royal Navy, so the operational Squadrons of the RAF represent the front line of operational duties, be they air defence, offensive bombing, air transportation or reconnaissance.

While researching the present book, as well as others dealing with various aspects of Royal Air Force history, this feeling has grown to conviction for, even allowing for a natural prejudice, the great majority of Service men and women (employed in the air and on the ground) to whom I have spoken, and with whom I have corresponded, have expressed strong feelings of privilege in having served with this or that Squadron. Almost everyone looks back on one Squadron or another with special pride and admiration. They recall being at ease with their peers and their duties, and a pervading sense of integrity, fairness, trust and mutual respect. All this, in long retrospect, recalls a period of enjoyment – in short *joie de vivre*. With this came a realisation that the Squadron had excelled in the function for which it had been trained to perform.

There are countless explanations for this phenomenon – some no longer fashionable to express, simply because they may be read out of context and therefore likely to be misunderstood. The Air Staff has very rarely gone out of its way to encourage any attitude of élitism among its fighting echelons (yet in all likelihood admitting to itself a quiet satisfaction if such élitism has been justified). Such élitism is a fact of life, particularly in the healthiest society, as competition always creates the winners and the losers.

In introducing the subject of this work I must declare an interest, in having served on No.25 (Fighter) Squadron for slightly over two years (the average length of a 'tour'), some fifty years ago. I was a pilot and, I hope, an inconspicuous one, for No.25 was my first Squadron and I was a fledgling. I don't think I perceptibly overstepped the bounds of decorum, except under certain acceptable circumstances. It was, of course, an unwritten law that for indiscretions, if committed to the detriment or inconvenience of the civilian populace, the miscreant would answer in person to the law of the land, after which the Service would impose its own Regulations and retribution. Neither did I knowingly offend my peers to any lasting extent. Fifty years later I regularly meet with a dozen or so surviving colleagues of those years, including my Squadron Commander, Flight Commander and my Navigator, and I revel in the fact that we still speak to each other! I know that they were the most exhilarating years of my life. I will say no more in this work about this personal association – except that its was a *privilege* to have experienced those salad days with No.25 (Fighter) Squadron.

I have read a dozen or so books by authors who, having served with No.25, went on to gain high rank and honour; each and all affirm that they were never happier and more content than when they were with '25'. And *they* were the true professional 'career' officers and airmen.

It may therefore be asked how it came about that this particular Squadron acquired and retained its distinctive aura. The Guards Regiments can point to long lists of Battle Honours, gained over centuries; their battles representing vital struggles to sustain Great Britain's position of power and authority in the days of Empire. No longer do these events represent more than yesterday's adventures and achievements, but they signify a tradition of duty to Sovereign and Country, and to each Regiment this tradition is instilled into succeeding generations as a measure of excellence, loyalty and devotion to duty.

In the Royal Air Force, still with less than a century of history behind it, custom and tradition have flourished, their origins sometimes obscure, sometimes tenuous, nevertheless tending toward the esoteric. In the case of No.25 Squadron the nature of its incarnation, though baldly announced in official records, has obscured the train of events that led to the conception, birth and infancy of a fighting unit whose existence and survival can only be described as extraordinary, if not unique. This was due largely to the character and achievement of the Squadron's first commanding officer, a young man who only served with No.25 for a period of some four months – its nursery days, to extend the analogy.

It probably goes without saying that of all those who have served on a Squadron, the most influential member must have been its first commanding officer for, once the decision has been made to create the new Unit to undertake a given task, it is its first leader who is entrusted to mould it in such a manner as to ensure its ability to pursue that task successfully. In those early days of the Royal Flying Corps it possessed very limited resources in men with combat experience. Felton Vesey Holt was one such man, young in age yet already decorated for gallantry: he was, after all, credited with being the first pilot in history to have shot down an enemy aeroplane in air combat! He never led the Squadron into battle for, having successfully prepared No.25 for operational duties, he was whisked away to repeat the process elsewhere. The very attributes demonstrated by such a man were quickly recognised and exploited thereafter in such a way that he was seldom in the limelight, but invariably Master of Ceremonies behind the scenes. His career during the first dozen, formative years of the Royal Air Force were such as to recommend him for the very highest appointments in the Service, had he not tragically lost his life in a flying accident in 1931.

Nevertheless it was the manner in which Holt created and nurtured No.25 Squadron, his ability to exploit the skills of his officers to the full, imbued the young squadron with the confidence and pride in achievement that attracted those with initiative and self-confidence. Thereafter it began to attract more than its fair share of young men who, through background, style of living and innate individualism, exactly suited them to become 'fighter pilots' – for air fighting was intended to be the Squadron's *raison d'être.* Even though, through no fault of its own, No.25 Squadron was obliged to undertake duties of a less spectacular nature, it was always pre-eminent in its field, and this excellence sustained its aura of élitism This aura ebbed and flowed throughout the First World War, and was to a great extent responsible for the Squadron's survival while so many others were disbanded during the post-war years.

Of course luck played an important part in that continuing survival and on occasion almost became something of a *cause célèbre,* such was the symbol which the Squadron had come to represent on account of its regular attendance and flying displays given at the annual Hendon air pageants between the Wars. Among those who chose to make the Royal Air Force their lifelong careers and were fortunate enough to be granted Permanent Commissions, one choice of Squadron stood out beyond the rest for which to apply. Time and again, while researching this book, I have come across frequent recollections, long cherished by authors and correspondents at all levels of seniority who look back on their service with No.25 Squadron as being 'the most rewarding', 'the happiest', or simply 'the best' years of their lives. Once more the Squadron was fortunate in having a succession of outstanding COs and flight commanders, most of them veterans of the First World War – men who had acquired a mixture of fighting experience and a deep understanding of their responsibilities.

A combination of circumstances, over which No.25 Squadron had no control, prevented it from continuing in the day fighter rôle during the Second World War yet, in changing to night fighting, it did much to pioneer that demanding rôle – from being the first squadron in the world to carry radar into the air to being the first to be equipped with jet-powered night fighters six years after the War ended.

Such was the lack of understanding, amongst a succession of post-war politicians (of all persuasions) of the need to keep abreast of technology, that the Royal Air Force was obliged to fly a whole generation of second-rate aircraft. So by the time No.25 Squadron received the transonic Javelin in 1959, both it and the Hunter had been eclipsed by such fighters as the American F-104, while the Mach 2 Lightning (which was handicapped by technology already five years out of date) proved from the day of its introduction to be inferior to new European fighters

In one of those seemingly endless cut-backs in defence expenditure following publication of the thoroughly flawed Sandys Defence White Paper of 1957, which sought to end the use of all manned fighter aircraft, like so many other famous Squadrons, No.25's rôle was changed to that of a Bloodhound surface-to-air missile launch squadron, deployed to protect the RAF's bomber bases. This task occupied the Squadron until 1989 when, once more, No.25 Squadron changed rôles, returning to that of the interceptor fighter, now to fly the tri-national Tornado from Leeming in Yorkshire, once again to be led by a succession of outstanding commanding officers. Under their leadership the Squadron quickly established itself as a key element in Britain's air defence structure, characteristically 'putting up' a tight formation of nine aircraft for photographic purposes within a few days of being re-formed. Yet, while the Squadron had been 'on the ground' an entirely new generation of young men has come of age, many of whom already hold University degrees before they even start their flying training. They are more mature than their predecessors, and their aircraft, equipment and fighting techniques demand an entirely new degree of professionalism – if for no other reason (and there *are* many others) than the fact that a single Tornado fighter costs no less than £20m, the cost of, for instance, a fully-equipped medium-sized hospital. Tradition and competition, however, survive – if only to foster a pride in the Squadron on account of its perceived excellence.

Since its reincarnation in 1989 the Squadron, with relatively few opportunities to participate in public flying displays (other than providing the RAF's official Tornado display crew, in fine tradition), has been kept exceptionally busy with duties overseas. These have ranged from Combat Air Patrols over the Persian Gulf during Operations *Desert Shield* and *Desert Storm* in the short but intense war against Iraq in 1991, to operations in the Near East and the Balkans, as well as frequent defence exercises at home and in the Far East and *Red Flag* participation in North America. In 1996 and 1997 No.25 won the Dacre Trophy – Strike Command's equivalent of the old Sassoon trophy which No.25 Squadron had won outright in the mid-1930s.

Flying (and air fighting) has changed out of all recognition during the past ninety years. In 1915 pilots fought almost hand-to-hand, as it were, and could certainly see the opposing pilot; today's pilot may never see the opposing aircraft, but the criteria dictating the basic facets of the fighter squadron and the men (and women) who serve on it have much in common. The Squadron is still deployed in much the same manner, its purpose being to deny a would-be aggressor the freedom of the skies from which to strike. When No.25 (Fighter) Squadron was officially granted its distinctive Badge and Motto by the Sovereign in 1936, it was flying fighters in an air force preparing for war against a totalitarian European Power; sixty-five years later the same Squadron may be called at very short notice to undertake the same task anywhere in the world. One surely cannot deny that history and tradition play significant parts in strengthening that responsibility.

CHAPTER 1

(From Montrose to 'Bloody April')

"Gentlemen, the days of Fokker Fodder are over"

IN THIS YEAR of AD2001 – with the first man on the moon already a matter of history – it is well-nigh impossible to visualise mankind's early, faltering efforts to achieve sustained, powered flight, let alone to translate the achievement into some vestige of benefit to Mankind.

Prior to the outbreak of the Kaiser's War fewer than one thousand men (and women) had learned to fly in Great Britain. In practical terms, being recognised as having gained a rudimentary ability to leave the ground, execute a gentle figure of eight and return to earth without serious injury was sufficient, provided the feat was witnessed by a qualified instructor, to gain the prized award of a numbered Aviator's Certificate by the Royal Aero Club – a sort of Jockey Club of the air, which had issued its first such Certificate in March 1910 (to one 'Mr J T C Moore-Brabazon').

The first, somewhat half-hearted, attempt to employ aeroplanes in warfare occurred in October 1911 during the Italo-Turkish campaign in Libya, when a handful of Italian airmen dropped a handful of 20lb 'bombs' from French- and German-built aeroplanes on enemy positions. It is, however, unlikely that this event did much to concentrate the minds at the War Department or Admiralty in London as to the practical value of the aeroplane as a weapon of war. If anything it more likely struck a familiar chord in the minds of retired Victorian generals thoroughly familiar with nasty little campaigns waged against recalcitrant desert tribes. Would-be aviators in Great Britain, whose numbers were to some extent composed of relatively moneyed members of the middle-class sporting fraternity and sorority, were intent solely on an acceptably dangerous sport, namely aviating – which was still blissfully devoid of serious regulation.

There was, after all, as one might expect, an element of the dramatic about the entire concept of 'slipping the surly bonds of earth' – all too familiar among Frenchmen, who had been drifting about the skies in hot-air balloons for more than a century, the Germans who almost predictably had been busy developing huge gas-filled sausage-shaped Zeppelins for a decade, and the Americans who had succeeded where all others had failed in getting a 'proper aeroplane' to first fly several hundred yards.

Britain had lagged behind the French in the development of the aeroplane, but when a *Frenchman,* Louis Blériot, had become the first pilot to succeed in flying non-stop across the *English* Channel, the penny had dropped. In effect Britain was no longer an island, at least in the nautical sense. Spurred on by the media, to wit Lord Northcliffe, press baron of the *Daily Mail* who offered huge prizes for various achievements (the first to fly from X to Y, the winner of this or that race, and so on), the public's attention was aroused. One had only to read breathless accounts of the almost monthly flying meetings at such aerodromes as Hendon and Brooklands, for tens of thousands of spectators to witness this or that now-famous aviator perform. Indeed, one has to admit that men like Northcliffe did more than any government department to sponsor the development of the aeroplane up until 1911. The prizes for successful pilots and constructors (men such as T O M Sopwith were both) were enormous for those days – but then so were the increases in circulation.

Altruism or not, the War Department (and Admiralty) were, however, by 1911 beginning to stir. More significantly, as much from sporting instincts as for any professional spur, soldiers and sailors (commissioned as well as non-commissioned) were lining up at the civilian flying clubs to learn to fly – at their own expense, and during their off-duty periods. Perhaps not unexpectedly, officers and men of the Royal Engineers featured fairly prominently among the hopeful soldiers; after all, the R.E. had been dabbling with man-carrying kites and balloons for almost a decade.

Yet the R.E. by no means monopolised the soldiers' queue for flying instruction (though the cavalry remained reluctant to join: 'The flying machines frighten the horses'). Infantry officers, if not yet flocking to the flying clubs, were certainly represented by a broad cross-section of the foot regiments, not altogether surprising having regard to the value placed on the military family tradition. And this is where the history of No.25 (Fighter) Squadron begins.

No.25 SQUADRON'S FIRST COMMANDING OFFICER

Born on 23rd February 1886, Lieutenant Felton Vesey Holt, Eton-educated third son of Sir Vesey Holt, KBE, had graduated at Sandhurst in 1906, and was commissioned into the Oxfordshire and Buckinghamshire Light Infantry. Felton's eldest brother, also Eton and Sandhurst, had been commissioned into the Black Watch, while the second son (traditionally persuaded from becoming a soldier, lest the first heir should be killed) became a banker for Glyn, Mills & Co – bankers to the Armed Services nevertheless – his sole martial claim to fame, apart from being a champion sporting gun, being a member of the British Olympic Epée team in 1908, 1912, 1920 and 1924 – shades of the traditional commercial aristocracy's penchant for duelling? This was a familiar pattern among military families during the early years of the twentieth century. It had served the Crown and society with reliability and loyalty for about a hundred years but, in four years of carnage on the Western Front, it was to be totally destroyed. Last born of the Holt brothers, Reginald Vesey chose the Royal Navy and rose to become a Rear Admiral after the Second World War. Between them the brothers were thrice appointed to the DSO, twice to the MVO, to the French *Légion d'Honneur* and awarded *Croix de Guerre* with Palms.

Shortly after joining the Ox and Bucks' regimental depot, Felton took a course in military ballooning and kiting at Farnborough and, incidentally, became well acquainted with Samuel Cody while doing so. It is likely that this association had much to do with Felton's 'air enthusiasm', even though, in 1908, no one in Britain had yet succeeded in achieving sustained flight in an aeroplane over much more than the length of a cricket pitch. Two years later Holt purchased a Blériot monoplane on which he intended to learn to fly. Word of the purchase reached the ears of his regiment and he was summoned before his commanding officer who told him in uncompromising terms 'to get rid of that thing forthwith'. Being of the Victorian military mould, Felton reluctantly obeyed – without having had the chance to sample the machine. Notwithstanding this rebuff, the idea of young army officers learning to fly gradually became respectable and, at their own expense, they began taking flying lessons.

Felton, who had evidently harboured a yearning as a young man to learn to fly, entered an application for transfer to the Royal Flying Corps in mid-1912, and was told by his Commanding Officer that, provided he was accepted by the newly-opened Central Flying School (CFS), his secondment to the Corps would be approved without delay. His application was, however, held in abeyance by the School owing to the stipulation that all entrants must have undergone prior flying training at Eastchurch, a Royal Naval Air Station, and the only Service training unit that had evolved a military flying discipline prior to the CFS. As this school was already over-subscribed, Felton had to remain with his regiment. He was however advised to seek flying training with a civilian flying club on the grounds that if he obtained a Royal Aero Club's Aviator's Certificate, his chances of 'jumping the queue' would be improved.

Felton Vesey Holt, Lieutenant, Oxfordshire and Buckinghamshire Light Infantry. Photograph taken on 1st October 1912 on being awarded The Royal Aero Club's Aviator's Certificate No.312. He then applied for transfer on attachment to the Royal Flying Corps in 1913 and joined No.4 Squadron, RFC. Awarded an immediate DSO in January 1915 for air combat over Dunkirk. In September 1915 he formed No.25 Squadron as Major (Temporary) and took this squadron to France, equipped with F.E.2bs.

(Photo: courtesy of the Holt Family Estate)

Accordingly he joined the Bristol Flying Club at Brooklands during September 1912, attending instruction periods at weekends, for which he was obliged to pay out of his own pocket. This was a difficult time for the Club as, earlier in the month it had suffered a fatal flying accident in which its Chief Instructor (a pilot of considerable experience) and an army observer had been killed when a Bristol monoplane crashed at Port Meadow, Oxford. This proved to be the latest in a series of much-publicised accidents involving monoplanes, and resulted in a War Department ban on army personnel flying monoplanes being imposed. Although the ban was partially lifted in due course, the stigma (which was ill-founded) lingered in the minds of senior army officers long after the Royal Flying Corps had become the Royal Air Force in April 1918.

The immediate result of the accident was the grounding of all the Bristol Club's monoplanes, and their replacement by some rather elderly Bristol Boxkites, and it was on this aeroplane that Lieutenant Holt qualified for RAeC Certificate No.312 on 1st October 1912 – only the fifteenth to be issued after that of the great Harry Hawker. Of the 311 Certificates before Felton's, 109 had been granted to Service officers, and of these recipients fifteen would later command RFC Squadrons. Of those who survived the Great War, many would attain senior rank in the Royal Air Force. Felton Vesey Holt would be one of them.

However, for the time being, it was back to regimental duties. In 1913, Felton was promoted Captain (Temporary), then in mid-1914 his secondment to the RFC came through, then in due course he was posted to No.4 Squadron at Netheravon. It was while the Squadron was transferring to Dover at the beginning of August that year that the First World War broke out. On 16th August the Squadron flew to Mauberge in France and, for the next three months moved from airfield to airfield, such was the instability of the front line. Pilots of No.4 were in action about a dozen times during the period October 1914 until the following January but, owing to the reliance on small arms (pistols, cavalry carbines and rifles), these 'combats' were usually fruitless, although the squadron lost a flight commander killed in action. Then on 22nd January a dozen German aircraft were spotted making for Dunkirk. A number of British and French pilots took off to attack the raiders, including Felton Holt – then based at St.Omer. Without rational thought, the lone pilot of No.4 Squadron, armed only with a rifle, made straight for the enemy formation and engaged it single handed. This proved difficult to say the least for, not only did he contrive to coax his B.E.2c into an attacking position but had to aim his rifle at an enemy aeroplane. He was soon joined by two other pilots of No.4 Squadron, and in due course one of the German raiders was forced down by rifle fire. It was later decided that the enemy aircraft had fallen to either Holt or Lt R P Mills (also of No.4 Squadron), the Distinguished Service Order being bestowed on Holt owing to his initial leadership of the attack, this being an immediate award. Confirmation of his Captaincy followed quickly.

There is no doubt that, despite his relatively small stature (he was no more than some 5ft 8in tall), Felton's service with No.4 Squadron had not gone unnoticed, and it was not long before he was recalled to England for a searching interview at the War Department. As the result of this, with the rank of Major (Temporary) he was ordered to Scotland to take command of No.6 Reserve Squadron, a training unit being formed at Montrose, Angus.

Montrose had been the scene of private flying since 1911 and after the creation of the RFC had been purchased by the military for conversion into a training station for the RFC. The first squadron to be stationed there was No.2, which undertook a number of very long distance flights (for those days) as part of the general training in reconnaissance duties.

No.6 Reserve Squadron was formed from a nucleus of ex-CFS flying instructors, trainee pilots and ground personnel who had been assembling at Montrose for several weeks. Indeed, a fair amount of *ad hoc* flying (that is to say without formal authority) had been taking place – on the pretext of getting to know the local area – in a heterogeneous assemblage of Maurice Farman Longhorns and Shorthorns, Caudron G.IIIs and B.E.2s. The first Avro 504 arrived in August, and was damaged in an accident almost immediately.

When Holt arrived from a short spell of leave he found a unit in being in all but name. Some of the students had flown solo, and an air of enthusiastic independence pervaded the station, a circumstance that could not be ignored among those who had been enjoying uninhibited flying. On the ground it was another matter, and all ranks observed strict decorum according to army regulations and the jaundiced eyes of a hardcore of seasoned NCOs, including two sergeant majors, seconded from the Guards. One of these was a fearsomely-moustached mountain of a man who had been flying for three years on the unsanctioned basis of an early RAeC pilot's Certificate; one of the diminutive Holt's first actions was to have the sergeant major posted away – to the CFS. He was to return to his erstwhile Montrose colleagues two years later as a lieutenant, sporting a well-won MC, and facial hair now conforming to the accepted military officer's neat rectangular patch of bristles on the upper lip!

Montrose had constituted an example of 'out-of-sight out-of-mind'. However, if there was one aspect of Montrose that remained implanted in the memories of every pilot who served there, it was for its consistently poor and apparently unpredictable weather. The result was that the training schedules tended to fall behind. So far no one had broken an aeroplane 'very seriously', but accidents would be bound to occur, probably sooner than later. Holt therefore prepared his first Notes for Instructors, dated in August 1915. Couched in quaint terms (even by later standards of flying vernacular) these guidelines were designed to curb any thoughtless excesses by as-yet unblooded youngsters, apt to regard with enthusiasm any new piece of machinery whose capabilities were simply waiting to be discovered, and certainly not restrained. Holt was at pains to avoid curbing the

During the three weeks prior to the formation of No.25 Squadron this Avro 504 biplane trainer was undergoing extensive repair after an accident at Montrose. When instructions were received by No.6 Reserve Squadron to prepare to form a combat squadron from its personnel and aircraft the Avro, which had been on the strength of No.6 (R) Squadron, was transferred to the embryo unit, thereby benefiting from the increased personnel establishment. Indeed, on 25th September, the day on which No.25 Squadron came into being, the charge list included one aircraft – 'Avro tractor biplane No.750'. (Photo: via the late Owen Thetford)

young pilots' enthusiasm, but rather to nurture a respect for the unknown – and in particular the onset of difficult flying weather conditions. Having regard for the fact that the aircraft industry was still feeling its way among the very basics of aerodynamics and flying structures, it was quite remarkable that the number of fatal accidents in those early days of military flying was relatively low, a matter that speaks volumes for the quality of instructor training at the CFS.

Although, in an old army tradition, it was customary for a commanding officer to lead his men from the front, it perhaps goes without saying that Felton was at pains to take every available opportunity to fly, and did so – studiously observing the rules which he himself had posted, taking as much advice as he could from the experienced ex-CFS instructors. The urgency to do so increased rapidly when orders were received in August by No.6 Reserve Squadron that it would shortly assume the status of a 'battle squadron' and might be required to go to France. It perhaps also goes without saying that (having regard for the action that had earned the DSO), Felton pursued a doctrine of aggression among his student pilots, a doctrine that was eagerly emulated with increasing enthusiasm. Despite the absence of cavalry officers, it was a growing characteristic among Holt's pilots to be at home with horse and hounds. Yet it should be emphasised that, in August 1915, there was still no such thing as a 'fighter' – let alone fighter squadrons. Every one of the score of squadrons that had been already been formed in the RFC had been tasked with reconnaissance, artillery spotting and general ground support duties.

What was not generally realised at the time at Montrose was that the War Office, recognising that the difficulties in meeting the training schedules owing to the adverse weather conditions that prevailed there, could only post the student pilots (who had yet to complete the greater part of their training) to flying schools further south. It made good sense to create a new operational squadron by employing the flying instructors of No.6 (Reserve) Squadron and the handful of student pilots nearing the end of their training course. As such, the new unit effectively become the world's 'first all-weather fighter squadron'. Whether that is strictly accurate or not, its pilots were certainly used to coping with the vagaries of persistent bad flying weather, probably more so than any other RFC Squadron yet formed.

By 1st August 1915 No.6 Reserve Squadron boasted a strength of twenty-two officer pilots (instructors) and a similar number of student pilots. All but two of the latter were 2nd Lieutenants (Temporary); the two exceptions were 'flight corporals awaiting commissioning'. On the ground the Squadron possessed no fewer than fifteen officers and 132 NCOs and other ranks. Many of them performed station as well as squadron duties. It is also interesting to note that among the student pilots were at least four who held Royal Aero Club Aviator's Certificates, granted shortly before the start of the War. While it would be wrong to over-estimate the value of these Certificates in terms of applied flying, they nevertheless provided evidence of a young man's wish to master the ability to fly (without killing himself), thereby relieving the RFC of the job of creating that essential determination.

Montrose suffered particularly bad weather during August 1915, such that would undoubtedly have caused the cancellation of all flying for days or even weeks on end at other training stations. Yet, mindful of the urgency to increase the supply of new pilots to France, Holt was forever encouraging his pilots into the air whenever the winds and rain let up, be it only for thirty minutes at a time. His own 'advice notes' for his instructors ensured that, while common sense would dictate whether or not it was really safe to fly, reasonable visibility and moderate wind strength were the obvious limiting criteria. He made it clear to all that he would not penalise any pilot who, having lost sight of the aerodrome, chose to force land in a convenient field while he still had sufficient fuel, rather than be faced with real difficulties when his fuel ran out. Indeed, the flying hours returned by No.6 Reserve Squadron for August were only marginally lower than those of other training units which enjoyed much better weather in the South. This fact had not gone unnoticed at the War Department.

Reflecting the very short pilot training courses of those early months, all but three students had completed the set syllabus satisfactorily by the third week in August, and most had probably amassed about 20-30 hours' total flying time (officially). This probably averaged out at around fifty training sorties per student pilot, none of whom ventured much beyond the horizon at Montrose. At a normal flying speed of little more than 45-50 mph, no one was going far away.

Holt himself had been informed that he would shortly return to France with, or in command of, a line squadron. Then he received news that he was to prepare to move to France with all or most of the personnel already under his command.

Thus far, Montrose had seemed very remote from the war in France, with only the newspapers (heavily doctored for civilian consumption) to report the conditions on the Western Front. Yet with the war already a year old, the Fokker Scourge had been widely, and very inaccurately reported. To begin with, Fleet Street had brushed aside the nimble Fokker fighting scouts as little better than German copies of the French Blériot which had first flown the Channel six years earlier. Habitués of West End bars and hotels, frequented by RFC pilots, home on leave from France, told a different story. 'Carbonised' – the early airman's euphemism for being shot down in flames – was a term now widely bandied by men who, for the first time in their short experience, had tasted the discomfort of being outflown and outfought by aeroplanes that seemed years in advance of anything conceived by the RFC. With the benefit of these new 'fighters', the enemy pilots themselves seemed to possess superior flying abilities. Already the names of Max Immelmann and Oswald Boelcke were known among the RFC pilots in France; they were men who, it was said, actually flew with the sole purpose of shooting down Allied aeroplanes, and were doing so with increasing success. Whether or not it was considered 'the done thing', the fox was fighting back at the hounds. . .

Those 'in the know' confirmed that no British aeroplane factory – least of all the Government's Royal Aircraft Factory at Farnborough – had anything remotely capable of matching the new German fighters. The secret of the enemy machines' superiority seemed to be their ability to fire a *machine gun* through the aircraft's propeller without smashing the blades. The French had come up with some little monoplanes with a forward-firing gun, but preferred to attach deflector plates to the propeller blades to swat the bullets aside, on the assumption that quite a lot of bullets would pass between the blades and therefore continue on towards their intended target.

In truth, the British *were* developing true machine gun interrupter systems, but it would be months before these reached the squadrons in aeroplanes designed to accommodate them. In the meantime it was necessary to adapt the existing aircraft configuration to counter the new German fighting scouts. So was born the first British fighter and the first fighter squadrons.

Thus far, by August 1915, as new RFC squadrons had been formed to some extent in numerical order, about a score of such squadrons were in existence, most of them now in France, operating in the battlefield reconnaissance rôle. From the earliest months of the RFC in 1912, this type of reconnaissance had been considered to be the Corps' *raison d'être.* After all, the army had for about thirty years included observation balloons from which observers could report the movement of enemy forces, otherwise invisible from the ground. The advent of the aeroplane (apart from 'frightening the horses') had simply introduced improved mobility to the means of reconnaissance. The mere idea of one aeronaut being employed for the purpose of shooting down another was only slowly entering the sphere of understanding of the military man. That is until the early summer of 1915 and the advent of the Fokker *Eindekker* (literally 'one wing').

By 1915 it had been tacitly agreed that all targets behind the enemy's front line would be of a strategic nature and therefore were the responsibility of the Royal Navy by means of the airmen of the Royal Naval Air Service. The RFC and RNAS had accordingly carved up the nascent aircraft industry from which to acquire aircraft for their respective needs. Shorts, in particular, supplied seaplanes to the RNAS, while the War Office (perhaps naturally) relied largely on the Royal Aircraft Factory to provide the designs and prototypes of reconnaissance aeroplanes; these would be built in quantity under sub-contract by numerous commercial manufacturers (few of them with any experience in constructing aeroplanes) throughout the country. These manufacturers were springing up all the time while others, such as Sopwith, were already beginning to produce designs according to their own ideas, and it was the product of this spirit of private enterprise and ingenuity that was to make available a fighting scout, the Sopwith Pup, that could meet enemy fighters on equal terms.

A new aircraft builder that came into being in 1915 was the Aircraft Manufacturing Company (Airco), which had been joined by Capt Geoffrey de Havilland, the outstanding pioneer pilot-designer who had recently left the Factory at Farnborough. At the time of the Fokker Monoplane's appearance over the Western Front, de Havilland had been working on a single-seat fighter with a front gun. Unfortunately, the army's preference was for the 'pusher' biplane configuration (that is, the pilot being situated *in front of* the engine and propeller, thereby affording untrammelled view forward for reconnaissance purposes). It had been de Havilland's idea to mount a machine gun in the nose of the pilot's nacelle, thereby, and by restricting the overall size of the aeroplane, he produced an aircraft, the D.H.2, that was sufficiently manœuvrable to be regarded as a fighting scout. As this impressed the army authorities during evaluation, it was hurriedly selected as the RFC's answer to the Fokker.

In July 1915 four new squadrons (Nos.24, 25, 29 and 32) were therefore authorised for formation during the remainder of that year, equipped with D.H.2s. No.24 was accordingly established on 1st September at Hounslow Heath, equipped initially with the usual miscellany of training aeroplanes, and shortly afterwards with the Vickers F.B.5 Gunbus. In December the first D.H.2s arrived, and on 7th February 1916 No.24 Squadron moved to France.

At Montrose, Holt had been ordered to assemble all serviceable aircraft and all qualified pilots (instructors and ex-pupils*), together with a ground echelon, for movement south to Thetford in Norfolk whence it was planned, in due course, to move south to Hounslow where it would take delivery of D.H.2s and subsequently deploy to France. Owing to delays in the production of D.H.2s, these plans had to be abandoned. However, when the situation was explained to Holt, he at once pointed out that an embryonic squadron now existed in everything but name or number, and was ready to move anywhere if required, with or without aircraft. It is also on record that Holt expressed his opinion that, having achieved the required flying abilities – despite the atrocious weather at Montrose during August – his group of trainee pilots had acquired an almost instinctive capability of flying in poor weather, and stated his belief that this ability must be a valuable asset in a war theatre. It took only three days for Wing Headquarters to make the necessary arrangements and on 25th September Holt's unit was formalised by the confirmation of No.25 as its identity.

The move south to Thetford was however delayed until December and on account of further difficulties with the D.H.2, a decision was taken to equip No.25 Squadron with F.E.2bs in the fighter rôle. This met with some derision among the pilots who, while not possessing first hand flying experience in the Factory's pusher, expressed justifiable apprehension at the thought of meeting the Fokkers in combat in an aircraft that was basically of much earlier design (albeit a product of de Havilland while he was at Farnborough). With a wing span about 20 feet greater than the D.H.2 and well over twice as heavy – and a two-seater at that – it was argued that the F.E. would be just another meal of 'Fokker fodder'. Holt was apparently anxious that such sentiments should not be expressed within earshot of 'out-

* One of the former students, who now became founder members of No.25 Squadron, was one Lieutenant Brian Edmund Baker. He accompanied the Squadron to France, and later served with No.48 Squadron (among others) on the Western Front, being credited with destroying a total of ten enemy aircraft. He was commissioned into the new Royal Air Force, and finally retired as an Air Marshal, KBE, CB, DSO, MC, AFC, in May 1950 (See Appendix 7)

Two very early and rare air-to-air photographs of No.25 Squadron F.E.2bs being flown by Captain W A Grattan-Bellew, MC, early in January 1916, probably over Norfolk shortly before moving to France. It has not proved possible to identify the machines with any certainty.

(Photos: courtesy of Lady Bettina Grattan-Bellew)

siders' lest they be misconstrued as an unwillingness by the squadron to fight in France, and felt obliged to deliver a fairly stern rebuke, without expressing a personal opinion on the matter. His outlook appears to have been consistent with an attitude of 'Let's wait and see what happens when we get there' (i.e. France). In short, Holt was content to leave the flying training to his flight commanders while he concentrated on the essential administrative work, not only to ensure that all personnel were fully aware of their duties and carried them out with efficiency, but were fully catered for in matters of accommodation, health, welfare and leave.

The squadron duly moved south just after Christmas, the Avro 504s, Martinsydes and Curtisses being flown down and the Farmans being left behind. Within a week the first of the F.E.2bs were delivered, being some of the first production aeroplanes built by G & J Weir Ltd, of Cathcart, Glasgow. Expecting to be ordered over to France at any moment, Holt decided to send the entire squadron on a week's leave before starting an intensive working up on the new aircraft. This began in about the third week of January 1916 with some rudimentary mock air fighting, the pilots now being joined by their observer-gunners – mostly NCOs and other ranks, few of whom had previously spent more than an hour or so in the air. Nevertheless, after having learned to cope with incipient airsickness, most of the gunners began to get some sort of idea of what was expected of them. It should be explained that the gunner was situated in a separate cockpit in the nose of the nacelle immediately *forward* of the pilot's windscreen, his Lewis gun perched on a pillar mounting in front of him; the ammunition drums were carried in racks on the sides of his cockpit, each drum loaded with 97 rounds of 0.303in ammunition. A most important task which the gunners had to master was to reload these drums on to the gun spigot which was open to the slipstream and quite possibly while the pilot was pulling manoeuvres in combat. Although gunners found it difficult to replace the drums without releasing their safety strap, there was a marked reluctance by most gunners to undo their strap when the pilot was twisting and turning. Most men came to an understanding with their pilot that, when it was necessary to make a drum change, they would hold an arm up vertically as a signal not to do anything that might pitch him into the void. There were no parachutes in the RFC. (There is a note in the old records of the RFC flying field at Santon Downham, in Thetford Forest, that two 'soldiers' had fallen from their aeroplanes to their deaths early in 1916, but no indication as to what unit suffered these casualties can be found, and it probably was not No.25 as the squadron personnel records at this time were fairly comprehensive, and no mention is made of these deaths.)

No.25 Squadron finally received its orders to fly to France in mid-February, the pilots and observers taking their aircraft across to St.Omer (the station almost invariably used to 'process' squadrons newly arrived on their way to the Front). Some squadrons were plundered of their more experienced pilots as replacements. The ground echelon obviously travelled by sea, about half of them sailing in a destroyer and the remainder in a commandeered paddle steamer. It was customary for new arrivals to remain at St.Omer for about six weeks to find their feet in France, to await motor transport allocated to the squadron and to carry out local flying 'to get the lie of the land'. It was during this time that Felton Holt was posted away from No.25. When the air echelon had left for France, No.25 Squadron's headquarters staff remained behind for the time being to ensure that trained replacement pilots and observers were 'processed' through to the Squadron when the occasion demanded. The actual flying training was provided by No.9 Reserve Squadron, also at Thetford using various Farman aircraft, Avro 500s and, from December, F.E.2bs.

There is no doubt but that young Holt had not only been very popular among all ranks, but highly respected as a leader who led by example. There is a story, probably not apocryphal, that on one occasion up at Montrose, while half a dozen of his pilots were in the air a report came in that fog was rolling in off the sea towards the aerodrome. He immediately took off and found each one of his pilots, to whom he signalled with his arms that they were to land immediately. This they all did safely, albeit scattered around in nearby fields. Holt managed to find and put down on Montrose aerodrome in visibility of less than

No.25 Squadron, Royal Flying Corps at Montrose in December 1915. (Photo: Francis K Mason collection)

Among a heterogeneous assembly of training aircraft collected by the embryonic No.25 Squadron during its early weeks at Montrose and Thetford were some ex-No.24 Squadron Vickers F.B.5 Gunbus 'pushers' (above), *generally regarded as useful and solid stepping-stones to the F.E.2b. Other types included French Caudron GIIIs, American Curtiss J.N.3 ('Jennies') and at least two Martinsyde S.1s. After the fully-trained members of the Squadron moved to France with its F.E.2bs, training continued at Thetford until about April 1916, the F.B.5s having been joined by Bristol Scout Cs.* (Photo: Francis K Mason collection)

100 yards. This was of course achieved without any of the flying instruments which later came to be accepted as essential.

Felton Holt had unquestionably laid the foundation of No.25 Squadron as a potentially efficient fighting unit, and in four short months had created a closely-knit Squadron that would take its place with little difficulty within the Royal Flying Corps operational structure that now existed in France. The Squadron's birth and early life in Scotland had in itself contributed to an air of self-dependence and *esprit* that was to become quickly evident on arrival in the war zone. He subsequently commanded two other fledgling squadrons and distinguished himself in home defence operations during 1916, being Mentioned in Despatches on at least four further occasions as well as receiving promotion to brevet Major in the field. In 1917 he was promoted Lieutenant-Colonel and given command of No.3 Wing, RFC, in France (in which No.25 was to become a component Squadron). During the final year of the War, he was a firm advocate of the 'fighter circus' as well as the 'stepped-up' fighter Wing escort for RAF bomber formations. As such he was probably the principal mentor of such men as Major William Sholto Douglas (then a squadron commander and later Marshal of the Royal Air Force The Lord Douglas of Kirtleside who, during the Second World War employed 'Big Wing tactics', though with varying degrees of success).

Holt held various senior staff appointments at the Air Ministry after the Armistice, being made CMG in 1919, as an Air Commodore was appointed Commandant of the Central Flying School in 1925, and in 1929 was Senior Air Staff Officer of Air Defence of Great Britain, being promoted Air Vice-Marshal. He died in a flying accident on 23rd April 1931 at the relatively early age of 44. His advance from subaltern to Air Rank in fifteen years had been ample testimony to the high esteem in which he was held during the formative years of the Royal Air Force. It has been fairly widely suggested that, had he lived, he would have been well placed to head one of the Royal Air Force's great Commands during the Second World War. He certainly possessed all the necessary experience of Command and Appointment.

OUT OF THE NURSERY. . .

It was not customary (nor ever has been in the RFC or RAF) for a squadron's senior flight commander to assume command of the squadron after the previous CO was posted away – except in very rare circumstances (such as those that existed on No.25 Squadron during 1941). Even when the CO had been killed in an accident or in action, the senior flight commander would normally only command the squadron temporarily, although he might be made up in temporary rank of major or squadron leader. This was simply because, before taking command of a squadron, the assumption of permanent squadron leader's rank usually followed a junior staff college or squadron commander's training course. The promotion to permanent squadron leader depended on successful negotiation of a promotion exam.

The senior flight commander of No.25 Squadron at the time of Holt's departure was Capt A W Grattan-Bellew (on a temporary posting), and there are indications that, with feeling running high at the apparent delays in ordering the Squadron forward from St.Omer, word reached Headquarters BEF – and in due course Hugh Trenchard himself – that the frustration was beginning to affect the Squadron's morale. Accordingly the great man decided that he would pay St.Omer an unannounced visit. This was to give rise to one of the favourite RFC anecdotes of the time.

One day in March there arrived a very large open staff car on the threshold of St.Omer's picket gate. With the appearance of a plethora of red tabs in evidence, the guard was called out, whereupon a loud bass voice was heard to enquire 'Which way to No.25 Squadron?' Simultaneously, a quick-witted subaltern, who had remained unseen in the guard hut, frantically called No.25's field office on the landline, gave his news, and was told 'to hold the General in conversation until Grattan-Bellew could make the journey to the picket to 'meet the visitors' according to military etiquette.

Now Grattan-Bellew, a man of some means, had in the short period so far spent in France acquired a fairly sportive Spyker motor car, and it was in this vehicle that he made the relatively short journey to the picket gate. Having been parked unintentionally on a particularly soggy patch of ground, Trenchard's large staff car was seen to have sunk up to its wheel hubs in mud. Without further observation of etiquette, Grattan-Bellew hailed the General, suggesting that it might be more comfortable if he were to transfer to the Spyker. Trenchard began the walk, arriving at the firmer ground on which the Dutch sports car was standing. Unfortunately, as Grattan-Bellew dismounted in order to arrange the seating plan, the Spyker's braking system let go and the car rolled forward and came to rest on one of the general's sparkling boots which accommodated one of the general's feet. Now a Spyker weighed about 30 cwt, and officers' boots were fashioned in pliable leather of the finest quality, but without significant load-bearing properties. Unaware of his motor car's act of *lèse majesté,* Gratten-Bellew called to suggest that his Very Important Passenger should mount the car and get into the front passenger seat. Only when the said VIP managed to recover his voice and roared an unrepeatable expletive did Grattan-Bellew realise that his motor car was imprisoning his guest. Not being equipped with a reverse gear, there was no alternative but to move forward, and no car of that period would do so without a fairly sudden jerk. There is no need to give any account of what followed; it is best left to the imagination. However, it can be inferred that No.25 Squadron's acting flight commander must have brought considerable tact to bear, for records show that not only did he remain on No.25 Squadron for some time, but was later to be awarded the Military Cross – duly endorsed by none other than Trenchard himself.

Records show that this very early F.E.2b was among the No.25 Squadron aircraft which flew to France on 20th February 1916. Despite being powered by the 120hp Beardmore, driving a two-blade propeller, these early F.Es – with a top speed of about 75 mph – acquitted themselves remarkably well, their gunners shooting down a dozen German aircraft during the period of the Battle of the Somme.

While No.25 Squadron was kicking its heels at St.Omer, its full complement of flying personnel and aircraft was gradually being achieved by a trickle of trained pilots and observers, as well as brand new F.E.2b aircraft flown in from Thetford. Among these was an unassuming young man who first reported to Thetford in January 1916 and who would, in the distant future attain the rank of Marshal of the Royal Air Force, the appointment of Chief of the Air Staff (the first of two members of No.25 Squadron to do so), and become a household name during the Second World War. That name was Arthur Tedder.

Tedder had been educated at Whitgift and gained a Second in History at Cambridge. Despite evincing some interest in a career in the Army (having joined the Cambridge Officers' Training Corps) and a brief spell in the Diplomatic Corps – being posted to Fiji in a very junior post – he returned home to England on the outbreak of war and joined the Dorset Regiment, being commissioned 2nd Lieutenant. However, when he injured a knee during a night exercise, he missed the Regiment's first draft to France, and was told that he would have to apply to re-join when he was fully fit once more. Week followed week of inactivity (other than getting married) and, after a comedy of administrative rituals, Tedder finally answered the call for volunteers to join the Royal Flying Corps as an observer, seeing this as likely to be the quickest way to reach France. Further delays ensued (during which he attended a course in Electricity, Morse and Telegraphy at the Marconi School) before he was posted to Thetford for training but – never fully explained – as a pilot. His knee now fully serviceable, Tedder underwent a month's instruction in engines, 'theory of flight', the elements of an aeroplane (including instruments and cameras), culminating in a very brief flying training stint. There being no such thing as an F.E.2b with dual control, he was taken aloft in an Avro 504 by an instructor of No.9 Reserve Squadron before being 'shown the cockpit' of the F.E. and sent off solo for a circuit and landing. Further ventures into the air, including a cross-country or two, followed without detectable difficulty, and in May he was gazetted Captain (Temporary) and posted to join No.25 Squadron in France.

In the meantime the Squadron had moved from St.Omer to Auchel, about 20 miles to the south, near Béthune, where it was to be based for the next eighteen months. Auchel was a mining village and the flying field was bordered by two prominent slag heaps – which proved to be useful landmarks for pilots lost and short of fuel. Morale on the Squadron was high, and Tedder found himself among a band of high-spirited young men – the majority younger than he – which seemed to be leavened by more than a sprinkling of the junior aristocracy, a feature of the Squadron that remained to varying extents throughout the War (Arthur Tedder himself was the son of a Knight of the Realm). A prominent 25-year-old Lieutenant pilot on the Squadron at this time was Lord Francis Douglas Stuart Doune, transferred to the RFC from the Scottish Horse (Yeomanry) and heir to the Earldom of Moray; he was to feature fairly often in the Squadron's records and won an MC for shooting down a Fokker EIII. It is said that he seldom walked out to his aircraft, having arranged to purchase his own four-footed transport. This led to the sobriquet *Burke's Squadron,* widely used by others, but never by the Squadron itself. The Squadron's mere mortals soon became accustomed to the whims of title.

. . .INTO THE FRONT LINE

On 31st March 1916 No.25 Squadron was ordered to make ready to move to Auchel on the following day. It was, however, on the 31st that No.25 suffered its first combat casualty in action. While flying as escort for a reconnaissance machine Lieutenant Norris was attacked by a Fokker EIII over Gheluwe; the attack was apparently somewhat half-hearted. Norris was unhurt, but his observer, Capt H Seagrave, was wounded in the leg. The aircraft was brought back to St.Omer without further ado.

On moving to Auchel on 1st April, No.25 Squadron, formerly under General Headquarters, transferred to the 4th Brigade, RFC, its sector of operations being the front of the British First Army. Its *modus operandi* was to fly daily patrols over this sector, to prevent German aircraft from spotting for the enemy's artillery and to protect British aircraft engaged in similar pursuits. This was also the period of the Fokker Eindekker's worst depredations but, with the arrival of No.24 Squadron's D.H.2s, the end of heavy losses among Allied aircraft seemed to be in sight.

As far as can be judged, the Squadron was fairly satisfied with its F.E.2bs, although most of the pilots preferred to continue gaining flying experience when not called to fly patrols. Apart from the F.E.2bs, there were still several other aircraft with No.25 (including a handful of Bristol Scouts, probably on loan from No.12 Squadron), but these were only flown by the more experienced pilots and probably not exposed to combat. The early F.E.2bs featured an out-rigged 'nosewheel' undercarriage, which tended to be unpopular, calling for extra care when landing, the aircraft being brought in nose-up in order to avoid digging the nosewheel into the ground on touch-down – but not 'too nose-up' otherwise the empennage (tail unit) would take the brunt of the landing shock! Other F.E. squadrons, operating from rougher airfields that Auchel, had experienced some nasty accidents, but it was felt that sooner or later No.25 would follow suit. However, on his own initiative No.25 Squadron's new Commanding Officer, Major R G Cherry (of whom more later), decided to remove the offending nosewheel and supporting struts and ordered one of his flight commanders 'to suck it and see'. The verdict was that the aeroplane's landing characteristics were much improved, although the resulting slight rearward shift of the centre of gravity meant that the aeroplane needed to be flown on to the ground with some throttle to avoid ballooning and stalling. Within a week or so, the other F.E. squadrons had followed suit, and almost all F.E.s delivered after mid-April were without nosewheels from the outset.

No.25 Squadron had not been involved in the Battle of Verdun on account of the Germans concentrating most of their front line aircraft around the great fortress to the south. This preoccupation by the enemy air force provided some relief for the RFC, not least from the Fokker monoplanes. It also provided No.25 Squadron with the opportunity to begin flying 'armed reconnaissance' patrols over the front lines

This F.E.2b, A5478 (presentation aircraft 'Gold Coast No.10'), seen at Auchel with a load comprising one 230lb and eight 20lb Cooper bombs under the nacelle and wings. The extraordinarily exposed position adopted by the observer during combat is graphically illustrated.
(Photo: Francis K Mason collection)

without too much interference, and at the same time become thoroughly familiar with its sector of operations.

The Battle of Verdun had found the French totally unprepared to meet the new tactics being employed by the Germans, who had by then learned of the advantages of operating in formations of up to six or eight aircraft. Both the British and French, more often than not, preferred to limit their patrols to flights by two or three aircraft – including escort; bombing raids by more than six aircraft were the exception, not the rule. And the fighter pilots of the RFC had grown accustomed, or were accustomed by character, to fly singly or in pairs – and a young pilot named Albert Ball came to epitomise the successful 'loner'. Moreover, when such Squadrons as Nos.23 and 29 began to emulate the German formations, they did so with commensurate losses when met by similar numbers – simply because the Allies were slow to introduce the necessary training. This time-lag between the development of new front line fighting tactics, and the introduction into flying training courses at home in Britain of measures to cope with the tactics, was to grow to an alarming extent during the next nine months, and was to be a major cause of the Allies' loss of air superiority over the Western Front during the last few months of 1916.

However, for all the highly coloured newspaper accounts, which had given no indications of the RFC's predicament and increasing losses, one thing was all too obvious to No.25 Squadron. The Royal Aircraft Factory's F.E.2b (the F.E. standing for Farman Experimental, on account of the general similarity of configuration with the aircraft designed by the Farman company) was simply not a modern fighter. Inherently stable about all axes, it possessed none of the attributes of a 'dogfighter', and depended entirely on a keen-eyed pilot and observer/gunner, the permanent proximity of a large cloud into which to escape and, preferably, an escort of dedicated fighting scouts. Despite its lack of manœuvrability, however its one useful attribute was

An F.E.2b of No.25 Squadron seen at Auchel, France, carrying a 230lb bomb beneath the nacelle. It is also fitted with underwing racks for up to eight 20lb Cooper bombs, though these are not being carried.
(Photo: via J M Bruce)

This Royal Aircraft Factory-built F.E.2b, 6341, probably photographed in March 1916, is interesting in several respects. Apart from being a fairly early example, retaining the unpopular nosewheel (which was probably removed shortly after), it carries the presentation name 'Zanzibar No.1' on the port side of the nose, and 'The Scotch Express' on the starboard side. On 16th May 1916, flown by Capt Duncan Grinnell-Milne, with Cpl D McMaster as observer/gunner, this aircraft took off from Auchel at 07:55 hrs as escort for a reconnaissance patrol; after encountering some anti-aircraft fire, Grinnell-Milne was attacked by four enemy aircraft and shot down near Fournes; both crew members survived the subsequent crash landing and were made prisoners. Grinnell-Milne managed to escape on 1st April 1918 from German captivity into Holland, and returned to England soon afterwards. He was the author of the well-known book 'Wind In The Wires', in which he recounts his experiences on No.25 Squadron during the War.

The close-up view of the aircraft's nose well illustrates the position adopted by the observer who, having lifted his Lewis gun on to the gun mounting pillar is able to direct defensive fire to the rear over the pilot; the canvas bags suspended from the gun are to collect spent cartridge cases, so that the pilot and other vital parts of the aircraft are spared a cascade of brass. (Photo: G S Leslie collection)

its nose-mounted machine gun, which possessed a very wide field of fire and could be lifted off its front pillar spigot and re-mounted on either of two spigots situated behind the shoulders of the gunner; he was therefore also able to fire over a high, wide arc in the two rear sectors. The discomfort (and vulnerability), though, lay in the gunner's need to stand in his exposed cockpit to fire his gun, so that his whole body – from the knees upwards – was exposed to the slipstream and presented a prominent target for an enemy gunner!

In retrospect it can be seen that by the time No.25 Squadron pilots and gunner/observers were getting their first taste of combat, the peak of Fokker monoplane supremacy had passed. This was due not to the introduction of a superior British fighter, but rather to an increasing number of RFC squadrons, of which No.25 Squadron was one of those tasked with the rôle of 'fighting reconnaissance', and although many of the reconnaissance patrols (usually by two or three aircraft) were uneventful, there were a score of occasions during April when the enemy monoplanes were seen, but actual combat was avoided by one side or the other. Much depended on the location of the sighting. This circumstance was to remain a tactical consideration throughout the whole of the War, for it had to be remembered that the prevailing wind was from the west, that is to say that the Allied aircraft usually had to cope with a headwind on the return leg of their patrol, and any prolonged combat over or beyond the front lines could jeopardise their safe return owing to fuel shortage. There are numerous accounts in No.25's records of pilots force landing away from Auchel, either within artillery range of the front line or in some remote field nearer home.

No.25 Squadron's first victory was gained by Lieutenant Lord Doune and his observer/gunner 2/Lt R U Walker who destroyed a Fokker EIII between La Bassée and Hulluch, and several inconclusive actions followed during the next fortnight. On 16th May one of the Squadron's more experienced pilots, Captain Duncan Grinnell-Milne, was attacked by four enemy scouts and shot down at Fournes, managing to crash land safely, but behind enemy lines. His aircraft had already been damaged by ground fire and was hardly in shape to resist the enemy effectively. Both the pilot and his observer, Cpl D McMaster, were unwounded and were taken prisoner. He later escaped from captivity and returned home after a short, enforced stay in Holland.*

* Grinnell-Milne began putting together a book *Wind in the Wires* (publisher not known) during the 1930s in which he described his wartime experiences in a somewhat jaundiced manner. Later editions were largely re-written, placing more emphasis on his escape to Holland in 1918. His period of service with his first squadron – which he did not identify – was evidently frustrating, finding little to respect among his fellow pilots. Few dates are quoted, but at least he appears to have had little opportunity to find fault among his colleagues on No.25, none of whom is identifiable by name. As far as can be discovered, his last flight with No.25 was only about his fifth or sixth operational sortie.

It has been said that this very first generation of fighter pilots (as well as those of the German air force) were fully aware that they were the builders of a new fighting tradition, and were determined not to be found wanting. If there was one thing they firmly established it was that the fighter pilot, unlike the infantryman or the sailor, was primarily an individualist who, given the means and the opportunity, would undertake seemingly impossible feats of courage. Tedder, however, being somewhat more mature in years and outlook, was less hell-bent. He was, after all, by now a family man! Yet decades later Tedder was to recall that No.25 was regarded as a 'glamorous' unit, by no means composed of effete young men, but young men who were more afraid of letting down their colleagues than of air combat itself. In pursuit of this determination, they took terrible risks and all too often they paid the price. And what a price they paid. They frequently saw close friends shot down in fragile aeroplanes that had become flaming torches – and in those days no one wore a parachute. . .there were none. Some could not bear the prospect of being burned to death and leapt from their cockpits long before the remains of their aeroplanes reached the ground. In Squadron records the fate of an airman who died in such circumstances was simply 'Shot down – Jumped'.

That No.25 Squadron was something of a justifiably élitist band of young men was certainly recognised in high circles for, whenever civilian organisations adopted the practice of 'presenting' aircraft (that is subscribing money, ostensibly to pay for their manufacture), No.25 Squadron was constantly nominated as the recipient unit by the War Office; such aircraft proudly displayed attributions from as far afield as Trinidad, Australia, Canada and Zanzibar. Determined not to create an element of élitism as a matter of policy, other Squadrons were also 'awarded' presentation aircraft. But the label stuck to No.25 for many years to come. In the meantime the Squadron had yet to justify any sort of reputation as a 'crack' unit. The opportunity arrived on the afternoon of 18th June 1916.

On that day a flight of three 25 Squadron F.E.2bs was set on by a formation of seven Fokker EIIIs over Arras; one of the F.E.'s was shot down almost immediately, but then, instead of trying to make good their escape, the two remaining British pilots turned into their attackers so sharply that their gunners were quickly able to bring their Lewis guns to bear. 2nd Lieutenant G R McCubbin and his gunner, Corporal J H Waller, engaged one of the enemy and shot it down, while Capt Grattan-Bellew (already referred to) claimed another before the remaining Fokkers made off. McCubbin's victim turned out to be none other than Max Immelmann, the famous German Fokker pilot. The Germans have always contended that Immelmann's aircraft crashed as the result of his gun interrupter gear failing and the engine, minus a propeller, self-destructing, but have never substantiated the theory. This reluctance to admit that a German 'ace' had been shot down by an enemy was by no means uncommon. However in the circumstances of Manfred von Richthofen's death much later in the War, when it was claimed that he had not been shot down in aerial combat – even though a Canadian pilot was credited with the victory – it was to be about sixty years later that extensive research confirmed beyond reasonable doubt that the top-scoring German pilot was indeed shot down by ground fire. In the case of McCubbin and Waller, Immelmann's interrupter gear could just as easily have been damaged by the F.E.'s fire. Nevertheless, it was seldom the German habit to accept

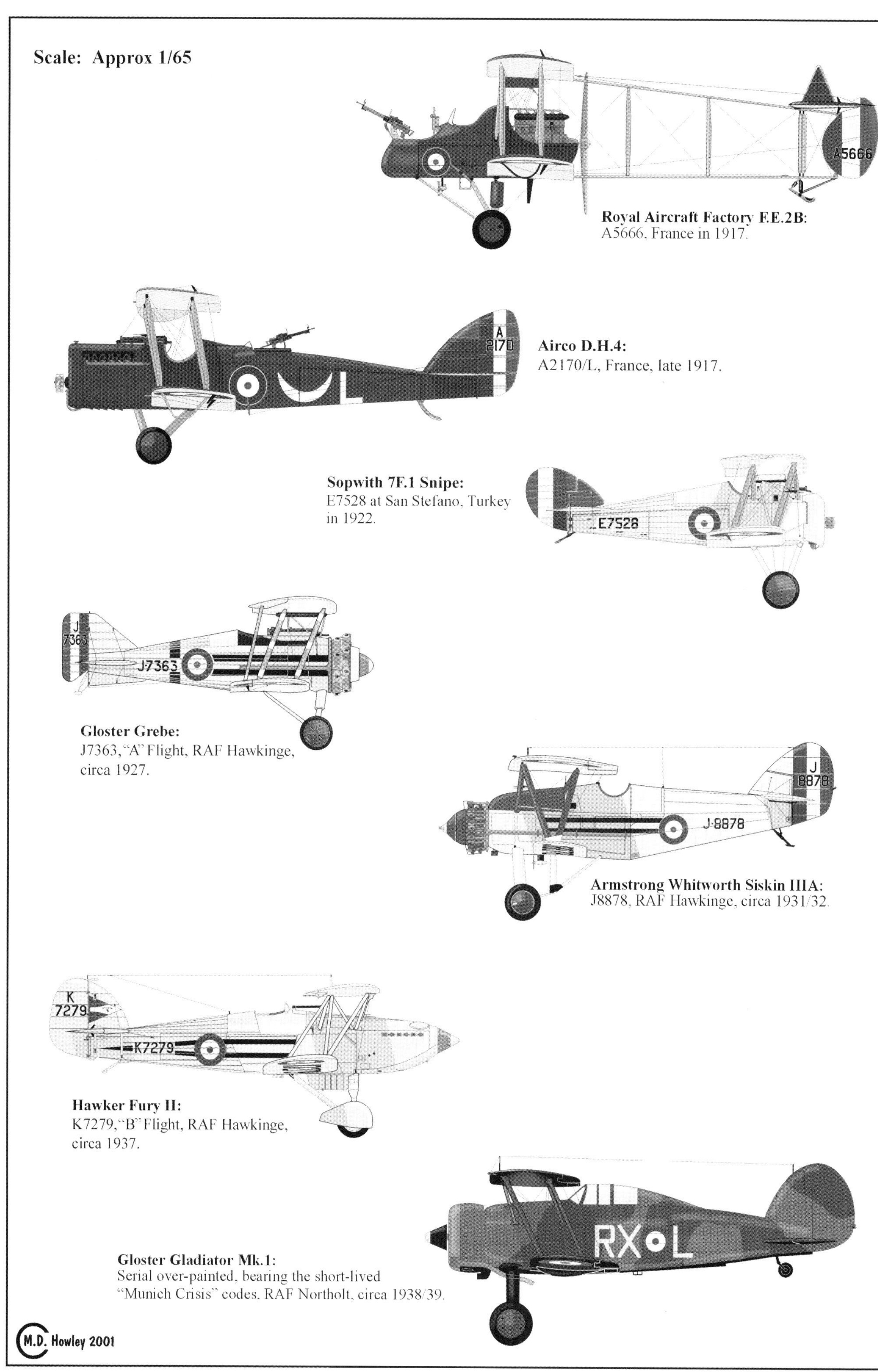

Scale: Approx 1/65

Royal Aircraft Factory F.E.2B:
A5666, France in 1917.

Airco D.H.4:
A2170/L, France, late 1917.

Sopwith 7F.1 Snipe:
E7528 at San Stefano, Turkey in 1922.

Gloster Grebe:
J7363, "A" Flight, RAF Hawkinge, circa 1927.

Armstrong Whitworth Siskin IIIA:
J8878, RAF Hawkinge, circa 1931/32.

Hawker Fury II:
K7279, "B" Flight, RAF Hawkinge, circa 1937.

Gloster Gladiator Mk.1:
Serial over-painted, bearing the short-lived "Munich Crisis" codes, RAF Northolt, circa 1938/39.

©M.D. Howley 2001

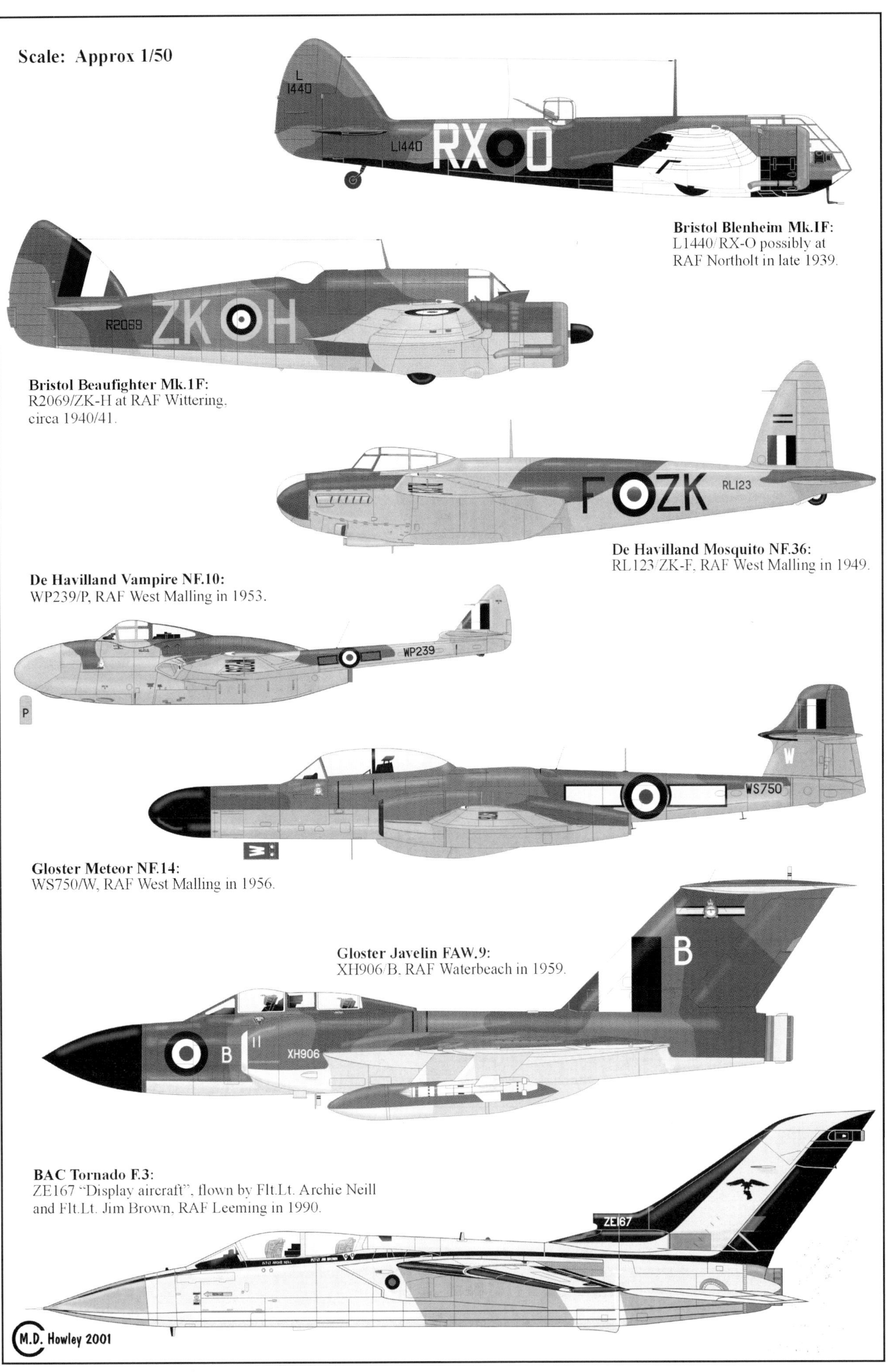

Scale: Approx 1/50

Bristol Blenheim Mk.IF:
L1440/RX-O possibly at
RAF Northolt in late 1939.

Bristol Beaufighter Mk.1F:
R2069/ZK-H at RAF Wittering,
circa 1940/41.

De Havilland Mosquito NF.36:
RL123/ZK-F, RAF West Malling in 1949.

De Havilland Vampire NF.10:
WP239/P, RAF West Malling in 1953.

Gloster Meteor NF.14:
WS750/W, RAF West Malling in 1956.

Gloster Javelin FAW.9:
XH906/B, RAF Waterbeach in 1959.

BAC Tornado F.3:
ZE167 "Display aircraft", flown by Flt.Lt. Archie Neill
and Flt.Lt. Jim Brown, RAF Leeming in 1990.

that their *Experten* were shot down by enemy aircraft, unless there was irrefutable evidence to the contrary. Grattan-Bellew was in action again several days later when, leading a formation of five F.E.2bs, he shot down two Fokkers of a formation of eight which had attacked them before the survivors made off. For this, and his previous success, Grattan-Bellew was awarded the Military Cross. Shortly afterwards he was promoted Major and appointed to command No.29 Squadron, flying F.E.8s from Abeele.

The sorties on which these combats occurred were among those being undertaken by No.25 Squadron, and many others, in preparation for a major offensive which was scheduled to begin at the end of June, and which in fact opened on 1st July. At this time No.25 Squadron was called on to give its views on a new version of the F.E.2, the F.E.2c, in which the pilot's and observer's cockpits were changed over, with the pilot in the extreme nose. This was a proposed night bomber version, it being contended that the pilot, who would actually release the bombs, would possess a better view of the ground. As far as can be determined, only a few examples were flown by No.25 before being delivered to another Squadron for more objective trials.

It was no secret either among the flying Squadrons or the Germans, that in June 1916 the British were preparing for a mighty offensive. During the last two weeks of that month the night skies lit up with gun flashes and the ground shook as the British artillery pounded away at the German lines, giving ample warning to the enemy that a big attack was on the way. During daylight, No.25 was ordered to fly over the enemy lines to report on the previous night's bombardment, or to provide cover for others similarly engaged. No.25 suffered half a dozen casualties, mostly involving either pilot or observer being hit by 'Archie' shrapnel, the vernacular for anti-aircraft gunfire. There was little or no attempt made to attack the German troops on the ground, for such was plainly suicidal in an aircraft whose speed was seldom over 70 mph, flying downwind.

The loss of Max Immelmann was keenly felt, not only throughout Germany, but among the enemy squadrons on the Western Front, for whom the loss of one of their acknowledged heroes was a catastrophe. By Imperial order, Oswald Boelcke, at that time the highest scoring German pilot, was forbidden to fly over the Front lest his loss should further erode morale; instead he spent the time touring other fronts to bolster spirits. Indeed the loss of Immelmann could not have occurred at a worse time. During the lead up to the Battle of the Somme, Allied pilots were displaying unusual aggression and confidence, and despite fairly heavy casualties on both sides, air combats were taking place further behind the German lines than had previously been the pattern, so that the absence of pilots like Immelmann and Boelcke seemed to bode ill for the coming battles. What was then not yet apparent was that a new star was gaining ascendancy. And No.25 Squadron was to feel its effect.

Beardmore-powered F.E.2b, A5666, photographed by its manufacturer, G & J Weir of Glasgow. This aircraft featured in No.25 Squadron records for a short time in 1917, though it is omitted from RFC charge lists in France. (Photo: via Leslie Hunt)

Summary of Squadron Combat Operations

From the Battle of Verdun to the First Battle of the Somme

(No.25 Squadron arrived in France on 20th February 1916)

31st March. Squadron's first casualty. While providing escort for a reconnaissance aircraft, F.E.2b 6342 was attacked by a Fokker EIII over Gheluwe. The observer, Capt H Seagrave, was wounded in the leg, but the unwounded pilot, Lt Norris, brought the aircraft home without further damage.

16th April. While on patrol over La Bassée, F.E.2b 6344 was damaged by AA fire but returned home safely. Pilot, Lt C J Hart; Observer, Cpl J H Waller both unhurt.

23rd April. During a patrol F.E.2b 5210 was attacked by a German scout flown by Ltn M Mülzer of FAb62 in the vicinity of Estaires. The pilot, Lt Collison, managed to disengage after his observer, 2/AM GF Atwell, had been killed, and returned to base.

29th April. F.E.2b 5209, flown by Lt Lord Doune, with observer 2/Lt R U Walker, engaged and destroyed a Fokker EIII in the area of Hulluch – La Bassée.

4th May. While on patrol near Fromelles F.E.2b 5212, flown by 2/Lt H Dixon, with Lt E R Davis, was hit in the radiator by ground fire and made a forced landing behind the British lines. It was repaired and recovered.

16th May. F.E.2b 6341, escorting reconnaissance aircraft, attacked by four enemy scouts and shot down near Fournes. Capt D Grinnell-Milne and Cpl D McMaster, observer, both made POW.

17th May. F.E.2b 5238, on reconnaissance sortie over La Bassée canal, in combat with German scouts. Pilot, Capt W Milne wounded in action; Observer, 2/Lt E R Davis unhurt. Aircraft returned safely.

26th May. F.E.2b 6932, on reconnaissance sortie, hit by AA near Arras; radiator damaged, but returned safely. Capt B A May and 2/Lt J C M Stewart unhurt.

27th May. F.E.2b 6932, on reconnaissance sortie, hit by AA fire. Pilot, Capt C J MacKay, wounded but brought aircraft back safely.

4th June. F.E.2b 6938, on reconnaissance sortie, hit by AA fire near Bethune and damaged. Observer, 2/Lt R U Walker, wounded; pilot, Lt Lord Doune, unhurt, brought aircraft back safely.

18th June. 1st combat. One of three F.E.2bs 6940, on patrol at 3,000ft near Arras in action against seven Fokkers led by Max Immelmann. 6940 shot down by Immelmann at Bucquoy (in German claim) at 16.00 hrs. Pilot, Lt C E Rogers killed in action; observer, Sgt H Taylor, wounded in action and made POW. Both the other F.E.2bs, one flown by Capt W A Grattan-Bellew, claimed one Fokker each).

18th June. 2nd combat. F.E.2b 4909 was one of 'several' aircraft on patrol that were in combat with two Fokker EIIIs at 19.45 hrs (British time), and claimed shot down by Lt M Mülzer over Wingles; pilot, 2/Lt J R B Savage, died of wounds; his observer, Air Mechanic Robinson, was wounded and made POW. The other Fokker was attacked by the F.E.2B flown by 2/Lt G R McCubbin, with Cpl J H Waller (observer) and claimed shot down; this was flown by Oblt Max Immelmann who was killed.

22nd June. 1st combat. F.E.2b 5209, on patrol over enemy lines, was in combat with a Fokker EIII and forced down near Hulloch in enemy territory; the pilot, 2/Lt J L P Armstrong was taken prisoner but died of wounds; the observer, Sgt G Topliffe was unhurt and made POW. Claimed shot down by Ltn. M Mülzer.

22nd June. 2nd combat. F.E.2b 6334, while on patrol was damaged by AA fire near Souchez; the pilot, 2/Lt L C Angstrom was wounded but brought the aircraft home, his observer 2/Lt H C Hardwick being unhurt.

23rd June. F.E.2b 4907, while on artillery spotting sortie over the Bois de Biez, was damaged by ground fire. The pilot, Lt H B Davey, was unhurt and force landed behind the Allied lines, but the observer, Lt S R P Walter, was wounded.

26th June. F.E.2b 5212 was one of a formation bombing raid which was engaged by Fokker EIIIs in a running battle. It was forced down near Mazingarbe, its pilot, Lt RCB Riley, having been wounded; the observer, Lt E H Bird, died of wounds. This aircraft was claimed shot down by Ltn Mülzer of the Kampfeinsitzer-Kommando (Nord).

26th June. Another F.E.2b, 6334, which took part in the above bombing raid, was shot down over Cambrai. The pilot, 2/Lt R Sherwell, was unhurt, but his observer, 2/AM H Chadwick, was killed.

26th June. A third F.E.2b, 6346, in the above bombing raid, was damaged in action against enemy scouts near Bouvrai. The pilot, 2/Lt McCubbin, was wounded in action, but brought his aircraft home safely; the observer, Cpl J H Waller, was unhurt.

F.E.2ds began arriving on No.25 Squadron in March 1917, being characterised by a switch to the 250hp Rolls-Royce Mk.III engine, which increased the speed performance by some ten per cent. Of about twenty-five examples known to have been issued to the Squadron, nine were lost to enemy action. The aircraft seen here is flying over Lens at 6,000 feet.

(Photo: G S Leslie / J M Bruce collection)

By the time No.25 Squadron had settled in at Auchel it was already becoming widely accepted that the F.E.2b with the 120hp Beardmore engine could no longer undertake the air fighting rôle as a primary function, and was increasingly called on to confine its activities to daylight reconnaissance and bombing, for which an escort would usually be provided, the escorts being increasingly flown by F.E.2bs with the 160hp Beardmore engine. Some examples of the more powerful aircraft were just arriving on the Squadron when the Battle of the Somme opened at the beginning of July 1916, but their initial reception was not enthusiastic. The new engine was somewhat heavier than the 120hp version, so that performance had not been increased, and it soon proved less reliable – resulting in more forced landings than previously. Added to this was the unexplained fact that the majority of the more powerful F.E.2bs delivered to No.25 still possessed the unpopular nosewheel, whether by design or in error is not clear (or even that stocks of the unmodified aircraft were still being used as replacements). There is some suggestion that Major Cherry again favoured simply removing the offending nosewheel as before, but was dissuaded by wiser counsels from issuing the order prematurely. It was pointed out that, with the heavier engine and four-blade propeller, the aircraft's centre of gravity was already dangerously close to the 'aft limit', and that removal of the nosewheel and mounting structure might render the aircraft uncontrollable when landing. A compromise was reached by racking the gunner's ammunition forward by about eighteen inches. When it was pointed out that, after combat, these racks might well be empty and the centre of gravity aft of its safe limit for landing, good sense prevailed, and the problem referred to the Aircraft Park in France. It was apparently ameliorated by amending the rigging instructions so as to reduce the angle of incidence of the upper wing by half a degree. However, because the F.E.2b had still to be 'wheeled-in' with plenty of throttle, landing accidents continued to be common.

By all accounts, morale on the Squadron was good, and there were occasions when 25 received congratulatory messages, both from RFC Field Headquarters and the troops in the front line. Tedder was promoted Temporary Captain and appointed a flight commander on 9th August. After the departure of Major Holt, command of No.25 Squadron had passed briefly to Major T W C Cartwright DSO (previously with Nos.2 and 4 Squadrons), but he had stayed for no more than about a fortnight before the arrival of Major R G Cherry MC, who was to remain in command for more than a year.

The new CO was something of an enigma. It is said that there are, or were, two types of 'acceptable' commanding officers: the 'ball of fire' who led from the front and let his adjutant get on with the paper-work; and the avuncular officer who, knowing his own limitations, occupied his office chair during daylight hours, bought drinks all round during the hours of darkness, and let his flight commanders command and lead their own flights. Cherry fitted neither of these categories exactly. For one thing, he seldom flew, if he could help it, yet his presence was felt throughout the Squadron all the time. Tedder believed that this was erring on the right side; others resented it, especially when casualties tended to be high. He appears at first to have been a poor judge of character among his pilots and allowed no tolerance among subordinate ranks, yet was supremely protective of the Squadron as a whole, and therein lay an unforgivable weakness – suspicion and distrust of experienced replacement pilots posted to No.25 from other squadrons, a suspicion that would persist, no matter how capable the 'outsider' proved to be. Nevertheless, Cherry would always defend his squadron from any criticism coming from outside – particularly by Wing Headquarters. Fortunately, pilots and observers (the latter frequently non-commissioned personnel) had the very highest regard for their flight commanders who, it must be said, were wholly responsible for the high morale that pervaded the Squadron as a fighting unit. And Cherry, it seems, was a proficient administrator when it came to report-writing and form-filling. One order, however, attracted deep-rooted resentment among the pilots and gunners alike, resentment due mainly to the CO's own apparent aversion to flying. This order forbade the wearing of seat belts while flying, on the grounds that in a crash or forced landing the crew had more chance of being thrown clear of the aircraft than being crushed by the engine, located aft of the crew, plunging forward into the cockpit. It never occurred to Cherry that in most cases the pilot and observer were the best judges of the relative risks involved. It should be remembered that, in combat, the F.E.2b's gunner was obliged to stand almost entirely unshielded in his cockpit as the pilot banked, climbed and dived. As already remarked, parachutes for flying men in the RFC (and the later RAF) were still some years away.

This F.E.2b, 4909, was in combat with a pair of Fokkers (probably EIII monoplanes) over Wingles and shot down at 19:45 hrs on 18th June 1916 during the run-up to the Battle of the Somme (possibly by Lieutenant Max Ritter von Mulzer of KEK Nord – Kampfeinsitzerkommando *North; this pilot shot down no fewer than five aircraft of No.25 Squadron during his combat career). It is said that the engine was probably hit and the pilot, 2/Lt J R B Savage managed to force land in enemy territory before succumbing to his wounds; his observer/gunner, Air Mechanic 2nd Class T N U Robinson was wounded but survived as a prisoner of war. The photograph (from German archives) bears the caption 'English aircraft shot down on 18th June 1916 near Noyelles'.*

(Photo: G S Leslie collection)

CHAPTER 2

From Bloody April to Victory

But it was *never* quiet on the Western Front

The Battles of the Somme continued, seldom with any respite, until the end of November 1916. On the ground the British armies had made what, in those months, constituted significant advances towards Peronne and Bapaume – but at a staggering cost in lives, said to be well over half a million men dead. In the air the RFC had gained the ascendancy while faced by such German fighting scouts as the Albatros DI and Fokker DII, the elderly Fokker Eindekkers gradually being taken out of service. The great German fighter exponent, Oswald Boelcke, had been killed in combat when his Albatros was struck by a colleague's machine. In the RFC the Sopwith 1½-Strutter, which had become obsolete, was also being phased out of service, and the excellent new Sopwith Pup single-seater with a forward-firing synchronised machine gun was due to start delivery to the RFC early in 1917 – while several RNAS squadrons were flying the aircraft some weeks before the end of 1916. However, the Germans also had new fighting scouts on the way to the Western Front, namely the Albatros DIII and the Fokker DIII; both aircraft possessed a maximum speed of about 103 mph and two fixed guns firing forward. Of the two, the Albatros was the superior, while the Fokker still employed wing-warping instead of ailerons and was without a fixed tail-fin.

No.25 Squadron (now without Captain Tedder, who had been posted on New Year's Day 1917 to command No.70 Squadron with Sopwith 1½-Strutters, recently arrived at Auchel), continued to fly the F.E.2b with the 160hp engine, but now the long-awaited F.E.2d was beginning deliveries to France. Powered by a 250hp Rolls-Royce engine (later developed to become the famous Eagle), the new F.E. arrived on No.25 in March 1917, being welcomed not so much for its slight increase in speed (to about 98 mph) but for the increase in combat ceiling from around 10,000ft to more than 16,000ft as well as its ability to carry two additional fixed, forward-firing guns on the sides of the nacelle, fired by the pilot. Nevertheless, there was no improvement in the old pusher's manœuvrability. Moreover, all chance of springing a surprise with the introduction of the new F.E. vanished when the pilot delivering the first example to France accidentally landed behind the German lines – thereby presenting the enemy with a brand-new Rolls-Royce Eagle engine as well. (This 'own goal' was by no means unique, one of the first Handley Page O/100 heavy bombers being delivered to France having accidentally landed intact behind the German lines on New Year's Day 1917!)

BLOODY APRIL

The F.E.2d arrived on No.25 Squadron just in time for what came to be known forever as 'bloody April'. Its arrival also coincided with a visit to the Squadron by Major The Hon Maurice Baring, Staff Equipment Officer of the RFC. This influential officer had, for some months, endorsed Trenchard's outspoken complaints to the War Department in London, pointing to the continued reliance by the RFC in France on wholly obsolete aircraft and the apparent absence of any new aircraft capable of matching the new German scouts. It seems that there had been a few instances among No.25's pilots of qualified refusals to continue flying the F.E.2b, derelictions that had been reported to HQ by Major Cherry, and passed on to Trenchard. With considerable tact – but treading on thin ice – Baring addressed the Squadron's assembled pilots, telling them that, in the event of further refusals, he would find it difficult to take any disciplinary action against such pilots. One can only guess at Major Cherry's reaction to this, as he possibly hadn't flown an F.E. for months. Baring's attitude was simply to deter the CO from forwarding any report of a refusal by a pilot to fly. The arrival of the F.E.2d on No.25 was almost certainly a direct result of Baring's visit, and there was no further known instance of refusal.

Indeed, shortly afterwards No.25 Squadron was 'asked' to carry out a photo reconnaissance of Vimy Ridge on 3rd April – likely to be little short of suicidal. Major Cherry asked for three volunteers for the task, and every pilot stepped forward. After three pilots had been selected, the F.E.2s took off and had completed their photographic task when they were approached from above and behind by about a dozen German scouts led, as it transpired, by Manfred von Richthofen. Apparently a fighter escort had been 'laid on', but did not appear. The F.E. pilots immediately went into a defensive circle, so as to guard each other's tail and to give the gunners a better chance of hitting some of the enemy. So confident were the German pilots of despatching the three F.E.s that von Richthofen led just two other aircraft into the attack by *Jasta* 11. He himself despatched the aircraft flown by 2/Lt D P McDonald with 2/Lt J I M O'Beirne as gunner; the latter was shot through the head and killed instantly, but the pilot managed to crash land the aircraft and was taken prisoner. This was von Richthofen's 34th air victory. The second aircraft shot down was sent crashing by Ltn Karl Emil Schaefer. The surviving F.E. returned safely with a set of the vital photographs. *

The loss of the two 25 Squadron aircraft on 4th April was no more than typical of that being experienced throughout the RFC. Not only were the British aircraft now thoroughly out-classed by the enemy's fighting scouts, but the whole gamut of the Germans' air fighting tactics had undergone fundamental change. Led in person by Manfred von Richthofen, these tactics, backed up by transformed training standards, employed large formations of modern aircraft

* Although von Richthofen kept a careful record of his 80 combat victories, recording the names of the crews of the aircraft shot down, wherever possible, he seems to have been unaware of the F.E.2's existence as such, recording all pusher biplanes as 'Vickers 2s'. Only one of his claims cannot be verified from Allied records. He had also shot down another 25 Squadron F.E. during September the previous year.

flying defensive patrols *over their own lines,* while the RFC, possessing a numerical superiority of outdated aircraft would be attacked on every possible occasion.

The German armies had, during the final stages of the Battles of the Somme, retired to a prepared defence line (the Ludendorf, or Hindenburg Line), in which greatly improved lines of communication had been given the utmost priority, while a line of defensive strongpoints, prepared in depth and at leisure, was regarded as impregnable.

On the Allied side, the French commander, General Joseph Joffre, had been discarded on account of the appalling waste of lives in the Somme battles, and was replaced by Robert Nivelle, whose creeping barrage advance tactics had achieved spectacular success (albeit against troops in the open); these tactics would now be tested against forces much more difficult to dislodge.

In the air, new British aircraft now appeared in service, not least of which was the Sopwith Pup, referred to earlier. The first Bristol Fighters and S.E.5s had arrived in France, but neither had been cleared of snags, and were withdrawn while the worst problems were rectified; the Sopwith Camel, expected to dominate the Western Front, was ready for delivery but was delayed at home, having met with a barricade of red tape which had come close to destroying the entire delivery programme for three vital months (partly due to wrangling between the Royal Naval Air Service and the RFC as to which was to be given priority for the new fighters). Finally, and to some extent posing a serious 'knock-on' problem for No.25 Squadron, there was the matter of the Factory's R.E.8 (known forever as the ''Arry Tate'), a corps reconnaissance aircraft that had started delivery to France before the end of 1916.

This badly-flawed aeroplane had first equipped No.52 Squadron in November, but so many accidents had occurred (as a result of the aircraft's dreadful handling qualities) that it was immediately withdrawn while the worst defects were addressed. The main problem stemmed from the Factory's traditional determination to produce aircraft that were inherently stable about all axes, resulting in a total absence of manœuvrability; such a fundamental flaw, however, proved insurmountable. On the other hand, another design fault in the R.E.8 resulted in a lamentable tendency to catch fire in a heavy, or forced, landing, the gravity fuel tank being located under the port upper wing root, just eighteen inches from the engine's exhaust stack! Added to these 'difficulties' was the R.E.8's apparent tendency to spin without warning buffet, a condition of flight from which RFC pilots had received only perfunctory instruction in recovery, a situation made somewhat worse owing to a marked deficiency of rudder control – even in straight and level flight; this potentially lethal handling problem was alleviated by a hurried enlargement of the tail fin.

With the approach of the large-scale British offensive, planned for 9th April 1917, it became essential for the R.E.8 to be introduced into service beforehand, come what may, it being decreed that all such reconnaissance and artillery spotting operations by the aircraft should be accompanied by a fighter escort, a job given, among others, to No.25 Squadron, in addition to reconnaissance work undertaken by the Squadron in its own right. However, such was the impact of the new German air fighting tactics, allied to the weaknesses among the British aircraft that, during the preparatory operations flown during the four days before the offensive, no fewer than 43 aircraft were lost in action and 67 men killed or missing; 26 other aircraft were lost in accidents. No.25 Squadron, despite being heavily engaged, but well escorted, lost only two aircraft, with two men killed and three made prisoners of war.

As air activity increased after 9th April, and British losses climbed rapidly, calls for heavier protection of the reconnaissance machines became increasingly difficult to provide, that is until the RNAS agreed to 'lend' squadrons of Sopwith Pups and Triplanes, far superior to the fighters immediately available to the RFC. These were greatly respected by the German pilots, even including von Richthofen and other high-scoring Germans, who frequently broke away from the fight, having discovered – often to their cost – the unaccustomed agility of these British fighting scouts.

For much of the early part of April the weather had been too poor for full use of the opposing air forces, but on the 13th the skies cleared somewhat, enabling the Germans to fly protective patrols against Allied forces seeking to interfere with enemy troop movements. In a concerted effort to attack the German rail-head at Henin-Lietard, no fewer than 38 aircraft from Nos.19, 25, 27 and 66 carried out a series of bombing raids during this day. A formation of about six F.E.s of No.25 Squadron, escorted by a similar number of Nieuports of No.40 Squadron, had successfully attacked the target when the escort departed from the scene, whereupon a large formation of German fighting scouts appeared. Believing that the new arrivals were the escort returning, the No.25 Squadron pilots turned to meet them, placing themselves at the mercy of *Jasta* 3, 4 and 11, led once more by Manfred Freiherr von Richthofen, who promptly shot down the F.E. flown by 2/Lt A H Bates, with Sgt W A Barnes his observer; Leutnant Hans Klein of *Jasta* 4 shot down the aircraft of Capt L L Richardson (an Australian on No.25), and Leutnant E Bauer of *Jasta* 3 despatched the aircraft of J Dempsey and 2/Lt W H Green, with such clinical precision that the Germans were later able to file all the details of the British crews and aircraft (and although Richthofen subsequently acquired part of his victim's aircraft as a souvenir and correctly recorded its serial number, he again identified it as a 'Vickers'). So economically executed was the initial German attack that, when No.40 Squadron's pilots rushed back to protect No.25's survivors, Richthofen had long since led his formation away. In this action No.25 lost two pilots and two observers killed, and one pilot and one observer taken prisoner.

As the Allied offensive stalled and the subsequent German 'push' made good lost ground, 'Bloody April' ended in a crescendo of air activity but, thanks to representations made to Brigade HQ about the frequent failure by RFC escorts to arrive at their planned rendezvous, Major Cherry himself declined to commit his crews and aircraft to what he saw as suicidal sorties unless the squadrons with reputations for missing their rendezvous were at the meeting point *in advance* of the planned time!

Despite being engaged in half a dozen combats during the last ten days of April, the pilots of No.25 Squadron felt that they had been sidelined on too many occasions, much of their flying being confined to patrolling *behind* the Allied lines, and only infrequently being called on to fly photographic sorties. On other occasions sections had been sent up to meet and escort home the photographic aircraft of *other* squadrons.

Then, during the first week in May, Major Cherry was informed that he was being posted home, news that was accompanied by a notice to the effect that the Squadron was to be re-equipped with D.H.4 light bombers, this latter being met with mixed feelings by the pilots and observers – most of whom regarded themselves primarily as 'fighter' men, occasionally employed as flying photographers'. With such aircraft as the Sopwith Pup and Triplane, S.E.5 and S.E.5A, and Bristol F.2b Fighter, now becoming firmly established in service, this could hardly be an accurate assessment by pilots of the F.E.2, whose origins lay more than two years in the past and which, if one was honest, had become obsolete well over a year previously. The Squadron's increasing use as escort for corps reconnaissance aircraft during April had usually been little more than a forlorn measure to put a few more machine guns into the air, in the hope that they just might occupy some of the nimble enemy fighting scouts. *Sic transit gloria mundi!*

It would be wrong to suggest that Cherry's departure came about as a result of any culpable shortcomings as the Squadron's commanding officer. He had held the Squadron together in some difficult situations, and had backed his all-important flight commanders in their operational capacities. He had done a great deal to improve the living conditions of flying and ground personnel alike (more than could be said of several other squadron commanders of the period). He was not over-generous in endorsing recommendations for gallantry decorations – as far as can be discovered he only recommended the award of four Military Crosses during his entire tenure of command, as well as about a score of Mentions in Despatches, by far the lowest number of any squadron in the Brigade. It is likely that, having been in command for about a year (rather longer than was usual) it was evidently considered that the change-over to the D.H.4 light bomber was a convenient time for a change of command.

Nevertheless the arrival and service of the D.H.4 was indicative of the War Department's assessment of air fighting, particularly on the Western Front. Whereas the Germans, after 1915, were constantly introducing new and improved aircraft, generally 'overlapping' older aircraft by only two or three months, the War Office seldom took account of a new aircraft's inevitable obsolescence, and once a new aircraft arrived in service, all thought of an eventual replacement was dismissed. The D.H.4 was an excellent example and, good though the aircraft was by the standards of mid-1917, it was becoming obsolete by the end of that year – and there was no immediate replacement in sight. When the hurriedly-prepared D.H.9 appeared about six months later, it was found to be, at best, no better that the D.H.4 in some respects, and a good deal worse in others. The R.E.8 was, of course another example of this lack of forethought, and that aeroplane, introduced shortly before 'bloody April' (suffering heavy casualties), continued in service with numerous squadrons until the end of the War.

Just how out-of-date the F.E.2b had become was evident when the first six D.H.4s arrived at Auchel late in May and early June 1917. Powered by the 250hp Rolls-Royce in-line engine, and capable of carrying either four 112lb or two 230lb bombs, the new aircraft possessed a top speed of 116 mph at sea level and was armed with a single synchronised machine gun and either one or two rotatable Lewis guns on the rear cockpit. It was a pleasant aircraft to fly, with few apparent vices, and was robustly designed. Indeed, in many experienced pilots' estimation, the D.H.4 was the best of all light bombers produced during the First World War. It certainly shouldered a very heavy responsibility during the last eighteen months of the Great War.

In the words of the Central Flying School, the D.H.4 was described as 'exceptionally comfortable to fly, easy to land and light on the controls; the tail-adjusting gear (in effect a variable incidence tailplane) enabled the pilot to fly or glide at any desired speed without effort'. Nevertheless, as will be shown, the D.H.4 was to become notorious for the very large number of aircraft destroyed or badly damaged in flying accidents. That most of these were easily attributable to pilot and servicing errors cannot be denied, yet their very occurrence may be interpreted as a reflection on the aeroplane's and engine's design. In truth, although an undoubted advance over current in-service aircraft in mid-1917, by the end of the year many of the aircraft and engines were worn out.

Cherry's replacement at the helm of No.25 Squadron was a man of very different outlook and character. Major The Hon Oscar Montague Guest was born the fifth son of the 1st Baron Wimbourne, and had joined the Lothian and Border Horse on the outbreak of war; he later transferred to the RFC while retaining his rank. By all accounts Guest was 'comfortably wealthy', and a man of considerable charm and energy, who took care to keep a stable of several horses within convenient reach of the aerodrome. He appears to have been a popular CO, without seeking popularity, and his habit of maintaining a good table in the Mess (*sic*) was no more than an extension of his accustomed life-style. He also took great care to get to know *all* his men and their circumstances. He always took his share of operations, beginning by flying as a subordinate in his two Flights. He seldom made out the operational flying roster, preferring to lead the Squadron only when asked out of deference by one of the Flight Commanders. Unfortunately it has not proved possible to discover the name of the Squadron adjutant at this time, for he must have been an officer possessed of considerable energy and tact.

Unless compelled to do so by army regulations, Guest seldom originated signals to higher authority, for such – being generally of a routine nature – were left to his adjutant. Instead, the CO preferred to arrange face-to-face meetings at No.3 Wing HQ to discuss out-of-the-ordinary matters, drawing attention to shortage of aircrew for instance. This was a subtle ploy on Guest's part, to obtain at first hand a better view of the Squadron's intended part in the operational affairs of the Wing's or Brigade's area of operations in advance of operational orders. In this manner he was able to assess his Squadron's ability to perform certain duties. Armed with this advance information, which he immediately passed on to his flight commanders, the Squadron was able –when opportunities arose – to concentrate the crews' minds on preparing themselves by means of 'operational training'. This would sometimes take the form of sending one flight out to carry out a mock bombing attack to the rear of the Allied front, and then ordering another flight off to intercept the 'bombers' on their return journey.

Guest had been a flight commander on No.7 Squadron on 14th December 1915 when, flying a B.E.2c on a reconnaissance over Ypres, he was attacked by a Fokker EIII monoplane and had to make a crash landing, being fairly seriously wounded. Several months in hospital were followed by a short ground appointment then after a refresher flying course, he was promoted Major and took command of No.25 Squadron in June 1917. Although he struggled to retain as many of the existing personnel, whom he felt could provide the nucleus of the Squadron as they strove to convert on to the D.H.4, he soon found that most of the 'old lags' were exhausted, some having flown almost 200 hours on operations in three months. Most had experienced difficult forced landings, and some of them were still suffering from minor wounds and slight injuries as a result. During his first month with the Squadron, therefore, he arranged for all but about half a dozen recent arrivals to be sent home for a rest; he also asked Wing HQ if three experienced D.H.4 pilots might be attached from other squadrons, supernumerary to No.25 for a month, to assist in the Squadron's working up on the new aircraft. Two such officers are said to have joined No.25, though it transpired that both had been due for rest in the United Kingdom and neither remained for more than about a fortnight, having done little more than give a number of impromptu talks on the D.H.4's vicissitudes. If they did little else, they were at least emphatic concerning the one fundamental difference between the D.H.4 and its pusher predecessor: whereas the old F.E. had to be flown 'with some determination' into every departure from straight and level flight, the D.H.4 was light on the controls, particularly about the directional axis and, provided the adjustable tailplane was accurately set, the aircraft was decidedly manœuvrable – to the point at which making a perfect landing demanded a finesse only acquired by plenty of experience. This weakness – if such it was – was to dog No.25 Squadron pilots for a long time, as witness the number of landing accidents experienced.

No.25 was only the fourth RFC Squadron in France to be equipped with the new light bomber (after Nos.55 in March, 57 in May and 18 in June) – No.25's first examples being delivered before the end of June. Compared with the old F.E.2b and F.E.2d, the D.H. was in a new class of its own. With its 250hp Rolls-Royce water-cooled twelve-cylinder in-line engine, the D.H.4 was, of course, a tractor biplane with two-bay wings. It possessed an endurance of about three to three-and-a-half hours, giving a safe combat radius of some 140 miles, assuming no necessity for air combat. Later, in 1918, some of No.25 Squadron's D.H.4s were provided with twin-yoked Lewis guns, and at least one of the aircraft being flown at the beginning of 1918 featured two forward-firing Vickers guns. It is thought likely that the heavier armament was confined to aircraft that were allocated for the bomber escort rôle, simply because a load of bombs, plus additional guns and ammunition, would severely reduce the aircraft's speed, climb and range performance.

THE THIRD BATTLE OF YPRES AND THE FLANDERS OFFENSIVE

July 1917 was spent by the Allied forces on the Flanders Front making concerted preparations for a major offensive in an effort to reach the Belgian coast, among its objects being to deprive the Germans of submarine and bomber bases, capable of launching air and sea attacks on British seaports and shipping in the English Channel at very short range. Already, German daylight bombing raids by *Kagohl* 3's Gothas, based around Ghent in Belgium, had been launched and found the British home defences sadly lacking. The daylight attacks on London brought about unconcealed public outcry and Parliamentary pressure on the War Department to put the defences in order. An immediate result was for the recall of No.56 Squadron, flying the new S.E.5s in France, to an airfield in Kent to counter the raids – a measure that was wasted as being a classic

D.H.4, A2170/L, was shot down during a bombing sortie during the Battle of Arras on 23rd November 1917; the crew members, 2/Lt R Main and 1/AM G P Leach, were taken prisoner. It is seen here under German scrutiny. (Photo: via Ray Sturtivant)

example of 'too little, too late', never being called into action against the Gothas.

The plans for the initial stages of the great offensive did not immediately involve No.25 Squadron as a whole, as it quickly became evident that the majority of the pilots needed a fairly lengthy working-up period. Indeed, although the flight commanders and one or two other experienced pilots were almost immediately at home in the new aircraft, the remainder required at least twenty hours to become acceptably proficient to undertake any of the operational tasks likely to be ordered. In the meantime the Squadron retained half a dozen F.E.2ds so that some semblance of an operational capability could be maintained.

The first combat success by a 25 Squadron D.H.4 was gained by the flight commander, Capt J Fitz-Morris, and his observer Lt D L Burgess who, during a brief reconnaissance patrol, shot down an Albatros DV out of control near Dorignies on 7th July. Four days later the last patrol by the remaining F.E.2ds was set on by three Fokker DVs of *Jasta* 12 near La Bassée; 2/Lt F H St C Sargant, with Lt J H Kirk, shot down one of the enemy; their aircraft was damaged and Sargant was wounded. He managed to force land safely without further trouble.

The preliminary Allied attack at Ypres got off to an untidy start and failed to herald the opening of the offensive, which had still to be given the go-ahead from London. Nevertheless some ground was gained, as the Germans fell back towards a much stronger defensive line. Few calls were made for air support, most of the air fighting being confined to fighter-versus-fighter combat. During ten days in mid-July, No.25 Squadron only flew some sixty short-range sorties, confined mainly to watching for the arrival of German reinforcements and trying to pinpoint the location of German artillery, for it was becoming clear that the enemy was well aware of the coming British attack. On the 27th, while on photo reconnaissance, No.25 lost a D.H.4 near Douai, both crew members, on their first operational sortie, being killed.

During the latter stages of the Battle around Ypres, it was seen that the Germans were employing even larger formations of fighter aircraft than hitherto and, from prisoners who disclosed their Units on capture, it was found that formations of up to thirty of the new Albatros DVs were being drawn from three *Jastas* at a time. This was, in effect, the beginning of the Fighter 'Circuses' – originally aimed at overwhelming the relatively small numbers of Allied escorts for the R.E.8s and other corps reconnaissance aircraft over the battlefields. It was perhaps ironic that, in one of the biggest air battles up to that time, the old F.E.2d was to gain one of its biggest victories. On the same day, but a couple of hours later, that No.25 Squadron lost the D.H.4 near Douai, No.20 Squadron was ordered to send eight F.E.2ds over the lines as a decoy, intended to attract German fighter formations and lead them towards Polygon Wood, near Menin. The bait was taken and, after a brief chase (during which the F.E.2ds themselves claimed five victories – without loss), an RNAS Squadron of Sopwith Triplanes, and No.56 Squadron with S.E.5s (newly returned from its fruitless stay in Kent) fell upon the German *Jastas.* A further thirty RFC fighters waited above, in case the Germans tried to escape. For some fifty minutes the one-sided battle continued, attracting numerous other aircraft to the area. Total losses amounted to sixteen Albatros DVs shot down out of twenty engaged, for the loss of one S.E.5A and one naval Triplane.

The great Allied offensive in Flanders was eventually scheduled to advance on 1st August, but then the heavens opened up, with low cloud and torrential rain which, for four days, effectively prevented any significant movement on the ground and any air activity – even had it been called for. Those four days, however, enabled the Germans to rush reinforcements up to the front.

It was not until 14th August that No.25 was called on to fly an armed reconnaissance, with three pilots ordered off to join a bombing attack on a German rail-head. They were met by a formation of twenty German aircraft of *Jasta* 37, and had time only to jettison their bombs and try to reach cloud cover. One didn't make it, and was shot down by Leutnant Ernst Udet, his seventh victory in a score which would rise to 62 by the end of the War – second only to that of Manfred von Richthofen.

The following day, No.25 Squadron joined Nos.10 and 27 Squadrons with an appropriate fighter escort in a very heavy raid on German troop concentrations behind the front; No.25 alone dropped twenty 112lb HE and more than fifty smaller fragmentation bombs. None of the British aircraft suffered damage.

While the tempo of battle increased around Ypres, it was the turn of the British to extend its air tactics, now employing aircraft in fairly large numbers to attack the German trenches with machine guns and light bombs from very low level, a hazardous and haphazard form of attack in the drifting smoke of the battlefield. Although possessing a speed not much different from the single-seat Camel and other fighters, which were adapted to carry light bombs for these attacks, the D.H.4 was not considered suitable for the rôle. This was on account of its one major criticism – the unusually large distance between the pilot's and observer's cockpits – which effectively prevented communication between the two, reliance being on a simple speaking tube. While the pilot, armed with but a single gun, could spot and choose his own target, his observer could only fire at fleeting targets if they happened to lie athwart the pilot's line of flight. It was considered more sensible to concentrate all armament and ammunition under the pilot's control; with fighter escorts now considerably strengthened, the D.H.4's rear gun had become superfluous in the trench strafing rôle.

Good sense prevailed, and the D.H.s were almost invariably tasked with bombing troop concentrations and rail-heads close-up behind the enemy's front line. When possible, the bombers were accompanied by at least one camera-equipped D.H. (frequently provided by No.25 Squadron), whose observer's main job was to record damage inflicted during the attack. However, bearing in mind that most attacks were carried out from 10,000ft or more, the photographs seldom proved to be of much value as smoke and low cloud often obscured the target. It was not long before the Germans established large batteries of anti-aircraft guns around the obvious rail-head targets; they also provided standing patrols by fighters during the critical de-training and dispersal of troops, while field telephones

An unidentified D.H.4 of No.25 Squadron, probably photographed in 1918. While the appearance of damage to one of the propeller blades suggests a failure of the gun interrupter gear, it is possible that the blades are covered with canvas sheaths. The significance of the letters 'RAA' on the fuselage is not known. (Photo: via Ray Sturtivant)

between observation posts and the railway stations gave warning of approaching bomber formations (a precaution advocated by Oswald Boelcke during the previous year). Despite these precautions, the D.H.4 raids achieved a remarkable degree of success, with surprisingly low casualties, most of which were suffered on the long return journey against the prevailing winds. It was No.25 Squadron's normal practice, after completing its bombing, to climb to 15,000 feet (or higher, if possible) where they were almost immune from German fighters and anti-aircraft gunfire. However, this constituted an unwelcome tactic among the Squadron's observer/gunners who, despite their thick leather flying coats, were often literally frozen stiff, a condition, they claimed, that could only be corrected by liberal consumption of French brandy!

However, with the hard evidence of a significant number of D.H.s having to force land during the return journey through shortage of fuel, and, with the likelihood of an Allied advance, not even the D.H.4's relatively long range would be adequate, especially as there were suggestions that future bombing targets might be selected further behind the German lines. It seemed obvious that No.25 Squadron would have to move its base eastwards, if indeed the advance into Belgium was to be achieved.

Be that as it may, September (after a three-day lull in air operations due to poor weather) was to bring about a marked increase in demands for bombing attacks by the D.H.4 squadrons. The most ferocious of No.25 Squadron's air battles occurred in the evening of the 4th when a flight of aircraft was ordered off on a bombing attack and ran into twelve Albatros DIIIs of *Jasta* 30 near La Bassée. Such were the determined attacks on the D.H.s that there was no alternative but to slug it out rather than attempt to find cloud cover. Resorting to the defensive circle, the 25 Squadron pilots, most of whom possessed a good deal of combat experience, found themselves forced into individual combats, and thereby lost two of their number, including the promising 2/Lt Charles Pullen, shot down by Obltn Bethge. Two pilots claimed an Albatros each; one of them, 2/Lt Pike (also claimed shot down by Bethge) in fact struggled home with a damaged aircraft and a mortally wounded gunner (2/Lt A T Williams). The remainder of September involved a dozen or so other bombing raids, but they were either heavily escorted or were not significantly engaged by German aircraft. Several D.H.s were damaged by 'Archie' – the RFC's vernacular for enemy anti-aircraft fire – which earned a healthy respect among the Allies. (One aircraft, not of No.25 Squadron, was said to have been hit and shot down from 20,000ft!).

Guest left No.25 Squadron in October 1917, later to occupy a staff appointment at the Air Ministry following the formation of the Royal Air Force (he became Member of Parliament for the Loughborough Division of Leicester (1918-1922) and for North West Camberwell (1935-1945)). His successor, Major C S Duffus, had joined No.22 Squadron in 1915 to fly F.E.2bs, but his stay with that unit had been uneventful (other than an occasion when, during combat in September that year, his observer, while changing the ammunition drum on his machine gun, accidentally lost his grip of the magazine which, being out of control, flew aft and damaged the F.E.'s propeller. Duffus broke off the combat and managed to bring the aircraft back home without too much difficulty).

Despite remaining in command of the Squadron from October 1917 until two months after the Armistice, his name does not once appear in the Squadron's operational records; indeed, it seems unlikely that he ever flew with the Squadron, relying entirely upon his flight commanders to take full charge of No.25's operations.

Once again, the change of command coincided with a move to another airfield, this time to Boisdinghem, and at the same time some of the older D.H.4s were returned to the Aircraft Park, to be replaced by a newer version of the aircraft, now powered by a more powerful Rolls-Royce engine (though not as powerful as the later 350hp Eagle VIII). Boisdinghem, however, was not in fact closer to the front lines, but ten miles west of St.Omer, a location which suggested that, for the foreseeable future the Squadron's rôle would be increasingly that of reconnaissance – and less of bombing on account of the amount of fuel required to reach enemy-held territory. It was anticipated that bombing sorties would only be carried out by 'staging' through a forward airfield.

With the creation of the 41st Wing (later to become VIII Brigade, and eventually the Independent Force, RAF, in 1918), the D.H.4s of No.55 Squadron joined the new Wing, and for several weeks it seemed likely that No.25 Squadron would follow suit. However, once it had become established at Boisdinghem, it joined the newly formed 9th Wing, now under orders to fly all reconnaissance sorties from between 13,000 and 15,000 feet.

By the time – early November – that No.25 Squadron had settled into its new base, and most pilots had had a chance to fly the new D.H.s, the Battle of Passchendaele had opened – constituting the final phase of the 'Flanders offensive' of that autumn. This, and the following two months were a frustrating period for No.25 Squadron, with an average of only one or two bombing raids attempted each week. The targets were usually small and difficult to make out from the height at which the pilots were ordered to attack. The Germans was almost certainly aware of the restrictions on the bomber pilots and, because the damage inflicted on military targets was usually slight, the enemy seldom bothered to engage the D.H.s – preferring to concentrate their efforts against the ground support fighters and tactical reconnaissance R.E.8s over the front line.

This pattern of operations continued well into the New Year, with a growing number of photographic reconnaissance sorties being flown – as being more productive than the bombing attacks. It is worth summarising here the fortunes of No.25 Squadron during the period July to December 1917. It should be borne in mind that the establishment of the Squadron was theoretically three flights, each of ten aircraft; in flying personnel the Squadron was established for sixteen pilots and sixteen observer/gunners. In practical terms, not more than six aircraft per flight were airworthy simultaneously ('serviceable' in later, less logical jargon), and this allowed for a surplus of personnel either sick, wounded or on leave – or in circumstances resulting in replacements pending.

Airco D.H.4 Operations, July – December 1917	
Killed in Action	7
Killed on Active Service	3
Died of Wounds Received in Action	1
Enemy aircraft confirmed as destroyed	9
D.H.4s lost in combat	12
Airco D.H.4s Written off in Accidents	
Engine failure on take-off	3
Engine failure in flight	4
Landing accidents, adjudged unavoidable	9
Landing accidents, adjudged avoidable	12
Other Causes	
Ran out of fuel and crashed	1
Collided with hangar on take-off	1
Disposal of other aircraft (repaired on site)	23
Damaged beyond repair on site	41
Hours flown	
Operational	4,522
Training and other non-operational	2,002

THE GREAT OFFENSIVES OF 1918

1918 witnessed the fiercest air battles of the whole War on the Western Front. The great German 'push' of March that year was an all-out attempt to defeat decisively the Western Allies before the Americans arrived in France in any strength. That nation had entered the War on 6th April 1917, but had not possessed the military wherewithal to contribute fighting forces of any significance on the Western Front for many months. Moreover, what amounted to a Russian withdrawal of forces from the Eastern front, resulting from the October Revolution, enabled the Germans to transfer a large proportion of their military strength to the West. To add to the Allies' discomfort were the terrible losses suffered by the French armies (and to a lesser extent the British and Empire forces) in the almost fruitless and enervating offensive adventures.

In anticipation of the approaching German offensive, No.25 Squadron was transferred on the 5th and 6th March to the Fifth Army, whose front lay to the south, moving its base to Villers-Brettoneux, about seven miles east of Amiens, and for the time being to engage in high level bombing of German troop concentration areas in addition to its photo reconnaissance work. It was but one of 31 squadrons deployed in support of the Third and Fifth Armies.

Bad weather delayed the opening of the German offensive, and reconnaissance behind the enemy lines during the crucial 18th, 19th and 20th March, had to be restricted. Then, before dawn on the 21st, the German preparatory bombardment opened, the like of which had never before been seen, deluging fire on a fifty-mile front and to a depth of twenty miles. Five hours later the Germans launched more than sixty divisions against the British Third and Fifth Armies – which could raise no more than half that number. In the south, where No.25 Squadron sent a succession of reconnaissance aircraft, pilots reported that thick fog had rolled in and persisted over almost all their area of operation. 28 sorties were flown on that first day, all keeping strictly to the mandatory 13,000ft altitude restriction. Not surprisingly, there were no combats, no casualties and few worthwhile photographs.

From the outset the Germans maintained the initiative and made considerable ground. By the 25th the situation faced by the two British armies had become desperate, and the Officer Commanding the RFC in the field, accepting that reconnaissance behind the enemy lines could now be regarded as superfluous, had intuitively moved Nos.25 and 27 Squadrons (the latter also flying D.H.4s) to switch base to Beauvois, forty miles north of Amiens, the previous day, and undertake to commence close support ground attack operations '. . .on to the line Grevillers – Martinpuich – Maricourt. . .these squadrons will bomb and shoot up everything they see on the enemy side of the line. . .very low flying is essential. . .all risks to be taken. . .Urgent'.

These attacks continued for four days, with No.25 Squadron flying a total of 229 sorties, expending no fewer than 53,000 rounds of ammunition and dropping about 160 light fragmentation bombs. There is no doubt that the D.H. squadrons, to which two others were later added, made a significant contribution to the Allied defences. By the 31st the German assault had begun to waver, the cumulative effects of air attacks of its lines of communication and reinforcement having seriously eroded its army's ability to sustain the offensive. By the evening of the 29th No.25 Squadron had moved its base northwards once again, this time to Ruisseavillle, to return to its more accustomed bombing attacks, but with a much lower height restriction. Those five days had brought about the loss of five D.H.4s in action: one on the 26th when 2/Lt Fitz-Gibbon was wounded by ground fire and had to force land in No Man's Land; together with his observer, he set fire to the aircraft before escaping back to the Allied lines. On the 27th 2/Lt B L Lindley crashed on landing at base after anti-aircraft fire had shot away part of his landing gear; on the same day another of the Squadron's D.H.4s was shot down in air combat, probably with *Jasta* 36; a third aircraft also force landed, damaged by ground fire, but both crew members were unhurt. On the following day Sgt A M Muff was wounded in action, but his pilot brought the D.H.4 back safely. There had been one unfortunate accident when on the 26th 2/Lt A W P Cumming swung badly on take-off and struck a hangar at Boisdinghem, killing two Air Mechanics (see Appendix 1); the D.H.'s crew members were unhurt.

No.25 Squadron took no further part in the ground battles that eventually halted the German offensive, although the Squadron was warned from time to time to hold a flight at readiness to join attacks on the German forward troops. More often then not, bad weather prevented such operations. On 21st April the Squadron lost two aircraft in separate engagements, one on a reconnaissance sortie and the other during a bombing raid; in the latter the pilot, 2/Lt J D Dingwall, was killed, and the observer, Lt C M Sinclair (who had been wounded), managed to crash land behind the British lines.

On the next day the great German fighter pilot, Manfred von Richthofen, was shot down and killed, an event that was

Probably not a battle casualty, No.25 Squadron D.H.4 N7482 has very likely taxied into soft ground and dug its propeller into the grass. Damage would have been minimal and could have been repaired on the Squadron. (Photo: via Ray Sturtivant)

to have a profound effect on morale amongst the *Jasta* pilots for weeks to come.

With the increasing tempo of operations by the strategic bomber squadrons (soon to become the Independent Force), the D.H.4 Squadrons were sent increasingly against relatively short-range targets once more, enabling them to load up with maximum bomb loads, and the use of 230lb bombs became the norm. So as to avoid having to jettison these weapons if attacked by German fighters, the bombers were increasingly provided with heavier fighter escorts, usually comprising Bristol Fighters and S.E.5as. It was not uncommon for a formation of eight D.H.4s to be accompanied by as many as 18-20 fighters.

So it was that during the summer of 1918, with ever-increasing Squadrons of Sopwith Camels, Bristol Fighters and S.E.5as, the new Royal Air Force (including the former RNAS fighter and bomber squadrons) gradually achieved air superiority over the Western Front, a vital prerequisite for the last great offensive, scheduled to be launched in August. And the Americans were just beginning to arrive in useful numbers. . .both in the air and on the ground.

In July the Germans launched their last offensive – against the French front on the Marne and, having regard to the further heavy casualties suffered by the French in the air (more than fifty per cent higher than the British), Haig was asked to provide reinforcements from the RAF, a request answered by the despatch south of ten squadrons (including four flying the new D.H.9).

No.25 Squadron remained in the north with its D.H.4s, now almost wholly engaged in long-range (*sic*) reconnaissance work, not to mention the training of newly-arrived pilots, who were still arriving in France – seldom with more than half a dozen flying hours on the D.H.4. Nor were the replacement aircraft all that might be desired. Given that the aircraft's performance was, by mid-1918, somewhat pedestrian, there was no excuse for new replacement aircraft being delivered that were so deficient in standard of workmanship that, even after only a single 'acceptance flight', it was necessary for the Squadron to return them to the Aircraft Park. Several aircraft were refused on account of serious flaws in the airframe manufacture or premature corrosion. One aircraft could not keep up with the rest of the Squadron, even at 10,000ft; another would not climb above 7,000ft! Major Duffus might have been justified in seeking a change to the new D.H.9. Fortunately this option did not arise, simply because this supposed 'improvement on the D.H.4' was itself already in deep trouble with the RAF.

The design of the D.H.9 addressed the criticism of the D.H.4's widely-spaced cockpits, the pilot's cockpit now being located about two feet further aft. This was the only basic improvement over the older aircraft, but at least enabled the pilot and observer to communicate with each other without having to rely on the inter-connecting speaking tube (which was almost useless owing to the noise of the engine in flight). The only other significant change from the D.H.4 lay in the engine, and therein lay the source of the D.H.9's major shortcomings.

The engine chosen for the D.H.9 was the 230hp BHP (Beardmore-Halford-Pullinger), selected as being the only mass-produced engine of adequate power available. The

D.H.9 was ordered on account of its manufacturer's claim that it could carry a heavier bomb load, but although this was borne out in test, it took no account of the considerable drop in performance and serious wear on the engine (in which there emerged all manner of design flaws, evident as a result of mass-production techniques).

These shortcomings (amounting to the fact that in operational terms the D.H.9 was in fact inferior to the D.H.4) were recognised by Geoffrey de Havilland, who wrote to Major General John Salmond admitting the fact as early as November 1917 – but by that time orders for 2,000 BHP engines had been placed and production was under way. Not surprisingly, Major-General Hugh Trenchard was furious, and let his feelings be known to the Air Board in no uncertain terms. The only concession he could obtain was to limit the number of D.H.9-equipped squadrons to fifteen; the others would retain their D.H.4s. No.25 Squadron, on account of its long, and relatively successful operational experience with the older aircraft, was fortunate in being among the latter.

In passing, it is perhaps worth recording some instances of the D.H.9's misfortunes, if only to demonstrate that despite No.25's continuing loss of D.H.4s in flying training and other accidents, they did not compare with those suffered by the D.H.9s. The first D.H.9s arrived in France with Nos.98, 206 and 211 Squadrons in April 1918, followed by Nos.49 and 103. The following losses were suffered by these five Squadron during the first five weeks of operations with D.H.9s (excluding those serving with the Independent Force).

Squadron	*98*	*206*	*49*	*211*	*103*	*Totals*
D.H.9s lost in action	21	10	9	4	4	*48*
Crew Members lost in action	10	14	4	4	5	*37*
Aircraft Damaged	11	2	6	4	6	*29*
Crew Members wounded	4	3	9	4	6	*26*
PoW	14	4	4	4	6	*32*

During the same period No.25 Squadron, flying D.H.4s on rather more operations than any of the above Squadrons, suffered the following losses.

D.H.4s lost in action	6
Crew Members lost in action	5
Aircraft Damaged	1
Crew Members wounded	6
PoW	4

In addition to No.98 Squadron's losses in combat and accidents, it was unfortunate in also losing five D.H.9s, damaged to varying extents, as the result of a German air raid on its base at Coudekerque on the night of 5th/6th June, one of a number of German retaliatory attacks launched following bombing raids on Zeebrugge.

Among the aircraft lost by No.25 Squadron, was a D.H.4 shot down on 20th May by German anti-aircraft fire near Aulnoye at 15,000 feet (both crew members being killed), a remarkable feat of artillery by any standards.

Finally in context of this aside, one may cite the worst catastrophe to befall a D.H.9-equipped Squadron, No.99, which, on 31st July sent twelve aircraft to bomb Mainz. Three aircraft had to turn back with engine trouble before even crossing the lines, and on reaching these, enemy scouts shot down another. Pushing on towards the target, the formation was assaulted by about forty German aircraft and lost a further three D.H.9s. The remaining five bombers reached Saarbrücken, where their leader decided to drop the bombs and turn for home. One D.H.9 crashed in the town, and two more fell on the homeward flight, leaving only the leader and one other pilot the sole survivors to land back at base.

Not surprisingly, in August, Trenchard proposed the total withdrawal of the D.H.9 from operations but, with Allied preparations well advanced for the final great offensive, this could not be achieved in time without effectively reducing the bombing force by fifteen squadrons, as stocks of D.H.4s had been allowed to dwindle. Nevertheless, tight restrictions were placed on D.H.9 operations with the result that the D.H.4 Squadrons, despite dwindling reserves for use as replacements, were ordered much more frequently than ever before.

As No.25 Squadron, still at Ruisseauville, sought to increase its pilot and observer establishments, and stepped up its 'operational' training programme so as to relieve the more experienced crews whenever possible, one might well wonder at the state of morale on the Squadron. Three times since the opening of the German offensive in March, the Squadron had been ordered to shift base at very short notice, and then maintain a high state of readiness for combat operations, with very little of the ground infrastructure yet in place. Yet Major Duffus met each crisis admirably and, with the support of his flight commanders, managed to maintain a speedy and surprisingly efficient system of communications (with no question of any authority from Brigade HQ). To this end he 'ran' a daily flight between Ruisseauville and the aerodrome at Boisdinghem (where the Squadron equipment stores had remained in March, as well as most of the Squadron administrative personnel); more important to the pilots at Ruisseauville was the daily collection of mail from home – still being delivered to Boisdinghem. Gradually these components of the Squadron, were able to acquire transport with which to join up with the Flights. Incidentally, Duffus employed two D.H.4s which, having suffered airframe 'distortion' and could not be cleared for operations, underwent a cursory inspection on a daily basis 'just to see that nothing was on the point of falling off'. Their pilots had all received wounds in combat, and there was no question of anyone being fit for operations. The system operated very well, even on the occasion when one of the 'taxis' suffered a fuel leak and had to force land about a dozen miles from Ruisseauville; the passenger, in fact a sergeant returning on recall to England, walked to the airfield, explained the situation and returned to his aircraft (which had been repaired by the pilot in the meantime) in a van carrying petrol in cans.

There was no paperwork to complete simply because, according to all relevant records, the aircraft 'was not airworthy, but AOG awaiting disposal'.

Duffus divided his time between the two aerodromes, and was tireless in ensuring that all ranks were well fed and accommodated as comfortably as possible. Most of the time since leaving Boisdinghem had been spent under canvas, the nearest Royal Engineers providing marquees in which to store aircraft parts and accommodate the flying personnel. Two unmarried Sergeants refused to take leave due to them in the interests of keeping the D.H.s flying whenever possible. One of them would disappear on the pretext of 'visiting a friend' at a nearby aerodrome, his reappearance the following morning coinciding with that of a brand-new D.H.4 tailskid or an equally pristine carburettor for a BHP engine. In short, morale on the Squadron remained extremely high. this being due in large part to the flight commanders, men who not only led their flight on long and difficult raids over the German homeland in daylight, but trained men in their Flights to lead in their absence, whether temporary or permanent.

By the summer of 1918, with the establishment of the Royal Air Force as an autonomous third fighting Service, some of No.25 Squadron's more senior officers still served on detachment from their Army regiments. With final victory over Germany becoming ever more conceivable and the number of trained American soldiers and airmen fast increasing, the Flight Commanders (and their deputies) were aware that they would soon be faced with the decision as to whether they would choose to return to their parent regiments to pursue a life-long career in the army (as had often been their original intention) or accept a commission as a Regular in the new Royal Air Force – whose rôle in peacetime had yet to be defined, and whose very survival was still by no means assured. In the meantime, however, they must survive the inevitable last great Allied offensive that loomed ever closer.

By August 1918, No.25 Squadron was finally reassembling all its personnel at Ruisseauville, the Flight Commanders trying every administrative trick to rid their Flights of their oldest and most tired D.H.4s in the hope of receiving the latest version (the superb D.H.9a) as replacements. One of the most experienced of the Squadron's Flight Commanders, Captain Eric Waterlow, MC, DFC, had, alas, been killed in air combat on 16th July during a reconnaissance sortie over Tournai. This loss that was keenly felt by the Squadron as, not being seconded from the Army, he had already been offered a substantive commission in the Royal Air Force, and had filed an application to be considered for a Regular ('permanent') commission in the new Service; both his decorations for gallantry had been won prior to his joining No.25.

Another Flight Commander, Captain Alexander Roulstone, had gained six air victories in F.E.2bs and early D.H.4s before being posted to No.57 Squadron. It was for his fighting with No.25 Squadron, however, that he received his Military Cross. He left the RAF in 1920.

Capt John Edward Pugh, although of British nationality, had left England for Canada shortly before the War. Back in England in 1916 with the 19th Alberta Dragoons, he was seconded to the RFC and joined No.25 Squadron in 1917 to fly D.H.4s. In March 1918 he became a Flight Commander, but was posted back to England on 12th June, having shot down five German aircraft and received the DFC. He died in Canada in May 1966, aged 76.

While on the subject of combat victories, it is perhaps appropriate to refer to the achievements of the Squadron's observer/gunners. Various attempts have been made to compile list of victories gained by the gunners (or observers as they were officially described). Such lists would be justifiable if only for the fact that in aircraft such as the F.E.2s and D.H.4s, it was usually only the observer who fired the gun(s) that destroyed an enemy aircraft. On the other hand, it was the pilot who flew his aircraft into a position from which the gunner could bring his gun to bear. Traditionally it has normally been the pilot (as captain of his aircraft) who has scored the combat victory – and reaped the reward in the form of medals. There were undoubtedly many a very skilled gunner who returned a relatively high score of enemy aircraft destroyed, irrespective of the pilot with whom he flew. As a corollary, it might be said that it was the pilot who scored the victory by his repeated skills in placing the aircraft in such a position that even the least skilled gunner couldn't miss the target! Nevertheless some gunners were clearly outstanding, and these can be identified fairly easily by a glance at the Squadron's victory 'scoreboard' (Appendix 3).

Finally, regarding the 'victories' that constituted a pilot's or an observer's tally during the First World War, there were arbitrary criteria by which to decide how to define a 'combat victory'. No one could question a victory if the enemy aircraft was seen to catch fire and crash. However, a victory was claimed if an enemy aircraft was 'forced down', that is to say that owing to damage inflicted the enemy pilot chose to land (or 'force land'); sometimes the enemy aircraft was seen to enter a spin, or for its engine to stop; in either case, if the enemy aircraft disappeared into cloud and was not seen again, it was defined as a 'victory'. Such a 'victory' constituted an addition to the pilot's score. There is no doubt that this was too arbitrary to be at all accurate, and on countless occasions on which enemy aircraft were simply seen to disappear from the fight they should not strictly have been the basis for comparison with a score of victories comprised solely of enemy aircraft seen to be 'destroyed'. This was obviously a distinct handicap for the pilots of bombers and reconnaissance aircraft (such as F.E.2bs and D.H.4s) who were not in a position to leave their formation and 'go looking for their victims wreckage' on the ground. The same difficulties persisted in the Second World War, although much tighter distinctions were made between enemy aircraft which where 'destroyed', 'probably destroyed' and 'damaged'. No.25 Squadron, seldom employed in the fighter 'rôle' despite its original *raison d'être,* achieved an exceptionally fine combat tally, having regard for its operational rôle and the aircraft it was obliged to fly, yet was far below the scores achieved by those squadrons whose job it was solely to shoot down enemy aircraft.

• • •

Preparations for the final great Allied offensive included the launching of a bombing campaign on an unprecedented scale, ranging from the heavy bombers (the Handley Page O/400s of the Independent Force, whose targets were industrial cities up to 180 miles behind the German lines), to the day and night raids over shorter distances by the D.H.4s and D.H.9s, now afforded powerful protection by entire Wings of fighters. It soon became obvious to the German Air Force that the D.H.9s were easier targets than the D.H.4s, their speed and altitude performance being appreciably inferior to that of the older aircraft. Moreover, the enemy fighter pilots had been briefed to look out for straggling D.H.9s – and aircraft whose pilots had decided to turn back on account of being unable to keep up with the main formation.

Overall the Allied plan, however, displayed a new and relatively sophisticated understanding of the manner in which the gaining of local air superiority could be progressively developed by forcing the enemy to concentrate much of his strength in relatively small and often tactically unimportant areas; by thus doing it enabled the Allied bombing strength to be sent against key objectives with a much reduced risk of substantial opposition. No.25 Squadron, now widely regarded as a vital and highly competent tactical *and* strategic reconnaissance asset and, on account of the D.H.4's superior performance when not weighed down by bombs – was now formally classified as a 'reconnaissance squadron'.

The offensive opened on 8th August with a devastating artillery barrage around Amiens, followed by an immediate advance by tanks and infantry. By mid-day, air reconnaissance disclosed that heavy German reinforcements were streaming towards the Somme and, as bombers were ordered against the eleven key bridges and as several *Jastas* waded in, nine squadrons of S.E.5as, Camels and Bristol Fighters arrived. Losses among the RAF squadrons quickly mounted and by the time darkness fell, 41 British fighters had been lost, as well as eleven D.H.9s and nine other aircraft. The following day, in further attempts to destroy the bridges, orders were given for the bombing to be stepped up, fighter squadrons being allocated to specific D.H.4 and D.H.9 bomber squadrons which, instead being used *en masse,* were ordered to bomb in succession. Once again, the enemy fighters concentrated on the D.H.9s and tended to keep clear of the D.H.4s, No.107 Sqn alone losing six D.H.9s compared with a single D.H.4; the fighters on the other hand suffered much higher losses. On the third day the British abandoned its attacks on the Somme bridges and switched instead to the railheads and troop concentrations behind the German lines. By then the German fighter efforts were beginning to dwindle, as the Allied armies made good their advance of a dozen miles into the enemy defence line.

No.25 Squadron had only been called on to join two bombing raids and were only fleetingly attacked by fighters. None of the D.H.4s were damaged, nor were those which continued to fly reconnaissance sorties over the German lines and beyond, completing 64 sorties during those three days – scarcely a single German aircraft being seen. By 16th August Amiens had been saved, and the day bombers were sent against targets further beyond the German lines. In an attack on Darmstadt No.55 Squadron, with D.H.4s, ran into twenty German fighters which shot down four bombers, for once without fighter escort. Two days later the British army in Flanders began its final advance.

No.25 Squadron, still at Ruisseauville, continued to fly reconnaissance patrols, most of the patrol lines forming a triangle, based on Lille, one edge of which ran roughly parallel to the line of advance and about fifteen miles ahead of the advancing army. Although few escorts were provided, the D.H.4s, usually flying at between 9.000 and 12,000ft, were seldom approached by enemy fighters which were constantly being engaged by RAF fighter patrols over the slowly advancing Allied armies. The Battle of Bapaume, which was fought between the 23rd and 28th August, did not involve No.25 directly, although two photo reconnaissance sorties were flown each day to watch for any major German reinforcements approaching the front.

Then, on 3rd September, the Squadron suffered its first death in action for three weeks. In the late evening that day, Lt S Crosfield, with 2/Lt Edward Francis Boyce, observer (a Canadian), took off for a practice combat exercise with an S.E.5a of another squadron. While over Dixmude, they were attacked by five enemy fighters which damaged the D.H.4 and forced it to crash land. The pilot was unhurt, but 2/Lt Boyce was killed.

This was a prelude to further combats in September, as German airmen fought ever more desperately while the Allied armies advanced on their homeland. Occasionally the Squadron was ordered to fly armed patrols, sometimes carrying anti-personnel bombs, on the look out for enemy troops and transport in the open. This was not so much a reversion to the Squadron's former bombing rôle as simply the need to resort to any means of attacking the German forces which, as yet, showed little evidence of decisive collapse. It was more an attempt to weaken and prevent them from occupying a strong defensive line in their rear. The weather, however, during the first fifteen days of September, was atrocious, and for much of this period scarcely any operations were possible. On the 16th, both sides embarked on air reconnaissance as well as resuming all-out support for the front line forces, the Allied armies now concentrating on obliterating the German salients from the Hindenburg Line – the enemy's mainline defence of its homeland. As casualties on the D.H.9 bombing squadrons continued to soar, reconnaissance sorties by No.25 Squadron's elderly D.H.4s concentrated on these front line salients. On that first day one of its aircraft failed to return from a photo sortie, the experienced Capt Reginald Livesey Whalley and his observer 2/Lt Eric Bernard Andrews being posted Killed in Action. During a reconnaissance sortie the aircraft flown by Lt C Brown was attacked by enemy fighters, and his observer, Lt Edward William Griffin, killed; Brown, however managed to make a forced landing in Allied territory.

As the German salients were gradually reduced, preparations to assault the Hindenburg Line began in earnest on the 24th. On that day the Squadron suffered a tragic and unusual accident. On return from a photographic sortie, one of the flight Commanders, Capt S Jones (himself wounded), who knew that his observer, 2/Lt John Pullar, had been severely – probably mortally – wounded, landed his aircraft

A D.H.9a of 'B' Flight, No.25 Squadron, H3452, at Bickendorf, Germany in July 1919. (Photo: Capt Chetwynd Stapleton, RAF)

and, leaving the engine idling, stopped and called to two orderlies to help him remove the wounded observer from the aircraft so that he could be carried away by stretcher, and to put ballast in the rear cockpit. As this was being done the engine throttle was accidentally opened and the aircraft surged forward and eventually overturned, injuring Jones, but the observer was found to be dead. The orderlies were unhurt.

The following day, during the preparations for the Battle of the Canal du Nord (which constituted the opening phase of the assault on the Hindenburg Line) a D.H.4 of 25 Squadron failed to return from an early morning reconnaissance of the German defences on the canal, most probably shot down by ground fire; both crew members, Lt Dudley Howard Hazell and his 18-year-old observer, 2/Lt David Brown Robertson, were later confirmed Killed in Action.

Amidst rumours that the Squadron was about to be re-equipped with the new version of the D.H.9 – the long-lived and greatly improved D.H.9a – it was clear that the British army was through the main Hindenburg defences on a front of more than five miles, and that victory was in sight. Interrogation of prisoners indicated that there was increasing unrest among ships of the Imperial German Navy, and outbreaks of rioting in some German cities. The German Air Force, however, still fought fiercely, though with a growling lack of cohesion. No.25 Squadron was now occupied on reconnaissance over German towns, sometimes as much as fifty miles behind the battle line. The Squadron lost an aircraft on 3rd October, and another the following day, the first near the French border with Belgium at Maubeuge and the second in unknown circumstances. All four crew members perished.

On the 27th the Squadron quit Ruisseauville for La Brayelles, just north of Douai and almost immediately started receiving new D.H.9as. Powered by the 400hp American Liberty 12 engine, the new aircraft possessed a maximum speed of 123mph at sea level and, when loaded with two 230lb bombs, could reach a ceiling of 18,000ft; its maximum bomb load was 600lb. Only one feature proved unpopular at the outset, namely its coil ignition, but once mastered by the pilot the engine ran well and was reliable.

It seems that No.25 Squadron received no more that about nine examples of the D.H.9a, such was the demand to replace as many of the disgraced D.H.9 as quickly as possible. (The new aircraft had, incidentally, been in service with the Independent Force for several months with considerable success.) No.25 began flying the new aircraft almost immediately.*

* A number of excellent and usually reliable works of reference state categorically that no D.H.9as reached the RAF in France before the Armistice. It has however been established without doubt that these aircraft began arriving in France before the end of August 1918, and that more than fifty examples were in action with Nos.205 and 207 Squadrons of the RAF fighting over the northern area of the Western Front, and with Nos.55 and 110 Squadrons of the Independent Force by the end of September; of these, twelve had been lost in combat. By the date of the Armistice the total number of D.H.9as delivered had reached 203, of which 29 had been lost in action, or written off as the result of combat. The heaviest casualties in a single raid were suffered by No.110 Squadron in a raid on Frankfurt on 21st October, with seven aircraft lost to enemy action out of the thirteen aircraft that set out. Eleven of the crew members were taken prisoner, one died of wounds and two were Killed in Action.

Just as the Allied armies were poised to launch their final great assault on Germany, some of the fiercest air battles raged, with fairly large formations of enemy fighters being encountered all along the Western Front. On 1st November the Squadron flew its first reconnaissance with one of its new aircraft shortly after mid-day, but was evidently intercepted by German fighters and forced to land in enemy territory; its crew, 2/Lt Richard Gray Dobeson and 2/Lt Frederick George Mills, being taken prisoner. Thereafter the Squadron was ordered to fly daily morning reconnaissance sorties in the area of Maubeuge. It was in the course of one such sortie, at around 9am on the 4th, that the D.H.9a being flown by Lt Lionel Liffard Kay Straw, with 2/Lt Pybus Cartwright, observer, was shot down and both crew members were killed – the last fatal casualties suffered by the Squadron in the First World War. An hour later, another D.H.9a, flown by Lt J H Latchford, with Lt H L Tate, was in combat with an Albatros C; they may have shot down the enemy aircraft, but were themselves forced to land with battle damage; neither was hurt.

No.25 had not moved from La Brayelle by the time of the Armistice on 11th November, and remained in France for several months, there being no further need for reconnaissance. Within days of the end of the War, flying and ground personnel were being posted home for demobilisation, while other squadrons – now being disbanded, transferred personnel to No.25, the Officers being those who had either been granted peacetime commissions or were not due for immediate release. Indeed the personnel strength returns show the Squadron staffed by almost as many Officers as other Ranks!

The Squadron, while obviously not achieving combat victories as numerous as those of the famous fighter squadrons, had lost fewer aircraft (from all causes) than most of the bomber squadrons. Yet, during the last two years of the War, during which by far the greater volume of work had been reconnaissance (with and without fighter escort), No.25 Squadron had gained a reputation second to none, and scarcely a month passed without a despatch being received expressing appreciation by the Army of the work carried out Indeed, it might be said, with much evidence, that No.25 Squadron was the forerunner of the Mosquito-equipped photographic reconnaissance squadrons of the RAF in the Second World War – quite apart from its early rôle as a fighter squadron. It was a return to the fighter rôle that occupied the minds of men who recalled those early days and now occupied positions of influence in the RAF's higher ranks.

Post-War photograph said variously to be of Bechtheim, Merheim and Bickendorf in Germany. No.25 Squadron records state that it is in fact Bickendorf, the photo having been taken early in July 1919. Two D.H.9s and a D.H.9a of No.25 Squadron, some Dolphins of No.79 Squadron, and the Snipes of No.43 (lined up in the background) are visible. Also identified is a Fokker DVII (at the near end of the hangar, and what appears to be a Fokker DrI triplane between the Snipes and the furthest hangar. (Photo: The RAF Museum)

CHAPTER 3

(From the Armistice to Siskins)

"Some Preferred Chicken-farming"

After remaining in Germany with the forces of occupation for some months after the Armistice, No.25 Squadron learnt on the grapevine that it was to return home 'shortly'. Rumour had it that it would probably be reduced to cadre, at least until the future status of the Royal Air Force had been thrashed out, as Trenchard confronted the Generals and Admirals – who were already jockeying for the lion's share of the post-war defence appropriations. This rumour reached the Squadron while it was still at Bickendorf in June 1919, and early in July it was ordered to Merheim, also fairly close to Cologne, there to have all its aircraft thoroughly inspected, for it was intended to fly the youngest D.H.9as home, and hand over the veteran D.H.4s to another squadron in Germany.

At this time the Squadron possessed seven D.H.4s and eight D.H.9as, as well as a Camel and two Avro 504Ks (the Camel having arrived with one of the succession of seven COs who commanded No.25 during 1919 – and got left behind as each was posted home for release). When No.25 reached Merheim, demobilisation had reduced the Squadron strength to fourteen officers (eight pilots, three observers, the adjutant, a medical officer and a padre), eighteen NCOs (of whom seven were NCO observers) and about 40 Other Ranks, of whom only three were armourers – presumably in the belief that guns and bombs were now superfluous. A moratorium had been declared on any further demobilisation in Germany; in compassionate and medical cases, men were to be flown home to end their military service. One of the latter was the Squadron intelligence officer, posted home with suspected malaria.

It was on account of the large number of technical personnel who had assembled at Merheim that the Squadron was moved there in preparation for its flight home. In the event, all the D.H.9as were deemed safe to fly home, the flight, via St.Omer, beginning on 4th September and finishing at South Carlton, Lincolnshire, two days later.

By then it was no secret that the CO, Major G G A Williams, was not a well man and, although he had technically retired from the RFC on 1st April 1918, he had been asked to transfer to the RAF with the rank of Squadron Leader, and then to remain in the Service until its future could be clarified. At some time during the autumn of 1919 he was called to attend a Board in London, and was officially Retired on Sickness Pension in December that year.

IT'S NOT WHAT YOU KNOW, BUT WHO

However, during the last four months of 1919 a train of events occurred that were to have a lasting influence on No.25 Squadron's future fortunes. It seems that Major Williams, on his return home from Germany, landed at the former RFC Depot at Hawkinge, near Folkestone, probably to refuel and drop in at the Mess hut for lunch. In the course of his brief visit he met an old friend, Sqn Ldr Sir Norman Leslie (8th Baronet, and a fairly wealthy man who, at the time, was about to leave his post as the British Aïr Attaché in Paris). It has been said that the latter officer had been privy to some decisions that had been taken at the Air Ministry for the almost complete disbandment of the RAF's home-based fighter squadrons, and the closure of the majority of the former Depot stations. Whether this was a price being paid by Trenchard to the Generals and Admirals so as to be able to keep the RAF's bomber arm, or whether it was forced on Trenchard by Sir Eric Geddes (of 'axing' fame), cannot be discovered – although it is known that Trenchard would have sacrificed almost any part of the young RAF (particularly the fighter arm) so long as he could keep what he felt was the *raison d'être* of his Service – namely the bomber arm. It should be recalled that No.25 Squadron ended the War classified as a reconnaissance unit, and as such was neither fish nor fowl in peacetime

Be that as it may, no evidence can be found that Williams informed anyone on the Squadron (which by now was resident at South Carlton) of his conversation with Sir Norman Leslie. The order was posted that a large number of RAF squadrons were to disband at 23.59hrs on 31st December 1919, their personnel being sent on leave while it was decided whether to offer re-engagement elsewhere in the Service or to discharge them on assisted retirement. The following day six of the officers and about a score of NCOs and Other Ranks, former members of No.25 Squadron arrived at Hawkinge where they were met by none other than Sir Norman Leslie, who told them that he had been appointed to take command of No.25 Squadron in place of Major Williams, *vide ante,* at least on a temporary basis. He explained that, although they were still technically serving members of the RAF and entitled to be on Government property, he hoped to be able to secure the re-formation of their Squadron in the near future, if possible at Hawkinge provided the Air Ministry could secure a further lease on the land. Certainly nothing was likely to be done in the near future to vacate the former Depot Station; the hangars still contained large quantities of aircraft components, fully equipped workshops, and an armoury. There was an adjutant in residence who was said to be trying to make up his mind whether to accept a Commission in the Royal Air Force or to take up chicken-farming – then said to be all the rage among demobilised officers. The War Department had commandeered huge tracts of land during the War, and many of the former owners appeared to have no interest in purchasing back land that had become fallow through disuse; the alternative choice was to offer the land for sale as smallholdings. Chicken-farming appeared to be the simplest means of scratching a living with unemployment rising swiftly as war industries were forced to lay off their surplus work forces.

To keep those of No.25 Squadron who opted to remain at Hawkinge 'in touch', he had arranged to have a few War-surplus Avro 504Ks delivered to Hawkinge, and explained

One of half a dozen Avro 504Ks used by No.25 Squadron for general training and night flying between 1920 and 1926, F8794 served on the Squadron from March 1924 until early in 1926.
(Photo: L H Weeks)

that he had already made arrangements for the fuel stocks held at the former Depot to be used as and when the pilots wanted to fly. *

* Whether all details of the situation regarding No.25 Squadron's status on arrival at Hawkinge can be authenticated (and they have been fairly widely recalled and recounted by some of those on the spot), the more 'official' version – and one that was quoted for statistical purposes during the following decade – is that No.25 Squadron was not, in fact, disbanded at all on 31st December 1919, but was simply moved to Hawkinge as a lodger unit (a term that was to undergo a different interpretation in later years) pending confirmation of its change of rôle to become a fighter squadron once more. Its establishment orders clearly refer to a single-seat fighter squadron, equipped at the outset with twelve Sopwith Snipes. The Author acknowledges the considerable assistance afforded by the late Air Vice-Marshal Foster McNeece Foster who prepared a long set of notes in which he recalled, from diaries, the train of events surrounding No.25 Squadron between leaving Germany after the War and becoming formally established at Hawkinge on 1st January 1920. As far as is known this officer, then serving as a Wing Commander, never served on No.25 Squadron, but occupied a staff appointment at the Air Ministry at the time of No.25 Squadron's move from South Carlton to Hawkinge.

What other wheels had been set in motion are open to conjecture. On 1st April 1920 the aeronautical Press published an Air Ministry Notice listing No.25 Squadron under the command of Squadron Leader Sir Norman Roderick Alexander Leslie Bt, at RAF Hawkinge, Kent. The Squadron was to be a fighter unit with an initial aircraft establishment of twelve, a total of 14 officers, nine NCOs and 70 Other Ranks. No trace has been found of an AMO setting out the Station's manning establishment, and it must be assumed that Sir Leslie was left to his own devices to create an *ad hoc* infrastructure until such time as a formal manning structure could be organised. Yet this process was by no means unique in the Royal Air Force between the Wars, namely that 'single-squadron stations' were to be commanded by the resident squadron commander and would in due course become responsible for the establishment of a headquarters section, messing and barrack accommodation, and sections for armament, motor transport (including crash and fire vehicles and an ambulance), fuel storage, and so on.* In a number of instances the officer pilots doubled as heads of these various Sections. In the pervading atmosphere of post-war austerity, it was anyone's guess when the Air Force Appropriations would be adequate to bear the cost of making more than a handful of stations suitable for permanent occupation by flying squadrons.

Later in April a couple of fairly new Avro 504Ks were delivered to Hawkinge, and these replaced two of those that had been in use since New Year's Day (which were by then showing their age). A number of new pilots also began arriving that month, and Leslie received notification that 'in due course' Sopwith Snipe fighters would be delivered to Hawkinge, together with four experienced officers who would take charge of training (a somewhat daunting task as two-seat Snipes were not yet available). In the event all the pilots were sent away in rotation to No.1 Flying Training School at Netheravon for a formal training course.

By the end of 1920, Hawkinge had been transformed. The wartime hangars had benefited from Air Ministry contracts for limited refurbishment by local builders; a small but by no means austere Officers' Mess with dining room, anteroom, three bedrooms for a duty officer and official guests and kitchen – in fact no more than a sound wooden structure not unlike a village cricket pavilion – had been erected, together with a hutted annex for squadron officers' accommodation; the MT Section possessed three widely-differing vehicles, loosely termed Station Transport (between them sharing such duties as crash tender, ambulance, personnel transport – for those with liberty in Folkestone or a railway warrant for leave). Some of the officers possessed motor cars or motor cycles – and these were 'looked after' by the MT Section in return for an occasional keg of beer or tins of cigarettes. Taking the place of what would later be the NAAFI was a shop-van, which was allowed on to the Station to offer for sale such necessities as beer, cigarettes, and confectionery. The Station Warrant Officer also managed a small store to provide the necessary items to maintain the personal appearance of the men – boot polish and laces, blanco, uniform rank insignia and the hundred and one everyday items required by men – effectively confined to camp by isolation and very low pay. An evening in Folkestone was a luxury that demanded several weeks of saving. A return bus trip into Folkestone – not five miles distant – would alone cost an airman three or four days' pay, assuming he had not invoked any 'stoppages'.

Morale throughout the Station was extraordinarily high during the 1920s. The average age among the NCOs and Other Ranks seems to have been in the upper twenties, and most snapshots that have survived show men with wartime medal ribbons and very few post-war recruits. Almost every

* No.25 Squadron was fortunate in boasting a corporal who had been a barber before enlisting during the War. On arrival at Hawkinge in 1920, when the adjutant noticed his former civilian occupation, the corporal was asked if he would undertake this as an extramural duty, to save personnel the expense of visiting a civilian establishment; the corporal agreed, subject to the payment by each 'customer' of one penny, which he should be allowed to pocket to cover 'his running costs'. The adjutant willingly agreed to this as being entirely reasonable; yet a 'captive' clientele of some 70 men returned a turnover not much less than a Pilot Officer's flying allowance, particularly during the days immediately preceding a Station Commander's inspection!

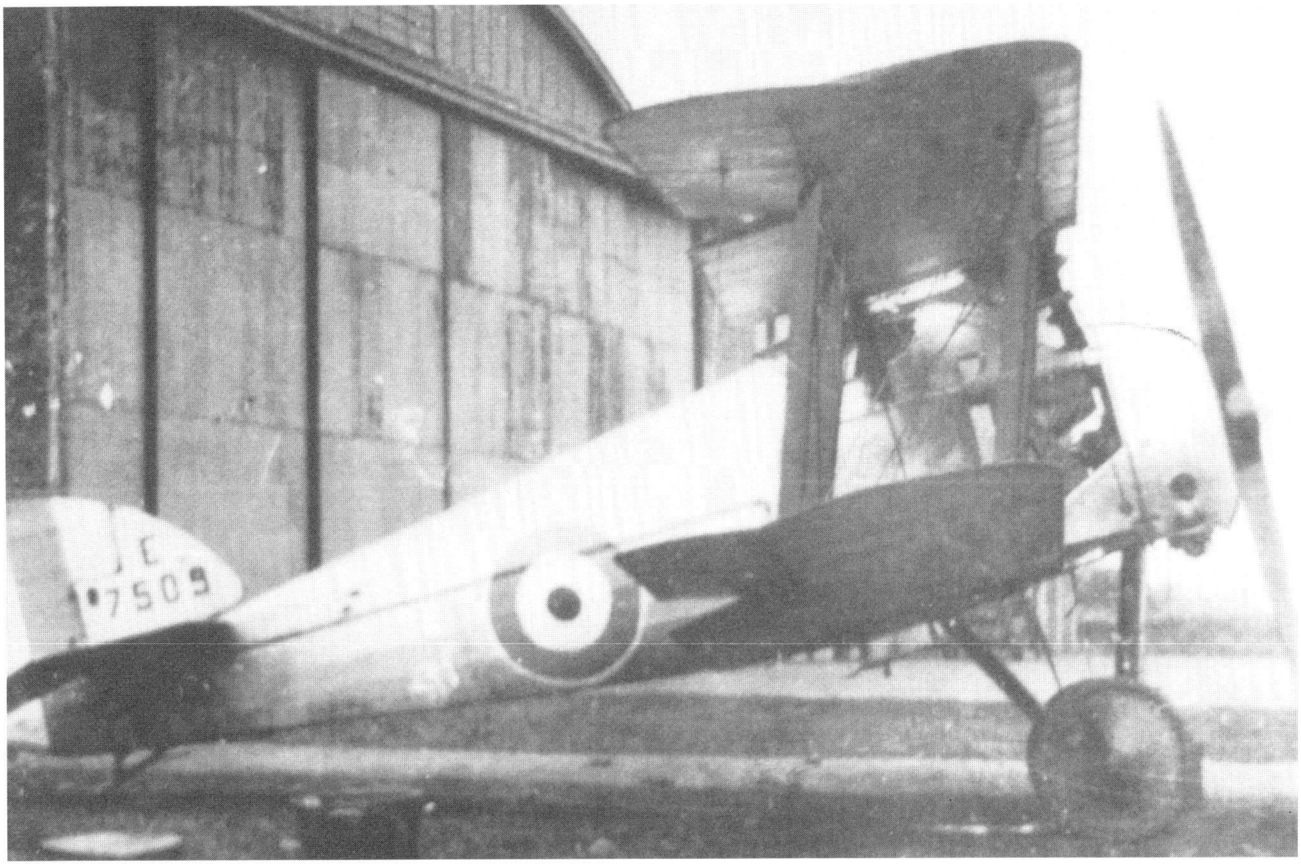

One of the Sopwith Snipes with which No.25 Squadron was first equipped at Hawkinge; this Ruston & Proctor-built example, E7509, served from April until November 1921. (Photo: L H Weeks)

Believed to be E7429, another Snipe of No.25 Squadron, pictured at Hawkinge early in 1922. This aircraft accompanied the Squadron to San Stefano, but suffered an engine failure on 25th January 1923; the pilot force landed at Haida Pasha and then set fire to the damaged aircraft. (Photo: via Roy S Humphreys)

one of the officers wore pilots 'wings', steadfastly retaining their old Royal Flying Corps pilots' badge. A photo taken in 1921 at Hawkinge shows eight out of fifteen officers wearing the ribbon of the DFC (at least three of them with the old horizontal stripes), and four with the MC.

One reason for the Squadron's high morale stemmed from the fact that, for several months No.25 Squadron was the RAF's only home-based fighter squadron, a situation that had arisen from the manner in which it had circumvented the otherwise universal process of cadre, terminal leave, preparation of operational stations and selection and posting of flying and ground personnel.

There was also the important matter of the RAF's command structure. Groups had been formed to administer the Stations and Squadrons, but many of the Stations (such as they were) were being de-commissioned and sold back into agriculture once more, and buildings demolished. Thus much of the RAF's early command structure had simply evaporated. For some weeks Hawkinge remained under the direct administrative control of the Air Ministry – a control that, on account of a somewhat rudimentary telephonic network, was tenuous indeed. Some of the administrative orders, which could only be passed in writing, arrived by telegram via the Post Office in Hawkinge village and a cyclist. The truth was that the "Geddes Axe", with its arbitrary cuts in all Government expenditure, bit deep and with a surprising suddenness; it caused something of a vacuum in the administrative officers' middle ranks – from Squadron Leader to Air Commodore. By April 1922 the entire Home-based (excluding Ireland) Order of Battle comprised no more than seven Squadrons:

No.2 Squadron	Digby	D.H.9a	Army Co-operation
No.4 Squadron	S. Farnborough	Bristol F2b	Army Co-operation
No.24 Squadron	Kenley	D.H.9a	Communications
No.25 Squadron	Hawkinge	Snipe	Fighter
No.39 Squadron	Spittalgate	D.H.9a	Light day bomber
No.100 Squadron	Spittalgate	Vimy	Heavy bomber
No.207 Squadron	Bircham Newton	D.H.9a	Light day bomber.

In addition there were two 'coastal' squadrons with Sopwith Cuckoo torpedo bombers and Felixstowe flying boats at Gosport and Cattewater (Mountbatten) respectively.

By contrast there were still a dozen Squadrons with Royal Air Force (Rhine), thirteen in the Middle East and six in India. Nor were there many fighters squadrons overseas – No.1 Squadron (with Snipes in Iraq) and No.56 (with Snipes in Egypt). It is as well to remember this extraordinary eclipse of the RAF's fighter arm when one recalls the urgency with which Dowding pleaded to retain his hard-won Fighter Command in the United Kingdom in 1940, whilst others (including Churchill) advocated sending ever more fighter squadrons to France. How many of the great fighter commanders have survived by the old adage 'Never send reinforcements to a lost cause'?

Returning to No.25 Squadron in splendid isolation at Hawkinge, it was at the beginning of 1922 that the Air Ministry began recreating a Group command structure, No.25 being included in No.1 Group whose headquarters were situated at Kenley. Indeed No.25 Squadron was the only 'combat' unit in the Group, No.24 Squadron being no more than the Group Communications unit; the other formations in this Group were the Armament and Gunnery School at Eastchurch, the Signals Co-operation Flight at Biggin Hill, and No.6 Flying Training School at Manston. It is little wonder that the personnel at Hawkinge 'felt a bit special'. An old member of the Squadron, George Chamberlain (of whom more later), on being asked what his preference of posting was on leaving the RAF College, he replied 'No.25 Squadron. Have I any choice?'. True, he graduated in 1925, but the Squadron – by its singularity – had earned itself an enviable reputation.

Later in 1922, as one by one, other Squadrons began re-forming (three of them), No.25 Squadron itself was ordered overseas as danger threatened in the Near East.

THE CHANAK CRISIS

As was to become increasingly apparent during the twentieth century, Britain (largely on account of her former Imperial domination of world affairs, and the proliferation of Republican factions the world over) became increasingly committed to a peace-keeping rôle, both by residual Treaty obligations and by Mandate. The ultimate defeat and

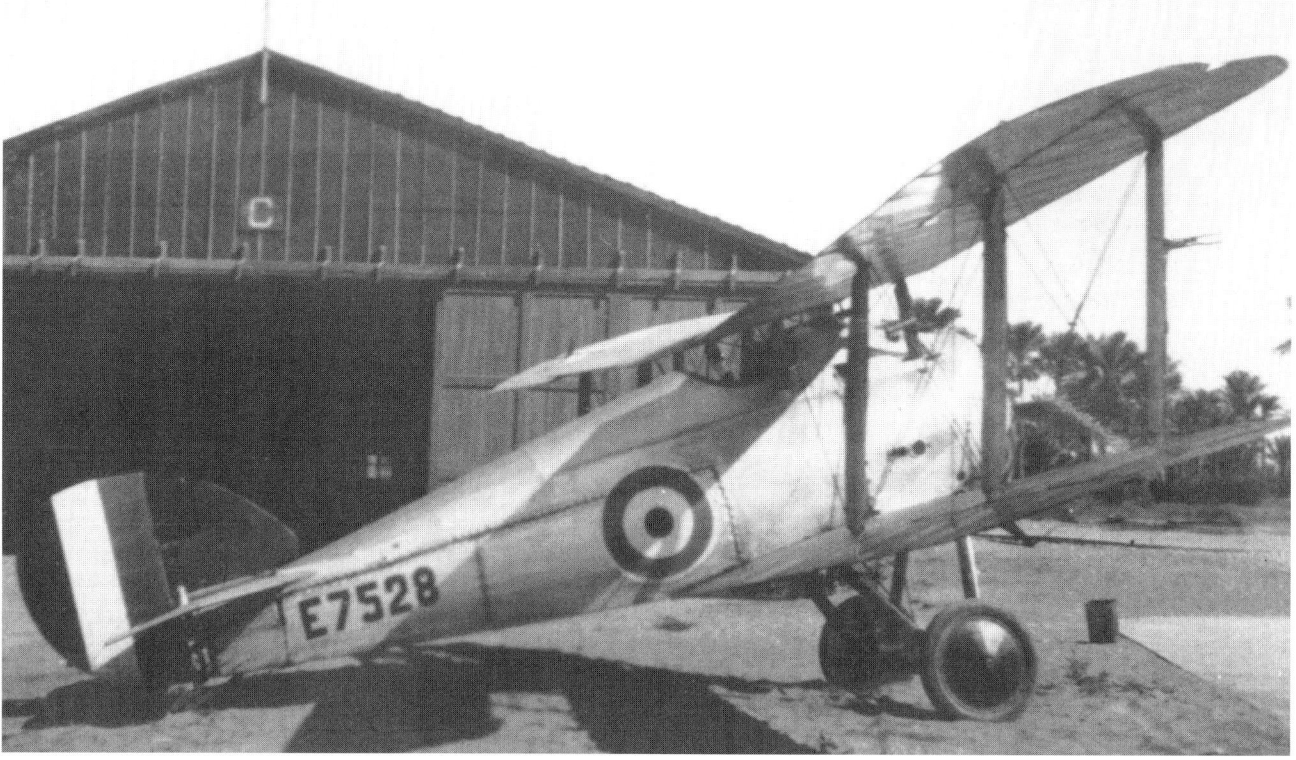

Sopwith Snipe E7528 was originally delivered to No.25 Squadron in about January 1922 at Hawkinge. It accompanied the Squadron to San Stefano in October, when this photo was taken, but was passed on to No.208 Squadron shortly afterwards. (Photo: The RAF Museum)

A pair of No.25 Squadron's Snipes, newly arrived at San Stefano, standing beside one of the primitive canvas hangars.

collapse of the old Ottoman Empire at the end of the First World War posed political problems which prompted the League of Nations to look to Great Britain and France, as the prominent and apparently best equipped Powers (politically and militarily), to intervene in the quarrels which seem endemic among newly-created republics.

As a result of the Treaty of Sèvres of 1921, a neutral zone had been established between Turkey and Greece, where trouble was expected, largely on account of age-old friction between the two nations. The security of this neutral zone became endangered when Mustafa Kemel rose against the Sultan of Turkey, prompting Greece to interfere on the Sultan's side. The Greeks suffered defeat at the battle of Smyrna in August 1922, prompting the Kemelist forces to advance on the Asiatic side of the Straits. French and Italian peace-keeping forces then withdrew, while Lloyd George, sadly underestimating the influence posed by the Turkish faction, decided to strengthen the relatively small British military presence. Initially effected by diverting a troopship *en route* for India – it was unfortunately loaded with non-combatant RAF personnel. This did little to improve the situation and, in part, led to the deployment of two RAF Squadrons, No.25 (with Snipes) and No.207 (with D.H.9as), to a small airfield at San Stefano which lies almost on the shore of the Sea of Marmara, about 30 miles from Istanbul, though on the south side of the Bosphorus*.

* One of the difficulties in tracing the events during the Chanak Crisis lies in the three different languages by which towns, rivers and other geographical features were known, namely Arabic, Anglicised Armenian and Turkish; San Stefano appears to be of the second. It seems that this variation in nomenclature was not recognised when RAF records and reports were prepared (with the result that references to the location of an accident that befell an RAF aircraft, appears to have occurred at three different places – a gaff that has apparently been overlooked in 'official' records of the Chanak Crisis!

Arriving to find both the military and political situations in some confusion, the two Squadrons took it upon themselves to engage in local area surveillance, on the look-out for any troop concentrations within a radius of about forty miles of the airfield, although as yet no information had been provided as to how to recognise a Kemelist threat. San Stefano was not wholly unfamiliar to the RAF for, as an element of the post-war forces of occupation, No.17

Seemingly incongruous in their post-War silver finish, these seven Snipes of No.25 Squadron are pictured at San Stefano, probably in January 1923. (Photo: via Peter Green)

Sopwith Snipe E7565 on the gun-butts at San Stefano, almost certainly during January 1923, soon after its arrival in Turkey. It had been built by Ruston & Proctor Ltd in 1918-1919. It later served with No.43 Squadron until 1926. (Photo: via Ray Sturtivant)

Squadron had spent ten months there in 1919, equipped with Sopwith Camels. When No.25 arrived, it seems that nothing had been done to tidy the place up since No.17 had left. Indeed, any visible semblance of order that had been achieved had long since reverted to nature. No.56 Squadron had also sent a detachment of Snipes from Aboukir in Egypt, accompanied by Bristol F.2b Fighters of No.208 Squadron in the army co-operation rôle, a term that replaced the former wartime corps reconnaissance duties (there being no Corps based in Turkey – but also precious little 'Army').

Both Squadrons from England arrived at San Stefano on 11th October 1922, although much of the support equipment, such as motor transport, spares, guns and ammunition, and stocks of clothing, being carried by chartered or other non-military vessels, arrived over the next three weeks. Indeed, as no duration of the deployment could be anticipated, No.25 Squadron, almost *in toto,* was packed up at Hawkinge, leaving no more than a skeleton staff and a bare minimum of ground and flying personnel to enable training of newly arrived pilots to continue. When the ships carrying the Squadron's equipment arrived at their destination port, it was discovered that little or no thought had been given by

Flying view of Snipe E6977 over Turkey. Records state that this was a dual-control aircraft, the conversion presumably being made later. Note the light bomb racks under the fuselage. It remained on the Squadron until April 1924. (Photo: via Ray Sturtivant)

Late-production Sopwith Snipe F2485. A rare flying photo taken in the vicinity of San Stefano late in 1922; the pilot is said to be the CO, Sqn Ldr Sir Norman Leslie Bt. (Photo: Air Ministry)

the loading authorities in England to enable important items likely to be needed quickly to be unloaded first, and there was a suspicion that the spares had been loaded in alphabetical order; Guns (Vickers) and Guns (mountings) were loaded in different ships. The ships had to be unloaded into lighters, but there appeared to be no tugs to tow the lighters to the quayside. Having loaded the railway trucks for the final journey to San Stefano, it was found *en route* that they had to be unloaded so as to enable the trucks to pass through tunnels. On arrival at the airfield the men found a sorry state of affairs – a few tents and inadequate marquees, flimsy hangars comprising canvas draped loosely over an iron framework. To make matters worse, a violent storm broke over the camp one night, and it was not long before four hangars were blown down or totally wrecked, as were the wireless marquee and many of the bell-tents. When the shelter over the power generator was blown away, the rain flooded the generators and all lighting failed on the camp. Fortunately only a small number of the aircraft had been uncrated and assembled, but these suffered some damage before they could be picketed adequately.

When the hostile elements abated, Sir Norman Leslie (who still commanded No.25, but was approaching the end of his tour with the Squadron) suggested that, in order to keep the men from dwelling too much on their misfortunes, a competition should be held immediately to see which Squadron could complete the assembly of all its aircraft first (the pilots joining the ground crews in the work – there was little else to do). No.25 Squadron won by about half an hour, but No.207's squadron commander entered an objection, pointing out that none of the Snipes had been fitted with guns. None had yet arrived from the port. No.207's Commanding Officer was none other than Arthur Tedder! He had evidently learned the benefits of democratic impartiality, if not sartorial elegance. Throughout his long and distinguished career, he never seemed to obtain uniforms that fitted him, his trousers inevitably being unfashionably short and his headgear always displaying evidence of a long life

View of San Stefano, showing the somewhat rudimentary 'facilities'. The aircraft in the foreground are the D.H.9as of No.207 Squadron which shared the airfield with No.25, four of the Snipes may be seen beyond. An attempt was made to provide trenches (as in the foreground) for cover in the event of air or ground attack, but none was experienced. (Photo: courtesy of No.25 (Fighter) Squadron)

'Hangars' for the aircraft at San Stefano were in reality no more than large tents – canvas on wooden and light metal frames. In the snow storm that hit the airfield, all the hangars collapsed, but with little damage to the aircraft inside. One of No.25 Squadron's Snipes is just visible in this collapsed shelter. (Photo: courtesy of No.25 (Fighter) Squadron)

of service. By contrast, his fellow CO was the picture of sartorial elegance, splendidly caparisoned as befitting an ex-Indian cavalry officer, also familiar with impeccable dress, appropriate to a former member of the British Diplomatic Corps in Paris. Sir Norman was also an enthusiastic pilot and loved the Snipe.

It took the men about a week to get the airfield ready for flying operations, although little could be done to improve to the 'field' itself which consisted of a moss-like growth on top of black cotton-soil which baked hard when the sun shone, but dissolved into glutinous mud at the first sign of rain. The 'domestic' tents were infested by centipedes and huge horseflies, while such bedding that existed in the semi-derelict 'Officers' Mess' was infested by bed bugs. Later, as winter set in, a powerful snow storm hit the airfield and considerable damage was suffered – including the wrecking of several aircraft; moreover where drifting occurred it was impossible to identify the airfield boundaries, which made for some interesting landings – despite having cleared a landing strip of snow.

Few orders had been issued as to what Nos. 25 and 207 Squadrons' operational rôles were to be, although the despatch of a D.H.9a squadron had implied the need for reconnaissance. This was carried out within a radius of about forty miles of the airfield, and it was necessary for Tedder to organise visits to the British Embassy to pick up some hints as how exactly No.207 Squadron crews were to recognise Kemelist forces from the air. When rumour had it that there was a possibility that some War-surplus German aircraft might be used by the Turks to attack San Stefano, No.25 Squadron's pilots were not slow to organise a system of patrols – although a suspicion existed that the 'rumour mongering' was no more than a ploy to permit almost unlimited flying by the Snipes. There were half-a-dozen instances of the Snipes being fired on by tiny groups of assumed Turkish soldiers, but only one aircraft may have succumbed to ground fire. On 19th February 1923, Snipe E7429 suffered engine failure and force landed on the Ismid peninsula. Acting on Standing Orders, the pilot set fire to the aircraft to prevent its capture, being soon picked up by a truck sent from the airfield. The station itself was always somewhat vulnerable in case the Kemelists decided to attack it, and a number of armed picket posts were set up around the assumed perimeter, until the services of a home-made armoured train, dubbed *Marlborough,* became available – being able to command the entire field with its arsenal of such guns as could be adapted for the purpose. Yet the danger of a Turkish commando-style raid was ever present, and could probably have destroyed every Snipe, D.H.9a and Brisfit in sight. However, they never attacked, even though the possibility kept the station on its toes.

As was perhaps to be expected, having regard for the state of San Stefano's landing ground, there were several flying accidents; these are recorded in Appendix 5.

Sir Norman Leslie returned home early in 1923 and handed over command to Squadron Leader Arthur Hicks Peck in February that year, on being appointed Assistant Secretary (Air), Committee of Imperial Defence, as a wing commander.

The political situation slowly degenerated into stalemate early in 1923. The Sultan fled to Malta, while Lloyd George had ill-advisedly sided with the Greeks and pitch-forked Britain into an untenable position at the Lausanne Conference as the Kemalists produced a list of forthright

An early Grebe, newly arrived at Hawkinge in 1925. Note the fuel tanks, situated under the upper wing. (Photo: The RAF Museum)

Snipes of No.25 Squadron during an exercise with the army, possibly at Upavon in 1925. (Photo: Francis K Mason collection)

demands. Only the election of a Conservative administration at home, and the ability of Lord Curzon as foreign secretary to extricate Britain by signing the Lausanne treaty with Turkey, saved the day; all the territorial demands by Turkey were agreed in return for the demilitarisation of the Straits (the Dardanelles and the Bosphorus). The RAF presence continued until September that year and Nos. 25 and 207 Squadrons returned to the United Kingdom, the former to Hawkinge once more; No.56 Squadron's detachment re-joined its headquarters – which itself had been established at Biggin Hill some months earlier.

Sqn Ldr Arthur Peck – known throughout the Service as 'Bushell' – had been an accomplished fighter pilot during the last year of the Great War, joining No.111 Squadron on its formation at Deir-el-Belah in Palestine in August 1917 as a Lieutenant. To start with he flew Bristol Scouts and D.H.2s before the Squadron received the S.E.5a. Promoted Captain and made a flight commander, he shot down eight German aircraft, his last victory with the Squadron being an Albatros DIII in March 1918. He retired from the RAF as a 55-year-old Group Captain in September 1944.

From the outset, Peck detected an air of élitism in No.25, both in the air and on the ground, and made no secret of the fact that he intended that that quality must be earned – and never taken for granted. He was a strict disciplinarian in all matters of duty, but was one of the first to join his pilots when high spirits were the order of the day. It goes almost without saying that he was a superb pilot, respected far beyond the confines of No.25 Squadron, and it was largely at his behest that every pilot should become highly

One of the first batch of Grebes issued to No.25 (Fighter) Squadron, seen here at Hawkinge in 1925. The Squadron markings, consisting of two black bars on the sides of the fuselage and at mid-chord on the upper surface of the wing, had been painted on the aircraft by the Gloucestershire Aircraft Company, but did not conform to Air Ministry instructions, being too narrow and too close together; however, they were allowed to remain until each aircraft became due for periodic maintenance work at Hawkinge when the markings were corrected. (Photo: via Ray Sturtivant)

A Grebe after having been repainted with the correct Squadron markings. Just visible in this photo are the 'wireless telegraphy' aerials, extending from the upper wing to the fin post; No.25 Squadron used W/T as a matter of course during air drill and routine training.

(Photo: via Ray Sturtivant)

proficient in close-formation air drill. He is on record, when entertaining the Aeronautical Press (in those days represented almost exclusively by the magazines *Flight* and *The Aeroplane*), as stating his belief that an excellence in precision formation flying instilled all the necessary skills demanded of a fighter pilot – instinctive and instantaneous reactions, 'eyes outside the cockpit', and complete confidence in one's fellow pilots. Another of his radical demands was that every pilot on the Squadron must, come what may, explore the furthermost extremes of his aeroplane's flight envelope, that is to say determine just what the aircraft was capable of achieving 'before it came to pieces'. This attitude was years ahead of its time – and was not formally recognised until adopted as a standard part of the flying syllabus at the Central Fighter Establishment after the Second World War! One of his favourite 'tricks' was to warn the Squadron pilots that if, while flying, they saw him approaching they were to formate on him and follow his manoeuvres in close company. He would in due course take off and surreptitiously climb as high as he could while on the lookout for an unsuspecting pilot. Having selected his 'target' he would roll into an almost vertical power dive, recovering several hundred feet behind the unsuspecting pilot. With his surplus excess speed he would shoot past the other aircraft, signalling the pilot to formate on him. He would then watch with some satisfaction as the other pilot tried every conceivable means of catching up-in vain. Number One lesson demonstrated: 'He who has the height has the combat advantage'. . .an elementary lesson perhaps, but it works wonders when one's commanding officer proves the point.

THE GREBE IS FLEDGED.

No.25 continued to fly its Snipes for another year, although the stock of War surplus aircraft had all but disappeared, and assembly of 'new' aircraft was running down as more modern types of fighters were undergoing Service trials and would soon join the RAF. No.17 Squadron was re-formed at Hawkinge on 1st April 1924, also flying Snipes, although it was expected that, owing to the station's limited amenities, it would soon be moved elsewhere. Peck therefore assumed the titular status of station commander, while continuing to lead No.25. A new form of training exercise had been introduced while the Squadron had been abroad, known as the Battle Camp, intended to provide a measure of mobility in the field. At short notice the whole complement of flying personnel (in the case of No.25 only pilots were thereby involved) would be ordered to another station where it would carry out exercises in support of the army in the field. As the Army's principal training ground in the south of England was on Salisbury Plain, No.25 Squadron was usually ordered to either Netheravon or Old Sarum (both stations being even more rudimentary in basic amenities than Hawkinge) for several days of concentrated flying, sometimes being given the opportunity of firing its guns at derelict army vehicles on orders passed by wireless from the ground. Shorter exercises were also flown over the South Coast, though without gunnery practice. On one occasion the Army carried out a mock attack on Hawkinge itself, although on this occasion the exercise fell somewhat flat as no one had thought fit to warn No.25 Squadron, most of whose pilots had been given the weekend off and were enjoying the attractions of Folkestone. On the Monday morning Peck was paid a visit by a 'somewhat jovial' brigadier who explained the significance of a number of coloured flags which had mysteriously sprouted up around the station. These, apparently, signified where 'grenades' had been thrown or shells had landed. All the station's aircraft had been safely locked away in the hangars. By mutual consent the 'exercise' was declared a non-event, and the parties repaired to be bar.

As Peck pursued his 'close flying' ambitions it became obvious that the Snipe was far from being an ideal aircraft on which to fly in formation. This was due to its Bentley rotary engine, which bestowed fierce torque characteristics and, unless constantly held in check, caused the aeroplane to turn in a direction contrary to that desired by the pilot, rendering close formation flying a thoroughly absorbing pastime. In fact, it is likely that few, if any, serious attempts by No.25 were made to perform aerobatics in formation on Snipes; much more likely were 'air drills' by up to five aircraft in echelon and vic, the aircraft remaining not less than fifty feet apart, the leading pilot giving hand signals which were easily visible up to 100 feet away. Such manoeuvres were normally confined to gently-banked turns through 90 degrees, dives in vic and echelon. Later these were tried in line abreast, but the Snipe was a difficult aeroplane to fly tidily in this formation. Most of the air drills were flown over Hawkinge itself, with a flight commander taking notes on the ground. There were variations, some of them, by all accounts somewhat hair-raising when seen from the ground, though simpler to execute in practice. These consisted of one vic of three Snipes flying head-on 'through' the other vic, aircraft apparently passing each other within a few feet; in fact the two vics had at least 200 feet vertical separation, while local regulations forbade such antics below 2,000 feet! In practice all formation flying, whether or not 'air drill', gave the pilots great confidence in, if not much knowledge of, their elderly Snipes.

Then, in October 1924, No.25 Squadron became the first line Squadron in the RAF to receive the Gloucestershire Grebe II (the famous manufacturer still at that time so named – it was to become the Gloster Aircraft Company on Armistice Day 1926)*. This attractive, if aggressive-looking little biplane possessed a top speed of 162 mph at sea level and was not, as it has so often been termed, a sesquiplane, though it is true that the upper wing possessed a larger span than the lower and, although the aerofoil section of the upper wing could in theory produce more lift than the lower, the net lift and drag of both wings were almost identical through more than 80 per cent of the speed range of the aircraft. Indeed, the aircraft was aerodynamically beautifully balanced, particularly if balance weights in the rear fuselage were exactly suited to the pilot flying the aircraft. The fuel tank, pilot, guns and ammunition were accommodated closely round the centre of gravity and combined centres of pressure (*à la* Sopwith Camel), so that using fuel and ammunition made little difference to the aircraft's handling. Almost gone were problems with propeller/engine torque, though these were always present to some degree in the biplane fighters.

* No.111 (Fighter) Squadron had received three prototype Grebe Mark Is at Northolt in 1923 for Service Trials, during which it was found that the aircraft needed a number of changes to be acceptable by the RAF. At the same time the Squadron was also flying early Siskins on similar trials, and the Grebe (warts and all, at that stage) was declared the better fighter; the irony of this verdict will be evident in due course.

Pilots of No.25 (Fighter) Squadron attending a battle camp at Odinham, Kent, in 1926 with Grebes. These exercises might be described roughly as an early equivalent of a cross between an armament practice camp and an ad hoc *army co-operation exercise. The then squadron commander, Sqn Ldr A H Peck,* DSO, MC, *is on the extreme right, and Flt Lt R J A ('Revver') Ford is eighth from the right. The wide variety of flying clothing is fascinating – the pilot, three from the right, appears to have secured his white scarf with his belt, and he appears to be wearing wellington boots over jodhpurs.* (Photo: Roy S Humphreys)

Fully-modified Grebe of No.25 Squadron with V-struts. Note the camera gun on the lower wing; it was customary to fly 'dogfight' training, using these cameras, directly over Hawkinge. The Grebes seldom flew anywhere without full film magazines, and any pilot who failed to keep a sharp lookout would be a legitimate target for a prowling flight commander. (Photo: The RAF Museum)

The Grebe became an immediate favourite among No.25 Squadron's pilots, the burly 14-cylinder, two-row Armstrong Siddeley Jaguar IV radial engine producing 400hp (compared to the Snipe's 230hp Bentley rotary engine).

Pending the completion of diving tests at Martlesham Heath, No.25 Squadron's early Grebes were limited to a diving speed of 180 mph, and this restriction was firmly expressed when twelve pilots flew (in Snipes) to the Gloucestershire company's Hucclecote factory airfield near Gloucester. Each pilot was given flying instruction in a factory-owned two-seat Grebe (which had been ordered in small numbers by the Air Ministry), as well as several hours instruction on the ground. Then it was back to Hawkinge where the new fighters caused much excitement and attention. Meanwhile the groundcrews were also arriving back, after having received basic servicing instruction from the manufacturers. Gone were the days when pilots were expected to carry out running repairs on their own aircraft if necessary, although they were still responsible for removing the cockpit clock after a forced landing – a traditional ritual intended to deny inquisitive civilians any temptation of acquiring a very accurate clock for their domestic mantelpiece.

Diving trials were proceeding at Martlesham Heath, where more than one pilot had reported what was at first called 'dithering' – but then hurriedly referred to as 'wing flutter' – a phenomenon about to be experienced by many biplane fighters in the mid-1920s. It was usually caused by too great an unbraced wing overhang – too great an area of wing outboard of the interplane struts. Indeed, No.25 Squadron pilots were quick to experience wing flutter at speeds somewhat lower than the limit set, simply because they were anxious to fly their 'new toys' to the limit, so that in mock dogfight practice the outer wing structure was being subjected to relatively high loads at speeds much closer to the Grebe's normal maximum level speed. After several fatal accidents elsewhere in the RAF, usually attributed to 'wing flutter' as being a convenient fault of the aircraft rather than what would later become referred to as 'pilot error', the Air Ministry sat up and took note. Various remedies were tried at Martlesham (including stronger flying wires), but without producing a cure, and it was the Royal Aircraft Establishment at Farnborough that eventually came up with Vee-struts to be added outboard of the interplane struts, thereby positively securing the upper wings' overhang to the lower wing. This transformed the Grebe into an excellent little dogfighter, which the squadron pilots could throw about without any 'dithering'. In due course the diving limit was to be set at 210 mph. (It should be mentioned in passing that the terminal velocity of those early biplane fighters was usually about 40-50 mph above the limit imposed on line squadrons, a limit that was dictated more by the engine's tendency to over-speed in a dive on account of the propeller's fixed pitch; serious and prolonged over-speeding could and frequently did cause calamitous engine damage.)

With manageable torque effect and plenty of power, aerobatics became every pilot's delight, and it was not long before loops were being flown by 3-vic formations, and more elaborate air drills were practised. There were still occasional flying accidents, usually mid-air collisions or misjudgement of landing speeds, but the Grebe tended to be forgiving in the latter instances, being provided with oleo strutted undercarriage. However, when one new pilot damaged his Grebe after a landing display of ever-increasing bounds across the airfield (ending with an incipient spin and little else), the order went out 'Just before you touch down cut the throttle and haul back on the stick – you can only break the tail skid' (This notice was brought out of storage and displayed again when the Squadron's next type of aircraft – the Siskin – displayed the same habits, but more vigorously).

By and large the Grebe was a forgiving little fighter and

No.25 became recognised as being the outstanding exponent of the aircraft, being much in demand to give public flying displays all over England, whatever the event or excuse. On one occasion the famous protagonist of flight re-fuelling and provider of flying trips at air displays, Alan Cobham, found that he had doubled-booked a Saturday appointment, but settled the dilemma by asking which of the two events was going to be attended by No.25's Grebes and chose to attend the 'other one', not wishing to be up-staged!

Eclipsing all these 'local' displays, however, the annual Hendon 'pageant' proved to be the opportunity, handed to No.25 on a plate during the summer of 1925, on which to demonstrate the Squadron's skill at formation flying in front of His Majesty King George V and enormous crowds of Londoners. To the accompaniment of twelve crackling Jaguar engines the crowd was treated to what seemed then to be an astonishing display of precision flying, led by 'Bushell' and quickly termed 'formation aerobatics', but which, apart from a huge loop in vic formation, was more accurately regarded by the Squadron as 'Air Drill' consisting as it did, of integrated dives and turns by three vics, each of three or four aircraft. Indeed the ultimate manoeuvre, initiated 'on the wireless' by His Majesty with the command 'Mosquito', involved two sections of four Grebes which dived and then climbed into a half-roll with a stall off the top, as the two remaining sections each of two Grebes in mirrored echelon, dived over the aerodrome side-by-side and then pulled up to break outwards into 180-degree turns before joining the flanks of the first two sections to form a large vic for the final salute before the Royal party. Executed at a speed of around 160 mph, this brought the crowd to its feet, seeming to become a blanket of white flowers as 20,000 people waved their programmes over their heads!' The national Press acknowledged that the Squadron had set a standard of professional flying that would be difficult to emulate. *

* The Squadron had previously practised trailing white smoke, but the Display organisers had decided against its use as being 'likely to create a dangerous fog in the sky, thereby endangering the public, should there be a mid-air collision'.

As for the members of No.25 Squadron during the 'Grebe era', a number of RAF pilots who would enjoy fame later (for one reason or another) had opted as a choice on leaving their flying training schools to join No.25, such was its growing prestige within the Service. Plt Off Richard James Alexander Ford – widely known as 'Revver' – joined the Squadron in 1924 on completing his flying training and, armed with a permanent commission, had clearly set his sights on a Service career. A contemporary of his, George Chamberlain, remembers that most of the young pilots who joined No.25 in the mid-1920s were struck by the apparent advance the Grebe represented over such aircraft as the Snipe (which most of them had had an opportunity of flying towards the end of their flying training), but 'Revver', who seemed more than a little ham-fisted in his early days at Hawkinge, appeared not the slightest overawed by the power of the Jaguar engine in front of him. As a result, and with the early discovery of wing flutter, he found the Grebe quite a handful. His ears tended to get blocked, possibly as he was unaccustomed to the Grebe's rate of climb from sea level (9 minutes to 10,000ft, compared with 14 minutes on the Snipe). A visit to the medical officer brought the advice 'hold your nose and blow hard', advice difficult to follow with one hand on the throttle and the other on the control column. Yet, within nine months Ford was master of the little fighter and became quite a display pilot in his own right, as well as being the pilot usually given the job of 'checking out' newcomers on the Squadron when a Grebe two-seater became available. By 1928 he had been promoted Flight Lieutenant.

Throughout 1925 and for much of 1926 Peck encouraged every pilot on the Squadron to exploit the Grebe's power to the full for, apart from its good acceleration (compared with that of the Snipe), it imparted much more positive control in formation flying, which in turn enabled the pilots to fly much tighter vics and echelons. And by all accounts, the sight of five Grebes tearing around the Kent skies was 'something worth watching'. Loops in 3-vic were now commonplace, and a succession of three slow rolls would result in relatively little loss of height – though Peck forbade any such attempt at less than 6,000 feet! Loops, though simple to perform, were not generally popular among the pilots, it being necessary to gain as much speed as possible on entry so as to maintain comfortable positioning throughout the loop. At least one Grebe (not on No.25 Squadron) crashed having experienced a fatal dose of flutter having in all likelihood exceeded 200 mph on the entry into a loop (albeit a solo loop).

To a pilot of to-day, all these early attempts at precision flying in formation, must appear so elementary as to be hardly worth describing. Yet the pilots of the 1920s were pioneers in their own right, flying aeroplanes to their limit with such a small margin of excess power available that the slightest deviation from handling precision could, and frequently did, result in the tidiest formation coming apart at the seams. One of those pilots recalls a split second's panic on losing sight of every other Grebe during a slow roll in vic, and not knowing in which direction to break away!

At last all the Squadron's Grebes had been modified with the 'RAE V-struts' and this happened to coincide with the end of 'Bushell's' stint as No.25's CO. As a pilot he was highly respected, and he went to great pains to leave almost all organisation of Squadron training and arrangement of flying duties to his flight commanders. Peck never forgot his happy association with No.25, and on every annual anniversary of the Squadron's founding – 25th September – he unfailingly sent a greetings card, no matter where No.25 was stationed – a tradition that was already being followed by former COs.

Meanwhile No.17 Squadron, still at Hawkinge with Snipes, had been warned to begin training as a night fighter unit and, somewhat cautiously began flying 'later and later in the evening', for the Snipe was probably one of the most difficult aeroplanes to land in the dark, for the pilot's view directly forward was almost non-existent. In March 1926, however, the squadron was re-equipped with the Hawker Woodcock, which was marginally better in this respect but which had originally been designed by an army officer and was rather unkindly judged by spectating pilots of No.25 as

Flt Lt Richard James Alexander Ford (later Group Capt, CBE) with his Grebe J7579 at Hawkinge. 'Revver' Ford flew Grebes at the height of their flutter problems. (Photo: Roy S Humphreys)

'an aeroplane which appeared to land rather in the same fashion as a Grand National racehorse alighting from a jump'. In fact, although the Grebe had scarcely diverged from the technology of the First World War, it was in fact a considerable advance in handling and agility, whereas the Woodcock seemed to have stood still since 1918. But then, no one really knew what the specific demands of a purpose-built night fighter were. Another dozen years would pass before anyone found out.

Elsewhere the fighter squadrons of the RAF, still convinced that the Grebe was fundamentally and critically flawed by wing flutter, were demonstrably reluctant to fly the aircraft anywhere near its safe limits. They were being re-equipped with the Gloster Gamecock, whose 425hp Bristol Jupiter engine bestowed a top speed only 2 mph more than that of the Grebe. Many pilots of the day swore that the Gamecock was streets ahead of the Grebe, yet it possessed its own unpleasant vices – of which its spinning characteristics were dreadful by any standard, a very high rate of spin to the right, which quickly flattened and a difficulty for the pilot to get the nose down to raise the speed for recovery (caused by the engine being uncomfortably close to the aircraft's centre of gravity.

However, the Gamecock was not for No.25, and without any suggestion of sour grapes it seems that the Squadron was perfectly content with its Grebes for the time being. This was, in fact highly beneficial for the Squadron in the long term – but less so in the short – as will be shown. The Gamecock was quickly recognised for what it was, little more than an attempt to soup-up the Grebe in order to placate other disgruntled squadrons, and disguise the fact by giving it a new name. When it was found that the Gamecock, despite the addition of RAE V-struts, still occasionally displayed noticeable wing-flutter (even though a Gloster test pilot dived a Gamecock to about 270 mph 'without *troublesome* flutter'), an entirely new fighter design, the Bristol Bulldog entered RAF service in 1928. This biplane fighter, with extensive metal construction, was hailed as the cornerstone of Britain's air defence for years to come, with its maximum speed of 174 mph, and remained in service for eight years, eventually equipping no fewer than eleven squadrons. By the time it was withdrawn in 1936 both the Hurricane and Spitfire had flown! But No.25 Squadron took a wholly different course. Who could have foreseen that, within three years of its introduction into service, the Bulldog would be rendered effectively impotent and obsolete by another fighter, and at the height (or rather depth) of the great Depression.

The year 1927 found No.25 back in sole occupation of Hawkinge once more and, despite the much trumpeted Gamecock's entry into service, it still attracted a very satisfactory stream of outstanding pilots. Pilot Officer Walter Karl Beisiegel graduated from Cranwell in December that year and joined No.25 Squadron, at once proving to be up to the standard expected. Within a year he was in the aerobatic team (the term 'air drill' having been discarded by No.25 as *de trop,* but still good enough for other squadrons if they wanted to keep it), although his landings occasionally left something to be desired, but then relatively few pilots completed a tour with a squadron without 'bending' an aircraft or two.

On 9th December 1926 an accident occurred on No.25 Squadron that demonstrated to Parliament itself the impartiality of death among those of the peacetime Royal Air Force. On that day Pilot Officer Purvis was taking part in gunnery practice over Hawkinge airfield (the ground target being a large circle of white chippings marked out in the centre of the flying field). While diving at the target Purvis probably encountered severe wing flutter and lost control, his Grebe crashing in a nearby field and bursting into flames. Despite the courage of a farm worker in dragging the pilot from the fire, Purvis had died instantly. It happened that the young pilot was the nephew of Sir John Gilmour, Secretary of State for Scotland, and the news reached him during a debate in the Commons of the increasing accident rate in the Royal Air Force. Yet what immediate course could be taken to prevent the occurrence of accidents, other than abandoning flying? It was pointed out, probably truthfully, that the Royal Air Force enjoyed one of the world air forces' lowest accident rates, in relation to the amount of flying it undertook – an achievement made possible by superior ground maintenance and flying training. The usual assurances could only be given to maintain and, where possible, improve these high standards but, like the costly development of military aircraft, it would be a slow process, and only just perceptibly did the flying accident rate decline during the inter-War years – to soar once more during the Second World War.

While on this subject, it is worthwhile mentioning that

an estimate of the cost of training a pilot of the RAF in the mid-twenties was widely quoted as being 'about £20,000', this taking account of accidents to, and depreciation of training aircraft and the consumption of fuel, oil and ammunition. The Grebe, with its engine, cost under £4,000 to build. The Bulldog was initially considered to be expensive, at about £4,400. With an annual Treasury allocation of about £16m to the Royal Air Force for all purposes – from pay to the purchase of all equipment, such considerations as aircraft wastage and replacement were of unaccustomed importance. Thus it was that the write-off of, or extensive damage to, one of His Majesty's aeroplanes through demonstrable carelessness or abuse of flying regulations invariably bypassed the formality of a Court of Enquiry direct to a Court Martial. Much depended (as always) on the Squadron Commander's statement for mitigation in the case of any doubt.

And it was in this respect that No.25 Squadron was particularly fortunate in its long line of Commanding Officers who, more often than not, were able to detect and express their belief in a miscreant's fundamental professionalism and skill – with the result that some of the pilots who were later to become the very cornerstone of the Royal Air Force ten years hence were saved from a guilty verdict and from future obscurity. Some, as will be shown, were less fortunate, such as the famous Douglas Bader of No.23 Squadron who suffered the loss of both legs in a crash while performing aerobatics at an illegally low altitude; at least one Commanding Officer of the time had forecast that Bader would come to a sticky end for his alleged frequent disregard of safety regulations. The same CO stated that he would have been court martialled long before his terrible accident if he had been on his squadron – and at least he would have kept his legs. But, as is well known, Bader was a very special sort of man, his determination to overcome his handicap was typical, and was confirmed by his outstanding power of leadership a decade later.

Squadron Leader W H ('Porky') Park, CO of No.25 (Fighter) Squadron, at Hawkinge in 1927 with his Bull-nose 'Doctor's' Morris. After he died the Squadron buried the car on the airfield.
(Photo: Roy S Humphreys)

It was in 1929 that another pilot's name, later to be associated with No.25 Squadron, was to distinguish himself with a Grebe, when Richard Atcherley (using the name R Llewellyn) flew a two-seat Grebe to victory in that year's King's Cup race, and in so doing established a new speed record for the race. His twin brother, David, was to command No.25 at the height of the German *Blitz* in 1941.

As for the Squadron's COs at this time, two names stand out and have become legendary in the Squadron's history. Both were intensely proud of their Squadron and, with a kind of paternal facade, ruled No.25 with a rod of iron while retaining a benevolent acquiescence to the attributes of youth; both were blessed with an innate sense of humour. In turn, their flagrant eccentricities were tolerated 'by head office' just so long as the Squadron's efficiency was never impaired. Such a man was 'Porky' Park.

Peck had left the Squadron in September 1926, after the

A Grebe in flight (not of No.25 Squadron), showing the newly introduced 'Farnborough-type' vee interplane struts.
(Photo: Francis K Mason collection)

The Grebe in which Fg Off Purvis lost his life on 9th December 1926 during air-to-ground firing over the airfield at Hawkinge, an incident referred to in a House of Commons debate on RAF casualties during training. Purvis was the nephew of Sir John Gilmour, Secretary of State for Scotland.

(Photo: C G Gulvin)

Plt Off Karl ('Bike') Beisiegel tries to appear nonchalant as he attends the evidence of a tête-bêche landing at Hawkinge in J7292.

(Photo: C G Gulvin)

longest incumbency of any of No.25's COs, to be followed by Squadron Leader E D Atkinson, who only stayed until April the following year, when he retired from the Service. Next came Squadron Leader W.H. Park, who had won an MC and DFC during the War. He proved to be an enthusiastic pilot, professing great enjoyment of the Grebe, although by all accounts his own ample dimensions made for difficulties in looking over his shoulders to keep watch for other aircraft – fortunately without mishap. His landings were also not beyond reproach, again without causing any culpable damage. He was a keen horseman, if only to maintain good relations with neighbouring gentry. His greatest attribute was, however his knack in spotting fledgling pilots with instinctive flying skills, believing that such Young Turks, *because of rather than in spite of* their junior status could well influence some of the more senior, but less assured men – always provided that they were kept fully aware of their formal status! Indeed, Porky was a stickler for the niceties of decorum and etiquette – for he had little influence over the recognised *status quo*.

There is an oft-quoted anecdote involving Park's habit of inviting local Kentish dignitaries with their wives to evening drinks with his officers in the Mess (which was still little more than an 'elaborate village cricket pavilion'). On one such occasion, amidst the rumble and press of senior sailors and soldiers from local establishments, Park spotted a particularly attractive young girl, seemingly lost and ignored by her seniors. Grabbing a convenient glass of

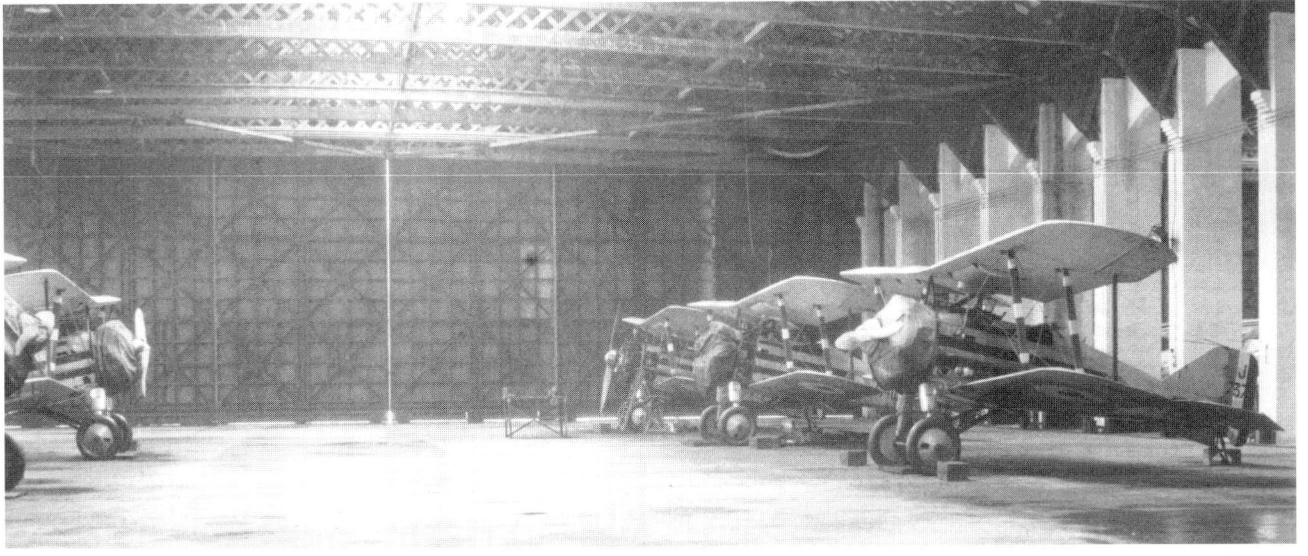

It is said that the collective noun for Starlings is a murmuring; a fluttering of Grebes would seem to be appropriate. These early aircraft of No.25 Squadron, in No.2 Hangar at Hawkinge, probably in 1926, have not been modified with the outboard V-struts to counter the chronic wing flutter to which the Grebe was prone. (Photo: Air Cdre W K Beisiegel, via Roy S Humphreys)

Gloster Grebe II J7569 was usually flown by Fg Off Walter Karl Beisiegel of No.25 Squadron at Hawkinge in 1928. 'Bike', as he was universally known in the RAF, was widely popular in the Service and, as a Wing Commander, commanded RAF Station Coltishall during the Second World War, one of No.25 Squadron's wartime bases. He retired as an Air Commodore, OBE, in April 1956.
(Photo: Air Cdre W K Beisiegel)

alcohol, Porky sidled over to make his favourite and wholly innocent form of welcome and introduction and, quite oblivious to a lull in the hubbub, began 'Ah, good even, m' dear. I don't think I've had the pleasure. . .', at which point the voice of someone who had perhaps partaken unwisely was heard to announce too loudly 'And I bet he never will'. Only moments later the Lord Lieutenant of Kent was seen, hurriedly leaving the Mess with his daughter.

On a slightly different level of humour, there is another story, apparently not apocryphal, that Park lodged in the care of his adjutant a sort of will with instructions that, in the event of his death, his Bull-nose Morris motor car, with a full fuel tank and an equally full bottle of brandy on the front seat, was to be interred close to the landing 'T' on the airfield. Porky, alas, did die in harness, following an emergency operation in 1928. His wishes were, by some quite independent accounts, carried out, with the Squadron personnel drawn up on parade and the Squadron's Grebes arranged in 'hollow square', pointing outwards. At a pre-ordained moment in the proceedings one of the Grebes opened fire and discharged all its ammunition into the void beyond, as being an appropriate salute to a lost friend.

Yet a third illustration of the light-hearted approach to life in general that existed at Hawkinge in those far-off days was provided by the 'famous departure of Gilbert Harcourt-Smith, MVO'. This extremely popular flight commander and a very good friend of 'Revver' Ford, on reaching the end of his tour with No.25 Squadron, was posted overseas and had opted to take the ferry at Dover. As seemed appropriate, the Squadron decided to give him a good send-off at the quayside. Unfortunately it seemed likely that Revver, being duty officer that day, would miss the event, but managed to persuade the most recent arrival on the Squadron, a young pilot officer (who happened to be teetotal), to stand in for him in his absence. The moment of departure from Hawkinge arrived and with a guard of honour accoutred with bayonets fixed lining the guardroom gate from the Station, a convoy of every squadron motor car set off with Harcourt-Smith for Dover where, arriving with some time to spare before the ferry's departure, it seemed equally appropriate to repair to the ship's bar to raise valedictory toasts. The duty-free inevitably had its effect as toast followed toast until someone noticed that Dover was moving past the bar's windows. Realising the predicament, someone was despatched to the Captain to negotiate a return to *terra firma* – to no avail, on account of a mere airman not fully understanding the science of tidal habits. The upshot was that final farewells were extended in French waters, before a group of dishevelled flying personnel, much the worse for wear after several hours of enforced incarceration in a bar, arrived back at Dover. It then occurred to Revver that perhaps the young teetotal officer who'd been left 'to mind the shop' might not have been equal to the absence of every other officer of the station, should it have been visited by someone very senior. Fortunately for 'Revver', all had been quiet on the home front, but a lesson had been learned

Flying Officer Walsh baled out safely from this Grebe, J7392, after colliding in cloud with J7372, another No.25 Squadron aircraft during a battle climb on 17th February 1928. Flt Lt Watson, in J7372, was killed, having failed to get clear of his aircraft. (Photo: C G Gulvin)

This replica of the Octave Chanute glider was built by Corporal W B Manuel of No.25 Squadron in 1927. One wonders whether the Corporal was an accurate replica of Chanute, as adjusting the cg range would have been a very delicate job to say the least.
(Photo: W B Manuel)

with no more than a score of very thick heads.

Squadron Leader Park's death was followed the same month by the arrival of Squadron Leader L G S Payne, MC, AFC (later Air Cdre, CB, MC, AFC), who later retired from the RAF to become the much respected and influential Air Correspondent to *The Daily Telegraph* for a couple of years before the Second World War and again shortly after. He also compiled what was to become a very widely used Chronology of Aviation, the book *Air Dates,* culled mainly from newspaper reports of both civil and military aviation achievements and events all over the World.

It was during Payne's period of command (September 1928 until February 1930) that No.25 Squadron was re-equipped as the popular little Grebes were consigned to history in favour of an aeroplane of a very different calibre and reputation, the Armstrong Siddeley Siskin, probably one of the most disliked fighters to join the RAF between the Wars. While the Service test pilots (that is, those pilots of the RAF who were charged with detailed examination of, and reporting on, the features and habits of aircraft before, or if ever they reached operational service) were not permitted to express personal opinions on an aircraft's general behaviour, they were charged with recording its measured performance and ability to meet those requirements originally set out in the Air Ministry's Specification. In the case of the Siskin, the aircraft *could* be landed safely; however, the pilots' reports could not record the grey hairs they accumulated while doing so. And they were some of the best pilots in the Service.

The Siskin had first appeared in 1919 (!), afflicted by a Dragonfly radial engine, and had been designed originally by the despised Royal Aircraft Factory. The ABC (All British Engine Company) Dragonfly engine itself proved to be an abject failure in that year, and the Siskin came to be damned by faint praise as 'the most successful fighter powered by that engine'. At full throttle, the aircraft might perhaps reach a speed of 145 mph provided that other things remained fairly equal. It has to be said, however, that despite development costs almost entirely dependent upon private philanthropy, rather than Treasury funding, the engine's eventual manufacturers produced the Jaguar engine, which had served the Grebe well for half a decade, and the same engine – albeit de-rated to 385hp – was selected for the Siskin Mk.III fighter as it first appeared in 1923. Little wonder that it proved some 7 mph slower than the Grebe. The reason that the Mk.IIIA version (first flown in 1925) was selected for mainline production for the RAF had little to do with performance, but on account of its predominantly metal construction, as plans were already afoot to adopt this type of aircraft structure and gradually to phase out the old wood-working trades in the Royal Air Force; this process – for no other reason than shortage of funds – occupied no less than fourteen years, a short-sighted attitude that, politically motivated, has periodically dogged the Armed Services during the past seven decades

Thus ended the first decade of peace since the first World War, a decade that had witnessed a modest growth of the Royal Air Force, as well as the establishment of traditions of which the young Service could be well satisfied. The fighting echelons had progressed within the limited resources available, while resourcefulness had been cultivated among young men whose individuality had contributed so much to the victory in 1918 and had now established the foundations of an air defence of Great Britain. The weapons for defence were yet far from adequate, but a much clearer understanding of what was required was being gained by those who would now reach the highest ranks of the Service*, while Europe chose to ignore or forget the terrible lessons of the Kaiser's War.

* One such officer was No.25 Squadron's founding CO, now Air Commodore, Felton Vesey Holt, CMG, DSO, appointed to the Directorate of Technical Development at the Air Ministry, and responsible to the Air Council for recommendations as to the RAF's future equipment.

The MT Section at Hawkinge in 1934 outside No.1 hangar, including four of No.25 Squadron's private vehicles. Second from the left is one of two vehicles that doubled as crash tenders and ambulances. The fire tender is absent. (Photo: via Roy S Humphreys)

'Daddy' Probyn's special Westland Widgeon III in which he led No.25 Squadron in its Siskins on the weekly battle climb. This aeroplane was unique in being powered by a 75hp Armstrong Siddeley Genet II and possessed a special wing centresection which increased the wing sweepback to cater for the lighter engine. Sqn Ldr Probyn flew G-EBRQ to victory in the 1928 Grosvenor Trophy race, and during the winter of 1928-29, accompanied by his wife, he made a 4,200-mile tour to Naples, Catania, Tunis, Seville, Madrid and Biaritz in a flying time of 60hrs 50min. Probyn also flew the Widgeon in the 1929 King's Cup race, but without success.

(Photo: Air Cdre H M Probyn, CB, CBE, DSO)

CHAPTER 4

'Flies on the Windscreen be Damned'

(1930 to 1936)

FOR THE ROYAL AIR FORCE the inter-War period may been seen in retrospect as conveniently falling into two ten-year parts, the first decade dominated by the Trenchard bomber philosophy, the second characterised by a determination, originally fostered by Air Chief Marshal Sir John Salmond – Trenchard's successor – to achieve a Service better balanced to suit the scenario of any future war. Trenchard had certainly achieved his own main aim, namely to establish an autonomous air force centred on the bomber, but unashamedly at the expense of other vital operational elements, particularly home defence, air mobility and maritime air security. On the other hand, he had conceived the structure of superb flying and ground training organisations. Many believe that in the latter enterprise lies the true value of Trenchard's leadership.

Be this as it may, it must be explained that, while France had remained the only major power in Europe with a significant military strength, and therefore Great Britain's only potential enemy, Trenchard's strategic 'bomber core' – for all the money spent on creating it during the 1920s – was only marginally capable of striking France in the unlikely event of a war against it. Yet, against whichever European nation the Royal Air Force might conceivably be called on to defend these shores, the RAF fighter arm in 1930 was unquestionably in very poor shape.

It must have been ordained on high that Salmond should take Trenchard's place at the helm of the Royal Air Force on 1st January 1930 for, as Air Officer Commanding-in-Chief, Air Defence of Great Britain (ADGB), and the senior of only two Air Chief Marshals in the Air Force List at that time, he had been able personally to follow and assess the neglect suffered by the air defences – occasioned by a parsimonious Treasury in the years leading up to the Great Depression. As long ago as 1925, it had been decreed that the Home-based RAF should consist of a minimum of 52 Squadrons: 35 with bombers, and 17 with fighters. By 1930 only twelve fighter squadrons had been re-formed since the post-war disbandments.* The arguments used to justify the shortfall were two-fold: Germany was beaten and forbidden to create an air force, and the Ten-Year Rule dominated the RAF's readiness for a future war. The latter was a politician's dream plan. In the belief that a British Government would always be capable of identifying any likelihood of serious aggression which might endanger Great Britain ten years before it materialised, the Royal Air Force would continue to exist at a level no more than just adequate to become strong enough to deal with that aggression ten years hence. In theory, the Ten Year Rule was up-dated every twenty-four hours, only to be abandoned outright in 1932 – with the Second World War only *seven* years hence. Moreover, Adolf Hitler had been in power for two of those years before any serious effort was made, through greatly increased defence appropriations, to commence expansion of the Royal Air Force and, in particular the fighter defences. In short, the Principles of War had not been re-written, merely shuffled – some would say, not before time. Indeed Trenchard abided by those Principles only so long as they matched his ambitions for the RAF. There is scarcely any suggestion that, for instance, Security of the Base, was permitted to cloud his vision. Thus can be seen that the assumption of the RAF's reins in 1930 by Sir John Salmond represented by far the most significant occurrence, and one on which far-sighted Air Officers could now plan the RAF's future. That they were able to begin doing so more than two years before Germany emerged as a likely future totalitarian and potential aggressor speaks volumes for the quality of Air Officers reaching the halls of influence, unfettered by sacred cows.

* At this half-way point in the inter-war years, just as the Royal Air Force was about to make important decisions with regard to its future modernisation in all aspects of Imperial defence, it is perhaps convenient here to list the Annual Air Estimates against the authorised manpower level of the Royal Air Force. The figures for the years 1935 to 1938 include the Supplementary Budgets to accommodate the various Expansion Programmes.

Year	*Personnel*	*Estimate*
1921	30,880	£18.4m.
1922	33,000	£12.5m.
1923	33,000	£12.0m.
1924	35,000	£14.5m.
1925	35,500	£15.5m.
1926	35,500	£16.0m.
1927	33,000	£15.5m.
1928	32,500	£16.3m.
1929	32,000	£17.0m.
1930	32,000	£17.9m.
1931	32,000	£18.1m.
1932	32,000	£17.4m.
1933	31,000	£17.4m.
1934	31,000	£17.7m.
1935	45,000	£27.6m.
1936	55,000	£50.7m.
1937	70,000	£56.5m.
1938	83,000	£73.5m.

The NAAFI and airmen's mess at Hawkinge, built in 1928; it still stands in use as a private residence.

(Photo: via Roy S Humphreys)

Delivered new to No.25 Squadron in April 1929, this Bristol-built Siskin IIIA, J9312, was badly damaged the following month while landing at Hawkinge in a gusty crosswind. It was repaired in due course and disposed of to No.56 Squadron.
(Photo: Wg Cdr F Landrey, AFC)

It is perhaps interesting to speculate on the effect the Ten Year Rule had on the Royal Air Force at 'combat' level, and worthy of note that, even before he took over from Trenchard, Salmond had personally paid visits to the Captains of industry, in particular those at Rolls-Royce, Bristol, Hawker and Gloster, to learn at first hand why the aircraft industry had repeatedly come up with fighter aircraft (and their engines) little better than those in service ten years earlier and whether, with adequate inducements, they could speed the development of significantly better fighters, and quickly. The universal answer was a pervading lack of funds for research. Bristols, in particular, pointed to the fact that for some six years the company had been engaged in producing all-metal aircraft as prototypes and, more recently building the Bulldog on a production line, the necessary research and production change-over having been underwritten entirely by commercial financing. This could only be recovered by amortising a long production line, hence continuation of Bulldog production long after it had become obsolete – a situation further aggravated by the effects of the Depression which would hit Britain hardest only two years hence. The presence in service of the metal Siskin, a deplorably out-dated aeroplane long before the end of the 1920s, was a similar case, although its exceptionally high accident wastage prompted the Air Ministry to terminate its service as soon as sufficient Bulldogs could be built to replace it. It is also worth mentioning here that the Director of Technical Development (DTD) at the Air Ministry was none other than Felton Vesey Holt, now one of only twelve Air Vice-Marshals in the Royal Air Force. However, there is no evidence that knowledge that No.25 Squadron was saddled with the Siskin in 1930 in any way influenced his recommendation to terminate that fighter's service life so abruptly!

This Siskin crashed on a sports field in Folkestone; the pilot, Sergeant Pearce, 'a most competent pilot', was killed after being seen to leave a No.25 Squadron formation without apparent reason. It was later concluded that he had been overcome by carbon monoxide fumes which had leaked from the cockpit heater.
(Photo: E Daniels)

With all the appearance of being a suitably robust aeroplane, though somewhat unattractive, the Siskin IIIA was an unpopular and unforgiving aircraft. The wingtip lamps suggest that night flying was not excluded from No.25 Squadron's activities. J8878's ultimate indignity was to be taxied into one of the Squadron's brand-new Hawker Furies (K2053) – which was parked – on the night of 10th March 1932. The Fury survived to be repaired, but the Siskin was summarily thrown away.
(Photo: Wg Cdr F Landrey, AFC)

An aerial photograph of Hawkinge airfield taken by Max Upton early in 1932 while he was flying a Siskin belonging to No.25 Squadron. Four other Siskins can be seen in front of No.2 Hangar, left of centre. No.4 Hangar, which was to be burned down the following year, is the largest of the three hangars on the right.
(Photo: Francis K Mason collection)

Notwithstanding the looming Depression, Salmond 'sponsored' the issue of a Specification for an advanced fighter almost before he'd reached his throne at Air Ministry, a sponsorship that was to be rendered realistic in its objectives by the appointment of a certain Air Vice-Marshal Hugh Dowding as Air Member for Supply and Research on the Air Council in September 1930. That this Specification proved impossible to meet in the short term is immaterial, but the appearance of new prototype fighters soon convinced those on the fighter squadrons that their years in the wilderness were coming to an end.

It is important here to refer to a subtle change that was occurring in the organisation of ADGB, initiated by Salmond. The Fighting Area was a deep coastal strip in the south and south-east of England in which the fighter squadrons were based, and over which enemy bombers would be fought by them. Salmond recognised that, by allowing enemy bombers to cross into British air space before being intercepted was to endanger all those forward fighter stations. The three fighter Squadrons, No.25 at Hawkinge, and Nos.1 and 43 at Tangmere, were now to become 'specialist' interceptor squadrons – the spearhead of the RAF's air defences – while other fighter squadrons, based on such 'inland' stations as Biggin Hill, Kenley, Hornchurch, North Weald and others, would engage such enemy aircraft that broke through or evaded the interceptors. This principal of fighter defence in depth was to undergo progressive development right up to the outbreak of, and for much of, the Second World War.

However, miracles could not be performed overnight. No.25 Squadron at Hawkinge appeared to have lost out by its perseverance with, and mastering of, the six-year-old Grebe to such an extent that, while other squadrons had been re-equipped with the Bristol Bulldog (top speed 174 mph) and Gloster Gamecock (157 mph), No.25 had to make do with the Armstrong Whitworth Siskin (156 mph) – the first of which arrived on the Squadron in May 1929. Yet morale on the Squadron remained as high as ever, tucked away in a corner of Kent in splendid isolation on a station where it was effectively master of it own destiny, if not a law unto itself. The Squadron's high morale was thus self-generated (and had been ever since its return home after the Chanak crisis). A succession of highly respected and experienced Commanding Officers had recognised that good morale and general efficiency were closely related. And word had spread among the flying training units that No.25 was not only an efficient, but also a supremely happy *interceptor fighter* squadron. So it continued to attract those pilots who headed the graduation lists at the training units. And No.25 continued to receive more than its 'fair share' of Cranwell graduates – fledgling officers who had decided on the Royal Air Force as a lifelong career.

During the 1920s a high proportion of the Squadron's personnel, ground and flying, had been veterans of the Kaiser's war, though those who had been granted short service commissions had either left the Service or were transferring to the Reserve of Officers. However, those who had already risen to the rank of Squadron Leader had received permanent commissions, and it was one of these, Squadron Leader Harold Melsome Probyn, DSO, (known universally in the Service as 'Daddy'), who arrived at Hawkinge to take over the Squadron from Robert Aitken in October 1930, having moved from No.2 (Army Co-operation) Squadron, based 'up the road' at Manston. Probyn had received his baptism of fire as a 2nd Lieutenant, having joined No.34 Squadron on its formation in 1916, and taken part in the Squadron's first combat on 23rd August that year flying a B.E.2e (during which he was wounded). As will be told much later in this work, 'Daddy' celebrated his 100th birthday in Kenya during the early 1990s, whither to-day's representatives of No.25 Squadron flew to honour the occasion.

Probyn was a strict disciplinarian yet, as recalled by those who later rose to Air Rank, was scrupulously fair in dealing with those who transgressed, never awarding unreasonable punishment and always equating the nature of such transgressions with any mitigating circumstances. In those days at Hawkinge, there were effectively only two levels of punitive legislation – a court martial or confinement to camp for a period, penalties a world apart; few officers possessed cars, and therefore left the Station on only relatively rare occasions in any case. On-Station amenities were just

The officers of No.25 (Fighter) Squadron outside the Officers' Mess at Hawkinge immediately after the change-over to Hawker Furies in 1932.

Back Row, left to right: *Fg Off (later Gp Capt) Leslie Frank Brown; Fg Off Arthur Edmund Clouston, AFC (later Air Cdre, CB, DSO, DFC, AFC*); Fg Off (later Gp Capt) Thomas Arthur Head, Engineering Officer; Fg Off Roland Gustave Harman (later Gp Capt, DFC); Fg Off Roy George Claringbould Arnold (later Sqn Ldr, DFC); Plt Off T A Hunter.*

Centre Row, left to right: *Fg Off (later Wg Cdr) Harry St George Burke; Fg Off (later Sqn Ldr) Miles Herbert Garnons-Williams; Fg Off (later Wg Cdr) George Peter Macdonald; Sqn Ldr Walter Edward George Bryant (later Gp Capt, MBE), Commanding Officer; Fg Off (later Sqn Ldr) Charles Ronald Hancock, DFC; Fg Off Felix Patrick Raphael Dunworth (later Wg Cdr, AFC); Fg Off Neill ('Michael') Daunt, RAFO; Fg Off John Nesbit-Dufort (later Wg Cdr, DSO).*

Front Row, left to right: *Fg Off (later Gp Capt) Eric Alfred Douglas-Jones; Fg Off Kenneth Brian Boyd Cross (later Air Chief Marshal Sir Kenneth, KCB, CBE, DSO, DFC).*

(Photo: 'FLIGHT')

adequate, but only just, even though Hawkinge had undergone some enlargement during the previous decade (mainly confined to the substitution of wood by bricks and mortar). Things like a new Officers' and Sergeants' Messes, purpose-built workshops, equipped sick quarters and a Station Headquarters were all considered.

'Daddy' Probyn possessed no fewer than three means of personal transportation – in addition to his Siskin. Being an avid 'private pilot' – a hobby he enthusiastically pursued for a further half century – he owned a rather special Westland Widgeon III (G-EBRQ), whose lightweight Genet engine had been 'breathed on' to provide 75 hp. The wing featured a special centre section which increased the sweep-back to offset the lighter engine. He had flown to victory in the 1928 Grosvenor Trophy race and, during the winter of 1928-29, accompanied by his wife, he made a 4,200-mile tour to Paris, Nice, Pisa, Naples, Catania, Tunis, Biskra, Algiers, Oran, Almeira, Seville, Madrid and Biarritz in a flying time of 60hr 50min. He had also flown the Widgeon in the 1929 King's Cup Race, gaining only 12th place – but with an engine firing on only four out of five cylinders and a broken rocker-arm. G-EBRQ continued to fly until 1936.

His second mode of transport was an ancient Trojan four-seater car, whose two-stroke engine exuded a singular wheezing noise, a most considerate warning note to any officer who had inadvertently opened the Mess bar slightly before the appointed hour – whereupon all evidence of illicit drinking could be concealed in good time. The car was, naturally, employed to convey Squadron members to and from the local watering holes, when needed. Probyn did however put an end to a habit which had recently edged into the hazy area that existed between the Law and good sense – that of visiting at least one of those watering holes by air; the outward journey and landing might at a pinch be defended as some sort of emergency, but the return flight could well

Classic air-to-air photo of No.25 (Fighter) Squadron, demonstrating one of the most difficult formations, three vics in line abreast; with so little surplus power available the secret was apparently for the two outside vic leaders to maintain accurate distance from the inner vic leader.

(Photo: Francis K Mason collection)

The first Fury to serve on No.25 Squadron, K2041, had previously flown with No.1 Squadron at Tangmere. It is seen here without serial number on the rear fuselage and no Squadron Badge on the fin. K2041 remained on No.25 Squadron until 1937!

(Photo: via Ray Sturtivant)

The second Fury, K2048, also without a rear fuselage serial number, the pennant on the fin discloses that it was the aircraft of the CO, Sqn Ldr W E G Bryant, MBE. It also survived on the Squadron until 1937.

(Photo: via Ray Sturtivant)

be marred by the presence of alcohol in the pilot's operational systems. Fortunately there had been no actual accidents during such 'local' flying, but the CO clearly wasn't prepared to tempt providence.

In the finest traditions of the Squadron, 'Daddy' also owned a pair of horses, being a keen member of the East Kent Hunt, and regularly each week could be seen departing Hawkinge, resplendent in pink, to hunt. His other horse, also 'maintained' on the Station, was ridden by the CO during his regular Station inspections, having gone to endless pains to standardise the necessary formal ritual to be observed by the various Section Officers and NCOs, on arrival at his dominions.

As was to be expected, all the RAF's fighter squadrons were required to conform to a rigid routine of flying commitments each week and month. For example, the whole Squadron was required to fly a weekly Battle Climb to 16,000ft (later increased to 20,000ft), followed by twenty minutes patrolling 'on the look-out for possible hostile aircraft'. The whole sortie would be carried out in vics of three or a single vic of nine, and it was customary for each flight to be led by its fight commander; occasionally the whole sortie, led by 'Daddy', would be flown as a single vic of however many Siskins were serviceable. On other occasions the CO might be encountered in his Widgeon, wielding a camera. Woe betide any pilot found (and proven) to be significantly out of formation.

In addition to the Battle Climbs, the flight commanders took care to include others forms of 'applied' flying, organising navigation sorties around Kent, practising forced landings, and use of R/T (then in general use and effective up to about forty miles air-to-air). Mock dog-fights using camera-gun, as well as local night flying sorties were carefully organised (so as to keep clear of commercial air traffic, plying between London and the continent).

Despite this very full flying routine, solo and formation aerobatics and air drill (now an *ad hoc* commitment), dominated No.25 Squadron's time in the air, and it was customary to do everything possible to avoid any serviceable aircraft remaining on the ground for any length of time. If no other exercise had been planned, every pilot was expected, as a matter of habit, to brush up any weak areas of his flying repertoire in a remote corner of the Kentish skies.

Probyn brought No.25 Squadron to new heights of efficiency with that rare skill of combining administrative responsibilities (remembering that he also commanded the Station) with his own enthusiasm for flying, and both Squadron and Station flourished under his command. Perhaps this was not such a difficult task, having mind of the quality of pilots then being posted to Hawkinge. The names Beamish, Cross, Daunt, Clouston, Nesbitt-Dufort were, with others, to resound through the halls of Service history for twenty or more years. Some have become legends.

A newcomer to the Squadron in 1930 might be mystified by a fairly common facial feature among his fellow pilots – unless he had already trained on the Siskin. In short, they displayed 'Siskin face', the evidence of having come into violent contact with the Aldis gunsight, a gun cocking handle or the front cockpit sill. For the Siskin was a tricky aeroplane to land (to say the least), even if only slightly out of wind direction or in only mildly gusty weather. Pilots recall their training days at flying schools when anything up to five Siskins at a time could be seen tipped up on their nose or lying upside down, following a 'tricky' landing. Fortunately the Siskin was a fairly simple aeroplane to repair on site – provided the metal parts had not been too badly bent. Its shortcomings were the result of the designer's quaint adherence to a belief that flawed theory is more reliable than demonstrated fact. Too many aircraft designers still tended to regard the pilot as an appendage, to be accommodated at a late stage in their design masterpiece.

The Siskin was what was known as a sesquiplane, that is, a biplane in which the very large upper wing provided much greater lift than the smaller lower wing. The trouble was that the upper wing was much thicker than the lower, and was disproportionately heavier. Thus on landing, the lower wing 'dumped its lift' somewhat sooner than the upper wing. The secret was evidently to fly the aircraft on to the ground with plenty of engine, yet with the stick fairly well back. However, a modest gust of wind had a habit of blowing the thing upside down, while the slightest undulation of the grass tended to dig the propeller into the ground. Either way, the pilot would be slammed forward in his cockpit, with facial evidence of collision with cockpit furniture.

No.25 received a motley selection of Siskins which had been manufactured by a number of different makers, each being associated with some quirk of behaviour in the air –

Cameo One. Pecking Order. The Squadron Commander (on the right) is about to fly and the adjutant offers him the authorisation book; the CO's flying overalls and parachute lie on the ground (!). When the signing ceremony is over, the CO will hand the adjutant his walking stick (in those days his badge of rank and authority), and will expect it to be handed back on landing.
(Photo: courtesy of No.25 (Fighter) Squadron)

Cameo Two. Pecking Order. A flight of three Furies (the fin tip of the third aircraft just visible over the rear fuselage of K2078) taxies out to take off, led by the Flight Commander whose fin and wheel discs are painted in Flight colours. A ground crewman holds one wing during taxying to assist manoeuvring (owing to the lack of forward vision on the ground and fixed tailskid); his Nos.2 and 3 pilots are expected to formate on him. The pilot of K2078 has omitted one Vital Action – his Sutton harness has not been secured and one strap dangles outside his cockpit! (Photo: courtesy of No.25 (Fighter) Squadron)

which made for interesting training and handling. One or two dual-control two-seat trainers were also delivered, while at least one Siskin was already six years old when it joined the Squadron in 1930; it had undergone the harsh tropical trials in India before serving with No.5 Squadron and returning home in 1929.

A letter home from an airframe fitter, Cpl Bill ('Blanco') Webber, of March 1930, says it all:

> '. . .At last the Squadron has got its dose of Siskins and the last of the dear old Grebes have gone. I don't think much of the new planes (and I don't think the flying boys like them very much either as they are much more tricky to land properly). My job is to see that they are rigged properly, among other things, but one of my kites was a real pig. We stripped off the covering on one wing and found that a spar joint was RUSTY. Jack, my sergeant pilot, told the CO that he thought it was unsafe to fly, and we don't have the right spares to put it right. The CO said he'd have the kite taken away. Then men from the makers arrived yesterday to look at it, and they said it was OUR fault that it was rusty. I thought our CO would have a fit, but told the men that we'd only had the kite for less than a week, and it was nearly brand new and if their planes went rusty in that time they were no b—— good. That caused red faces I can tell you. The pilots call them TWISTKINS, but on the whole they grin and bear it. With any luck we won't have to cope with them for long. Two of them tipped up on their noses on landing this morning, breaking their props, and we had to put new ones on. But it can't have done the engines much good, and there are more crates in for inspection than there are able to fly'

Some brief notes on the pilots of the Squadron during the Siskin years, may provide an insight into the character and aspirations of RAF fighter pilots of that era.

Flt Lt Victor Beamish, (later Gp Capt) was born in County Cork in 1903, and had graduated at the RAF College, Cranwell, in 1923. He was one of four brothers, all accomplished sportsmen, Victor playing rugger for the RAF (and was reserve for Ireland). When required for the RAF team, off he would fly in a Siskin on the Saturday morning, to return in time for colour hoisting on the following Monday. He was invalided out of the RAF some months after leaving No.25, diagnosed as having TB. Towards the end of the pre-war expansion period, he argued his way back into the Service as a Squadron Leader, and then back on to flying, wholly recovered from his illness. In due course he took over command of North Weald, and was Station Commander at the time No.25 Squadron was based there with night fighters during the Battle of Britain. On several occasions he jumped out of his office window to take off in a Hurricane and join 'his' pilots in combat. He was credited with several enemy aircraft shot down, later to be awarded the DSO. He it was who, while on a *Rhubarb* (an *ad hoc* offensive patrol over the French coast), was the first to spot the German battleships *Scharnhorst* and *Gneisenau* during their famous Channel dash on 12th February 1942. He was killed in action while leading the Kenley Wing only six weeks later.

Plt Off Kenneth Brian Boyd Cross, (later Air Chief Marshal Sir Kenneth, KCB, CBE, DSO, DFC), was born in October 1911. He joined No.25 Squadron from No.3 Flying Training School at Grantham in April 1931 during the Siskin era. Known throughout the RAF as 'Bing', he was selected to fly Furies in the Squadron formation aerobatic teams at the Hendon Air Display in 1933 and 1934, but left the Squadron later that year for a flying instructor's course at the Central Flying School, and became an instructor with No.5 Flying Training School at Sealand. He was also an outstanding rugger player for the Harlequins. He was appointed CO of No.46 Squadron (Hurricanes) at Digby in October 1939 and led this Squadron at Narvik during the second phase of the Norwegian campaign the following year. During the evacuation from Norway, Cross called for volunteers to land the Hurricanes aboard the carrier HMS *Glorious* (never previously attempted), a feat successfully achieved. Two days later the carrier was found and sunk by the German battleships, *Scharnhorst* and *Gneisenau.* Cross (and one of his flight commanders as well as five survivors

It has been stated (presumably by disciples of Nos.1 and 43 Squadrons) that it was not possible to perform tied-together air drill in Furies with nine aircraft all *joined. Evidence that No.25 achieved the 'impossible' is provided by this photo of a perfect 9-vic, showing the streamers intact between all nine aircraft. The normal squadron routine would be a fly-past in 9-vic, then 9-abreast, all aircraft connected. In the 'long displays' at Hendon, the leading 3-vic would dive away, breaking the elastic cords with the other two vics before executing a formation loop with vics-in-vic. On one occasion at Hendon (in Fury IIs) the Squadron looped in a 9-vic, but landed with one cord broken. The offending pilot swore that his cord had been broken by a bird. . .it should be pointed out that 'air-drill' did not include loops and rolls (which constituted 'aerobatics').* (Photo: Francis K Mason collection)

from the crew of the *Glorious*) were picked up after two days in an open boat – the only survivors from those aboard the carrier. After appointments in the Middle East, Cross became Director of Overseas Operations at Air Ministry in 1944, Officer Commanding Eastern Sector, Fighter Command in 1949; Air Officer Commanding, No.3 (Bomber) Group, 1956-1959; and AOC-in-C, Bomber Command, from 1959. He retired on 24th January 1967.

Plt Off John Nesbitt-Dufort (later Wg Cdr, DSO) joined No.25 Squadron in 1931 from No.3 Flying Training School, Grantham. After a short conversion course on Fleet Air Arm aircraft in 1932 he returned to No.25, by which time the Squadron had converted to Hawker Furies, an aircraft that evidently transformed Nesbitt-Dufort's prowess as a pilot, and in 1936 he was duly selected for the Hendon air display, led on that occasion by No.25's then Squadron Commander, Sqn Ldr W F Dickson, of whom more will be told later. The event was almost marred by a previous social engagement that had overrun, delaying Nesbitt-Dufort's arrival at Hendon, so much so that he was still climbing into his Fury as the remainder of the team was taxying out to start its routine! On the outbreak of war, Nesbitt-Dufort's flying career took a new course. After a spell with No.2 Service Flying Training School as a flying instructor, he was posted to a flying training school in Southern Rhodesia, a departure that was only cancelled as he was boarding the ship. Instead he was posted to No.23 Squadron at Ford to fly intruder operations in Blenheims. Unfortunately an indiscreet remark was overheard and led to his posting from No.23, to be followed by flying duties with No.1419 (Special Duties) Flight which, in 1941, was stationed at Stradishall, equipped with Lysanders and Whitleys, its job being to drop agents into France and, if all went well, to recover them. It is not the purpose of this work to go into detail about 25 Squadron members' careers in 'after years', and it must suffice to say that thereafter Nesbit-Dufort's flying career embraced some of the most hazardous operations that the RAF ever flew. Landing the Lysander in enemy-held territory, dropping agents from Whitleys, and even landing a Hudson deep inside France to pick up agents and other persons – any of whom might be late for their rendezvous – all with the knowledge of dire stories of torture and death if caught. Indeed, after running out of fuel on one occasion (due to waiting for an agent who did not arrive at the rendezvous and then encountering bad weather on the return flight), Nesbitt-Dufort was obliged to force land back in France where he was found and looked after for some days by Resistance members before being recovered by another pick-up Lysander and brought back to England. Ironically, the agent who failed to make contact on that ill-fated pick-up was bringing back details of the German plans for the break-out from Brest by the battleships *Scharnhorst* and *Gneisenau.* In his autobiography *Black Lysander,* John Nesbitt-Dufort describes his two periods at Hawkinge in the 1930s as the happiest days of his life.

Plt Off Nigel ('Michael') Daunt, who held a Short Service Commission on No.25 Squadron, is remembered as a brilliant pilot, and one who was selected to appear at two Hendon Displays in the early 1930s. On leaving the RAF, he was one of the earliest ex-Service pilots to spend a period with the Royal Aircraft Establishment, Farnborough, where he learned the rudiments of flight testing aircraft (there being no Empire Test Pilots School before the Second World War). After the Chief Test Pilot at Gloster Aircraft Company, Gerry Sayer, lost his life in a Typhoon, Daunt became responsible for the early testing of the Meteor, making the first historic flight by this, the first British jet fighter, at Cranwell on 5th March 1943. There was the occasion on which, while Daunt was standing beside an early Meteor, a ground engineer started one of the

Two interesting group photographs of the NCOs of No.25 (Fighter) Squadron/RAF Hawkinge, evidently taken about three years apart in the late 1920s and early 1930s, outside the Sergeants' Mess. The disciplinary Warrant Officer, in the centre of the seated men in the right hand picture reappears in every such group photo between 1927 and 1937, occasionally wearing an impressive array of medal ribbons, but never the same array! Unfortunately none of the men's names have been traced. (Photos: via Roy S Humphreys)

engines which sucked the unsuspecting pilot off his feet and wedged him firmly in the jet intake, an event corroborated by Daunt to the author. Thereafter the early Meteors were equipped with detachable grills over the intakes – unfeelingly nicknamed Anti-Daunt Guards. Some years before Nigel died in July 1991, the author wrote asking him for his recollections of his time on No.25 Squadron. In his reply, he stated that his time at Hawkinge 'were the salad days of his life, those in which he learned the somewhat 'unfeeling manner' in which Service pilots were wont to treat their aeroplanes!'

Pilot Officer Arthur Edmund Clouston, RAF and RAFO (later Air Cdre, DSO, DFC, AFC*) was born in New Zealand in 1908 and came to England in the late 1920s to join the RAF, bringing with him a letter addressed to Keith Park, a fellow New Zealander and the brilliant No.11 Group Commander who later took such a vital part in the Battle of Britain, asking him for advice as to how he should go about entering the Service. The upshot was that, on being accepted, he was posted to a Flying Training School and thence to No.25 Squadron late in 1930 (having completed the one year's training course in six months). After a brief and unhappy spell on Siskins, Clouston took to the Fury like a veteran, quickly gaining selection for the Squadron's display team, which not only participated in the annual Hendon shows, but also fly-pasts during State and other ceremonial events, such as the opening of Speke Airport, and the dedication of the R.101 Airship Memorial at Le Bourget. Clouston was involved in one of the very few accidents suffered during the Squadron's formation aerobatic practice flights. On this occasion his flight was in vic, inverted at the top of a loop, when another Fury was struck by Clouston's propeller. The other aircraft broke up in the air and the pilot was killed. Clouston immediately closed the throttle to prevent his engine from disintegrating, whereupon the Fury whipped into an inverted flat spin. Never having experienced this 'unusual attitude', Clouston decided that this was not the time to employ half measures and slammed on full rudder, this having the effect of un-stalling one wing and flipping the Fury right side up. Thereafter 'it was simple just to put the nose down and glide back to Hawkinge'. The accident did not prevent him from accompanying the team at Hendon a week or so later. Almost all the period of his Short Service Commission was spent with No.25, and he was offered a Permanent Commission, which he declined, planning to return to New Zealand. However an invitation to spend some time at the Royal Aircraft Establishment, Farnborough (like Michael Daunt, above) proved too much of a temptation, and in a short period of incredibly varied

Manhandling a Fury I with a tailskid dolly in about 1933. The aeroplane is adorned with the unofficial Squadron Badge with the motto "FERIENS TEGO" on the fin. The device became official in 1936. (Photo: Francis K Mason collection)

The pilot of this Fury (Flt Lt A E Clouston) made a forced landing on a rugby pitch on the outskirts of Folkestone, probably due to fuel starvation during a mock dogfight. An engine and airframe fitter arrived within half an hour from Hawkinge. The aircraft was undamaged and only required topping up with fuel from a nearby garage and an engine run before Clouston was able to fly the five miles back to the Station. Note the camera gun mounted on the Fury's lower wing. (Photo: Francis K Mason collection)

Furies of No.25 Squadron during their annual armament camp at Sutton Bridge on the Wash. Station amenities were somewhat primitive, and the term 'Summer Camp' was singularly appropriate, as both personnel and aircraft were accommodated under canvas (note the Bessoneau hangars). In his book STRAIGHT AND LEVEL, 'Bing' *Cross was scathing in his criticism of other fighter squadrons whose flying discipline (as well as their gunnery results) left much to be desired, and emphasised that it had become No.25 Squadron's habit to apply great care to do everything with precision, taking off and landing in immaculate formation, whether as one, two or three vics. Their consistently high competition results, year in, year out, confirmed the pilots' interpretation of the old phrase 'decorum only when it matters most'.* (Photo: The Lincolnshire Echo)

flying ventures both at the RAE and with small commercial flying companies, he began undertaking record-breaking flights, beginning with the 1936 Schlesinger Air Race from London to Johannesburg in an open Miles Hawk; he completed about 95 per cent of the course before crashing and destroying his aircraft. He subsequently established numerous point-to-point speed records in Europe and the Middle East, and became one of the most famous long-distance racing and record-breaking pilots of the late-1930s, creating new records to Australia and New Zealand. During the War he became Chief Instructor and Commandant of the new Empire Test Pilots School.

Another of the outstanding pilots on No.25 Squadron was Sgt D A ('Max') Upton and while referring to his time on the Squadron, it is worth making some observations on the matter of NCO fighter pilots between the Wars. Following the Armistice, the number of NCO pilots offered places in the peacetime RAF was very small indeed, probably on account of the number of distinguished commissioned pilots seeking a lifetime career in the Service. In due course, as the Service grew in size and the demand for new junior pilots could not be fully satisfied from the existing training schools, former wartime NCO pilots were offered the chance to attend the schools and ultimately to join Squadrons, and so a precedent was set. By 1927 some of the flying training courses were being dominated by NCO pilots on account of their previous distinguished service in the old RFC, and it was felt to be a logical step to offer airmen in ground trades the opportunity to transfer to flying duties. Max Upton was one of these, and he demonstrated from the outset that, despite his small stature (he was only 5ft 6in tall), he promised to be an outstanding pilot, and in due course joined No.25 at Hawkinge as a sergeant. Despite some initial apprehension among his fellow pilots, he was quickly accepted, not just 'one of the boys', but a highly intelligent extrovert and a brilliant aerobatic pilot – not the slightest overawed by the career officer pilots who, in turn, recognised his ability. With such commitment, experience and professionalism, it was inevitable that Max would gain a commission, and did so on 12th July 1940. He retired as a Wing Commander with an OBE on 23rd September 1957.

A SYMBOL OF UNSOLICITED ELITISM

Bearing in mind that the Sopwith Snipes, with which the Squadron had been equipped during the early 1920s, were almost without exception either elderly veterans, refurbished or rebuilt aircraft, it was not surprising that their rate of attrition was high, the more so having regard to the harsh and often primitive conditions in which the Snipes were flown while based at San Stefano in Turkey. With that in mind, it is worth comparing the rates of attrition experienced by No.25 Squadron's principal types of fighter flown between 1920 and 1937,

Aircraft Type	*Time on Squadron*	*Total Number Delivered*	*Aircraft Written off*	*Percentage Attrition*
Sopwith Snipe	4 yrs	40	13*	32.5
Gloster Grebe	4 yrs	56	9	16.0
AW Siskin	3 yrs	41	13	31.6
Hawker Fury I/II	5 yrs	53	5	9.5

* Including four at San Stefano

While no excuse can be offered for the Grebe's proclivity for wing flutter (in this context at any rate), the figures appear to emphasise the wisdom of the Air Ministry's decision to rid the RAF of the Siskin, particularly in view of the apparent inability of the manufacturer to offer any suggestion as how to eliminate the aircraft's shortcomings, other than to build an expensive new prototype – but still calling it a Siskin! Needless to say, it did not impress.

Fortunately an alternative fighter design had been prepared (as a private venture) by Hawker Aircraft Ltd, which in prototype form had shown considerable promise, even though it had fallen short of the Air Ministry's long-term fighter requirement, Specification F.7/30. This was the Hawker Hornet – soon to be re-named the Fury, an exceptionally attractive biplane – but one that was still only armed with the traditional pair of Vickers machine guns. Apart from close attention to design detail to reduce drag, the Fury owed its clean lines to the choice, made by Sydney Camm (Hawkers' illustrious designer) of a Rolls-Royce Kestrel engine. This had already been ordered into large-scale production for a new generation of *light bombers* based on the Hawker Hart; this possessed a top speed some 10 mph greater than that of the Bristol Bulldog fighter, with which

An unusual shot of No.25 Squadron's Furies at Brooklands, before delivery to Hawkinge and therefore without their distinctive markings.
(Photo: courtesy of No.25 (Fighter) Squadron)

Air Vice-Marshal F V Holt, **CMG, DSO.**
Commander-in-Chief, Fighting Area, Air Defence of Great Britain. A photograph taken shortly before his death on 23rd April 1931.
(Photo: Temple Press Ltd.)

the RAF was stuck for a further half dozen years (for the reasons given above).

Unfortunately the Hawker Fury was relatively expensive, at slightly over £5,000 per aircraft, for the anticipated number of aircraft ordered (between 60 and 70, to be delivered during 1931-32) – sufficient for just three fighter squadrons, these three squadrons being those stationed on the South Coast, namely at Hawkinge and Tangmere.

That No.25 was to be re-equipped last of the three came as a great disappointment at Hawkinge. There was however nothing sinister about the reasoning: and it was announced in the national Press that as the annual appropriations allowed for two Squadrons to re-equip during 1931 and one in 1932, it made better sense to concentrate the effort and cost at a single Station (i.e. Nos.1 and 43 Squadrons at Tangmere) during the first year, and No.25 at Hawkinge during the second. Sadly, it was a Siskin flown by a No.43 Squadron pilot that collided with the civilian Moth aircraft on 23rd April 1931 in which Air Vice-Marshal Felton Vesey Holt (No.25 Squadron's founding CO) was to lose his life. Even more ironic was the fact that Holt had been at least a party to the decision to get rid of the Siskin in the first place (as already stated).

Notwithstanding the above, No.25 Squadron flew its first two Hawker Furies in April 1931, but these were aircraft 'lent' for air experience flying only and, in the course of which, to confirm that Hawkinge airfield was suitable for the new fighters. Needless to say, at least half a dozen pilots got the chance to take the new fighters aloft, between them amassing 73 flying hours in the course of a month! (Many years later, Probyn confessed to having tried to pull numerous strings to extend their stay at Hawkinge, but to no avail.) Without exception every pilot who flew those early Furies was ecstatic in his verdict on the aircraft, some threatening never to fly a Siskin again. Five more of the old aircraft were to be written off before the rest were withdrawn. One of two Siamese pilots, serving 'courtesy' tours with No.25 Squadron, was killed when his Siskin failed to recover from a spin over the outskirts of Folkestone (See Appendix 1).

'Daddy' Probyn remained as CO just long enough to see his Squadron begin re-equipping with Furies in February 1932, although ironically, because there was no dual-control version of the Hawker fighter, two 'new' Siskin trainers were delivered to replace the two veteran examples used previously! Perhaps not surprisingly these aircraft were considered useless as trainers for Furies (except under the guidance of one pilot, namely 'Max' Upton, see below), especially as an increasing number of pilots who joined the Squadron in future were to get an opportunity to fly a Fury at a Flying Training School or at Cranwell, as four such aircraft were set aside for the purpose.

As stated above, Probyn left No.25 just as it was beginning to receive the long-awaited Fury fighter. Those who had flown the aircraft the previous year, and were still with the Squadron, were now able to give the other pilots the benefit of their brief experience. Not least of the former was 'Max' Upton who summoned up all his recollections of the fighter, and proved his expertise as well as an entirely unassuming modesty when instructing the uninitiated. One of his unique 'exercises' was to take up one of the new-to-Fury pilots in a dual Siskin and, by some deliberately ham-fisted use of the throttle and flying controls, reproduce what the Fury would do in the same circumstances – and *that* is 'real' flying.

With the delivery of Hawker Furies to No.25 Squadron at Hawkinge, the 'interceptor' force of ADGB was complete – the other squadrons, based further inland, continuing to fly Siskins and Bulldogs for some years.

In truth the advent of the Hawker Fury interceptor necessitated a fundamental revision of air combat tactics in the RAF. With a rate of climb so much better than that of the Siskin (about five minutes to 10,000ft, compared with the Siskin's twelve minutes) and a speed margin over current 'heavy bombers' also doubled, the emphasis on the fighter's rôle was on interception – that is to say, the engagement of a hostile bombing raid over the coast, if not while the hostiles were still out to sea – as distinct from a ponderous climb and a long tail chase *after* the hostile raid had crossed in over the coast. The trouble was that, in the past, there had been no means of warning the fighter pilots that a hostile raid was approaching the coast, other then to resort to the wasteful practice of employing standing patrols, flown some miles out to sea.

For some years experiments had been carried out with huge concrete, concave parabolic sound detectors, set into the cliffs of Kent's Channel coastline, with which it was hoped that microphones positioned at the focal point of the great bowls would enable listeners with earphones to detect and locate approaching aircraft. The experiments proved the system to be hopelessly inadequate for all practical purposes. The solution was still half a decade away – and did not depend on sound waves. No.25 Squadron was called upon to intercept any incoming 'hostile bombers' located by the coastal listeners. With eager anticipation three Fury pilots sat waiting for a call to take off and climb to meet the approaching raid. After a couple of hours waiting in the sun, with never a word on the telephone, the CO called a fitter over and told him to run across to the flight office and ask the duty pilot to phone the coast and find out if there were 'any problems'. Back came the answer 'unfortunately the noise of the traffic on the coast road has made it impossible to tell traffic from approaching bombers'. Needless to say, the exercise was terminated immediately – whether or not the bombers had in fact already flown in over the coast was not recorded. Yet it was the very failure of the sound detector system that focussed scientists' minds on the transmission of *radio* signals, and the tracking of the signals as they were reflected by an approaching aircraft that gave birth to 'radar' and the all-important solution of the early warning problem that enabled RAF fighters to intercept enemy bombers and win the daylight Battle of Britain seven short years later.

The new Commanding Officer arrived several days after Probyn had left Hawkinge, a tactful gesture as any ceremony to mark the much lamented departure of the former incum-

A full squadron group with a Fury visible in the hangar behind. (Photo: Francis K Mason collection)

An engine fitter ground running a Fury I at Hawkinge in 1932.
(Photo: via Roy S Humphreys)

bent might well have resulted in widespread embarrassment – not least among the line pilots. The Service grapevine had hinted that Squadron Leader Walter Edward George Bryant was widely thought to be a 'career' officer and a strict disciplinarian, having already commanded a squadron – which was said to have greatly benefited from his tight rein. One of his eccentricities however, contrary to expectations, was to result in his immediate 'acceptance' by the squadron.

It is said that in the course of a conference of Flight Commanders, called by Bryant, an invitation was given for the CO to witness from a two-seat Siskin a display of aerobatics by nine Furies (three vics). Bearing in mind that the Squadron had only just taken on charge its full complement of the new fighters, this was almost certainly tempting providence. Nevertheless the planned display (as such it certainly was) was duly flown, including a loop by vics in line astern. Now the lack of agility of the Squadron's former aeroplanes had demanded that three vics of Siskins maintained a healthy separation distance between them so as to enable each pilot to keep the aircraft ahead well in view. Unfortunately, No.25 was as yet unwilling to acknowledge that the Fury, with its long sleek nose stretching away in front, *did* possess blind spots from the cockpit. That first three-vic loop almost proved to be the Squadron's last, with at least two pilots opting to stall-turn out of formation on losing sight of their vic leaders, and a flight commander opting for an Immelmann on losing sight of the whole vic ahead of him.

On landing, the CO called the shame-faced pilots around him and, after a pregnant silence, Bryant, staring nonchalantly at a point in the far distance, offered the remark 'Strange. It all looks so different from the ground; I've obviously got a lot to learn.' He didn't fool anyone. That evening he posted a notice in the flight office to the effect that *all* pilots would report daily to the station parade ground, each in possession of a BICYCLE. Some wag pencilled at the bottom of the notice 'Sorry sir, I had a lot of dead flies on my windscreen'.

At the appointed hour, twelve pilots were to be seen assembled with a motley selection of bikes, awaiting the arrival of their leader. He duly arrived, clutching a large megaphone. . .and seated astride one of 'Daddy's' horses (presumably left behind while the former CO arranged alternative stabling). It soon became clear that the new CO had decided that, under his direction, the Squadron was to

Preparing Fury I K2062 for flight at Hawkinge. Both this aircraft and the one in the previous picture were disposed of to No.1 Squadron at Tangmere after service with No.25 (Fighter) Squadron.
(Photo: Francis K Mason collection)

return to first principles and since with only two dimensions available on the parade ground, formation aerobatics were out of the question, it was back to basic Air Drill.

As curious spectators assembled round the perimeter, they were treated to an entertainment involving cyclists attempting to turn left and right through 90 degrees in vic, the pilot on the inside of the turn trying hard not to fall off his mount, forced as he was to move at less than walking speed. The climax occurred when a voice from the cyclists was heard to call 'Would the pilot of the Siskin please move his horse as my twelve Furies need more air space to execute your orders without stalling?' Which request was greeted by a derisory cheer from the bystanders. To give him his due, the CO retained his composure, and had the good sense to enter into the spirit of the occasion with the order 'Parade, Dismiss'. Whereupon everyone dismounted to gather round for a de-briefing which was, indeed, brief: 'Thank you, gentlemen. I hope you will learn from your experiences yesterday and today that you would be well advised to take seriously your obvious need for plenty of practice on our new aeroplanes.'

It took very little time for Bryant to understand exactly what made the Squadron 'tick', but that bringing it to heel (by his standards) was not an option open to him. What he had diagnosed as quite unacceptable élitism was little more than a natural result of the Squadron's unique situation, alone on a station, well away from the customary, strictly determined infrastructure of almost every other operational Station in the RAF. The realisation of this was fortunate for Bryant as it strengthened his resolve to ensure that No.25 Squadron, in 'catching up' with Nos.1 and 43 Squadron – who had already been flying their Furies for some months – would regain its mantle of assumed superiority in double quick time. His target was to win as many of the various inter-squadron trophies, for which competitions were staged each year, for applied flying: Air Drill, Aerobatics, Gunnery, Navigation (day and night) and, eventually the Sassoon Trophy for all these disciplines combined. On explaining this target to his Flight Commanders, he not only earned their unqualified respect but demonstrated to them that only by a much more professional approach towards their flying

Sqn Ldr Paxton briefing the 1933 Hendon Display pilots. From left to right: *Sqn Ldr A L Paxton, Flt Lt C R Hancock, Sgt D A Upton, Sgt M Pearson, Flt Lt K B B Cross, Flt Lt Douglas-Jones, Flt Lt Blackburn, Flt Lt A E Clouston, Flt Lt N Daunt.*

(Photo: Wg Cdr D A Upton, OBE)

would they have the slightest chance of regaining any justifiable *élan*. Furthermore, as a measure of his grasp of the situation on the Squadron, Bryant took what seemed to be a radical step by appointing to an entirely unofficial post as Squadron Training Pilot an NCO – namely Sgt Max Upton! After a shocked silence, it suddenly dawned on the Flight Commanders that this could well put the Squadron on its mettle – without offending anyone, such was the respect held by all for this superb pilot. Many years later, when recalling his service on the Squadron, Max confessed that he always considered pilots of single-seat fighters as being of equal rank and of unequal qualities as pilots and, with this in mind, he would have declined a commission, had Bryant suggested he apply for one at the time. Bryant was sensible not to have done so.

In fairly quick time the Squadron made visible progress, and invitations began to come in for flying displays on a number of 'local' occasions up and down the country. These included the opening of municipal airports, the dedication of war memorials and even an occasional sporting event.

An unfortunate accident occurred at about this time. One of the more experienced pilots, R M ('Jock') Ross, who had joined the Squadron in 1930, was detailed to collect a new Fury from the Hawker works at Brooklands, having been given a lift in the two-seat Siskin. Arriving back at Hawkinge, he decided to celebrate his Fury's arrival by executing three slow rolls in succession; unfortunately, due to a dearth of altitude, he only managed to complete two and a half of these manoeuvres before landing upside-down in front a group of fascinated fellow pilots. Releasing his harness, Jock extricated himself by dropping gently out of his inverted cockpit, and walked away unscathed. Nevertheless, in due course the whole panoply of King's Regulations was arraigned at Court Martial, and Jock was busted on the spot. Nothing daunted, he climbed back up the ladder and by the outbreak of war in 1939 was flying once more as a Pilot Officer 'on probation'. He retired from the RAF after the War as a Squadron Leader and was one of the first to become a member of No.25 (Fighter) Squadron Association. Alas he died, widely mourned by the Royal Air Force he had served so ardently, aged 90, in 1999.

Returning to the cause of Jock's accident in his Fury, the Court simply recorded it as 'executing unauthorised aerobatics below the minimum height permitted for such manoeuvres with consequent damage to a Royal Air Force machine'. This was, in fact, only half the story. One of the few vicissitudes of the Fury, not yet fully mastered by any of the three squadrons equipped with the new fighter, was the tendency of the Rolls-Royce Kestrel engine to cut out in a slow roll due to fuel starvation, this manoeuvre imposing negative 'g' on the engine's carburettor float, thereby cutting off the fuel supply momentarily before regaining normal flight. In those few seconds the aircraft would lose height. Jock, in attempting three such rolls, had unwittingly been losing what little height he had started with, and the final roll was just too low when the Kestrel faltered. Jock's real fault, on his first flight in the Fury, was a lack of experience of fuel starvation – but no such grounds for mitigation existed.

Squadron Leader Bryant remained with No.25 Squadron for almost exactly a year, a period that brought with it the realisation of most of the CO's ambitions to blend the pilots' energies with skills in applied flying. He was soon able to take their prowess in close formation for granted and, like Peck a decade earlier, directed the precision that formation flying entailed to the skills of air combat and air firing. Navigation was simply a matter of mugging up the various 'triangles of velocities' – which everyone had been taught at the kindergarten in any case – and applying them to the control column.

The Squadron was selected once more to display at Hendon in June 1933*, a privilege that was to create something of a problem for the flight commanders. To begin with, Squadron Leader Bryant had been posted away to an appointment in Tokyo in March that year, his place being taken by Squadron Leader Anthony Lauderdale Paxton, DFC – another veteran of the War. He was a quiet man, unassuming and somehow not quite what one had come to expect as a fighter squadron commander. And he was bald! The flight commanders and other experienced members of the squadron expressed doubts among themselves as to whether the newcomer could adapt to and master the requirements of a display formation leader, performing the planned routine with smooth and accurate finesse. It had been assumed, immediately after Bryant had departed and before the arrival of Paxton, that either Flt Lt Edward Cecil Theodore Edwards, popularly known as 'Ted Squared', or Flt Lt Charles Ronald Hancock, the senior Flight Commander, would take over as formation leader; both were very experienced and skilled pilots, and universally respected by all; and, of course, they had led their respective flights in formation aerobatics on countless occasions.

Imagine everyone's surprise when, at the briefing for the first full squadron display practice, the entire meeting was led by the new CO, who proceeded to set out the complete routine – times and positions, changes of formation, degrees and rates of turn, and so on, the lot, and impeccably detailed. The old hands, of course, already knew it by heart anyway, but it was encouraging to realise that the new CO had also been doing a bit of practice in his own fashion.

* No.25 Squadron had been represented at Hendon in 1932 by a Sergeant Pilot, 'Jock' Bomar, who gave a scintillating display of solo aerobatics in a Fury, which many of the national newspapers hailed as the highlight of the whole Display (a display of precision flying low over spectator's heads and one that would today fill the law courts with corporate litigation until Doomsday.)

Everything went smoothly until it came to the first loop in vics of three; several pilots had to break formation; then there were aircraft all over the sky; and so it continued for the rest of the day. At first, the 'followers' concluded that the fault lay in the new CO, though no one could put their finger on what he was doing wrong. Then one day, Paxton was called away from the station when a practice was scheduled, and Hancock took over as leader; the resulting fiasco was worse than ever. And it began to dawn on the Squadron that the truth was that Paxton was almost certainly the best pilot on the Squadron and that he had been leading the formation faultlessly. The 'followers' realised that they had allowed the precision of their formation flying to deteriorate. On hearing this, Paxton decided that the only way to 'tighten up' the formation keeping was to *tie the aircraft together* ! By doing so, the cords, if they remained unbroken, would demonstrate how precisely the Squadron was keeping station. It now emerged that Paxton was an extremely experienced and proficient pilot, having been a qualified flying instructor and a 'graduate' of the Central Flying School.

It was then suggested that a roll by a vic of three aircraft should be included in the routine – a manoeuvre not hitherto achieved in public. After several attempts by Fg Off Bing Cross, Fg Off Harry Burke, and led by Flt Lt Hancock, the roll was accomplished with precision, and accepted as part of the display routine. As previously explained, it had to be a barrel roll in order to prevent the engines from cutting and the aircraft from losing height; a slow roll would have been more spectacular in more senses than one!

Sad to relate, the day of the Hendon Display, 24th June, brought with it rain and total cloud cover and although the Squadron performed an immaculate routine in front of 140,000 members of the public – it was confined to Air Drill, plus a loop or two and – the roll! Nevertheless that famed, but ascetic, aeronautical correspondent, C G Grey (editor of *The Aeroplane*) waxed lyrical. It seems that Grey always did have a soft spot for No.25, and once referred to them as 'that old, bold band of greatly accomplished aviators'!

The year 1933 was marked by an unusual entertainment at Hawkinge. For some years builders' trucks, cement

The Officers, Warrant Officers and Sergeant Pilot of No.25 (Fighter) Squadron at Hawkinge in 1935. The upholstered armchair is obviously an augury for the future of the booted figure of the CO, Sqn Ldr William Dickson, DSO, OBE, AFC, later to become Chief of the Air Staff. Those in civilian clothes are probably serving on the RAF Reserve of Officers and 'doing time' on the Squadron.

(Photo: via Roy S Humphreys)

Death of a Hawkinge hangar. On 7th August 1933 a Horsley of No.504 (County of Nottingham) Squadron, flown by Flt Lt Hartridge, suffered engine failure on the approach to land after a gunnery flight over Leysdown. With nowhere else to go, the pilot made a perfect landing on the roof of No.4 Hangar, rolling to a stop just feet from the brick parapet over the hangar doors. As the crew clambered from the roof down a hastily provided ladder, fuel from a ruptured tank seeped down the hangar walls and ignited. A full petrol bowser, with its paint blistering in the intense heat, was dragged clear by some airmen, but six Blackburn Dart aircraft stored in the hangar were totally destroyed. One of the onlookers was Major Arnold of the Royal Engineers, in charge of the building expansion at Hawkinge. It is unlikely that he was amused. The hangar was never re-built. (Photo: Gp Capt F Wiseman-Clarke)

mixers and scaffolding had been a common sight on the station, as gradually the hangars assumed brick and steel office extensions, while new barrack blocks, Messes, sick quarters and so on sprung up, many of the old wooden huts being replaced by more permanent structures. On 7th August, while No.504 (County of Nottingham) Squadron, Auxiliary Air Force, was in temporary residence at Hawkinge, one of its pilots, on approaching to land, realised that he was overshooting and attempted to stretch his glide, but only achieved a passable landing – on top of No.4 Hangar. Realising that nothing further could be achieved by remaining in their cockpits, the two crew members climbed out on to the hangar roof and then to ground level by means of an iron ladder, apparently affixed to the hangar for such an eventuality.

Unfortunately, unknown to anyone, the Horsley had ruptured a fuel tank, the contents of which dribbled on to the hangar roof and then down the inside of the walls and somehow ignited. A fire started and spread rapidly; despite the efforts, first of the station fire tender and shortly afterwards of the Folkestone fire brigade, the hangar was effectively destroyed. The local press got hold of the story and of the fact that six 'Harts' had been destroyed inside. The aeronautical press also got hold of the story but assumed that the local paper's reporter didn't know his Hart from his Fury and the nation was informed that 'six of No.25 Squadron's Furies had been destroyed'. Fortunately, nothing of the sort had occurred. There had been a misunderstanding somewhere: the aircraft were in fact six old Fleet Air Arm Blackburn Darts, which had been put into storage in the hangar, and they were the casualties. There was however also some confusion at the Air Ministry, and its contracts department went so far as to draft a contract for six 'replacement Furies' from Hawker Aircraft Ltd – this was cancelled almost as soon as the mistake was spotted!

There was one other result of this mishap. The Chief Engineer of the commercial building contractor was an enraged spectator at the conflagration, enraged on account of the re-building contract already being some weeks behind schedule. However, he evidently decided on a policy of silence, and awaited further instructions from the RAF 'Works and Bricks' department at the Air Ministry. The upshot was that the builders were authorised to remove all traces of the former hangar, other than its concrete base. It was never re-built.

In 1934 the Squadron was again selected to give the principal aerobatic display at Hendon at a time when it was awaiting the results of the annual Sassoon Trophy, the first time that it seemed it had a real chance of winning the coveted fighter competition, which included all the applied flying disciplines. If this could be achieved, it would silence those who looked upon display flying as no more than window dressing – being quite unaware of the precision flying it entailed, and the resulting in-bred precision that it produced when it came to the skills required in successful air combat, the *raison d'être* of a fighter squadron. Some of the old hands had by then left the Squadron, and it was necessary to move others between Flights so as to distribute those with the most experience; two of the three gaps in the display team were filled by those who had not been selected in 1933, the third being taken by a newcomer, Sergeant Pearson.

This time the weather was kind and all went well, except that Nigel Daunt's cord parted during a nine-vic loop. Such was the perfection aimed at by every pilot that some of them felt that the Squadron's entire display had been sullied and declined to join the celebrations held that evening in

Nine Fury IIs of No.25 Squadron in immaculate Vic near Hawkinge in 1937. (Photo: courtesy of No.25 (Fighter) Squadron)

London, but preferred to return to Hawkinge with their collective tail between their legs.

All was forgotten and forgiven when, about three weeks later, it transpired that the Squadron had indeed won the Sassoon Trophy, Daunt himself having achieved one of the highest individual gunnery scores of all 132 pilots of ADGB competing. Ironically, Daunt was one of the very few of those pilots who would never fire his guns in anger in the Second World War. He would be engaged in another sort of 'precision' flying! Another coincidental triumph was achieved by Clouston who, although he was a member of the Squadron's aerobatic display team at Hendon, won the Cross Country (navigation) competition – and later, as a member of the Reserve of Officers, achieved fame for his long-distance records, flown all over the world during the last years before the Second World War. 'Bing' Cross, as already noted, rose to become an Air Chief Marshal.

Meanwhile, No.25 Squadron had demonstrably reached the enviable position as the most professionally efficient fighter Squadron in the Royal Air Force at a critical stage in the affairs of the Service. Deterioration of the political situation in Europe, centred on the ambitions expressed to the world by Adolf Hitler, now established as the leader of the Nazi party of Germany. By the end of 1934 he had made no secret of his determination to make that nation the most powerful in Europe, a stance emulated by Hermann Wilhelm Göring, now appointed commissioner for aviation in Germany, and who trumpeted the creation of a new military air force, to be armed with aircraft already being developed by a resurgent aviation industry, evidence of which was already reaching the British Government.

To meet the potential threat to Great Britain, plans were being laid to embark on a huge expansion of the Armed Services, the greatest emphasis being on modernisation and expansion of the Royal Air Force. The old target of 52 fighter squadrons, originally announced long ago in 1925 was still far from realisation, a state of affairs that was now to become addressed as being of the highest priority.

Achieving this target was not simply a matter of increasing aircraft production, but of finding and training hundreds of new pilots and aircrews and – at least as important – of developing new fighter aircraft that no longer appeared to perpetuate a design formula that was not fundamentally different from that being pursued in 1918 – namely the single-bay biplane, armed with two rifle-calibre machine guns. In short, the days of 'the Best Flying Club in the World' and its highly polished and nimble little biplanes, were unquestionably numbered.

Thanks largely to the encouragement provided by Sir John Salmond, before he stepped down from the Air Ministry to join Imperial Airways in 1933, several aircraft designers had toyed with monoplane fighters but, without adequate funding for research, none had entered production. All the time the Royal Air Force remained primarily equipped with the Bristol Bulldog, now six years out of date.

The steps taken to put into effect expansion of the RAF's fighter arm were to have a growing influence on No.25 Squadron, as almost all its pilots were posted away to

Immaculate with their polished engine panels and wheelspats, two of No.25 (Fighter) Squadron's Hawker Fury IIs taxy out to begin their annual demonstration of nine-aircraft formation aerobatics at the 1937 Hendon Display. This was the only occasion on which the Squadron flew the much-improved Mark II Fury at Hendon. Within six months Fighter Command was receiving its first Hawker Hurricane monoplane fighters.
(Photo: Francis K Mason collection)

attend instructor courses at the Central Flying School, before being posted to the growing number of Flying Training Schools that were now being opened.

Squadron Leader Tony Paxton was promoted Wing Commander and posted away in January 1935, his place being taken by Squadron Leader William Forster Dickson, DSO, OBE, AFC, an officer whose Service career had already marked him down for senior commands.

Several old members of No.25 Squadron, pilots and ground personnel, recall that Bill Dickson was no less keen that, not only would No.25 Squadron win the Sassoon Trophy again but, so long as he commanded it, would go on winning it. He therefore set as a new target the winning of *each* of the five disciplines – something that no Squadron had ever achieved in a single year. According to one pilot, a photograph was taken towards the end of 1935 (when No.25 again won the Trophy) showing the entire Squadron arrayed behind a huge bank of silverware, among which stood all the major trophies, cups and *bric-à-brac* – in addition to the Squadron's other dining table accoutrements. As Dickson somewhat austerely remarked, 'It was an entertaining sight but in thoroughly bad taste! To have it photographed is only compounding the crime.'*

* Every effort to locate a copy of this photograph has failed, although Sqn Ldr Dickson's observation can be understood, for it was a very old tradition on No.25 that every officer, on being posted away, would donate a 'piece of silver table furniture' to the Squadron. The collection was certainly impressive, including silver 'genie lamps' as cigar lighters, tankards by the score, and all the trappings of smokers and drinkers, not to mention the odd candelabrum, bowls, cigar cutters, cigarette boxes, menu holders, cruets and so on; some pieces had obviously been begged from the officer's family, as being far beyond the scope of a Flying Officer's purse! Among the most attractive gifts were superbly fashioned solid silver models of every type of aircraft flown by the Squadron from the D.H.4 onwards; most of these had been presented by the aircraft manufacturers. Alas, much of this 'thoroughly bad taste' was mysteriously dispersed during the Second World War.

In July 1935 Hawkinge had opened its new headquarters building, and acquired an administrative personnel establishment. Yet it did not immediately become a Station, in that the officer commanding the resident Squadron was still also the station commander in the rank of Squadron Leader. Dickson continued to divide his time between leadership of No.25 Squadron and attending to station affairs until he was posted to the RAF Staff College in February 1936. His subsequent rise through the ranks of the Royal Air Force, though by no means meteoric, was steady and, to those who knew him well, inevitable, for in the mid-1950s he was to become Chief of the Air Staff – and No.25 Squadron's second Marshal of the Royal Air Force, after Arthur Tedder.

A Hawker Fury Mk.II of No.25 (Fighter) Squadron, Hawkinge, October 1936. (Photo: Francis K Mason collection)

Dickson's successor in command of No.25 was Squadron Leader Harold Hunter Down, AFC (later Air Commodore, CBE, AFC). Was there ever a more appropriately christened officer posted to command a fighter squadron, and one based not thirty miles from the battlefield of Hastings? Needless to say he quickly became known on No.25 Squadron as 'King Harold' – and throughout the Air Force, not as Harold Down, but Hunter Down. Those who were with No.25 Squadron at the time thought the world of their new CO, who proved to be an excellent leader in the air and on the ground. Alas, however, he was never able to achieve Dickson's target of a clean sweep of all flying disciplines in the Sassoon competition – although by winning the competition in 1936, ensured that No.25 Squadron became the outright and permanent custodian of the Trophy by the terms expressed by Sir Philip Sassoon, its donor and the Permanent Under-Secretary of state for Air. Be that as it may, Hunter Down was to be appointed Commandant of the Central Flying School in 1940-1941, the Squadron's third 'old boy' to join that illustrious list of famous airmen.

The year 1936 was the last in which No.25 Squadron appeared at Hendon flying the Fury Mark I. By the end of that year both the Hurricane and Spitfire eight-gun monoplane fighters were entering production (but would not appear in service for many months). Nevertheless, it had been realised that a dangerous gap in fighter equipment would exist between the demise of the eight-year-old Bulldog fighter and the arrival in service of the new monoplanes. Gloster had produced the two-gun Gauntlet biplane, but this was less of a stop-gap fighter than a convenient, and relatively inexpensive means of providing the RAF's newly-formed Fighter Command with an aircraft of modestly-improved performance. Hawker's design team had also been at work, trying to scrape the last, untapped potential from the Fury I – itself already half a decade old. For some three years the Company had been flying an aircraft, dubbed the Super Fury but, although it returned a speed of around 230 mph, it had employed the Rolls-Royce Goshawk steam-cooled engine, whose development had been halted (largely because it interfered with Rolls-Royce's vital work to get the new Merlin into production). Instead, Hawker came up with a less ambitious development of the former Fury I. Once this aircraft, which was capable of a maximum speed some 20 mph faster than the Mk.I, had completed its Service trials, it was a simple matter to run it off the existing production line with scarcely a day's delay.

The first of the new Fury Mk.IIs reached No.25 Squadron in October 1936.

THE END OF AN ERA.

On 14th July 1936 it was announced that Air Chief Marshal Sir Hugh Dowding had been appointed Air Officer Commanding-in-Chief of the new Fighter Command, which took the place of the former Air Defence of Great Britain. Within a few months the Command would assume a new Group structure, each Group organised geographically for the defence of a region of the British Isles, and the over-sea approaches to it. No.25 Squadron, based on the coast of Kent, became a component of No.11 Group, which itself was divided into Sectors; in due course Hawkinge would become a forward fighter base in the Biggin Hill Sector. Tactical operational control of all fighter squadrons based in the Sector would be exercised at an operations centre at Biggin Hill.

Outwardly, life on No.25 Squadron appeared to change little; formation flying still occupied the pilots fairly frequently, although there was already speculation that a change in the operational function of the Squadron was under consideration. When it was yet again announced that No.25 Squadron would be taking its new Furies to Hendon for the annual display, these rumours seemed to have been disproved. Yet much more time was being given to a series of 'wireless calibrations exercises', whose purpose was still obscure. Sections of three Furies would be ordered to fly very accurate 'patrol lines' parallel to, and about ten miles off the north and south coasts of Kent. Early in 1937, the Squadron received orders to fly a succession of single Furies on a direct approach towards the coasts, holding exact speed and height from points fifty miles out to sea. Heights of the approach varied from 15,000 to 22,000ft.

As was perhaps natural, speculation as to the true purpose of these wireless calibration flights was rife, more so because the pilots had orders to maintain strict radio silence. What earthly use, they asked, were such flights? How could anyone calibrate a wireless set on the ground when there was nothing to hear from an aeroplane in the air?

In truth, of course, these were the early efforts to discover the best location for coastal 'radio direction finding' (RDF) stations – later to become the all-important 'radar' chain, whose stations were intended to locate and track incoming enemy raiders. The 'listeners', with their huge concrete sound detectors set into the Channel shores, had long since packed their bags and moved away, so no one seems to have associated their purpose with that of the 'wireless calibration flights'. Just as extraordinary was the fact that the purpose of the tedious calibration flights was kept so secret, bearing in mind the number of air force personnel involved.

Secrecy had never been a wonted feature in the 'flying club' atmosphere that had pervaded fighter squadrons in the south of England since the Kaiser's War. The advent of the new restrictions heralded a new aura of professionalism that closed a chapter in the history of the Royal Air Force – the end of The Best Flying Club in the World!

The No.25 (Fighter) Squadron Hendon display team of 1937. Left to right: *Sgt W T Jeffrey, Sgt R C Haine, Sgt Walley, Flt Lt Cameron, Sqn Ldr H H Down, Flt Lt R J C Nedwill, Plt Off Robert Henry Lonsdale, Sgt T Blackburn, Sgt Aggett. It has not proved possible to discover why Lonsdale fought in the Battle of Britain three years later as a sergeant pilot.* (Photo: Sqn Ldr W T Jeffrey, AFC)

CHAPTER 5

'Sorry, Chaps, you'll have to imagine they're Hurricanes'

(The Months before Munich, 1937-1938)

IN HIS CAPACITY as station commander Squadron Leader Hunter Down was kept informed as to the importance attached to the location of Hawkinge – the fighter station closest to the French coast. Although there was no longer any question that France represented any threat to the British Isles, both nations being equally aware of the danger of, and militarily deploying to oppose, a resurgent and fast re-arming Germany. In any case, no one on No.25 Squadron could be unaware of Hawkinge's potential importance in the air defence of south-east England. The Squadron was still one of only three in the RAF officially referred to as interceptor fighter squadrons, although this was to change during 1936 as more and more squadrons re-equipped with the Gauntlet; and early in 1937 No.72 Squadron was re-formed at Tangmere (from a nucleus provided by No.1 Squadron) equipped with the four-gun Gladiator, which had been belatedly adjudged the eventual winner of Salmond's F.7/30 Specification, issued to the aircraft industry in 1930-31.

The first flight by the Hawker Hurricane in November 1935 and the Spitfire in March 1936, both aircraft being capable of speeds of over 300 mph, a service ceiling of around 30,000ft, and an armament of no fewer than eight machine guns, brought about a fundamental reappraisal of fighter squadron deployment by the new Command. Could Hawkinge continue to be regarded as a suitable location for fighter squadrons? Indeed, if fighters with the performance of the Hurricane and Spitfire were based at, say, Biggin Hill, Kenley and Croydon, did an airfield like Hawkinge represent a significant asset or a sitting target? That is not to say that Hawkinge might not continue to represent a useful forward landing ground for re-fuelling and emergency use. Be that as it may, as war plans began to be examined and adjusted in the light of a yet likely war against Germany, it was now planned that, in the event of war, whatever No.25 Squadron's future operational rôle, the Squadron would be pulled back to a 'War Station' – in this instance Northolt.

As No.25 Squadron continued flying the beautiful Hawker Fury Mk.II biplane fighter in 1937, members of the Squadron yearned for the day when they would receive either Hurricanes or Spitfires. Indeed there cannot have been a single squadron in Fighter Command that didn't share that yearning. However, in mid-1937 it was discovered by Rolls-Royce that the Merlin engine required a fundamental modification to the valve rocker boxes, itself a straightforward and relatively 'local' design change, but one that demanded an alteration in the aircraft nose profile in the Hurricane and Spitfire. This change, discovered after Hawker had almost completed the jigs for the Hurricane production line, delayed the completion of the first production examples by more than three months, and reduced the rate of Merlin engine production by an overall 20% for a further three months.

While Rolls-Royce toiled to set up the Merlin II production lines in September 1937 – bombarded by Air Ministry memoranda seeking clarification as to the anticipated delivery dates, deliveries of the unmodified Merlin I went ahead, destined for the ill-fated Fairey Battle light bomber. The company was also continuing to turn out huge numbers of Kestrel engines – principally for Hawker Harts, Audaxes, Demons and Hinds (which between them constituted more than half the numerical strength of the RAF) as well as for further orders for the Fury II, as Nos.41, 73 and 87 Squadrons followed No.25 Squadron in equipping or re-equipping with the fighter.

Meanwhile, putting an end to No.25 Squadron's agonising as to whether or when it was going to receive Hurricanes, Hunter Down was warned to ensure that all the Fury IIs were serviceable, preparatory to their transfer to No.41 Squadron at Catterick in Yorkshire early in October. No sooner had the CO been given these instructions than he himself was promoted Wing Commander and posted from the Squadron, his place being taken by Squadron Leader Donald Malcolm Fleming, DFC. His first task was to convey to the Squadron the news that, in due course, it was to become a dedicated night fighter squadron – a specialist combat rôle not exclusively undertaken by an RAF Squadron since 1918*.

* Both Nos.3 and 17 Squadrons had undertaken night fighter training at Upavon in the late 1920s in Hawker Woodcocks. They also assumed a secondary day fighter rôle, both being for the defence of the industrial Midlands when, theoretically at least, this vital heart of Britain could be threatened by a bomber force based in France.

Throughout October 1937, as the beloved Furies flew off to Catterick, two-seat Hawker Demon fighters began arriving at Hawkinge from Nos.41 and 29 Squadrons, and observer/gunners were posted in. During the first month, the latter comprised two pilot officers, a flight sergeant, five sergeants and eight 'airmen gunners' – most of them leading aircraftmen (LACs); some were posted in from the above former Demon Squadrons, while others arrived direct from training units. The non-commissioned aircrew, at that time, received a flat fourpence a day 'flying allowance' in addition to the pay appropriate to their rank.

The Hawker Demon had already been in service in the RAF since 1931. Following the air exercises of 1930, when Hart light bombers had outpaced every Bulldog squadron sent up to intercept them, Sydney Camm had suggested to the Air Ministry modifying a small pilot batch of Harts 'as fighters' – a logical step to ensure that at least there was a chance of catching the bombers. Known initially as Hart Fighters, these equipped one Flight of No.23 Squadron (the other two flights retaining their Bulldogs). Whereas the Hart bomber possessed a top speed of 184 mph, the fighter version, with all the bomb racks and other *impedimenta* removed, but with twin Vickers machine guns firing forward (plus a Lewis gun on the rear cockpit) could manage about

186-188 mph! Nevertheless the Hart Fighters could out-fly and out-fight the Bulldogs on No.23 Squadron, and it was not long before its remaining Bulldogs were also discarded in favour of the Hart Fighter, now re-named the Demon and ordered into quantity production. Within three years over ninety aircraft had been built, as sub-contracting of the Hart variants was spread throughout the aircraft industry. Indeed, by 1935, production of Sydney Camm's Hawker designs, undertaken by such manufacturers as Armstrong-Whitworth, Avro, Boulton Paul, Bristol, Gloster, Vickers and Westland, had enabled these large and vital elements of the British aircraft industry to survive the great Depression for, without these orders, most of them would have gone into liquidation, with the subsequent loss of hundreds of design staff and thousands of skilled factory workers. As it was, there were still large numbers of Demons available to equip fighter squadrons and training units in 1937.

As a fighter the Demon could not, in 1937, be regarded as anything but a stopgap, and a poor one at that. Quite what it was intended to achieve in service with No.25 Squadron is difficult to imagine, unless it was to demonstrate to experienced Fury pilots what it was like to be carrying a passenger in the back. Certainly it was not an 'interceptor' fighter (and had never been intended as such), and for a squadron, with an established reputation – within the Service – for precision flying, particularly during formation flying and aerobatics, it must have been galling to read accounts of the Empire Air Day displays, held annually at aerodromes throughout Britain, and attended by relatively small and inexperienced display teams which concealed their mediocrity with lots of coloured smoke!

This said, the reality was perhaps slow to dawn on those fighter squadrons which, like No.25, had constituted the cutting edge of the Royal Air Force throughout the inter-war years. Slow, perhaps, to realise the change that had come about with the approach of another war against Germany. Yet those few squadrons had performed a vital task, in spite of the pervading parsimony of a wholly disinterested succession of governments – protected by the flawed 10-year Rule – whose leaders had paid little attention (and *nothing* else) to the importance of technical design continuity and the maintenance of military capability to match evolving threats to the *status quo*. The oft-quoted statement by Stanley Baldwin, 'The bomber will always get through', were empty words for all the notice taken by his government. If there is one attribute which a dismal procession of governments (of all political hues) has ignored, usually to the Nation's peril, it is that Defence is seldom the job of the armed forces *today*, but rather *tomorrow*. And one can't start digging trenches when the enemy is already charging!

While the re-equipping of No.25 Squadron with Demons continued up to the end of 1937, No.111 Squadron started receiving its first few Hurricanes at Northolt a few days before Christmas, becoming – quite justifiably – the first of the RAF's new élite first-line interceptor monoplane squadrons. No.25 Squadron drifted away from the public gaze as more than half its pilots were posted to other fighter squadrons – several to the Middle East, and some to the

A different view of Hawkinge in about 1937, after the decision had been taken to enlarge it to accommodate two squadrons. The new, enlarged Officers' Mess, with tennis courts and elaborate approach driveway, is in the centre of the picture, and the tented accommodation for No.2 (Army Co-operation) Squadron can be seen on the left. The two large buildings in the foreground are the Station Commander's and CO No.25 Squadron's married quarters; however, as these two posts were held by the same officer, the second house was occupied by the CO of No.2 Squadron. The Sergeant's Mess and the two large barrack blocks flank the parade ground beyond the Officer's Mess. The site originally occupied by No.4 Hangar, which was not re-built after the fire, is simply a large rectangle of concrete hardstanding.

(Photo: The RAF Museum)

Hawkinge Wireless Section personnel checking their equipment prior to carting it off to Hendon for the 1937 Display; HM King George VI passed 'instructions' to No.25 Squadron during its Air Drill and aerobatic display on that occasion.

(Photo: via Roy S Humphreys)

CFS to receive training as instructors.

True, the Squadron continued to practice formation flying, as well as all the other disciplines, with night flying taking an increased share of No.25's effort. However, the very fact that Fighter Command had introduced a two-seat fighter, and one with a very pedestrian performance, into service represented a sinister trend that was to have disastrous results two years hence.

The history of the two-seat dedicated fighters began effectively with the introduction of the Bristol F.2b Fighter into service with the RFC in 1917, with considerable success – once the fighting tactics had evolved and the co-ordination of pilot and gunner had been worked out by trial and error. In effect the pilot, with his two machine guns was still the offensive element, and the gunner, with his rotatable machine gun in the rear cockpit could defend the aircraft from any enemy fighter attacking from the rear. The 'Brisfit' remained in front line service with the RAF, long after the Armistice, the last examples being withdrawn from squadrons overseas in the early 1930s. It remained in service for so long simply because it continued to give sterling service when not opposed by enemy aircraft of any sort; there was very little money available, or need, to replace it as a *fighter*. Trenchard had made sure of *that*.

At home the Demon had entered service, as has been shown, not so much because there was a requirement for it, but simply because nothing could catch the Hart light bomber – except the Fury, which only served with three interceptor squadrons. And the Demon simply stayed in service because it was a *fighter*. The folly was committed when it came for the Demon to be replaced, assuming that there was a need for this type of fighter. And it was in 1935 that the Air Ministry assumed that the need existed. A scenario was imagined in which Germany might conceivably attempt to attack England using bombers with a fighter escort, and at once minds went back to the Brisfit of the First World War, with its gunner defending the fighter's tail. At once the Demon was seen as a useful stopgap, and its manufacturer evolved a curious folding shield to protect the Demon's gunner from the slipstream, in the interests of improving his aim! The 'lobster claw' shield was fitted to some Demons in service, but was unpopular among the gunners simply because it reduced their field of view by half.

Fortunately this contraption didn't reach No.25, simply because the Squadron was seldom used in an air defence capacity. Instead the pilots found themselves being called upon to fly all manner of exercises – scarcely any of them involving air combat. During daylight hours, between the traditional limited formation practices, air drill and battle climbs, they collaborated with local infantry units based in Kent, flying over the 'battlefield' to simulate attacks on opposing forces. Cross-country navigation training flights were frequent and fairly popular as it gave the pilots an opportunity to visit other stations in No.11 Group to 'see how the other half lived'. Ironically, the most unpopular of all the training, bearing in mind the supposed future night fighting rôle, were the night exercises, and later the searchlight co-operation flights. To begin with, landing away from their own familiar airfield at night posed something of a hazard, as those Stations in No.11 Group, unaccustomed to illuminating their grass runways, tended not to worry over

Hawker Hind K4544 at Sutton after its collision with K3983 on 5th November 1937, displaying the damage to its wings.
(Photo: P Jarrett)

much about laying a flarepath into wind, thereby tending to overtax the Hawkinge pilots' ability to land a Demon out of wind, and at night. One pilot recorded the fact that he made seven attempts to land at Biggin Hill at night and each time overshot 'because I kept coming across vehicles on the flarepath'. On enquiry, after the Demon landed, Biggin Hill flight office denied that any vehicles were motoring about the airfield; the Demon had arrived before the runway flares were lit and the pilot had been trying to land on the Bromley-Westerham road. The watch office staff admitted that no one was manning the radio transmitter, but confessed they had been outside, waiting with bated breath to see exactly where the Demon pilot finally chose to land.

The Demon, despite its name, was a very forgiving aeroplane, with scarcely anything approaching a vice. The worst hazard was provided by the engine exhaust pipes which extended aft along both sides of the fuselage as far as the pilot's cockpit about three feet below the cockpit coming. These pipes retained a considerable amount of heat for many minutes after landing and woe betide any pilot who grasped one to steady himself as he vacated the 'office', or allowed his parachute to brush it as he climbed out! These lengthened pipes were fitted to the Demon (and seldom on any of the other Hart variants) simply to prevent glare from the engine exhaust blinding the pilot during night flying.

No.25 Squadron suffered only one serious flying accident while equipped with Demons. On 5th November 1937 – while the Squadron was still receiving its initial quota of Demons – several pilots were authorised to carry out some practice formation flying on the new aircraft in the vicinity of Dover. During the course of this flight two aircraft collided, the tail of K3983 being cut off by the wing of K4544. The pilot of K3983, Plt Off John Geoffrey Cave (who had arrived on No.25 Squadron from Flying Training School three months earlier) managed to bale out safely, but his passenger, AC1 James Dale, was killed when the aircraft crashed at Tilmanstone Colliery, near Dover. The other pilot managed to force land in a field at Sutton, near Deal, without further damage to his aircraft. It seems that the pilots, used to close formation flying in Furies, had not yet realised that the Demon's reserve of power was inadequate to enable such close separation flying to be safely undertaken. It was not established at the subsequent enquiry why Dale did not bale out of the stricken aircraft, although it is most likely that he was not equipped with a parachute, or had not been instructed in its use.

• • •

As the international situation in Europe continued to deteriorate with the annexation of Austria by Germany early in the New Year, the Air Ministry announced in January 1938 that no further Hendon air displays would be held. The reason given was that the airfield was now considered too small for modern aircraft, the emphasis in future being to increase the scope of the Annual Empire Air Days held at most of the principal RAF stations throughout the country. Much later it transpired that the real reasons for the discontinuation of the Hendon display were threefold, namely the presence of important prototype aircraft in the traditional New Types Park during the period of the Display (causing too much disruption to the manufacturers' flight trials), delays in delivering new aircraft to the Squadrons, and a tightening of security regarding the use and capabilities of new aircraft already entering service. Being 'local affairs', the Empire Air Day displays had not only fostered good relations among the neighbouring community but constituted a powerful opportunity to bolster recruiting for the RAF during those Expansion years.

Certainly such considerations did not concern No.25 Squadron which, if it had been invited to attend a Hendon display that year would, in all likelihood, have abandoned its Demons there. For young enthusiastic fighter pilots, now joining their first operational squadrons in fast growing numbers, the thought of being called on to fly aircraft incapable of reaching 200 mph was unpalatable, when everyone was talking about the Hurricane and Spitfire. And salt was rubbed into the wound when No.111 Squadron's CO, Sqn Ldr John Gillan, flew a Hurricane from Edinburgh to London, covering 327 miles in just 48 minutes – an average ground speed of no less than 408 mph. Even though no one thought it necessary to mention the strong tail wind, it was undoubtedly a tremendous fillip to the nation's morale and pride in the Royal Air Force.

As the interminable searchlight and army co-operation exercises dragged on (with fewer and fewer opportunities to indulge in occasional formation flying), and almost meaningless attempts at 'dog-fighting' were authorised as a standing item in the Squadron's allocation of operational training effort, morale on No.25 took a perceptible dip. It would have been surprising if the Squadron's commanding officer, Sqn Ldr Donald Fleming, did not seize any opportunity that presented itself to report the situation to Group headquarters, explaining that the pilots felt that they were simply being used 'to keep the grass cut' at Hawkinge, just in case war broke out.

Early in 1938 Hawkinge was spruced up for the annual inspection by the Air Officer Commanding No.11 Group, Air Vice-Marshal Ernest Leslie Gossage, CB, CVO, DSO, MC. Arrayed in a neat line in front of the hangars were the twelve serviceable Demons of No.25 Squadron, as well as a similar number of Hawker Hectors of No.2 (Army Co-operation) Squadron, then sharing the station with No.25, but living under canvas. Before leaving Hawkinge, Gossage addressed the Demon pilots with a conciliatory and informal talk, giving them an overall picture of No.11 Group's progress in re-equipping with modern fighters – so far one Squadron of Hurricanes and two more planned for 1938, three with Gladiators and four with Gauntlets – but none with Spitfires, these not being expected in No.11 Group until 1939. He held out hope that, by the end of the year No.25 Squadron, would be re-equipped, but declined to state what aircraft it might expect to receive; and the AOC would not be drawn on the question as to whether it was still planned for No.25 Squadron to become a night fighter unit.

This did little to reassure the Squadron, and did not address the vexed problem, already apparent, of the use of airmen gunners. This was not centred so much on the widely acknowledged injustice of absurdly low pay and flying allowance, but on the matter of ground duties and discipline, some of the less imaginative ground NCOs being unwilling to take account of the fatigue and discomfort of several hours' in a draughty and noisy cockpit (often at night), and with seldom more than a sandwich and cup of tea on landing. Several palliatives were tried (such as airmen on night flying being excused all further duties until noon the following day). This aggravating problem persisted until late in the Battle of Britain in 1940 when it was decided to promote all airmen gunners to the paid rank of sergeant, and to increase the daily flying allowance by an average of about ninepence (to one shilling and threepence, about 6p in decimal coinage – just adequate to buy a pint of beer and a packet of five small cigarettes! If an airman was free of an evening to visit Folkestone, the return bus fare cost most of his daily flying allowance. . .

No.25 Squadron's Hawker Demons in line abreast formation; it was normal practice to fly half a wing span apart within Flights. The Demon was under-powered compared with, say, the Fury and the Gladiator. (Photo: Francis K Mason collection)

THE GLADIATOR

In June 1938 everything changed on No.25 Squadron once more as the Demons started being flown away – mainly destined for Squadrons of the Auxiliary Air Force. Such was the continuing shortfall in the number of squadrons in Fighter Command that most of the former Auxiliary bomber squadrons were declared to become day fighter squadrons, a metamorphosis that was to be less radical than it sounded, being re-equipped with Hawker Demons in place of Hawker Hinds, and learning the skills of air-to-air combat in place of dropping bombs.

In place of the Demons, No.25 Squadron now welcomed its full establishment of sixteen Gloster Gladiators, all but two of them arriving from No.56

Evocative picture of the biplane era. Air-to-air with No.25 Squadron Demons. Contrary to previous beliefs that the military establishment in the background was Hawkinge, it is in fact Shorncliffe Camp near Folkestone, which had been the unlucky recipient of a heavy aerial raid by Gothas during the Kaiser's War. (Photo: The RAF Museum)

Squadron, which was to become the third to receive Hurricanes.* At long last the first trickle of Spitfires had started arriving on No.19 Squadron at Duxford, but with a list of flying limitations which would occupy almost a year to rectify.

The low pay offered to those who considered volunteering to fight in what seemed to be an inevitable war – those whose fathers (if they had survived) recalled the horrors of the Kaiser's War – seemed to represent no deterrent. The after-effects of the Depression were still apparent throughout Britain in the mid-1930s with unemployment rampant. The chance of a job and comradeship in what was being portrayed as a glamorous Service, with all living expenses provided, and a possible chance 'to see the world', seemed the perfect means to escape the hardship and uncertainties of life as a civilian.

* This must be qualified. The second Squadron to receive Hurricanes, No.3, was stationed at Kenley, but it soon became all too obvious that, with considerable enlargement, Kenley airfield was too small for Hurricanes and, after receiving the new fighters in March, had to give them up again in July and return to Gladiators, while the Kenley airfield was enlarged and the station buildings modernised and extended. No.3 did not get Hurricanes once more until July 1939, by which time the squadron had moved to Biggin Hill! No.56 Squadron, however, was effectively the second squadron to become *fully operational* on the Hurricane – after No.111.

• • •

The manner in which the Gloster Gladiator biplane reached the Royal Air Force via the Gauntlet has already been touched on. By the time it entered squadron service with the new Fighter Command, with a top speed of slightly over 250 mph, Germany's new *Luftwaffe* was already making plans to send its first 24 examples of the Messerschmitt Bf 109B single-seat monoplane fighter (maximum speed 320 mph) to Spain where it would join the *Legion Cóndor* fighting in the Civil War).

The Gladiator Mk.II, with which No.25 Squadron was re-equipped, was powered by an 830hp Bristol Mercury VIII air-cooled radial engine (compared with the 640hp of the Fury IIs in-line Kestrel VI). As such, the Gladiator proved to be a useful stopgap pending the arrival in service of the Hurricane and Spitfire (as originally intended). Though still a biplane, it nevertheless introduced a number of features that were new to the fighter squadrons with which it served, most important of which were landing flaps which served to reduce the landing speed and improve control of the aircraft right down to the touch-down speed. The enclosed cockpit came as a surprise to most pilots – long used to flying 'in the fresh air' – but proved to be essential while attempting to keep a target in the gunsight, such was the increasing turbulence in the pilot's cockpit as speeds of 250 mph, and more, were now to become commonplace. Yet, many of the 'older' pilots still preferred to keep their cockpit hoods open for take-off and landing, as well as much of their cruising flight.

On the subject of the big radial engine of the Gladiator, this feature considerably reduced the forward field of view, and demanded that, while taxying, the aircraft was weaved

Such a precocious display of air power can only herald an imminent AOC's Inspection. Either that or the CO wanted to check that no one had pinched one of his aircraft during the night. Nineteen Demons in line abreast certainly occupied quite a lot of space. A photograph taken at Hawkinge in about April 1938. (Photo: Hawker Aircraft Ltd.)

from side to side to ensure it would clear any obstacles. To many young fledgling pilots, this had to become second nature as both the Hurricane and Spitfire, with their big Merlin engines, demanded constant weaving if the pilot was to avoid collisions.

Another break with tradition was the Gladiator's armament of four machine guns, two of which were mounted under the lower wings, outboard of the propeller arc, and therefore free-firing; the other two guns were mounted in the sides of the fuselage and, firing through the propeller, were therefore synchronised. The aircraft flown by No.25 Squadron were armed with four Browning rifle-calibre guns, the license-built version of the brilliant American Colt; this was a light and compact gun which proved to be about four times as reliable as the age-old Vickers; needless to say the Colt-Brownings equipped the new eight-gun monoplane fighters.

Though not blessed with a retractable undercarriage, the new Dowty cantilever, single-oleo strut landing gear of the Gladiator proved exceptionally strong, yet absorbed much of the touch-down energy and made for much smoother and positive landings.

In general, the pilots on No.25 enjoyed flying the Gladiator. For those who still had memories of the Fury, it did represent a marked step forward. The Gladiator possessed adequate surplus power to enable formation aerobatics to be flown but, as most of the veteran Fury pilots had by mid-June already left No.25 Squadron, such formation flying was confined to air drill, and practice dogfighting – still based on the old 'Fighting Area' tactics. That is to say the initial approach to an enemy being flown in fairly close formation, followed by a diving attack in line astern before re-forming and repeating the same tactic. Variations of this included a head-on charge in line abreast and a diving attack from a rear quarter in close vic, before breaking downwards. These tactics were also pursued by the Hurricane and Spitfire squadrons well into 1940, when the Hurricane pilots were the first during the Battle of France to realise that they were almost invariably suicidal in combat with the German Messerschmitts, and pilots quickly abandoned the Fighting Area Attacks (FAA) to adopt much smaller and agile sections of two or four fighters as the basic attacking element.

All this training proved to be academic when at the end of 1938, after only six months with Gladiators, No.25 was informed that it was to be re-equipped with the Blenheim. The old-established tradition, which had taken the Squadron to the forefront of Britain's fighters defences, was apparently at an end. It is true that there had been some speculation that the posting away of the gunners had been necessary for further training in air gunnery; this was now confirmed with the arrival of the first Blenheims – equipped with a dorsal turret. Indeed, when the original plan to use the early Blenheims as night fighters had been suggested, fairly lengthy tests had to be carried out to ensure that they were suitable, while conversion to the fighter rôle also entailed the manufacture of a four-gun 'tray' to be added under the Blenheim's fuselage; this entailed removing all the bomb-rack equipment from the bomb bay to make space for the gun magazines, these guns being fired by the pilot. It happened that these gun trays were to be manufactured in the railway workshops at Ashford – scarcely 20 miles from Hawkinge.

The early Blenheims, which had joined Bomber Command in 1937, although over-optimistically claimed to be the fastest light bomber in the world, proved to be disappointing in service to say the least, being capable of carrying no more than four 250lb bombs over a radius of about 300 miles. In hitting on the idea to use the Blenheim as a night fighter – because of its 'adequate' speed for a short period of service – no account was taken of the layout of the pilot's cockpit and his field of vision, which was quickly found to be badly restricted by structural members criss-crossing the transparent nose panels of the cockpit. Furthermore, the two big Bristol Mercury engines, located just four feet on either side of the pilot's seat, effectively reduced the lateral field of

Subject of long-standing controversy, this Gladiator II, N5902, carried the Munich-style code letters of No.25 Squadron, and yet was never on the Squadron strength. The aircraft was in fact flown by the Hawkinge station commander, who was also CO of No.25 Squadron. (Photo: Air Ministry)

One of No.25 Squadron's Gladiators at the time of the Munich Crisis showing the hasty application of camouflage, which had obscured the aircraft's serial number. The Squadron's 'RX' codes were changed to 'ZK' shortly after this photo was taken.

vision to an arc of about 70 degrees on either side of the centreline. In its favour, the Blenheim possessed a good forward view for night landings.

Although, in 'official' circles, the Blenheim's adaptation was generally regarded as yet another stopgap, there were two reasons why such an opinion was not released for public consumption (apart from the obvious reluctance to admit to any suggestion of unpreparedness during the Expansion period). To begin with, the Blenheim had, only the previous year, been trumpeted as the world's fastest light bomber; if this was so, why was the fighter version only a stopgap when there was nothing in sight to take its place? And the Air Ministry did not wish to emphasise that the 'new' Blenheim fighter was converted from Blenheims which were already outdated by what now was seen to be a somewhat pedestrian performance. In truth, the Air Ministry was well aware that the Bristol Aeroplane Company was already committed to a new, dedicated night fighter developed, not from the Blenheim, but from the more advanced Beaufort torpedo-bomber. No Air Ministry Specification had been issued to cover the new Bristol night fighter, and it was still proceeding as a Private Venture – though in close collaboration with the R & D department at the Air Ministry. Though far from being an accepted reality, and certainly nowhere near ready for flight, progress was already being made with an airborne form of radar which, it was intended, would eventually be carried by an aircraft such as the new Bristol night fighter.

While this aid to night interception was still very much in the future, and before the Gladiators finally left No.25 Squadron, unbeknown to the Squadron's pilots, they were taking part in a new phase in the development of the coastal 'radio direction finding' plan, aimed at gaining early warning of approaching hostile aircraft. In July 1937 an RDF station had been opened at Dover – the first such station to be tasked with operational duties within the jurisdiction of Fighter Command, and as such participated in the major annual air defence exercises. Known as AMES1 (Air Ministry Experimental Station 1) – later CH (or Chain Home) – and characterised by a cluster of steel lattice masts as well as a few rudimentary wooden huts – this station began work to perfect its task of locating and reporting the position of incoming aircraft, although until other similar stations were opened further round the coast it remained impossible to do more than provide a bearing and an approximate height of an approaching aircraft.

When the CH station at Rye opened in 1938, Gladiators of No.25 Squadron were ordered off, usually in pairs, from Hawkinge, to fly carefully prepared 'patrol' sorties, usually beginning with a course to approach the coast near Folkestone from a point about 20 miles out to sea, before setting course for a point east of Deal from which the pilots would fly south and west along the south Kent coast, about 20 to 30 miles off the shore line for about 50 miles before returning to Hawkinge. As before, no wireless transmissions would be made during the sorties, and the pilots were not as a rule 'de-briefed', such was the secrecy surrounding the exercises. The sorties were always entered in the pilots' logbooks as 'Patrols'. If questions were raised and reached the CO, they were shrugged off as being for calibration of the sound detectors being introduced with searchlight units near coastal towns. The reason for wireless silence was simply given as the ground units not being equipped with wireless. This was accepted as being entirely logical!

The Munich crisis occurred in September 1938 (the same month in which another former 25 Squadron member, George Ranald Macfarlane, DSO, DFC, who had served with it during the First World War and had reached the rank of Air Vice-Marshal, was appointed AOC British Forces in Aden).

As Germany demanded the right of self-determination for over three million Germans living in Czechoslovakia, the British Prime Minister, Neville Chamberlain, flew to Munich to a meeting between German, French and Italian leaders, at which Germany was 'allowed' to occupy the predominantly Sudetan German territories of Czechoslovakia. No one in Britain was under any misapprehension that this climb-down was anything but a prelude to an inevitable war – despite reassurances voiced by Chamberlain to the contrary on his return to London. At the first signs of danger, Fighter Command had ordered its squadrons to deploy to their War stations, and No.25 had moved away from Hawkinge to Northolt – where, ironically, it joined No.111 Squadron's Hurricanes! With the apparent ending of the crisis, No.25 returned to Hawkinge on 10th October with the feeling that the Blenheims could not now arrive soon enough. . .

CHAPTER 6

"I know you are married, but it's not all that dark tonight"

(Night Fighter Squadron and 'Radar' – 1939-1940)

THE LAST SERVICEABLE GLADIATOR had left Hawkinge by the time the first Blenheim (K7058) arrived in mid-December 1938 at Hawkinge, destined for No.25 (Fighter) Squadron. Eight of the former Gladiator pilots were sent on generous leave so as to include Christmas before their posting away – no fewer than six of them due to join Hurricane and Spitfire squadrons elsewhere. Only one pilot, Fg Off Alastair McLaren Lyall, remained who could remember flying the Fury II with No.25, having joined the Squadron as an Acting Pilot Officer on 7th August 1937, and had subsequently flown Demons and Gladiators and then completed a three-day 'crash' conversion course at a training unit to convert on to twin-engine aircraft. Now a Flying Officer and regarded as an 'experienced' Blenheim pilot (though in fact he had not yet flown one), he was charged with checking out K7058 as being acceptable by the Squadron (not least because it was only temporarily on loan from the School of Army Co-operation, and there lurked a suspicion that this aircraft might have been selected for disposal as a rogue aircraft!). All appears to have passed off smoothly, and three more Blenheims (this time brand-new aircraft) arrived before Christmas. All were then locked away while No.25 Squadron evaporated on Christmas leave to await the arrival of replacement aircrews and ground staff.

The former CO, Sqn Ldr Donald Fleming, DFC, was posted away early in the New Year, his place being taken by Sqn Ldr John Robert Hallings-Pott (who later rose to Air-Vice Marshal, CBE, DSO, AFC), and it may be worth mentioning those former Gladiator pilots who remained with No.25 when the Blenheims began arriving in numbers in the New Year, for, whether they realised the fact or not, it was on these few men that the continuity and traditions of the old squadron now rested – such was the profound change wrought by the nature of the new night fighting rôle.

Flying Officer Alastair McLaren Lyall. Joined No.25 Squadron on 7th August 1937 from No.10 Flying Training School as an Acting Plt Off; (flew Fury IIs, Demons, Gladiators and Blenheims). Participated in the attack on Borkum on 28th November 1939. Posted away as a Flight Lieutenant on 14th September 1940. Released from the Royal Air Force in 1946.

Flying Officer Hugh Michael Stamford Lambert. Joined No.25 Squadron on 4th September 1937 as an Acting Plt Off; (flew Fury IIs, Demons, Gladiators and Blenheims). Was killed in a flying accident on 15th September 1940.

Flight Lieutenant William Alexander Coote Emmett. Joined No.25 Squadron 1st January 1938 from No.2 Flying Training School at Brize Norton as an Acting Pilot Officer (flew Demons, Gladiators and Blenheims, and served on the Squadron throughout

The first six Blenheims to be delivered to No.25 Squadron at Hawkinge. Note the black and white undersurfaces.
(Photo: via Roy S Humphreys)

the Battle of Britain. He retired from the RAF on 30th April 1958 as a Squadron Leader.

Flying Officer Miles John Miley. Joined No.25 Squadron as a Pilot Officer on 30th July 1938 after graduating from the RAF College, Cranwell; flew Demons, Gladiators, Blenheims and Beaufighters. Participated in the attack on Borkum of 28th November 1939. Was killed in a flying accident on 15th September 1940.

Flying Officer Ernest Cassidy. Joined No.25 Squadron as an Acting Pilot Officer on a short service commission from No.7 Flying Training School, Peterborough, on 17th September 1938, and flew Gladiators and Blenheims. He flew with the Squadron throughout the Battle of Britain, and on 21st October 1940 was posted to No.249 Squadron. During later service in the Mediterranean theatre shot down two enemy aircraft and damaged three others, being awarded the DFC in January 1942 and the AFC in June 1952. He retired from the RAF on 1st June 1958 in the rank of Wing Commander.

Flying Officer Beresford Gwynne Hooper. Joined No.25 Squadron as a Pilot Officer on a short service commission in December 1938 from No.11 Flying Training School, Shawbury; flew Gladiators, Blenheims and Beaufighters. Was the only survivor from the accident in which Lambert and Miley (see above) were killed on 15th September 1940. Later served in the Administrative and Fighter Control Branches, leaving the Service during the 1950s as a Flight Lieutenant.

No.25 Squadron was by no means the only one to undergo the change from the day to night fighting rôle at the end of 1938, for it was the original intention that each of the Groups in Fighter Command would deploy one such squadron to begin with; others would follow once the planned day fighter strength had been achieved. No.23 Squadron had been relieved of its Bulldogs in 1933, these being replaced by Demons which soldiered on until December 1938 when the first Blenheims were delivered to the Squadron which had, in the meantime moved to Wittering. No.29 Squadron, at Debden, had also followed the Bulldog/Demon route, becoming the third of those early Blenheim night fighter squadrons. Indeed this august trio was to represent the core of the RAF's night fighter force, as well as Britain's much later 'all-weather' air defence, for the next sixty years.

FUMBLING IN THE DARK

The nine months immediately prior to the outbreak of war in September 1939 were a period of feverish activity for the Royal Air Force. For Fighter Command in particular it was seen as a race against time, as most thinking people saw a European war as inevitable. It was unthinkable, indeed illogical, that a dictator at large with powerful military forces, would be content with a few peripheral territorial seizures. Adolf Hitler had, after all, made no secret of his philosophy of *Lebensraum* and his intention to display the German nation as the Master Race.

For the squadrons of day fighters and light bombers – the Hurricanes, Battles and Blenheims – contingency plans had been drawn up for the eventuality of war with Germany, involving the movement of the Advanced Air Striking Force and an Air Component of the British Expeditionary Force to assume support of the British sector of the Western Front to the north of the Maginot Line.

The night fighter arm of the Command, however, was in a state of flux, and with it, perhaps more than any other night fighter squadron, No.25. While the Hurricane and Spitfire

Taxying accident (1). Blenheim RX-A caught its main wheels in the rut at the side of a taxy-track; in trying to extricate himself by use of throttle the pilot was too heavy-handed and the Blenheim swung on one wheel, which then collapsed, causing fairly heavy damage.
(Photo: Bruce Robertson)

had, since 1936, been afforded the highest priority for development, production and introduction into service (Hawkers, incidentally, producing more Hurricanes than the RAF knew what to do with), the dedicated night fighter had, until late 1937, been left 'sucking hind tit'. Moreover, despite great efforts being made to create a chain of coastal radar stations to keep watch for approaching enemy raiders, precious little thought had been given to their interception at night.

When the Blenheim had first appeared as a commercial prototype (*'Britain First'*) in the mid-1930s, it took the RAF by surprise as it was far in advance of any twin-engine aircraft under consideration for the Service. And when Lord Rothermere, sponsor of the aircraft and architect of his newspapers' "Wake Up Britain" campaign following Hitler's rise to power, offered the aircraft to the Air Ministry for evaluation, not only was the offer gladly accepted but plans were put in hand to develop a light bomber version for the RAF. The only other 'new' light bomber destined to join the Service was the Fairey Battle which, having been under development since 1932, proved disappointing to say the least – being underpowered, under-armed and unable to carry any worthwhile bomb load. Otherwise it was an excellent aeroplane.

Unfortunately the Blenheim itself came to be developed at a time when technology in aircraft design was making giant strides, so that, when the Mark I (short-nose) version entered service in 1937 as a light bomber, it was already obsolescent. Had it been powered by Rolls-Royce Merlin engines its performance would have been quite acceptable; it was, however, an unwritten rule at the Bristol company that Bristol aeroplanes would always be powered by Bristol engines. In any case, all Merlin engines in 1936-37 were reserved for Hurricanes, Spitfires and Battles. The Blenheim therefore was powered by a pair of 840hp Bristol Mercury radial engines (themselves constituting six-year-old engine technology) and, with an all-up weight well over twice that of the Hurricane and Spitfire, it only possessed about 40% more power.

Thus it was that little over one year after joining the RAF as a light bomber, the Mark I Blenheim came to be considered as a night fighter. It was being argued that, notwithstanding its poor performance (a maximum speed of about 285 mph in a following wind), it was better than anything else available as a night fighter.

Moreover, by the time Blenheims reached No.25 Squadron (armed with but a single forward-firing machine gun, and another in a midships gun turret), the Air Ministry was already considering a new fighter, being offered by Bristol and which, within two years, would enter operational service as the Beaufighter. As a night fighter, therefore, the Blenheim was only ever regarded as yet another stopgap. Yet for two crucial years it was effectively the *only* night fighter available to the RAF, and one that was quite unable to match the performance of the *Luftwaffe's* modern bombers – let alone its fighters.

These observations, and their implied ramifications, are legitimate in long retrospect, but the true situation was rigorously concealed from the public at large, for nothing would be gained by divulging the unpleasant truth at a time when Britain was fast approaching a showdown with the growing might of Nazi Germany. After all, when the Blenheim began equipping Fighter Command's night fighter squadrons, only a year had elapsed since the first Blenheim bombers had joined Bomber Command amidst much trumpeting as the 'fastest bomber in the world'. Suffice it to say that there was no great enthusiasm among the fighter squadron's for this aircraft, even though it was at least a monoplane.

No.25 had scarcely completed its Summer Camp in 1938 when Hitler's sabre-rattling turned to the sinister demand that over three million Germans, resident in Czechoslovakia, be given self-determination, thereby provoking the Munich Crisis. No.25 Squadron, still commanded by Donald Fleming, hurriedly slapped drab camouflage paint on its pristine Gladiators and flew them to its war station at Northolt, twelve miles west of the capital. It had been decided that, when the chips were down, Hawkinge just was not the right place to base a fighter squadron, now that it seemed very likely that a coastal radar chain might be built that would enable fighters to take off from bases further inland and still have time to intercept before enemy bombers reached the English coast. Of course, the whole theory of radar was a most closely guarded secret, to which No.25 Squadron was to become privy before any other in Fighter Command. But more of that in due course.

The Squadron's hurried visit to Northolt during the Munich crisis was short-lived, and lasted from 12th September until 10th October 1938; adequate time for all the Gladiator pilots to fly a number of sector patrols to get the lie of the land and line up their aircraft for a visit by 'Stuffy' Dowding himself.

During the remainder of 1938, back at Hawkinge, all pilots flew locally at night – given the added task of 'black-out spotting'; this entailed flying over Ashford, Canterbury, Dover, Folkestone, Margate, and Ramsgate, and then making reports on the effectiveness of these towns' preliminary attempts at night-time black-outs. Judging by some of the reports, the pilots were not impressed, one newly arrived fledgling pilot reporting that, while flying at 15,000 feet over Dover (clearly visible below him), he could simultaneously identify Deal, Margate, Ramsgate and Canterbury, not to mention most of the main roads in East Kent (private car owners had not yet been issued with headlight masks). Of course, full air raid precautions had yet to be introduced, and much of the early black-out 'exercises' were voluntary affairs, few air raid wardens having yet been appointed in the towns.

All the mastering of the Gladiator at night was to prove academic. Only a fortnight after arriving back at Hawkinge, a Blenheim 'dropped in' from Filton to give the CO and the flight commanders some air experience and an opportunity to get the feel of the controls (though of course the aircraft was not fitted with dual controls). This aircraft, K7113, is recorded as having flown 22.15 hours in three days – and remained fully serviceable (under the watchful eyes of a small working party attached for the purpose from Harwell – home of Blenheim bomber squadrons).

Reading between the lines of several reports, prepared by No.25 (as well as Nos.23 and 29 Squadrons), no one was impressed with the Blenheim's potential as a fighter. With a crew of three (including a rear gunner manning a dorsal turret with a single machine gun and doubling as wireless operator), the aircraft lacked adequate manœuvrability, speed performance and armament. However, it was quickly pointed out that plans were in hand to add the ventral gun pack, referred to above.

None of the initial 13 Blenheim fighters delivered to Hawkinge between 12th December 1938 and the end of the following March, was equipped with the four-gun pack, and doubts were raised as to whether they would be of any value, one pilot recalling the general feeling that with only a single forward-firing gun the Blenheim would be hard put to shoot down a modern bomber, and that the four-gun pack would slow the Blenheim so much as to prevent it from catching one. (Moreover, the first reports were coming out of Spain that modern German bombers possessed speeds of around 300 miles per hour!)

While most pilots converted to the Blenheim on the Squadron (without the benefit of any prior twin-engine dual instruction), some were detached to No.11 Flying Training School, and at least three attended the Central Flying School for an *ad hoc* two-week conversion course (gaining formal dual training on Airspeed Oxfords or Avro Ansons).

After the departure of Donald Fleming, Squadron Leader John Hallings-Pott guided No.25 through the difficult working-up period with the Blenheim, all the time trying to arrive at some sort of night patrol and combat routine which was entirely dependent on collaboration with ground searchlights. Such patrols would presumably be flown by single aircraft, each negotiating its patrol by dead reckoning, temporarily assisted by identification of towns with – as yet – inadequate black-out, for the new radar chain was still working to obtain both range and height interpretation. Over the land, the Observer Corps could also contribute some assistance, provided that there was very little flying (which would confuse the 'picture'), but this would progressively improve as the reporting network was completed.

Regarding the 'combat' tactics to be employed in attacking an enemy bomber at night, everything depended on the target's exposure and holding by searchlight, and this in itself almost invariably resulted in any interception being confined to over-land locations. By mid-1939, however, the CH radar chain had been completed to a sufficient degree to enable adjacent coastal stations, working together, to provide target location in range, bearing and height – although the latter, to be anywhere near accurate, demanded considerable experience and skill in the personnel using the very rudimentary radar displays then available. In theory this would enable the night fighter to locate an approaching enemy bomber while still over the sea; provided the fighter's pilot had a fairly accurate idea of his own position, and the information of the enemy aircraft's calculated position and course had been transmitted to the fighter very quickly (after all, a bomber flying at only 200 mph covers about 17 miles in five minutes), there was just a chance that the raider might be spotted. Such 'practice interceptions' using another Blenheim as a 'target', were very infrequently attempted but, in the last resort, any sighting was only possible in condition of bright moonlight and possible assistance by searchlights.

In an attempt to gain a fractional increase in the Blenheim's speed and climb performance, some sorties were flown without the navigator, but with the number of ventral machine guns reduced to two and the ammunition also reduced by half, the improvement was so small that it was difficult to determine with any certainty whether or not other circumstances might have been responsible!

With regard to the Blenheim's 'safety' record, No.25 Squadron was fortunate in not suffering any loss of life during the last nine months before the outbreak of War. The first accident occurred on 14th May 1939 when L1436 suffered engine failure and crashed while making a forced landing near Dartford, the occupants being little hurt. In L1423, the pilot was unable to correct a swing on take-off and crashed in the overshoot area on 9th July. Four days later L1510 crashed while landing at Hawkinge and the aircraft was badly damaged, though the crew members were unhurt.

On 1st August the pilot of L1241 aborted a night landing, but opened the throttles too quickly to overshoot; both engines cut and the aircraft crashed in the overshoot area. Again no one was seriously injured.

The Squadron attended a shortened armament practice camp early in August, during which, on the 6th, a pilot committed what was a fairly common error in those days – he forgot to lower his wheels before landing at Sutton Bridge (this despite his warning klaxon sounding its plaintive scream)! Unfortunately the Blenheim, L1436, was damaged beyond economical repair, and was carted off to a Maintenance Unit for disposal.

No record can be found of the air firing results achieved during the armament camp, and only about half the pilots gained any experience in firing the Blenheim guns at night. However Hallings-Pott made a point of giving the Squadron armourers plenty of practice in re-arming the Blenheims at night, with the minimum of illumination – by no means an easy job. Nevertheless, despite plenty of cuts and bruises, as well as an aura of doubtful language, the Squadron's armament officer could express some satisfaction with improvement in re-arming times, this being as much the purpose of the Camp as improving air firing skills.

• • •

Thus No.25 (Fighter) Squadron, in the few short months that remained before the outbreak of the Second World War, was poised in the very front line of Britain's defences, stationed precariously on the Channel coast, working feverishly to master the skills of night flying in aircraft whose capabilities left much to be desired. A few of the Blenheims at Hawkinge were still ostensibly bombers, but gradually these underwent the necessary modifications to fit the new four-gun armament.

The first of the coastal radar stations (the Chain Home stations, which had a medium altitude range of about 120 miles) were now in service, their purpose at this time being purely the reporting and tracking of approaching aircraft. No attempt had yet been made to introduce any measure of fighter control – this was still more than a year away. Instead, the coastal stations simply reported the positions of

Taxying accident (2). Having hardly been on the Squadron for more than a week, this Blenheim also failed to climb from the grass on to the hardstanding and simply tipped on to its nose. The figure in silhouette under the wing seems to be about to lasso the tail. If successful, he would have probably broken the Blenheim's back.

approaching aircraft to a Fighter Operations Centre, whose Controller warned the various Sector Operations Centres, where orders would be passed to fighter pilots waiting to take off to intercept possible enemy aircraft approaching. Similar procedures were in theory used by both day and night, but in practice patrolling Blenheim night fighter pilots were still very much in the dark, metaphorically and literally. They carried no radar of their own, and in any attempt to achieve night interceptions they had to rely on such expedients as searchlight concentrations, and in the final analysis, the human eyeball – not the most reliable piece of equipment on a dark night. Navigation lights, invariably used at night in peacetime, were just as invariably switched off after take-off during the War. Just as the glow of engine exhaust pipes were usually just visible on Blenheims, it was hoped that German aircraft were equally so. Time would tell.

The 'aircrew' establishment of No.25 Squadron in July 1939 comprised of thirteen officers, seven NCO aircrew (pilots and WOp/AGs) and eleven airmen aircrew (corporals and LACs). The Squadron's Unit Establishment (UE) stood at fourteen Blenheims at first line availability and two Blenheims at 'War Reserve'. Most of the other night fighter Blenheim squadrons possessed a slightly lower establishment. It had been proposed as long ago as 1936 that the respective UE and Reserve should be 18+4, and in fact No.25 Squadron reached these figures early in 1939.

Records show that by the beginning of July 1939, all No.25's pilots had been assessed as 'operational by day', and all but three 'operational by night'. These assessments were confirmed in several air exercises involving aircraft of the French *Armée de l'Air,* the first of which approached the South Coast in far from perfect flying weather. It is not known exactly how many French aircraft were involved, but of the 21 daylight interceptions achieved by Fighter Command during one exercise, about a dozen occurred before the 'raiders' crossed the coast, of which three were obtained by No.25. One of the 'umpires' qualified this achievement with the throwaway remark that all three were gained almost overhead Hawkinge. More important from the Squadron's viewpoint was the estimate that of the six night interceptions, no fewer than four were gained by the Blenheims from Hawkinge – though it is not explained what exactly was meant by an 'interception', as the pilots concerned merely reported having obtained 'fleeting glimpses' of an unidentified aircraft flying in the reported area! With unilluminated gunsights, it is difficult to guess exactly how the pilots were expected to bring their guns to bear at night.

AIRBORNE RADAR EXPERIMENTS

A much more interesting time was being enjoyed during this period by a number of No.25 Squadron's crews, temporarily detached elsewhere. Why No.25 Squadron was selected for this work is uncertain. As the Squadron was required to detach four Blenheim crews for an undetermined period, the Squadron may have been chosen simply because it was the only Blenheim fighter squadron that had reached its wartime first line and reserve establishment in personnel and aircraft, and could therefore afford to establish a third Flight for the purpose of the new task.

Well-known, yet evocative photograph of a No.25 Squadron Blenheim taken in mid-1939. The fin 'arrow' marking was a relic of more peaceful times when it would have carried the Squadron Badge; this marking was ordered to be removed soon after (probably when the Squadron changed its code letters to 'ZK'). (Photo: courtesy of No.25 (Fighter) Squadron)

Very little was divulged to the Squadron as a whole; nor were there any rumours – there was nothing particularly dramatic about forming and detaching an extra Flight; perhaps the only unusual aspect of the formation of 'C' Flight was that its Blenheims were not delivered to Hawkinge (and indeed were never seen, as far as anyone can recollect, by anyone else on the Squadron). The task to be undertaken by 'C' Flight was to fly Blenheims (the Mark IV 'long-nose' variety) from Martlesham Heath on the Suffolk Coast on courses passed to the pilot from a ground controller towards approaching RAF aircraft (usually Ansons or Oxfords – aircraft of fairly pedestrian speed capabilities – but occasionally the odd Whitley). A special operator, situated in the Blenheim amidships – using equipment about which no one but the operator seemed to know anything – was to sing out and inform the pilot that he would endeavour to give him instructions as how to continue the interception. This equipment was, of course, very rudimentary airborne radar, and the operators themselves, if asked what exactly their gear was doing, would reply rather sheepishly that they weren't too sure, but that if a certain 'picture came up on the screen' they could tell the pilot whether to turn left or right.

Although various post-war commentators have sought to describe those early airborne radar sets, no one with first-hand knowledge or recollection has described in detail the equipment used by those early Blenheims of No.25 Squadron between August and November 1939, and it has not even proved possible beyond doubt to name the pilots of 25 Squadron involved. It has been suggested that the equipment installed in the Blenheims was 'AI Mark III', but it is much more likely that no two sets were identical, being what were known at the time as 'bread-board' sets, with all components set out on portable open boards so that they were fully accessible to the operators who, incidentally, were all civilians. As no detailed account of 'C' Flight's activities ever reached the Squadron's records (and it is believed that at least three of the four pilots involved did not return to the main body of the Squadron when the trials were completed), one may only speculate that the various radar 'sets' carried aloft differed fairly fundamentally from each other. They probably therefore featured different aerial arrays, but one version probably showed more promise than the others and it was this that provided the basis of AI Mk.III, the first version to achieve anything approaching series production – and then probably only about a dozen or so sets.

What is now almost certain is that the 'C' Flight Blenheims operated from Martlesham Heath (the Aeroplane and Armament Experimental Establishment having moved from there to Boscombe Down on the outbreak of War). Under instructions passed to the Blenheim pilots by a controller situated at the most secret and experimental coastal radar station (CH) at nearby Bawdsey Manor, near Felixstowe, in Suffolk, where almost all the development of the new ground coastal radar had been undertaken, and would continue to be for much of the War.

It has however proved possible to assemble a few anecdotes from among some of the NCOs and airmen who were serving at Martlesham Heath, whence the 25 Squadron Blenheims flew the majority of their 'interception' sorties. The Wireless Section at Martlesham was 'host' to the civilians who, with little regard for Service routine, persisted in laying out their 'bread-boards' on any available table – the term 'bread-board' incidentally originating from the term given by a 25 Squadron corporal Wireless Operator, and which gained universal usage for any 'unboxed' component of radar equipment. Another term which entered the mysterious vocabulary of the new equipment was 'Black Box'. It is said that, as the trials began to bear fruit, some attempt was made to sort out all the 'bread-board' components into self-contained units – if for no other reason than the restriction of space in the operator's position in the Blenheim. These units were apparently first made of plywood and, inevitably in keeping with the best traditions of the Service, as 'it' didn't move, the order was given to 'paint it'. It so happened that there was an abundance of black paint – for it had been anticipated that night fighters would shortly be painted black overall – and all the boxes of tricks (the favourite term used by the pilots for many years to come) came to be given that colour. In fact, by the time radar sets were being issued to line squadrons, most radar component casings were of metal sheet, painted black – and the 'Black Box' has survived to this day to describe almost any esoteric electronic equipment – including modern flight recorders used for analysing flight conditions immediately prior to an aircraft accident.

One should bear in mind that in the early days of the coastal radar chain, employing the Chain Home (CH) radar, while the geographical position of a 'target' aircraft could be determined fairly accurately (provided that at least one neighbouring radar was also operating so as to give accurate bearing 'cuts'), the determination of the target's height was far less reliable, and required considerable skill from the operator. This is borne out by examining some of the occasional reports filed by pilots of RAF Bomber and Coastal Command aircraft that they had been 'intercepted' by Blenheims while returning from exercise sorties over the North Sea. They had been warned that this might happen and one detects an air of surprise that Blenheims did indeed put in an appearance at roughly the right time, but quite a number of these reports stated that the Blenheims arrived at a much higher or lower altitude than that at which the Whitley or Anson was flying. One is, however, left with the verdict on these trials that they must have been considered a success. The trials themselves petered out in about January or February 1940, at least as far as the Blenheim pilots of No.25 Squadron were directly involved, to be followed shortly afterwards by the formation of the Fighter Interception Unit (FIU) – its first Commanding Officer being none other than George Chamberlain who had served as a junior pilot on No.25 Squadron way back in the 1920s but was now an Air Commodore. The astonishing progress made during and after the No.25 Squadron trials and by the FIU in 1940 resulted in the first operational airborne interception radar-equipped (AI) Blenheims joining Fighter Command before the end of the Battle of Britain, not to mention the radar-equipped purpose-designed Beaufighter.

The final moves towards war were apparently acted upon by Fighter Command rather earlier than those during the Munich scare of the previous year, and No.25 Squadron

Blenheim L1440/RX-O landing at Hawkinge. The red and blue roundel on the fuselage was a token attempt at low visibility markings (particularly among night fighters), which was rather pointless in the presence of 'high visibility' code letters and black and white undersurfaces! (Photo: via Roy S Humphreys)

was ordered to take up its wartime station at Northolt as early as 22nd August 1939, the ground party arriving by road and rail during that and the following day. Sixteen Blenheims flew in to Northolt at that time, followed by the pair of war reserve aircraft on the 24th. Much of the time during those early weeks was spent flying daylight patrols off the South and East Coasts, occasionally being called on by a ground controller to fly set patterns for no immediately apparent reason. It was now that the Squadron's pilots were briefed, in broad outline, on the purpose of the coastal 'radio direction finding' stations, and that these required aircraft flying accurate courses so as to calibrate their equipment.

On 15th September No.25 was ordered to Filton, Bristol, where it remained until 4th October; bearing in mind that the Blenheim's manufacturers were situated at Filton, it is not known whether the move was made to enable some modification to be made to the aircraft or whether it was for the air defence of that important factory. The latter seems unlikely as No.501 (County of Gloucester) Squadron was already (and had been for ten years) stationed at Filton, being now equipped with Hurricanes. An old member of No.25 Squadron has recorded his belief that the aircraft were taken to Filton to have equipment known as IFF (Identification of Friend or Foe) installed, although there appears to be no reference to this in Squadron records. This seems be the most likely reason, simply because the Maintenance Unit, located at St.Athan in South Wales, was already engaged in fitting this equipment in aircraft already in service in the RAF, and had detached a working party to the Bristol factory at Filton to equip new Blenheims coming off the production line. There is some suggestion (quoted in other works) that a No.25 Squadron Blenheim collided with another aircraft over the Bristol Channel while on an 'air test', but no such incident appears in No.25's records, and no casualties are recorded in the Squadron's Roll of Honour at this time.

As was to become readily apparent in examining Squadron records (as well as those of the many units of what later became Signals Command) the utmost secrecy surrounded radar equipment being introduced into Service in the RAF, its purpose, efficiency and performance – for obvious reasons – and such reticence is a hallmark of such matters to this day.

However, it is necessary here to explain that the purpose of IFF was to enable the ground radar to identify with certainty the appearance of friendly aircraft which appeared on their display screens. IFF in those early days was, in itself, not a component of airborne radar (as yet no operational fighter aircraft in the RAF carried such radar); it was simply a separate radio transmitter which transmitted a signal on a special frequency which the ground station was tuned to receive. When called on by the ground operator to 'switch Canary', the pilot would simply activate a switch in his cockpit. The signal transmitted would be displayed as a blurred 'halo' round the radar response being given on the ground radar display, thus identifying it as friendly.

THE SEA MINING THREAT

No.25 Squadron returned to Northolt early in October 1939 at about the time when German minelaying aircraft were causing a serious threat to shipping in the seas around Britain's coasts. As these aircraft only operated at night and singly, and necessarily flew at very low level, they were never seen by observers and, because the CH radar was unable to 'see' targets at very low altitude, the aircraft were not detected on radar for some weeks; indeed, their presence was not confirmed until a ship activated a mine while steaming in a swept channel. It was also confirmed that a high proportion of the German mines were of the acoustic type and these alone were inflicting most of the shipping casualties.

Fortunately the Admiralty had been aware of the magnetic mine for some time (and indeed a similar British weapon was being developed). However, it was not until a naval officer, Lieut-Cdr J G D Ouvry, at considerable personal risk, managed to recover an air-dropped mine off Shoeburyness on 23rd November 1939, that it was confirmed that aircraft had been sowing the mines and that the polarity of the mine's detonating mechanism differed from that of the surface-sown weapons. This coincided with an Intelligence report which suggested that the aircraft responsible for mining were based at the German seaplane station on the East Frisian island of Borkum in the mouth of the River Ems, close to the junction of German and Dutch territorial waters. That day the following signal was sent from HQ Coastal Command to HQ Fighter Command:

> IMMEDIATE. Information indicates that enemy aircraft which engaged in mine laying in the Thames Estuary last night were operating from a Seaplane Base at Borkum. You should arrange for a force of Blenheim fighters to search for and attack enemy seaplanes or flying boats at Borkum which may be preparing or taking off for attacks against this country towards dusk.
>
> Nov. 23rd. Only aircraft on the water or in the air should be attacked. Arrangements should be made with C-in-C Coastal Command for the provision of observers to navigate fighter sections. Greatest care should be taken not to infringe neutral territory or territorial waters.

Thus was set in motion the first British fighter attack of the Second World War against a target in Germany. Alas, the urgency of the situation took no account of the fact that the nature of such an attack was entirely outside the scope of Fighter Command's training. Air Commodore Keith Rodney Park, MC, DFC, AOC, No.11 Group, warned No.25 Squadron at Northolt to prepare for the attack, and all leave for the Squadron was cancelled from 10.00hrs on the 23rd.

At Northolt none of the Blenheims were equipped with dinghies; their gunsights were not suitable for air-to-ground aiming; and their short-range radio sets were quite unable to cover the 270-mile distance over which the aircraft would be operating. Then it was found that suitable dinghies did not appear to have been supplied to any Fighter Command station; also the necessary radio sets were only held at a Maintenance Unit at Carlisle and would take three days to reach Northolt. Frustrated by these delays, Park sent a signal on the 24th demanding a report on the reasons for these delays. A further snag was found when it became clear that the Coastal Command navigators were experiencing considerable difficulty in coming to terms with unfamiliar aircraft, flying at much greater speeds than those to which they were accustomed.

On the afternoon of the 26th, Sqn Ldr Hallings-Pott took off from Northolt with four Blenheims and set course for Borkum. The navigators, however, erred on the safe side in over-estimating the effect of a headwind on the return flight and when, after a perfect close-formation outward flight, the pilots failed to find the enemy coast on ETA, they decided to turn back; most of the Blenheims landed with sufficient fuel for about another twenty minutes' flight. Nevertheless, Hallings-Pott pointed out in his report of the abortive flight that, had the formation been intercepted by enemy fighters, there would have been insufficient fuel to return to Northolt; he accordingly suggested that any subsequent attack should involve refuelling at a forward airfield on the outward leg. When ordered by Fighter Command to make a second attempt later the same night, Hallings-Pott signalled No.11 Group headquarters

> 'Sweep by No.25 Squadron will not, repeat not take place today. One aircraft fitted with W/T is US. W/T on third aircraft is US, leaving two only – considered too few. When additional W/T sets arrive more aircraft should be serviceable.'

With characteristic forthrightness, 'Stuffy' Dowding now took a hand and, countermanding the request for radio sets from Carlisle, appealed direct to Bomber Command for the loan of a dozen W/T sets and a number of navigators, and ordered No.601 (County of London) Squadron, Auxiliary Air Force, to provide six additional aircraft and crews, these to join No.25 Squadron at Northolt.

Late in the afternoon of the 28th, the twelve Blenheim fighters took off for Bircham Newton to refuel; their Order of Battle was as follows:

Pilot / Navigator / Air Gunner

First Section (No.25 Squadron)

Sqn Ldr John Robert Hallings-Pott
/ Sqn Ldr Gordon Ernest Hawkins / Aircraftman Serase
Fg Off Richard Cummins Haine / Sgt Belfit
/ Sgt John Edward Bignell
Fg Off Alastair McLaren Lyall / Sgt Baker
/ Aircraftman McCarthey

Second Section (No.601 Squadron)

Flt Lt Michael Fitzwilliam Peacock / Sgt Hollam
/ Ldg Aircraftman Dean
Fg Off Cecil Halford Davis (USA) / Sgt Hurn
/ Aircraftman Haggett
Fg Off Sir Archibald Philip Hope / Sgt Nichols
/ Aircraftman Elves

Third Section (No.25 Squadron)

Flt Lt Cecil Halford Bull / Plt Off John Bernard Ensor
/ Aircraftman Mortimer

Plt Off John Harold Gilbert Walker / Sgt Battle / Aircraftman Strode
Plt Off Miles John Miley / Sgt Bowmer / Aircraftman Taylor

Fourth Section (No.601 Squadron)

Fg Off The Hon John William Maxwell Aitken / Fg Off Denis Leplastrier Vercoe / Corporal King
Fg Off William Henry Rhodes-Moorhouse / Sgt Joyce / Aircraftman Makin
Fg Off Thomas Edward Hubbard / Sgt William David McAdam / Aircraftman Guest

Led by Hallings-Pott from Bircham Newton, the four Sections flew in echelon port, about 300 yards separating each Section, crossing out near Great Yarmouth at low level under roughly half-cloud cover in patchy rain and mist. As they arrived off the Frisian Islands, the formation altered course slightly to port and the Sections opened out to long line astern as they began their approach to Borkum. In the gathering dusk, Hallings-Pott's Section swept low over the harbour mole, opening fire on a Heinkel He 115, drawn up on a slipway, before passing over the main hangar and firing on three further seaplanes on other slipways.

Evidently warned of the approaching Blenheims, the ground machine gunners were seen to open up with heavy fire on the leading Section, and Peacock's pilots concentrated their fire on gun positions on top of the main hangar, before turning to attack a ship anchored close to the mole. Flt Lt Bull's Section also attacked the defending gun positions then sighting a Heinkel, which had apparently escaped attention and now received the fire from twelve Blenheim machine guns. The last Section gave attention to the moored ship.

The whole attack probably lasted no more than two or three minutes before the twelve Blenheims took up their formation positions for the return home. Scarcely any damage had been suffered from the ground defences, and the Blenheim crews had no difficulty in landing at Debden. German losses are now known to have amounted to three He 115s destroyed and three damaged – a fairly spectacular feat bearing in mind the slow tempo of the war at that time, not to mention the Blenheim's lightweight weaponry. Hallings-Pott was awarded the DSO for his leadership of the attack, and Michael Peacock received the DFC; the other two Section leaders were both Mentioned in Despatches. In adition, despite the lack of preparedness that so delayed the attack in the first place, the ultimate achievement was hailed as a great success, from which valuable experience was gained for future fighter sweeps a year or so hence. Sadly, more than a dozen of the crew members, who took part in this first offensive fighter strike of the war against the German homeland, were to lose their lives before the war was another year older. The youngest participant, the promising John Miley, yet to reach his twentieth birthday, was killed while flying in a Beaufighter (one of the first to enter RAF service) on 15th September. On No.601 Squadron, both Rhodes-Moorhouse and Carl Davis (a South African-born American) were shot down and killed in the same air combat near Tunbridge Wells on 6th September 1940. Flight Lieutenant Bull died in a tragic shooting accident while on leave on 8th August 1940. Plt Off Walker was to be killed in action while serving as a Squadron Leader with No.118 Squadron on 9th May 1942, aged just 23.

Bristol Blenheim IVF, N6239/WR-L, of No.248 Squadron, of the type used by No.25 (Fighter) Squadron for its pioneering work with airborne radar. As far as is known no photograph of these aircraft was ever taken, they were only identifiable by a tiny 'broad-arrow' antenna on the tip of the nose – easily removable by a censor. (Photo: Bristol Aeroplane Company Ltd.)

• • •

The Borkum raid proved to be the only significant combat action in which No.25 Squadron was involved during the first six months of the war. It served to demonstrate that, although the Blenheim squadrons of Fighter Command were apparently able to undertake operations successfully, beneath the surface the Command's infrastructure still left much to be desired. A glance at the Operational Record Books of each of the night fighter squadrons discloses that only a relatively small proportion of the pilots and crews of the Blenheims were truly experienced in night flying, much of their time at night being spent on searchlight co-operation and blackout checking exercises, and on 'circuits and bumps'. The more demanding cross country flights (with relatively few beacons to assist navigation) highlighted the dependence on 'running fixes' which frequently resulted in aircraft having to land anything up to fifty miles from base, short of fuel! With the onset of a particularly severe winter, the Squadron's flight commanders showed a reluctance to authorise night flying by the majority of the less experienced crews. Another difficulty that had to be overcome was the tendency of CH radar stations' operators to pass ambiguous positions of aircraft, owing to 'back error', not yet fully understood.

This 'back error' was caused by the performance characteristics of the big metric-wavelength aerials which consisted of massive arrays suspended between 300-foot high masts. Normally used to survey the seaward approaches to the coast, these arrays possessed reflectors positioned on the landward side of the transmitter aerials. If only the seaward surveillance was being employed, the reflectors were switched on, thereby cutting out duplicated signals on the landward side. However, if a night flying Blenheim pilot called up from the landward side of the CH station, in order to receive his true position the CH operator had to remember to switch out his reflector arrays, otherwise the pilot would be given a position over the sea! This characteristic had led to the famous 'Battle of Barking Creek' in September 1939, in which several RAF day fighters were shot down by 'friendly fire'. An entirely innocent friendly aircraft was reported to be approaching the coast and was accordingly plotted. As an ad hoc training exercise, a section of Spitfires was scrambled to carry out a practice interception. However, a neighbouring CH operator had forgotten to switch out his reflectors, so that the friendly fighters appeared to be approaching the coast from a seaward direction. These were reported by the first CH station and caused the fighter controller to scramble more fighters, and so it continued for several minutes with an apparently large formation of aircraft coming in over the coast. In the ensuing confusion, it was not long before the Spitfires were diving out of the sun on a squadron of unsuspecting Hurricanes, shooting down two of them.

This feature of CH operation, together with the very considerable practice required to achieve accurate height estimation of approaching raiders, led to the opportunity being taken to combine convoy patrols with calibration flights off the East Coast during the early months of 1940. Gradually the Blenheim crews acquired a considerable degree of confidence, not only in their ability to operate at night and in fairly unpleasant weather conditions but later to use GEE in conjunction with the navigational facilities offered by the CH stations. In March 1940 No.25 Squadron began sending some of the navigators away on short detachments to attend rudimentary airborne radar introduction courses, even though it was emphasised that the first 'operational' airborne sets were still some months away.

Meanwhile the actual location of potentially hostile aircraft at night continued to baffle the pilots of the Blenheim squadrons. Searchlight exposure of aircraft continued to represent the basis of any lucky interception. This in itself lent a further hazard to the operations which claimed the lives of several Fighter Command Blenheim crews, including one from No.25 Squadron. Unable to distinguish friend from foe at night, the ground searchlight crews were just as likely to expose friend as foe, and while the night fighter crews had become familiar with the need to develop and protect their night vision (such as by avoiding bright lights in crew rooms prior to night sorties), the sudden flash of brilliant light in a cockpit as some searchlight beam latched on to the Blenheim was quite literally blinding. In an instant the pilot would be quite unable to read his cockpit instruments, and occasionally resulted in his being completely disorientated with disastrous results.

That winter of 1939-40 brought home another of the Blenheim's weaknesses to its crews, namely the lack of any crew or cabin heating, either by warm air ducts or by electrically-heated flying clothing. The Blenheim was an exceptionally draughty aircraft, particularly for the navigator and midships gunner. The gun turret, by the nature of its purpose to mount a machine gun capable of being moved in azimuth and elevation, resulted in a host of cracks and crevices through which a howling blast of icy wind blew on the unfortunate turret occupant. No matter how many layers of exotic silk, woollen garments, sheepskin and leather jackets and flying boots the gunners donned, by the time the aircraft reached its patrol height the unfortunate man was, and remained, almost petrified by the intense cold – which would instantly freeze any superfluous grease that had not previously been removed from the gun mounting. It has been said (with some authority) that by far the most common reason offered by gunners for their requests to re-muster in another 'trade' was the stupefying cold of those gun turrets. The navigators' lot was little better. (The unpleasant conclusion reached after examining numerous flight reports prepared by aircraft manufacturers and the experimental establishments is that, as flight testing of prototype multi-crew aircraft was usually confined to a pilot only, scarcely any attention was ever paid to the welfare of other crew positions in the aircraft, until the Lancaster bomber entered service. Compared to the majority of American aircraft, British aircraft were notorious among aircrew members until serious *frostbite* began to constitute a source of Squadron attrition.)

Fortunately the *Luftwaffe* exercised its bomber crews very little over Britain during the first winter of the war. Not only were the harsh weather conditions also affecting the German airfields, but the *Luftwaffe* was engaged in preparing for new conquests in the coming spring. Nevertheless, it

Famous as one of the Irish international rugger-playing brothers, Victor Beamish had served as a junior officer with No.25 Squadron in the mid-1920's. Seen here as a wing commander and station commander of North Weald during the Battle of Britain, Beamish on hearing his Hurricane squadrons being scrambled for combat, would grab his flying helmet and vacate his office – often by the window – and sprint for his own Hurricane, rushing to join up for take-off. (Photo: The late Air Commodore E M Donaldson)

was perhaps ironic that in all these preparations little or no thought had been given by the German High Command to the creation of a night fighting arm – in the belief that no one else in Europe possessed the wherewithal to attack the Fatherland by day or night. There *were* night fighter pilots in the *Luftwaffe,* but they simply formed one or two *Staffeln* (each of about half a dozen aircraft) of night-flying day fighters on some of the *Jagdgeschwader* (fighter wings). By the beginning of 1940 it is unlikely that there were more than 40-50 single-seat Messerschmitt Bf 109s in the entire *Luftwaffe,* set aside for night flying, fewer still of their pilots being trained in night *fighting.* By contrast the RAF probably possessed more than 80 night fighter Blenheims and a similar number of trained night crews.

The German attack in the West, which burst against France and the Low Countries on 10th May 1940 found No.25 Squadron then stationed at North Weald whither it had moved from Northolt on 10th January. The original intention had been to move the night fighters closer to the Thames Estuary to provide them with a better chance of intercepting the night mine-layers. Despite, however, flying these off-shore sorties whenever the weather permitted, the Squadron was unable to bring any fleeting glimpse of the Heinkels to a successful conclusion. The enemy seaplanes were flying well below 100 feet at between four and ten miles off shore and were thus well below the CH radar's minimum detection limits. On several occasions during those early months of 1940 attempts were made to deploy some of the larger searchlights on the Estuary coasts in an attempt to illuminate the minelayers for the benefit of the patrolling Blenheims, but on most occasions poor visibility reduced the range of the beams, while the same weather conditions prevented the Blenheims from being flown at the necessary low altitude, the radio altimeter not yet being in use.

These activities were brought to an abrupt end by the German invasions of Holland and Belgium, as the Squadron was called upon to fly shipping protection sorties over traffic plying back and forth evacuating those nations' soldiers who had been isolated by the Germans' drives towards the sea. As May approached its end, so the great evacuation of Dunkirk got underway and, with the German navy poised to attack the ships bringing back the British Expeditionary Force and the *Luftwaffe* occupying airfields ever closer to the Dunkirk pocket, all available Fighter and Coastal Command aircrews were ordered to provide what air cover they could. For once, No.25 sensed that it was able to make a valuable contribution by flying night patrols, sending up single aircraft on specified patrol lines. With so many fires burning along the French coast, not to mention the glare in the sky produced by these fires, patrolling pilots were well able to spot other aircraft silhouetted against the ground and sky alike. Enemy air activity at night was however on a very small scale as the majority of the available *Luftwaffe* ground support aircraft and crews were saving their energies for daytime activity. Most of the night air activity was confined to the aircraft of Coastal Command and the Fleet Air Arm in their attempts to locate and attack German E-boats which posed the greatest threat to the evacuation at night.

During the period of 10th May to 17th June, which effectively encompassed the Battle of France, No.25 Squadron flew a total of 980 'war' sorties, totalling just over 2,000 flying hours, all without the loss of a single aircraft; this was remarkable testimony to the level of proficiency achieved during the months of trial and error. The Squadron's much respected CO, John Hallings-Pott, was posted away in May to take command of No.7 Operational Training Unit at Hawarden. He enjoyed a distinguished career in the Royal Air Force, retiring from the Service in 1957 as an Air Vice-Marshal. His command of No.25 Squadron then passed to Sqn Ldr Kenneth McEwan, who remained for no more than one month.

No.25 Squadron remained based at North Weald until 19th June, sending frequent Flight detachments to Debden and forward to Martlesham Heath, the latter station being employed as the forward airfield from which the Blenheims flew their coastal patrols; the night patrols had been flown from all three airfields and all were to come under frequent heavy attack by the *Luftwaffe* during the great Battle of Britain. No.25 was thus still at North Weald when command of the Station passed to that legendary RAF officer, Victor Beamish, who had served on the Squadron early in the 1930s before being invalided out of the Service with tuberculosis. Invigorated by being reunited with his beloved Service, Victor (now a Wing Commander) set about stamping his character indelibly on this important fighter station, although it was to be several months before he renewed acquaintanceship with his old squadron. Indeed, it was at his suggestion that No.25 Squadron should be moved away from North Weald to a more permanent deployment at Debden. He argued that North Weald would likely come under daylight attack when many of the night fighters would be on the ground and highly vulnerable targets. Little did he guess that the Squadron would only escape annihilation at Debden and Martlesham Heath (Debden's forward airfield) by the skin of its teeth!

Thus, on 19th June, the Squadron moved out of North Weald, its Flights taking turns for deployments between Debden and Martlesham Heath. This was the situation when the Battle of Britain opened early in July. It has to be said that No.25 Squadron was not a vital element of Britain's air defences during the Battle, even though its pilots and crew members rightly qualified for the Battle of Britain Clasp by reason of having flown operational sorties under Fighter Command's orders. The reason for this was obvious. Until the final stages of the Battle, the *Luftwaffe* scarcely operated at night, and therefore the night fighter squadrons were seldom called upon to fight. Indeed, like one or two other Squadrons, No.25 Squadron suffered the loss of almost as many of its aircraft to the guns of friendly fighters as to those of the enemy. This was due in almost every case to mistaken identity, for the Blenheim had as many engines as the German bombers, and the Junkers 88 also had a single fin and rudder. To many of the RAF pilots, any aircraft that possessed two engines and a single rudder was unquestionably a Junkers Ju 88 and should be treated as such. The Canadians, most of whom had never before seen either Blenheims or Ju 88s, found the 'Ju 88' a piece of cake, and the 'German gunners' unable to make their guns fire – oblivious of the possibility that the gunner concerned had correctly identified the Canadians for who they were. Long before the end of the Battle, No.25 Squadron was far from being the only Blenheim squadron that adopted the practice of carrying a stock of Very cartridges for the sole purpose of discharging them at the first sight of a formation of Hurricanes. There is a favourite anecdote (probably apocryphal) which went the rounds of Blenheim squadrons in 1940: A young British Blenheim pilot accosted a rugged Canuck, wearing the DFC, in a bar and enquired whether he had been awarded the decoration for destroying five of the enemy or one Blenheim. . .and the Canadians tended to take their combat claims rather seriously!

• • •

Looked at dispassionately, No.25 Squadron's participation in the Battle of Britain was distinctly 'low key' in comparison with that of the great majority of the day fighter squadrons, but marginally more eventful than the other Blenheim night fighter squadrons. Indeed, the total number of enemy aircraft shot down *at night* by day fighter pilots exceeded the number shot down by all the night fighter squadrons combined. This rather strange statistic implies no reflection on the capabilities of the night fighter squadrons; there were, after all, no more than six operational Blenheim night fighter squadrons in the whole of Fighter Command (usually deployed as two in No.11 Group, two in No.12 Group, and one in each of Nos.10 and 13 Groups). The enemy aircraft which were shot down by the day fighters at night came about as the result of either *ad hoc* patrols flown by experienced pilots who obtained permission to do some 'freelancing', or on certain occasions (particularly in the West Country) when experienced pilots were called on to fly night patrols when there were intelligence suggestions that night raids might be flown against factories and ports, and insufficient Blenheims were available to cover all the likely approaches to these targets. (Of the four occasions on which Spitfire pilots claimed night victories, two of the pilots crashed on landing – though without injury to themselves. The Spitfire was notoriously difficult to land at night on grass.)

In contrast to the hectic tempo of the daylight battle, life on No.25 Squadron was, more often than not dictated by routine – the routine of daylight coastal convoy patrols and the 'calibration flights', and the repetitive night patrols. A 'scramble' was almost unheard of on No.25 Squadron, and as far as can be discovered, only occurred four times, twice at Martlesham Heath, once at North Weald and once at Debden. And on each occasion the order to get airborne was given so as to reduce the number of aircraft on the ground during what appeared to be an imminent bombing attack on the station. In each case the Blenheim pilots were ordered away from the approaching raiders so as to reduce the risk of the Blenheims being misidentified as Junkers Ju 88s!

In the famous attack on Martlesham Heath of 15th August, carried out by *Erprobungsgruppe 210* and led by that astonishing Swiss pilot, Walter Rubensdörffer, six of No.25 Squadron's Blenheims were away on patrol and two were undergoing repair in a hangar. The German unit comprised two *Staffeln* of Bf 109s (about sixteen aircraft each carrying a 250kg bomb), and one Staffel of Bf 110s (nine aircraft) each carrying two 500kg bombs or two 250kg and four 50kg fragmentation bombs. The formation appeared at very low level, the Bf 109s well ahead of the 110s; the 109s made a single pass, each dropping its bomb before pulling up to provide protection for the 110s, each of which made two bombing passes. Having regard for the relatively small number of bombs dropped, the damage caused was proportionately heavy, and the only aircraft remaining on the ground (a Fairey Battle) was hit by a 50kg bomb and blew up with such force that it destroyed the watch office and severely damaged No.25 Squadron's equipment store and two hangars. The Station workshops and Officers' Mess were also hit, and the telephones and water supplies to the station put out of action for two days. Rubensdörffer had already carried out one raid (on radar stations on the South Coast) that day, and would carry out two more (being shot down and killed by Sqn Ldr John Thompson of No.111 Squadron in an evening attack on Croydon).

The Squadron experienced a flurry of excitement at the

While still wholly equipped with Blenheims, No.25 Squadron eagerly awaited the Beaufighter. Before the first examples of this very advanced night fighter equipped the Squadron in September 1940, two early production aircraft (such as R2186 shown here) were 'lent' to the Squadron in advance for reports by Service pilots; they carried no AI radar or armament. No.25's verdict was 'a superb aircraft, though a trifle tricky to land'. (Photo: The Bristol Aeroplane Co, Ltd.)

beginning of September, although in part there was tragedy. Following six nights of increasing activity by the *Luftwaffe* with progressively greater numbers of German bombers roaming about South-East England and the Midlands, Park had decided to withdraw his two night fighter squadrons from their forward stations, No.25 from Martlesham Heath to North Weald, and No.600 from Manston to Hornchurch, so that in the event that the Germans decided to attack the capital in any strength the Blenheims would be closer at hand.

The first day of September was a red letter day for Nos.25 and 604 Squadrons, the first two Beaufighters being delivered to these squadrons, No.604 Squadron being located at Middle Wallop. Although generally referred to as 'production aircraft', these two machines were regarded as trainers, although the Beaufighter could not be equipped with dual controls. The radar was fitted but the wing machine guns were not, and although about six pilots on No.25 Squadron took turns to get the feel of the impressive new night fighter, no attempt was made to use the radar until the first three navigators returned from their necessarily brief radar training course, on or about the 10th.

It was, however, on the 3rd that Essex felt the weight of a major *Luftwaffe* assault as 54 Dorniers, escorted by 80 Messerschmitt Bf 110s, made for North Weald. As six squadrons of Hurricanes were scrambled to engage the large formation as it crossed the coast around Southend, No.25 Squadron was scrambled but ordered to climb to the west. As usual this suggested that the Controller at North Weald wanted the Blenheims 'out of harm's way'. The Blenheims took off hurriedly, three by three, the last trio just clearing the airfield as the first Dorniers arrived. Despite being harassed by the Hurricanes, the Dorniers carried out a text book pattern bombing attack from about 15,000ft. About 200 bombs fell on the airfield (many of them delayed action), hitting all the hangars (two of which were gutted); the Messes were all hit, as were the station headquarters and the operations block (though fortunately the latter was not destroyed). The airfield itself was heavily cratered, but only four personnel were killed.

As the German formations withdrew and the harassed controllers struggled to marshal their scattered fighters, the three Blenheim pilots of No.25 who had left the ground last now returned over North Weald – and were promptly attacked out of the sun by the Hurricanes of No.46 Squadron. The Squadron Record Book takes up the sorry story.

> "Plt Off Douglas Hogg was killed; Plt Off Ernest Cassidy force landed at Hatfield, and Sqn Ldr Wilfrid Loxton landed safely at base. Sgt Edward Powell, who was Hogg's gunner, was instructed to jump by the pilot before he died. Powell crawled forward to the cockpit, found the pilot dead over the controls, returned aft and jumped. The aircraft crashed about a mile from North Weald." *

* As evidence of the confusion that could arise under combat conditions, three No.46 Squadron pilots claimed one Ju 88 destroyed and three damaged between them. There were no Ju 88s in the area, and an examination of times and locations clearly shows that their victims were indeed the No.25 Squadron Blenheims.

For the remainder of daylight that day, as army bomb disposal teams cleared away the dozens of unexploded bombs, the station personnel set about filling the craters on the airfield, and No.25 Squadron put up three Blenheims to patrol the coast shortly after dusk to look for any of Kesselring's night bombers that might be intent on following up the successful daylight raid. The experimental Ground Controlled Interception (GCI) section at Bawdsey – with whom No.25 Squadron frequently worked, both on operations and for calibration – instructed Fg Off Rofe to turn towards Harwich as there were indications that a small trickle of German aircraft was approaching that port. The pilot caught sight of an aircraft crossing from left to right and dived beneath it so as to have the enemy aircraft outlined against the moon. As he pulled up in a rear quarter attack and opened fire (evidently damaging the aircraft, a Heinkel He 111), the Harwich guns also opened fire, hitting Rofe's Blenheim and throwing it into a spin. Only with considerable skill was the pilot able to recover and nurse his crippled aircraft back to North Weald. The Heinkel was seen to crash, but Rofe learned later that night that it had been credited to the Harwich gunners.

Shortly after Rofe landed, operations informed No.25 Squadron that its New Zealander, Plt Off Michael Herrick, accompanied by Sgt John Pugh, had shot down two Heinkels, both of which were known to have crashed on land. The first to be destroyed at 02.15hrs was an aircraft of the Staff Flight of *I.Gruppe, Kampfgeschwader I*, carrying the *Gruppenkommandeur,* Major Maier; the entire crew of five was killed. Half an hour later Herrick shot down a second He 111, this time of *4.Staffeln, Kampfgeschwader 26;* the four-man crew were also all killed. Bearing in mind that Herrick's Blenheim was not one of those fitted with AI radar, and therefore depended wholly on his eyesight, his economy of ammunition to be able to shoot down two Heinkels (generally regarded as particularly hard to destroy with rifle-calibre guns) must have been extraordinary. His second victim broke up after he had opened fire at a range of 'less than 30 yards'.

On this briefly-held high note in the Squadron's fortunes, it is convenient here to take stock of the stage about to be reached in the Battle of Britain. The casualties being suffered by the hard-pressed day fighter squadrons during the last week in August and the first in September would, had they continued for three more weeks, have brought Fighter Command to its knees, with the equivalent in pilots and aircraft of two whole squadrons being lost *each day.* As is well known, it was on the evening of 7th September that Hermann Göring, believing that Fighter Command was already down to its last few squadrons, decided to change direction and go all out against London itself, as well as Britain's other major cities. Although what was to become known as the Night *Blitz* began with the massive attack on London's Dockland during the evening and night of the 7th, the daylight Battle of Britain continued until the end of October. During that autumn London endured no fewer than 52 consecutive nights of air attack. No.25 Squadron remained at North Weald until 8th October when it moved to Debden. Herrick was awarded the DFC on 24th September.

During the last month in which it flew principally from North Weald, eight of its Blenheims were exchanged for aircraft equipped with AI Mk.III and two with AI Mk.IV. Beaufighters arrived at the rate of one or two each week, all fitted with AI Mk.IV, and all were now fully armed with four cannon and six machine guns, the most heavily-armed fighter in service anywhere in the world. And one final tragedy was to occur during the North Weald period.

It has not proved possible to discover exactly what happened when a Beaufighter and a Blenheim, both of No.25 Squadron, appear to have collided during the night of 15th September at or near the airfield at Biggin Hill. The Squadron's original Beaufighter R2067, being flown by Fg Off. Beresford Hooper, with John Miley as a passenger (the aircraft still not carrying serviceable radar), had been sent off to act as target for practice interceptions for a radar-equipped Blenheim flown by Fg Off Hugh Lambert, accompanied by 'Observer Airman' Leading Aircraftman John Wyatt. Both pilots had been instructed to land at Biggin Hill, possibly on account of enemy aircraft in the vicinity, and the collision appears to have occurred about a mile from the station. What is not known is whether Wyatt was operating the Blenheim's radar or whether the aircraft was carrying a civilian technician (as has been suggested); it is known that Wyatt, despite his lack of Sergeant aircrew rank, had attended an introductory course on radar during the summer. One is left with the conclusion that Wyatt was indeed the radar operator, as his Sergeant's rank would have been ratified within the next week or so, and that he was, despite his humble rank at the time of his death, one of the more proficient radar operators on the Squadron. Of the crews of these two aircraft only Hooper survived (with injuries), but never flew again with No.25 Squadron.

During the remainder of September, the Squadron gained three further victories at night, including another by Herrick, and reported inconclusive sightings of eight or nine enemy night raiders.

No.25 Squadron's association with Victor Beamish was renewed when it returned to North Weald. During the summer this remarkable man had found no regulation that forbade him from accompanying one or other of the Hurricane squadrons stationed under his command. On these 'occasional' sorties he was credited with the destruction of seven enemy aircraft, with another nine probably destroyed. His aircraft was damaged on three occasions, but he brought the Hurricane back safely to North Weald. Not a bad record for a 37-year-old who had received no formal flying training since the 1920s, and flown nothing more modern than Hawker Demon biplanes with No.64 Squadron shortly before the war. He was awarded both the DSO and the DFC for his actions during this period as Station Commander at North Weald.

CHAPTER 7

Getting the Hang of Things
(Wittering and Ballyhalbert – 1941-1942)

As the great daylight battle reached its climax in mid-September 1940, and thereafter declined (although the West Country was to experience some very heavy attacks over several weeks), London now began to suffer raids on more than 50 consecutive nights, some of little more than nuisance attacks but many causing widespread devastation. Operating at very short range from their bases in northern France and the Low Countries, the German bombers were able to carry their maximum loads of bombs, sometimes flying at 20,000ft or more. There was precious little that Fighter Command could do to counter them at that time.

Apart from a general lack of experience in mastering the new and still unreliable intercept radar in the handful of Beaufighters which had reached a few night fighter Squadrons, No.25 Squadron in particular found difficulty in reaching the raiders, unless they were already on patrol over London. North Weald lay almost on the northern outskirts of London's gun and balloon defences and the Squadron's pilots were forced to gain altitude after take-off by flying a northerly course before turning back to begin their patrols. The very small number of enemy aircraft successfully attacked had almost invariably been illuminated by searchlights and held while a night fighter (usually a Defiant or Hurricane) positioned itself for attack. Scarcely any assistance could be provided by ground radar, other than to give warning of the approach of raiders over the coasts of the South East Counties. The Observer Corps posts, dotted about the countryside in their hundreds, could frequently hear the raiders above them, but do no more than report either enemy bombers or friendly fighters to be flying 'in the vicinity'.

The Squadron was getting nowhere. The Blenheims were of no operational value whatsoever, and the trickle of new Beaufighters was, in October, amounting to less than a dozen aircraft per month to the four Squadrons which by then were under orders to re-equip with the new night fighter.

A few words should be said of the Beaufighter, for it was by any standards an advanced aircraft. It was a twin-engine aircraft of typically robust Bristol design. The pilot's cockpit was located in the very short nose, under which were installed four 20-mm Hispano Mk.1 cannon, the heavy gun bodies extending to the rear of the pilot where the radar operator had the difficult and somewhat hazardous job of lifting empty magazines off the guns and replacing them with loaded drums in the very confined space available, possibly as the pilot was twisting and turning to gain a favourable attack position on his target. There were also six rifle-calibre Browning machine guns, four in the starboard wing and two in the port, outboard of the engines. Together these guns constituted an extremely heavy armament at the time the Beaufighter entered service and, indeed for its five-year operational life. The two engines, Bristol Hercules, each developing 1,000hp, bestowed a normal maximum speed of about 330mph at 15,000ft. By and large, the Beaufighter came as a very pleasant surprise to pilots and navigators alike. It possessed a fairly high acceleration – important in those early days of night interceptions which, almost invariably developed into a long stern chase.

Before the general introduction of Ground Controlled Interception radar stations (the first of which started operation in mid-1941), it demanded a highly skilled radar operator on the ground to 'set up' an interception. The coastal CH radar stations were only just being equipped with goniometers, a means by which the operator switched his vertically 'stacked' aerial arrays in turn as an enemy aircraft approached the coast; by comparing the signals from each of his four aerial arrays, he could estimate the height of the aircraft according to its position in the array displays. This height estimation required exceedingly experienced operators, but was even then seldom more accurate than 2,000-5,000 feet (more accurate low down than above about 12,000ft.). The ground operator could then pass to the operations centre a fairly accurate approach course and height, and the ground controller would simply transmit this information to the pilot, who would endeavour to steer a reciprocal, or head-on course in the hope that his radar operator would spot the target approaching on the aircraft's radar. If the ground reporting of the height and course of the enemy aircraft was moderately accurate, the pilot stood a reasonable chance of turning to one side of the approaching target in a 'parallel head-on' attack; the radar operator would read off the fast diminishing 'off-set' ranges and, depending on the offset distance, the pilot would decide the moment to turn in on the target, and this would in all likelihood be the moment at which the pilot might spot his target – a dim silhouette, engine exhaust glow or a sudden moon glint on metal. The pilot would try to carry out a rear quarter attack, so that the enemy aircraft would fly through his gun fire. If the speed performance of fighter and bomber were not greatly different, a long stern chase would follow. Too often, the German aircraft would pull ahead in a shallow dive and seek safety in a large cloud. And it would then be too late to set up a new attack pattern.

Until the performance and range of the AI Mk.IV radar could be improved in the Beaufighter, night combat successes for Fighter Command would remain low. Only by frequent day and night practice interceptions would the radar operators become competent in judging the moment at which to tell the pilot to turn towards the target. Too soon, and the Beaufighter would finish up in the path of the raider, too late and the pilot might be too far astern of his target; despite the long ensuing stern chase, the operator had a better chance of regaining contact on his target, hoping that the Beaufighter's speed margin was adequate to retain radar contact and eventually visual contact by the pilot. In short, the ground radar was still only of value in placing the Beaufighter somewhere in the path of an approaching raider.

Everything depended on the CH station detecting an incoming raid when it was still well out to sea. By and large the Heinkel He 111 and the Dornier Do 17 were the German aircraft more frequently engaged, owing to their lower cruising speeds, than the Junkers Ju 88 which, with bomb load was only about 30 mph slower than the Beaufighter at combat rating. Of course, once the radar operator had a steady signal from the Junkers he would open the throttles and accelerate fairly quickly. Until the Beaufighter was fitted with more efficient flash reducers on its engine exhaust pipes, the latter glowed brightly at anything like full throttle and might well be spotted by the German rear gunner.

By dint of constant training exercises, continual assessment of pilots and radar operators, it proved possible to 'pair off crews', each member becoming familiar with the other's strengths and weaknesses during the course of setting up interceptions, and honing their procedures to an effective degree. In the event of a successful interception – real or simulated – the pilot and operator would go over the reasons why it had been successful, and then repeat it to ensure it was no fluke!

Gradually it became normal practice for pilots and radar operators to 'team up', flying together whenever practicable – according to exigencies of leave, illness and so on (as always, it was inadvisable to fly if one had a heavy cold, simply because rapid changes in flying altitude could, and sometimes did cause serious injury to the eardrums, for the Beaufighter was not pressurised). Likewise, pilot and radar operators preferred, whenever possible, to stick to one aircraft, each becoming familiar with that aircraft's and radar's operating behaviour. However, in 1941, the AI Mk.IV was still very temperamental and this might only be discovered in the course of the night flying test (NFT) which had already become almost mandatory during the afternoon before night stand-by or patrol. Aircraft would take off in pairs and one would act as target for the other and then 'change sides'. The nav-rad would go though the intercept pattern, watching for any particular idiosyncrasies of the radar equipment, and ensuring that the range indications were reliable (achieved by 'calibrating' against the pilot's reflector-sight-on-wing span). Once set up for the night, the radar would be switched off prior to landing with the hope that switching on again during the night sortie would not upset the careful work done during the NFT. Getting to know the vagaries of any one set would inspire confidence in that particular set.

Unfortunately there was little 'trade' among German aircraft during No.25 Squadron's brief stay at Debden, and on 27th December 1940 it pulled up its roots once more and transferred northwards to the RAF Station at Wittering in Northamptonshire, about ten miles north-west of Peterborough. This was far from being a random choice by Fighter Command for, by then, the *Luftwaffe* had switched its bombing effort away from London to the provinces, and the Industrial Midlands were frequently being attacked. The move was, however, too late for the Squadron to meet the disastrous night raid on Coventry on 14th/15th November, in which 437 German bombers approached their target from several directions. Ironically the greater number of successful interceptions that night were achieved by some day fighters whose pilots caught sight of enemy bombers silhouetted against the blazing inferno below and were able to deliver the *coups de grace* out of the darkness above.

Third production Beaufighter, R2059, delivered to No.25 Squadron at North Weald towards the end of September 1940; though painted with the Squadron code letters ZK, it has not yet been given its individual aircraft letter. This aircraft is armed with the four nose 20mm Hispano cannon, but the wing machine guns have not been fitted, nor has any AI radar – the pilot being provided with the pillar-type foresight for general training purposes. This was almost certainly the replacement Beaufighter for the aircraft lost in the accident on 15th September. Just visible in the background are some of the Squadron's 'old' Blenheim fighters. (Photo: Bunny Druce Bennett)

On the night of 9th April 1941 Fg Off Bunny Druce Bennett and his radar operator, Sgt Frank Curtis in 'B' Flight's Beaufighter R2122, flying from Wittering, destroyed a Junkers Ju 88C-2 night intruder (Wkr Nr 0766/R4+CM of 4.Staffel, Nachtjagdgeschwader 2). The pilot, Gefreiter Frank Brötz, was killed, but Unteroffizier Willi Lindla (radio operator) and Gefreiter Ewald Gaelt (gunner) survived to be taken prisoner. This was the first confirmed victory by a No.25 Squadron Beaufighter. The photo above-left shows Druce Bennett (on the left) and Sgt Curtis, and above-right the nose of X7546 showing their 'Felix the Cat' motif. This is a very rare photo as any picture taken 'privately' at that time, showing the AI Mk.IV nose aerial, was strictly forbidden. This Beaufighter was to become Bennett's 'own' aircraft for a long period of time

(Photos: Bunny Druce Bennett)

DOWN TO BRASS TACKS

It can be said that No.25 Squadron became an accomplished night fighter squadron during its fourteen-month stay at Wittering. As is so often the case, the likelihood of increased combat, with the opportunity to demonstrate crew skills, brought about a return of the old 'squadron spirit', an honest belief that the time had come to show once more that No.25 was as good as the best. This process was assisted beyond question by the quality of the various levels of leadership. Beginning, not illogically, with the Station Commanders at Wittering.

When No.25 arrived at Wittering, the Station was commanded by Group Capt Harry Broadhurst who, at the age of 25 had been a flight commander on No.41 Squadron, flying Bulldogs at Northolt in the early 1930s. He would later rise to lead Bomber Command and Second Tactical Air Force as an Air Chief Marshal. He had a powerful personality, which he stamped on every appointment he ever held, not least that at Wittering. He it was who quickly identified the innate differences between the day and night fighter personnel that existed during the early years of the night fighter arm, and he commanded plenty of useful guinea pigs on whom to base his views, for Wittering was also home to No.151 Squadron, a Defiant night fighter squadron. Although the Defiant had begun its Service life as a two-seat day fighter, its suitability for day combat in the presence of superior enemy day fighters was quickly shown to be fatally flawed, possessing no forward-firing guns and depending on a large four-gun turret amidships. After crippling losses had been suffered by the two day fighter Defiant squadrons at the height of the Battle of Britain, its rôle had been changed to that of night fighter. Being at that time without AI radar, it was at a disadvantage when compared with an aircraft such as the Beaufighter, and effectively little more use than the Blenheims. Nevertheless, the Defiant had its trickle of successes – which soon far outnumbered that of the Blenheim night fighters. It has been said that most Defiant crews were made up of a day fighter pilot and a gunner with outstanding eyesight! Indeed, No.151 Squadron's highest-scoring pilot, Plt Off Richard Stevens, preferred to fly a Hurricane at night rather than the Defiant, and eventually amassed a total of 14 night combat victories before his death in December 1941. But he was the exception that proved the rule – or so thought Harry Broadhurst.

Indeed, while curbing excesses of high spirits among the air (and ground) personnel, Broadhurst, on his own admission, found it necessary 'to light the occasional squib under some of the more reserved gentlemen on his Squadrons'. The lesson was seldom forgotten, and was to a great extent nurtured by Broadhurst's successor, none other than Group Captain Basil Embry – another legendary figure in the Royal Air Force annals. When command of No.25 Squadron passed in January 1941 to none other than Wg Cdr David Atcherley (twin brother of Richard – universally known as 'Batchy' – for David in his early years had been 'Atchy'), the amalgam was daunting, for all three officers were experts at creating their own 'independent air forces' within the Royal one. There was seldom anything unlawful in this, usually provided that the end result was an improvement over the former *status quo*. Batchy was the 'thinker', David was the 'instrument', although the distinction was seldom so clear-cut. Perhaps fortunately for the RAF, they never served together.

When Embry and Atcherley arrived, almost together – for it is said that Embry arranged for David Atcherley to take command of No.25 (once more a case of 'who you know') at Wittering, it was not long before they discussed the fundamental problem facing the night fighter squadrons, this being summarised as follows. It was one thing to teach a radar operator how to get the best performance from his 'black boxes' under ideal conditions, namely that the equipment is fully serviceable, the weather not too bad, and the 'enemy' conforming to the same conditions as those being employed in training (in terms of flying straight and level, at a constant speed, and so on). The AI equipment obviously could be made to cope with minor variations, but it needed realistic training, both in the air and on the ground. And on the ground, the training had hitherto been little more than class-room theory. Richard, it was, who put the problem in a nutshell. 'What we need are people who are absolutely brilliant at electrical gadgetry, radio and their theories, who regard divergences from the norm as being problems to overcome, not ignored, but otherwise completely unaware of such inconveniences as hazard, air sickness and other human failings. Which of the two officers hit on the solution is not known (though one could guess).

The upshot was, so the legend goes, that fairly soon after the above conference, two officers of the RAF visited the University of Cambridge, to seek a casual meeting with certain graduates (or even undergraduates) to discuss a hypothesis which touched only briefly on the matter of radio waves, but which were causing a number of problems the Royal Air Force was having difficulty in solving. The upshot of this visit was, quite simply, that the following day a small number of 'temporary, unpaid, acting sergeants' found themselves at Wittering, inspecting radio equipment and discussing all manner of problems being experienced in its operation. The next step was to provide practical demonstrations in the air. Little is known of what became of these 'sergeants', although once they had forced themselves to accept the discomfort of the Beaufighter's compartment behind the pilot, with the bodies of four 20mm cannon set into the floor – not to mention the often unexpected and violent manoeuvres being made by the pilot in the dark – they might just be able to pay attention to the problems of solving the actions the pilot needed to take and, of much greater importance how best to formulate a teaching process for the would-be RAF experts whose critical task it was to detect enemy aircraft and shoot them down at night. It should be remembered that almost all the training that the RAF had, so far, undertaken had been confined to the ground trades, how to keep the radar in working condition and to rectify the many faults which in those early days occurred with depressing regularity.

One of the first practices to come under scrutiny throughout the operational night fighter squadrons was the NFT. Unfortunately, it became all too apparent that merely switching the set off after an NFT, and then switching it on again two or three hours later, had the effect of changing the settings – in particular the range calibration – with the result that time was often wasted while rectifying some minor 'fault'.

It is said that these 'boffins' later underwent a process of persuasion to encourage them to undergo more formal induction into the RAF, and they, or others like them, soon became familiar figures at other night fighter stations – their job to bring a touch of sympathetic understanding to the radar operators' difficult tasks. Such superfluous niceties as wearing any sort of uniform correctly was set aside (to the consternation of the Station Warrant Officer) in the interests of increasing the number of German bombers shot down by Beaufighters during the *Blitz* of 1940-41. It also just happened that at Wittering, Atcherley had foreseen the need for a first-class radar operator of his own, and had obtained permission to bring with him the Group Technical Officer as his own radar operator, then a flight lieutenant and already a man of outstanding technical abilities and possessed of exceptional intelligence. (He later reached Air Marshal rank as Sir John Hunter-Tod, KBE, CB, MA, retiring from the Service in 1973.) The wisdom in selecting 'Hunter' as

The shot-down remains of Heinkel He 111H, 5J+CD, of Kampfgeschwader *4* 'General Wever', *based at Leeuwarden, Holland. On the night of 24th/25th June 1941, during a sortie to drop sea mines in the Mersey, it was intercepted and shot down over Lincolnshire by Beaufighter R2082, flown by Plt Off D W Thompson with Plt Off L D Britain (navigator/radar operator) of No.25 (Fighter) Squadron, then stationed at Wittering.* (Photo: by courtesy of Ernest Sutton)

David's R/O was quickly apparent when, on almost their first night patrol together, they destroyed a German bomber. Crewroom cries of 'fluke' were quickly stifled when Hunter's almost instinctive ability to set up an interception with great speed and accuracy came to be realised and, when David Atcherley was otherwise engaged, was eagerly sought by No.25's flight commanders keen to take the expert with them on patrol! It goes without saying that David's R/O spent much of his time in discussion with, not only the 'impressed' boffins, but also the Squadron's harassed operators. This powerful element of professionalism slowly but surely replaced the otherwise 'blind leading the blind' attitude that had pervaded the flight crew room on No.25 Squadron. In passing, it should be mentioned here that, despite being David's R/O, Hunter-Tod's appointment was Station Technical Officer, and was officially a member of Wittering's Station Flight; this device also enabled Hunter to pay attention to the difficulties being experienced when No.151 Squadron began receiving a few AI-equipped Defiants.

The war situation at Wittering as winter gave way to spring in 1941 centred on the *Luftwaffe's* night attacks on the industrial Midlands, attacks most frequently carried out by small batches of bombers flying across from Holland (and Germany), their crews often briefed to attack such targets as Derby, Manchester, Birmingham, Coventry (again), and so on. A glance at German records of those months show that the majority of those raids resulted in haphazard attacks on many much smaller towns and, when no obvious target could be spotted on ETA, the bombs were simply jettisoned on some other likely target. Training airfields suffered many such attacks, especially with aircraft in the landing circuit with their navigation lights on, and a delay in dousing the runway lights.

Wittering itself came under attack on a number of occasions, and it was on one such night that yet another Atcherley legend was born. The event is clear in numerous minds, and many eye-witness accounts are to hand, none better than that of Sqn Ldr J B Wray, then visiting a friend on the Squadron, (and soon to be appointed OC 'A' Flight, later Gp Capt, CBE, DFC)

> I seem to recall it was about February/March 1941 *(15th March – FKM)*. The Squadron had received orders from Group that aircraft were no longer to be kept in hangars unless they were undergoing major servicing. Needless to say, this instruction was not being complied with to the letter and, on this occasion there were still one or two Beaufighters in the hangar that should, rightfully, have been dispersed on the airfield. No.25, at least, was still operating from the hangar.
>
> We were in the crewroom that night, listening to the radio, and I think David Atcherley was there at the time. Suddenly, bang, crash, wallop, and it was all too clear that the airfield was under attack. All our lights went out and it was equally obvious that our hangar was on fire, and we were all thrown to the floor. Our immediate concern was for the safety of the Beaufighters. Picking ourselves up, we all rushed into the main body of the hangar to find various fires dotted about, obviously caused by incendiaries. Well, a Beaufighter weighed ten tons and was not easily moved by human pushing alone; and the hangar doors, closed because of the blackout, were difficult to open with the winding handle, even when one was sane and rational. In those conditions of utter panic, moving the Beaufighter and opening the doors was going to be a monumental task. It was eventually achieved, not without many four-letter words – often between the best of friends.
>
> The fires were eventually put out and at last we could repair to the Mess which we found had received a bomb; this had destroyed parked cars and blown in the Ladies' Room. The only casualty had been a visiting officer who had been sitting in his room when a bomb splinter came in through the window and killed him.*

* Sadly, among the other casualties at Wittering that night was one, widely known as 'Timbertoes' Carlin. Carlin had been a farmer in Yorkshire before the First World War and had fought in the trenches early in that War, winning the Military Medal. He lost a leg, but then joined the RFC, becoming a pilot on No.74 Squadron in France and shooting down eleven of the enemy. He returned to farming 'twixt the Wars, but joined up again and became a Defiant gunner, fighting in the Battle of Britain. His Defiant was dispersed on the airfield at Wittering, and it is thought that he was hobbling out to the aircraft to offer some defence in its gun turret, but was killed instantly by a bomb. He had won a DSO and MC to add to his Military Medal.

> In the morning we returned to the hangar to examine the damage in a more rational light. The first thing we noticed was that one of the Beaufighters had about six feet missing from one wing. Had we hit it on the hangar door when pushing the aircraft out? The panic at the time suggested that this had been the cause. However, the real cause of the damage became evident when we moved into the hangar; there, beside the piece of wing, was a large hole in the ground, at the bottom of which was an unexploded bomb of about 500lb. Needless to say, we all made off at high speed. Except for one person, David Atcherley. (At this point I need to say that if you haven't served with an Atcherley, and I have served with both, then you haven't lived, nor are you familiar with their unusual thought processes, of which this account may be considered typical.)
>
> David stood there looking down into the hole while we, at some distance stood looking at him. Suddenly he turned round and called for the Squadron Adjutant, a chap called Meek (and meek by nature). 'Look, Meek' David said, 'We'll get this thing out of here and empty it, then we'll cut a slot in it, paint it red, and use it as the Squadron post box.' An idea which, in the circumstances, would never have occurred to a rational person. David continued, 'Go and get some airmen and some rope and we'll pull it out. Meek tried to remonstrate, but to no avail, and went off to do as bidden. As the

> rope was produced, however, a Bomb Disposal Unit arrived, saw what was about to occur, expressed considerable opposition to the venture, and ordered everyone well away from the site – an order welcomed by all, except of course David.
>
> The following day, David was arraigned before Basil Embry, who expressed a few home truths – long since familiar to the Atcherley twins. However, quite unfairly, the unfortunate Meek was also summoned before the Station Commander, who said, 'Look here, Meek, if you want to fiddle about with unexploded bombs, I'll have you posted to a Bomb Disposal Unit'.
>
> Needless to say, when I returned (now posted to the Squadron), there in the Orderly Room was the bomb, painted red with a slot cut in the front for posting letters.'

Witness to another occurrence at Wittering at about this time was Henry ('Knocker') West, a Flight Mechanic (Engines), who recalls

> It was at Wittering that I saw my first crash. It was frightening and a sad experience. The aircraft was a visiting Westland Whirlwind. It took off after an hour or two, and the pilot obviously wanted to show what a Whirlwind could do, so he made a fast, low flypast before going on his way. As he flashed past the control tower we distinctly saw something fly off the tailplane. The aircraft immediately went out of control, shot across the Great North Road and dived into a field with a terrific explosion, which ended in a pall of smoke and flame.'

When John Wray returned to Wittering as a Squadron Leader, his arrival coincided with that of Sqn Ldr Alington, both promoted to take command of Flights on No.25 Squadron. However, as only one vacancy existed, Atcherly referred to the Air Force List on the matter of seniority and, seeing that Wray was in fact the senior, appointed him to take over 'A' Flight, with the remark that, as there's been no flight commander for a week or so 'the Flight has been run by a sort of Soviet, and that state of affairs cannot be allowed to continue'. Alington joined 'B' Flight, but not then as Flight Commander, the post being already filled by Sqn Ldr Harold Percival ('Flash') Pleasance – who would in due course take over command of the Squadron from David Atcherley, when Alington would succeed him as flight commander. This seems to have sparked a fierce rivalry between 'A' and 'B' Flights – which, for no logical reason, seems to have persisted for many months. More of that in due course.

During No.25 Squadron's unusually long stay at Wittering, it appears that, although it was constantly called on to fly night patrols, and occasionally scrambled at night (not a normal procedure unless an attack on the station was anticipated), night contacts with German bombers were fairly rare. It has only proved possible to trace a total of eighteen such contacts during the first six months of 1941, with a total of four aircraft confirmed shot down. Such a proportion of successes to radar contacts was, at the time about

Friedrich Ertsinger (left), *the wireless operator/gunner, was the only survivor from the crew of the He 111H, shown in the previous picture. He was invited to visit No.25 (Fighter) Squadron at Leeming on 12th November 1998. He is seen here in the Squadron crew room with Hauptmann Werner Theisen (the German Air Force Liaison Officer to No.25 (Fighter) Squadron), examining documents relating to the action in which the Heinkel was shot down in 1941. As befits the date, Herr Ertsinger is wearing the Armistice Day poppy in his lapel.*
(Photo: by courtesy of Ernest Sutton)

par for the course, the main difficulty arising from the lack of ground radar coverage. The use of early mobile ground radar fighter control units was only in its early stages of operational development at that time, and dependence upon searchlights was also fairly rare in the Midlands. The aircraft shot down by David Atcherley, during the period of the night *Blitz,* appears to have been a fairly regular visitor to the Wittering area, as it had been reported at the same time on several consecutive nights and had been the cause of some disruption to the night flying programme. David had been given several good contacts by 'Hunter' but without seeing anything until at last he saw the target some distance below him. Without waiting for further instructions from his R/O, he threw the Beaufighter into a thundering dive and opened fire with all his guns. The next moment he found himself flying through the wreckage (which fell over a wide area). The next day, on close inspection of his aircraft, the ground crew found evidence of his success with a number of dents and traces of blood and flesh on the nose and wings of the Beaufighter. On enquiring whether this should be removed, David replied 'No, leave it; it'll come off in due course.' He was considerably more distressed to hear that some of the bomber's wreckage had fallen on a local pub, killing a sailor home on leave.

Wing Commander David Francis William Atcherley (later Air Vice-Marshall), the memorable Commanding Officer of No.25 (Fighter) Squadron at RAF Station Wittering in 1941 – the formative year of the Bristol Beaufighter night fighter.

(Original portrait by Eric Kennington)

On another occasion *(28th August 1941 – FKM)*, David, fortunately without an R/O in his haste to take off after a raider, narrowly missed a Defiant on the unlit runway (the lights had been extinguished owing to the proximity of the enemy), and in his avoiding action flew through some trees and crashed in a neighbouring field, totally destroying his Beaufighter, and aggravating an old Officers' Mess Rugby injury to his neck. Shortly after this, he was awarded a DFC, and there is a photograph of the investiture by HM King George VI at Wittering, in which David appears with a large plaster-cast encasing his torso! This injury, incidentally, put paid to an imminent posting to the Middle East in command of its first Beaufighter squadron.

Whether this or other near misses on the runway at Wittering prompted action by Basil Embry is not known, but post-war, in the winter of 1945-46, Wittering's runway was considerably lengthened by joining it with that of Collyweston, situated just to the north of the station. It was to transform Wittering into a much larger station and obviate the need to employ Collyweston as a separate satellite airfield, which had itself caused problems in the Wittering landing circuit.

The gradual run-down of the German night *Blitz* on Britain, which eventually petered out in May 1941, resulted in scarcely any significant night combat for No.25 Squadron during the second half of the year, other than routine night interception training, now being tentatively controlled by the first of the GCI stations, of which about half a dozen were being sited.

There is no doubt but that Basil Embry achieved an enormous improvement in the air defence of the Midlands in 1941. His *modus operandi* appears to have been, when confronted by a suggestion for improvement in the station's operational efficiency, 'give it a try, and if it works, we'll adopt it'. He had the means at his disposal, possessing his own Sector Operations Centre, a day fighter squadron, two night fighter squadrons, and another day fighter Squadron (No.266) at Collyweston. No.25 Squadron was certainly transformed into a very efficient and, on the whole, satisfied fighting unit.

ULSTER INTERLUDE

Whatever the reason for No.25 Squadron's transfer from Wittering to Northern Ireland in January 1942, it would not have been on account of its prowess as a night fighter unit. The most likely explanation seems to have been America's entry into the War, and the anticipation of an increase in Atlantic convoys arriving at and sailing from Liverpool and the Clyde, not to mention the likelihood of increased maritime reconnaissance activity in support of these convoys. In both, there would be a need to provide shipping and airfield protection from German air and submarine activity in the approaches to the ports. It was also to provide night defence of Belfast, although this city was not attacked in any great strength.

No.25 Squadron arrived on 24th January 1942 at Ballyhalbert, situated on the coast of the Ards Peninsula in County Down, and about 20 miles due east of Belfast. By all accounts it was a desolate place, swept by cold east winds, prone to frequent sea mists off the Irish Sea, and only accessible by a coast road that wound its way between Donaghadee to the north and Portaferry to the south. Accommodation was almost entirely confined to wooden huts – marginally waterproof but certainly prone to icy draughts.

Fortunately the Squadron's sojourn at Ballyhalbert lasted only about three months, during which coastal and convoy patrols were the order of the day (and night). The Squadron moved in as No.504 (County of Nottingham) Squadron moved out with Spitfires. The long-stay Squadron, No.153, also a night fighter Squadron with Beaufighters, had been at Ballyhalbert since the previous October, and was to remain there until January 1943. Needless to relate, that Squadron had appropriated all the better accommodation and amenities, but No.25 Squadron soon learned the art of acquisition.

Night patrols began within a week of arrival, while three new crews flew night training sorties, with practice interceptions over the sea (an innovation for the Squadron as few had been possible at Wittering). Unfortunately the Squadron lost an aircraft on 11th February 1942, when it crashed into the sea while on such a training flight. Another Beaufighter crashed on take-off at Ballyhalbert on 16th April, killing both crew members.

Perhaps one of the episodes of life at Ballyhalbert most frequently recalled by members of No.25 was the enrolment on to the ration strength of a native quadruped. . .

"We landed at Ballyhalbert and as the aircrew stood around chatting, waiting for the Dakotas that would bring the groundcrew and certain of our equipment, we became aware that we were not alone for, standing a few yards away was a large Billy goat with a fine set of horns and a rather splendid beard. We did not immediately take much notice of him as we had always understood that goats are fairly common in Ireland, and so we assumed that he had come through one of the hedgerows from the fields that surrounded us, and that in due course he would leave us.

Having sized us up he proceeded to crop the grass that was in abundance around our dispersal, but as the day wore on it became apparent that he was in no hurry to leave. Once the groundcrew arrived, several of them attempted to make friendly gestures towards him, but these were rejected, not by any retreat by the goat, who firmly held his ground, but by a look from two beady eyes which said THESE HORNS ARE NOT COSMETIC DECORATION! So we went about our business, and he went about his.

After a few days it became all too clear that the goat had no intention of leaving, so we made enquiries among local farms to try to find out who had mislaid a splendid Billy goat. However, no one claimed ownership, and it appeared that farmers in that area did not keep goats anyway.

A fully-armed Beaufighter IIF with AI Mk.IV radar was received by No.25 Squadron at Wittering from No.604 Squadron on 24th May 1941 for brief operational assessment before being passed on to No.600 Squadron on 26th June 1941. It was not popular with No.25 as the Merlin engine cut out on several occasions during simulated evasive manoeuvres. It was also deemed to be about 20 mph slower than the standard Beaufighter I, while directional control at low airspeed required even coarser use of rudder.

(Photo: Bristol Aeroplane Company Ltd.)

The goat was now beginning to take an interest in our activities, and followed people around, watching them perform their various tasks. He kept well clear of the aircraft when engines were running but, this apart, he became more of a participant than an observer. So we decided that we had no option but to absorb him on the Flight strength where, naturally, he was recorded as Billy Goat.

Very soon we were able to stroke him and to talk to him as familiarity created a more friendly atmosphere. However, we soon discovered one act of familiarity that he would not abide, and this was anyone getting hold of his horns. This was not helped by a habit he had of coming up and, in friendly gesture, rubbing his head on legs and thighs. Automatically, the recipient, in defence of his jewellery, put a hand on Billy's horns. A violent shaking of the goat's head caused the horn-holder, with self-preservation now in mind to hold on tighter or even grab the other horn. It was at this stage that bystanders understood the meaning of being caught on the horns of a dilemma, for what was the now desperate horn-holder to do? Either he could hope to hang on to this violently gyrating goat forever, or choose the alternative of pushing the goat away and then make a run for it. Unfortunately, none of us was capable of covering a hundred yards in ten seconds, and in any case Billy could do it in about eight. So the concluding scene of this drama, to be re-enacted so many times during the next few months, was a fleeing ex-horn-holder pursued by a very agile goat and rapidly being caught and receiving two or three butts up the backside, rarely more. In 'A' Flight, if you hadn't been butted at least once by Billy, you were not an initiated member.

We always had great fun with new arrivals. 'Oh, look!' they would exclaim, 'a goat'. 'Yes', would be the reply, 'That's Billy – why not go and say Hello to him?' The drama would then be acted before a most appreciative audience, made the more exciting because the new arrival had no idea what was about to befall him.

Billy's official score of confirmed butts was never recorded but, in comparison to the air aces, he must have been well up the list. He had no 'Probables' as escape was almost impossible. However, he recorded two 'Damaged' when a visiting Air Commodore and Group Captain thought they knew all about goats and, having received a butt each when making their escape, were saved from further punishment by the heroic action of an airman who threw himself between

Late production Bristol Beaufighter Mk.IF as flown by No.25 (Fighter) Squadron in 1942, equipped with AI Mk.IV radar.
(Photo: Bristol Aeroplane Company Ltd.)

pursuer and pursued, thereby taking the remaining butts himself. He was, however, an old hand himself to whom the experience was not new.

Very soon the goat made a practice of coming into the aircrew restroom to sit with us. By this time we had become so accustomed to him that his arrival was only noted with a polite greeting. However, one day, he arrived to find one of the rather battered armchairs unoccupied, so he climbed into it and settled himself down. From that moment that chair was regarded as belonging to Billy, and when the sun was shining we used to put it out for him to sit in and enjoy the sun.

During these visits to the crewroom, or others in the Flight, he never made messes. But, occasionally, he would wander down to 'B' Flight about 400 yards away, go into their crewroom, leave his card, and then saunter back to 'A' Flight. As there already existed severe disagreement between the two Flights, their chagrin was only matched by our delight.

Another activity in which Billy would indulge was to go into the room where our flying clothing and parachutes were kept in tall green lockers, and assault these lockers with a violence that had to be seen to be believed. The attacks would seldom last more than a few minutes, but during that time we chose not to require our parachutes and flying clothing.

Eventually the rapport between man and beast became so close that one of the airmen constructed a harness, and persuaded Billy to pull starter trolleys when he felt like it. He seemed to enjoy this and participated willingly, though during the fitting of the harness 'horn touching' was still strictly 'off limits'.

At night we had to mount armed guards on the aircraft; this was usually in the ratio of one guard to two, or possibly three aircraft, depending on how far apart they were dispersed. This was a demanding job, and so the aircrew were pressed into service.

For those who have never mounted guard at night in a hostile environment, the reader may be assured that it can be a lonely and scary experience. All kinds of night sounds become accentuated in the minds of the guards, and converted into a variety of sinister and immediate threats. It has not been unknown for a guard to shoot a cow when his three-times uttered 'Halt, who goes there?' has gone ignored, the heavy rustling gets closer and closer. So, in this rather eerie environment it really was a comfort when Billy came wandering round. His obvious lack of fear and the knowledge that an intruder would get very short shrift should they tangle with him inspired the courage and confidence we needed.

So life went on, the aircrew carrying out patrols and chasing Germans, while the groundcrew ensured that the aircraft were kept at the peak of efficiency. Billy, of course, went about his business of keeping everyone on their toes and keeping us all entertained with his own unique brand of humour.

Suddenly in May a signal arrived ordering the Squadron to re-deploy to Church Fenton in Yorkshire. Immediately the cry went up 'What about Billy?' for a move had never occurred to us, and if it had, we put it out of our minds like a bad dream.

A Flight meeting was called, which everybody attended, and very quickly it became apparent that overwhelming opinion supported the view that Billy should come with us. But how? Loading him in one of the Dakotas, which would lift the groundcrew and part of our equipment seemed the only answer, once we had rejected a suggestion that he might be carried in one of our Beaufighters because the flight would be much shorter.

Having accepted that this was the only course open to us, I felt unsure of what the reaction of the Captain of the Dakota would be when he was informed that he would have a big live Billy goat among his passengers. Neither was I certain that Billy's enthusiasm for flying would match ours. Then someone had a brainwave, 'Get the Doc to give him a shot to put him out for the period of the flight to Church Fenton. If necessary, we can smuggle him aboard while he's asleep as part of the

Flight Lieutenant Joe Singleton's groundcrew standing with his Beaufighter in 1942, known as the 'Three Gs', their names all beginning with that letter. However Joe died before he could pass their names to the Author, but they were an Engine Fitter, Airframe Fitter and a Radio/Radar Mechanic. He always took a keen interest in their work, and never ascribed any blame if he should suffer any malfunction in the air. (Photo: Sqn Ldr Joe Singleton)

ground equipment.' This suggestion was welcomed with a loud 'Yes, that's what we'll do'. . .

These are the occasions when the weight of responsibility presses heavily. It was now necessary to persuade the Squadron Medical Officer to administer a knock-out dose to an Irish Billy goat. All this had to be achieved without the knowledge of the Squadron Commander (still 'Flash' Pleasance), whose aircraft was serviced by 'B' Flight, and who, as a result, tended to share the antagonism 'B' Flight had for 'A' Flight.

That night, in the quiet of my room, removed from the heady emotions of the morning meeting, my thoughts turned to Billy. Was it fair on him? Had we not perhaps allowed our own feelings to dominate to the detriment of his? In time, postings and casualties would bring changes to the Flight, and those who replaced us might not give Billy the friendship and the respect he had received from us. He would then be alone in a foreign environment, and goodness knows what might become of him. I was utterly convinced that it was not in Billy's interests to be taken to England.

I immediately drove down to the Flight, where I found Billy on his nightly patrol, boosting the morale of the guards. I knelt down and he came over and rubbed his chin on my shoulder. I said to him 'I wonder what you would like to do, Billy.' But as I looked at him I knew my decision to be the right one, and that his future happiness and security was more likely to be assured here in Ireland than if he were to be transported away to foreign pastures.

In the morning, the day we were to leave, I gathered the Flight together and announced my decision, and gave my reasons. The response was very sullen, with only one or two muttering 'I suppose that is best'. In fact, the atmosphere suggested that, had this scene taken place in former times, a nearby tree and rope would have been put to good use.

The Dakotas were to take off first, so all the ground crew gathered round to say their farewells to Billy. He obviously sensed that something was afoot because not only did he allow himself to be hugged and stroked, but his horns were 'on limits' on this sad occasion. There were not many dry eyes as the groundcrew lined up to board the Dakotas.

When the time came for the Beaufighters to depart, I put Billy's chair outside in the sun. Then I took his head between my hands and said 'Well, Billy, this is it. Goodbye old friend, and thank you for bringing so much laughter and happiness into our lives. We'll never forget you.' I turned on my heel and climbed into my Beaufighter, started engines, taxied out and took off. Not a word passed between 'Griff', my R/O, and myself.

I circled the airfield and there he was, standing alone in an empty Flight, with his splendid horns and his beard silhouetted as he looked up at us. With a heavy heart and a lump in my throat, I set course for Church Fenton. That was the last I ever saw or heard of Billy Goat of 'A' Flight, No.25 (Fighter) Squadron."

(A slightly abbreviated extract from a letter received from John Wray.)

Billy Goat, the greatly respected non-flying, temporary member of 'A' Flight, No.25 (Fighter) Squadron, at ease in his allotted chair outside the crew room at Ballyhalbert in 1942. John Wray has contributed entertaining recollections of this Ulster goat's attachment to the Squadron.

(Photo: by courtesy of John Wray)

CHAPTER 8

Beaufighters at Church Fenton and Mosquitos at Coltishall

'My Weapon's Bent' – 'Well, try Kicking it'

TO MANY ON THE SQUADRON the brief visit to Northern Ireland had been something of an anti-climax after the occasional excitements at Wittering (not to mention the 'Atcherley experience'). Some crews, in the air and on the ground, felt that the spell at Ballyhalbert had been useful in coming to terms with the improved AI Mk.IV radar in the Beaufighter, and the rather low-key patrols had served to demonstrate the equipment's potential, as well as its limitations. It is certain, however, that the crews were anxious to get going once more against German night bombers. Moreover, it soon became clear that the extent of East Coast radar cover and the quality of ground control, on which No.25 would be entirely dependent, had improved immeasurably during the Squadron's short absence.

The morale of the ground personnel, which had been tested to the full at Ballyhalbert (largely owing to the remoteness of the station), climbed once more, the feeling being generally one of relief at being 'at home' again in a relatively familiar environment – both operational and recreational – Church Fenton being within roughly a dozen miles of both Leeds and York. The county was rapidly becoming accustomed to large numbers of RAF and Canadian personnel, with the result that once the traditional antipathy that existed between the 'fighter and bomber boys' had been moderately assuaged, there was always a wide range of cinemas, pubs and cafés in which men off duty could relax. In short, the long-suffering Yorkshire folk were friendly and hospitable.

The bulk of the Squadron arrived with its Beaufighters at Church Fenton on 16th May 1942. This was a period of relative inactivity by the *Luftwaffe,* and the few fairly heavy enemy raids launched at that time were mostly confined to the south of England. Typical of these was a heavy raid on Canterbury which caused heavy damage on the night of 30th May.

Of much greater importance for the night fighters in the North of England was the huge effort being made by Bomber Command to extend its deployment, No.4 Group being mainly based in Yorkshire (predominantly equipped with Whitleys, Wellingtons and Halifaxes), and Nos.3 and 5 Groups further south with Wellingtons, Stirlings, Manchesters and Lancasters. Indeed new Bomber Stations

No.25 (Fighter) Squadron, Church Fenton, 1943 – Mosquito FB Mk.VI Intruders.

Back Row, left to right: *Sgt Eddie Butler, Sgt Don Forryan, Sgt (unknown), Sgt (unknown), Sgt McCausland, Sgt (unknown), Plt Off (unknown), Plt Off (unknown), Sgt A W Patterson, Sgt Bert Mogg, F/Sgt Nicholson, Sgt (unknown), Fg Off Lilwall (?), Sgt Barney Travers.*

Middle Row, left to right: *F/Sgt Brocklehurst, Sgt (unknown), F/Sgt Tony Hay, Plt Off (unknown), Fg Off Brett-Young, Fg Off Geoff Haslam, Plt Off (unknown), Plt Off (unknown), F/Sgt Keith Panter, Plt Off Henry Cook, Plt Off Jock Henderson, Fg Off Cox, Plt Off Reg Skinner, Flt Lt Gunn (Eng Off), Sgt (unknown), Plt Off Jack Lilwall (?), Plt Off Alvar Liddell (Int Off), Plt Off (unknown).*

Front Row, left to right: *Fg Off Quinn RCAF, Fg Off (unknown), Fg Off Grey, Fg Off George Hogarth, Sqn Ldr 'Butch' Baker (OC 'A' Flight), Flt Lt Peters (Adjutant), Wg Cdr Maude (Sqn Cdr), Sqn Ldr Matthews (OC 'B' Flight), Flt Lt Bill Bailey, Flt Lt Johnny Limbert, Fg Off J F R Jones, Fg Off Linthune, Fg Off (unknown).*

were opening at an average rate of slightly more than one every week, with new heavy bomber squadrons being formed at a rate slightly above this. This was also the period of Harris's three great '1,000-bomber' raids against Cologne on 30th-31st May, on Essen two nights later, and on Bremen on the night of 25th-26th June. It was never much of a secret that the operational squadrons of Bomber Command did not then possess anything like '1,000 bombers', and the magic number was made up by using aircraft from the Operational Training Units (some of which were also situated in the Midlands) and Coastal Command. But the propaganda value of these raids was immense. A great deal of damage was done, and Bomber Command's losses were not prohibitive. Compared to Britain, Germany had been rather slower in creating a night fighter arm of the *Luftwaffe* – largely in the belief that there was no air force in Europe capable of discharging any significant weight of bombs on the German fatherland.

One of the results of the increasing bomber strength of the RAF was the growing likelihood of attacks on Bomber Command airfields in Yorkshire, Lincolnshire and Norfolk, flown by *Luftwaffe* intruder aircraft against the bomber bases, which also included a number of bomber Operational Training Units (OTUs) dotted about the same area of England. Not that Germany deployed a large number of bombers in Western Europe (the majority of which were then being deployed on the Eastern Front). Yet a growing number of Junkers Ju 88s, usually operating singly, were reported over and around these stations.

One of a number of Canadian groundcrew members who served on No.25 (Fighter) Squadron during the War, Radar Mechanic Finkle in a Mosquito at Church Fenton. (Photo: Steve Stevens)

No.25 Squadron's move to Church Fenton may have been as much part of the constant rotation of night fighter squadrons from Sector to Sector, as to meet the gradual increase in enemy intruder attacks against the bomber airfields, as well as the occasional attacks on coastal convoys off the East Coast, and the routine German mining operations off such ports as Bridlington, Newcastle and in the Humber estuary.

These threats had been recognised as early as 1941, with the result that the CH coastal radar chain had been progressively strengthened, and now included several new CHL (Chain Home Low) and CHEL (Chain Home Extra Low) stations, as well half a dozen GCI (Ground Control Interception) stations. All these radar stations reported air activities, through Filter Rooms, to the numerous operations centres located at Group and Sector headquarters. Because each GCI's radar cover overlapped those of neighbouring stations by a substantial margin, it was possible to hand over the control of a night fighter from one GCI to another, thereby preventing one station from being swamped by air activity. In theory at least, this would enable a Beaufighter of No.25 Squadron to be controlled by a GCI station located in Durham in the North, all the way down Neatishead in Norfolk during a single intercept sortie.

There is some evidence which suggests that it had been intended to move No.25 Squadron to Church Fenton much earlier, but the move was evidently delayed by the decision to make this station into a Sector Night Fighter base, and as such there was a need to lay concrete runways and perime-

The Squadron Radar Workshop at Church Fenton in 1943. Left to right: *Sam Roddan (later Fg Off), Leslie Palfrey, and Ron Penny.* (Photo: Steve Stevens)

ter tracks, with improved airfield and runway lighting, together with a Sector Operations Centre on the station. In the event, this work occupied more than six months and No.25 was deployed to Northern Ireland before arriving at Church Fenton in May 1942, being the only operational unit there until joined by No.600 Squadron, also with Beaufighters, in September. This squadron, however, only remained for two months before being ordered overseas (to accompany the *Torch* landings in North Africa). Its place was taken by No.183 Squadron, a day fighter squadron formed at Church Fenton with Typhoons. Normally this squadron would have moved away to an airfield in the south fairly quickly, but the Typhoon was giving considerable technical trouble so its departure was delayed until the following spring.

Squadron Leader Pleasance remained in command of No.25 Squadron until September 1942. During the last sixteen weeks which he spent with the Squadron at Church Fenton it flew 507 operational sorties, amounting to 1,310 flying hours, in the course of which six enemy aircraft were shot down and five damaged. No Beaufighters were lost though enemy action, though two other Beaufighters failed to return. The first, on 23rd July, apparently being flown solo by Plt Off Gerald Pizey, was shot down by another Beaufighter (not of No.25 Squadron) off Bridlington. It seems that this came about as a result of Pizey's IFF being unserviceable, and therefore causing some confusion at the GCI, so that the ground controller vectored another aircraft into a combat situation, with tragic results.

A Beaufighter of No.25 Squadron was lost on 8th September following engine failure over the sea; the pilot radioed that one engine had failed and that he was returning to base. Nothing more was heard, and it is assumed that the other engine also failed, as the Beaufighter was perfectly capable of maintaining height on one engine. In this instance both crew members' bodies were recovered, which suggests that they had managed to bale out.

Of those enemy aircraft shot down by the Squadron during this period, two were shot down by Squadron Leader Pleasance (who was promoted to Wing Commander while still commanding No.25). Both were Dornier Do 217s and on both occasions his radar operator was Flt Lt L D Britain, whose family firm had been famous as the manufacturers of the familiar toy 'tin soldiers', collected by successive generations of young boys. Whilst with No.25 Squadron, Squadron Leader Pleasance had destroyed five German aircraft, probably destroyed one and damaged two.

During the period at Church Fenton following the Squadron's arrival from Ballyhalbert, another 'star' pilot was emerging. Flying Officer Joseph Singleton opened his score by damaging a Dornier Do 217 on 23rd August 1942 over South Lincolnshire in an action which resulted from a stern chase under the control of the GCI at Neatishead; on this occasion, the Neatishead controller was just about to discontinue the interception as passing out of radar cover when Singleton called 'Contact' and opened fire, his last sight of the Dornier being as it entered cloud, flying east with an engine on fire; it did not crash on land. His radar operator was Plt Off C J Bradshaw.*

* It is perhaps convenient here to explain the radio vernacular which had come into general use among the night fighter fraternity and continued in vogue for many years; it was introduced primarily to keep radio messages brief in the crowded time-span of air combat:
'I have trade' (GCI call) = I have an indication that suspected enemy aircraft are approaching you.
'Vector. . .' (GCI call) = Change course to . . .
'Contact' (Pilot call) = We have located the target on our radar; please continue instructions.
'Judy' (Pilot call) = We have visual contact with the target and are setting up an attack. . .
'Tally Ho' (Pilot call) = We are about to attack .
'Switch Canary' (GCI call) = Switch on your IFF transmitter.
'Canary Singing' (Pilot's reply) = IFF switched on.
'Strangle Canary' (GCI call) = I have identified you on my screen; switch off your IFF.
'What is your gravy?' (GCI call) = Have you sufficient fuel to return to your base?
'Gravy plus'/'Gravy Minus' (Pilot's reply) = I have sufficient/insufficient fuel.
'Query Ammo?' (GCI call) = Have you still got sufficient ammunition for further combat?
'Ammo Plus/Minus' (Pilot call) = I have sufficient/insufficient ammunition.
'My Weapon's Bent' (Pilot call) = My radar has become unserviceable.

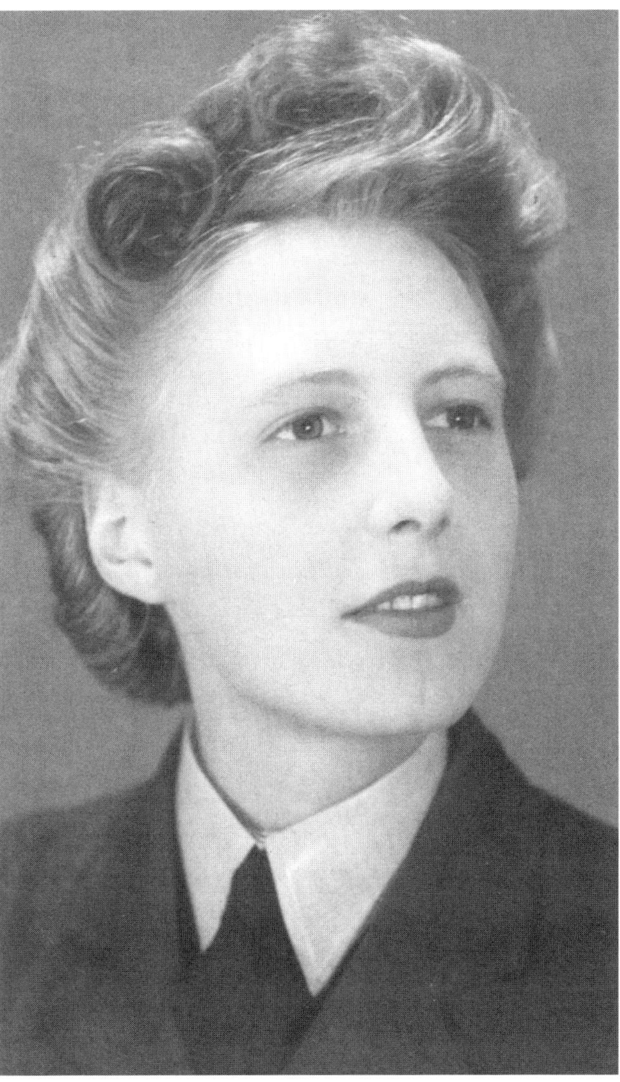

Lasting love blossomed on No.25 Squadron (more than once). Corporal Steve Stevens met and married this beautiful WAAF on Active Service while at Church Fenton. Both Steve and Marjorie continue to grace the Squadron reunions more than fifty years later! (Photo: Steve Stevens)

~~SECRET~~ **Form "F"**

I N T E L L I G E N C E

COMBAT REPORT

Sector Serial No.........................Date.......................... (A) Night 20/21/ May 1943

~~Serial No. of Order detailing Flight or Squadron to Patrol~~ UNIT (B) 25 Squadron

~~Date~~............ Type and Mark of our Aircraft (C) Mosquito IIF

~~Flight, Squadron~~.... Time attack was delivered (D) 00.56-02.00 hours

~~Number of Enemy Aircraft~~ Place of Attack and/or Target (E) (1) Train, Station Buildings, signal Box at (?*)

~~Type of Enemy Aircraft~~.. (2) Train and Station Buildings at Raber

~~Time Attack was Delivered~~.................................... (3) Two trains North of ULZEN

~~Height of Enemy~~... (4) Three searchlight sites in vicinity of Bremen

WEATHER............. (F) West Of Dortmund-Ems - 4-6 miles,6/10ths cloud at 6000ft dispersing. East of Dortmund-Ems, no cloud. Visibility unlimited.

~~Enemy Casualties~~...

Our Casualties - Aircraft.. (G) Nil (one .303 bullet hole in port wing)

Our Casualties - Personnel.. (H) Nil

Enemy Casualties in Combat.................................... (J) Nil

Enemy Casualties - Ground or Sea........................... (K) Four locomotives & coaches damaged; one signal box set on fire and two station buildings at RABER and DRENTEWEDE damaged. Three searchlight positions shot up,

GENERAL REPORT: One Mosquito IIF, 25 Squadron, Pilot F/O Davies, Navigator W/O Bent, took off from COLTISHALL at 23.25 hours to attack transportation targets on Ranger Route No 19. Crossed Dutch Coast at TEXEL at 23.54 hours at 3,000 feet and set course for MEPPEN and, when over the railway one mile North of the town about 20 searchlights exposed, several of them illuminating and holding the Mosquito for approximately 30 seconds. Violent evasive action evaded them. Considerable light flak, accurate for height but not direction, was also experienced. Set course for NEUSTADT and at 00.40 hours at DRENTEWEDE a train on BREMEN/OSNABRUCK line) was sighted at 00.56 hours in the Station and was attacked twice. The first attack was made from abeam with a three seconds burst with Cannon and M/Gs, opening from 2000 feet and closing to 300 feet.

Strikes were seen on the engine which emited clouds of steam. The second attack was carried out from astern and the entire train (engine and coaches) was raked with a 6 secs burst from Cannon and M/Gs, opening at 2000 feet and closing at 400 feet. Strikes were seen on the engine and coaches, Station buildings and Signal Box. The engine emitted considerable steam and vivid blue and green flashes followed by a dull red glow were observed from the Signal Box. Course was then set for GIFTHORN at 01.00 hours and ULZEN at 01.00 hours. A train was seen at RABER (on the HANOVER - ULZEN line at 01.26 hours which was attacked from astern with a 4 secs burst with Cannon and M/Gs opening at 1500 ft and closing to 500 feet. Strikes were observed on the engine and one coach which was set on fire. Strikes were also seen on the Station Buildings and a small fire was seen to start. At 01.40 hours two to three miles North of ULZEN (on ULZEN - HAMBURG line) another train going North was sighted and attacked from astern with a 4 secs burst from Cannon and M/Gs, opening at 1500 feet and closing to 600 feet. The entire length of the train was raked and strikes were seen on the coaches and the engine which emitted clouds of steam, and the train stopped. Two minutes later, at 01.42 hours, a Southbound train in approx. the same vicinity, and travelling very fast, was attacked from abeam with a three secs burst with Cannon and M/Gs, opening at 1,500 feet closing to 300 feet. The engine and coaches were seen to be hit, and the former emitted large volumes of steam and appeared to explode. The train stopped. No further targets being sighted, a course of 270 degs. was set for Base, and, it is believed, arrived over BREMEN at 02.00 hours at 1000 feet. Numerous searchlights exposed and illuminated Mosquito and intense and accurate light flak was experienced. Violent evasive action was taken and three of the searchlight positions were attacked with a 2 secs. burst against each position from Cannon and M/Gs, opening at 500 feet and closing to 300 feet. Strikes were seen around the searchlight positions which doused. At this time the aircraft electrical equipment became u/s (with the exception of the intercom). Having cleared the area a course of 270 degrees was set for Base, intending to cross the coast of VLIELAND. About ten minutes after E.T.A. the coast was reached and we pinpointed ourselves over the SCHELT Estuary. It appears the the Compass was seriously affected (possibly by the firing of the M/Gs) thus causing the Mosquito to be well South of its intended track. The Dutch Coast was crossed at NOORDAL at 3000 ft. at 02.50 hours, landfall being made over MARTLESHAM HEATH, which was identified by the characteristics flashed by its beacon. A Northerly course was then steered for COLTISHALL where aerodrome beacon was again identified. Mosquito flashed the letter of the period, S.O.S. followed by the letter "Q" in response to which a "green" was fired at 03.00 hours, pancaking at COLTISHALL. Patrol was carried out between 1500 and 3000 feet.

Enemy Casualties:- Four locomotives and coaches damaged. One Signal Box set on fire and Station buildings at RABER and DRENTWEDE damaged. Three searchlight positions were shot up.

Our Casualties:- Nil (One bullet hole in Port wing)

(Signed) E. Davies

Facsimile of a Combat Report that was filed by No.25 (Fighter) Squadron's Intelligence Officer (Fg Off Alvar Lidell, later well known as a BBC news reader) which follows a Ranger *on the night of 21st/22nd May 1943. This was a diversionary patrol carried out over north-west Germany while fourteen Lancasters were minelaying off the Frisian Islands (in an area that was codenamed 'Xeranthemums'). Not one Lancaster was lost, and such was the frequency with which these* Rangers *were flown that their benefit to Bomber Command cannot be underestimated at all.*

Bradshaw was again his operator on 2nd September when they were vectored on to an enemy aircraft twenty miles off the Yorkshire coast at Filey, again under Neatishead control. This time Bradshaw had set up a good parallel head-on and Singleton turned into a perfect quarter attack on a Heinkel He 111, pulling through with a six-second burst from four cannon and six machine guns; both engines burst into flames, soon consuming the whole aircraft. No crew were seen to bale out before the wreckage fell into the sea.

Singleton and Bradshaw damaged another Dornier Do 217 on 17th September, again under Neatishead control, the action taking place near Hunstanton; on this occasion the German aircraft probably escaped at very low level as it faded from radar view at about 1,000ft over land, but no wreckage was found. This was to be Singleton's last combat in a Beaufighter.

ENTER THE MOSQUITO

It is often said that flying instructors used to introduce a student pilot to his first Mosquito with the tactless remark 'Well, young man, this aeroplane sorts the men from the boys!' Such a remark was entirely unnecessary, although it *did* possess a few snares which, unless watched with ordinary attention, could 'turn nasty'.

The Mosquito was, from the outset, famous as possessing a wooden airframe – predominantly a balsawood ply, bonded cross-grain for strength. Power was provided initially by a pair of Merlins, each delivering 1,460hp. Such a marriage between this power and the lightweight airframe resulted in the night fighter possessing a maximum speed of 382 mph, and a service ceiling of 36,000ft. Compared with the Beaufighter's all-up weight of around 21,000lb, the Mosquito night fighter weighed in at about 18,500lb. Its armament comprised four 20mm cannon and four 0.303in Browning machine guns clustered in the nose into which, unlike the Beaufighter, the pilot and radar operator were crammed side-by-side. (Later, with the introduction of the bulkier American AI Mk.X radar in the nose, the four machine guns were omitted.)

There were two habits of the 'Mossie' which could be embarrassing. The first stemmed from the positioning of the relatively small engine radiators in the wing leading edge between the fuselage and engine nacelle. If, while taxying prior to take-off) the wind was light or blowing from the rear, and the ambient temperature was high, the engine

No.25 (Fighter) Squadron, Church Fenton, 16th June 1943 – de Havilland Mosquito NF.II.

At the time the above photo was taken the Squadron was operating a detachment in Cornwall, involving six crews; three days earlier, on 13th June 1943, four officers were Killed in Action while operating over the Bay of Biscay, said to have been shot down by Junkers Ju 88C fighters. Of the personnel seen above, Fg Off Cooke and F/Sgt Ellacott were to be killed over the North Sea on 30th July; Sgt Kendall (later W/Off) and F/Sgt Nowak (absent from the photo) were killed in a flying accident on 12th August; and Plt Off Grey (later Fg Off) was Killed in Action on 9th July 1944.

Back Row, left to right: *Plt Off Franklin, Plt Off Cooke, Fg Off N Underdown, Fg Off P Sewell, F/Sgt Ellacott, Sgt Booth, Sgt D Skinner, Sgt Kendall, Sgt A Wilson, Fg Off F Charman.*

Middle Row, left to right: *W/O Bent, Plt Off T Gibbs, Plt Off W Cummings, Fg Off G Hogarth, Fg Off F Haigh, Fg Off Cairns, Fg Off Norris, Plt Off Grey, Fg Off H Gallagher, Fg Off Guthrie, Sgt Hampson, Plt Off Patterson.*

Front Row, left to right: *Fg Off L Davies, Sqn Ldr F Snell, Wg Cdr S Maude DFC (OC Squadron), Gp Capt F Stannard (Station Commander), Flt Lt J Singleton, Fg Off R Cooke.*

coolant could and usually did boil; this could only be rectified by quickly turning into wind and opening the throttle fully against the wheelbrakes, or simply shutting down the engines and allowing them to cool.

Failure to carry out some action to cool an overheating engine before take-off could lead to the Mosquito's only other suicidal trick. The aircraft's single rudder, being partly blanked from the engine slipstream and of relatively low keel area, gave poor directional control at low speeds, and this resulted in a high critical speed (the minimum safe speed at which the aircraft could be controlled after failure of one engine). Thus, if the Mosquito suffered a single engine failure during take-off before reaching the critical speed, there was no other course open to the pilot but to close the other throttle immediately and push the stick forward to crash-land straight ahead. To attempt to continue climbing, with a dead engine and virtually no rudder control would be to invite one wing to drop like a stone.

These 'vices' were not wholly unique to the Mosquito, although it was a powerful fighter, and during take-off the engines were providing considerable thrust, so that asymmetric loads were unusually powerful and any loss of aerodynamic balance was converted into an uncontrollable sequence of events. However, once the various vital handling demands were met instinctively, the Mosquito was a true thoroughbred aeroplane and a delight to fly. Few pilots will ever forget their first night take-off, with those powerful Merlins roaring away some six feet from the cockpit windows, and the glowing exhaust flames being ejected from the red-hot manifolds.

Flash Pleasance stepped aside from command of No.25 about a week before the first Mosquito II arrived on the

No.25 (Fighter) Squadron, Coltishall, 28th February 1944.

Front Row, seated or kneeling, left to right: *Plt Off B Travers, Flt Sgt R Pickles, Plt Off A N Wilson, Fg Off J R Brockbank, Fg Off Butt, Plt Off Franklin, Flt Sgt Hutchings, Fg Off Carne, Fg Off Hamilton, Sub-Lt Adams RNVR.*

Second Row, standing, left to right: *Flt Sgt G T Glossop, Flt Sgt B W Christian, Flt Sgt Tait RAAF, Flt Sgt Greenwell, Flt Lt D H Grieves DFC, Sgt Noble, Flt Sgt Hitchcock, Fg Off Young, Flt Lt Irwin, Sqn Ldr Mitchell, Fg Off Cox, Wg Cdr C M Wight Boycott DSO (Commanding Officer), Sqn Ldr Baker, W/Off E C Barnard, Lt Toynbee RNVR, Flt Lt R H Saunders DFC, Fg Off Saunderson DFC, Plt Off George, Fg Off Melville.*

On Starboard Engine: *Fg Off Jack Stuart Henderson* (left; *Missing in Action, 7th October 1944, on air defence ops, Prisoner of War*), *Flt Lt J Singleton DFC* (right).

Between Starboard Engine and Fuselage, in front, left to right: *Sub-Lt Smith RNVR, Fg Off Robins DFC, Flt Sgt (unknown), Sub-Lt Franck RNVR.* Behind, left to right: *Fg Off T A Gibbs, Fg Off D Harwood (Killed in Action, 9th June 1944, on bomber support ops), Lt Green, Fg Off K W Gray (Killed in Action, 9th June 1944, on bomber support ops), Fg Off D McCausland.*

Standing in Cockpit: *Fg Off W G Haslam with 'Popski'.*

Between Port Engine and Fuselage, in front: *Flt Sgt Patterson* (left), *Plt Off George* (right). Centre Row: *Plt Off (unknown, left), W/Off Cragg* (right). Back Row, left to right: *Flt Lt Carr, Flt Lt A S H Baillie (Killed in Action, 13th June 1944, on bomber support ops), Plt Off J M Simpson (Killed in Action, 13th June 1944, on bomber support ops), Plt Off Carter (?).*

On Port Engine: *Fg Off Cumbers DFM.*

(Photo: courtesy of No.25 (Fighter) Squadron)

Squadron, his place being taken by Squadron Leader Edward Watkins, AFC. And who but Joe Singleton was the first to celebrate the Squadron's first combat success in a Mosquito, although it was to be about three months before this event came about.

After the Beaufighters were flown away, the Squadron began training in a new operational rôle – described broadly as bomber support, but more accurately as intruder operations. ('Bomber Support', though continuing to include intruder work, came to embrace a much wider *tranche* of duties, including flying inside the bomber streams over Germany, radio countermeasures, patrolling over enemy night fighter airfields, diversionary attacks – any operations designed to keep German night fighters away from the huge Main Force bomber streams that would shortly constitute Bomber Command's principal *modus operandi* in taking the War to the German cities and factories.)

Indeed by January 1943 roughly eighty per cent of No.25 Squadron's operational flying was confined to these night intruder sweeps, which were flown over Belgium, the Netherlands and Northern Germany. It is known that No.25 kept a tally board of ground targets attacked and either destroyed or damaged, but this has not apparently survived; however, the Squadron Operational Record Book (Form 540) does record that Joe Singleton (by then a Flight Lieutenant and flight commander) led the field by a wide margin, in terms of locomotives, trains, railway stations, bridges, road vehicles and aircraft on the ground attacked and destroyed.

The first air combat claim, was a Dornier Do 217, claimed damaged by Singleton (still with Bradshaw, also now a Flight Lieutenant) during an intruder sortie over the Netherlands on 15th January 1943. Flt Lt Bradshaw was posted away shortly afterwards, his place being taken by Fg Off Geoff Haslam as Joe's radar operator. One of this crew's most notable night air-to-air intruder sortie occurred on 11th June, when they tangled with a Ju 88 night fighter, which had in all likelihood been ordered off to attack a Bomber Command stream over Germany, and shot it down off the Danish coast.

These bomber-support/intruder operations continued throughout 1943, accounting for several enemy aircraft destroyed and damaged, but a much larger tally of ground targets was attacked and destroyed. In September that year No.25 received eight Mosquito FB.VI fighter-bombers (without radar) but capable of carrying two 500lb bombs under the wings and two in the rear half of the bomb-bay (the front half being occupied by the gun-bodies of the four 20mm Hispano cannon). These aircraft, though flown by 25 Squadron crews, were detached to a Bomber Command airfield in Norfolk for about a month, and no record of their operations appears to have been saved. At least one of them is recorded as having been lost on operations, but no mention of crew members losing their lives, as been traced, and it is likely that both survived.

It is perhaps of interest here to set down the operational responsibilities of the personnel that existed after command of the Squadron passed to Wing Commander S N L Maude in April 1943.

ORGANISATION: No.25 (Fighter) Squadron

Squadron Callsign – MANOR

Officer Commanding	Wg Cdr S N L Maude, DFC
Adjutant	Flt Lt E J Peters
Officer Commanding 'A' Flight	Sqn Ldr V R Snell
NCO i/c	F/Sgt Verity
Officer Commanding 'B' Flight	Flt Lt A S H Baillie († 13-6-44)
NCO i/c	F/Sgt Hitchcock
Officer Commanding 'C' Flight	Sqn Ldr F N Brinsden
NCO i/c	Cpl Kerrod
SPECIALIST OFFICERS	
Medical Officer	Fg Off M P Nelson
Intelligence Officer	Plt Off T A Q Lidell
Engineer Officer	Flt Lt A E Gunn
Signals Officer	Plt Off E F Smith
Signals (Radar) Officer	Plt Off E F Smith
Navigation Officer	Fg Off D Bruce
Gunnery Officer	Sqn Ldr F N Brinsden
Cine Camera Assessment	Sqn Ldr F N Brinsden
Parachute Officer 'A' Flight	Plt Off W E Cummings
Parachute Officer 'B' Flight	Plt Off H S Cook
Senior Nav/Rad	Fg Off J P Cairns
Air/Sea Rescue Officer	(Temporarily vacant)
Special Navigation Officer	Fg Off W G Haslam
NCO i/c Orderly Room	Cpl Clifton
NCO i/c Armoury	Sgt Turbayne
NCO i/c Echelon	F/Sgt Philpott
NCO i/c Instruments	Sgt Boyle
NCO i/d Signals	F/Sgt Bullous
NCO i/c Signals (radar)	F/Sgt Basill
NCO i/c Squadron Discipline	F/Sgt Holness
OPERATIONAL PERSONNEL	
Pilots	*Nav/Rad*
Wg Cdr Maude, DFC (CO)	Fg Off Cairns
'A' Flight	
Sqn Ldr Snell ('A' Flt CO)	Plt Off Cummings
Sqn Ldr Brinsden (i/c Ranger)	Fg Off Sewell
Sgt Brockbank	Sgt McCausland
Fg Off Norris	Sgt Booth
Flt Lt Baker	Fg Off Young
Fg Off Bridges	Fg Off Hampson
Plt Off Quinn († 2-10-43)	Sgt Carter († 2-10-43)
Fg Off Hogarth	Fg Off Haslam
Plt Off Gray († 9-6-44)	Plt Off Harwood († 9-6-44)
F/Sgt Nowak († 12-8-43)	W/O Kendall († 12-8-43)
F/Sgt Wilson	Sgt Davies
'B' Flight	
Flt Lt A S H Baillie ('B' Flight CO) († 13-6-44)	Fg Off Burrow († 13-6-44)
Flt Lt Davies ('B' Flt Deputy CO)	Plt Off Bent
Fg Off Jones	Plt Off Skinner
Fg Off Gibbs	Fg Off Franklin
F/Sgt Panter	W/O Mogg
Fg Off Limbert († 24-9-44)	Plt Off Cook († 24-9-44)
Fg Off Gallagher	Fg Off Bruce
Fg Off Linthune	W/O Paine
Fg Off Lilwall	Sgt Lilwall
Sgt Travers	Sgt Patterson

Corporal Steve Stevens at work on an AI Mk.X in No.25 Squadron's Radar Workshop at Coltishall in 1944.
(Photo: Steve Stevens)

Corporal Steve Stevens uses leg muscles and a car foot pump to pressurise the radar transmitter unit of a Mosquito at Coltishall.
(Photo: Steve Stevens)

THE PERRANPORTH DETACHMENT

Full records of another operation involving No.25 Squadron Mosquitos and crews also seem to have disappeared, and only a few sparse details ever reached the Squadron. Sometime early in June 1943, Coastal Command requested Fighter Command (or Air Defence of Great Britain as the Command would be termed during the build-up of the Second Tactical Air Force for the invasion of Europe) to detach a Flight of Mosquito fighters to Perranporth in Cornwall for the purpose of providing protection for maritime reconnaissance Sunderland and Catalina flying boats patrolling the Bay of Biscay. These big long-range aircraft had been flying constant patrols covering Allied convoys sailing between the United Kingdom and Gibraltar, watching for German submarines and blockade runners attempting to reach French ports. In recent weeks, in an attempt to curtail these patrols, the *Luftwaffe* had countered them by sending small groups of Junkers Ju 88s on patrol to shoot down the flying boats.

Although there are unconfirmed recollections that several of No.25 Squadron's pilots succeeded in engaging the Ju 88s (with or without success is not known), it is recorded that on June 13th a patrol by four Mosquitos was engaged by a *Staffel* of about eight Focke-Wulf Fw 190s. No details of the combat can be traced, but two of the Mosquitos failed to return to Perranporth, and all four crew members were posted Missing Believed Killed, their names being recorded on the Runnymede Memorial (See Appendix 1).

There was no record of this detachment in the Squadron Form 540, and on account of this omission it is surmised that no formal application was ever made for the Battle Honour 'Biscay 1943' to be accorded to No.25 Squadron, although there can be no doubt as to the entitlement. (Three of the Mosquitos' Travelling Forms 700 confirm their inclusion in the Detachment to Perranporth).

On 12th December the Squadron lost a flight commander in tragic circumstances. No.25 had been warned that it might be required to fly towards the Danish coast to meet, and provide fighter protection for a force of RAF bombers, then expected to be returning from a raid on Peenemünde on the Baltic coast at dawn the following day. Not being accustomed to day fighting tactics, the pilots of No.25 Squadron were ordered off to practice some mock combats in pairs, as much as anything to discover how the Mosquito behaved 'when thrown around like a dogfighter'. While leading a section of Mosquitos, 'B' Flight Commander, Sqn Ldr Colin Robertson suddenly called 'Break Port, GO' as he pulled his Mosquito into a violent turn. Other pilots saw the aircraft pitch up violently and start spinning. He was evidently unable to recover fully from the spin and crash landed into marshy ground near Filey (south of Scarborough). It is thought that he and his navigator (Fg Off Ernest Bartholomew) were still alive when aircraft came down, but were unable to extricate themselves from the cockpit before the aircraft was engulfed in the quagmire. The raid that was proposed on Peenemünde is believed to have been cancelled on account of bad weather.

On 19th December 1943 No.25 Squadron was ordered to leave Church Fenton and move north to Acklington in Northumberland. This proved to be very unpopular among the personnel, particularly those who had been granted Christmas leave – which was cancelled; also cancelled were arrangements for the traditional festivities – limited and frugal though these were in wartime. As usual these would have included a dinner held in the Airmen's Mess, at which the Officers served the Other Ranks. This had become a occasion when everyone let their hair down.

Instead a brave attempt was made to organise a similar event on the new station and, judging from long-held memories, someone had succeeded in surreptitiously transferring much of the food, intended for consumption at Church Fenton, northwards with the Mosquitos!

The reason for this sudden move was not divulged in advance and the stay at Acklington was short-lived. On 5th February 1944, after only seven weeks, No.25 flew south to Coltishall in Norfolk, where it was to remain for fifteen months.

THE ARRIVAL IN SERVICE OF AI MARK X RADAR

Only three days after No.25 arrived at Acklington, three new Mosquito NF.XVII night fighters were delivered, followed by about six more during the remainder of December 1943. All these aircraft carried the enigmatic letter 'G' as a suffix to their serial numbers – it being explained that this denoted a mandatory guard to be placed on the aircraft 'at all times' – signifying that it carried secret equipment.

A Mosquito NF.XVII of No.25 Squadron at Coltishall in 1944. (Photo: Steve Stevens)

The secret equipment in this instance turned out to be the new American AI Mk.X – the first efficient centimetric intercept radar to reach the RAF, the British AI Mk.VIII having proved unsatisfactory and unwieldy. Employing a rotating hemispherical scanner (which resulted in enlarged nose contours to accommodate a large radome and deletion of the Mosquito's four rifle-calibre machine guns), the new radar possessed a much improved performance in almost every respect – range (maximum and minimum), relative target height, and enhanced definition of low flying targets, the latter having previously been lost in the radar's 'ground clutter'.

The two bandaged figures in this picture are, left, *Flt Lt Joe Singleton (pilot) and,* right, *his Nav/Rad, Fg Off W Haslam, enjoying a night-flying supper in the Officers' Mess at Coltishall at about 1am on 20th March 1944. Two hours earlier they had together destroyed three Ju 188s. Their slight head injuries were received in the subsequent landing, but they were quickly discharged from sick quarters. The above photo appeared in the next morning's national newspapers.* (Photo: via the late Wg Cdr Joe Singleton)

Strict limitations on the use of this equipment were imposed, including a total ban on its use over enemy-held territory or within range of possible German electronic intelligence sensors. However, No.25 was in fact the second Squadron to receive Mosquito NF.XVIIs, No.85 having been re-equipped with the aircraft a month earlier, while based at West Malling in Kent, itself bordering on the area of likely enemy signal surveillance.

There is little doubt but that the arrival in service of this centimetric radar marked a turning point in the efficiency of the RAF's night fighter defences, remaining in service for almost a decade after the end of the War. Nevertheless the deliveries of the equipment from America were slow and erratic to begin with (one entire consignment of twenty sets being lost at sea early in 1944). The first 100 Mosquito NF.XVIIs were converted from the early Mosquito NF.IIs, but were fractionally slower than the earlier aircraft – owing mainly to the heavier radar.

Having received seventeen NF.XVIIs at Acklington, No.25 again moved south, this time to the famous airfield at Coltishall, a few miles north of Norwich, on 5th February 1944. The immediate task was to begin defensive patrols off the Norfolk coast, almost exclusively under the control of Neatishead GCI. Most of the crews were given the opportunity to visit this station (then equipped with a mobile Type 7 radar, as well as a pair of Type 13 height finders). Several of the squadron's pilots and navigators – who had never been given the opportunity to watch the GCIs at work – recall being very impressed by the efficiency of the ground reporting and control teams, and on one occasion watched a fighter controller set up a perfect 'parallel head-on' attack which resulted in a Junkers Ju 88 being shot down (not by a No.25 Squadron aircraft) after less than five minutes under the GCI's control.

Once again the first No.25 Squadron crew to claim an enemy aircraft shot down in their NF.XVII were Joe Singleton and Geoff Haslam, who despatched a Dornier Do 217 into the sea off Lowestoft on 20th February, and the same night Plt Off J R Brockbank, with Plt Off D McCausland, shot a Junkers Ju 188 down over Braintree, Essex, this time under Bawdsey control. Three nights later Flt Lt A S H Baillie, with Fg Off J M Simpson, were vectored on to a Heinkel He 177 and shot it down over Yoxford in East Sussex; this was a 'rare bird', not frequently used over Britain. The aircraft belonged to the *Luftwaffe's I./Gruppe, Kampfgeschwader* 40, flying from Châteaudun under General Major Peltz, *Angriffsführer England* (Attack Leader England) as part of Operation *Steinbock* – a series of fire raids against the City of London.

March was a busy month for the Squadron, no fewer than nine enemy aircraft being shot down, of which four were destroyed by Joe Singleton and Geoff Haslam. On the 14th they had been vectored on to a Junkers Ju 188 and shot it down just off the coast at Southwold, Suffolk. On the night of the 19th they were flying over the Humber Estuary when they were vectored eastwards towards what looked like a small stream of approaching enemy aircraft. Singleton had no sooner called 'Contact' and shot down a Ju 188, when the controller quickly directed him towards another, and yet a third – all of which were despatched into the sea – the entire

Some of No.25 Squadron's officers outside the Officers' Mess at Church Fenton in September 1942. Left to right: *'Flash' Pleasance, Fg Off Rodger RAAF, Joe Alington, Nobby Clarke, Joe Singleton, John Wray, 'Ron' MacLaughlan, Allan Pinknett, Chris Bradshaw, 'Inky' Inkster, 'Norry' Norris, and 'Guy' Guyton. The Nav/Rad on the extreme right has not been identified.*

(Photo: via the late Wg Cdr Joe Singleton)

combat occupying just thirteen minutes.

For something like twenty minutes Singleton's Merlins had been at 'combat rating' (full throttle), and soon after the last of his victims had fallen into the North Sea, one engine began to run roughly, with its radiator temperature hovering around 140 degrees, the other one climbing fast. Calling up Happisburgh GCI on the Norfolk coast, Singleton was given a course to steer and told to call Neatishead. As the Mosquito crossed the coast, with sparks streaking from the engine exhausts, Singleton called up Coltishall on its local frequency and asked for the beacon and runway light to be turned on so that he could locate the airfield and make a straight-in approach. For some minutes he'd been flying with flaps down and radiator shutters open, but as soon as he spotted Coltishall's lights he decided to land with wheels and flaps up.

When still at about 1,000ft and two or three miles from the runway, the Mosquito's right-hand engine burst into flames. Now needing more power from the other engine, the pilot gradually opened the left throttle and feathered the blazing engine's propeller. Suddenly that engine seized. There was no alternative to an immediate crash landing. As Singleton began to ease back on the stick and Geoff Haslam jettisoned the top hatch, the aircraft struck the ground at around 140 mph about half a mile from the runway threshold. Without further delay, both men made their escape from the cockpit and sprinted away from the Mosquito. As it gave no signs of being about to blow up, Singleton searched for but could not locate the other fire extinguisher so, with Haslam, set about throwing lumps of earth on the melting engines and had succeeded in putting out the fire on the starboard Merlin by the time the station crash tender and ambulance arrived.

It was decided, on subsequent examination of the wreckage, that one of Singleton's victims had disintegrated at such short range that debris had probably damaged one or both the engine radiators, which then began to lose glycol so that, reverting to type, the engines quickly overheated. 'Things didn't go too badly, and it soon seemed possible that we'd just about get down OK at Coltishall. In due course we spotted the beacon at base and started to begin our approach. Unfortunately things started to come apart after we touched down short of the runway, and the Mossie caught fire as it scraped along the ground; when it stopped Geoff and I left

Rare close-up photo of a No.25 Squadron Mosquito NF.XVII (on account of its new and secret AI Mk.X radar) HK322/ZK-M at Coltishall in 1944 with its air- and groundcrew, left to right, *Fg Off Benny Bent (Nav/Rad), LAC Tom Paris, LAC Harry Corns, and Flt Lt Robert Lloyd Rees Davies. The relative height of the pilot prompts the obvious question: How* did *he manage to enter and leave the cockpit through the hatch? This is just visible above Corns' head, and was disturbingly adjacent to the starboard propeller! This crew was the subject of the Combat Report on page 114 (before the arrival of Mosquito XVIIs).* (Photo: Benny Bent)

An early Mosquito NF.XXX, delivered to No.25 Squadron at Coltishall on 23rd September 1944 was MM810/ZK-Y. In due course it became the aircraft regularly flown by newly commissioned Plt Offs George Glossop (left) *and Bernard Christian.*

(Photo: George Glossop)

the office very smartly, suffering little more than a few cuts and bruises about the head. A short call at Station Sick Quarters and then back to the Mess for supper. I was more tired than sore.' (These were to be Joe Singleton's last victories of the War, but not his last tour on No.25 Squadron.)

Coltishall was a popular station with No.25 Squadron, being within cycling distance of Norwich, famous throughout the RAF as the city with a church for every Sunday in the year, and with a pub for every day! Coltishall village had a number of friendly pubs, which had all become thoroughly Royal Air Force 'orientated'. The Station had, after all, been commanded during the early War years by a former pilot on No.25 – none other than 'Bike' Beiseigel (of the early 'twenties). The station had been built largely in peacetime and was well catered for in the matter of comfortable Messes, a large NAAFI, and so on. It was always alive with flying activity, not least with frequent visits by USAAF fighters and bombers, diverted in on account of bad weather or blocked runways at the mass of American bases in East Anglia, not to mention those of RAF Bomber and Fighter Commands.

From an operational viewpoint, Coltishall was also very close to the important GCI Station at Neatishead, whose personnel lived and messed at the airfield. There were thus frequent occasions when a Mosquito pilot, returning to the Mess for his 'night flying supper' (invariably fried eggs and bacon), would find himself chatting with the Controller who had been directing him in the air. This all contributed to a well-knit team and the common purpose: to find and shoot down enemy aircraft. Joe Singleton recalled that he could recognise all the Neatishead Controllers on his R/T.

On the same night that Singleton and Haslam shot down three Junkers Ju 88s, another crew, Flt Lt Douglas Haig Greaves and Fg Off F M Robbins, shot down two other night raiders, also in quick succession, this time a Do 217 and a Heinkel He 177, about thirty miles north of Cromer – but again being controlled by Neatishead. And another double victory was gained three nights later by Flt Lt R L E Davies and Fg Off Benny Bent, shooting down a pair of Ju 188s at the southern end of Coltishall's sector into the sea off Lowestoft and Southwold.

And so it went on through April. The Germans continued to fly Ju 188s and Do 217s, but with the relaxation of the ban on flying the Mosquito NF.XVII near enemy-held territory, pilots were allowed to chase enemy aircraft over the Dutch and Belgian coasts, and started to encounter the Messerschmitt Me 410; this proved to be a very fast and awkward customer, suspected of carrying tail warning radar. Several pilot reported stalking these aircraft from astern so as to close the range, only being prevented from firing at the last moment when the enemy pilot started firing his remotely controlled guns mounted in rotatable barbettes on the sides of the rear fuselage. The secret was to remain just in radar contact until, on reaching the supposed safety of the enemy coast, the enemy pilot would shut off his radar and start descending towards his home base. At this moment the Mosquito pilot would open the throttle and, when in range, open fire. These tactics were used with success by Plt Off K V Panter and W/Off A W Mogg who shot down their first Me 410 on 19th April, their victim falling in the sea just off the Dutch coast.

The privilege of shooting down the first German aircraft on D-Day has been claimed by three different pilots, depending on the definition. It seems that the first enemy aircraft downed *on D-Day* fell to the guns of Flt Lt R L R Davies and Fg Off Benny Bent, of No.25 Squadron, who shot down a Messerschmitt Bf 110 night fighter west of Schiermonnikoog, Holland, at 00.43hrs on 6th June 1944. The other claimants' whose victims fell shortly afterwards were claimed *as the first victories in Operation Overlord* – the invasion of France. The distinction is obvious, but necessary.

THE AIR-LAUNCHED FLYING BOMBS

On the night of 15th June 1944 the Germans began their long-awaited assault on southern England with their V-1 flying bombs. Fortunately the Hawker Tempest fighter, at that time the fastest in the British and American air forces, had entered service and the Tempest Wing immediately went into action against these most unpleasant weapons, backed up by Spitfires and ground defences. However, No.25 Squadron, being responsible for the night defence of the East Coast of England, was not immediately called on to combat the bombs, which were falling on Kent and London. Nevertheless, the crews continued their nightly patrols. As far as can be determined (despite one or two suggestions to the contrary), no trace of a combat report or claim, involving a ground-launched V-1, by a No.25 Squadron crew can be found.

This phase of the flying bomb assault on southern England, petered out on 15th September as the British and Canadian Armies in France, having broken out of the Normandy invasion pocket, began a swift advance alongside the Americans to the south, and swept into the Pas de Calais, where the majority of V-1 launch sites had been constructed. Meanwhile No.25 Squadron had continued defensive patrols off the coast of East Anglia, as well as fairly frequent 'bomber support' sorties over Belgium and Holland, and on 28th August Plt Off Barney Travers, with Plt Off 'Pat' Patterson, got a visual on a Messerschmitt Bf 109G at night – something no one on the Squadron had ever encountered. After a short stern chase the Mosquito closed from astern and quickly despatched the unsuspecting enemy. In due course this was confirmed as a likely *Wilde Sau,* one of the widely-used German day fighters, which carried no radar and which were sent up against RAF heavy bomber streams at night on the off chance of picking off stragglers. So intent were the *Luftwaffe* pilots on setting up their attacks on the stream that they paid little attention to the possibility of a Mosquito sneaking up at six o'clock, and a three-second burst from four 20mm cannons from a steady gun-platform like a Mosquito didn't leave much opportunity for compromise.

No.25 Squadron's air war was resumed when, on the night of 24th/25th September Wg Cdr L J C Mitchell, RAFVR, recently appointed squadron commander, with Flt Lt D L Cox as nav/rad, spotted a Heinkel He 111 some forty miles off Great Yarmouth, apparently launching a flying bomb while flying at about 3,500ft above the sea. Such a tactic was wholly unexpected, as no advance

A pulsejet-powered Fiesler Fi 103 V-1 flying bomb mounted beneath the port wing-root of a Heinkel He 111H-20. The low altitude at which these stand-off weapons were carried at night made them very difficult targets for RAF night fighters on patrol over the sea. The weapon itself proved extremely inaccurate when air-launched. (Photo: via Wg Cdr R W Leggett)

warning had been given to night fighter squadrons (although the 'Y' Service had been aware that such a form of attack was in the offing). The GCI warned Mitchell that the Heinkel, having released its flying bomb was turning and diving, and the Mosquito regained contact at a height of 600ft, continuing to drop to 200ft and obtaining visual contact at a range of 1,300ft. Quickly grabbing his night glasses, Mitchell confirmed the target's identity, then closed to 400 feet and gave a short burst from his cannons. The Heinkel exploded, hurling fragments over a wide area before plunging into the sea. A new phase in the flying bomb attacks had started. It was later learned that these Heinkels belonged to III.*Gruppe, Kampfgeschwader* 3 (at that time equipped with about fifty of the modified bombers.

Wg Cdr Mitchell had taken over command of No.25 Squadron in August from Wg Cdr M W Wight-Boycott, who was still supernumerary on the Squadron, awaiting his posting. On the night of 26th/27th September Michael Wight-Boycott was airborne with his former nav/rad, Flt Lt D M Reid, when they were vectored by Neatishead on to a Junkers Ju 188 a few miles off Lowestoft and, after a short stern chase, shot it down into the sea.

Not to be outdone by his predecessor, Wing Command Mitchell took off the following night with Flt Lt Cox and, after taking up their patrol line were vectored out to sea in the direction of some likely 'trade'. This interception followed almost exactly the same pattern as that of the pilot's first success three nights earlier; having obtained a visual on the target, he again used his night binoculars to confirm the enemy's identity, before delivering the *coup de grace.* No sooner had the Heinkel blown up and Mitchell set course to rejoin his patrol line when he saw the flash of another Heinkel launching its flying bomb. The diverging tracks of the launcher and bomb were quickly identified by the GCI, which then passed a course to intercept the Heinkel. Flt Lt Cox was able to set up a perfect 'parallel head-on' and Mitchell turned into a tail chase only 500 yards astern of the target. Obviously unaware of the fighter behind, the German pilot was sauntering homewards at about 200ft above the waves; Mitchell, down to only 150ft, quickly caught up with the bomber and fired a short burst at 200 yards, hitting the Heinkel's right wing; closing to about 150 yards he now fired at the left engine, which burst into flames. The aircraft crashed into the sea and Mitchell then spent more than half an hour searching the area for signs of survivors. There were none.

During the next six weeks No.25 Squadron shot down a further half dozen flying bomb launchers – all of them off the Norfolk, Suffolk and Essex coasts. Nor was No.25 by any means the only Mosquito squadron involved, coming third in the 'league table' of Heinkels destroyed. All the leading squadrons were equipped with AI Mk.X radar, thereby demonstrating its superiority against enemy aircraft flying at low altitudes. At the same time III. *Gruppe,* KG3, had been re-named III.*Gruppe,* KG53 – whose other two *Gruppen* were now re- equipped with the He 111-H22 (the V-1 carrier version). It is believed that at the peak of the attacks this *Kampfgeschwader* was equipped with as many as 90 aircraft. In the final analysis these air-launched V-1s were wholly random weapons and, of those that managed to cross the English coast, almost all fell in open countryside. It is said that only one landed in the town intended as its target.

NEW MOSQUITOS, NEW HOME.

On 27th October 1944, under the command of Wing Commander Mitchell, No.25 Squadron left Coltishall – and never regretted a move more. It is believed that the transfer to Castle Camps – a dozen miles south-east of Cambridge – was again made on account of the Squadron being warned to receive a new version of the Mosquito – which would entail a working-up period. Such flying could interfere with the operational efficiency of Coltishall which, after all, had come to represent a front line station in the defence against the air-launched flying bombs. Castle Camps was succinctly summed up by Barney Travers as 'Dire', and by his navigator as 'worse than that'. In an attempt to bolster morale, bus-loads of nurses were ferried over from Addenbrooks hospital in Cambridge to social functions on the station. And many a dreary afternoon was spent wandering around Cambridge to admire the fine University buildings.

The new Mosquitos, which began arriving at Castle Camps were Mk.XXXs, still equipped with AI Mk.X, but now provided with pressure cabins and powered by 1,690hp Merlins (Mk.72/73s, 76/77s or 113/114s, in each case the second Mark of engine driving the cabin blower). With these engines rated at about 1,680hp, the Mosquito possessed a maximum speed of 404mph and a service ceiling of 38,000ft. – representing an overall ten percent performance improvement of around 5 per cent over the original Mk.II night fighter – apart from its greatly enhanced AI radar. Also introduced was improved GEE navigation equipment. The new night fighter was also some 3,000lb heavier (all up) than the NF.II.

No.25 Squadron remained at Castle Camps for the rest of the War, its working-up period being marred by a number of fatal accidents, most of them during training for intruder and bomber support operations. The first, however, occurred during an air test on 27th November 1944 when the aircraft of Flt Lt Alfred Marshall, DFC, DFM (flying with Fg Off Charles Allen) was seen to enter a dive over the airfield and break up during the attempted recovery; both crew members were killed. LAC 'Knocker' West, one of the fitters on the aircraft, remembers the event vividly.

'The aircraft had been up for about ten minutes when we saw it approaching the 'drome in a slight dive. As it was almost overhead the pilot pulled it up into a fast steep climb and we distinctly saw something fly off the wing, after which the wings began to disintegrate. It had gained quite a lot of height when we saw that there was hardly any wing left outboard of the engines. The aircraft then seem to just fall out of the sky as it continued to break up. It fell in a field nearby and later on that evening we went over to see it, but found only an engine and a wheel and a large amount of splintered wood.

'After an inspection of the wreckage by the plane's makers it was decided that a tear in the wing skin might have caused the airstream to get inside the wing causing the rest of the skin to come adrift and then cause the aircraft to break up. After that, we always had to wear canvas shoes when climbing on to the Mossies. '

On 23rd January 1945 two Mosquitos were lost in a collision during practice night interceptions over land; all four crew members were killed (including a flight commander, Sqn Ldr John Arnsby, and the Squadron navigator leader, Flt Lt Douglas Reid, and two other flight lieutenants). The aircraft all crashed at Camps Hall, not far from the station. On 9th February Flight Lieutenant Michael Corrie, believed to have been flying solo, hit some trees on take-off; one of his engines lost power and, after struggling unsuccessfully to reach the critical speed, crash landed at Radwinter, near Saffron Walden and was killed. A fifth Mosquito crashed during an attempted forced landing on 6th March after losing power on both engines, both occupants being killed.

Nevertheless, not all was gloom during this period. On 9th November 1944 Flt Lt J M Lomas, with Flt Lt N B Fleet, found and destroyed a Heinkel flying bomb launcher off the Essex coast, and two nights later Flt Lt Douglas Haig Greaves and Fg Off F M Robbins destroyed another Heinkel 70 miles east of Lowestoft.

The Squadron's final victory of the Second World War was another rare bird. On 1st February 1945, shortly after Mosquito NF.XXXs were released for bomber support operations over Germany, as Bomber Command was attacking Mainz, Berlin and Ludwigshafen, Flight Lieutenants Lomas and Fleet found a prowling Heinkel He 219 and shot it down ten miles east of Bonn. This was the *Luftwaffe's* most potent night fighter, heavily armed with 30mm cannon and equipped with very capable radar, so Lomas must have exercised considerable skill to bring his guns into a lethal firing position. The He 219 was employed almost exclusively by the Germans for the defence of the fatherland.

And so ended the War in Europe. There was never any intention to re-deploy No.25 Squadron to the Far East, even though at the time of Germany's final defeat No.25 possessed no fewer than 22 NF.XXXs on strength. Other Mosquitos (of several variations) had been despatched to South-East Asia, but prolonged trouble had been experienced in the hot and humid environment with its effects on the aircraft's wooden construction, and more than a year's delay in overcoming this problem had limited its employment – and this did not include general use as a night fighter.

The cockpit of a Mosquito NF.XXX as seen by the Navigator/Radar Operator – not what one might describe fifty years later as 'user friendly'. An indication of how cramped it was may be gained by the pilot's gunsight (upper left, above the blind flying panel) and the operator's display unit (centre). The latter folded forward – slightly – for the two occupants to gain access to the entry/escape hatch (bottom right). As the pilot had to wait for the navigator to leave the cockpit, before leaving his own seat to crawl across the floor to reach the hatch, the risk of snagging his parachute on some protruding object was high, and successful emergency escapes from Mosquito night fighters were the exception rather than the rule! (Photo: by courtesy of 'Tommy' Knight)

CHAPTER 9

Mosquitos after the War

'Peace with Parsimony'

PEACE AND CONFUSION

Following the signing of the unconditional surrender of German armed forces on 8th May 1945, events moved quickly and smoothly towards the complete occupation of the defeated nation, according to the agreed conditions signed previously by the Allies. This entailed a re-arrangement for immediate post-war deployment of Royal Air Force squadrons that had, under combat conditions, occupied many former *Luftwaffe* stations and airfields, as the Second Allied Tactical Air Force took its place among the armies of occupation. This did not directly affect No.25 (Fighter) Squadron, which had fought over but had not been based on the Continent, nor indeed been a component of the Second Allied Tactical Air Force (2ATAF).

Indeed, precious little realistic thought had been given to the likely strength and deployment of the peacetime Service; after all, there was still the War against Japan to be fought and won, a war that seemed likely to continue for many months, if not years. Although the Air Ministry's immediate task was to implement the release of squadrons of fighter, bombers and other aircraft for transfer to the Far East, a large number of wartime units were, however, seen to be surplus to requirements in the Far East; these were some of the first to be disbanded, and many of their personnel demobilised. With no plans to send No.25 Squadron to the Far East, the questions arose (as it did with every other operational squadron), what would be the strength of the operational Commands, and how many squadrons could be disbanded? What were the criteria for retaining squadrons? What would be the minimum safe personnel strength for a peacetime Royal Air Force? It was already fairly clear that the Soviet Union was determined to impose a powerful Communist influence over its occupied territories.

Regarding the level of aviation technology, Britain had led the Western world in 'gas turbine' (later re-named 'turbojet') technology, having had already introduced a jet fighter – the Meteor – into operational service, about a year ahead of America. Germany was ahead in sonic flight exploration, and in transonic aerodynamics, but within six months of the end of the War the picture was changing as the leading German aviation scientists and technicians were being offered influential and secure positions within the American and Soviet aircraft industries. In other words these nations were committed to an undisguised arms race. Once the American people recognised that powerful armed services were essential in order to maintain peace (and to avoid the lasting trauma of another Pearl Harbor), aviation technology continued to advance without any significant check in the impetus reached at the end of the War.

Britain's priorities were introverted; a Labour administration had assumed power from the wartime National Government; many of the nation's industries had to be rebuilt to meet the demands of peacetime, servicemen mobilised into the fighting services for the duration of the War were now being demobilised largely on the principle of 'first in, first out', with married men and women also returning to civilian life. The nation's whole infrastructure was in need of reconstruction – demanding huge sums of money.

Air Vice-Marshal S D Macdonald, CB, CBE, DFC, Air Officer Commanding No.11 Group, Fighter Command, meets the air- and groundcrews of No.25 (Fighter) Squadron during the 1947 AOC's Inspection at RAF West Malling. The aircraft are Mosquito NF.36s.

(Photo: via the late Wg Cdr Joe Singleton)

On top of this the Attlee government had committed itself to creating a Welfare State, and this would impose a colossal burden on the Exchequer.

For those directly involved in maintaining Britain's military responsibilities, not only in terms of home defence, but in the defence of the Commonwealth – still in effect structurally the same as the old Empire and Dominions – the nation could barely support adequate Defence appropriations to meet these commitments, let alone underwrite expensive research in its most basic requirements. In almost every aspect of aviation research Britain fell further and further behind America and the Soviet Union.

The British aircraft industry kept its head above water by exporting the first generation of jet aircraft (the Meteor and Vampire) to the smaller air forces of the world, but this revenue was quite inadequate to support extensive research into supersonic flight and the engine technology this would demand.

As a result of this, the Air Ministry's operational requirement staff was constrained to think in terms of developing the existing aircraft. No one could realistically put forward a demand for an aircraft to match American fighters and bombers expected to fly at transonic speeds within a couple of years of the end of the War. The finance demanded for such advances simply did not exist. There were far more important demands to meet the cost of merely getting Britain on its feet once more.

In the field of night fighters, no one at the Air Ministry was in a position to prepare a Requirement or Specification for a replacement for the Mosquito, simply because it would presumably have to be powered by turbojet engines, and without the necessary advance into transonic technology, the resulting aircraft would hardly represent an advance on the Mosquito. In due course it was decided to issue a requirement for a two-seat night fighter development of the Meteor single-seat day fighter.

Another line of thought, originating at this time, was emerging; it was so radical – yet apparently logically argued – that it was addressed by a manufacturer that was effectively unfettered by traditional philosophies. This was the concept that, given the necessary technology to locate a target, be it by day, by night or *in bad weather* by day or night, one type of fighter was all that was needed to equip an entire defence system. This line of thought brought into being the English Electric Lightning – although financing the technology needed to reach this goal would not become available for another half decade.

Thus it was that the Royal Air Force had to make do with the existing Mosquito night fighter, based on the Mk.XXX – with only 'cosmetic' changes.

• • •

MAKING DO WITH THE MINIMUM

Wing Commander Mitchell relinquished command of No.25 Squadron in April 1945, a month before the end of the War, almost certainly on account of his being an RAFVR officer, who could expect to leave the Service fairly soon after the ending of hostilities. His period with the Squadron had been eventful and one of distinction, and the officers and men were sad to see him leave. His successor, Wing Commander William Hoy, DFC, AFC, had been commissioned in October 1939, having entered the Service as a Regular before the outbreak of War. He could therefore expect his Permanent Commission to continue with the peacetime RAF, although his wartime substantive rank was, in 1945, still temporary squadron leader. Furthermore, as had occurred at the end of the First World War, the Squadron was to have no fewer than four COs in the first two years of peace.

Such was the increasing rate of demobilisation in the RAF, the personnel strength of No.25 Squadron was reduced by 50 per cent during its remaining seven months at Castle Camps. The Unit Establishment of Mosquitos was reduced from 18 plus War reserve of four aircraft to 12 plus two. In practice this soon became a *total* of twelve Mosquitos, with seldom more than nine or ten aircraft serviceable. Each of the two Flights possessed about eight crews, each frequently having to 'borrow' armourers and engine fitters from the other from time to time. In effect, the Squadron was

As recalled by Geoff Smythe, the snowstorm at West Malling in 1947 did its best to disrupt flying but knowing that sooner or later all aircraft would have to fly away, if only to another airfield, it was necessary for the engine fitters to start up and run all engines, much to the discomfort of the long-suffering groundcrews. Unfortunately, the Merlins in the Mosquito were prone to overheat very quickly on the ground, and so the engine runs had to be short but frequent. (Photo: Fred Embleton)

Mosquito NF.36s lined up at West Malling for the AOC's Inspection in 1947. Propellers were then already old hat among the day fighter squadrons; little did the night fighter squadrons suspect that another four years would elapse before they would get jets.

(Photo: Fred Embleton)

bordering on limited cadre status, which would remain in being for more than two years.

For a short time, when the release of aircrew members threatened to outpace the expectation of replacements, there was a tendency for pilots to undertake practice interceptions (still the staple diet of the night fighter squadron), knowing that some piece of equipment should, because of unserviceability, have grounded an aircraft, such was the requirement of individual pilots to reach a minimum number of flying hours each month – except when the weather was particularly bad over a period of time.

This practice was halted on threat of disciplinary action being taken, fortunately before any serious accident occurred.

From time to time Fighter Command took part in rudimentary defence exercises, their somewhat unimaginative nature reflecting not only the general run-down of aircrew and aircraft strength, but also the gradual de-commissioning of radar and GCI stations.

In short, Fighter Command was engaged in maintaining the status quo, at least until the whole pattern of Europe's attitude towards defence had been fully defined. Germany (or at least the Allied-occupied zone, then known as West Germany) was disarmed, possessing no military forces. The former occupied countries struggled to come to terms with rebuilding their towns and communities, without which they were politically and strategically vulnerable. Some, such as France, Belgium, Holland, Denmark and Norway, began building their air forces around squadrons that had, during the War, been formed within the RAF and now returned home.

Sharing Castle Camps with No.25 Squadron was No.85, also flying Mosquito XXXs, and it was natural that there would be a degree of friendly rivalry between the two, an association – if not rivalry – that was to re-occur on several occasions during the next half century. However, no one was surprised to learn that Castle Camps was not to continue as one of the RAF's peacetime stations. The ravages of war had gone unchecked and, to quote another 'inmate' had reached the status of 'an alfresco slum'. Aircraft were dispersed on hardstandings that quickly flooded at no more than a hint of rain; flight offices possessed windows without full complements of glass, and rats constituted the 'permanent staff'.

Accordingly No.85 Squadron left Castle Camps for Tangmere in December 1945, while No.25 moved to Boxted, on the outskirts of Colchester, Essex, the following month. This move, however, only served to emphasise a growing suspicion that Fighter Command had still not made up its mind whether night fighter squadrons were to continue in being. Though nothing could be as bad as Castle Camps,

An embarrassing rendezvous. Sqn Ldr Joe Singleton extends a formal welcome to Air Vice-Marshal MacDonald, at the 1947 AOC's Inspection, West Malling. The temporary hangar in the background is referred to in the text.

(Photo: via the late Wg Cdr Joe Singleton)

Boxted was clearly not on a list of priorities for post-war renovation, and rumours that Castle Camps had been ear-marked to become a motor racing venue also surfaced in and around No.25 Squadron's new home. (Regarding the news-papers' preoccupation with Britain's post-war return to motor racing, it was being suggested that plans were already being hatched to create a race track at the Crystal Palace, but that the Ministry of Town and Country Planning could not make up its mind whether this was an appropriate priority when so much needed to be done to rebuild London's bomb-shattered buildings. Thoughts had therefore been voiced as to alternative venues, such as semi-derelict, 'war-surplus' airfields within reach of the Metropolis.)

All this was far from conducive to soaring morale among the personnel of the Squadron. The Mosquito XXXs, were beginning to show signs of senile decay, despite possessing relatively low cumulative flying hours. During one month at Boxted the total hours spent on air tests exceeded that on applied flying. The normal availability of fully serviceable aircraft on No.25 was about four or five, with an equal number undergoing repair or prolonged servicing. Morale was not noticeably poor as leave was fairly plentiful and London was only a short bus and train journey away. Continuing petrol rationing severely limited the number of cars on the Squadron, and one of the favourite means of 'getting about' was the motor cycle (of which huge numbers of ex-military Royal Enfield mo-bikes were on the market at little more than £30). Food rationing was gradually disappearing, but the occasion of a Guest Night in the Officers' Mess demanded considerable ingenuity from the catering staff, not to mention the skill of members with a 12-bore. Austerity was a word (and an excuse) for any hardship suffered.

Such occurrences as Britain's extending the World's Absolute Air Speed Record in September 1946 (in a Meteor) did much to hearten those involved in the nation's aviation world, be it in the armed Services or the manufacturing industry. Here was tangible evidence that, at least at that time, the RAF was about to be equipped with a World beating fighter – or so it seemed. It demonstrated that the Royal Air Force had retained a determination to sustain a modern and capable fighting strength. That confidence would take a number of years to be eroded. Unfortunately, no one in the pacifist government or at the near-destitute Air Ministry understood the artificial implications of these World Speed Records; technically the racing Meteors were scarcely more than highly polished two-year-old bangers that concealed the unpleasant fact that this was about as far as Britain's aircraft designers would ever get, without a great deal of finance for research. The appearance of the North American P-86 Sabre, which would appear in less than a year represented a leap forward of five years *ahead* of Britain, during which the Meteor should have been discarded; instead, it became a night fighter!

That same month No.25 Squadron picked up its bags and moved to West Malling, an airfield in the 'Garden of England' near Maidstone. Built just before the Second World War and gaining operational status during the Battle of Britain, this station had become famous as the premier night fighter station for the defence of London, from the 1940-41 *Blitz* onwards. No.25 Squadron was at last based at a station already recognised as a permanent fixture in the

Fly-past by No.25 (Fighter) Squadron at West Malling. No one would pretend that the formation keeping was up to the Squadron's traditional quality, although it should be said that maintaining close and accurate station-keeping in the Mosquito was by no means simple: the pilot was offset to the left hand side of the cockpit, and the proximity of the engines severely resticted his field of view. The centre line of aircraft in this picture is beyond reproach, for keeping position in line astern, albeit well stepped down to avoid turbulence, was relatively simple. (Photo: Francis K Mason collection)

Fairly early post-War photograph of a Mosquito NF.36 of No.25 (Fighter) Squadron, probably during its first months at West Malling, Kent. The AI Mk.X radar was originally enclosed under a transparent nose fairing, this remaining standard until late in 1948 when it was replaced by an opaque dielectric fairing that was overpainted to match the normal camouflage scheme. Although the wartime squadron codes 'ZK' were retained for several years, the Squadron's horizontal parallel black bars appear on the Mosquito's fin; these were later to be painted on the front of the nose. For a short time the spinners were painted in Flight colours – red, blue and yellow, but this was discontinued owing to confusion with aircraft of various training units.

(Photo: courtesy of No.25 (Fighter) Squadron records, via MAP)

post-war RAF. Situated in the midst of apple orchards and hop fields, the airfield had already acquired that aura of permanency, with large modern Messes, numerous married quarters, and large hangars; it also possessed a large concrete runway and taxytracks. Needless to say there were several pubs in the immediate neighbourhood which 'fitted the taste' of night fighter squadrons – not least 'The Startled Saint'.

THE MOSQUITO NF.36

The same month that No.25 Squadron moved to West Malling it was also re-equipped with a new version of the Mosquito. As someone remarked, 'The NF.36* may differ very slightly from the NF.30, but the main difference as far as I'm concerned is that the aircraft are *new*, that is to say they were build yesterday, not five years ago'. The real difference was that both engines were Merlin 113s.

* Prior to June 1948 it had been customary for succeeding versions (or Marks) of aircraft serving in the RAF to use Roman numerals; this became farcical when aircraft such as the Mosquito XXXVI (and the planned XXXVIII) arrived in service, so that a changeover to Arabic numerals was adopted universally from that month onward.

Things, however, got off to a bad start. During October 1947, while the Squadron was still finding its way around the new station, the Americans announced that they were going to make an attempt at the World's Long Distance Record (without in-flight refuelling). The route was to be from Hawaii to Frankfurt, via the North Pole. As this entailed flying a north to south flight through British air space, the Air Ministry felt that this would be a fine opportunity to exercise the air defences. Orders were issued for Nos.25 and 29 Squadrons to stand by. However, the American aircraft, named the *'Pacusan Dreamboat'*, delayed take-off while good weather conditions were awaited, and, standing by at the end of the runway at West Malling, the Mosquitos also waited. And waited. And waited. Then, quite suddenly, the 'dreamboat' appeared out of the night and serenely flew the length of Britain – and flew directly over West Malling, while Nos.25 and 29 Squadrons, still at standby, waited. At least no known heads rolled at West Malling.

With a complement of ten new Mosquitos, a comfortable station with new distractions in nearby Maidstone and elsewhere, morale among air and ground crews began to climb. The Squadron was still well below manning level, but there was an air of being a full and effective member unit of Fighter Command's No.11 Group. However, nature decided to take a hand and during February 1947 the worst winter in living memory struck the south of England. Kent was to be one of the worst-hit counties as very heavy falls of snow blanketed West Malling, which was sited on fairly high ground. Fg Off Geoff Smythe, a nav/rad and a recent arrival on No.25 Squadron recalls:

> "Unfortunately the onset of the storm coincided with a critical date in No.25's calendar. We had a Royal Task to perform, namely to escort their Majesties as they sailed down the English Channel in the battleship *HMS Vanguard* on their way to a State Visit to South Africa. This was due to take place on Thursday.
>
> However when Monday of that week dawned, our world was covered with some six inches of snow. Instantly West Malling went to panic stations to clear the runway, and all day every man, woman, officer, NCO and airman toiled with shovel and brush (there being no mechanical aids in those

days). A grateful hierarchy issued liberal tots of rum throughout the day. At the end of Monday, as darkness fell, the taxyways were clear, and 6,000 feet of black tarmac was there for all to see. We retired, aching but well satisfied to our beds.

Some of us had noticed that, throughout the day, it had remained bloody cold. But the significance had escaped us entirely.

During the night a strong wind got up. The next morning (Tuesday) we were greeted by one of the weirdest sights ever. The world had been transformed again. The whiteness of the previous day had all but vanished. The wind had blown the powdery snow away. The roads were clear. The airfield was back to nearly its normal green. But the snow had not gone far. It had drifted into every gully and corner it could find. It found a convenient 'gully' between the 6,000ft-long heaps of snow on either side of the runway. The net result was *a mound of snow some four feet deep at its mid point and occupying the whole of the runway from end to end.*

The annoying thing was that, had we done nothing at all on the previous day, the runway would have been completely clear. As it was we were faced with an even greater task than before!

You can imagine, the panic was ever greater.

All day that Tuesday, we slaved and slaved and slaved. The task was too great however. We were ordered to clear just sufficient surface to enable the aircraft to be flown off. This was achieved late in the day when all the required aircraft were despatched to Tangmere where conditions were (momentarily) better.

The Royal Task was performed from there."

THE RETURN OF AN OLD FRIEND

On the 1st April (when all good things occur in the Services) command of No.25 Squadron again changed – to none other than Joe Singleton, now a substantive Squadron Leader. To many of the younger members of the Squadron, his was just another name. To those who had flown night fighters during the War, Joe had been a pilot to be reckoned with. Things had got done. Pilot Officers were encouraged to read through the wartime Forms 540, and the penny dropped. Joe had come back to his favourite Squadron. At once No.25's establishment increased to its full (*sic*) strength of twelve Mosquitos, with more promised.

However, the good news was tempered with bad. There was to be an AOC's inspection of West Malling. Now these annual inspections send shivers down the spines (or used to) of everyone from the Station Commander to the most junior airman, depending on your viewpoint. Essentially they serve the purpose to demonstrate to the Commander-in-Chief of the Group to which the Station belongs that it is being efficiently commanded and that, when called on, will be able to carry out its operational duties to the standard expected. Anything extraneous and visible may come under scrutiny, from the food served in the Messes and the ability to keep in step while on parade, to the outward cleanliness of the aeroplanes and the ability of the pilots to fly.

West Malling, for all its homely atmosphere among the hop fields and blossoms of Kent, had still not completed its post-war refurbishing. Some of the wartime 'blister' hangars displayed the worst characteristics of *Anno Domini,* and no one had gone out of their way to enquire just what was stored in them. Apart from tattered shreds of canvas, formerly constituting part of their roofing and various rust-lined holes elsewhere, there were frequently signs that hop-pickers and other nomads found it more convenient to pitch their tents on the airfield than in the undergrowth. It proved extremely difficult for the Station Warrant Officer to persuade these bucolic squatters to break with generations of tradition. The Official Secrets Act and Defence of the Realm meant nothing to them. It was therefore agreed among the Station authorities that all that could be done on The Day was to arrange for the AOC's itinerary to be kept well away from these flaws.

In due course the Day dawned. After the customary ceremony of welcoming the AOC and his entourage, and a quick walk through one of the barrack blocks as well as Parachute Section, MT Section, workshops and so on, it was the turn of the Squadrons. It had been intended that the AOC's car would drive up to the Flight Offices, situated alongside the large main hangars, where the AOC would be introduced to the officers and men of the Squadron. At the

Mosquito NF.36 RL125, coded ZK-G, seen around September 1949. (Photo: via Ray Sturtivant)

No.25 (Fighter) Squadron – May 1949.

Winner of Fighter Command Night Fighter Gunnery Trophy.

Participating Aircrew – Seated, left to right: *Pilot 1 Sellers, Fg Off Webster, Flt Lt Winton, Sqn Ldr McGlashan, Flt Lt Cameron Cox, Pilot 1 Steinke.* Standing, left to right: *Navigator 2 Petrie, Navigator 2 Millar, Navigator 1 Wanstall, Pilot 2 Gardner, Navigator 2 Smethurst.*

(Photo: by courtesy of Ludwik Steinke)

appointed time Joe and No.25's personnel were lined up outside the offices, when the adjutant spotted the be-flagged staff car travelling round the airfield in the 'wrong' direction. It then stopped on the far side of the airfield, and the AOC was seen to alight and move towards the boundary fence. Joe now showed his mettle. Calling his flight sergeant, he gave orders for the whole Squadron to fall in and march towards one end of the line of Mosquitos, drawn up ready for their later inspection. However, when the AOC eventually arrived, his car came to rest only yards away from one of the station's most dishevelled blister hangars. After several minutes gazing at the ageing artefact, he turned to find Joe Singleton awaiting him, rooted to the ground at the salute. Joe recalled that the AOC simply said 'Good morning, Singleton. That's an interesting building you've got there. Do you find it useful?' To which Joe replied, 'I'm sorry to say I don't know, sir. As far as I know, it belongs to No.85 Squadron.'

Later that day, the Mosquitos of the two squadrons flew past in formation, each managing to put up twelve aircraft (their full complement), a fact that was commented on favourably to the Station Commander who then spoilt everything by replying 'Of course, sir, most of their radar is unserviceable'. A matter that was taken up with the two Squadron COs over the customary cup of tea in the Officers' Mess.

Regarding the contents of the blister hangars, this prompts mention of extra-mural activities, not only of the two night fighter squadrons at West Malling, but throughout most squadrons of the home based Royal Air Force.

As in pre-war years, the annual Armament Practice Camp was a welcome break in the everyday ritual of flying training. During these early years following the end of the War, Lübeck in West Germany was the chosen location for Fighter Command's Armament detachment. The prevailing 'currency' of that period comprised cigarettes and coffee; goods available in Germany were watches and cameras. Smythe takes up his recollections,

> "A healthy two-way traffic was maintained. Customs never discovered the means – although they tried! The means was the excellent AI Mk.X radar fitted in our Mosquitos. Two of the system's units, the modulator and RF unit, were large 'dustbin' shaped boxes. A set was maintained which consisted of empty boxes – room for thousands of cigarettes and many pounds of coffee. And for the return, dozens of cameras and hundreds of watches.
>
> The boxes were camouflaged by being sealed and then heavily labelled 'High Voltage' and 'Pressurized'. It worked because of the ignorance prevailing and the awe in which radar matters were held."

MASTERS AT ARMS

As some of the Officers and others became due for release from the Service (having joined up only shortly before the end of the War), so post-war volunteers and other Short Service aircrew officers and NCOs began arriving on No.25 Squadron, including some who were obviously very gifted. Among those who arrived on the Squadron in 1948 were a number of Poles who, when given the choice of returning to their native countries, chose to remain in Britain with the Royal Air Force – simply because, without family ties in those countries, they had no wish to be subservient to the Soviet Union. This was the time in which the sinister 'wall' was built across Europe, and the onset of the Cold War.

Among those who joined No.25 at that time was Pilot II Ludwik Steinke, a Pole who had fought with the RAF during the War and who, with Joe Singleton and half a dozen other experienced Flight Commanders and their deputies, and two or three NCO aircrew (now ranked as Pilots and Navigators I, II and III, and Master Pilots and Navigators), all of whom had opted to remain in the Service and make a career of it, constituted a hard core of experienced and dedicated men. This proficiency was quickly demonstrated when No.25 Squadron began by winning the No.11 Group Night Fighter air gunnery trophy, and followed this with the Fighter Command gunnery trophy (Night Fighter Squadrons) in 1949 – and in doing so also beat the gunnery scores of almost all the day fighter squadrons as well, in each case Steinke easily topping No.25's score. In 1950, the Squadron repeated its achievement as Steinke, now promoted Master Pilot, increased his own score by about 30 per cent.

Joe Singleton left the Squadron for the last time in November 1948 having brought it a long way along the road to self-esteem, which had been lacking during the year or so after the War. Once more the Squadron could hold its head up and feel instinctively that it was as good as the best, an attitude of mind that reached throughout the RAF. Cadets at Cranwell, who were determined to join a night fighter squadron when they graduated, and those passing through Advanced Flying Schools, put No.25 at the top of their preferred postings – just as they had in the 1920s and 1930s; West Malling itself got a limited face-lift, as more and more redundant buildings and huts were swept away.

The Mosquito was, however, now something of an anachronism, in a world of jet day fighters, and approaching the age of the jet bomber. The major Defence Exercises, held two or three times each year, showed that Mosquitos were no more able to counter aircraft such as the Lincoln (largely on account of the growing use of radio and radar countermeasures) than they had been half a decade earlier. The radar equipment at the GCIs had also undergone little or no improvement since the War, the old CH radar chain still being in everyday use and nearing the end of its useful life.

Squadron Leader K B McGlashan, who took over command of No.25 from Singleton in November 1948, was the last CO to lead the Squadron exclusively with Mosquitos. His successor, Squadron Leader R W Leggett, who took command in July 1950, himself a wartime night fighter pilot, would experience the onset of an entirely new world – the world of the jet night fighter and the jet bomber.

No.25 (Fighter) Squadron – March 1950.

Third-time Winner of Fighter Command Night Fighter Gunnery Trophy.

Participating Pilots – Seated, left to right: *Flt Lt Young, Flt Lt Cameron Cox, Sqn Ldr McGlashan, Flt Lt D Leete, Master Pilot Ludwik Steinke (record highest score).* Standing, left to right: *(Pilot 1, New Zealander, name not recorded), Pilot 1 Gardner, Pilot 1 Sellers, Pilot 1 Radwanski, (Flt Lt Winton absent).* (Photo: Francis K Mason collection)

CHAPTER 10

(Vampires, Meteors and Javelins, 1951-1962)

'We are called All-Weather Fighters' – 'Oh yeah'

IT WAS FAIRLY widely known in 1950 that the de Havilland Aircraft Co Ltd had been working on a two-seat version of the Vampire to an order placed with the Company by Egypt which – like so many foreign countries around the world – looked to either Britain or the USA to equip their post-war air forces with modern aircraft. DH had already built a prototype of this aircraft, which evidently met the Egyptians' requirement, and an order for twelve production aircraft was put in hand and completed early in 1951. However, diplomatic relations became strained between Egypt and a number of Western countries (including Great Britain), owing to apparent strengthening of ties between Egypt and the Soviet Union, which were considered dangerous on account of the security of the Suez Canal, and improving relations between Israel and America. This resulted in the Vampire order being cancelled by the British Government, an advance payment on the order having to be repaid, leaving de Havilland considerably out of pocket, until the Attlee government agreed to purchase the twelve existing Vampire NF.10s, and added a further order for 83 aircraft for the RAF. In the event, those Vampires (now termed Vampire NF.10s) originally destined for Egypt were delivered to No.25 Squadron at West Malling during July 1951. The Squadron thereby became the first regularly established jet night fighter squadron in the world*.

* The same claim has been made by several other RAF Squadrons, which were about to receive the new Armstrong Whitworth Meteor NF.11 twin-jet night fighter. The first three Meteor-equipped RAF Squadrons were No.29 Squadron (in August 1951), No.85 Squadron (in September 1951) and No.264 Squadron (in December 1951). There is evidence to suggest that No.25 Squadron had been warned much earlier in 1951 that it would be receiving Vampire two-seat night fighters, the first of several single-seat Vampire FB.5s being delivered to the Squadron as early as February that year for 'single-jet conversion' by former Mosquito pilots. (One of these was flown by the author).

The First Jet Night Fighter Squadron In The World.
An unposed photograph taken at West Malling in 1951, said to have been of the late Flight Lieutenant C C Smith (or his navigator) climbing aboard a Vampire NF.10 on the first night flying occasion with these aircraft (note the absence of drop tanks).
(Photo: Francis K Mason collection)

There was some disappointment on No.25 Squadron that it had been selected to receive Vampires, owing largely to their inferior performance to that of the Meteor night fighter. It was however made clear that the Vampires were only temporary equipment, and that in due course a Venom night fighter would replace them. (This never occurred on No.25 Squadron.)

Indeed the Vampire NF.10 was substantially slower and more sluggish than any of the single-seat versions. It accommodated the normal two-man crew, side-by-side in a much enlarged nacelle, as well as the bulky and weighty AI Mk.X radar. To cope with this much greater all-up weight, the thrust of the Goblin turbojet in the NF.10 had only been increased to 3,350lb thrust, compared with the single-seat Mk.5's Goblin which had a thrust of 3,100lb thrust. The quoted maximum speed of the NF.10 was 538mph but when, as was normally the case, the aircraft carried two large fuel tanks under the wings its maximum speed was reduced to no more than 480mph at the same height. Such a speed did not even register on the Vampire's Machmeter!

The NF.10 was a pleasant enough little aeroplane to fly, with few flaws or vices. Although the cockpit was in some respects similar to, but smaller than, that of the Mosquito NF.36 in that pilot and nav/rad sat side-by-side, and the radar was still the AI Mk.X; the four 20mm cannon were again located directly below the cockpit, but in one important respect Vampire and Mosquito cockpits differed: there was no escape hatch in front of the navigator's right foot! The only means of vacating the cockpit in flight was to jettison the upper transparent canopy panel, invert the Vampire, release one's seat straps and simply drop out (navigator first) – in the hope that the tailplane did not strike either crew member *en passant*. In short the NF.10 was a very simple aeroplane to fly; there were none of the unpleasant habits of the Mosquito, no critical speed, no swing on take-off or landing, no overheating radiators (although if the jet pipe temperature rose too high the throttle had to be reduced fairly quickly). There was no nosewheel steering and all ground steering had to be accomplished by differential wheel braking.

In the air, owing to the low power/weight ratio, the Vampire was extremely slow to accelerate and, thanks to a pair of diminutive trailing-edge air brakes (half the necessary area) the rate of maximum deceleration was very slow. Because the internal fuel tanks were also small, it was always necessary to carry the two large underwing drop tanks to make the sortie worthwhile.

After most of the pilots and navigators had flown half a dozen practice daylight interception sorties on the new fighters, the first night flying programme was arranged for the night of 16th August. One of the flight commanders and an exceptionally experienced pilot, Flt Lt Roy Winton had put himself down to take off first, carry out a quick weather check, and then be joined by another Vampire for PI's over the Thames Estuary. He had rolled on to the runway, paused for routine take-off checks and then started off. Watchers in the control tower were horrified to see the aircraft apparently make no effort to lift off, but to disappear over the over-shoot area, followed by a great gust of fire on the horizon. By the time anyone reached the scene, the aircraft's cockpit nacelle and engine were completely gutted. Both Winton and his navigator, Sgt Thomas Petrie had died in the blaze. What was left of the Vampire failed to disclose any reason why the aircraft had failed to unstick. Naturally, all further night flying was cancelled, and at once shock and gloom pervaded the Squadron, for both crew were very popular men. At first it was thought possible that a wing drop tank had started to jettison and the pilot may have attempted to abort the take-off without adequate time to prevent the aircraft from running into the overshoot area; this theory was only partly supported by the fact that both tanks were found well behind the wreckage – but could easily have been torn adrift when the aircraft ran onto the relatively rough ground.

Nevertheless, after about a week, night flying restarted and continued without problems. A set pattern of PIs was adopted, the only criteria limiting the frequency of night flying being that there should always be a diversionary airfield available (usually Manston, with its enormous runway) and that weather limitations – according to whether the pilots held a white, green or master green instrument rating card (these cards limited the pilot to flying in set visibility criteria). Those with a Master Green were, in theory, permitted to fly in a London fog!

During the autumn of 1951, the National Press visited the 'first jet Night Fighter Squadron in the World' at West Malling. In this strangely-posed picture of the Author and his navigator embarking in their Vampire NF.10 preparatory for a sortie in the 'wide black yonder', no one explained that pilots of fighters, day or night, seldom wore their flat 'ats on board their aeroplanes, nor that, with all those powerful arc lights eroding eyeballs, their night vision would be so impaired as to prevent them from seeing anything anyway. (Photo: Francis K Mason collection)

A daylight assembly of approximately half No.25 Squadron's initial establishment of Vampire NF.10s aligned on the hardstanding for inspection by the Press. (Photo: Francis K Mason collection)

LIGHTSTRIKE EXERCISES

Early in 1952 No.25 Squadron was selected to join a programme of exercises in conjunction with Lancaster maritime reconnaissance aircraft in simulated attacks on small coastal launches and other small ships, usually in the Thames Estuary. While the Lancaster went about its search for the 'target' vessel, employing its ASV search radar, two (or more) Vampires would be standing by near the end of the runway at West Malling, awaiting a summons from the Lancaster.

Once a target was spotted by the Lancaster, a course to steer was passed to the Vampire whose pilot would immediately set course under surveillance by ASV. On seeing the Vampire reach a pre-determined point the Lancaster, which would have positioned itself on the far side of the target, dropped an 'indicator' flare to show the position of the target to the Vampire pilot, who would then set up his timed attack. Assuming that the ASV continued to track the approaching Vampire, the Lancaster would have circled the target and now dropped an 'illuminator' flare on the attack side of the target, but offset from the line of attack, thereby enabling the Vampire pilot to attack a brightly lit target without being blinded by the glare; this also prevented any 'gunners' from seeing the attacking Vampire on account of the glare. After the first attack a second was set up similarly, the attack pattern being designed to keep the Vampire out of sight from the target, and the attack being carried out from a quarter 90 degrees from that of the first.

A continuous plot would be recorded in the Lancaster and this would be given to the Vampire squadron at West Malling so that pilots could examine their attack pattern.

It was during one of these Lightstrikes on the night of 21st May 1952 that No.25 Squadron lost another of its most popular members in a spectacular accident at West Malling. It happened that arrangements had been made for Flight Lieutenant John King to fly in the Coastal Command Lancaster as a passenger during a Lightstrike exercise to see for himself the attack pattern being set up from the air; also travelling as passengers were three of the Lancaster squadron's ground personnel.

The Lancaster had taken off from West Malling en route for the exercise area, and a number of Vampires were awaiting their turn to take off at the end of the runway. A radio call from the Lancaster pilot was heard saying that he was returning to West Malling as one of the flares in the Lancaster's bomb bay had ignited and that it could neither be extinguished nor jettisoned. The Lancaster was soon to the north seen flying low towards the airfield, an ominous glow clearly visible in the lower part of the fuselage. The big aircraft came in low and flew down the length of the runway, and watchers saw the glow of navigation lights disappear over neighbouring woodland, followed by the noise of the Lancaster crashing. It was some time before the crash vehicles could get close to the crash site, where they found the Lancaster in one piece but with its back broken and extensive damage to the rear fuselage. All its crew members appeared to be unhurt, but Flt Lt King and the three other passengers had been killed. The regular crew members had taken up their prescribed crash positions, which had saved their lives. However, no such positions existed for other occupants and they had evidently sought safety with their backs to the aircraft's mainspar, facing aft. Unfortunately the Lancaster had swung round through 180 degrees on colliding with a tree and travelled some 100 yards tail first,

Nice air-to-air study of Vampire NF.10 WP239 being flown solo and without those drop tanks. (Photo: Francis K Mason collection)

placing the passengers facing all the debris of the rear fuselage being demolished and thrown towards them.

AIRBRAKES AND THAT AOC's INSPECTION, 1952.

As usual the 1952 AOC's inspection of West Malling involved a flypast by the three resident Squadrons, namely No.500 (County of Kent) Squadron, RAuxAF (flying 12 Meteor 8 day fighters), No.85 (Fighter) Squadron (flying 12 Meteor NF.11s) and No.25 (Fighter) Squadron (flying 12 Vampire NF.10s), in that order. Because of the disparity of speeds, it was necessary to set up the Squadrons some miles down wind. The leading Meteor 8s would throttle back slightly, enabling the squadrons to space themselves comfortably behind, then the formation leader (the Wing Commander Flying at West Malling, Wg Cdr A P ('Falsh') Dottridge), in a Meteor 11, would call on the R/T 'Airbrakes, Airbrakes, GO', whereupon all three Squadrons would select their airbrakes, and the entire formation would pass the saluting base at a fairly respectable speed, though decelerating. That was the theory.

Come the time for the flypast and the Wing could be seen fast approaching in a nice tight stream. At that critical moment 'Flash' called those fatal words, and out went 37 sets of airbrakes. No.25 Squadron flew *through* the entire formation – such was the inefficacy of those absurd little airbrakes. Whether the AOC thought that this was all part of the programme or that No.25 Squadron had taken umbrage at being placed at the back of the flypast will never be known.

BATTLE OF BRITAIN STUFF

If the *Lightstrike* exercises seemed somewhat extraneous for night fighters, some of the major Fighter Command defence exercises were intended to emphasise the air defence responsibilities of its fighters. Geoff Smythe, who had returned to No.25 Squadron for a second tour, recollects –

"October 1952 brought the first major exercise which made use of the new concept of the 'all weather fighter'. Unfortunately the concept, which we had borrowed from the Americans, did not mean that at all. It meant 'dual rôle' – day and night fighter. Our masters, who controlled the exercise, knew this very well, but there was a lot they didn't know. They did not know, for instance, that No.25 Squadron had only sufficient 'operational' crews to fill the number of aircraft available. This allowed no rest interval for crews between being 'on state'.

'The first phase of the exercise was due to start at 18.00hrs on the Friday, and the Squadron's day was planned around that time. Those not involved with the exercise had a virtual day off. The selected crews reported for briefing at 08.30hrs, being told that, after completing an NFT on their allotted aircraft, they would be stood down until a weather

The owner of this 1921 Blue Label 3-litre Bentley wishes to remain anonymous. Having been purchased for about £60, it was frequently employed to assist Squadron members to convenient watering holes in Kent. Being No.84, it was said to be the third oldest Bentley extant; it is also said that the car now resides in Kenya, possibly the oldest of its ilk, and that it last changed hands for some £180,000.
(Photo: Francis K Mason collection)

Led by the Squadron Commander, Sqn Ldr Dick Leggett, eight Vampire NF.10s taxy past the squadron offices at Leeming early in 1952, for an air drill sortie in preparation for a forthcoming AOC's inspection. Although this usually comprised a fairly stately fly-past, the Vampire two-seater was badly under-powered, particularly when weighed down by underwing drop tanks, and the so-called airbrakes were virtually ineffective. However, if used while flying in formation, it was ages before the Goblin engine could stoke up enough energy to catch up.
(Photo: courtesy of No.25 (Fighter) Squadron)

Vampire NF.10, WM673, of No.25 (Fighter) Squadron at West Malling, collided with a naval Oxford training aircraft in 1953 over north Kent. The pilot of the Vampire brought his aircraft back to West Malling, albeit through the trees on the airfield boundary and despite considerable damage to its nose and wings. Neither crew NCO crew member was injured, but the Fleet Air Arm pilot and two trainee navigators were killed. F K M attended their funeral, representing the RAF. (Photo: Francis K Mason collection)

brief at 17.00hrs. It was, as intended, all very casual. The crews made their way to the Squadron, checked on the state of their aircraft, and prepared to do the NFT. I was briefed to fly with Roy Bowie* and got airborne around 11.00hrs; it was a beautiful day.

* Flight Lieutenant Bowie had recently arrived on No.25 Squadron from No.54 at Odiham, one of the first Vampire day fighter squadrons which had made a name for itself as the first Fighter Squadron to specialise on formation aerobatic displays-no mean feat with the Vampire's slender power margin. Despite that margin being even less in the Vampire NF.10, Bowie was made responsible for 'organising' similar activities on No.25, by all recollections a rather tame achievement-despite Bowie's very real expertise. He was also very adept at concealing his frustration at the NF.10's obvious shortcomings!

'Suddenly everything changed – but at that point we had no way of knowing by how much. Malling sent out a Recall; all aircraft were to return to base. After landing we were told that we'd been 're-deployed' (a word we were soon to hate) to Leuchars, at the northern end of the British Isles. Departure was to be ASAP. One by one, and routing individually, the aircraft took off and departed. Bowie and I aborted and were delayed a couple of hours. We eventually arrived at Leuchars at about 13.00hrs to be told that we would go 'on state' at 18.00hrs, with briefing an hour beforehand. In the meantime we spent a miserable time in the Mess ante-room.

After briefing, we went into the 'on state' sequence, the first crews assuming Stand-by (at 2 minutes) at 18.00hrs.

We 'fought the battle' throughout that Friday night repeatedly, as individual crews went through the sequence of Readiness, Standby to Scramble. Never for a moment were we off-state. It was a long and busy night, and we looked forward to our tour of duty coming to an end when the day boys took over at 07.00hrs.

But it was not to be. At about 06.30hrs Operations told us that we would have to take on the 'day battle', because the Meteor 8s *had their cockpit canopies iced-up!*

So we 'fought on' (to be honest, with a feeling of smugness). I was airborne with Bowie about 09.00hrs when Leuchars recalled us. We had been re-deployed, and on landing were told that we were to re-deploy to West Malling.

Arriving at Malling at about 10.30hrs, we were informed that we were 'on State' immediately. There was a touch of 'where the hell have you been' about the message'. So we continued to fight the 'day battle', repeatedly going through the state

All that is known about this Vampire is that it was being flown by Flt Lt 'Jimmy' James. Was he checking on the thickness of the runway's boundary layer? Or had he just noticed that he hadn't got 'three greens'. Both would have made plausible defences had it gone further. But 'Jim' had the Royal Air Force in his pocket! (Photo: Francis K Mason collection)

Letting off steam – In 'The Startled Saint'. . .
(Photo: Francis K Mason collection)

. . .or at Ladies' Night in the Mess.
(Photo: Francis K Mason collection)

sequence and scrambling to 'deal with the enemy'. This went on all that Saturday.

Then (again I was airborne at the time) we were recalled and redeployed, this time to Linton-on-Ouse up in Yorkshire. Again it was all ASAP. Bowie and I landed at Linton just after 17.00hrs, to learn we were on-state as from 17.30hrs. We 'fought the night battle' throughout that Saturday night. At about 02.00hrs the 'big event' developed, and we had the pleasure of dealing with a traditional Bomber Command 'stream' of targets – in our decidedly weary state of health, it was quite hairy. . . At no time during the night was there a let-up, and we continually hopped on and off the scramble sequence. Dawn finally came but, with it, came the same message from Ops as the previous day – the day fighters were 'suffering' from iced-up canopies, and we would have to continue. We did.

Again, about 08.00hrs, came the now-familiar message. 'Redeployed to West Malling'. This time we did not assume or hope that the word was a mistake. We rushed (to avoid the charge of 'where have you been?) back home to find ourselves, as we fully expected, immediately on state.

We 'fought the day battle again', as crews continually passed through the scramble sequence. Surprisingly, despite the fact that it was now Sunday and our last night's sleep had been that on Thursday night, everyone had held up very well, treating it all as a kind of a joke. However, we were beginning to worry because we were faced with yet another night phase that Sunday night. There had been no accidents, or serious incidents, so far, but we thought that fate was being overstretched .

Late that Sunday afternoon, the Battle of Britain was effectively re-enacted. The skies over Kent and Sussex were laced with contrails, and those of us involved with the 'battle' were given unending trade. Bowie was in his element!

Finally, at something after 17.00hrs, it was announced over the R/T that the weekend's phase of the exercise was being terminated. The planned night bit was cancelled. We returned to Malling, weary but jubilant (and very relieved). We landed just before 18.00hrs.

We had been operating continuously for 57 hours. A record, certainly a peacetime one, but I would guess rare even in wartime. Makes the legally-enforced 15-hour working day of the airline operators look very sick!

Did we all collapse in a heap. No, as a Squadron, we went out to a pub to celebrate (our survival?)."

'JIMMY JAMES'

One of the new arrivals on No.25 Squadron at West Malling early in the Vampire era was Flight Lieutenant H G James, AFC* DFM, who became a flight commander under the incumbency of Sqn Ldr Dick Leggett. Universally known as

On the last day of No.25 Squadron's tenure of Vampires, one aircraft HAD to go unserviceable, and the groundcrew felt that this was a justifiable opportunity to record the fact for posterity.
(Photo: via F R Cunningham)

Looking somehow suggestive of a boy wearing his school cap, this Vampire was adorned in the colour scheme as part of a private venture by the Squadron Commander to ensure that everyone knew that he was flying. In all likelihood the Wing Commander (Flying) caught sight of it, and the aircraft reverted to normal within about a week. (Photo: via F R Cunningham)

Three-Vic of Meteor NF.12s of No.25 Squadron photographed in 1955. (Photo: courtesy of Bruce Robertson)

Jimmy, he had volunteered for service with the RAF at the age of 17, early in the Second World War and by the time he had reached 19 he was a sergeant pilot with No.216 Squadron, flying Bristol Bombay 'bomber transports' over the Western Desert.

Jimmy it was who was flying a Bombay, carrying General 'Strafer' Gott to take command of the Eighth Army, accompanied by his full staff, when it was attacked by a *Staffel* of Messerschmitt Bf 109s far out over the desert and shot down. The Bombay force landed, the army officers all being killed when they scattered after leaving the crashed aircraft. James was found, still in his cockpit, some three days later little the worse for wear and returned to No.216 Squadron. He later became the personal pilot to the Commander-in-Chief, Transport Command, flying almost every conceivable VIP to and from the various Allied Chiefs of Staff conferences as well as meetings by the Allied Heads of State at Casablanca and Yalta.

At the age of 29, Jimmy decided to seek a new strain of Service flying, applying for night fighters, in due course arriving as a Flight Lieutenant at the Mosquito Night Fighter Operational Conversion Unit at Leeming in 1950 (joining the same course as the author). Even before completing the course, he was again leaving his mark on the Royal Air Force; having begged permission to accompany a sergeant pilot, who was to carry out an air test on a Meteor T7 trainer. In the course of a Mach Run (simply a full throttle speed run up to the limiting Mach number) at fairly high altitude, the huge cockpit canopy flew off the aircraft, leaving the occupants at the mercy of a violent blast of fresh air. The Meteor also suffered damage. The Sergeant had been injured and, though this was his first flight in a jet aircraft, Jimmy succeeded in making a perfectly good landing back at Leeming.

His appearance was always somewhat misleading for,

Close formation study of the NF.12, showing the enormous 'greenhouse' cockpit canopy, a relic of the T.7 trainer. (Photo: courtesy of Bruce Robertson)

Four NF.12s in echelon right, showing the considerably lengthened nose radome, and the compensating tailplane/fin fillets. All the Squadron's Meteor NF.12s carried the 'plain bar' style of fuselage marking until late in 1955; after that it was changed to the 'outlined rectangle' style. (Photo: courtesy of No.25 (Fighter) Squadron)

as a result of his desert brush with the Messerschmitts, Jimmy had acquired a dense white head of hair, and casual acquaintances might have been forgiven for believing that he was perhaps a semi-retired septuagenarian. Until he got into an aeroplane. And particularly a Vampire.

In due course on No.25 Squadron, it was discovered by his navigator, Flt Lt 'Chalky' White, an outsized ex-policeman (who must have been by far the largest Vampire navigator ever), that Jimmy was approaching his 5,000th flying hour. Accordingly, as that landmark arrived, the Squadron held a mock – but wholly serious – parade on the hardstanding, complete with march-past (a hunting horn providing an appropriate accompaniment), to seal the occasion.

Some months after this, Jimmy was taking off in an NF.10 at night from West Malling when one the Vampire's large wing drop tanks fell off shortly after unstick. An immediate attempt to jettison the tank on the other side failed, threatening to render the aircraft uncontrollable. Without second thought Jimmy hauled the aircraft round on to a reciprocal compass bearing and, without being able to see the runway lights (being on the wrong side of them) landed the aircraft, down-wind, wheels-up on the grass beside the runway, scarcely scratching the Vampire's paint. Such a manoeuvre was taught as being the biggest crime a pilot could commit, simply because it was always fatal. Not when Jimmy was flying… For this feat of flying he was awarded the Queen's Commendation for Valuable Service in the Air. When he eventually left the Squadron, he received an exchange posting to the United States Air Force, to fly McDonnell F-89D Scorpions in Alaska. One further anecdote links Jimmy with Geoff who recalls one very near miss –

> 'I was with Jimmy on a minor exercise. We led a 'four' on a milk run where we had to simulate ground attacks on several different targets. The weather was not bad, but there was a layer of strato-cumulus at around 1,000ft, and thick gloom beneath.

Line-up of the Squadron's NF.14s (and a T.7) displaying the outlined rectangle fuselage markings. (Photo: 'T')

The Meteor NF.14's AI radar revealed by removal of the nose radome, allowing servicing in situ by technicians working at ground level. (Photo: 'T')

Although the majority of pilots of the Squadron had originally flown Mosquitos before the spell with Vampire NF.10s, those who had no experience in twin-engine aircraft were sent on a short conversion course when the Squadron was re-equipped with Meteor night fighters. The Squadron was also issued with a single Meteor T.7 two-seater trainer (VZ638) for routine checks, instrument flying and so on. It is seen here at West Malling in 1954 wearing the Squadron markings. (Photo: Francis K Mason collection)

A Meteor NF.14 of No.25 Squadron WS781/J at West Malling in 1956. In the background is a Meteor T.7, almost certainly an aircraft of the Instrument Training Squadron, which periodically visited the operational Squadrons to check line pilots' Instrument Rating Cards (the means by which pilots were classified as to weather minima in which they were permitted to fly). (Photo: via Ray Sturtivant)

We made a pass at the tip of Portland Bill in line astern. Having made one pass heading out to sea, we turned around and attacked again, heading north-easterly, cunningly lined up and heading for our next target, which was a radar station on the coast. But, as we approached the coast, the gloom thickened and Jimmy decided to abort the attack. He ordered the formation to reform 'box' for the transit home. He then told me to let him know when No.2 was in position. I watched him closely and was about to say he was there when there was a violent BANG! Out of the corner of my eye I had a momentary glimpse of the tails of two Meteor 8s before they vanished into the gloom. There was a cry from Pete Lee (No.4) saying 'I've just hit another aircraft!'

As it happened, no one had hit anything or anyone. Those two Meteors had passed through our Box Four formation, behind us and in front of No.4. Where, in relation to our Nos 2 and 3, no one could say. What we could say was that the miss factor as it affected all four of us had been a matter of inches. We had all experienced a loud, pistol shot-like explosion.

We guessed that the Meteors were from Tangmere, but no one there knew anything about a near-miss!'

Some forty years later Jimmy James was to become one of the first members of No.25 (Fighter) Squadron Association, being the Committee Member responsible for organising the twice-yearly Reunions – by no means a simple task. He hasn't changed one iota and, if no one was looking, he'd be trying his hand at a Tornado! Undoubtedly a 'twenty-fiver' of the old stamp.

A SHORT, SHARP WAR

Meanwhile Dick Leggett commanded the Squadron with

August 1958. Meteor NF Mk.14s. Squadron detachmentto Akrotiri, Cyprus, for thirteen weeks during another Middle Eastern bust-up. At this time No.153 Squadron became No.25 (Fighter) Squadron once more.

Standing, left to right: *Flt Lt Ray Tyler, Flt Lt Bif Bifield, Flt Lt Bob Stringer, Flt Lt Ray Hardy, Flt Lt Ernie Coppard, Flt Lt Bill Page, Fg Off Paul Rundell, (unknown), (unknown), (unknown), (unknown), Fg Off Mike Rollings, Fg Off Jack O'Dowd.*

Seated, left to right: *Flt Lt Ken Foster (Adjutant), Wt Off Young (Engineering Officer), (unknown), Sqn Ldr Pip Piper (OC 'A' Flight), Wg Cdr Ken Cook (CO), Sqn Boss Breed (Nav/Rad Leader), Flt Lt Dave Stringer (OC 'B' Flight), Flt Lt Al Hilton, Flt Lt Bob Reekie.*

Front, left to right: *Sgt Roy Evans, Sgt Mick Monks, Sgt Pete Holmes.*

(Those marked *(unknown)* cannot be named positively.) (Photo: courtesy of Ken Foster)

August 1958. The CO's NF.14, WS723/T, staging through Luqa, Malta, en route *for Cyprus.* (Photo: courtesy of Ken Foster)

firmness but understanding; he was particularly quick to recognise his officers' strengths and weaknesses. He always seemed to be 'there' when one or other of his junior officers needed a few friendly words of advice, yet was always determined to delegate authority to his very able flight commanders. Above all, he possessed a wicked sense of humour which was capable of defusing any threatening disaster.

'Soon after my appointment as CO in July 1950, Sqn Ldr Bill Griffiths arrived to command our deadly rival at West Malling – No.85 (Fighter) Squadron. Soon after this we were preparing our Mosquitos to taxy out for NFTs when suddenly a Mosquito of No.85 Squadron fired a large number of 20mm cannon shells at us. It was exciting and a pleasant break from our peacetime routine; our splendid groundcrew were particularly impressed and sensibly prostrated themselves on the grass outside the Squadron dispersal, waiting for the fun to continue. Our Fitter I was quick to ask my permission to return their 'friendly' fire with extra interest and much better accuracy. He was most despondent when I explained our shortage of ammunition would not allow a return contest!

The event was, of course, an accidental firing from an 85 Mosquito parked outside their dispersal on the opposite side of the airfield from No.25 Squadron. However, next day I was delighted when HQ No.11 Group appointed me as the official investigating officer. Fortunately, the Press did not get hold of the *faux pas,* and I was unable to discover where the 20mm shells came to rest. Nevertheless it was a great bonus for us as my unofficial deal with Bill Griffiths demanded lots of medicinal refreshment for all ranks of No.25 Squadron.'

Another of Dick Leggett's exceptionally experienced Flight Commanders was Flt Lt C C Smith (always known simply as 'CC'); most ex-members of the Squadron remember him as being totally 'unflappable'. To him there was no such event as a disaster, but merely an isolated deviation from the norm. He always introduced himself to a newly arrived member of his Flight with the invitation to the new pilot to take him for a short trip in a Vampire 'round Kent'; CC would apparently be engrossed in pointing out landmarks, railways and rivers etc – while all the while quietly keeping his eye open for any slight weakness in the new arrival's flying ability or attention to important details. He also had a keen sense of humour but, unusually, he could see nothing funny in anything concerned with the practice of flying an aeroplane. Amusing stories would be told but, if they centred around a pilot's ignorance or a failing in an aircraft, 'CC' could seldom bring himself to see anything humorous in such a situation. He was a fairly outspoken critic of the Vampire, seeing in it failures by senior officers at the Air Ministry, and felt ashamed that No.25 Squadron

August 1958. No.25 Squadron's Meteor NF.12s and 14s refuel at Decimomannu, Sardinia, en route *to Cyprus.*
(Photo: courtesy of Ken Foster)

August 1958. Squadron's hutted accommodation during detachment to Akrotiri. The CO (Ken Cook) stands outside the Squadron's HQ. (Note the picket fence in the foreground, made from 30lb concrete rocket heads.) (Photo: courtesy of Ken Foster)

should be equipped with what he considered to be a bad adaptation of a poor original.

Sadly, CC was to lose his life in a Vampire. Owing to more than average bad flying weather during December 1952, the Squadron had come nowhere near completing the various applied flying exercises set down by No.11 Group for the month – and with Christmas approaching, the figures looked 'bad'; this was regarded as important (and by some as unnecessary bureaucracy) as it did provide for HQ No.11 Group a measure of the strength and ability of a particular squadron in the Group to undertake defence exercises and so on. In this particular instance, No.25 Squadron had frequently been unable to fly at night owing to continuing bad weather. This had placed something of a strain on those pilots on the Squadron with Green and Master Green Instrument Rating Cards.

The night of 18th December was windy but clear; it also happened that the Sergeants' Mess was holding its Christmas Party to which some of the Officers were invited (for a short stay). Knowing that this was a very popular function, and so that no sergeant pilot or navigator would miss the party, CC voluntarily put himself down for night flying – and decided on low level practice interceptions over the Channel with another of his crews.

Around midnight the Station Air Traffic tower duty officer rang the Sergeants' Mess to speak to Sqn Ldr Denis Furse (Dick Leggett's successor as No.25's CO) to say that there was a report that a Vampire had gone in over the sea near Dungeness, and that it was believed to be CC's. There being no regular Air-Sea Rescue patrols available at short notice, the coast guards had been warned. At once the CO and Jimmy James (with their navigators) hurried down to the airfield and were soon airborne to see if they could spot any dinghy lights on the sea in the area. Nothing was seen, either

1958. The Squadron displays its 'trademark' – the 'Swan' formation – during the USAF Armed Forces Day at Lakenheath, Suffolk. (Photo: courtesy of Ken Foster)

then or the following day, and it was assumed that CC's Vampire had hit the sea and broken up. Later some wreckage was thrown up on the shore.

The loss of these two men was keenly felt throughout West Malling; CC was well-known and much respected on the Station, not least by all ranks on his Flight. (This incident added fuel to the argument, which had surfaced from time to time, not only among the Vampire squadrons but those of Meteor night fighters, concerning the lack of windscreen wipers on these aircraft; surely, it was argued, if one was aiming at operations in 'all weathers' it was a logical and simple piece of equipment for these aircraft; the request had been, and continued to be refused on *the grounds of cost,* said to be £150!).

THE DEMISE OF THE VAMPIRE NIGHT FIGHTER

Accidents, fatal and not fatal, in relation to the number of NF.10s, not only on No.25 Squadron but on Nos 23 and 151 Squadrons, similarly equipped, had much to do with the withdrawal of the aircraft from service, No.25 disposing of its Vampires in April 1954. The aircraft had never been regarded as more than a stopgap until the Venom NF.2 was ready for service. Unfortunately, after this aircraft began re-equipping No.23 Squadron during 1953, it encountered all manner of problems resulting from design faults, pointing a finger at lack of understanding of compressibility effects approaching the speed of sound; pending searching tests, the aircraft was limited to a maximum speed lower than that of the Vampire NF.10, and was soon removed from the RAF.

However, the most pressing need for the speedy withdrawal of the Vampire from the night fighter squadrons was the fact that the last RAF bombers which the Vampire could (sometimes) intercept, namely the Lincoln, were being replaced by bombers, such as the Canberra, and shortly the Valiant – aircraft which, theoretically could operate above the ceiling of the first generation of jet night fighters. In other words, the Fighter Command air defence exercises were becoming meaningless, a situation that was further aggravated by the failure of the early Venoms, from which so much had been expected. That aircraft had been trumpeted as Britain's first swept-wing fighter, an empty claim as

August 1958. Squadron party visits Episkopi, Cyprus. From left to right: *Flt Lt Ken Foster, Flt Lt Bill Page, Sqn Ldr Pip Piper, Flt Lt Colin Bainbridge and Flt Lt Ray Tyler. The Sten gun and sidearms being carried were indicative of the tensions pervading the island at that time.* (Photo: courtesy of Ken Foster)

Waterbeach, October 1958. The CO, Wg Cdr Ken Cook prepares to embark in Javelin FAW Mk.7 XH905/A for night high-level practice interceptions (HLPIs). (Photo: courtesy of Ken Foster)

October 1958. Squadron Officers and NCO aircrews at Waterbeach shortly before re-equipping with Javelin FAW Mk.7s. (Photo: courtesy of Ken Foster)

1960. Five-ship Vic formation over Javelin FAW.7 'P' at Waterbeach.

the wing was not swept back in the aerodynamic sense of the term, but merely possessed a greater angle of sweepback on its leading edge!

Accordingly, No.25 Squadron was allocated Meteor night fighters in 1954 – an aircraft that had also been regarded as temporary equipment back in 1951! This all went to prove just how little coherent thought had been given to the special requirements of the new generation of jet night fighters during the late 1940s. The Meteor NF.11, for instance (as well as the Venom) still retained the old AI Mk.X radar. Fortunately No.25 Squadron was not destined to receive the Meteor NF.11, but the NF.12, equipped with more advanced AI radar.

The final weeks of the NF.10 on No.25 Squadron coincided with the arrival of a new Commanding Officer, Sqn Ldr John Cameron Cox, who joined them at West Malling in March 1954. This was to be his second tour with the Squadron as he had served as a flight commander under Joe Singleton, Sqn Ldr McGlashan and Dick Leggett between 1948 and 1951.

Cameron Cox was pitched in 'at the deep end' as soon as he arrived for, not only did he have to contend with an AOC's inspection – which always tended to cause tempers to fray – but also an infinitely more significant event for the Squadron, the presentation of a Squadron Standard.

The idea of awarding Standards to Squadrons, which had completed long and distinguished service to the Nation, was originated by HM King George VI early in the Second World War, and one of the first to be nominated to receive a Standard was No.25 (Fighter) Squadron, at that time engaged in the night fighter defence of Britain. It was, however, decided that because some of the other qualifying Squadrons were serving overseas (it being originally

September 1959. No.25 Squadron Javelin FAW.7s in 'Swan' over the Suffolk coast. Crews: *1 - Flt Lt Foster / Wg Cdr Cook, 2 - Flt Lt Alderson / Fg Off Whorwood, 3 - Flt Lt Bassett / Flt Lt Woods, 4 - Flt Lt Bainbridge / Sgt Evans, 5 - Flt Lt Willey, Sgt Edwards.*

(Photo: courtesy of Ken Foster)

Javelin FAW.7, XH961/R, of No.25 Squadron awaits its turn to fly during a Battle of Britain Display in 1989.
(Photo: via Ray Sturtivant)

intended that the King himself would actually present the Standards) the presentation ceremonies would have to await a return to peace. Owing to the time needed to produce these beautifully crafted Standards – which not only feature the Squadron's recognised Battle Honours but also the Squadron Badge, the whole device being framed in a border comprising the English Rose, Scotland's Thistle, Wales' Leak and Ireland's Shamrock – it was not until the early 1950s that the first Presentation Parades were held. No.25 Squadron's ceremony had been scheduled for 1953, but owing the organising of the Coronation ceremonies that year, it was delayed until 1954. It had also been arranged that the presentation would be made by Marshal of the Royal Air Force Sir William Dickson (the former Commanding Officer of No.25 Squadron) but, at a late stage in the preparations, this Officer stated that he would be unable to officiate, his place being taken by Air Marshal Sir Dermot Boyle, the then Commander-in-Chief of Fighter Command.

These Standards represent the visible symbol of pride of the Unit in its achievements in war, and are always paraded at formal functions attended by the Squadron, ranging from Guest Nights in the Officers' Mess and weekly Church Parades, to local civic parades and those held annually on Remembrance Sunday. From time to time, owing to deterioration from fair wear and tear, the Standard is replaced, and the opportunity may be taken to substitute other Battle Honours which had not previously been emblazoned (the number of such Honours being limited on each Standard. When a Standard is renewed, the old one is laid up, usually in the nearest Cathedral Church to the station at which the Squadron is currently serving; when a Squadron is only temporarily disbanded, it is laid up in the entrance hall at the RAF College, Cranwell, or, if permanently disbanded, in the Royal Air Force Church of St Clement Danes in London. No.25 Squadron currently parades its third Standard.

When Cameron Cox took over No.25 Squadron, his flight commanders were Flt Lts Peter Lea and R Easterbrook. The aircraft establishment was raised from 12 (as with Vampires) to 14, and 14 Meteor NF.12s were duly delivered. Almost immediately the Squadron was notified that its establishment was being increased to 22 and, with little warning, 8 Meteor NF.14s arrived at West Malling within the next fortnight, as had additional pilots, navigators and groundcrews – the radar technicians having received the necessary training to manage the new American-built APS-21. This radar was significantly more bulky than the AI Mk.X in the Meteor NF.11, and demanded a considerably lengthened nose compared to that of the NF.11. Rolls-Royce

Javelin FAW.9, XH767/A, showing its re-heat jet nozzles, the determining feature of this version. Around 1960 the all-weather squadrons were only permitted to display their Unit markings discreetly concealed at the top of the fin. (Photo: via Ray Sturtivant)

Waterbeach, December 1959. No.25 Squadron Javelin on Quick Reaction Alert (QRA); a wet and windy winter's night on runway 23 ORP.
(Photo: courtesy of Ken Foster)

Derwent 9 turbojets replaced Derwent 8s in the NF.11, with the improved nose profile, increased the limiting Mach number to 0.81. The increased keel area of the nose was compensated by increased fin area, with the addition of small fillets the fin at its junction with the tailplane. Some structural strengthening of the wing was necessary to enable the Meteor NF.12 to withstand the loads experienced while manoeuvring at the increased Mach number. Compared with the earlier NF.11, the NF.12 was a significantly improved aircraft. The NF.14, which in due course replaced most of the NF.12s was further improved by the replacement of the old side-hinged, heavily framed 'cage-style' cockpit canopy with a rearward-sliding single-piece blown canopy.

In short, the 'second-generation' Meteor night fighters, which joined Fighter Command from 1953 onwards, represented a considerable step forward, particularly for No.25 Squadron, which had been equipped with Vampires.

WINDS OF CHANGE

This very slow progress forward, however, did very little to enhance confidence in the British aircraft industry which, at the time of No.25 Squadrons change to Meteors, had yet to deliver a transonic fighter to the RAF. The Hawker Hunter, pleasing to the eye, was soon to be delivered to the day fighter squadrons, as was the Supermarine Swift; the former was to experience all manner of serious setbacks, inadequate range and endurance, a chronic tendency for its Rolls-Royce Avon to surge and flame-out when firing its guns, and inadequate airbrake (!). Fortunately all these serious shortcomings were fairly quickly and successfully addressed, but the Swift was less lucky and, although its problems were similar to those of the Hunter, the remedies necessary were impossible without major alterations to the aircraft's design. Although the Hunter went on to become one of the most popular fighters ever flown by Fighter Command, it was rendered almost superfluous by an ill-conceived policy adopted by the British government after the Suez Crisis on 1956. As long ago as 1953, work on a genuinely supersonic version of the Hunter had been cancelled.

Of immediate concern to the Royal Air Force in 1954, was one of those unsettling defence cut-backs that have plagued the Services fairly frequently ever since the Second World War, thwarting Britain's attempts to maintain *technical* parity with the United States.

Beginning in 1950, on the outbreak of the Korean War, efforts were made to strengthen the British armed forces. In the RAF, Fighter Command re-formed a relatively large number of fighter squadrons – these being equipped with Meteors and Venom day fighters, as well as ordering large numbers of Canadian-built American F-86 Sabres – most of which equipped RAF squadrons in Germany. Bomber Command, while gradually disposing of the Lincoln heavy bomber, had opted to lease a number of B-29 Washington heavy bombers (but failed to obtain sufficient spares and

Waterbeach, July 1960. Squadron Scramble from runway 05 ORP. The first aircraft rolling fifty seconds from 'Scramble' order, the others follow in sequence at five second intervals.
(Photo: courtesy of Ken Foster)

Javelin FAW Mk.7s, Waterbeach, December 1959.

Rear, left to right: *Fg Off Pete Simpson, Flt Lt Jack O'Dowd, Flt Lt Pete Brunskill, Flt Lt Tony Smythe, Flt Lt 'Moby' Dick, Sgt Dave Garfoot, Sgt Laurie Manns, Sgt 'Cobber' Edwards, Flt Lt Richard Willey, Flt Lt Ray Tyler, Flt Lt Pete Pascoe.*

Centre, left to right: *Fg Off Paul Rundell, Flt Lt Bill Akister, Flt Lt Terry Dixon, Flt Lt Norman Glass, Flt Lt Mike Rollins, Flt Lt Brian Whiteley, Flt Lt Guy Woods, Flt Lt Colin Bainbridge, Flt Lt Ken Bassett, Fg Off Dave Bexley (Engineering Officer), Flt Lt 'Pop' Parsons, Flt Lt John Lucking.*

Seated, left to right: *Flt Lt Larry Parkin RCAF, Flt Lt Mike Holmes, Flt Lt 'Hank' Hemming RCAF, Sqn Ldr 'Paddy' MacIlrath (Nav/Rad Leader), Sqn Ldr Ken Hutchings (OC 'A' Flight), Wg Cdr Ken Cook (CO), Sqn Ldr John Chick (OC 'B' Flight), Sqn Ldr Ted King (Engineering Officer), Flt Lt Tony Shepherd, Flt Lt Olly Anderson, Flt Lt Ken Foster (Adjutant).*

(Photo: courtesy of Ken Foster)

Waterbeach, July 1960. No.25 Squadron Officers and aircrew.

Standing, left to right: *Sgt Laurie Manns, Flt Lt Bill Akister, Flt Lt Larry Parkin, Fg Lt Paul Rundell, Flt Lt Jack O'Dowd, Flt Lt Mike Rollins, Sgt Dave Garfoot, Fg Off Pete Gunns (Engineering Officer), Fg Off Dave Bexley (Engineering Officer), Flt Lt Alan Mawby, Flt Lt Al Vosloo, Flt Lt Guy Woods, Flt Lt Ken Bassett, Flt Lt Ray Tyler, Flt Lt Colin Bainbridge, Flt Lt Ken Foster (Adjutant), Sgt 'Cobber' Edwards, F/Sgt Bob Kelly, Sgt Roy Evans.*

Seated, left to right: *Flt Lt Tony Smythe, Flt Lt Terry Dixon, Flt Lt Norman Glass, Flt Lt Mike Holmes, Flt Lt Hank Hemming, Sqn Ldr Ken Hutchings (OC 'A' Flight), Wg Cdr Jim Walton (CO), Sqn Ldr Ted King (Engineering Officer), Flt Lt Tony Shepherd, Flt Lt 'Pop' Parsons, Flt Lt Derek Hall, Flt Lt Pete Pascoe, Fg Off Bas Whorwood.*

(Photo: courtesy of Ken Foster)

July 1960. Javelin FAW.9s fan break left.

create the necessary back-up infrastructure demanded by these aircraft). The Canberra had entered service and, although this transformed Bomber Command's tactical capabilities, its value was limited in not being capable of significant performance advance – its fundamental design already being outdated. In some rôles, however, the Canberra, quite fortuitously, reigned supreme.

After the end of the Korean War, in which the RAF was not significantly involved owing to its inability to match the Soviet-inspired transonic MiG-15 swept-wing transonic fighter, the Treasury began reducing the Defence appropriations (in real terms), with growing emphasis being placed on development of the coming V-force – the Valiant, Vulcan and Victor (all enormously expensive by the standards of the time. Also being developed, with some relevance, was a much more efficient early warning radar system, expensive though essential in view of growing Soviet long-range striking power.

Much had being made in the Aviation press in Britain

July 1960. CO Jim Walton includes ATC cadets in an exercise briefing. Left rear to left front: *Flt Lt Colin Bainbridge, Flt Lt Ken Foster, Sgt Roy Evans, Flt Lt Ken Bassett.*

of the forthcoming English Electric P.1 (later to be named the Lightning), heralded as the Royal Air Force's first Mach 2 fighter. First flown in prototype form in August 1954, this employed a sharply sweptback wing of low thickness chord ratio. Given engines of adequate power, there was no reason to doubt that it would eventually be capable of reaching Mach 2. More significant, although the Lightning was envisaged as remaining a single-seat fighter, it was eventually assumed that it would become an all-weather fighter (or, more accurately, an all-weather air-to-air missile launcher). At last it appeared that the Air Ministry appeared to be in sight of a true 'All Weather' fighter. However, many important questions had to be addressed, some not even anticipated.

LIFE WITH THE METEOR NIGHT FIGHTERS

Every day (and night) life on No.25 (Fighter) Squadron at West Malling continued much as it had done in the Vampire years. Fighter Command engaged in periodic Air Defence Exercises although, with growing numbers of Canberras (and the first Valiants) participating, the number of successful interceptions was falling exercise by exercise, though radar contacts (with the new American AI radar) were on the increase, only to be thwarted by the target's altitude and speed. Air-to-air missiles for fighters were under development, though no serious thought had yet been given to any such use on the Meteor night fighters. Such missiles were still some three or four years away in 1955.

Unlike the Vampire night fighters, the NF.12 and NF.14 squadrons did go abroad, either to join NATO exercises or annual armament 'camps'. (In the days of the Vampire night fighters, few facilities existed overseas in the event of radar and engines needing replacement, its engine and most of its radar installation being uniquely confined to the three home-based NF.10 squadrons.)

The Squadron suffered a single fatal accident while equipped with Meteors. On 4th February 1957 Squadron

Waterbeach, July 1961. Squadron hangar busy through the night. (Photo: courtesy of Ken Foster)

Leader Alan Hall, DFC, (flight commander of 'B' Flight, was flying a cross-county, with his navigator Flying Officer Arthur Levett, in an NF.14, when some sort of emergency occurred; whether or not the crew decided to abandon the aircraft is not clear. The pilot, in attempting to force land, crashed about four miles west of Oxford, and both pilot and navigator were killed. Some trouble with the cockpit canopy has been mentioned, but whether this jammed when the crew attempted to bale out, or whether the canopy detached in flight and damaged the aircraft (causing the pilot no alternative but to attempt a forced landing), is not known and is not clarified in the accident documentation.

Among the groundcrews on No.25 Squadron was a Junior (later Cpl) Technician Norton Thirumalai, who must have been one of the longest-serving members of the Squadron at this time; an extract from a letter gives an excellent indication of the degree of professionalism that existed among the lesser known (and so often overlooked) Squadron members.

July 1960. Cheers! Flt Lt Olly Alderson and Flt Lt 'Pop' Parsons enjoy a thirst quencher on arrival at Nicosia in Javelin FAW.9 'K' for a six week detachment. (Photo: courtesy of Ken Foster)

'I arrived at West Malling in September 1954 as a Junior Technician after completing an Air Radar Fitter's course at No.12 Radio School, RAF Yatesbury. After some months in the Radio Servicing Flight, I was transferred to No.25 Squadron, where I remained until we moved to

Leuchars, March 1962. Flt Lts Ken Foster and Derek Hall, clad in immersion suits, are removing Firestreak window covers whilst preflighting. (Photo: courtesy of Ken Foster)

Waterbeach, July 1961. Introduction of 'Progressive Maintenance': Javelin FAW.9 pressure switch change at around 03:00 hrs.
(Photo: courtesy of Ken Foster)

RAF Tangmere in 1957. I worked on Meteor NF.12s and NF.14s, Vampire NF.10s, Hunters, Javelin FAW.7s and 9s and on Javelin Simulators.

The Squadron went on detachments to Waterbeach, Wattisham, St.Mawgan and Aldergrove. All I remember of Wattisham was that we had eggs for breakfast, eggs for lunch and eggs for dinner!

I returned to Yatesbury on three occasions on courses for AI Mk.21, in 1956, and was promoted to Corporal, AI Mk.22 and converting to Air Radar Fitter (Fighter Command) in 1957, and promoted to Corporal Technician and AI Mk.17 in 1959, after which I was posted to Leuchars where I was demobbed in June 1960.

I was married to Ratna on 18th March 1957 in London, and the Squadron sent us a telegram which we still possess. We never qualified for married quarters, so Ratna didn't see much of the Squadron.

There was a Queen's Regulation which stated that an elder brother could request for his younger brothers to join him. So Douglas joined the Squadron as an engine fitter in 1956, then Eddie joined as a Radio Mechanic in 1957.

My first car was a limousine, an Armstrong Siddeley Sapphire (1935 vintage) which I bought in 1955 for £30. . . My next car was a 1928 Austin Seven with cable brakes, which I bought for £25. (It had 'Danger Ejector Seat' painted on the doors.) The cable brakes were always giving trouble,

Javelin FAW.9s fan break right; as a matter of routine, the four Firestreak SRAAMs were carried on the majority of training sorties.
(Photo: courtesy of No.25 (Fighter) Squadron)

Javelin FAW.9 XH881/M at about 40,000 ft.
(Photo: Francis K Mason collection)

Leuchars, 1962. Javelin FAW.9 being flown by Flt Lt Ken Bassett and Flt Lt Roy Houghton.

particularly when descending Wrotham Hill. I was travelling to London one night, after night flying at Malling, and had reached Burdett Road in the East End, when a policeman, who was directing traffic, stopped me having observed a brake cable trailing on the road. After questioning me, he made a telephone call and within minutes a police car arrived with an Inspector, Sergeant and two constables. I was expecting to be put in the 'Clink' or fined. Instead, they suggested I go across the road for a cup of tea; when I came out I found that they had got under the car and repaired my brake cable. I never had any more trouble with it!

I remember doing guard duty on a Meteor of one of the other West Malling squadrons which had crashed in a neighbouring fruit fields, killing at least one fruit picker.

Douglas and I played cricket for the Squadron.

West Malling was a small village, yet it had 13 pubs. It took a number of days to do a 'pub crawl! 'These were the best years of my life. (After he left the Service, 'T' – as he was known – qualified as an Electronics Engineer and a Chartered Engineer. He is a Member of the Squadron Association and regularly attends reunions!)

No.25 remained at West Malling until 30th September 1957 when it finally left the station for ever (the famous night fighter station then being closed), moving to Tangmere in Sussex. The move had only been intended as temporary, but the Suez Crisis had an immediate and profound effect on the whole future of the Royal Air Force, and in particular of Fighter Command. The government White Paper on Defence was published, throwing into doubt the size, deployment, manning and equipment of the Command. The Javelin all-weather fighter was already being delivered to the Service, and No.25 Squadron anticipated that this big fighter would, in due course, replace the Meteor night fighters.

In the event, No.25 only remained at Tangmere until the end of June 1958 and was disbanded on the 30th. On the following day it was reformed at Waterbeach in Cambridgeshire, No.153 Squadron being disbanded simultaneously; the majority of No.25 Squadron's former personnel and aircraft moved to Waterbeach under the command of Wg Cdr Kenneth H H Cook, who had taken over from Wg Cdr G H Melville-Jackson, DFC (the Squadron's *fifth* CO in four years) at Tangmere on 23rd June. Thus the future of No.25 was effectively guaranteed as Waterbeach had already undergone modernisation adequate to cater for Javelins. Nevertheless, these aircraft were still some months away.

Leuchars, August 1962. Aircrew group.

Left to right: *Fg Off John Rust, Flt Lt Ken Foster, Flt Lt Ken Bassett, Flt Lt Bill Akister, Plt Off Tony Craig (Engineering Officer), (Fg Off Roger Lloyd *), Flt Lt Mike Gautrey, Sqn Ldr Colin Bidie, Flt Lt Norman Glass, Flt Lt Brian Bullock, Flt Lt Roy Houghton, (Flt Lt Bob Taylor *), Flt Lt Derek Hall.*

Note: (*) - unsure if names are correct.

Exercise Matador, September 1962. Detached Javelin FAW.9s of No.25 Squadron on apron at Middleton St.George.

(Photo: courtesy of Ken Foster)

ALMOST ON WAR FOOTING

The island of Cyprus had, since the Convention of 1878, been occupied by the British as a base for the defence of Ottoman Asia against Russia as well as protection for the routes to India. This situation was to become increasingly difficult to justify during and after the Second World War, with the predominantly Greek Cypriot population demanding union with Greece in opposition to the traditional rule by the Turks. The situation soon became an embarrassment to the British who were under pressure (largely led by powerful American world-wide influences) for de-colonisation of the British Empire, but who had come to regard the Cyprus bases as a substitute for those formerly in Palestine. However, when the Suez Crisis had emphasised the value of Cyprus as an important air base (but without any suitable naval base), Britain, with the support of NATO, proposed a tripartite settlement that sought, among other matters, the ending of Greek and Turkish terrorism, and safety for the British air bases.

As a measure of protection of these bases, as well as to establish a NATO presence on the island (Turkey at that time not being a member of NATO), the British gradually strengthened their presence on the island and, among the RAF units despatched on detachment, was No.25 Squadron, sent to Akrotiri in August 1958, each of its Flights sending six aircraft (mostly NF.14s) for a period of six weeks. Akrotiri itself was on war readiness, being on the alert for any terrorist activity, while RAF personnel venturing outside the base, whether on duty or not, always travelled in small groups and carrying side arms for self protection. Otherwise, normal flying training and the occasional exercise, continued without any significant interference.

Exercise Matador, September 1962. Javelin FAW.9 XH776 'P' on apron at Middleton St.George.

After returning to Waterbeach at the end of the Cyprus detachment, the Meteors were finally discarded in March 1959, and No.25 (Fighter) Squadron moved firmly, and not before time, into genuine transonic flight by re-equipping with the Gloster Javelin FAW (fighter all-weather) Mark 7.

THE JAVELIN WAS A LOT OF AEROPLANE

The Gloster Javelin Mk.7, at norm take-off weight, tipped the scales at 35,700lb – almost exactly twice the normal all-up weight of the single-seat Hunter in its ground-attack configuration. Powered by a pair of 11,000lb thrust Armstrong Siddeley Sapphire Sa7 axial-flow turbojets, it was marginally supersonic in a shallow dive, and was equipped with the American-built AI Mk.22 radar. Its flying control system, an advance on previous versions of the aircraft, included pitch auto-stabilisation, fully-powered hydraulic rudder control with yaw stabiliser, and electro-hydraulic three-axes control auto-pilot with automatic approach and altitude control. In these respects, the Javelin 7 was as technically advanced as the Lightning fighter (at that time about to enter service with the day fighter squadrons, but not yet a 'Mach 2 fighter')

It was designed to carry four Firestreak infra-red homing short-range air-to-air missiles (SRAAM) under the wings, as well as two 30mm Aden guns. Aircraft usually flew with two large 250-gallon fuel tanks under the fuselage, and for long distance sorties, four 100-gallon drop tanks under the wings. At maximum load, the Javelin 7 weighed just over 40,000lb. The Firestreak missiles were not fully operational when the Squadron's Javelins were delivered and, for the first few months the Squadron (the first to receive the weapons) had to be content with carrying Firestreaks with concrete warheads! These warheads were what were known as the 'continuous rod' variety, namely a long metal bar with hundreds of deep notches along its length. The bar was wound round the explosive charge which, when detonated, blew the bar into a cloud of lethal fragments, capable of causing fatal damage to a target aircraft – such was the energy released.

Flt Lt Peter Pascoe recalls the first Javelin six-week detachment to Cyprus, by all accounts a memorable event:

> 'This visit created an international incident with France by flying the whole Squadron (12 Javelins) there in one formation – which France accused us as being an act of war! One Javelin went unserviceable

Waterbeach, June 1961. AOC's Inspection Day.

Rear, left to right: *Flt Lt Gordon Turner, Flt Lt Bob Rogers, Flt Lt Bas Whorwood, Fg Off John Rust, Flt Lt Bill Hustwaite, Flt Lt Chris Cowper, Flt Lt Ken Bassett, Fg Off Pete Gunns (Engineering Officer), Fg Off Mel Evans, Flt Lt Mike Gautrey.*

Centre, left to right: *Flt Lt Bill Akister, Flt Lt Keith McRobb, Fg Off Mike Harris, Flt Lt Ken Foster (Adjutant), Fg Off Ivan Symonds, Sgt 'Cobber' Edwards, Sgt Laurie Manns, Fg Off Fred Bates, Fg Off Bob Arnott, Flt Lt Paul Hobson, Flt Lt 'Pop' Parsons, Flt Lt Brian Whiteley.*

Front, left to right: *Flt Lt Roy Houghton, Flt Lt Norman Glass, Sqn Ldr Ted King (Engineering Officer), Sqn Ldr Keith Mossman ('A' Flt Cdr), Wg Cdr Jim Walton (CO), Sqn Ldr John Chick ('B' Flt Cdr), Sqn Ldr 'Paddy' McIlwrath (Nav/Rad Leader), Flt Lt John Lucking, Flt Lt 'Moby' Dick.* (Photo: courtesy of Ken Foster)

Akrotiri, November 1961, for Operation Leprechaun.

Standing, left to right: *Flt Lt Ken Bassett, Fg Off Ivan Symonds, Flt Lt Paddy Pratt, Flt Lt John Galley, Fg Off Roger Lloyd, Fg Off Dennis Pike, Flt Lt Hamish Cook, Flt Lt Fred Richardson, Flt Lt Jock Shields, Flt Lt Derek Hall, F/Sgt Bob Kelly, Sgt Roy Evans, Flt Lt Mike Gautrey, Fg Off Bob Arnott, Sgt Laurie Manns, Flt Lt Bas Whorwood, Fg Off Pete Goodwin, Flt Lt Terry Dixon, Fg Off Pete Gunns (Engineering Officer), Fg Off Mike Harris, Fg Off Mel Evans.*

Seated, left to right: *Flt Roy Houghton, Flt Lt Bill Akister, Flt Lt Fred Bates, Sqn Ldr Colin Bidie ('B' Flt Cdr), Sqn Ldr Phil Hyson (Nav/Rad Leader), Wg Cdr Jim Walton (CO), Sqn Ldr Keith Mossman ('A' Flt Cdr), Sqn Ldr D A P Saunders-Davies (attached officer), Flt Lt Ken Foster (Adjutant), Fg Off Taff Evans, Flt Lt Chris Cowper.* (Photo: courtesy of Ken Foster)

'Arrow' formations were particularly appropriate for Javelin squadrons, while the two 'wing' aircraft had only to ease back to form No.25's own characteristic 'Swan' formation.
(Photo: courtesy of Ken Foster)

at Orange in the South, and Ray Tyler and I were detailed to remain, and follow on to Cyprus when the fault had been rectified. (After a night on the town) I had great difficulty the next day in flying on to Luqa (Malta), and the rest of the flight to Akrotiri.

'After night flying we used to go to the beach club at Kyrenia the next day in an old RAF one-tonner with a crash gearbox, which our adjutant, Ken Foster, used to drive. We sat in the back, passing round a demi-john of Cyprus sherry to keep ourselves lubricated.

'We were scrambled one night to intercept an intruder – which, on interception, nearly blinded us with a searchlight, and turned out to be an American ELINT snooper.

'On our way home to the UK, it was found that the leg from Luqa to Orange was somewhat critical with regard to fuel (which the navigators had pointed out before take-off), with the result that the pilots flew in very loose formation to avoid constant throttle movement. Arriving at Orange the pilots found 8/8ths cloud, but were committed to landing on account of fuel shortage. Everyone let down, hoping for the best. On breaking cloud, we found Javelins emerging from all directions. Everyone landed OK, but without sufficient fuel for an over-shoot.

'I felt terribly ill, and had to be helped from the aircraft and put to bed in the sick quarters where I was found to have dysentery. The support Hastings, carrying the groundcrews, eventually picked me up and brought me back to Waterbeach.'

(I left No.25 Squadron at the end of 1960 to complete the Guided Weapons Course. In 1965, after completing a tour in the Far East on heli-copters, I was again posted to No.25 Squadron, this time as an Engagement Controller/Instructor at North Coates; I enjoyed the instructional aspects of the job, and subsequently became the Operations Flight Commander.)

Representing an enormous step forward from the Meteor, the Javelin gave back to the old-established night fighter squadrons well-deserved self-esteem. In possessing a service ceiling of about 53,000ft, the new fighter was able to match the usual operating altitudes of the V-bombers being flown in the late 1950s and early 1960s in the course of the Fighter/Bomber Command air defence exercises, and inter-ception claims by the Javelin crews at last began to have some significance, even though doubts still lingered as to the true effectiveness of the Firestreak missile (which was still limited to a narrow 'aft-cone' lock-on – a weakness that would not be addressed until the arrival of AI Mk.23B and the Red Top SRAAM, eventually carried in the later Lightnings).

On the matter of the Javelin's Firestreaks an incident is recalled by a Flight Sergeant pilot on No.25 Squadron,

'We were due to go to Akrotiri as Quick Reaction Alert (QRA) Squadron, which meant that we had to take our own live Firestreaks on the aircraft (none being available at Akrotiri). Several cross-country sorties were flown to check range figures with a full war load (four Firestreaks and two Aden guns).

'I and my crew (Sgt Ray Evans) were detailed for one of these sorties. The day was very blustery and turbulence was forecast at low level. Take-off and initial climb seemed normal except that the turbulence was very marked for the first few hundred feet of the climb. The climb was continued to 40,000ft on the first leg. All seemed normal as we levelled out and continued the leg.

'With my seat in its usual position it was im-possible for me to see the inboard missiles and pylons as the engine intake obscured the view; therefore it was not until some minutes after Top of Climb when I eased my weight off the seat that I saw that only the two outboard missiles were still on the aircraft! Check all switches – all off? – Yes! When did they go? In the turbulence after take-off?

'Inform Area Radar' – 'Reverse course' – 'Divert or return to Waterbeach'. Waterbeach want us back. (No one else knew much about the Firestreak at that time).

'Never was there such a welcoming committee for a Flight Sergeant pilot and his Sergeant radar operator! Everyone from the Station Commander down, all looking as if they wanted to hang us.

'To our relief, when the armourers checked, there was still power at the plugs to the inboard jettison units.

'The cause. A small fragment of metal swarf in the missile jettison switch. The turbulence after take-off had moved it so that it completed the circuit to the inboard units.

'The very bent missiles were recovered after some considerable effort from a field of carrots just off the end of the runway!'

The Javelin referred to above was in fact a new version of the Javelin, XH898, a Mark 9. Beginning late in 1960, Mark 7s were being flown away from the Squadron in small groups back to the Manufacturers for extensive up-grading, and then returned to No.25. The result was a somewhat improved aircraft.

The older Mk.7 had been found to lack manœuvrability at 50,000ft, this was remedied by adding re-heat nozzles to the engines to provide an additional thrust of some 1,300lb at heights above 20,000ft. In due course almost all the Javelin 7s underwent this modification, and were returned during the summer of 1961. Meanwhile, Wg Cdr Cook had continued to command the Squadron until January 1960 when his place was taken by Wg Cdr John Walton, AFC, and it was under his leadership that No.25 settled down once more with the Mark 9s.

Close-up view of the Javelin FAW.9's tail, showing the Squadron markings and the re-heat nozzles which characterised the Mk.9.
(Photo: courtesy of Ken Foster)

THE SOVIET THREAT FROM THE NORTH

During 1961, NATO and Royal Navy ships, exercising in the North Sea, were found to be shadowed by Russian aircraft, and it was realised that, in reaching that area, they were outflanking the Norwegian radar and maritime reconnaissance patrols by flying far to the north before changing to a southerly course which would bring them over the seas between the north of Scotland and southern Norway. As the Soviet Union now evidently possessed maritime reconnaissance aircraft of considerable range, other similar aircraft would pose a major threat to the British Isles.

With the onset of this threat, and the likelihood that such long-range Soviet bombers would, like the Vulcans and Victors of Bomber Command, employ long-range stand-off missiles, the Ministry of Defence undertook a major redeployment of the RAF's air defences, with much greater emphasis being placed on manned fighters based in the north of the British Isles, in particular Leuchars and later Lossiemouth. Moreover, the short range defence of the vital V-Bomber bases, grouped in England's East Midlands –which represented Britain's contribution to the Western Nations' deterrent against a possible nuclear war, constantly threatened by the Soviet Union – would soon be undertaken by ground-to-air missiles, sited throughout Yorkshire, Lincolnshire and Norfolk.

Accordingly, No.25 Squadron, with its Javelins, left Waterbeach on 23rd October 1961 and flew to Leuchars in Fife, Scotland, thereby renewing its original Caledonian association for the first time since the Squadron's formation in 1915.

At once the Javelins' crews undertook increased QRA duties, as well as long patrol sorties on the look-out for Soviet aircraft engaged in covert ELINT gathering and maritime reconnaissance, a task for which the Javelin was far from ideal, largely on account of its short-range gun and missile armament. Moreover, no long-range in-flight refuelling tanker aircraft were regularly available (even had No.25's Javelins been equipped for this).

The Squadron persisted in these duties at Leuchars for a year as rumours abounded that its stay in the north was soon to end. The axe fell on 30th November 1962 when No.25 was disbanded, and this time almost every member, air- and groundcrew alike, received postings – not to a single Squadron or unit (as would have been the case had another Squadron been re-numbered 25), but distributed to other Squadrons in the RAF.

Yet, on the very next day, a new No.25 Squadron came into being at North Coates on the coast of Lincolnshire, now to be equipped with Bloodhound ground-to-air missiles. The age-old air defence rôle continued in being and the transfer of the Squadron Standard to North Weald was evidence that the traditions were to be maintained – only the nature of its weapons and those who delivered them were to change.

CHAPTER 11

The Bloodhound Era, 1962-1989

Light the Blue Touchpaper and . . .

THE SUEZ CRISIS, WHICH OCCURRED in the autumn of 1956 precipitated something of a long-term crisis at home in Britain. What had started in the minds of some politicians as an aggravating incident, demanding little more than gunboat diplomacy, quickly emerged as a premeditated test of the West's true attitude towards the Middle East, and in particular the Arab world. Egypt, under Colonel Gamil Nasser, unilaterally declared shipping restrictions in the Suez Canal, in contravention of long-standing treaties, an action that unified the Arab nations not only against the new state of Israel but against the Imperial countries of Western Europe, notably Great Britain and France.

Ultimata were announced against Egypt to rescind the Canal restrictions and, when these were ignored, Britain and France sailed a naval task force through the Mediterranean to seize and take control of the Suez Canal. At the same time the RAF deployed two Hunter fighter squadrons in Cyprus and moved Canberra light bombers and Valiant four-jet strategic bombers to Malta.

Against a background of implied opposition by the United States of America (influenced by a Jewish lobby that feared for the safety of Israel), the task force landed troops at the northern end of the Canal and these began to advance southwards. The landings were covered by British and French land and carrier-based air forces, while Canberras and Valiants attacked Cairo, mainly by night. The Egyptian Air Force, equipped with Russian MiG-15s and Il-28s, however, avoided air combat, preferring to withdraw to bases in the south of the country, its government claiming the British and French attack was unprovoked. At a critical stage in the advance southwards, the US government began exerting diplomatic pressure in London and Paris to halt the military operation. The result was a humiliation for the Western forces, which had no alternative but to withdraw – without achieving the object of securing a guarantee of freedom of passage by international shipping through the Canal.

Though losses in men and materiel were negligible, the

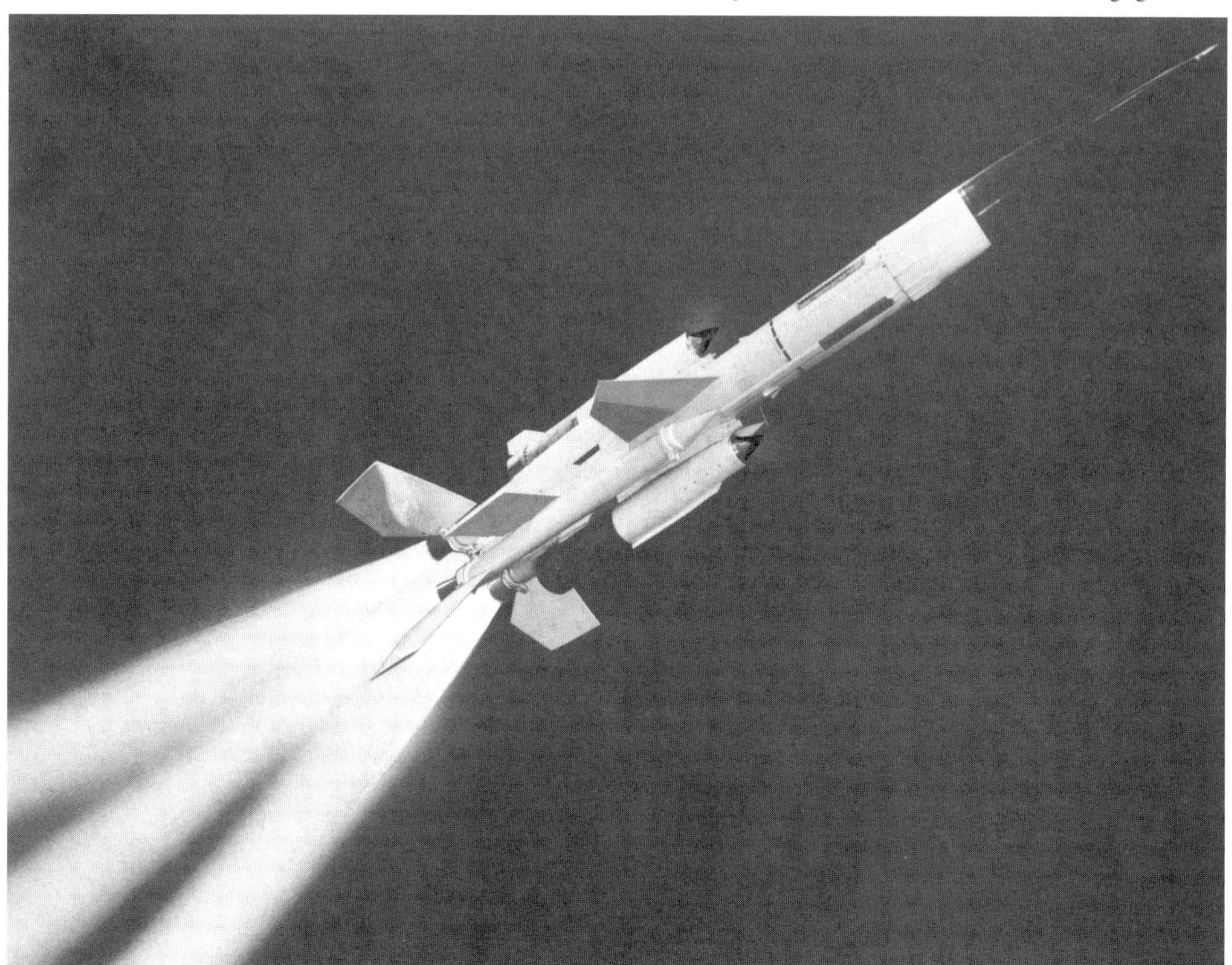

The Bloodhound surface-to-air missile, as it equipped No.25 (Fighter) Squadron, having been precipitated into service as the result of the ill-conceived 1957 Defence White Paper, thereby causing lasting damage to the British Aircraft Industry by effectively stifling the long-term research and development of advanced fast-jet military aircraft in Britain. (Photo: via Wg Cdr M R S Cunningham, MBE)

A general view of No.25 Squadron at North Coates with Bloodhound Mk.2s on their launchers.

cost of mounting the operation was disproportionately high. What was more disturbing for the RAF was that, in comparison with the naval and ground forces, the air operations had failed to influence the result of the campaign. Seen in the context of the RAF's principal purpose in war – that of providing an effective contribution to NATO's defence of Western Europe against a possible attack by the Soviet Union, the whole strategy of the Royal Air Force came under searching scrutiny, not only by the Service Chiefs themselves but by the British Government.

When the cost of up-grading the Services to the status of a major World power was contemplated, both Government and Treasury retreated. Priorities underwent radical change, with the emphasis being placed on the growing strength of the V-bomber force – armed with British nuclear weapons. (The early tests of these weapons had already begun, and it was expected that these would become available before the end of the 1950s).

For RAF Fighter Command, the results of early post-war parsimony (by the Government and Treasury of those years), the damage had been done. Britain was dropping further and further behind the Americans, equipped with transonic Hunters, and still awaiting the Lightning supersonic fighter, already compromised by eight-year-old technology. There *were* options available, of which some commentators favoured the purchase of modern fighter aircraft from America, in order that the British aircraft industry might acquire the technology to develop aircraft with which to catch up. This was anathema to the Treasury and aircraft industry alike, with the result that the British Government issued its ill-advised, and fundamentally flawed Defence White Paper early in 1957. By setting its aim as the progressive replacement of the manned interceptor fighter by surface-to-air missiles (SAMs), its aim was militarily pacifist. Fighter defences in the West would eventually become the responsibility of the American elements of NATO. The SAMs would be deployed solely for the air defence of the V-bomber stations, until a British

The personnel of No.25 Squadron in the mid-1960s. Of the 79 Squadron members here, 17 are commissioned officers, of whom 12 are aircrew, either serving a ground tour or transferred to the General Duties (Fighter Control) Branch.

(Photo: via Wg Cdr M R S Cunningham, MBE)

intermediate-range ballistic missile (Blue Streak) could be brought into service. It was specifically stated that only the Lightning would continue development and equip the Squadrons of Fighter Command, until it eventually became outdated and retired. The aircraft was to be regarded as an 'all-weather' fighter, thereby replacing the Meteor, Venom and Javelin night fighters.

Over the next half-dozen years Squadrons equipped with Meteor NF.14s and Venom NF.3s were either disbanded or re-equipped with the Javelin – itself now defined as an all-weather fighter.

The flaws in the Sandys White Paper soon became apparent. Britain still possessed responsibilities overseas, and the Lightning proved not only difficult to operate efficiently in the all-weather rôle but slow to achieve its hoped-for performance. The British medium-range SAM, the Bloodhound, was strictly of 'first generation' technology. It was not then, in 1957, realised that the entire gamut of missile technology was fast-moving, and therefore extremely costly to keep abreast of either the Americans or Russians.

• • •

The 50th Anniversary of the formation of No.25 (Fighter) Squadron occurred on 25th September 1965. A parade was mounted on the 28th at which the salute was taken by Air Marshal Sir Douglas Morris, KCB, CBE, DSO, DFC, A-O-C-in-C Fighter Command. The Squadron Standard was trooped, and the Colour Party, seen here, included Flt Lt (later Sqn Ldr) C Cureton, the Standard bearer.

(Photo: via Wg Cdr M R S Cunningham, MBE)

No.25 (Fighter) Squadron was fortunate in not being one of those to be disbanded in the short or medium term. In 1957 it had already been scheduled to be re-equipped with Javelins, and these were retained until 1962, when the blow fell. The Squadron might have retained its Javelins had the aircraft's attrition rate been lower elsewhere in the Service and production of the aircraft continued. As it was, with a number of overseas commitments (notably at Singapore), the last Javelins were withdrawn from service with No.60 Squadron six years later.

Despite the forthright terms of the 1957 Defence White Paper, the first British surface-to-air missiles were relatively slow to enter operational service, and although the first Fighter Command Squadron to be equipped received its weapons in 1958, No.25 had to wait four years, hoping against hope that it would escape the axe, a hope kept alive by the increasing realisation that the White Paper had been premature, to say the least. Ironically, only about a month after the Squadron had settled into its Bloodhound base, it became all too clear that a defence against enemy bombers relying on SAM was a fool's errand – the more so as year by year the Lightning fell further and further behind the Americans, French, Swedish and indeed all those air forces that had equipped with, or ordered the F-104 Starfighter.

No.25 Squadron closed as a Javelin squadron on 31st October 1962 at Leuchars, but re-appeared at North Coates, a former operational RAF flying Station, on the Lincolnshire coast the following day, destined to be equipped with the Bristol-Ferranti Bloodhound Mk.1, thereby becoming one of fifteen Fighter Command Air Defence Missile Squadrons (ADMS), which formed a surface-to-air missile shield whose primary task was to defend the RAF's V-bomber bases in Lincolnshire and Yorkshire against possible Soviet air attack from across the North Sea.

THE BLOODHOUND MISSILE.

The 25ft long Bloodhound Mk.1 weapon was originally developed under the codename *Yellow Duster*. It was launched from semi-mobile launchers and was boosted to Mach 2 by four rocket-boost Gosling motors, at which speed two Bristol-Siddeley Thor ramjets took over for the flight towards the target. being directed by high-powered Metro-Vick three-dimensional radars and AEI target-illuminating radars, the nuclear warhead being detonated proximity fuse.

Beginning in 1964, the Bloodhound Mk.1 was replaced by the Mk.2, which also equipped No.25 Squadron. This weapon was air transportable (by Argosy, and later Hercules aircraft) and was much less susceptible to countermeasures, employing continuous-wave radar in place of the former pulse radar.

THE SQUADRON.

On becoming a Bloodhound squadron, No.25 was commanded at the outset by Wg Cdr P G K Williamson, DFC (a former General Duties (Flying) officer) with an establishment of about 16 officers and some 70 NCOs and Other Ranks. The officers included three TIR (Target Illuminating Radar) commanders, adjutant, missile controllers and Technical Branch officers, while the NCOs and Other Ranks comprised mainly technicians, MT and catering personnel.

Each TIR worked with a Launch Control Post (LCP) and 'controlled' eight missile launchers, dispersed approximately 300 yards apart, being located around its radar/control tower. The Squadron thus comprised sixteen missiles on their launchers, each with one reload missile. Other than this tower and the launchers, there were no others buildings, the workshops, missile stores, Messes, MT and other sections being located well away from the launch site. Being open to the elements at all times, and subject to frequent operational checks and simulated firing, the Bloodhounds underwent regular examination, involving de-mounting the missile and substituting a reload weapon, while the former underwent detailed system checks and inspection, this operation often being used to practice quick re-arming of the launcher. Every so often replacement missiles would be delivered from the maintenance unit to enable major overhauls and component replacement to be carried out.

At the time No.25 Squadron joined the Bloodhound network, there were four area Type 82 radars, one of which was also sited at North Coates, which included a Tactical Control Centre (TCC), its task being to assess any incoming threat, and to allocate it to one of its Missile Squadrons; these were sited at Dunholme Lodge, Woodhall Spa, and No.25 – co-located at North Coates. However, soon after No.25 came 'on line', the Type 82 radars were phased out of service, and the Master Radar Stations at Patrington in Yorkshire, and Bawdsey in Suffolk, assumed the task of allocating targets to the eleven squadrons (equipped with a total of 352 Bloodhounds) which then constituted the RAF's point defence system in the United Kingdom.

Ironically (for No.25 Squadron) no sooner had this re-

50th Anniversary Luncheon,
No.25 (Fighter) Squadron – September 1965, North Coates.
Back Row, left to right: *Wg Cdr K Cook (1958-1960); Wg Cdr R W Leggett (1950-1952); Air Cdre C M Wight-Boycott, CBE, DSO AND BAR; Wg Cdr J Cameron Cox (1954-1955); Sqn Ldr R T Goucher, DFC (1945-1946).*
Centre Row, left to right: *Wg Cdr J H Walton, AFC (1960-1961); Air Vice-Marshal C E H Allen, CB, DFC (1919, served on, but did not command Squadron); Marshal of the Royal Air Force Sir William Dickson, GCB, KBE, DSO, AFC (1935-1936); Gp Capt A H Peck, DSO, MC (1923-1926); Wg Cdr J Singleton, DSO, DFC, AFC (1947-1948).*
Front Row, left to right: *Sqn Ldr M J Bridges (1964-1965); Sqn Ldr M R S Cunningham, MBE (1965-1966); Sqn Ldr D J Fowler, AFC (1963-1964).* (Photo: via Wg Cdr M R S Cunningham, MBE)

As part of RAF Swinderby's Battle of Britain annual display and Open Day in September 1966, No.25 Squadron, then deployed at North Coates (also in Lincolnshire), provided a quartet of Bloodhound Mk.2 SAMs, complete with their support and operations vehicles. Each missile was painted with the Squadron Badge just aft of the radar nose cone. (Photo: via Wg Cdr M R S Cunningham, MBE)

Group photo of No.25 Squadron technical personnel in Germany, taken during the 1970s.

(Photo: courtesy of No.25 (Fighter) Squadron)

allocation of target task to just two Master Radar Station been accomplished than it was realised that the Mk.1 Bloodhound system had already been rendered obsolete by the Soviet bomber threat, which now included stand-off weapons, not to mention fairly sophisticated electronic countermeasures capable of rendering the pulse radar ineffective. Accordingly the Bloodhound Mk.1 system began being phased out of service, No.25 Squadron being the first to be re-equipped with the Bloodhound Mk.2 system, still at North Coates, in October 1963.

The Mark 2 system that equipped No.25 Squadron employed the Type 86 ('Firelight') TIR with an air transportable wheeled control cabin, which could be carried by a transport aircraft without being dismantled (the Type 87 'Stingray' TIR, which equipped some other Squadrons, possessed a greater range, but had to be dismantled for air movement).

While other Mk.2 Bloodhound Squadrons began moving or forming overseas (Cyprus, Singapore and Malaysia), No.25 remained at North Coates, now with three Flights, until 1970, when it transferred to Germany, deploying its missile sites to Bruggen (A Flight), Wildenrath (B Flight) and Laarbruch (C Flight), with its headquarters at Bruggen. Each Flight possessed two Type 86 radars – -mounted on a 20ft tower for better low-looking – and eight missiles. This deployment remained in being for the remainder of the 1970s until the RAF Regiment began assuming the point defence rôle with Rapier missiles.

No.25 Squadron began returning to the United Kingdom when C Flight at Laarbruch became E Flight of No.85 Squadron at Wattisham in November 1981 – but then reverted to C Flight, No.25, once more in April 1983. HQ No.25 Squadron, together with B Flight, had returned to Britain, being established at Wyton, while A Flight was relocated at Barkston Heath in Lincolnshire – retaining their Type 86 radars, but reduced to six missiles per Flight.

Thus, with No.85 Squadron the only other Bloodhound unit in the United Kingdom, Britain's missile defence system comprised a total of 116 weapons at six locations (with at least a 100% reload ability). Then, in the mid-1980s, as foreign nations – which had purchased Bloodhounds – began to dismantle their missile networks and revert exclusively to manned fighters, Britain re-purchased large numbers of Bloodhounds, leading to plans for a major refurbishment and greater dependence on SAMs, it being intended to retain a Bloodhound-based defence system until at least the year 2006. However, closer costing of the work involved (coming at a time when the Soviet threat appeared to be diminishing) led to this plan being dropped and a decision to abandon the entire Bloodhound defence system. This began in July 1989 as No.25 Squadron at West Raynham started to run down and dispose of its equipment. It was not until the following month that a new Squadron, assembling at Leeming in Yorkshire with Tornado F.3 fighters, was officially confirmed as being the reincarnation of No.25 (Fighter) Squadron.

LIFE AS DOG HANDLERS

So much for the bare historical details, movements and technicalities of this twenty-eight year period in which the nature of No.25 Squadron's existence had strayed from the traditions which had been jealously nurtured for almost half a century.

Yet it must be stated here that No.25 Squadron was by no means the only former fighter squadron in the Royal Air Force to suffer what was regarded by many as the indignity of being 'grounded' – shot but not killed. A total of thirteen other well-known fighter squadrons had suffered similar fates; about half of them have since gone, perhaps forever.

Whether or not those Squadrons survived depended to a great extent on the care with which the officers involved were, or took the trouble to become, aware of their Squadrons' former traditions. No.25 Squadron was extremely fortunate in this, and its possession of a Standard, with Battle Honours won during the First World War, provided the evidence of a long tradition.

The first two years as a SAM squadron could scarcely be regarded as entertaining, for much of the time was spent in changing over to the Bloodhound Mk.2, a technical commitment that must have seemed hardly conducive to the outwardly visible evidence of a fine fighting tradition, but with the arrival of Sqn Ldr Russ Cunningham and the approach of the Squadron's 50th Anniversary, the opportunity presented itself to demonstrate that, when possible, No.25 could show itself to be aware of its long and distinguished history. In September 1965 the Squadron Standard was paraded at North Coates before the Air Officer Commanding-in-Chief, Fighter Command, Air Marshal Sir Douglas Morris, KCB, CBE, DSO, DFC, who took the Salute, and a luncheon was afterwards held in the Officers' Mess, attended by no fewer than a dozen former Commanding Officers, including Marshal of the Royal Air Force Sir William Dickson, GCB, KBE, DSO, AFC, as well as Sqn Ldr, later Wg Cdr Cunningham, MBE, the serving Commanding Officer at the time. Russ Cunningham was at pains to keep a record of the event as part of his own contribution to the Squadron's colourful history.

The Squadron was also able to display its wares to the public when, at the annual Battle of Britain Open Day at Swinderby in 1966, No.25 provided a Section of four Bloodhound 2s on their launchers, complete with their support equipment and vehicles. The Squadron Badge was emblazoned on each missile to emphasise the fact that this famous Squadron of the RAF was still, as it had been in the Battle of Britain, engaged in defending the United Kingdom from enemy air attack.

After the Squadron moved to Germany, with three Flights dispersed at different Royal Air Force Station, the nature of everyday life changed to some extent. For one thing, much of the training in identifying and tracking of aircraft involved commercial airliners, as it was realised that any surprise attack by the Soviet Union might well be launched by bombers flying 'commercially' along the recognised air lanes, while exercises by NATO air forces, after giving notice of the areas in which military aircraft would be flying, would be carefully tracked so that no opportunity could be taken by the Soviets to launch covert reconnaissance aircraft.

Equipment support in Germany was little different from that at home, although replacement Bloodhounds were frequently flown in Hercules transports to the airfields on which No.25's Flights were deployed, as was much support equipment. This procedure prompted the posting of a notice by a Squadron wisecrack, following accidental damage to one of the Hercules –

A Bloodhound Mk.2 on its launcher.
(Photo: courtesy of No.25 (Fighter) Squadron)

> *Question:* 'How do you know when a Herkybird is cooked?'
> *Answer:* 'Stick a fork-lift into it!'

Life for the Squadron in Germany was, as many a British Serviceman discovered, no great hardship, and the standards of living and Service amenities were, if anything, perceptibly better that in Britain, especially among the married personnel, although perhaps the operational pressures could be, and sometimes were, more demanding. The state of readiness was usually somewhat higher owing to the proximity of the potential enemy. Exercises involving the NATO air forces were more frequent, but hardships in the 1970s were not demanding.

When, eventually, the RAF Regiment, with its Rapiers, assumed the rôle of the Bloodhounds, and No.25 Squadron moved home, its arrival was tainted by future uncertainties, as explained above. Yet, after the reappearance of the Squadron in its traditional manned fighter rôle, and the creation of a Squadron Association – open to all past members of No.25 – it was noticeable that an agreeable number of past 'dog handlers' applied for membership and found a warm welcome (as well as sympathy, possibly interpreted as patronising) awaiting them! As time passed, it soon became evident that the Bloodhound had been, after all, just another type of aircraft. The Squadron's traditions were untarnished.

CHAPTER 12

Tornados in the 1990s

Like the Mosquito, they spell them without the 'e'

WHEN (AND WHY) NO.25 (FIGHTER) SQUADRON WAS RE-FORMED

No.25 (Fighter) Squadron re-formed one minute after the dissolution of the Bloodhound Squadron on 2nd July 1989. It had been nearly thirty years since the Squadron had flown fighters. Anyone who had been with the old Squadron and had not flown fighters since the 'Javelin' days, would have been awe-struck by the extraordinary changes that had come about in the meantime, both in the increase in the complexity of modern technology and by the operational procedures that had come about in the meantime.

However, before describing the manner in which the Fighter squadron had changed, it should be explained that, in the instance of No.25, the reincarnation was not immediate and clear-cut. To begin with, while it is accurate to record that the Squadron was re-formed on 2nd July 1989, only the new Commanding Officer (and perhaps an adjutant) actually arrived at Leeming in North Yorkshire on that day, thereby representing the 'arrival of personnel'. There were no aircraft, and, indeed, the *identity of the new Squadron* had yet to be decided 'higher up'. These things took time.

Slowly, but surely, a 'squadron' began to take shape. A Panavia Tornado F.3 aeroplane was taken on charge by the unit, as were a growing number of personnel, including a member, presumably in the trade of Fitter (Exterior Decorator). The Commanding Officer, of whom more later, anxious to know something of the history and tradition of the Squadron which he commanded – was prevented from having Squadron code insignia painted on his Tornado, as required by RAF regulations, simply because he still was in ignorance of the Squadron's identity. The procedure in vogue required that Tornados in squadron service displayed a two-letter identity code on their empennage, the first letter denoting the Squadron, and the second its identity on the Squadron. The new Unit, being the sixth Tornado fighter squadron to be formed, would logically carry a code beginning 'F', and, for the reason that its identity on the squadron was somewhat academic, the CO, at no more than random, chose 'K' as the second letter. And this device was applied forthwith. As the resulting device could be interpreted as indecorous, depending on the broadmindedness of the viewer, the order came down from on high for the second letter to be removed. The CO accordingly substituted a large question mark. While no offence could possibly be taken at this, it must have appealed to a very senior Sense of Humour and History, and left no doubt as to the choice of Squadron identity. With thoughts turning to the 1930s, No.25 (Fighter) Squadron was inevitably that choice. And so, at a stroke, a great tradition was perpetuated.

At first sight, the Squadron's operational base appeared as clusters of concrete buildings, apparently dispersed in haphazard groups, and dominated by a dozen or so hardened aircraft shelters. Gone were the brick or wooden 'huts' nestling around huge hangars whose basic design was at least half a century old. One might be lucky to spot even a single aircraft in the open, unless there was a flying commitment in progress; otherwise the Tornados were enclosed in their shelters.

On entering the 'traditional' crewroom, one could hardly fail to be aware of the ranks and ages of No.25's aircrew (pilots and navigators). All were of at least Flight Lieutenant rank, with no fewer than eight squadron leaders (nine with the senior Squadron Technical Officer). On enquiry one would learn that all had completed at least two 'fast jet' tours prior to coming to No.25, some having flown Lightnings, Phantoms, Harriers, Buccaneers, Hawks and Jaguars on other squadrons. Most would have completed a course on the Tornado Conversion Unit, some (almost certainly the Flight Commanders) would probably have already served with a Tornado squadron, and most would have accumulated at least 1,000 hours on fast jets, either in Britain or Germany. They were, by any criteria, a highly experienced assembly of pilots and navigators, already well-versed in air defence procedures and tactics. One or two of the pilots had already amassed 2,000 fast jet hours!

As was the normal practice in the RAF, pilots and navigators of other air forces served on exchange postings with No.25 Squadron, and as will be seen from the accompanying list, it included a pilot of the Fleet Air Arm and another from the Royal Netherlands Air Force. During the next decade Americans, Danes and Germans followed this practice. It might also have surprised those, who were ignorant of more recent changes in the 'customs' of the Service, to discover that No.25 Squadron was commanded by a Navigator, rather than a Pilot (in fact Wg Cdr Mick Martin had qualified as a Pilot early in his service, but had then gone on to train as a Navigator). In due course, women pilots and navigators of the RAF also served on No.25 – a phenomenon that caused some surprise (somewhat illogically in the new age of equal opportunities) among visitors to the Squadron of older generations of males. Before a decade had passed, a No.25 Squadron Tornado would be crewed by two young women.

In short, the past quarter century had brought an entirely new professionalism to Strike Command, rendered essential in the environment of Cold War. No longer could Western nations afford to abide by the 'Ten Year Rule' syndrome – 'We'll be alright if the balloon goes up'. By the skin of British teeth, and by an extraordinary sequence of circumstances (certainly not by forward planning), Britain's armed forces had achieved an astonishing *tour de force* in the Falkland Islands conflict of the early 1980s, principally by the gallantry, determination and professionalism of those forces, but also to a series of entirely fortuitous circumstances. The Falkland Islands conflict, by its very nature and outcome (and despite being no more than a minor incident on the world stage), demonstrated unequivocally that expert training, professionalism and very high quality of technology is a necessary burden of the national exchequer, so long as the nation retains international responsibilities for helping to maintain world-wide peaceful co-existence. Alas, the world has still not discovered how to deal with dictatorships and totalitarianism.

THE TORNADO F.3

When the Tornado F.3 joined No.25 Squadron in 1989, the aircraft was still relatively new in the Royal Air Force – although the strike (bomber) version, GR.1, had been in service for more than half a decade.

Representing the fruits of technology already more than fifteen years old, the Tornado – originally referred to as the Multi-Rôle Combat Aircraft (MRCA) – was first conceived as a replacement for the Lockheed F-104 Starfighter which, in the 1960s, equipped half a dozen NATO air forces. By attempting to produce a common airframe capable of being adapted as a fighter, strike and reconnaissance aircraft, it was hoped to reduce development and production costs by amortisation over much larger production orders, as well as to spread the production throughout the NATO nations. As the planned development costs emerged, the majority of participating nations withdrew – as well they might, since the Tornado was soon seen to be a true replacement, not for the F-104, but for the Canberra (which in fact only equipped the RAF among the NATO nations!).

Thus during the late 1960s, only Britain, Germany and Italy continued to participate in the MRCA programme, which at that time was conceived primarily as a tactical strike/reconnaissance aircraft with a Mach 2 potential employing variable-geometry (the so-called swing-wing, then a favourite configuration among aircraft manufacturers).

By the end of the 1970s production was in motion in Britain, Germany and Italy, and several prototypes were flying in these countries. Thus far, the concept of shared production between them had proved surprisingly successful. British Aerospace Corporation at Warton built the front fuselage, the tail unit and the engine installation, Turbo Union at Bristol (Rolls-Royce) supplied the engines, RB199 turbofans. MBB of Munich contributed the centre fuselage and Aeritalia of Turin supplied the wings. Each country developed its own weapons and weapons systems, according to their particular requirements.

However, before any of these strike-reconnaissance Tornados had been delivered, the RAF had for some years been endeavouring to replace the old Lightning fighter (in effect employing 25-year-old technology that was, by the mid-1970s, wholly outdated by aircraft in service with a score of world air forces). For Britain to have resorted to importing up-to-date American fighters to replace the Lightning would have destroyed all remaining vestiges of an indigenous aircraft industry at a stroke and created widespread unemployment, with all the political ramifications that would follow. Indeed, without an indigenous ability to manufacture its own military aircraft would render the United Kingdom helpless in the event of a war in Europe.

Pursuing the widely accepted creed that the modern fighter is primarily no more than an efficient, secure and reliable vehicle, capable of carrying a wide range of high performance weapons and their associated detection and discharge systems, within an overall national defence system, the Tornado was unilaterally selected by Britain as its foremost air defence fighter. While the adaptation of the basic Tornado airframe and engine proved to be a fairly straightforward task, the development of the new AI Mk.24 Foxhunter long-range target air-intercept radar was dogged by difficulties that had not been anticipated. In its original production state, this radar was to have been capable of detecting and tracking approaching targets at a range of 120 miles, with a look-down/shoot down capability. The aircraft would use an ECM-resistant data link system as a necessary element of the Joint Tactical Information Distribution System (JTIDS) to gain access to target data provided by Airborne Early Warning and Control (AWACS) aircraft. The latter was intended to be a modified version of the British Aerospace Nimrod, the AEW.3, but when the avionics of this aircraft repeatedly failed to meet the operational requirements, the RAF opted to purchase a small number of Boeing E-3A Sentry AEW aircraft for the RAF, and the Nimrod programme was cancelled.

The Tornado first appeared as the F.2 in service with No.229 Operational Conversion Unit at Coningsby in November 1984 but, owing to continuing problems with the AI Mk.24, these only carried ballast in the nose, and remained exclusively trainers. The first operational version, the Tornado F.3, first joined No.29 Squadron, also at Coningsby, in April 1987, followed by Nos.11 and 23 Squadrons at Leeming, No.43 Squadron at Leuchars in July 1989, and No.25 Squadron at Leeming in September 1989. (No.111 Squadron had been scheduled to re-equip early in 1989, but did not dispose of its Phantoms and receive Tornados at Leuchars for another year).

Within a week of receiving its fighter establishment during September, No.25 pilots flew a tight but immaculate six-ship formation as if to celebrate the Squadron's return to interceptor fighters (perhaps even after a glance back at No.25's pre-war speciality), but also providing evidence of the unusually high level of fast-jet experience possessed by the Squadron's original Tornado crews. Under the command of Wing Commander Martin, the Squadron was declared operational, assuming its place in No.11 Group's Quick Reaction Alert (QRA) roster. At other times its operational rôle was its share of long-duration standing patrols, far-out over the North Sea, on watch for Soviet long-range aircraft engaged in intelligence gathering over international waters.

A few words should be said here about Wg Cdr Mick Martin. No stranger visiting No.25 Squadron during the few years following the Squadron's reincarnation at Leeming could fail to be unaware of the apparently instinctive and wholehearted respect held by all member of the Squadron for their CO. It seems that Martin had done his homework in coming to terms with No.25's history, and had gone to some trouble to instil the importance of a pride in the Squadron and its inheritance. That is not to say that he fostered any sort of élitism, but simply that he and the Squadron had a reputation to live up to. And the Squadron responded wholeheartedly. To become 'the best' would take time and effort and, with the galaxy of experience among the Squadron's personnel, there would be little excuse if that end was not achieved in good time.

Someone in the Ministry of Defence must have correctly assessed Mick Martin as being 'just the man' to create the new Squadron in the image of the old – possibly the more so on account of the unintended assistance described above. It is difficult to imagine that on leaving No.25 at the end of his tour that he would not have continued on his way to very senior rank. But it was not to be. Instead, he opted to retire from the Service to accept an appointment in the avionics industry. Asked about this difficult decision he replied that he could not visualise any posting or appointment that could ever match the quality of life that he had enjoyed with the Squadron, nor the mutual respect which had existed during those formative years. He felt that any subsequent appointment within the Service might well come as an unbearable anti-climax. The Royal Air Force was poorer on the day he left No.25. Some six years later he was to become the Squadron Association's President, an appointment that resulted from a ballot of the Association's membership – such was the man's dynamism that it had also been widely recognised and appreciated by the Squadron's *past* members. (See Appendix 8).

All this is not to say that the Commanding Officers who have followed in Mick Martin's footsteps have been in any way less auspicious; indeed all appear to have had the same personal and professional influence throughout the Squadron. And it says much for the Royal Air Force that it can spot such officers when they are required. The fact that all Britain's fighting Services appear able to prepare such officers speaks volumes for the sort of young men determined on a career with the Colours.

OFFICERS ON SQUADRON AT RE-FORMATION 1989-1990

Commanding Officer: Wg Cdr A M Martin

A Flight	*B Flight*
Sqn Ldr I McG G Howe	Sqn Ldr G M Viney
Sqn Ldr P Barrett	Sqn Ldr S P Ayers
Sqn Ldr M C Johnson	Sqn Ldr R A Cole
Sqn Ldr A L Parker	Sqn Ldr F J O'Flynn
Flt Lt M Bennett	Sqn Ldr M Swan
Flt Lt R W Birtwistle	Flt Lt P J Beach
Flt Lt I C Black	Flt Lt P Boyle
Flt Lt M R Cobb	Flt Lt J E Brown
Flt Lt R M Goodrum	Flt Lt I H Cassely
Flt Lt J P Hutchings	Flt Lt S Clayton
Flt Lt R Jones	Capt S Huf, RNETHAF
Flt Lt D Morrison	Flt Lt A Neill
Flt Lt J C Prescott	Flt Lt A McK Pemberton
Flt Lt R G Price	Flt Lt P J Roberts
Flt Lt P J Siddall	Flt Lt P J Shenton
Flt Lt A J Simmons	Flt Lt R Walters-Morgan
Flt Lt T J Taylor	Flt Lt R A Watts
Sub-Lt N G Paine, RN	Flt Lt E G Wright

Engineering Officers:
Sqn Ldr S P Sanderson
Flt Lt A W Balderstone
Flt Lt N Matthews
W/Off R Hall

£190 million-worth of Tornados in diamond-nine formation pays its respects to RAF Leeming in traditional 25 Squadron manner, being also the last flight in a Tornado by Wg Cdr Mick Martin on 20th November 1992 before leaving the Squadron. His aircraft was flown by Sqn Ldr Mark Swan (who at the time of writing is a Group Captain at the Ministry of Defence).

(Photo: courtesy of No.25 (Fighter) Squadron)

A fine sense of history! One of a set of postage stamps issued in the year 2000 by the Guernsey Post Office to commemorate the 60th anniversary of the Battle of Britain. It depicts a Blenheim night fighter ZK-P (complete with radar aerial under the wing) of No.25 Squadron over St. Peter Port. The Channel Islands were the only sovereign territories of the British Isles on which the German Wehrmacht *set foot, and suffered five long years of ruthless enemy occupation.* (Photo: via Peter Williams)

Armed with four AIM-9 Sidewinder SRAAMs, a Tornado of No.25 Squadron breaks the 'surly bonds of Earth' as a setting sun silhouettes it against approaching night.

Javelin FAW.9 XH767 'A' of No.25 Squadron around 1960. (Photo: via Ray Sturtivant)

The first Tornado, ZE858, delivered to No.25 (Fighter) Squadron at Leeming in 1989. As told in the text, although the new CO had arrived, the identity of the new Squadron had not been announced, and some ingenuity had to be exercised in fin identity emblems, including the letter denoting the individual letter marking and a Squadron fin emblem. (Photo: Wg Cdr A M Martin)

The 75th Anniversary Tornado, ZE838, in its early 'muted' scheme (with Battle Honours on the side of the nose), taken on 25th September 1990 (the actual anniversary). All ranks gathered round the aircraft to raise the elbow and drink the Squadron's good health. Mick Martin is slightly right of centre, in front, wearing a black leather jacket over his flying overalls. Only about half the Squadron was present, the other half being detached to the Persian Gulf during Desert Shield. (Photo: courtesy of No.25 (Fighter) Squadron)

A three-quarter rear view of ZE203 'A'. (Photo: Francis K Mason collection)

Within a week of being re-equipped with the Tornado F.3 in 1989, No.25 Squadron put up this tight six-ship formation from Leeming; the aircraft are painted with the Squadron's traditional black and silver bars on their fins. In little over a year the Squadron provided Strike Command's solo aerobatic display crew. (Photo: courtesy of No.25 (Fighter) Squadron)

November 1991, and No.25 Squadron was sunning itself on armament detachment to Akrotiri, Cyprus. This was an unusual sight with all nine Tornados lined up on the hardstanding – with not a hardened aircraft shelter in sight. If there was one characteristic detrimental to the elegance of the Tornado, it was the exhaust staining at the base of the fin, aft of the discharge vent.

(Photo: Wg Cdr A M Martin)

When under stand-by orders for likely detachment overseas, all Tornados had their Squadron identity letter obliterated on the fin, leaving only the aircraft's own identity letter. This photo was taken in 1993, prior to detachment to Gioia del Colle in south-west Italy for operations over Bosnia. Note the very large ferry fuel tanks under the wings, and the hardened aircraft shelter in the background.

(Photo: Francis K Mason collection)

Another aircraft, ZE982 'P', awaiting the detachment to Italy. Unlike the Tornado GR1s, which fought in the Gulf War, the fighter squadrons refrained from applying ad hoc decorative devices on the exterior of their aircraft.

(Photo: Francis K Mason collection)

Nine Tornados up from Leeming; all the crews are of No.25 Squadron, but the aircraft on the extreme left of the photo has been borrowed from No.11 Squadron, as disclosed by its fin marking. (Photo: courtesy of No.25 (Fighter) Squadron)

A Tornado F.3 of No.25 (Fighter) Squadron in its hardened shelter at Leeming during the 1990s. These shelters are equipped to enable all first-line servicing, system checking, re-arming and fuelling to be carried out under cover – a pair of Skyflash MRAAMs (the Tornado's primary armament) can be seen on their cradles on the extreme left and right of the photo. The sliding doors at the rear of the shelter allow engine starting and running, thereby reducing the time before take-off. Crews on standby area also accommodated within the shelters, which are also proof against all but direct hits from enemy weapons and can be sealed against nuclear fallout.
(Photo: Wg Cdr A M Martin)

Close-up of the tail section of ZE858. (Photo: Wg Cdr A M Martin)

ZE858 with all fin markings now according to the book. (Photo: Wg Cdr A M Martin)

The 75th Anniversary Tornado, ZE838, with the final version of tail insignia flown late in 1990. This formed the basis of the Display Tornado's livery in 1991. (Photo: Wg Cdr A M Martin)

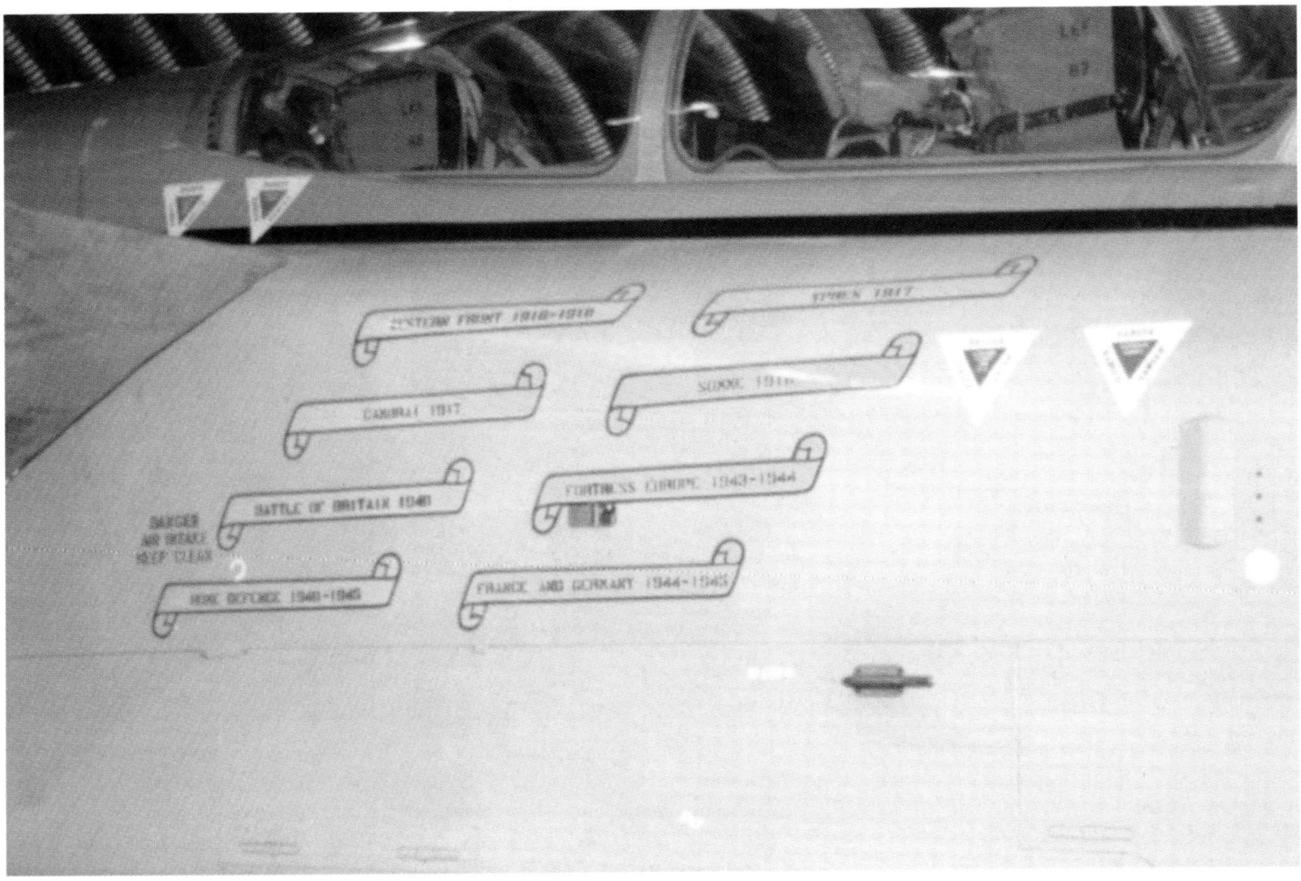

The Squadron Battle Honours (those that were permitted to be emblazoned on the current Squadron Standard) as painted on the nose of the Anniversary Tornado, ZE838. (Photo: Wg Cdr A M Martin)

A diamond-nine of No.25 Squadron makes a decorous but noisy pass 'near' RAF Station, Leeming, studiously avoiding buildings of authority!

(Photo: Wg Cdr Andy Dey)

A group photograph taken at Flying Training School in 1929, showing Airmen Flying Trainees during the newly introduced scheme to enable Other Ranks to transfer from Ground Trades to become NCO pilots. Two pilots shown here, Jock Ross in the centre, and Max Upton on his left, became prominent pilots on No.25 (Fighter) Squadron during the next two years, both later being commissioned. Jock stated that the other three trainee pilots in this photo all completed the course successfully and all gave valuable service in later years, and all were keen sportsmen.

(Photo: The late Sqn Ldr Jock Ross)

Jock Ross in his 90th year while attending a Squadron Association Reunion with No.25 Squadron at Leeming in the late 1990s. His sharp wit, keen memory and mobility astounded everyone, even two hours after midnight.

(Photo: 'T')

25TH SEPTEMBER 1990
Seventy-five years ago on this date, No.25 Squadron had been formed at Montrose in Scotland and, as far as can be ascertained, is the oldest Squadron in the Royal Air Force to have served on every day since its original formation. This is not to say that the Squadron has not been disbanded on half a dozen occasions, but on each occasion the Squadron has re-formed on the following day. The Service practice is to disband a Squadron with effect from 23.59hrs and form or re-form a Squadron with effect from 00.00hrs on the following day. There is an old Service chestnut that suggests that a soldier, sailor or airman may transgress during the sixty seconds before midnight and maybe escape retribution because, it has been argued that, as that single minute does not exist in the Service, the villain does not belong to any Unit, and therefore cannot be in the Service. It is unlikely that this hypothesis has ever been put to the test!

About a dozen other Squadrons, which had been formed before 25th September 1915, and were in existence in 1990, had each celebrated their own 75th anniversary by application of 'birthday clothes' – a distinctive colour scheme – to one of their aircraft, and this aircraft would be selected to visit public air displays at home and overseas as a symbol of pride in their achievements during three-quarters of a century. No.25 Squadron conformed to this practice, but then went one better when one of its Tornado crews, Flight Lieutenants Archie Neill (pilot) and Jim Brown (navigator) were selected as Strike Command's Tornado display crew, their aircraft being tastefully liveried in the Squadron's black and silver colours for a large number of set-piece aerobatic displays throughout the country.

THE GULF WAR
No.25 (Fighter) Squadron had been flying Tornados for less than a year when Iraqi forces invaded neighbouring Kuwait, a relatively small, but strategically important oil-producing state, which was in effect under United Nations protection. An ultimatum was served on the Iraqi government for the withdrawal of the invaders, and a multi-national military build-up, Operation *Granby*, began in Saudi Arabia, in case the ultimatum should be ignored. Although the United States of America contributed by far the largest proportion of this build-up, Britain assembled the second largest, sending army, naval and air force contingents.

Be that as it may, such was the massive build up by the USAF, US Navy and Marine Corps in the Gulf theatre, RAF Tornado fighters were not deployed in the forward combat zone, being tasked to fly Combat Air Patrols primarily over the Gulf itself, keeping watch for any air activity by the Iraqi air force on their long-range (*sic*) search radar so that interception by American fighters could be effected. (This was widely interpreted as a political decision for the USA, to be seen as justifying the enormous cost of deploying such strength; it cannot have been related to specific technical or tactical considerations.)

No.25 Squadron was not yet fully equipped for hot climate operations and a number of modifications still remained to be completed to its weapons system. The first Tornado F.3s to arrive in the Gulf were therefore aircraft from Nos.5, 29 and 43, which operated together as a 'Composite' squadron, first flying CAPs along the Kuwaiti/Saudi border on 12th August 1990 to bolster the Saudis' air defence network.

Meanwhile, at home, No.25 Squadron's crews underwent a work-up process as their aircraft were up-graded to a level known as Improved Stage 1 Plus F.3s, to allow reduced base heights and introducing night vision goggles (NVG). The first aircraft and crew accompanied twelve aircraft of No.29 Squadron's B Flight to Dhahran. Other aircraft made the journey out later and continued to fly CAPs, until 10th January 1991, but without threat from Iraqi aircraft.

A SHORT OVERSEAS VISIT
It was in 1991 that the eye of someone at the Ministry of Defence or the Records Office, whose job it is to scan the pages of the Air Force List periodically, was caught by the name of an Air Commodore who was approaching his 100th birthday. A quick check on this Officer's Service Records showed that he had commanded a Squadron in the RAF over half a century earlier. 'Daddy' Probyn, of Hawkinge fame, was now domiciled in Kenya in comfortable old-age retirement. What is more someone, who was aware that No.25 Squadron was still in being, and still flying fighters, caused this intelligence to be transmitted to the Squadron at Leeming.

In good time it was suggested that the present commanding incumbent might consider paying a semi-official visit to 'Daddy' on behalf of the Royal Air Force to help him to celebrate the event and demonstrate that he had not been forgotten by those who help to carry on the traditions which were being fostered all those years ago.

Accordingly Mick Martin and another officer flew out to Nairobi, compliments of the Ministry of Defence, to attend the celebrations. It was a pleasant surprise to find that waiting for them was another old member of the Squadron, also a well-known member of the No.25 Squadron Association, none other than one 'Dick' Whittingham, who acted as assistant host to the visitors. It transpired that 'Daddy' Probyn had, until very recently continued his old pastime of private flying, and had even built his own private aircraft in which he had done a good deal of flying. They found him is good fettle, though becoming increasingly frail. Alas, he was to die less than two years later.

Mention of 'Dick' Whittingham would not be complete without the aside that this elderly gentleman has, until only recently, attended almost every 25 Squadron reunion in the United Kingdom, travelling from Kenya, sometimes as part of a world tour of his other former squadrons. He is a perky octogenarian. Like so many others, he has always maintained that his service with No.25 were some of the happiest of his life.

JOIN THE AIR FORCE AND SEE THE WORLD, 1990s – NO.25 STYLE.

Wing Commander Phil Goodman was still at the helm at Leeming in 1996 after a Christmas spent at home by all members of the Squadron, following a perceptible improvement (though short-lived) in the war situation in Bosnia.

The first Squadron detachment was therefore an armament training visit to Valley in Anglesey to fire air-to-air missiles over the Cardigan Bay range. There was apparently only one missile discharge of any significance; one of the CO's missiles adopted a training sortie of its own when, instead of following electronic instructions as planned – to continue on a flightpath towards an assumed target somewhere around 12 o'clock when fired – it decided on an easier option, successfully giving all the indications of appearing at the Tornado's 'six' (i.e. immediately astern). However, after a short spell of the vernacular and remedial steps taken, the missile (to quote a Squadron source), decided to go away to look for an easier target!

In May the Squadron detached to Coningsby for a spell of training over the North Sea combat range, with sorties involving mock combat with fighter units of the USAF, the Dutch and – unusually – the Swiss.

The following month No.25 deployed to Eilson Air Force Base in Alaska to participate in Exercise *Distant Frontier*. The weather, however, took a hand and frustrated much of the USAF's participation, leaving No.25 Squadron to admire the sun not setting at sunset. The trip home also failed to go according to plan when, on meeting up with a Tristar for the first in-flight refuelling, it was found that the tanker had developed a fuel leak, and had to turn back. The second tanker arrived but then suffered a major failure in its central engine 'which caused a large amount of noise, accompanied by several falling panels'. This time, therefore, the Squadron was also obliged to turn back to Eilson for a further day.

In September the Squadron split into two flights, one going out to the Falklands, its main object being to exchange two Tornados with the Squadron then based in the South Atlantic. The trip out and back each involved two ten-hour flights and half a dozen rendezvous with tankers, one of which went unserviceable during the return flight, necessitating a diversion to Tenerife for the night.

Meanwhile, the other flight flew to Ankara in Turkey to participate in a NATO exercise against the Turkish air force. The first week seems to have gone according to plan, but then the Turks opted to withdraw from the exercise, followed by the Norwegians, Americans and Canadians, leaving No.25 Squadron to sample Hilton-style accommodation, just in case the exercise could restart.

One final overseas detachment remained in 1996 a brief visit to the NATO facility at Decimommanu in Italy to provide support for some Tornado GR.1 strike aircraft in an exercise.

As can be judged from that year's demands on No.25 Squadron's crews and aircraft, the recent reductions in the RAF's strength had placed a considerable burden on the few remaining fighter squadrons. It was, however, rewarded in well-deserved manner when, shortly before Christmas, it was announced that No.25 had been awarded the Dacre Trophy, the modern successor to the old Sassoon Trophy, which the Squadron had won outright between the wars. The new trophy was awarded to the best fighter squadron in the Royal Air Force, a fine reward for a squadron that had only returned to its traditional rôle six years earlier.

1998 – AND THE DAWN OF A NEW DEY.

The year began with the news that one of the other Tornado fighter squadrons was to be disbanded, the intention being to increase the establishment of the remaining units. Accordingly, the year brought no fewer than nineteen new aircrew members, while eleven reached the end of their tour. Fortunately the arrival of newcomers was spread fairly evenly throughout the year, so that bringing them up to operational status did not pose too much of a burden at any one time.

Among the veteran pilots at this time was Flt Lt Willy Hackett, yet another member of No.25 Squadron granted the privilege of selection as Strike Command's solo aerobatic display pilot. In the words of Flt Lt Paul Eves:

> "Willy has done a splendid job wowing the crowds, including the show at the Shepway (Folkestone) Festival, as well as numerous displays all over Europe. Unfortunately, going upside down at high speed and so close to the ground has had its effect on the navigators, with Willy wearing out two so far (Flight Lieutenants Al Taylor and Mario Puzey). The current incumbent is Flight Lieutenant John Shields."

One of the first of the new arrivals in 1998 was Wg Cdr Andy Dey, who took over as Commanding Officer from Wg Cdr Phil Goodman (who left, on promotion to Group Captain and a posting to the Ministry of Defence), his arrival almost coinciding with the Squadron flying to Nevada, USA, for the periodic Exercise *Red Flag,* at Nellis Air Force Base, Las Vegas, Nevada. This constituted an opportunity for the air forces of Western nations to hone their tactical skill (over a range of roughly the size of Wales) against such aircraft as F-15s, F-16s, Mirage 2000s, B-1s, and B-52s in an environment of widespread electronic countermeasures.

Back at Leeming, this was followed by the dreaded visit by the Standards and Evaluation Team from RAF Coningsby. Predictably announced by the unpleasant truism as being 'for the good of every member of the Squadron', the pilots and navigators are rigorously assessed in all manner of flight and combat situations in order to assess the instinctive manner in which they react, both in terms of safety and operational efficiency, and by these results ensure that all squadrons of the Tornado Fighter Wing succeed in achieving a common and optimum standard. To everyone's relief No.25 was 'passed fit'. Meanwhile the Tornado F.3 Display Team, namely Flt Lts Willy Hacket and Johnny Shields, were hard at work practising their aerobatic display routine, and in due course this gained approval by the Air Officer Commanding No.11/18 Group. They then went on to give no fewer than 41 flying displays all over the world – from Nancy in France to Santiago in Chile, the latter being participation in that nation's celebratory *Fidae 98,* an event also attended by twenty groundcrew members.

An Exercise that was entirely new to No.25 Squadron took place in May. Exercise *Brilliant Foil* involved the movement of air and ground personnel, lock, stock and barrel, of No.25 Squadron (and No.11, the other Tornado Squadron at Leeming) to RAF St.Mawgan in Cornwall. Representing the Royal Air Force's Immediate Reaction Force, the two Squadrons adopted a simulated war status, being assessed both in the air and on the ground, this time by the Operational Evaluation Team, in a range of war situations. No.25's flying was assessed as being 'of a very high standard'. It should be said that, such was the Squadron's length and depth of experience in recent years, visiting so many foreign nations under varying circumstances, adaptability rates high among the Squadron's attributes.

The following month, No.25 Squadron contributed three aircraft to Exercise *Co-operative Chance,* staged in Slovakia alongside aircraft and flying personnel of the French, German and Dutch air forces. As a preliminary to the operational functions of the detachment, the Slovaks hosted a hangar party for guest nations, each being asked to contribute food and drink appropriate to their native country. No.25 came up with Stilton on Yorkshire pudding with gravy, washed down with a glass of port; this proved to be a highlight for all the participants in the Exercise!

The 80th Anniversary of the creation of the Polish Air Force was celebrated by an international air display at Debden (Poland, not Essex) to which No.25 Squadron was invited to send two Tornados, one of which was to be flown by Willy Hackett and Johnny Shields. Imagine their astonishment when, who should welcome them, but a well-known ex- No.25 pilot, Ludwik Steinke (who had returned to his native land to join in the celebrations). Their pleasure at meeting was mutual.

Wing Commander Andy Dey had had a difficult year to say the least. After manning a desk for some six years, returning to operational flying brought with it the realisation that technology and tactics had undergone a considerable advance. Although he had flown twelve sorties in Tornados with the Operational Conversion Unit, arriving on the Squadron he found that the Joint Tactical Information Distribution System (JTIDS), increased and improved radar, night vision goggles (NVG) had become realities while his back had been turned. Thus, while getting to grips with the responsibilities of command, he was faced with a major job to become adept at speaking the same 'new language' as the most junior officers on the Squadron!

He had no sooner mastered these hurdles when his annual medical board discovered that he had a heart problem, for which the prognosis was far from favourable, with the end to flying a real possibility. He was grounded. Fortunately a spell on the ground and a self-imposed attitude of relaxation whenever possible (while retaining command) brought a just reward, as a medical examination in November showed that his heart rhythm had returned to normal, and he was cleared to fly once more – only to be faced with more 'catching up'. A measure of the man may be understood from the fact that he remained in command of No.25 (Fighter) Squadron for a further eighteen months! Moreover, he was to be rewarded with the news that No.25 had been awarded the Dacre Trophy for the second year running. Mick Martin's foundations had been well and truly laid.

In the same month that Andy Dey received his good news, the Squadron was host to an unusual visitor. Frederick Ertsinger had been a radio operator on a night visit to England on 24th June 1941 when his Heinkel He 111 was welcomed by a Beaufighter of No.25 Squadron, flown by Plt Off D W Thompson (pilot) and Plt Off L D Britain (radar operator). A brief action followed and the Heinkel crashed in Lincolnshire, Herr Ertsinger being the only survivor. The crash site had been traced by the Lincolnshire Aircraft Recovery Group, who contacted the author and provided photographic evidence of the Heinkel's demise. Close collaboration between LARG and the Squadron resulted in a courtesy invitation for Herr Ertsinger to pay a visit to No.25 and look over one of its Tornados.

TO THE GULF IN EARNEST – 1999

With continuing frustration of attempts by the Western Powers to achieve normal peaceful conditions in Iraq, there were rumours that the Tornado GR.1s at the Prince Sultan's Air Base in Saudi Arabia were to be replaced by Tornado F.3s shortly before Christmas 1998. It therefore came as little surprise that, with precious little time to make the necessary preparations, No.25 Squadron was selected to deploy to the Gulf. This involved modifying all the aircraft for desert service, issuing tropical kit to all personnel as well as providing all the necessary inoculations. Although much of the support equipment was already in theatre, the balance had to be airlifted out in advance.

On arrival in Saudi Arabia, the Squadron was tasked with patrolling the No Fly Zone over Southern Iraq, it being a condition of the fragile cease-fire that no attempt would be made by Saddam Hussein to harass the indigenous dissident population from the air. There was always the danger that, so as to conceal covert use of helicopters against the civilian populace, the Iraqi defences might react with surface-to-air weapons, or even attempt to engage the Tornados with fighters.

No sooner had the Squadron returned to the United Kingdom in April 1999 than it was ordered to be ready to return to Saudi Arabia in August that year. There was just time for a hurried spot of leave, then it was back to more preparations. Although these deployments could be regarded as the Squadron's operational *raison d'être,* and therefore welcomed as a means of applying the fruits of its constant training, there was considerable regret that 25's participation in the annual *Red Flag* detachment to

Nevada (always popular on account of its highly professional and searching demands) had to be cancelled, as was its visit to New Mexico for Exercise *Roving Sands* in May that year.

The year 2000 arrived with news that No.25 would deploy for a third time in fourteen months to Saudi Arabia in July, this in all probability being Andy Dey's last duty as the Squadron's commanding officer, albeit with a hectic engagement list beforehand – deploying once again to Leewarden in Holland, to Nevada for *Red Flag*, to Bodø in Norway, and Monte Real in Portugal!

At the time of writing (October 2000) the Squadron is preparing to detach to Akrotiri, Cyprus, for its routine air-to-air gunnery training, after which six Tornados and a support Hercules with their air and ground personnel will deploy to Azraq Air Base in Jordan alongside aircraft of the Royal Jordanian Air Force in the combat rôle as part of Exercise *Desert Thunder 2000*; afterwards the detachment will return to Leeming with a night's stop-over at Akrotiri.

As to the future, various reports have appeared to suggest that No.25 (Fighter) Squadron will remain in being for the foreseeable future, continuing to fly the Tornado F.3 until 2004 when, it is said, the Leeming-based Tornado Squadrons' turn will come to be re-equipped with the Eurofighter, by all accounts a worthy aeroplane with which No.25 can continue its long traditions of service to the nation, professionalism and esprit. A tradition second to none, hard won and jealously nurtured.

• • •

Squadron Battle Honours

'Home Defence, 1916'
'Western Front 1916-1918' (*)
'Somme 1916' (*)
'Arras'
'Ypres, 1917' (*)
'Cambrai, 1917' (*)
'Somme, 1918' (*)
'Lys'
'Hindenburg Line, 1918' (*)
'Channel and North Sea, 1939-1940' (*)
'Battle of Britain, 1940' (*)
'Home Defence, 1940-1945' (*)
'Biscay, 1943' (**)
'Fortress Europe, 1943-1944' (*)
'France and Germany, 1944-1945' (*)

(*) = Battle Honours Emblazoned

(**) = Battle Honour Entitled to be Emblazoned. No record can be found of any application for entitlement to this Battle Honour, despite the hard evidence that No.25 Squadron conformed to the necessary criteria, namely the detachment to Perranporth, Cornwall of the Squadron's Mosquitos for such combat operations in June 1943, with the loss of four aircrew lives in action on 13th June 1943 over the Bay of Biscay. See Roll of Honour – Appendix 1.

APPENDIX 1

ROLL OF HONOUR

No.25 Squadron, Royal Flying Corps and Royal Air Force

KILLED IN ACTION AND KILLED ON ACTIVE SERVICE

The First World War

23rd April 1916	7194 2/Air Mech Geoffrey Foster ATWELL, RFC. Observer, of Willesden Green, Middlesex. Killed in action in F.E.2b 5210. (Lt Collinson unhurt). Lapugnoy Military Cemetery, France
18th June 1916	2/Lt Clarence Elias ROGERS, RFC. Pilot. Aged 24, Died of Wounds 19th June, suffered on this day in F.E.2b 6940 (Sgt H Taylor made POW). Cabaret-Rouge British Cemetery, France.
18th June 1916	2/Lt John Raymond Boscawen SAVAGE, RFC. Pilot. Aged 17, of Bradford, Yorkshire. Killed in Action in F.E.2b 4909. (2/Air Mech T N U Robinson made POW). Sallaumines Memorial, Bully-Grenay, France.
22nd June 1916	2/Lt John Lewis Pasteur ARMSTRONG. Army Service Corp (Territorial) and RFC. Pilot. Aged 25 of Felsted, Essex. Killed in Action in F.E.2b 5209 (Sgt G Topcliffe made POW). Cabaret-Rouge British Cemetery, France.
26th June 1916	8651 2/Air Mech Herbert CHADWICK, RFC. Observer. Aged 20, Died of Wounds received on 22nd June 1916 in F.E.2b 6334 (Pilot, 2/Lt R Sherwell, unhurt). Lapugnoy Military Cemetery, France.
27th June 1916	Lt Eric Hinks BIRD. 1st Battalion, Royal Fusiliers and RFC. Pilot. Aged 22. Lapugnoy Military Military Cemetery, France.
3rd July 1916	2/Lt Rex SHERWELL. Pilot, 3rd Battalion, Lincolnshire Regt and RFC. Aged 18, of Brondesbury, Middlesex. Killed in Action in F.E.2b, 6339. Lapugnoy Military Cemetery, France.
27th July 1916	Lt Martyn Tulloch VAUGHAN-LEWES, RFC. Observer. Aged 21 of West Lulworth. Dorset. Died of Wounds received on 15th July 1916 in F.E.2b 4283. Formerly of 3rd Battalion, Welsh Regt. Bailleul Communal Cemetery, British Extension, France.
3rd August 1916	Sapper Eric Merril Des BRISAY. Canadian Infantry and RFC. Aged 23 of Vancouver, BC. Killed in Action in F.E.2b 4272 (Lt K Mathewson also killed). Cabaret-Rouge British Cemetery, France.
3rd August 1916	Lt Kenneth MATHEWSON, RFC. Pilot. Aged 22 of Montreal, PQ., Killed in Action in F.E.2b 4272. Bully-Grenay Communal Cemetery British Extension, France
9th August 1916	Capt (Temporary) Clifford John HART. Pilot, 5th Battalion, Bedfordshire Regt; 5th Battalion, Worcestershire Regt, and RFC. Aged 30, of Streatham, London. Killed in Action with J A Mann in F.E.2b 6996. Rue-Petillon Cemetery, Fleurbaix, France.
9th August 1916	Lt John Anderson MANN, MC. 5th Battalion, Cameronians and RFC. Aged 21 of Glasgow. Killed in Action with Capt C J Hart (see above). Rue-Petillon Military Cemetery, Fleurbaix, France.
16th August 1916	2/Lt Archibald Stanley BUTLER. 2nd/4th Battalion (South Midland) Howitzer Brigade, Royal Field Artillery, and RFC. Aged 26 of Thames Ditton, Surrey. Killed in flying accident at St Vevient. Buried at Lapugnoy Military Cemetery, France.
6th September 1916	Lt Ernest Charles KEMP. Observer, 9th Battalion, Yorkshire Regt, and RFC. Aged 24, of Brixton Hill, London. Killed in air combat (Pilot, 2/Lt J L Roberton, see below) in F.E.2b 5238 near Lens. Arras Memorial.
6th September 1916	2/Lt James Leslie ROBERTON. Pilot, 4th Battalion, Yorkshire Regt (Territorial) and RFC. Aged 21 of Stoke Golding Lodge, Nuneaton, Warwickshire. Killed in Action in F.E.2b 5238. Arras Memorial.
10th October 1916	2/Lt Moreton HAYNE. Pilot, Lancashire Fusiliers and RFC. Aged 18 of Richmond. Surrey. Killed in Action in F.E.2b 4292 (Lt A H M Copeland made POW). According to officer records, he died whilst in captivity. Brown's Copse Cemetery, Rouex, France.
10th November 1916	Lt Charles Hugh BIDMEAD. Observer, General List and RFC. Aged 27 of Long Wittenham, Berkshire. Killed while flying with Lt E S P Hynes in F.E.2b 4841. Lapugnoy Military Cemetery, France.
10th November 1916	Lt Ernest Stanley Patrick HYNES. Pilot, East Kent Regt (The Buffs) and RFC. Aged 18, of Penzance, Cornwall. Killed while flying with Lt C H Bidmead (see above). Lapugnoy Military Cemetery, France.
4th December 1916	Lt Ivan HEALD, MC, RN. Observer, Royal Naval Division and RFC. Aged 33. Killed in Action (Pilot, Lt D S Johnson) in F.E.2b 7022. Cabaret-Rouge British Cemetery, France.
4th December 1916	Lt Derek Sivewright JOHNSON. Pilot, Home Counties Divisional Cyclists (Territorials); Army Cyclist Corps and RFC. Aged 21, of Hove, Sussex. Killed in Action. (Observer, Lt I Heald, see above) in F.E.2b 7022. Cabaret-Rouge British Cemetery, France.
2nd March 1917	Lt Gerald Richard Francis WANER, RFC. Pilot. Aged 23 of London and Buenos Aires, Argentina. Died of Wounds received on 1st March 1917. Formerly of the Royal Engineers. Lapugnoy British Cemetery, France.
16th March 1917	14345 Sgt Clifford William Boiteux BUCHANAN, ASC. Pilot, 1st Battalion, Royal Dublin Fusiliers and RFC. Aged 25, of Stockwell, London. Killed while flying in F.E.2b 4847. Lapugnoy British Cemetery, France.
17th March 1917	Lt Arthur Elsdale BOULTBEE. Pilot, 3rd Battalion, Northamptonshire Regt and RFC. Aged 19, of Hargrave Rectory, Huntingdon, and Bath, Somerset. Killed in Action (Observer, 2/Air Mech F King, see below) in F.E.2b A5439. Arras Memorial. Now known to be buried in Canadian Cemetery No.2, Neuville St Vaast, France.

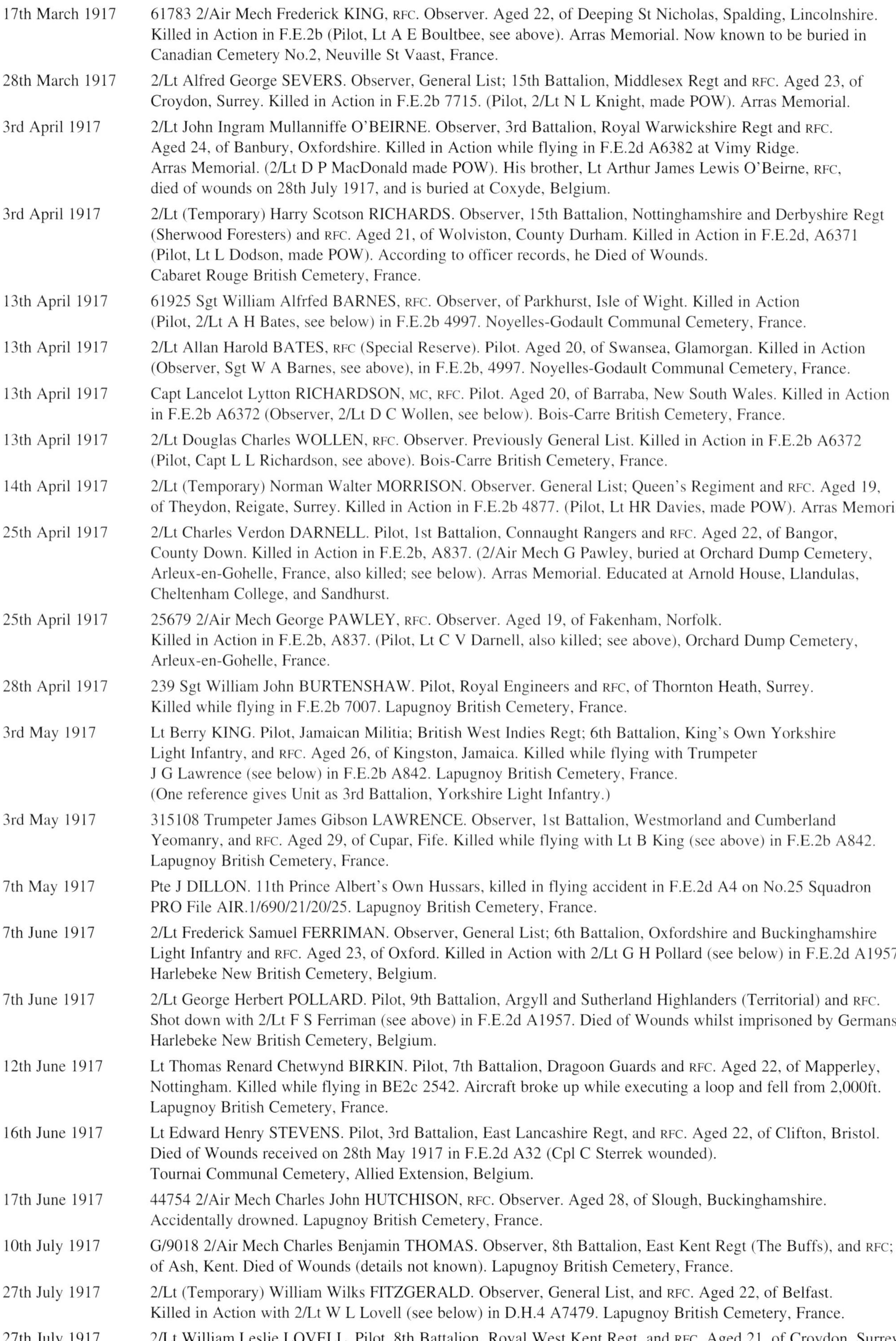

17th March 1917	61783 2/Air Mech Frederick KING, RFC. Observer. Aged 22, of Deeping St Nicholas, Spalding, Lincolnshire. Killed in Action in F.E.2b (Pilot, Lt A E Boultbee, see above). Arras Memorial. Now known to be buried in Canadian Cemetery No.2, Neuville St Vaast, France.
28th March 1917	2/Lt Alfred George SEVERS. Observer, General List; 15th Battalion, Middlesex Regt and RFC. Aged 23, of Croydon, Surrey. Killed in Action in F.E.2b 7715. (Pilot, 2/Lt N L Knight, made POW). Arras Memorial.
3rd April 1917	2/Lt John Ingram Mullanniffe O'BEIRNE. Observer, 3rd Battalion, Royal Warwickshire Regt and RFC. Aged 24, of Banbury, Oxfordshire. Killed in Action while flying in F.E.2d A6382 at Vimy Ridge. Arras Memorial. (2/Lt D P MacDonald made POW). His brother, Lt Arthur James Lewis O'Beirne, RFC, died of wounds on 28th July 1917, and is buried at Coxyde, Belgium.
3rd April 1917	2/Lt (Temporary) Harry Scotson RICHARDS. Observer, 15th Battalion, Nottinghamshire and Derbyshire Regt (Sherwood Foresters) and RFC. Aged 21, of Wolviston, County Durham. Killed in Action in F.E.2d, A6371 (Pilot, Lt L Dodson, made POW). According to officer records, he Died of Wounds. Cabaret Rouge British Cemetery, France.
13th April 1917	61925 Sgt William Alfrfed BARNES, RFC. Observer, of Parkhurst, Isle of Wight. Killed in Action (Pilot, 2/Lt A H Bates, see below) in F.E.2b 4997. Noyelles-Godault Communal Cemetery, France.
13th April 1917	2/Lt Allan Harold BATES, RFC (Special Reserve). Pilot. Aged 20, of Swansea, Glamorgan. Killed in Action (Observer, Sgt W A Barnes, see above), in F.E.2b, 4997. Noyelles-Godault Communal Cemetery, France.
13th April 1917	Capt Lancelot Lytton RICHARDSON, MC, RFC. Pilot. Aged 20, of Barraba, New South Wales. Killed in Action in F.E.2b A6372 (Observer, 2/Lt D C Wollen, see below). Bois-Carre British Cemetery, France.
13th April 1917	2/Lt Douglas Charles WOLLEN, RFC. Observer. Previously General List. Killed in Action in F.E.2b A6372 (Pilot, Capt L L Richardson, see above). Bois-Carre British Cemetery, France.
14th April 1917	2/Lt (Temporary) Norman Walter MORRISON. Observer. General List; Queen's Regiment and RFC. Aged 19, of Theydon, Reigate, Surrey. Killed in Action in F.E.2b 4877. (Pilot, Lt HR Davies, made POW). Arras Memorial.
25th April 1917	2/Lt Charles Verdon DARNELL. Pilot, 1st Battalion, Connaught Rangers and RFC. Aged 22, of Bangor, County Down. Killed in Action in F.E.2b, A837. (2/Air Mech G Pawley, buried at Orchard Dump Cemetery, Arleux-en-Gohelle, France, also killed; see below). Arras Memorial. Educated at Arnold House, Llandulas, Cheltenham College, and Sandhurst.
25th April 1917	25679 2/Air Mech George PAWLEY, RFC. Observer. Aged 19, of Fakenham, Norfolk. Killed in Action in F.E.2b, A837. (Pilot, Lt C V Darnell, also killed; see above), Orchard Dump Cemetery, Arleux-en-Gohelle, France.
28th April 1917	239 Sgt William John BURTENSHAW. Pilot, Royal Engineers and RFC, of Thornton Heath, Surrey. Killed while flying in F.E.2b 7007. Lapugnoy British Cemetery, France.
3rd May 1917	Lt Berry KING. Pilot, Jamaican Militia; British West Indies Regt; 6th Battalion, King's Own Yorkshire Light Infantry, and RFC. Aged 26, of Kingston, Jamaica. Killed while flying with Trumpeter J G Lawrence (see below) in F.E.2b A842. Lapugnoy British Cemetery, France. (One reference gives Unit as 3rd Battalion, Yorkshire Light Infantry.)
3rd May 1917	315108 Trumpeter James Gibson LAWRENCE. Observer, 1st Battalion, Westmorland and Cumberland Yeomanry, and RFC. Aged 29, of Cupar, Fife. Killed while flying with Lt B King (see above) in F.E.2b A842. Lapugnoy British Cemetery, France.
7th May 1917	Pte J DILLON. 11th Prince Albert's Own Hussars, killed in flying accident in F.E.2d A4 on No.25 Squadron PRO File AIR.1/690/21/20/25. Lapugnoy British Cemetery, France.
7th June 1917	2/Lt Frederick Samuel FERRIMAN. Observer, General List; 6th Battalion, Oxfordshire and Buckinghamshire Light Infantry and RFC. Aged 23, of Oxford. Killed in Action with 2/Lt G H Pollard (see below) in F.E.2d A1957. Harlebeke New British Cemetery, Belgium.
7th June 1917	2/Lt George Herbert POLLARD. Pilot, 9th Battalion, Argyll and Sutherland Highlanders (Territorial) and RFC. Shot down with 2/Lt F S Ferriman (see above) in F.E.2d A1957. Died of Wounds whilst imprisoned by Germans. Harlebeke New British Cemetery, Belgium.
12th June 1917	Lt Thomas Renard Chetwynd BIRKIN. Pilot, 7th Battalion, Dragoon Guards and RFC. Aged 22, of Mapperley, Nottingham. Killed while flying in BE2c 2542. Aircraft broke up while executing a loop and fell from 2,000ft. Lapugnoy British Cemetery, France.
16th June 1917	Lt Edward Henry STEVENS. Pilot, 3rd Battalion, East Lancashire Regt, and RFC. Aged 22, of Clifton, Bristol. Died of Wounds received on 28th May 1917 in F.E.2d A32 (Cpl C Sterrek wounded). Tournai Communal Cemetery, Allied Extension, Belgium.
17th June 1917	44754 2/Air Mech Charles John HUTCHISON, RFC. Observer. Aged 28, of Slough, Buckinghamshire. Accidentally drowned. Lapugnoy British Cemetery, France.
10th July 1917	G/9018 2/Air Mech Charles Benjamin THOMAS. Observer, 8th Battalion, East Kent Regt (The Buffs), and RFC; of Ash, Kent. Died of Wounds (details not known). Lapugnoy British Cemetery, France.
27th July 1917	2/Lt (Temporary) William Wilks FITZGERALD. Observer, General List, and RFC. Aged 22, of Belfast. Killed in Action with 2/Lt W L Lovell (see below) in D.H.4 A7479. Lapugnoy British Cemetery, France.
27th July 1917	2/Lt William Leslie LOVELL. Pilot, 8th Battalion, Royal West Kent Regt, and RFC. Aged 21, of Croydon, Surrey. Killed in Action while flying with 2/Lt W W Fitzgerald in D.H.4 A7479. Lapugnoy British Cemetery, France.

28th July 1917	2/Lt (Temporary) Herbert Alfred HOPE, RFC. Pilot. Killed while flying in D.H.4, A7463. (May have Died of Wounds). Lapugnoy British Cemetery, France.
14th August 1917	Lt Norman FIELD. Observer, 5th Battalion, Manchester Regt (Territorial) and RFC. Aged 24 of Skelmanthorpe, Yorkshire. Killed in Action (Pilot, 2/Lt P L McGavin) in D.H.4 A2159. Cabaret-Rouge British Cemetery, France.
4th September 1917	Lt Charles Jesse PULLEN. Pilot, Royal Garrison Artillery (Territorial) and RFC. Aged 24, of Wanstead, Essex. Killed in Action in D.H.4 A7480 (Observer, 2/Lt E D S Robinson, see below) near La Bassée. Commemmorated on Arras Memorial, and now thought to be buried at Cabaret-Rouge British Cemetery, France.
4th September 1917	2/Lt Eustace Dixon Sharper ROBINSON, RFC. Observer. Aged 19, of West Hartlepool, County Durham. Killed in Action in D.H.4 A7480 (Pilot, Lt C J Pullen, see above). Commemmorated on Arras Memorial; now thought to be buried at Cabaret-Rouge British Cemetery, France.
4th September 1917	2/Lt (Temporary) Arthur Trevor WILLIAMS, RFC. Observer. Aged 21, of Liverpool. Wounded while flying in D.H.4 A7487, but Died of Wounds. Formerly of 15th Battalion, Royal Welsh Fusiliers. Lapugnoy British Cemetery, France.
1st October 1917	Lt (Temporary) John Lawrence HUGHES. Observer, 17th Battalion, Welsh Regt, and RFC. Aged 25, of Swansea, Glamorgan. Killed in Action in D.H.4 A7405 (Pilot, 2/Lt C O Rayner, see below). Lapugnoy British Cemetery, France.
1st October 1917	2/Lt (Temporary) Charles Oliver RAYNER. Pilot, General List and RFC. Aged 26, of Vancouver, BC, Canada. Killed in Action in D.H.4 A7405 (Observer, Lt J L Hughes, see above). Lapugnoy British Cemetery, France.
9th November 1917	2/Lt (Temporary) Sydney Bolton CRAGG, RFC. Pilot. Aged 27, of Melbourne, Victoria, Australia. Killed in D.H.4 A7543 while attempting force landing on beach at Le Crotoy. Buried at Le Crotoy Communal Cemetery, France.
4th January 1918	2/Lt John Shaw MACAULAY, RFC. Pilot. Aged 19, of Inverness. Killed while flying in D.H.4, A7527 (Observer, 2/Lt A Thornhill, injured). Also stated to have Died of Wounds. Longuenesse (St Omer) Souvenir British Cemetery, France.
29th January 1918	2/Lt (Temporary) William John BORTHISTLE. Observer, 3rd Battalion, Royal Munster Fusiliers and RFC. Aged 23, of Dublin, Ireland. Killed in Action in D.H.4 A7600 (Pilot, Capt A G Whitehead, see below). Grand-Seraucourt British Cemetery, France.
29th January 1918	Capt Alfred Gordon WHITEHEAD, RFC. Pilot. Aged 25, of Baildon, Yorkshire. Killed in Action in D.H.4 A7600 (Observer, 2/Lt J Borthistle, see above). Formerly 6th Battalion, West Yorkshire Regt (Territorial). Grand-Seraucourt British Cemetery, France. His brother, 2/Lt Geoffrey Nield Whitehead, RFC (No.47 Kite Balloon Squadron) had been Killed in Action on 15th October 1917, and lies buried at Ypres, Belgium.
30th January 1918	106098 2/Air Mech Charles Norman HARVEY, RFC. Observer. Aged 21, of West Hartlepool, County Durham (no further details known). Longuenesse (St Omer) Souvenir British Cemetery, France.
5th February 1918	114348 2/Air Mech Roy IRELAND. Observer, Army Service Corps and RFC. Aged 27, of St Eleanors, Prince Edward Island. Killed in Action in D.H.4 A7865 (Pilot, 2/Lt R P Pohlmann, see below). Harlebeke New British Cemetery, France.
5th February 1918	2/Lt Reginald Peel POHLMANN, RFC. Pilot. Aged 19, of Hipperholme, Yorkshire. Killed in Action in D.H.4 A7865 (Observer, 2/Air Mech R Ireland, see above). Harlebeke New British Cemetery, France.
26th February 1918	2/Lt Ernest William GUEST. Pilot, Royal Lancashire Regt, and RFC. Aged 36, of Northenden, Cheshire. Killed in Action in D.H.4 A7642 (Capt H G Ashton, Observer?, Died of Wounds on 11th March 1918; see below). Lapugnoy British Cemetery, France.
27th February 1918	Lt Maurice Wilfred DICKENS, RFC. Pilot. Aged 22, of Kensworth, Bedfordshire. Killed in Action in D.H.4 A7733 (Observer, Sgt F J Swain, also killed; see below). Etaples Military Cemetery, France.
27th February 1918	75078 Sgt Frederick James SWAIN, RFC. Observer. Aged 19, of Wokingham, Berkshire. Killed in Action in D.H.4 A7733 (Pilot, Lt M W Dickens, also killed; see above). Arras Memorial, France.
11th March 1918	Capt Hadric Grey ASHTON. Observer?, East Lancashire Regt; 2/11 London Regt (Territorial) and RFC. Aged 23, of Preston, Lancashire. Died of Wounds suffered on 26th February 1918 in D.H.4 A7642. Lapugnoy British Cemetery, France.
26th March 1918	22360 2/Air Mech Frank WHITEHEAD, RFC. Observer. Aged 37, of Wimbledon, Surrey. Killed in taxying accident by D.H.4 A7823. Hesdin Communal Cemetery, France.
26th March 1918	1/Air Mech Thomas Henry STEPHENS, RFC. Killed in taxying accident by D.H.4 A7823. Hesdin Communal Cemetery, France.
27th March 1918	2/Lt Charles Gordon PENTECOST, RFC. Pilot. Killed in Action in D.H.4 A7664 (Oberserver, Lt A Rentoul, also killed; see below). Arras Memorial, France.
27th March 1918	Lt Alexander RENTOUL. Observer, Yorkshire Hussars Yeomanry, and RFC. Killed in Action in D.H.4 A7664 (Pilot, 2/Lt C G Pentecost, also killed; see above). Queens Road Cemetery, Bucquoy, France.
3rd April 1918	Lt John MITCHELL, RAF. Observer, 7th Battalion, Scottish Rifles (Cameronians). Aged 23, of Bothwell, Lanarkshire. Died of Wounds suffered in D.H. 4 on 26th March 1918. Attached to No.25 Squadron, possibly from No.27 Squadron. (No further details of circumstances). Abbeville Communal Cemetery, France.
21st April 1918	2/Lt John David DINGWALL, RAF. Aged 19, of Glasgow. Formerly on General List. Killed in Action in D.H.4 A8078 (Observer, Lt C M Sinclair, wounded). Aire Communal Cemetery, France.

20th May 1918	Lt Albert Henry HERRING, RAF. Pilot. Aged 20, of Ilford, Essex. Killed in Action in D.H.4 D9239 (Observer, 2/Lt R S Lasker, also killed; see below). Aulnoye Communal Cemetery, France.
20th May 1918	2/Lt Robert Sydney LASKER, RAF. Observer. Aged 22, of Newcastle, New South Wales, Australia. Killed in Action in D.H.4 D9239 (Pilot, Lt A H Herring, also killed; see above). Aulnoye Communal Cemetery, France.
23rd June 1918	2/Lt William H DIXON, RAF. Observer. Aged 22, of Birmingham. Died of wounds suffered on 8th June 1918 while on reconnaissance sortie. Formerly of 3rd Battalion, Seaforth Highlanders. Etaples Military Cemetery, France.
29th June 1918	Lt Bryant Lutellus LINDLEY, MC, RAF. Pilot. Aged 19, of Claremont, Cape Province, South Africa. Killed in Action on photosortie in D.H.4 A7913. (Observer, 2/Lt D Boe, made POW). Larch Wood Railway Cutting Cemetery, Belgium.
1st July 1918	Lt George Edward DOBESON, RAF. Aged 20, of Hebburn, County Durham. Killed in Action during photographic sortie in D.H.4 A8054. Claimed shot down by Vizefeldwebel F Piechulek of *Jasta* 56 at Ruddervoorde. (Observer, 2/Lt J E Pilling, also killed; see below). Ruddervoorde Communal Cemetery, Belgium.
1st July 1918	2/Lt John Elliott PILLING, RAF. Observer. Shot down and Killed in Action with Lt G E Dobeson in D.H.4 A8054 (see above). Previously 5th Battalion, King's Liverpool Regt (Territorial). Ruddervoorde Communal Cemetery, Belgium.
16th July 1918	Lt James Matthew MACKIE, DCM. Observer, Manitoba Regt and RAF. Aged 25, of Winnipeg, Manitoba, Canada. Killed in Action in D.H.4 D8380 (Capt E Waterlow, Pilot, also killed; see below). Possible claim to have been shot down by Vizefeldwebel F Piechulek of *Jasta* 56. Arras Memorial.
16th July 1918	Capt Eric WATERLOW, MC, DFC, RAF. Pilot. Of Hyde Park, London. Killed in Action in D.H.4 D8380 (with Lt J M Mackie, see above). Ypres Reservoir Cemetery, Belgium.
15th August 1918	56080 Sgt William Blackstock GRAY, RAF. Aged 19, of Belfast, County Antrim. Died of gas poisoning. Huby-St Leu British Cemetery, France.
3rd September 1918	2/Lt Edward Francis BOYCE, RAF. Observer. Aged 20, of Toronto, Ontario, Canada. Killed in Action with five enemy aircraft over Dixmude in D.H.4 D9235. (Pilot, Lt S Crosfield, unhurt). Huby-St Leu Cemetery, France.
16th September 1918	2/Lt Eric Bernard ANDREWS, RAF. Observer. Aged 20, of Hove, Sussex. Killed in Action during photographic sortie in D.H.4 A7784 (Pilot, Capt R L Whalley, also killed; see below). Formerly of Royal Field Artillery. Denain Communal Cemetery, France.
16th September 1918	Capt Reginald Livesey WHALLEY, RAF. Pilot. Aged 22, of Blackburn, Lancashire. Killed in Action in D.H.4 A7784 (Observer, 2/Lt E B Andrews, also killed; see above). Previously 4th Battalion, East Lancashire Regt. Cambrai East Military Cemetery, France.
16th September 1918	Lt Edward William GRIFFIN, RAF. Observer. Formerly of 6th Battalion, Gloucestershire Regt. Killed in Action in D.H.4 D8378 (Pilot, Lt C Brown, unhurt). Huby-St Leu British Cemetery.
24th September 1918	2/Lt John PULLAR, RAF. Observer. Aged 19, of Dundee, Angus. Killed while flying in D.H.4 A8051. (Pilot, Capt S Jones, injured).
27th September 1918	Lt Dudley Howard HAZELL, RAF. Pilot. Formerly 2nd Battalion, Royal Lancaster Regiment. Aged 23, of Frinton-on-Sea, Essex. Killed in Action in D.H.4 A8031 during reconnaissance prior to the Battle of the Canal du Nord (Observer, 2/Lt D B Robertson, also killed; see below). Cabaret-Rouge British Cemetery, France.
27th September 1918	2/Lt David Brown ROBERTSON, RAF. Observer. Aged 18, of Glasgow. Killed in Action in D.H.4 A8031 (Pilot, Lt D H Hazell, also killed; see above). Cabaret-Rouge British Cemetery, France.
3rd October 1918	65384 Sgt Frederick Percival CLARK, Croix de Guerre Belge, RAF. Pilot. Aged 21, of Plumstead, London. Killed in Action during reconnaissance sortie in D.H.4 A8052 (Observer, Lt W A G Middlecote, also killed; see below). Rumilly Communal Cemetery Extension, France.
3rd October 1918	Lt Edwin William Alfred George MIDDLECOTE, RAF. Observer. Formerly 16th Battalion, King's Royal Rifle Corps. Aged 21, of Burton-on-Trent, Staffordshire. Killed in Action in D.H.4 A8052 while on reconnaissance sortie (Pilot, Sgt F P Clark, also killed; see above). Cambrai East Military Cemetery, France.
4th October 1918	P/94255 Sgt Mech Harry Esmond WHITEHEAD, RAF. Observer. Aged 19, of New Chilwell, Nottinghamshire. Killed in Action during reconnaissance sortie in D.H.4 A8057. (Pilot, Lt L Young, also killed; see below). Cambrai East Military Cemetery, France.
4th October 1918	Lt Leslie YOUNG, RAF. Pilot. Aged 19, of Streatham, London. Killed in Action in D.H.4 A8057 (Observer, Sgt H E Whitehead, also killed; see above). Cambrai East Military Cemetery, France.
4th November 1918	2/Lt Pybus CARTWRIGHT, RAF. Observer. Of Thirsk, Yorkshire. Formerly of King's Own Yorkshire Light Infantry. Killed in Action in D.H.9a E9705 during photo reconnaissance sortie (Pilot, Lt L L K Straw, also killed; see below). Villers-sur-Nicole Communal Cemetery, France.
4th November 1918	Lt Lionel Liffard Kay STRAW, RAF. Pilot. Formerly with South African Horse. Aged 20, of Hill Crest, Natal, South Africa. Killed in Action during photo reconnaissance sortie in D.H.9a E9705 (Observer, 2/Lt P Cartwright, also killed; see above). Rouveroy Communal Cemetery, Belgium.

Between the World Wars

9th March 1919	125000 AC1 Stanley Charles SCHLAMP, RAF. Aged 29, of Ramsgate, Kent. Arras Memorial. (No further details of circumstances traced).
24th June 1921	Fg Off Henry Marinus STRUBEN, RAF. Pilot. Aged 23, of Redhill, Surrey. Killed when Snipe E6156 turned over on practice landing at Hawkinge. SS Mary and Eadburg Churchyard, Hawkinge, Kent.
24th July 1922	327181 AC1 Frank KERSHAW, RAF. Aged 21. Killed when Snipe E6600 stalled and spun in off steep turn at 2,000ft near Folkestone, Kent. (Pilot, Fg Off H E Walker, MC, AFC, seriously injured).
15th February 1924	Flt Lt George Howard Homer SCUTT, MC, RAF. Pilot. Aged 24. Killed when his Snipe E7601 struck the leading aircraft in a formation dive and crashed at Hawkinge after losing control at 500ft.
9th December 1926	Fg Off John Henry Campbell PURVIS, RAF. Pilot. Aged 20. Killed when his Grebe was in collision with another. His aircraft crashed at Terlingham Manor Farm, near Hawkinge.
17th February 1928	Fg Off Eric James WATSON, RAF. Pilot. Aged 21. Killed when Grebes J7372 and J7392 collided during mock dogfight training over Capel, near Folkestone. The other pilot baled out unhurt.
19th October 1928	Sqn Ldr W H PARK, MC, DFC, RAF went into Shorncliffe Military Hospital on 6th September 1928 and died there on 19th October 1928
18th February 1929	Sgt John William PEARCE, RAF. Pilot. Aged 28. Siskin left formation battle climb and crashed on sports field at Folkestone, killing pilot. Court of Enquiry gave opinion that the pilot was overcome by carbon monoxide fumes leaking from a cockpit heating pipe.
8th August 1930	Sgt Owen Herbert MCNAIR, RAF. Pilot. Aged 23. Killed while flying Siskin J9325; stalled in steep turn at low level after mock attack on troops of the 167th Infantry Brigade at Falmer, Sussex, and crashed.
29th October 1931	Lt Aat SUCHARITKUL; Siamese officer with the RAF. Aged 21. Pilot. While on air-to-ground firing practice at Hawkinge in Siskin J8881, pilot took evasive action to avoid another aircraft, stalled and spun from 700ft and crashed on side of hill near Folkestone, and was killed. (Note: Another source gives the date of accident as 27th October.)
5th November 1937	AC1 James DALE, RAF. Aged 19. Was passenger in Demon K3983, flown by Plt Off John Geoffry Cave, which was in collision with another Demon during formation practice and entered spin. The pilot baled out safely, but Dale died when K3983 crashed at Tilmanstone Colliery, near Dover. The other Demon landed safely.
18th May 1939	Blenheim L1439. AC F R JONES, RAF (full name not known) was killed after the pilot lost control in cloud and the aircraft crashed near Dartford, Kent. The pilot, Sgt Lingard, baled out safely.

The Second World War

27th March 1940	42046 Plt Off. Peter Darrell Walter BRIERLEY, RAF. Pilot. Aged 24. Circumstances of death not known. (One source states that a 'propeller accident' occurred involving a Blenheim at North Weald at about this time). This officer was interred at Cheltenham Cemetery, Gloucestershire.
31st July 1940	556058 Sgt Joseph Beckett THOMPSON, RAF. Pilot. Aged 24 of Magheragall, County Antrim, Northern Ireland. Circumstances of death not known. (One source states that Blenheim L1408 crashed on solo night flying test close to Martlesham Heath on this date. Body of pilot recovered). This officer was interred at the churchyard of Magheragall Church of Ireland.
8th August 1940	37594 Flt Lt Cecil Halford BULL, RAF. Pilot. Aged 24, of Monkton, Pembrokeshire. Squadron records state that this officer died in a shooting accident while on home leave. St David Churchyard, Monkton.
3rd September 1940	77977 Plt Off Douglas William HOGG, RAFVR. Pilot. Aged 23, of Thornliebank, Glasgow. Flying from North Weald in Blenheim L1512, was shot down in daylight by Hurricanes and killed. Aircraft crashed at Greensted Green, near Ongar, Essex. Glasgow (Eastwood), Cemetery.
15th September 1940	39419 Fg Off Hugh Michael Stanford LAMBERT, RAF. Pilot. Aged 22, of Reading, Berks. Was pilot of Blenheim R2067, reported Missing after night patrol over North Kent and Thames Estuary. Pilot may have lost control while avoiding another aircraft (possibly a Beaufighter) in the vicinity of Biggin Hill (Fg Off M J Miley and LAC J P Wyatt also killed; see below). Henley Road Crematorium, Reading.
15th September 1940	33345 Fg Off Miles John MILEY, RAF. Pilot. Aged 22, of Felixstowe, Suffolk. Killed in Blenheim R2067, captained by Fg Off H M S Lambert (killed, as well as LAC J P Wyatt, also killed; see above). St Andrew Church Churchyard, North Weald Bassett, Essex.
15th September 1940	915837 LAC John Pile WYATT, RAFVR. Aged 32, of Rodwell, Weymouth, Dorset. Killed in Blenheim R2067, captained by Fg Off H M S Lambert (killed, as well as Fg Off M J Miley, also killed; see above). Christ Church Churchyard, Melplash, Dorset.
16th November 1940	751715 Sgt Andrew Lunn ROMANIS, RAFVR. Wireless Operator/Air Gunner. Aged 24, of Edinburgh. Was a crew member of Blenheim L6679, captained by Sgt P L T Winter, with Sgt A J Theasby, which crashed on a night patrol near Ingatestone, near Billericay, Essex, while flying from Debden. All three men were killed. Sgt Romanis lies buried at Saffron Walden Cemetery, Essex.

16th November 1940 748949 Sgt Leonard Thomas WINTER, RAFVR. Pilot. Aged 22, of Coventry. Was Captain of Blenheim L6679, flying from Debden on night patrol, which crashed near Ingatestone with the loss of all three crew members (see above). St Michael Church Churchyard, Stoke, Coventry.

16th November 1940 1161473 Sgt Alec John THEASBY, RAFVR. Radio Operator (Air). Aged 23, of Norton, Yorkshire. Was a crew member of Blenheim L6679, flying from Debden on night patrol, which crashed near Ingatestone with the loss of all on board. Sgt Theasby lies buried in Norton Cemetery, Yorkshire.

21st November 1940 44403 Plt Off Ernest William John MONK, RAF. Pilot. Aged 26, of Borstal, Kent. While flying Beaufighter R2068, crashed into the sea after take off from Tangmere, and was killed. Remembered on Runnymede Memorial.

21st November 1940 548950 Sgt Edwin POWELL, RAF. Navigator/Radar Operator. Was flying in Beaufighter R2068 when it crashed into the sea after taking off from Tangmere, and was killed. Remembered on Runnymede Memorial.

7th December 1940 904234 Sgt Jack Richard FRIEND, RAFVR. Air Gunner. Aged 26, of Norwich, Norfolk. Was a crew member of Blenheim L1235, flying from Wittering on a blackout check over Peterborough; the pilot evidently lost control and crashed near Elton, Northamptonshire, the aircraft being extensively damaged; Sgt Friend and the pilot, Flt Lt J M M Hughes (see below) were killed. Sgt Friend was buried in All Saints Churchyard, Wittering.

7th December 1940 33191 Flt Lt John McCullough Middlemore HUGHES, DFC, RAF. Pilot. Aged 23, of Chilworth, Hampshire. Was killed in Blenheim L1235, flying from Wittering, which crashed during a blackout check over Peterborough. He and Sgt J R Friend were killed (see above). Flt Lt Hughes lies buried in Chilworth Churchyard, Hampshire.

24th December 1940 1940767 Sapper Arthur Mortimer COOPER, Royal Engineers, attached to No.25 Squadron at Wittering. Aged 30. No further details as to purpose of attachment, nor of circumstances of death. Interred at St John The Baptist Churchyard, Enderby, Leicestershire.

5th March 1941 60525 Plt Off Thomas Fairgrieve DORWARD, RAFVR. Pilot. Aged 24, of Galashiels, Selkirk. Pilot of Blenheim IF L6602 which hit a tree near Cottesmore in fog during flight from Wittering to Digby. Buried at Galashiels (Eastlands) Cemetery, Selkirk.

5th March 1941 84162 Fg Off John Austin STRONG, RAFVR. Signals Officer. Aged 31. Killed when Blenheim IF L6602, flown by Plt Off T F Dorward, hit a tree near Cottesmore (see above) in fog during flight from Wittering to Digby. Buried at Stamford, Lincolnshire. (May have been on attachment to No.25 Squadron).

3rd April 1941 748582 Sgt Harold Ian MAXWELL, RAFVR. Pilot. Aged 25 of Bromley, Kent. Killed flying Beaufighter X7541; stalled on landing approach at Wittering and spun in (Wireless Operator, Flt Sgt D F Roberts, also killed; see below). Buried at Bromley Hill Cemetery, Kent.

3rd April 1941 965482 F/Sgt David Francis ROBERTS, RAFVR. Wireless Operator. Aged 32, of Penylan, Cardiff. Was killed while flying in Beaufighter X7541 at Wittering (Pilot, Sgt H I Maxwell, also killed; see above). Wittering All Saints Churchyard, Wittering, Northamptonshire.

8th May 1941 923881 AC1 John Barclay MONTGOMERIE, RAFVR. Aged 27, of Parbrook, Somerset. Died on Active Service. Circumstances not known. Lies buried in St Mary's Churchyard, Billingshurst, Sussex.

8th July 1941 746701 F/Sgt Richard George CROSSMAN, RAFVR. Wireless Operator/Air Gunner. Killed in Beaufighter R2245, circumstances not known, but Pilot D W Thompson survived (see below). F/Sgt Crossman lies buried in Watford Cemetery, Hertfordshire.

8th July 1941 Plt Off 60528 David William THOMPSON, RAFVR. Pilot. Buried in All Saints Churchyard, Wittering

7th August 1941 Flt Lt Thomas Hovenden WORTH, RNVR. Pilot. Missing in Beaufighter R2157 on night patrol 6/7th August 1941, probably attacked by another Beaufighter. Commemorated on Panel 20 of the Runnydale Memorial.

7th August 1941 1182423 Sgt Frederick Peter NEKLUDOW, RAFVR. Observer. Missing in Beaufighter R2157 on night patrol 6/7th August 1941. Commemorated on Panel 49 of the Runnydale Memorial. (See above)

12th October 1941 930142 Sgt Harry Clifford WINDETT, RAFVR. Navigator/Radar Operator. Aged 30. Crashed and was killed while approaching to land at Wittering in Beaufighter X7620. Buried at Bournemouth East Cemetery, Hampshire. His pilot, Fg Off R G Setchell, survived.

9th December 1941 J/5496 Plt Off Ralph Ellard HOLDER, RCAF. Pilot. Aged 20, of Sault Ste Marie, Ontario, Canada. Pilot of Beaufighter X7580, stalled and crashed on take-off at Wittering (Wireless Operator/Air Gunner, Fg Off G G Waddington, also killed; see below). Interred in All Saints Churchyard, Wittering, Northamptonshire.

9th December 1941 85712 Fg Off George Guy WADDINGTON, RAFVR. Wireless Operator/Air Gunner. Killed in Beaufighter X7580 which stalled and crashed on take-off at Wittering. (Pilot, Plt Off R E Holder, RCAF, also killed; see above). Interred in All Saints Churchyard, Wittering, Northamptonshire.

11th February 1942 1157375 Sgt Anthony Wilson LAVENDER, RAFVR. Pilot. Killed or drowned when Beaufighter X7625 crashed into sea off Irish coast during night training flight from Ballyhalbert. Body not recovered. Remembered on Runnymede Memorial.

11th February 1942 1291581 Sgt Nagu RANGANATHA, RAFVR. Wireless Operator/Air Gunner. Aged 20 of Golders Green, Middlesex. Killed or drowned when Beaufighter X7625 crashed into sea off Irish coast, flying from Ballyhalbert. Body not recovered. Remembered on Runnymede Memorial.

23rd July 1942 116693 Plt Off Gerald George PIZEY, RAFVR. Pilot. Aged 20, of Blackpool, Lancashire. Killed when Beaufighter R2254 was shot down in error by Beaufighter X7941 (not of No.25 Squadron) off Bridlington. Body may not have been recovered as no reference is made in Commonwealth War Graves Commission records. Nor can the name be found on Runnymede Memorial.

8th September 1942	655283 F/Sgt Kenneth GILL, RAF. Pilot. Aged 21, of Blackburn, Lancashire. Abandoned Beaufighter R2205 over the North Sea following engine failure. Body not recovered. Remembered on Runnymede Memorial.
8th September 1942	658178 Sgt Reginald William CATLIN, RAF. Navigator/Radar Operator. Aged 22, of Hampton Hill, Middlesex. Abandoned Beaufighter R2205 over the North Sea following engine failure. Body not recovered. Remembered on Runnymede Memorial.
8th October 1942	1284380 F/Sgt Henry Lyons MIDDLEMAST, RAFVR. Pilot. Aged 22, of Stanley, County Durham. Killed when Beaufighter X7569 suffered engine failure when approaching to land at Church Fenton and struck buildings. (Navigator/ Radar Operator, F/Sgt Cracken, injured). Stanley New Cemetery, County Durham.
7th November 1942	1171174 Sgt Michael Harold GRIFFITH, RAFVR. Pilot. Aged 20, of Torquay, Devon. After one engine had failed, he crashed in Beaufighter X7698 while approaching to land at Pocklington and was killed. Buried at St Catherine Churchyard, Barmby Moor, Yorkshire.
30th November 1942	116101 Plt Off Raymond PEAKE, RAFVR. Pilot. Aged 22, of Higher Poynton, Stockport, Cheshire. Flying Mosquito II DD782, crashed and killed while attempting to overshoot on one engine at Church Fenton. (Navigator Radar Operator, Sgt T R Parry, also killed; see below). Buried at St George Churchyard, Poynton, Stockport.
30th November 1942	1134677 Sgt Thomas Richardson PARRY, RAFVR. Navigator/Radar Operator. Aged 20, of Wallasey. Mortally injured while flying in Mosquito II DD782 when it crashed overshooting on one engine at Church Fenton (Pilot, Plt Off R Peake, also killed; see above). Buried at Rake Lane Cemetery, Wallasey, Cheshire,
5th February 1943	90157 Acting Sqn Ldr William Fleming CARNABY, RAF, AUXAF. Pilot. Aged 29, of Newmarket, Suffolk. Was flying Mosquito HJ918 when it broke up in cloud, 2 miles from Church Fenton, killing him and his navigator/radar operator, Fg Off J H L Kemp (see below). Buried in Newmarket Cemetery, Suffolk.
5th February 1943	125946 Fg Off James Hector Lennox KEMP, RAFVR. Navigator/Radar Operator. Aged 26. Was killed in Mosquito HJ918 when it broke up in cloud near Church Fenton (Pilot, Sqn Ldr W F Carnaby, also killed; see above). Buried in New Kilpatrick Cemetery, Dumbartonshire.
22nd March 1943	656008 Sgt John Hudson STAPLES, RAFVR. Pilot. Aged 28, of Llaniestyn, Anglesey. Killed in Mosquito flying from Church Fenton. Records appear to be contradictory. Sgt Staples may have been the pilot of Mosquito DD750 which had been reported Missing on 2nd March 1943, and was later found to have crashed into a remote hillside at White Craig, Silsden, near Keighley. Sgt Staples lies buried in St Iestyn Churchyard, Llaniesztyn, Anglesey.
22nd March 1943	1576326 Sgt Ralph Ernest ANDREWS, RAFVR. Navigator/Radar Operator. Aged 20. Records contradictory. Sgt Andrews may have been killed in Mosquito DD750 which was later found to have crashed at White Craig and had been reported Missing on 2nd March 1943 (Pilot, Sgt J Hudson, also killed; see above). He was ward of Alfred and Beatrice Oldacre of Etruria, Stoke-on-Trent, and was buried at Hartshill Cemetery, Staffs.
8th April 1943	1294007 F/Sgt Terence Emile PROCUREUR, RAFVR. Pilot. Aged 21 of Ipswich, Suffolk. Killed when Mosquito DD747 broke up in the air and crashed at Airmyn, South Yorkshire (Navigator/Radar Operator, Sgt G H Wheatland, also killed; see below). Buried in Ipswich Cemetery, Suffolk.
8th April 1943	1338437 Sgt Gerald Henry WHEATLAND, RAFVR. Navigator/Radar Operator. Aged 21 of Hounslow. Killed when Mosquito DD747 broke up in the air and crashed at Airmyn, South Yorkshire (Pilot, F/Sgt T E Procureur, also killed; see above). Buried in St Leonard Churchyard, Heston, Middlesex.
28th May 1943	42491 Sqn Ldr David EVANS, RAF. Pilot. Aged 24, of Bebington, Cheshire. Killed flying Mosquito DZ264 which crashed during a single-engine landing at Church Fenton. Was probably flying alone. Lies buried in St Andrew Churchyard, Bebington, Cheshire.
13th June 1943	138510 Fg Off James Kenneth MYCOCK, RAFVR. Aged 22, of Royton, Lancashire. Posted Missing from patrol over Bay of Biscay in Mosquito DZ688. (Fg Off J Cheney, also Missing; see below). Reported to have been shot down by Focke-Wulf FW 190s. Remembered on Runnymede Memorial.
13th June 1943	122306 Fg Off Jack CHENEY, RAFVR. Aged 21, of Spalding, Lincolnshire. Posted Missing from patrol over Bay of Biscay in Mosquito DZ688. (Fg Off J K Mycock, also Missing; see above). Reported to have been shot down by Focke-Wulf FW 190s. Remembered on Runnymede Memorial.
13th June 1943	117154 Fg Off James Edward WOOTTON, RAFVR. Navigator/Radar Operator. Aged 23, of Hornsey, Middlesex. Posted Missing from patrol over Bay of Biscay in Mosquito DZ685 (Plt Off J Grundy also posted Missing; see below). Reported to have been shot down by Focke-Wulf FW 190s. Remembered on Runnymede Memorial.
13th June 1943	141016 Plt Off John Meikle DYMOCK, RAFVR. Aged 33. Posted Missing from patrol over the Bay of Biscay in Mosquito DZ685 (Plt Off J E Wootton also posted Missing; see above). Reported to have been shot down by Focke-Wulf FW 190s. Remembered on Runnymede Memorial.
13th July 1943	144280 Plt Off Jack GRUNDY, RAFVR. Pilot. Aged 20, of Sneinton, Nottingham. Killed flying Mosquito HJ921 which stalled and spun off steep turn and crashed at Weardale Road, Sherwood, Nottingham. Lies buried in Nottingham Southern Cemetery.
30th July 1943	109361 Flt Lt Edred Rodney Fitzpatrick COOKE, RAFVR. Pilot. Killed in Mosquito DD748 which crashed into the sea 10 miles off Flamborough Head during a patrol over the North Sea on the night of 29th/30th July 1943. Body not recovered. Remembered on Runnymede Memorial.
30th July 1943	1283359 F/Sgt Frederick Herbert ELLACOTT, RAFVR. Navigator/Radar Operator. Aged 27, of Hathersage, Derbyshire. Was flying in Mosquito DD748 which crashed into the sea 10 miles off Flamborough Head during the night of 29th/30th July 1943 (see Flt Lt E R F Cooke, above). Body recovered off Danish coast and buried in Kirkeby Cemetery on the island of Rømø, Denmark.

12th August 1943	783577 Pchor Juliam NOWAK, Polish Air Force. Aged 36. Killed in Mosquito DD637 which dived into the ground at Sigglesthorne, East Yorkshire (cause unknown). (Navigator/Radar Operator, W/Off C G Kendall, also killed; see below). Interred at St Mary Churchyard, Brandesburton, Yorkshire.
12th August 1943	1293123 W/Off Charles Godfrey KENDALL, RAFVR. Aged 34, of Cheam, Surrey. Killed in Mosquito DD637 which crashed at Sigglesthorne, East Yorkshire (Pilot, Pchor Julian Nowak, Polish Air Force, also killed; see above). Interred in Cheam Cemetery, Surrey.
2nd October 1943	953382 Sgt Herbert Anthony HAY, RAFVR. Pilot. Aged 21, of Castletown, County Durham. Killed in Mosquito DD738 which was in collision with Mosquito HK713 on night intruder training flight and crashed at Holme Lane, Shipton Thorpe, Market Weighton, Shropshire. (Sgt J C Scammell also killed; see below). Buried at Hylton Cemetery, Castletown, County Durham.
2nd October 1943	1681770 Sgt John Cosson SCAMMELL, RAFVR. Navigator/Radar Operator. Aged 33, of Charlton-cum-Hardy, Manchester. Killed in Mosquito DD738 on night intruder training flight and crashed at Shipton Thorpe, Shropshire (Pilot, Sgt H A HAY, also killed; see above). Cremated at Manchester Crematorium.
2nd October 1943	J/17904 Plt Off Thomas Patrick QUINN, RCAF. Pilot. Aged 21, of Bainsville, Ontario, Canada. Killed in Mosquito HK713 on night intruder training flight and crashed at Shipton Thorpe, Shropshire (Air Bomber, F/Sgt S A Carter, also killed; see below). Buried at Stonefall Cemetery, Harrogate, Yorkshire.
2nd October 1943	1585185 F/Sgt Stanley Albert CARTER, RAFVR. Air Bomber. Aged 20, of Ilford, Essex. Killed when Mosquito HK713 was in collision with Mosquito DD738 during night intruder training flight (Pilot, Plt Off T P Quinn, also killed; see above). Buried at Stonefall Cemetery, Harrogate, Yorkshire.
20th October 1943	82954 Sqn Ldr Kenneth MATHEWS, RAFVR. Was in Mosquito DZ689 which failed to return from a bomber support sortie. Buried in Sneek General Cemetery, Friesland, Netherlands. His Observer, Flg Off D C Burrow was taken prisoner.
12th December 1943	33412 Sqn Ldr Colin ROBERTSON, RAF. Pilot. Aged 26, of Falkirk, Stirlingshire. Died when Mosquito DD754 spun and crashed near Filey on the Yorkshire coast, being unable to extricate himself from marshy ground. Buried at Falkirk Cemetery, Stirlingshire.
12th December 1943	145496 Fg Off Ernest BARTHOLOMEW, RAFVR. Navigator/Radar Operator. Of Brynamman, Glamorgan. Died when Mosquito DD754 spun and crashed near Filey, being unable to extricate himself from marshy ground. Buried in Siloam Baptist Chapelyard, Lower Brynamman.
9th June 1944	127525 Fg Off Kenneth William GRAY, RAFVR. Pilot. Aged 23, of Basford, Newcastle-under-Lyme. Pilot of Mosquito HK354, killed on Bomber Support operation. No known grave. Remembered on Runnymede Memorial.
9th June 1944	145849 Fg Off Douglas Arthur HARWOOD, RAFVR. Navigator/Radar Operator. Aged 24, of Sherwood, Nottingham. Crew member of Mosquito HK354, killed on Bomber Support sortie (see above). No known grave. Remembered on Runnymede Memorial.
13th June 1944	88430 Flt Lt Alastair Stuart Hamilton BAILLIE, RAFVR. Pilot. Aged 30, of Moidart, Renfrewshire. Killed flying Mosquito HK288 on Bomber Support operation to Deelen, and crashed at Eupen (Fg Off J M Simpson also killed; see below). Buried at Brummen General Cemetery, Netherlands.
13th June 1944	136337 Fg Off John Milne SIMPSON, RAFVR. Pilot. Aged 22, of Montrose, Angus. Killed flying in Mosquito HK288 on Bomber Support operation to Deelen, and crashed at Eupen (Flt Lt A S H Baillie, also killed; see above). Buried at Brummen General Cemetery, Netherlands.
24th September 1944	102156 Flt Lt John Sharper LIMBERT, RAFVR. Pilot. Aged 23, of Finchley, Middlesex. While flying Mosquito NF.XVII HK300, was Killed in Action whilst attacking a V-1 flying bomb. No known grave. Remembered on Runnymede Memorial
24th September 1944	142132 Fg Off Henry Spencer COOK, RAFVR. Navigator/Radar Operator. Aged 20, of Barnes, Surrey. While flying in Mosquito NF.XVII HK300, was killed in attack on V-1 flying bomb. No known grave. Remembered on Runnymede Memorial.
26th September 1944	1377058 W/Off William Henry WATTS, RAFVR. Pilot (?). Aged 32. Was killed when Mosquito NF.XVII HK305 crashed into the sea off Wareham during drogue firing practice. Body not recovered. Remembered on Runnymede Memorial.
26th September 1944	1543012 F/Sgt Eric Armitage WALKER, RAFVR. Navigator/Radar Operator (?). Aged 23, of Warrington, Lancashire. Was killed when Mosquito NF.XVII HK305 crashed into the sea off Wareham during drogue firing practice. Body not recovered. Remembered on Runnymede Memorial.
7th October 1944	156605 Fg Off Roland Alfred NICHOLLS, RAFVR. Navigator/Radar Operator. Is believed to have been killed when Mosquito NF.XVII HK256 hit the sea while attacking a Hainkel He 111 carrying a V-1 flying bomb. Body not recovered. Remembered on Runnymede Memorial.
27th November 1944	47124 Flt Lt Alfred Ernest MARSHALL, DFC, DFM, RAF. Pilot. Aged 29, of Hitchin, Hertfordshire. Killed when Mosquito NF.XXX MT472 broke up in the air while recovering from dive during air test over Castle Camps. Interred in Hitchin Cemetery.
27th November 1944	149496 Fg Off Charles Arnold ALLEN, RAFVR. Navigator/Radar Operator. Aged 24, of Harrogate, Yorkshire. Killed when Mosquito NF.XXX MT472 broke up in the air while recovering from dive during air test over Castle Camps. Interred in the RAF Regional Cemetery within Harrogate (Stonefall) Cemetery, Yorkshire.

23rd January 1945	89635 Sqn Ldr John ARNSBY, RAFVR. Pilot. Aged 29, of Petts Wood, Kent. Killed in Mosquito NF.XXX MT494 which collided with Mosquito NF.XXX MV529 during practice interception and crashed at Camps Hall, Cambridgeshire. Cremated at the South London Crematorium.
23rd January 1945	129126 Flt Lt Douglas Mitchell REID, DFC, RAFVR. Navigation/Radar Operator. Aged 29, of Hyndland, Glasgow. Killed in Mosquito MT494 in collision with MT529 during practice interception; crashed at Camps Hall, Cambridgeshire. Buried in New Kilpatrick Cemetery, Dunbartonshire.
23rd January 1945	106851 Flt Lt Donald Leslie WARD, DFC, RAFVR. Aged 25, of Walsgrave-on-Sowe, Warwickshire. Killed in Mosquito NF.XXX MV529, in collision with Mosquito MT494 during practice interception, and crashed at Camps Hall, Cambridgeshire. Buried at Walsgrave-on-Sowe Cemetery, Warwickshire.
23rd January 1945	116703 Flt Lt Ernest Derek EYLES, DFC, RFVR. Navigator/Radar Operator. Aged 31, of Wellingborough, Northamptonshire. Was killed in Mosquito NF.XXX which was in collision with Mosquito MT494 during practice interception exercise; aircraft crashed at Camps Hall, Cambridgeshire. Buried in Doddington Road Cemetery, Wellingborough, Northamptonshire.
9th February 1945	116053 Flt Lt Michael CORRIE, DFM, RAFVR. Pilot. Aged 27 of Saffron Walden, Essex. Was killed when Mosquito NF.XXX MT489 struck trees on take-off and crashed at Bendish Hall, Radwinter, Essex. Buried at Saffron Walden Cemetery, Essex.
6th March 1945	116559 Flt Lt Edward Guy SHEPPARD, RAFVR. Pilot. Aged 25. Was killed flying an air test in Mosquito NF.XXX, MT470, when it lost power and struck trees in forced landing at Brookhall Farm, near Borley, Essex. Interred at Brentwood (London Road) Cemetery, Essex.
6th March 1945	1585748 F/Sgt Frederick George WARD, RAFVR. Navigator/Radar Operator. Aged 20, of Buckland Ripers, Dorset. Killed when Mosquito NF.XXX, MT470, lost power during air test and struck trees while making forced landing at Brookhall Farm, near Borley, Essex. (Pilot, Flt Lt E G Sheppard, also killed; see above). Interred at RAF Regional Cemetery, Cambridge.

Post Second World War

13th September 1948	55151 Flt Lt Eric N HART, RAFVR. Aged 35. Pilot of Mosquito NF.36 RL117 which collided while in formation with VT612 of No.85 Squadron and crashed at West Malling. (Navigator, Fg Off R L PALMER, was also killed).
13th September 1948	1454521 Pilot(2) S J BOUCHIER, RAFVR. Pilot of Mosquito T3, VT612, which collided while in formation with Mosquito RL117 and crashed near West Malling (see above).
7th June 1949	Fg Off R J WILKIE. Pilot of Mosquito RL204 crashed during single-engine landing four miles west of West Malling. Was flying solo.
16th August 1951	Flt Lt Roy Alexander Keats WINTON, RAF. Pilot, aged 31. Was pilot of Vampire NF.10 WP237 which failed to take-off at West Malling, crashed in the overshoot area and was burned out.
16th August 1951	Sgt Thomas Greig PETRIE. Navigator/Radar Operator, aged 25. Killed when the Vampire NF.10 WP237 piloted by Flt Lt Winton, failed to become airborne, crashed and was burned out (see above).
21st May 1952	Flt Lt Harry John KING, RAF. Navigator/Radar Operator, and Squadron Adjutant. Aged 29. Was flying as an exercise observer from No.25 Squadron in Lancaster ASR III, RE200, of No.204 Squadron; he and three others (members of No.204 Squadron) were killed when the Lancaster crashed at West Malling following a fire in the aircraft's bomb-bay. The Lancaster's crew escaped with slight injuries. (There were no regular crash positions for non-crew members).
18th December 1952	Flt Lt Cecil Conelius William SMITH, RAF. Aged 33. Flight Commander. Pilot of Vampire NF.10 WM669 which hit the sea and sank six miles east of Dungeness during low-level practice interception at night. Body not recovered.
18th December 1952	Fg Off James McNicol ADAMS, RAF. Navigator/Radar Operator of Vampire WM669 which hit the sea and sank six miles east of Dungeness during low-level practice interception at night (see above). Body not recovered.
19th October 1953	Fg Off John Albert DIDMON-WHITE, RAF. Aged 28. Pilot of Vampire NF.10, WP252, abandoned aircraft in a spin 10 miles south-east of South Foreland, but did not survive.
4th February 1957	Sqn Ldr Alan Edward HALL, DFC, RAF. Aged 33. Pilot and Flight Commander of 'B' Flight. Killed when his Meteor NF.14 WS753 suffered a canopy structural failure and crashed into high ground four miles west of Oxford while apparently attempting a forced landing. He lies buried at West Malling.
4th February 1957	Fg Off Arthur Geoffrey LEVETT, RAF. Aged 28. Nav/Rad. Killed when flying in the above Meteor NF.14 which suffered a canopy structural failure and crashed four miles west of Oxford (see Sqn Ldr A E Hall, above). Buried at West Malling.
26th October 1961	Flt Lt John Harry MORRIS, RAF. Aged 28. Navigator of Javelin FAW.9 XH906, killed when it collided with Canberra WD995 of No.32 Squadron during practice night interception and abandoned two miles north of Akrotiri, Cyprus. (Pilot, Flt Lt R H Lloyd, survived)

APPENDIX 2

PRISONERS OF WAR

NO.25 (FIGHTER) SQUADRON

Name	*Date*	*Aircraft*	*Serial*
ACKERS, Lt Cyril Holland Shakerley	26th February 1918	D.H.4	A7697
ARTHUR, Lt Thomas James	15th August 1918	D.H.4	A7891
ARMSTRONG, John Lewis Pasteur (Died of wounds)	22nd June 1916	F.E.2b	5209
BELL, 2/Lt Evelyn Victor Allen	8th April 1917	F.E.2b	A813
BLACKALL, 2/Lt John Fenwick Walker	21st May 1917	D.H.4	A6447
BOE, 2/Lt David	29th June 1918	D.H.4	A7913
CAMPBELL-MARTIN, Lt Pierre Clifford	3rd February 1918	D.H.4	A7873
CLEAR, Sgt A L	12th October 1917	D.H.4	A7426
COPELAND, Lt Arthur Harold Madill	10th October 1916	F.E.2b	4292
COTTON, Lt Henry	28th May 1917	D.H.4	A6378
CUDMORE, 2/Lt Ernest Osmond	5th February 1918	D.H.4	A7680
De SELINCOURT, Capt Aubrey	28th May 1917	D.H.4	A6378
DEMPSEY, Sgt John	13th April 1917	F.E.2b	A784
DOBESON, 2/Lt Richard Gray	1st November 1918	D.H.9a	F1068
DODSON, Lt Leonard	3rd April 1917	F.E.2d	A6371
ELLIOTT, Sgt W C	7th June 1918	D.H.4	D9266
FITZ-GIBBON, 2/Lt Cyril Joseph	21st April 1918	D.H.4	A7563
FRENCH, Lt Gerald Sidney	1st May 1917	F.E.2b	A815
GRAY, 2/Lt George Morgan	27th June 1918	D.H.4	A7670
GREEN, 2/Lt William Henry	13th April 1917	F.E.2b	A784
GREEN, Lt Ernest George, MC	3rd February 1918	D.H.4	A7873
GREIG, Capt Oscar	24th January 1917	F.E.2b	6997
GRINNELL-MILNE, Capt Duncan	16th May 1916	F.E.2B	6341
HACKLETT, Lt Leslie Arnold	7th June 1918	D.H.4	D9266
HARDING, Lt Geoffrey Parker, MC (escaped) ‡	1st May 1917	F.E.2b	A815
HILLS, 2Lt Oswald Marchant	21st October 1917	D.H.4	A7503
HUNT, 2/Lt Keith Flashman	22nd September 1916	F.E.2b	6993
KNIGHT, 2/Lt Norman Leslie	28th March 1917	F.E.2b	7715
LAW, 1/Air Mech L O	22nd September 1916	F.E.2b	6693
LAWE, 2/Lt Alfred George	11th August 1919	D.H.4	A7891
LEACH, 1/Air Mech G P	22nd November 1917	D.H.4	A2170
LOUPINSKY, 2/Lt Jacob	10th July 1918	D.H.4	D7279
McCALLUM, 2/Lt A H K	8th April 1917	F.E.2b	A813
MacDONALD, 2/Lt Donald Peter	3rd April 1917	F.E.2d	A6382
McLAURIN, 2/Lt Dougald	21st October 1917	D.H.4	A7503
MacLENNAN, Lt J E	24th January 1917	F.E.2b	6997
McMASTERS, Cpl D	126th May 1916	F.E.2b	6341

MAIN, 1/Air Mech L J W	3rd February 1918	D.H.4	A7680
MAIN, 2/Lt Robert	23rd November 1917	D.H.4	A2170
MATSON, 2/Lt Arthur William	18th March 1918	D.H.4	A2171
MILLS, 2/Lt Frederick George	1st November1918	D.H.9a	F1068
MOODY, 2/Lt Beverley Charles	21st May 1917	D.H.4	A6447
ROBINSON, 2/Air Mech T	18th June 1916	F.E.2b	4909
RUDMAN, 2/Lt Walter, MC	21st April 1918	D.H.4	A7563
SHAW, Lt George Mydhope	26th January 1918	D.H.4	A7697
SMITH, Lt Vivian	28th May 1917	F.E.2d	A6410
SOUTHORN, Lt Thomas Noble	28th May 1917	F.E.2d	A6410
STURROCK, L/Cpl C	28th May 1917	F.E.2d	A32
TALBOT, 2/Lt Fred William	12th October 1917	D.H.4	A7426
TANNENBAUM, 2/Lt Harold	2nd June 1918	D.H.4	A7882
TAYLOR, Sgt H	18th June 1916	F.E.2b	6940
TOPLIFFE, Sgt G	22nd June 1916	F.E.2b	5209
WEBSTER, Lt J	27th June 1918	D.H.4	A7670
WENSLEY, Lt James Haywood	18th March 1918	D.H.4	A2171
WRIGHT, Sgt J R	10th July 1918	D.H.4	D2879
ZIEMAN, Lt John Robert	2nd June 1918	D.H.4	A7882

Second World War

BRINSDEN, Sqn Ldr Francis Noel	17th August 1943	Mosquito FB.VI	HX826
SEWELL, Fg Off Peter Gordon Fane	17th August 1943	Mosquito FB.VI	HX826
BURROW, Fg Off Derek Charles	21st October 1943	Mosquito NF.II	DZ689
HENDERSON, Fg Off Jack Stuart	7th October 1944	Mosquito NF.XVII	HK256

‡ *This Officer excaped from captivity and returned to England on 22nd October 1917.*

APPENDIX 3

Squadron Victory Scoreboard

No.25 (Fighter) Squadron

FIRST WORLD WAR

Fokker EIII	29th April 1916	Lt Lord Doune (pilot) and 2/Lt R U Walker (observer) in F.E.2b 5209.
Albatros DII(?)	16th May 1916	Lt H B Davey (pilot) and Lt J A Mann (observer) in F.E.2b 5209.
Aviatik	16th May 1916	2/Lt G R M Reid (pilot) and Lt J A Mann (observer) in F.E.2b 6330.
Fokker EIII	19th May 1916	2/Lt G R M Reid (pilot) and Lt J A Mann (observer) in F.E.2b 6330.
(Unidentified)	21st May 1916	2/Lt G R M Reid (pilot) and Lt J A Mann (observer) in F.E.2b 6330.
Fokker EIII	18th June 1916	2/Lt G R McCubbin (pilot) and Cpl J H Waller (observer) in F.E.2b (No. not known).
Roland C	22nd June 1916	Capt C T McLean (pilot) and 2/Lt J C Barraclough (observer) in F.E.2b 6336.
Fokker EIII	2nd July 1916	Lt H B Davey (pilot) and Cpl W Paull (observer) in F.E.2b 5238.
Fokker EIII	19th July 1916	2/Lt N W Webb (pilot) and Lt J A Mann (observer) in F.E.2b 5245.
Two Fokker EIIIs	20th July 1916	Lt H B Balfour (pilot) and Capt H C Morley (observer) in F.E.2b 5238, *shared with* 2/Lt L I Richardson (pilot) and 1/Air Mech L S Court (observer) in F.E.2b 6932.
Roland CII	8th August 1916	2/Lt C H C Woolven (pilot) and Lt C Nelson (observer) in F.E.2b 6991.
Albatros C	9th August 1916	2/Lt N W W Ward (pilot) and Lt C S Workman (observer) in F.E.2b 4839.
Fokker EIII	7th September 1916	2/Lt A T Lloyd (pilot) and 2/Lt C S Workman (observer) in F.E.2b 6993, *shared with* Capt C H Dixon (pilot) and Air Mech J H Booth (observer) in F.E.2b 6997.
Fokker EIII	15th September 1916	2/Lt N W W Ward (pilot) and Lt C S Workman (observer) in F.E.2b 4841.
Roland D	16th October 1916	2/Lt J L N Bennett-Boggs (pilot) and 2/Lt A E Godfrey (observer) in F.E.2b 4847.
(Unidentified)	22nd October 1916	2/Lt D S Johnson (pilot) and 2/Lt W G Meggitt (observer) in F.E.2b 4877.
(Unidentified)	22nd October 1916	Sgt W D Matheson (pilot) and 2/Lt W G Meggitt (observer) in F.E.2b 7007.
(Unidentified)	26th October 1916	Lt J L Leith (pilot) and Sgt L S Court (observer) in F.E.2b, 7693.
Fokker DII	9th November 1916	Lt J L Leith (pilot) and 2/Lt E L Chadwick (observer) in F.E.2b 7693.
Albatros DI	16th November 1916	Lt C H C Woolven (pilot) and 2/Lt C H Marchant (observer) in F.E.2b 7024.
(Unidentified)	17th November 1916	Sgt J H R Green (pilot) and Cpl A G Bower (observer) in F.E.2B 4877 – *shared with four other aircraft.*

LVG C	22nd November 1916	Lt H B Balfour (pilot) and Lt A L Harrow-Bunn (observer) in F.E.2b 7694.
Albatros DI	23rd November 1916	Lt C H C Woolven (pilot) and Sgt G R Horrocks (observer) in F.E.2b 7024.
Albatros DII	23rd November 1916	Sgt J H R Green (pilot) and Capt A G Bower (observer) in F.E.2b 7672.
Albatros DII	23rd November 1916	Capt J L Leith (pilot) and 2/Air Mech L Emsden (observer) in F.E.2b 7683.
Halberstadt	23rd January 1917	2/Lt B Mews (pilot) and 2/Lt A V Blenkiron (observer) in F.E.2b 4925.
Albatros DII	24th January 1917	Lt J L Leigth (pilot) and 2/Lt A G Severs (observer) in F.E.2b 4946.
Albatros DII	29th January 1917	Lt J L Leith (pilot) and 2/Lt D C Wollen (observer) in F.E.2b 7693.
Albatros DII	29th January 1917	2/Lt A W Shirtcliffe (pilot) and Lt A V Blenkiron (observer) in F.E.2b A784.
(Unidentified)	15th February 1917	Capt L L Richardson (pilot) and 2/Lt W G Meggitt (observer) in F.E.2b 7686.
Albatros DIII	1st March 1917	Capt J L Leith (pilot) and Lt G M S Hobart-Hampden (observer) in F.E.2b A782.
LVG C	4th March 1917	Lt R G George (pilot) and Cpl E Emsden (observer) in F.E.2b 7693, *shared with* 7025, A780 and A5439.
Albatros	4th March 1917	Lt R G Malcolm (pilot) and Cpl L Lumsden (observer) in F.E.2b 4839.
(Unidentified)	16th March 1917	Lt J Whittaker (pilot) and 2/Air Mech F King (observer) in F.E.2b A5484.
Albatros DII	17th March 1917	Capt J L Leith (pilot) and 2/Air Mech L Emsden (observer) in F.E.2b 7693.
Albatros DII	17th March 1917	Lt R G Malcom (pilot) and Lt C W Wilson (observer) in F.E.2b A782.
Albatros DIII	17th March 1917	Lt C H C Chapman (pilot) and Sgt J H Booth (observer) in F.E.2b A5484.
(Unidentified)	6th April 1917	2/Lt A Roulstone (pilot) and 2/Lt E G Green (observer) in F.E.2c, 7686.
Albatros DIII	7th April 1917	2/Lt C Brown (pilot) and 2/Lt D P Walter (observer) in F.E.2b 7025.
Albatros DIII	9th April 1917	Lt T N Southorn (pilot) and 2/Lt H E Freeman-Smith (observer) in F.E.2b 7683.
Albatros DIII	13th April 1917	Sgt W A Burtenshaw (pilot) and Sgt J H Brown (observer) in F.E.2b 7003, *shared with* Capt J L Leith (pilot) and Lt G M S Hobart-Hampden in F.E.2b A782.
Albatros DIII	13th April 1917	Lt R G Malcom (pilot) and Cpl L Emsden (observer) in F.E.2d A6385.
Albatros DIII	14th April 1917	Sgt W A Burtenshaw (pilot) and Sgt J H Brown (observer) in F.E.2b 7003, *shared with* Lt R G Malcom (pilot) and 2/Lt J B Weir (observer) in F.E.2d 6383.
Albatros DIII	21st April 1917	Lt R G Malcom (pilot) and 2/Lt J B Weir (observer) in F.E.2d A6373.
Albatros DIII	22nd April 1917	Sgt W Green (pilot) and Cpl L Emsden (observer) in F.E.2b A797.
Albatros DIII	24th April 1917	2/Lt A Roulstone (pilot) and 2/Lt E G Green (observer) in F.E.2b 5247.

Albatros DIII	26th April 1917	Sgt J H R Green (pilot) and 2/Lt H E Freeman-Smith (observer) in F.E.2b 5427.
Albatros	26th April 1917	Lt C Dunlop (pilot) and Lt J B Weir (observer) in F.E.2b 4839.
Albatros DIII	26th April 1917	Lt C Dunlop (pilot) and Lt J B Weir (observer) in F.E.2d A5152.
Two Albatros DIIIs	1st May 1917	Lt R G Malcom (pilot) and Cpl L Emsden (observer) in F.E.2b 7672.
Albatros DIII	6th June 1917	Sgt J H R Green (pilot) and Pte H Else (observer) in F.E.2d A6365, *shared with* A6401 and A6500.
Two Albatros D IIIs	7th June 1917	Lt C T Lally (pilot) and 2/Lt L F Williams (observer) in F.E.2d A6417.
Albatros DIII	8th June 1917	Sgt R Mann (pilot) and 2/Air Mech J Harris (observer) in F.E.2d A6360.
Albatros DIII	24th June 1917	Sgt A N Stretton (pilot) and 1/Air Mech W Trezise (observer) in F.E.2d A6419.
Albatros DV	7th July 1917	Capt J Fitz-Morris (pilot) and Lt D L Burgess (observer) in D.H.4 A7505.
Albatros DV	11th July 1917	2/Lt F H Sargent (pilot) and Lt J Kirk (observer) in F.E.2d A6370.
Albatros DV	20th July 1917	Capt A Roulstone (pilot) in D.H.4 A7482.
Albatros DV	22nd July 1917	Capt J Fitz-Morris (pilot) and Lt D L Burgess (observer) in D.H.4 A7505.
Albatros DV	5th August 1917	Lt C T Lally (pilot) in D.H.4 A7477.
Albatros DIII	22nd August 1917	Lt A Roulstone (pilot) and Lt D Taylor-Fox (observer) in D.H.4 A7547.
Albatros DIII	4th September 1917	Lt D G E Jardine (pilot) and 2/Lt G Bliss (observer) in D.H.4 A7405.
Albatros DIII	4th September 1917	Lt C A Pike (pilot) and 2/Lt A T Williams (observer) in D.H.4 A7487. 2/Lt Williams died of wounds.
(Unidentified)	27th October 1917	Lt J A McCudden (pilot) and Air Mech J Harris (observer) in D.H.4 A7487.
Siemens Schukert DIII	27th March 1918	Capt J E Pugh (pilot) and 2/Lt W L Dixon (observer) in D.H.4 A7913.
(Unidentified)	29th March 1918	2/Lt S Jones (pilot) in D.H.4 A8078.
Fokker DrI	8th June 1918	Lt W H G Milnes (pilot) in D.H.4 A7626.
Pfalz DIII	4th August 1918	Lt J A Latchford (pilot) and 2/Lt H Pullen (observer) in D.H.4 A7637.
Pfalz DIII	4th August 1918	Lt L Young (pilot) and 2/Lt H Pullen (observer) in D.H.4 D9271.

THE SECOND WORLD WAR

	(Dest = Destroyed)	*(Dam = Damaged) (Prob Dest = Probably Destroyed)*
Heinkel He 115 (Dest)	20th July 1940	F/Sgt John Granville Lingard (pilot) gunner not known in Blenheim If, off Walton on-the-Naze.
Heinkel He 111H (Dest)	5th September 1940	Plt Off Michael James Herrick (New Zealand) (pilot) and Sgt John Stewart Pugh (gunner) in Blenheim If, near Braintree, Essex

Dornier Do 17 (Dest)	5th September 1940	Plt Off Michael James Herrick (New Zealand) (pilot) and Sgt John Stewart Pugh (gunner) in Blenheim If, near Rendlesham, Suffolk.
Heinkel He 111H (Dest)	14th September 1940	Plt Off Michael James Herrick (New Zealand) (pilot), Plt Off Archibald Wilkinson Brown (gunner) and Air Gunner Frank Files (radar operator) in Blenheim If, near Sheering, Essex.
Heinkel He 111H (Dest)	15th November 1940	Sgt Sydney Victor Holloway (pilot), Sgt James Douglas Culmer (observer) and Aircraftman Fields (gunner) in Blenheim, west of Chelmsford.
Dornier Do 17 (Dam)	16th January 1941	Flt Lt Christopher Dermont Salmond Smith (pilot) and Sgt Charles Alexander Johnson (observer) in Beaufighter If R2158, near Stowmarket, Suffolk.
Junkers Ju 88 (Dest)	9th April 1941	Sgt S Bennett (pilot) and Sgt Frank William Curtis (observer) in Beaufighter If R2122, near Cottesmore, Rutland.
(Unidentified) (Prob.Dest)	27th April 1941	Flt Lt J F Inkster (pilot) and Sgt Charles Alexander Johnson (observer) in Beaufighter If, over the area of the Wash.
Heinkel He 111H (Dest)	4th May 1941	Sgt Arnold Maurice Hill (pilot) and Sgt Ernest James Hollis (radar operator) in Beaufighter If, 7 miles south-east of Derby.
Junkers Ju 88 (Prob. Dest)	4th May 1941	Sgt Sydney Victor Holloway (pilot) and Sgt Richard George Crossman (observer) in Beaufighter If R2156, north of the Wash.
Junkers Ju 88? (Prob Dest)	4th May 1941	Wg Cdr David Francis William Atcherley (pilot) and Flt Lt John Hunter Hunter-Tod (radar operator) in Beaufighter If R2251, between Bourne and Market Deeping, Lincolnshire.
(Unidentified) (Dam)	5th May 1941	Sgt Sydney Victor Holloway (pilot) and Sgt Richard George Crossman (radar operator) in Beaufighter If R2156, location of combat not recorded.
(Unidentified) (Dam)	5th May 1941	Sqn Ldr Harold Percival Pleasance (pilot) and Sgt Benjamin Bent (radar operator) in Beaufighter If T2629, near Aldeburgh, Suffolk.
Junkers Ju 88 (Dam)	6th May 1941	Sgt Sydney Victor Holloway (pilot) and Sgt Reginald Robert Charles Pound (radar operator) in Beaufighter If R2197, near Watton, Norfolk.
Dornier Do 17Z (Dest)	8th May 1941	Sqn Ldr Harold Percival Pleasance (pilot) and Sgt Benjamin Bent (radar operator) in Beaufighter If T4634, near Skegness, Lincolnshire.
Dornier Do 17Z (Dest)	8th May 1941	Plt Off D W Thompson (pilot) and Plt Off L D Britain (radar operator) in Beaufighter If R2181, 10 miles north of Boston, Lincolnshire.
Junkers Ju 88 (Dam)	8th May 1941	Sgt Arnold Maurice Hill (pilot) and Sgt Ernest James Hollis (radar operator) in Beaufighter If R2247, near Holt, Norfolk.
Junkers Ju 88 (Dam)	8th May 1941	Plt Off Michael James Herrick (New Zealand) (pilot) and Sgt John Lewis (radar operator) in Beaufighter If R2209, south of Hull.
Junkers Ju 88 (Dam)	9th May 1941	Sgt Sydney Victor Holloway (pilot) and Sgt Reginald Robert Charles Pound (radar operator) in Beaufighter If R2198, near Grantham.
Dornier Do 17Z (Dest)	9th May 1941	Sqn Ldr Percival Pleasance (pilot) and Sgt Benjamin Bent (radar operator) in Beaufighter If T4634, over the coast about 15 miles north of Holt, Norfolk.
Heinkel He 111H? (Dam)	9th May 1941	Plt Off D W Thompson (pilot) and Plt Off L D Britain (radar operator) in Beaufighter If R2181, between Grantham and the East coast.

Focke-Wulf Fw 200 (Dest)	10th May 1941	Plt Off A J Picknett (pilot) and Plt Off G F Sellick (radar operator) in Beaufighter If T4636, south-east of Boston, over the Wash.
Heinkel He 111H (Dam)	12th May 1941	Plt Off D W Thompson (pilot) and Plt Off L D Britain (radar operator) in Beaufighter If R2181, inland from Skegness, Lincolnshire.
Heinkel He 111H (Dam)	12th May 1941	Sqn Ldr Harold Percival Pleasance (pilot) and Sgt Benjamin Bent (radar operator) in Beaufighter If T4634, about 10 miles north-west of Wells, Norfolk.
Heinkel He 111H (Dest)	17th May 1941	Sgt Kenneth Bruce Holloway (pilot) and Sgt Richard George Crossman (radar operator) in Beaufighter R2156, over the sea near West Runton, Norfolk.
Heinkel He 111H (Dest)	5th June 1941	Sgt H A H Gigney (pilot) and Sgt Gerard Chamock (radar operator) in Beaufighter If R2157, near Louth, Lincolnshire.
Heinkel He 111H (Dest)	5th June 1941	Sgt Kenneth Bruce Holloway (pilot) and Sgt Richard George Crossman (radar operator) in Beaufighter R2154, over the Wash.
Junkers Ju 88 (Dest)	14th June 1941	Sqn Ldr Harold Percival Pleasance (pilot) and Sgt Benjamin Bent (radar operator) in Beaufighter If T1634, near Swaffham, Norfolk.
Heinkel He 111H (Dest)	14th June 1941	Plt Off D W Thompson (pilot) and Plt Off L D Britain (radar operator) in Beaufighter If R2157, at Terrington, King's Lynn, Norfolk.
Junkers Ju 88? (Dest)	17th June 1941	Wg Cdr David Francis William Atcherley (pilot) and Flt Lt John Hunter Hunter-Tod (radar operator) in Beaufighter Ib R2251, near Sheringham, Norfolk.
Junkers Ju 88 (Dest)	22nd June 1941	Fg Off Michael James Herrick (New Zealand) (pilot) and Plt Off L Yeomans (radar operator) in Beaufighter R2277, near Market Deeping, Lincolnshire.
Heinkel He 111H (Dest)	25th June 1941	Plt Off D W Thompson (pilot) and Plt Off L D Britain (radar operator) in Beaufighter If R2082, over south Lincolnshire.
Junkers Ju 88 (Dest)	5th July 1941	Wg Cdr David Francis William Atcherley (pilot) and Flt Lt John Hunter Hunter-Tod (radar operator) in Beaufighter R2251, 21 miles east of Wells, Norfolk.
Junkers Ju 88 (Prob Dest)	1st October 1941	Sqn Ldr Harold Percival Pleasance (pilot) and Plt Off L D Britain (radar operator) in Beaufighter If X7621, near the Norfolk coast north of Wells.
Dornier Do 217 (Dest)	30th May 1942	Fg Off A J Picknett (pilot) and Plt Off H D Rodgers (radar operator) in Beaufighter If X7711, 15 miles ENE of Withernsea, South Yorkshire coast.
(Unidentified) (Dam)	5th June 1942	Flt Lt J F Inkster (pilot) and Fg Off L Yeomans (radar operator) in Beaufighter If X7876, off the coast at Whitby, Yorkshire.
Dornier Do 217 (Dest)	24th June 1942	Pilot and Nav Rad not named. Beaufighter If. Over the Humber Estuary.
Dornier Do 217 (Dam)	30th July 1942	Fg Off A J Picknett (pilot) Plt Off H D Rodgers and Sgt Patterson (nav rads) in Beaufighter If X7711, three miles east of Mablethorpe, Lincolnshire.
Dornier Do 217 (Dest)	9th August 1942	Wg Cdr Harold Percival Pleasance (pilot) Flt Lt L D Britain (nav rad) in Beaufighter If V8326, over the sea, 20 miles east of Hornsea, Yorkshire.
Junkers Ju 88 (Dam)	12th August 1942	Flt Sgt H L Middlemast (pilot) and Flt Sgt D McCracken (nav rad) in Beaufighter If X7569, 9 miles west of Selby, Yorkshire.

Dornier Do 217 (Dam)	23rd August 1942	Fg Off Joseph Singleton (pilot) and Plt Off C J Bradshaw (nav rad) in Beaufighter If X7643, 15 miles east of Bourne, South Lincolnshire.
Dornier Do 217 (Dest)	23rd August 1942	Sqn Ldr C J Alington (pilot) Fg Off DB Keith (nav rad) in Beaufighter If V8329, east of Sutton Bridge.
Dornier Do 217 (Dest)	23rd August 1942	Wg Cdr Harold Percival Pleasance (pilot) and Flt Lt L B Britain (nav rad) in Beaufighter If V8326, 20 miles east of Mablethorpe, Lincolnshire.
Heinkel He 111H (Dest)	2nd September 1942	Fg Off Joseph Singleton (pilot) and Plt Off C J Bradshaw (nav rad) in Beaufighter If X7824, over the sea 20 miles east of Filey, Yorkshire.
Heinkel He 111H (Dam)	6th September 1942	Flt Lt J L Shaw (pilot) and W/Off C Guthrie (nav rad) in Beaufighter If X7705, over the sea 10-15 miles east of Flamborough Head.
Dornier Do 217 (Dest)	15th September 1942	Sqn Ldr C J Alington (pilot) and Fg Off D B Keith (nav rad) in Beaufighter If V8329, over the sea 7 miles north of Sheringham, Norfolk.
Dornier Do 217 (Dam)	17th September 1942	Fg Off Joseph Singleton (pilot) and Plt Off C J Bradshaw (nav rad) in Beaufighter If X7824, near Hunstanton, north Norfolk.
Dornier Do 217 (Prob Dest)	19th September 1942	Sgt J H Staples (pilot) and Sgt J S D Gravell (nav rad) in Beaufighter If X7814, over the sea 45 miles north-east of Flamborough Head, Yorkshire.
Dornier Do 217 (Prob Dest)	19th September 1942	Plt Off J L B Norris (pilot) and Plt Off J R F Guyton (nav rad) in Beaufighter If R2081, over the sea about 70 miles north-east of Flamborough Head, Yorkshire.
Dornier Do 217 (Dest)	24th September 1942	Plt Off R Peake (pilot) and Sgt T R Parry (nav rad) in Beaufighter If X7814, over the sea 15 miles north-east of Flamborough Head.
Dornier Do 217 (Dam)	15th January 1943	Flt Lt Joseph Singleton (pilot) and Flt Lt C J Bradshaw (nav rad) in Mosquito NF.II DD752, on intruder operations over Holland.
(Unidentified) (Dam)	14th May 1943	Pilot and radar operator not recorded, in Mosquito NF.II over Twente, Holland.
Junkers Ju 88 (Dest)	11th June 1943	Flt Lt Joseph Singleton (pilot) and Fg Off William Geoffrey Haslam (radar operator) in Mosquito NF.II, off the Danish coast.
Junkers Ju 88 (Dam)	11th June 1943	Fg Off J E Wootton (pilot), radar operator not recorded, in Mosquito NF.II, probably on bomber support operations.
Junkers Ju 88 (Dest)	24th July 1943	Flt Lt E R F Cooke (pilot) and Flt Sgt F M Ellacott (radar operator) in Mosquito NF.II DD738, 4 miles south-west of Westland.
Junkers Ju 88 (Dest)	3rd October 1943	Fg Off V H Linthune (pilot) and W/Off J L Paine (radar operator) in Mosquito NF.II over Elgershausen, 5 miles south-west of Kassel, while on bomber support/intruder operations.
Junkers Ju 188 (Dest)	20th February 1944	Plt Off J R Brockbank (pilot) and Plt Off D McCausland (nav rad) in Mosquito NF.XVII HK285, over Braintree, Essex.
Dornier Do 217 (Dest)	20th February 1944	Flt Lt Joseph Singleton (pilot) and Fg Off William Geoffrey Haslam (nav rad) in Mosquito NF.XVII HK255, over the sea 50 miles east of Lowestoft, Suffolk.
Heinkel He 177 (Dest)	23rd February 1944	Flt Lt A S H Baillie (pilot) and Fg Off J M Simpson (nav rad) in Mosquito NF.XVII HK255, over Yoxford, East Suffolk.

Junkers Ju 188 (Dest)	14th March 1944	Flt Lt Joseph Singleton (pilot) and Fg Off William Geoffrey Haslam (nav rad) in Mosquito NF.XVII HK255, over the sea 4-5 miles east of Southwold, Suffolk.
Junkers Ju 188 (Dest)	19th March 1944	Flt Lt Joseph Singleton (pilot) and Fg Off William Geoffrey Haslam (nav rad) in Mosquito NF.XVII HK255, over the sea 55 miles NNE of Cromer, Norfolk.
Junkers Ju 188 (Dest)	19th March 1944	Flt Lt Joseph Singleton (pilot) and Fg Off William Geoffrey Haslam (nav rad) in Mosquito NF.XVII HK255, over the sea 65 miles NNE of Cromer, Norfolk.
Junkers Ju 188 (Dest)	19th March 1944	Flt Lt Joseph Singleton (pilot) and Fg Off William Geoffrey Haslam (nav rad) in Mosquito NF.XVII HK255, over the sea 50 (?) miles NNE of Cromer, Norfolk.
Dornier Do 217 (Dest)	19th March 1944	Flt Lt Douglas Haig Greaves (pilot) and Fg Off F M Robbins (nav rad) in Mosquito NF.XVII HK278, over the sea 35 miles NNE of Cromer, Norfolk.
Heinkel He 177 (Dest)	19th March 1944	Flt Lt Douglas Haig Greaves (pilot) and Fg Off F M Robbins (nav rad) in Mosquito NF.XVII HK278, over the sea 30 miles NNW of Cromer, Norfolk.
Junkers Ju 188 (Dest)	22nd March 1944	Flt Lt R L E Davies (pilot) and Fg Off Benjamin Bent (nav rad) in Mosquito NF.XVII HK322, 35 miles south-west of Lowestoft, Suffolk.
Junkers Ju 188 (Dest)	22nd March 1944	Flt Lt R L R Davies (pilot) and Fg Off Benjamin Bent (nav rad) in Mosquito NF.XVII HK322, 25 miles south-west of Southwold, Suffolk.
Junkers Ju 188 (Dest)	25th March 1944	Flt Lt V H Linthune (pilot) and Fg Off Alfred Bernard Cumbers (nav-rad) in Mosquito NF.XVII HK293, over the sea 45 miles east of Lowestoft, Suffolk.
Junkers Ju 88 (Prob Dest)	19th April 1944	Flt Lt R M Carr (pilot) and Flt Lt Saunderson (nav rad) in Mosquito NF.XVII HK288, in Map Ref H1295 (over the North Sea).
Junkers Ju 188 (Dest)	19th April 1944	Flt Lt R M Carr (pilot) and Flt Lt Saunderson (nav rad) in Mosquito NF.XVII HK288, over Suffolk coast 3 miles south of Southwold.
Dornier Do 217 (Prob Dest)	19th April 1944	Plt Off B Travers (pilot) and Plt Off A H C W Patterson (nav rad) in Mosquito NF.XVII HK304, over the sea 60 miles east of Great Yarmouth, Norfolk.
Messerschmitt Me 410 (Dest)	19th April 1944	Plt Off K V Panter (pilot) and W/Off A W Mogg (nav rad) in Mosquito NF.XVII HK237, over the sea 15-20 miles west of Ijmuiden, Holland.
Junkers Ju 188 (Dest)	20th April 1944	Flt Sgt D J Carter (pilot) and Sgt W J Hutchings (nav rad) in Mosquito NF.XVII HK354, off the Suffolk coast.
Messerschmitt Me 410 (Dest)	29th May 1944	Wg Cdr Cathcart Michael Wight-Boycott (pilot) and Flt Lt D M Reid (nav rad) in Mosquito NF.XVII HK257, over the sea north-east of Cromer, Norfolk.
Messerschmitt Bf110 (Dest)	6th June 1944 (00:43hrs)	Flt Lt R L R Davies (pilot) and Fg Off Benjamin Bent (nav rad) in Mosquito NF.XVII HK322, over the sea west of Schiermonnikoog, Holland.
Messerschmitt Me 410 (Dest)	8th June 1944	Flt Lt Douglas Haig Greaves (pilot) and Fg Off F M Robbins (nav rad) in Mosquito NF.XVII HK354, over the sea off the Norfolk coast at Great Yarmouth.
Junkers Ju 188 (Dest)	23rd June 1944	Wg Cdr Cathcart Michael Wight-Boycott (pilot) and Flt Lt D M Reid (nav rad) in Mosquito NF.XVII HK257, north-west of Orfordness, Suffolk.

Messerschmitt Bf109G? (Dest)	28th August 1944	Plt Off B Travers (pilot) and Plt Off A H C W Patterson (nav rad) in Mosquito NF.XVII HK304, Location not known, but Belgium likely.
Heinkel He 111 (Prob Dest)	24th September 1944	Fg Off R A Henley (pilot) and Flt Sgt J R Hope (nav rad) in Mosquito NF.XVII, over the sea probably off Suffolk.*
Heinkel He 111 (Prob Dest)	25th September 1944	Wg Cdr L J C Mitchell (pilot) and Flt Lt D L Cox (nav rad) in Mosquito NF.XVII HK357, over the sea 60 miles east of Coltishall.*
Junkers Ju 188 (Dest)	26th September 1944	Wg Cdr Cathcart Michael Wight-Boycott (pilot) and Flt Lt D M Reid (nav rad) in Mosquito NF.XVII (identity not recorded), over the sea about 30 miles south-west of Lowestoft. Suffolk.
Heinkel He 111 (Dest)	29th September 1944	Wg Cdr L J C Mitchell (pilot) and Flt Lt D L Cox (nav rad) in Mosquito NF.XVII HK357, over the sea 40 miles east of Grest Yarmouth, Norfolk.*
Heinkel He 111 (Dest)	29th September 1944	Wg Cdr L J C Mitchell (pilot) and Flt Lt D L Cox (nav rad) in Mosquito NF.XVII HK357, over the sea 50 miles east of Great Yarmouth, Norfolk.*
Heinkel He 111 (Dest)	5th October 1944	Flt Lt J F R Jones (pilot) and Fg Off R Skinner (nav rad) in Mosquito NF.XVIII HK239, over the sea off the Norfolk coast.*
Heinkel He 111 (Deat)	6th October 1944	Flt Lt Alfred Ernest Marshall (pilot) and Fg Off C A Allen (nav rad) in Mosquito NF.XVII HK257, over the sea 40 miles east of Southwold, Suffolk.*
Heinkel He 111 (Dest)	7th October 1944	Plt Off B Travers (pilot) and Plt Off A H C W Patterson (nav rad) in Mosquito NF.XVII HK285, over the sea off the Norfolk coast.*
Heinkel He 111 (Dest)	9th November 1944	Flt Lt J M Lomas (pilot) and Flt Lt N B Fleet (nav rad) in Mosquito NF.XXX MV521, over the sea 35 miles east of Clacton-on-Sea, Essex.*
Heinkel He 111 (Dest)	11th November 1944	Flt Lt Douglas Haig Greaves (pilot) and Fg Off F M Robbins (nav rad) in Mosquito NF.XXX MT492, over the sea 70 miles east of Lowestoft, Suffolk.*
Heinkel He 219 (Dest)	1st February 1945	Flt Lt J M Lomas (pilot) and Flt Lt N B Fleet (nav rad) in Mosquito NF.XXX MV521, 10 miles east of Bonn, Germany, on bomber support operations.

* Target aircraft probably V-1 flying bomb launch aircraft.

The primary sources for the above Victory claims filed during the Second World War have been the Forms 1152 (Combat Reports) held at the Public Record Office under AIR 50/13, with alterations notified by DDI (Tech), whose teams visited many of the crash sites on land soon after the German aircraft were shot down. These alterations have, in the main, confirmed the identity of an aircraft, but often located the crash site some miles from the location of the combat recorded in the Combat Reports.

The purpose of DDI Tech, Department of the Director of Intelligence (Technical) was to gather Intelligence concerning enemy aircraft, their equipment and armament, as well as technical Intelligence gathering during interrogation of captured German aircrew members. Some documents relating to the work of this Department are still considered sensitive and remain classified.

APPENDIX 4

COMMANDING OFFICERS

NO.25 (FIGHTER) SQUADRON

Major (Temporary) F.V. Holt, DSO (later Air Vice-Marshal, CMG, DSO, RAF)	Sept 1915 – Mar 1916
Major Thomas Walter Colby Carthew (later Lieut-Col, DSO, MC)	Mar 1916
Major R.G. Cherry	Mar 1916 – May 1917
Major the Hon Oscar Montague Guest	June 1917 – Oct 1917
Major C.S. Duffus	Oct 1917 – Jan 1919
Captain J.B. Fox	Jan 1919 – Feb 1919
Captain S. Jones	Feb 1919 – Mar 1919
Captain George Maxwell Lawson, MC (later Air Cdre, CBE, MC)	Mar 1919
Captain Charles Edward Hamilton, DFC (later Air Vice-Marshal, CB, DFC)	Mar 1919
Captain J.B. Fox	Mar 1919 – Apr 1919
Captain C.T. Lally	Apr 1919
Major C.S. Duffus	Apr 1919
Captain C.T. Lally	Apr 1919
Major G.G.A. Williams	Apr 1919 – Dec 1919
Squadron Leader Sir Norman Roderick Alexander Leslie, BT, CBE (8th Baronet, later Wg Cdr, Air Attaché, Paris, 1924)	Apr 1920 – Feb 1923
Squadron Leader Arthur Hicks Peck, DSO, MC (later Group Captain, DSO, MC)	Feb 1923 – Sept 1926
Squadron Leader E.D. Atkinson, DFC, AFC (Retired, RAF, 1927)	Sept 1926 – Apr 1927
Squadron Leader W.H. Park, MC, DFC (Retired, RAF, 1928?)	Apr 1927 – Sept 1928
Squadron Leader L.G.S. Payne, MC, AFC (Retired as Air Cdre, CB, MC, AFC, 10-12-45)	Sept 1928 – Feb 1930
Squadron Leader Robert Stanley Aitken, MC, AFC (Retired as Air Vice-Marshal, CB, CBE, MC, AFC, 20-7-46)	Feb 1930 – Oct 1930
Squadron Leader Harold Melsome Probyn, DSO (Retired as Air Cdre, CB, CBE, DSO, 25-9-44)*	Oct 1930 – Feb 1932
Squadron Leader Walter Edward George Bryant, MBE (Retired as Gp Capt, MBE)	Feb 1932 – Feb 1933
Squadron Leader Anthony Lauderdale Paxton, DFC (Retired (?) as Wg Cdr, DFC)	Feb 1933 – Jan 1935
Squadron Leader William Forster Dickson, DSO, OBE, AFC (later appointed Chief of the Air Staff, and rose to Marshal of the Royal Air Force Sir William, GCB, KBE, DSO, AFC)	Jan 1935 – Feb 1936

Squadron Leader Harold Hunter Down, AFC (Retired as Air Cdre, CBE, AFC, 2-11-45)	Feb 1936 – Sept 1937
Squadron Leader Donald Malcolm Fleming, DFC (later Wg Cdr, DFC)	Sept 1937 – Jan 1939
Squadron Leader John Robert Hallings-Pott, DSO (Retired as Air Vice-Marshal, CBE, DSO, AFC, 13-7-57)	Jan 1939 – May 1940
Squadron Leader Kenneth Alexander Keswick McEwan (Did not survive the War)	May 1940 – June 1940
Squadron Leader Wilfred William Loxton (Retired as Wg Cdr, AFC, 31-5-57; *fl.* 1990)	June 1940 – Sept 1940
Squadron Leader Henry Maynard Mitchell, DFC, AAF (Retired from RAF as Wg Cdr, DFC, 1946)	Sept 1940 – Jan 1941
Wing Commander David Francis William Atcherley, DFC (later Air Vice Marshal, CB, CBE, DSO, DFC)	Jan 1941 – Aug 1941
Squadron Leader Harold Percival Pleasance, DFC AND BAR (Retired from RAF as Gp Capt, OBE, DFC AND BAR, 1-12-60)*	Aug 1941 – Sept 1942
Squadron Leader Edward George (?) Watkins, AFC (later Gp Capt, CBE, AFC, 1962)	Sept 1942 – Mar 1943
Squadron Leader John Leslie Shaw, RAFVR	Mar 1943 – Apr 1943
Wing Commander Simon Napier Leslie Maude, DFC	Apr 1943 – Oct 1943
Wing Commander Cathcart Michael Wight-Boycott, DSO (Retired from RAF as Air Cdre, CBE, DSO AND BAR, 1-7-64)*	Oct 1943 – Aug 1944
Wing Commander Leicester John Cecil Mitchell, RAFVR	Aug 1944 – Apr 1945
Wing Commander W. Hoy, DFC (Retired from RAF as Wg Cdr, DFC, AFC, 5-4-66)*	Apr 1945 – Dec 1945
Squadron Leader R.T. Goucher, DFC	Dec 1945 – May 1946
Flight Lieutenant J. Lomas, AFC	May 1946
Squadron Leader I Hardiman, DFC	May 1946 – Apr 1947
Squadron Leader J Singleton, DSO, DFC, AFC (Retired from RAF as Wg Cdr, DSO, DFC, AFC, 22-5-58)*	Apr 1947 – Nov 1948
Squadron Leader K.B. McGlashan, AFC	Nov 1948 – July 1950
Squadron Leader Richard W Leggett (Retired from RAF as Wg Cdr, 1-4-68)*	July 1950 – Jan 1952
Squadron Leader D.C. Furse, DFC (Retired from RAF as Wg Cdr, DFC, 1-5-72)	Jan 1952 – Mar 1954
Squadron Leader J. Cameron Cox (Retired from RAF as Wg Cdr, MBIM, 15-7-68)*	Mar 1954 – May 1955
Wing Commander P.W. Jamieson, AFC AND BAR (Retired from RAF as Gp Capt, AFC AND BAR, 1-7-69)	May 1955 – Nov 1956
Wing Commander D.A. Trotman, AFC (Retired from RAF as Air Cdre, AFC, FBIM, 28-11-76)	Nov 1956 – Oct 1957
Wing Commander G.H. Melville-Jackson, DFC (Retired from RAF as Wg Cdr DFC, 29-9-68)	Oct 1957 – July 1958
Wing Command Kenneth H.H. Cook, DFC (Retired from RAF as Wg Cdr, DFC, 13-1-68)*	July 1958 – Jan 1960

Wing Commander J.H. Walton, AFC (Retired from RAF as Gp Capt, AFC, 5-4-72)	Jan 1960 – Oct 1961
Wing Commander P.G.K. Williamson, DFC	Oct 1961 – Oct 1963
Squadron Leader D.J. Fowler, AFC (Retired from RAF as Sqn Ldr, AFC, 19-3-69)	Oct 1963 – Aug 1964
Squadron Leader M.J. Bridges	Aug 1964 – July 1965
Squadron Leader M.R.S. Cunningham, MBE (Retired from RAF as Wg Cdr, MBE)*	July 1965 – Oct 1966
Wing Commander G. Middlebrook, MBE (Retired from RAF as Wg Cdr, MBE, 11-9-76)*	Oct 1966 – Feb 1969
Wing Commander H.D. Costain, MBE (Retired from RAF as Wg Cdr, MBE, MBIM, 27-3-77)	Feb 1969 – Mar 1973
Wing Commander J. Broughton (Retired from RAF as Air Cdre, FBIM, 1-1-89)*	Mar 1973 – Apr 1975
Wing Commander G.A. Massie (Retired from RAF as Wg Cdr, 14-5-83)	Apr 1975 – May 1977
Wing Commander E. Durham (Retired from RAF as Wg Cdr, 17-7-89)	May 1977 – Dec 1978
Wing Commander J. Ault, DFC (Retired from RAF as Wg Cdr, DFC, 29-1-87)	Dec 1978 – Nov 1981
Wing Commander A.C. Collins	Nov 1981 – Nov 1984
Wing Commander G.C. Smith, AFC	Nov 1984 – July 1987
Wing Commander J.P. Anderson	July 1987 – July 1989
Wing Commander A.M. Martin (Retired from RAF as Wg Cdr, 10-92)*	July 1989 – Oct 1992
Wing Commander J. Middleton*	Oct 1992 – July 1995
Wing Commander Philip C. Goodman, MBE, BSC (later Gp Capt)*	July 1995 – July 1998
Wing Commander Andrew Dey*	July 1998 – July 2000
Wing Commander Ian Morrison*	July 2000 –

** Past or present member of No.25 (Fighter) Squadron Association*

APPENDIX 5

Squadron Aircraft

No.25 (Fighter) Squadron

Prior to January 1916, while stationed at Montrose, Angus, and Thetford, Norfolk, No.25 Squadron pilots underwent training in a heterogeneous collection of aeroplanes, including Maurice Farmans, Caudron G.IIIs, R.A.F. B.E.2Cs, Avro 504s, Martinsyde G.100s and eight Curtiss JN.4s. Prior to moving to St Omer, France, on 20th February 1916, the Squadron was issued with a total of 24 Royal Aircraft Factory F.E.2bs which were delivered to its camp at Thetford direct from the manufacturers (G & J Weir Ltd, Cathcart, Glasgow, and Boulton & Paul Ltd, Norwich, Norfolk).

Avro 504 (80hp Gnome engine)

750 Formerly No.6 Reserve Squadron. Taken on charge 25th September 1915. The earliest known aircraft on No.25 Squadron charge. To No.32 Sqn., 1st January 1916.

Maurice Farman S7 Longhorn

2974 Formerly on charge of No.6 Reserve Squadron and transferred to No.25 Squadron in September 1915. Known to have been flown by Lieut. A.F. Somerset-Leeke on the Squadron. Struck off Squadron charge when moved to Thetford, Norfolk.

Caudron G.III

1887 Formerly with No.6 Reserve Squadron and transferred to No.25 Squadron in September 1915.

1900 Formerly with No.6 Reserve Squadron and transferred to No.25 Squadron in September 1915.

5255 Taken on charge, 1st October 1915; Struck off charge, 15th November 1915.

5256 Taken on charge, 1st October 1915; transferred to No. 19 Sqn., 12th November 1915.

Curtiss J.N.3

Eight of these aircraft were delivered new to No.25 Squadron and taken on charge on 1st October 1915.

5625 Transferred to No.32 Sqn., 1st January 1916.

5626 Transferred to No.32 Sqn., 1st January 1916.

5627 Transferred to No.32 Sqn., 1st January 1916.

5628 Transferred to No.32 Sqn., 1st January 1916.

5629 Transferred to No.32 Sqn., 1st January 1916.

5630 Struck off following accident, 3rd November 1915.

5631 Transferred to No.32 Sqn., 1st January 1916.

5632 Transferred to No.32 Sqn., 1st January 1916.

Martinsyde S.1

At least two examples of this lesser-known single-seater were delivered to Montrose, and taken over by No.25 Squadron, but were discarded when, following the failure of the D.H.2 to meet the Squadron's delivery schedule and the decision to equip it with the two-seat F.E.2b, the Martinsydes were passed on to No.32 Sqn.

4247 Taken on charge, October 1915; transferred to No.32 Sqn., 1st January 1916.

4248 Taken on charge, October 1915; transferred to No.32 Sqn., 1st January 1916.

Royal Aircraft Factory B.E.2c

2106 Received from No. 12 Sqn., 22nd February 1916; remained at Thetford until disposed of to 19th Wing Assembly Station Montrose, 11th July 1916.

2613 On temporary charge from A.R.S. No.1 A.D., 6th - 10th March 1916.

2615 On temporary charge from A.R.S. No.1 A.D., 20th - 21st March 1916.

4121 Taken on charge from Home Defence Flight, Cramlingham, 13th December 1915; to No.32 Sqn., 1st January 1916.

4310 Taken on charge for Home Defence duties, December 1915; to No.32 Sqn., 1st January 1916.

4313 Taken on charge, c. 15th December 1915; to No.32 Sqn., 1st January 1916.

4502 Received from A.R.S. No.1 A.D., 11th March 1916, for training.

4513 Received from A.R.S. No.1 A.D., 22nd February 1916; returned there 1st April 1916.

5384 Taken on charge from No. 17 Sqn., 26th October 1915; to No.32 Sqn., 1st January 1916.

5390 Taken on charge, 15th November 1915; written off 7th December 1915.

5394 On temporary charge from No.22 Sqn., 1st February 1915; returned to No.22 Sqn, soon after.

5397 Taken on charge, c. November 1915; to No.32 Sqn., 1st January 1916.

5399 Taken on charge, c. November 1915; to No.32 Sqn., 1st January 1916.

Vickers F.B.5 Gunbus

1629 Vickers-built; Received from No.24 Sqn., 5th January 1916; Still with Squadron February 1916.

2341 Vickers-built; Received from No.24 Sqn., 5th January 1916; Still with Squadron February 1916.

2342 Vickers-built; Received from No.24 Sqn., 5th January 1916; Still with Squadron February 1916.

5620 Vickers-built; Received from No.24 Sqn., 5th January 1916; Still with Squadron February 1916.

Morane-Saulnier Type L

One aircraft briefly on charge.

5056 Received from No.12 Sqn., February 1916; Later with No.1 Reserve Squadron.

Bristol Scout C

A small number of these small single-seat tractor biplanes were issued to No.25 Squadron on arrival in France.

4671 From A.R.S. No.1 A.D., 13th March 1916; Fate unknown.

4675 From A.R.S. No.1 A.D., 27th February 1916; Returned A.R.S. No.1 A.D., 13th March 1916.

4677 From No. 12 Sqn., 22nd February 1916; Wrecked, to A.R.S. No.1 A.D., 25th February 1916.

5298 From A.R.S. No.1 A.D., 25th February 1916; Crashed, 5th April 1916; To A.R.S. No.1 A.D., 6th April 1916.

5301 From A.R.S. No.1 A.D., February 1916; Fate unknown.

5303 From A.R.S. No.1 A.D., 22nd February 1916; Damaged landing 27th May 1916.

5304 From A.R.S. No.1 A.D., 28th March 1916; Crashed 14th May 1916; To A.R.S. No.1 A.D., 23rd May 1916.

5310 From A.R.S. No.1 A.D., 6th April 1916; To A.R.S. No.1 A.D., 5th June 1916.

5563 From A.R.S. No.1 A.D., 28th May 1916; To A.R.S. No.1 A.D., 5th June 1916.

Royal Aircraft Factory F.E.2b

Built by G & J Weir Ltd, Cathcart, Glasgow.

4269 From A.R.S. No.1 A.D., 22nd May 1916; To A.R.S. No.1 A.D., 4th Jûne 1916.

4272 From No.18 Sqn, 3rd June 1916; Shot down in flames by Fokker over Lens at 16.35hrs on 3rd August 1916 over Lens; 2/Lt K Matheson, pilot, and Sapper E M des Brisay, observer, both killed.

4280 Returned No.1 A.D., 29th April 1916; Fate unknown.

4281 From A.R.S. No.1 A.D., 18th July 1916; Wrecked, 31st August 1916; To A.R.S. No.1 A.D., 1st Sept 1916.

4283 From A.R.S. No.1 A.D., 24th June 1916; Crashed Bailleul, 15th July 1916, due to fuel shortage; Lt M T Vaughan, died of injuries, 27th July 1916.

4288 From A.R.S. No.1 A.D., 28th July 1916; Retd 1 A.D., 29th April 1916.

4289 From A.R.S. No.1 A.D., 24th June 1916; Fate unknown.

4292 From A.R.S. No.1 A.D., 6th August 1916; Shot down in combat in afternoon of 10th October 1916 during raid on Oppy. Crash landed behind German lines. 2/Lt M Hayne, pilot, killed; Lt A H M Copeland, observer, wounded and made PoW.

Built by G & J Weir Ltd, Cathcart, Glasgow.

4839 From A.R.S. No.1 A.D., 29 July 1916; 2/Lt N W W Ward, pilot, and Lt C S Workman, observer, forced down an Albatros C at Beaumont at 12.15hrs on 9th August 1916. On 27th September 1916, this aircraft was itself forced down near Tourmignies by Ltn Albert Dossenbach of *Flieger Abteilung* 22; 2/Lt V W Harrison, pilot, and Sgt L S Court, observer, unhurt. Aircraft repaired. On 4th March 1917 Lt R G Malcom, pilot, and Cpl L Emsden, observer, shot down an Albatros in flames at Bois Bernard; and on 26th April 1917 Lt C Dunlop, pilot, and 2/Lt J B Weir, observer, shot down an Albatros in flames at Izel-lès-Équerchin.

4840 From A.R.S. No.1 A.D., 8th August 1916; crashed from spinning nose dive at St Veviant, 16th August 1918. 2/Lt A S Butler, pilot, killed, and 2/Air Mech E B Brotherton, observer, seriously injured.

4841 From A.R.S. No.1 A.D., 16th August 1916; On 15th September 1916, 2/Lt N W W Ward and Lt C S Workman shot down a Fokker EIII at Fresnoy. On 10th November 1916, while on patrol, the propeller disintegrated and severed the tail booms; the aircraft crashed killing 2/Lt E S P Hynes, pilot, and 2/Lt C H Bidmead, observer. Wreckage to No.1 A.D., 11th November 1916.

4845 From A.R.S. No.1 A.D., 19th August 1916; Fate unknown.

4847 From A.R.S. 1 A.D., 2nd August 1916; On 16th October 1916, 2/Lt J L N Bennett-Boggs, pilot, and 2/Lt A E Godfrey forced down a Roland D out of control west of Douai at 11.20hrs on 16th October 1916. 10.45hrs on 6th April 1917 crashed near Vimy. 2/Lt B King, pilot, and Cpl L Emsden, observer, safe.

4857 From A.R.S. No.1 A.D., 28th March 1917; Returned to A.R.S. No.1 A.D., 31st March 1917.

4859 From A.R.S. No.1 A.D., 17th September 1916; SOC 1st October 1916.

4866 From A.R.S. No.1 A.D., 19th September 1916; SOC 3rd October 1916.

4877 From A.R.S. No.1 A.D., 14th October 1916; On 22nd October 1916 at 16.20hrs 2/Lt D S Johnson, pilot, and 2/Lt W G Meggitt, observer, shot down a German scout north-west of Lille. On 17th November 1916 Sgt J H R Green, pilot, and Cpl A G Bower, observer, shared the destruction of an enemy aircraft at Vitry with four other aircraft of the Squadron (6990, 7022, 7024 & 7025). To A.R.S. 1 A.D., 2nd April 1917; From A.R.S. No.1 A.D., 7th April 1917; At 16.44hrs on 14th April 1917 2/Lt W E Davies, pilot, wounded, and Lt N W Morrison, observer, killed when shot down in flames near Lievin, probably by Ltn K Schaefer of *Jasta* 11.

4907 From No.18 Sqn, 3rd June 1916; Damaged by ground fire over the Bois de Biez, 23rd June 1916, Lt H B Davey, pilot, unhurt, brought aircraft home; Lt S R P Walter, observer, wounded. Crashed 20 August 1916.

4908 From 18 Sqn, 3 June 1916; To A.R.S. No.1 A.D., 24th June 1916.

4909 From A.R.S. 1 A.D., 29th May 1916; In combat with 2 Fokkers, engine believed hit, shot down over Wingles 19.45 18th June 1916 (2/Lt JRB Savage, pilot, died of wounds & 2/Air Mech T Robinson, observer, PoW wounded) [shot down near Lens by Ltn Max Ritter von Mülzer KEK Nord].

4914 From A.R.S. No.1 A.D., 4th July 1916; Unserviceable, 6th August 1916 (SOC).

4922 From A.R.S. No.1 A.D., 23rd July 1916; Forced down by ground fire south-west of Haubourdin on 3rd Aug 1916; 2/Lt W H Rilett, pilot, and 1/Air Mech L S Court, observer, both unhurt. Aircraft wreckage shelled.

4925 From A.R.S. No.1 A.D., 10th August 1916; 2/Lt B Mews, pilot, and 2/Lt A V Blenkiron, observer, shot down a Halberstadt near Lens at 11.30hrs on 23rd January 1917. Wrecked, 10th April 1917; To A.R.S. No.1 A.D., 12th April 1917.

4929 From A.R.S. No.1 A.D., 29th July 1916; Delivered to Squadron, 29th July 1916. An old aircraft found to be incapable of climbing and disposed of to A.R.S. No.1 A.D., on 25th September 1916.

4932 From A.R.S. No.1 A.D., 29th July 1916; crashed and written off charge, 2nd August 1916.

4946 From A.R.S. No.1 A.D., 27th September 1916; Lt J L Leigh, pilot, and 2/Lt A G Severs, observer, shot down an Albatros DII Lievens-Lens at 15.00hrs on 24th January 1917.

4997 From A.R.S. No.1 A.D., 21st March 1917; Bombing raid on Henin Lietard, shot down by Manfred von Richthofen, *Jasta* 11, at 19.30hrs on 13th April 1917, near Noyelle-Godault (his 43rd victory). 2/Lt Allan Harold Bates, pilot, and Sgt William Alfred Barnes, observer, both killed in action.

Built by Boulton & Paul Ltd, Norwich, Norfolk.

5201 By 5th March 1916; Fokker E, shared with 5938 at 11.30hrs on 17th June 1916 (2/Lt J R B Savage & 2/Air Mech T Robinson); Unserviceable, 16th August 1916.

5209 By 5th March 1916; Lt Lord Doune, pilot, and 2/Lt R U Walker, observer, shot down a Fokker EIII at 11.05hrs on 29th April 1916 near La Bassée. Lt H B Davey, pilot, and Lt J A Mann, observer, shot down an Albatros near Lille at 09.25hrs on 16th May 1916. Shot down by Fokker at 07.30hrs on 22nd June 1916 near Loos by Leutnant Max Ritter von Mülzer of KEK Nord. 2/Lt J L P Armstrong, pilot, died of wounds in captivity; Sgt G Topliffe, observer, made PoW.

5210 In combat with enemy aircraft flown by Ltn Max Mülzer of *Fliegerabteilung* 62 near Estaires at 11.30hrs on 23rd April 1916, and was then engaged by ground fire which killed the observer, 2/Air Mech G F Atwell. Lt W E Collinson, pilot, force landed near Estaires during return flight. To A.R.S. No.1 A.D., 25th April 1916.

5211 Delivered by 5th March 1916; Crashed, 8th April 1916; To A.R.S. No.1 A.D., 9th April 1916.

5212 Delivered by 5th March 1916; Hit by ground fire and with damaged radiator 2/Lt Dixon made safe forced landing behind British lines, 4th May 1916. Aircraft recovered and repaired. In running fight with Fokker EIIIs on 26th June 1916; Lt R C B Riley, pilot, wounded, Lt Eric Hinks Bird, observer, died of wounds on 27th June.

5238 From A.R.S. No.1 A.D., 18th April 1916; Damaged in air combat on 17th May 1916 over La Bassée canal (Capt W Milne, pilot, wounded; 2/Lt E R Davis, observer, unhurt); aircraft returned safely. At 19.30hrs on 2nd July 1916 Lt H B Davey, pilot, and Cpl W Paull, observer, shot down a Fokker EIII over Lille. At

18.30hrs on 20th July 1916 Lt H B Balfour, pilot, and Capt H C Morley, observer, shared in the destruction of two Fokker EIIIs with 2/Lt L I Richardson, pilot, and 1/Air Mech L S Court, observer, in F.E.2b 6932. On 6th September 1916 aircraft was shot down in flames by Fokker over Allied territory; 2/Lt J L Roberton, pilot, jumped and was killed; 2/Lt E C Kemp, observer, killed when aircraft crashed.

5245 From A.R.S. 1 A.D., 19th June 1916. On 19th July 1916 at 06.45hrs 2/Lt N W Webb, pilot, and Lt J A Mann, observer, shot down Fokker EIII which crashed east of Provin. Crashed 26th August 1916.

5247 From A.R.S. No.1 A.D., 19th April 1917; On 24th April 1917 at 17.50hrs 2/Lt A Roulstone, pilot, and 2/Lt E G Green, observer, caused an Albatros to break up in the air near Fosse de Drocourt. At 17.20hrs on 26th April 1917, Sgt J H R Green, pilot, and 2/Lt H E Freeman-Smith, observer, shot down an Albatros DIII in flames east of Bois Bernard.

Built by the Royal Aircraft Factory, Farnborough, Hants.

6330 From A.R.S. No.1 A.D., 25 February 1916; On 16th May at 08.40hrs Lt G R M Reid, pilot, and Lt J A Mann, observer, drove down an Aviatik, which crashed and overturned at Souchez; the same crew shot down a Fokker EIII at Henin-Lietard on 19th May 1916; and the same crew shot down a German two-seater near Lens at 18.05hrs on 21st May 1916. To A.R.S. No.1 A.D., 1st August 1916.

6334 On strength by 5th March 1916; Damaged on 22nd June 1916 by ground fire; pilot, 2/Lt L C Angstrom, wounded, brought aircraft home safely; 2/Lt H C Hardwick, observer, unhurt. Shot down in air combat over Cambrai, 26th June 1916; 2/Lt R Sherwell, pilot, unhurt, but observer 2/Air Mech H Chadwick, was killed.

6335 On strength by 5th March 1916; Damaged, to A.R.S. No.1 A.D., 1st April 1916.

6337 From No.18 Sqn, 3rd June 1916; Aircraft failed to rise on take-off on 19th July 1916 and hit firing butts adjoining the airfield. Capt M G B Copeman, pilot, and Cpl A Reed, observer, both slightly injured.

6339 From No.20 Sqn, 27th June 1916; Bombing raid on La Bassée, destroyed by AA gunfire Festubert, 3rd July 1916. 2/Lt R Sherwell, pilot, & 2/Lt J C M Stewart, observer, both killed.

6341 TOC 18th January 1916. Aviatik C forced to land Herlies 07.00 27th April 1916, 2/Lt R S Maxwell, pilot, & 2/Lt S A Sharpe, observer, unhurt. While escorting a morning reconnaissance patrol on 16th May 1916 the aircraft encountered ground fire and was then engaged by four German aircraft, being forced down near Fournes. Capt Duncan Grinell-Milne, pilot, and Cpl D McMaster, observer, both unhurt and made PoW, the former later escaping from captivity to Holland.

6342 On strength by 5th March 1916; observer, Capt H Seagrave, wounded in leg in combat with Fokker EIII while escorting photographic patrol by F.E.2bs over Gheluwe on 31st March 1916; aircraft returned safely, pilot, Lt Norris, unhurt; crashed 18th July 1916.

6342 Force landed near Delette in snowstorm on 22nd February 1917; pilot unhurt, but 2/Lt J C Barraclough, observer, injured.

6344 On strength by 5th March 1916; damaged by AA fire over La Bassée, 16th April, 1916; Lt C J Hart, pilot, and Cpl J H Waller, observer, unhurt. Crashed on take-off from forced landing, 28th May 1916; To A.R.S. No.1 A.D., 29th May 1916.

6346 From 18th January 1916; Left squadron, date unknown; From No.20 Sqn, 11th June 1916; Left at 07.15, damaged in air combat near Beauvray, 26th June 1916; aircraft returned safely, but 2/Lt G R McCubbin, pilot, wounded; Cpl J H Waller, observer, unhurt. To A.R.S. No.1 A.D., 10th August 1916.

6347 Flown to France with No.25 Sqn., 28th February 1916. Wrecked 6th May 1917; To A.R.S. No.1 A.D., 12th May 1916.

6366 From A.R.S. No.1 A.D., 28th March 1916. Capt C T McLean, pilot, and 2/Lt J C Barraclough, observer, drove down a Roland near Lens at 08.00hrs on 22nd June 1916. To A.R.S. No.1 A.D., 1st August 1916.

6369 From 20 Sqn, 8th June 1916; Unserviceable, 11th June 1916 (SOC).

6371 Overshot while landing, 17th July 1916; crashed and overturned in cornfield; Capt B M Hay, pilot, and 1/Air Mech M H Brown, observer, both seriously injured; aircraft written off.

6374 From No.20 Sqn, 2nd June 1916; Hit and damaged by ground fire, 16th July 1916. Lt W L Chadwick, pilot, unhurt; Private W H Truesdale wounded. To A.R.S. No.1 A.D., 1st August 1916.

6376 From A.R.S. No.1 A.D., 7th May 1916; Wrecked 16th May 1916; To A.R.S. No.1 A.D., 23rd May 1916.

Built by Boulton & Paul Ltd, Norwich, Norfolk.

6932 From A.R.S. No.1 A.D., 7th May 1916; Radiator damaged by AA fire north of Arras, 26th May 1916; Capt B M Hay, pilot, and 2/Lt J C M Stewart, observer, unhurt. Aircraft returned and repaired. At 18.30hrs on 20th July 1916 2/Lt L L Richardson, pilot, and 1/Air Mech L S Court, observer, shared with 5238 the destruction of two Fokker EIIIs east of Lens. 2/Lt Richardson wounded but brought aircraft home; Air Mech Court unhurt. Crashed 20th August 1916.

6936 Shot down by Allied ground fire on 28th February 1916; crew unhurt. No.25 Squadron's first aircraft loss in war theatre.

6938 From A.R.S. No.1 A.D., 17th May 1916; Hit and damaged by AA fire at Bethune, 7th June 1916. Lt Lord Doune, pilot, unhurt, brought aircraft safely back to base. 2/Lt R U Walker, observer, wounded; Fokker E sent down out of control at Don, shared with 5201 11.30hrs 17th June 1916 (Lt H B Davey & 2/Lt J B Hinchcliffe); To A.R.S. No.1 A.D., 29th April 1916.

6940 From No.20 Sqn, 15th June 1916; Left 14.35hrs, in combat at 3,000ft with enemy aircraft north-east of Arras on 18th June 1916 (Lt C E Rogers, pilot, died of wounds on following day; Sgt H Taylor, observer, wounded and made PoW). Probably shot down by Obltn. Max Immelmann of FAb62.

6967 From A.R.S. No.1 A.D., 27th June 1916; Wrecked 12th October 1916; To A.R.S. No.1 A.D., 14th Oct 1916.

6978 From A.R.S. No.1 A.D., 18th July 1916; Crashed and written off, 10th August 1916. No casualties.

6990 From A.R.S. No.1 A.D., 29th July 1916; On 1st August 1916 was damaged by ground fire between Fromelles and La Bassée. Capt C H Dixon, pilot, unhurt, 2/Lt J B Hinchcliffe, observer, wounded. An enemy scout shot down east of Lille at 15.15hrs on 20th October 1916 (Sgt J H R Green, pilot, and Cpl W P Gilbert, observer). An enemy aircraft, shot down near Vitry at 19.30hrs on 17th November 1916, was shared by 2/Lt D S Johnson, pilot, and 2/Lt I Heald, observer, in 6990 with four other F.E.2bs of No.25 Squadron (4877, 7022, 7024 & 7025). Hit by AA shell on photographic sortie 4th December 1916; Sgt J H R Green, pilot, unhurt and Cpl A G Bower, observer, wounded; To A.R.S. No.1 A.D., 31st March 1917.

6991 From A.R.S. No.1 A.D., 1st August 1916; At 06.40hrs on 8th August 1916, 2/Lt C H C Woolven, pilot, and Lt C Nelson, observer, shot down a Roland CII out of control at Don. Wrecked, 28th February 1917; To A.R.S. No.1 A.D., 2nd March 1917.

6993 From A.R.S. No.1 A.D., 6th August 1916; On 7th September 1916 at 17.50hrs, 2/Lt A T Lloyd, pilot, and 2/Lt C S Workman, observer, shared in the destruction of a Fokker EIII at Pont-à-Vendin with F.E.2b 6997 and 7003 (see below). Scout crashed nr Pont-à-Vendin 16.00hrs 9th September 1916 (2/Lt N W Webb, pilot, and Cpl L S Court, observer). On 22nd September 1916, left at at 06.40hrs, while flying low east of Douai was shot down by ground fire (2/Lt K F Hunt, pilot, and 1/Air Mech L O Low, observer, both unhurt and made PoW).

6995 From A.R.S. No.1 A.D., 1st August 1916; Crashed, 9th August 1916.

6996 From A.R.S. No.1 A.D., 4th August 1916; On 9th August 1916, while on patrol was shot down at about 19.00hrs and burnt out (circumstances not known). Lt C J Hart, pilot, and Lt J A Mann, observer, both killed.

6997 From A.R.S. No.1 A.D., 8th August 1916; On 7th September 1916 at 17.50hrs Capt C H Dixon, pilot, and Air Mech J H Booth, observer, shared in the destruction of a Fokker EIII at Pont-à-Vendin with F.E.2bs 6993 and 7003. In combat with Albatros over Rouvroy, shot down and force landed on 24th January 1917 west of Vimy by Rittmeister Manfred Freiherr von Richthofen of *Jasta* 11 – his 18th victory. Capt Oscar Grieg, pilot, and 2/Lt J E MacLennan, observer, unhurt but made PoW.

6998 From A.R.S. No.1 A.D., 1st August 1916; Wrecked, 18th October 1916; To A.R.S. No.1 A.D., for reconstruction, 20th October 1918.

7002 From A.R.S. No.1 A.D., 17 August 1916; On 24th August 1916 left at 17.30hrs, aircraft was hit by ground fire and forced to land among the trenches south of Armentières, where it came under artillery fire. 2/Lt M T Baines, pilot, and Lt W E Harper, observer, both slightly wounded.

7003 From A.R.S. No.1 A.D., 11th August 1916; On 7th September 1916 this F.E.2b (2/Lt N W W Webb, pilot, and Cpl H Brown, observer) shared with 6993 and 6997 (see above) in the destruction of a Fokker EIII at Pont-à-Vendin. On 16th November 1916, while returning from a bombing raid on Somain rail junction was hit by ground fire but returned safely (2/Lt H Sellers, pilot, unhurt; 2/Lt W W Fitzgerald, observer, severely wounded). On 13th April 1917 shared with A782 (see below) in shooting down an Albatros DIII at Sallaumines (Sgt W J Burtenshaw, pilot, and Sgt J H Brown, observer). On 14th April 1917 the same crew shared with F.E.2d A6383 in shooting down an Albatros DIII at Henin-Lietard. On 1st May 1917 Lt C H C Woolven, pilot, and Sgt J H Brown, observer, shot down an Albatros DIII south-east of Fresnoy.

7007 From A.R.S. No.1 A.D., 25th August 1916; Shot down a German scout south-west of Seclin at 09.00hrs on 22nd October 1916 (Sgt W D Matheson, pilot, and 2/Lt W G Meggitt). To A.R.S. No.1 A.D., 3rd April 1917; Returned to sqn 10th April 1917. During an engine test on 28th April 1917, the aircraft crashed just outside Lozinghem airfield and was completely destroyed. Sgt W J Burtenshaw, pilot of No.25 Sqn., and Lt P Smith, observer of No. 12 Sqn., both killed.

7011 From A.R.S. No.1 A.D., 7th September 1916; During night flying practice on 16th September 1916, the pilot failed to flatten out on landing and crashed; 2/Lt H W Sellars being slightly injured. To A.R.S. No.1 A.D., 19th September 1916.

7015 From A.R.S. No.1 A.D., 1st September 1916; Wrecked 19th September 1916; To A.R.S. No.1 A.D., 20th September 1916.

7022 From A.R.S. No.1 A.D., 12th September 1916; During a bombing raid on Douai, aircraft was engaged by two Fokkers, Lt R Speirs, observer, slightly wounded, but returned safely, pilot unhurt. On 17th November 1916 at 19.30hrs shared with 4877, 6990, 7024 and 7025 in shooting down an enemy aircraft near Vitry (Capt R Chadwick, pilot, and Lt W G Meggitt, observer). On 4th December 1916 was shot down by Ltn Otto Splitgerber of *Jasta* 12 at Farbus. 2/Lt D S Johnson, pilot, and Lt I Heald, observer, both killed.

7024 On strength by 17th September 1916; Shot down an Albatros DI in flames at 13.00hrs on 16th November 1916 (Lt C H C Woolven, pilot, and 2/Lt C H Marchant, observer). On 17th November 1916 at 19.30hrs shared in the destruction of an enemy aircraft with 4877, 6990, 7022 and 7025 over Vitry (Lt C Dunlop, pilot, and 2/Lt H Scandrett, observer). On 23rd November 1916 Lt C H C Woolven, pilot, and Sgt G R Horrocks, observer, shot down an Albatros DI east of Oppy at 15.45hrs. On 28th April 1917 the aircraft crashed on a test flight, injuring 2/Lt H F Walker.

7025 From A.R.S. No.1 A.D., 16th October 1916; Shared with 4877, 6990, 7022 and 7024 in the destruction of an enemy aircraft at 19.30hrs on 17th November 1916 over Vitry (2/Lt H L Chadwick, pilot, and 2/Lt C J Butler, observer). Shared with 7693, A780 and A5439 in shooting down an LVG C over Courriéres at 11.15hrs on 4th March 1917. On 6th April 1917, while escorting B.E. reconnaissance aircraft, was in combat at 08.55hrs near Arras and caused an Albatros to spin down out of control; 7025 was hit and wrecked in forced landing at Grosville; pilot, 2/Lt D P Walter wounded; observer, 2/Lt C Brown, unhurt. To A.R.S. No.1 A.D., 8th April 1917.

7672 On strength by 6th October 1916; On 23rd November 1916 at 15.45hrs forced down an Albatros DII out of control east of Oppy (Sgt J H R Green, pilot, and Cpl A G Bower, observer). On 1st May 1917 Lieut R G Malcolm, pilot, and Cpl L Emsden, observer, shot down an Albatros DIII over Izel-lès-Équerchin at 06.20hrs and at 06.45hrs forced another to land west of Lens, where it and its crew were captured.

7683 From A.R.S. No.1 A.D., 1st October 1916; During offensive patrol on 23rd November 1916 2/Lt F S Moller, pilot, wounded, and Sgt C Butler, observer, unhurt; aircraft returned safely. Later, at 17.25hrs, Capt J L Leith, pilot, and 2/Air Mech L Emsden, observer, drove down an Albatros in a spin east of Arras. On 9th April 1917 at 19.05hrs Lt T N Southom, pilot, and 2/Lt H E Freeman-Smith, observer, drove down an Albatros west of Lievin. On 14th April 1917 at 17.25hrs 2/Lt B King, pilot, and Cpl H G Taylor, observer, drove down a Halberstadt over Lens. To A.R.S. No.1 A.D., 24th April 1917.

7686 From A.R.S. No.1 A.D., 1st October 1916; On 15th February 1917 at 16.30hrs, Capt L L Richardson, pilot, and 2/Lt W G Meggitt, observer, shot down a German two-seater out of control over Avion. On 6th April 1917 at 10.30hrs 2/Lt A Roulstone, pilot, and 2/Lt E G Green, observer, shot down an enemy aircraft which crashed in flames east of Givenchy. To A.R.S. No.1 A.D., 11th April 1917.

7693 From A.R.S. No.1 A.D., 20th October 1916; On 26th October 1916 at 09.04hrs Lt J L Leith, pilot, and Sgt L S Court, observer, shot down an enemy scout over Seclin. On 9th November 1916 at 08.30hrs Lt J L Leith, pilot, and 2/Lt E L Chadwick, observer, shot down a Fokker DII out of control over Henin-Lietard. On 29th January 1917 at 10.50hrs Lt J L Leith, pilot, and 2/Lt D C Wollen, observer, shot down an Albatros DII out of control at Harnes. On 4th March 1917 at 11.15hrs Lt R G George, pilot, and

Cpl E Emsden, observer, shared with 7025, A780 and A5439 in the destruction of an LVG C over Courriéres. On 16th March 1917, after combat at 15.30hrs, was forced to land near Cambrai (2/Lt R N L Munro, pilot, wounded; Sgt C H Nunn, observer, unhurt, and aircraft undamaged). On 17th March 1917 at 17.25hrs, Capt J L Leith, pilot, and 2/Air Mech L Emsden, observer, shot down an Albatros DII out of control near Arras. Wrecked 18th March 1917; To A.R.S. No.1 A.D., 20th March 1917.

7694 On 22nd November 1916 Lt H B Balfour, pilot, and Lt A L Harrow-Bunn, observer, shot down an LVG C east of Arras (German crew, Flgr Friedrich Simon and Ltn Ewald Fischer, both killed).

7715 From A.R.S. No.1 A.D., 21st March 1917; Was forced down east of Vimy by Obltn Lothar Freiherr von Richthofen of *Jasta* 11, at 17.15hrs on 28th March 1917. 2/Lt N L Knight, pilot, wounded and made PoW; 2/Lt A G Severs, observer, killed. (This was the first of 40 air combat victories by this pilot, brother of Manfred von Richthofen).

7880 Delivered from No.2 A.D., 23rd July 1916; no further information.

Built by G & J Weir Ltd, Cathcart, Glasgow.

A780 From A.R.S. No.1 A.D., 6th February 1917; On 4th March 1917 at 11.15hrs, 2/Lt W D Matheson, pilot, and Sgt W A Barnes, observer, shared with 7025, 7693 and A5439 in shooting down an LVG C at Courriéres. After combat during an offensive patrol on 15th March 1917, was forced to land at Bray and was wrecked; 2/Lt W D Matheson, pilot, and Sgt G Goodman, observer, both wounded. To A.R.S. No.1 A.D., 20th March 1917.

A782 From A.R.S. No.1 A.D., 26th January 1917; On 29th January 1917 during photo reconnaissance over Henin Lietard, was in combat with twelve Halberstadts; forced one down out of control, but engine was then hit by ground fire over Harnes; aircraft returned safely (2/Lt A W Shirtcliffe, pilot, unhurt, and 2/Lt AV Blenkiron, observer, wounded). On 1st March 1917 shot down an Albatros DIII at Mericourt at 15.00hrs (Capt J L Leith, pilot, and Lt G M A Hobart-Hampden, observer). On 17th March 1917 at c. 11.30hrs, Lt R G Malcom, pilot, and Lt C W Wilson, observer, shot down an Albatros near Oppy. On 13th April 1917 at 19.30hrs shared in the destruction of an Albatros DIII with 7003 over Sallaumines (Capt J L Leith, pilot, and Lt G M S Hobart-Hampden, observer). On 1st May 1917 at 18.15hrs was in combat with four enemy aircraft and was forced to land on Arras racecourse (2/Lt B King, pilot, unhurt; Sgt H G Taylor, observer, seriously wounded).

A784 From A.R.S. No.1 A.D., 2nd January 1917; On 29th January 1917 at 10.50hrs shot down an Albatros DII over Hames (2/Lt A W Shirtcliffe, pilot, and Lt A V Blenkiron, observer). Shot down on 13th April 1917 on return from bombing raid over Harnes at 19.30hrs by Vizefeldwebel Sebastian Festner of *Jasta* 11. Pilot, Sgt John Dempsey, and observer, 2/Lt William Henry Green wounded, both made PoW.

A797 On 22nd April 1917 at 17.30hrs drove down an Albatros near Noyell Godault (Sgt W H Green, pilot, and Cpl L Emsden, observer). Wrecked, 25th April 1917; To A.R.S. No.1 A.D., 26th April 1917.

A802 From A.R.S. No.1 A.D., 18th March 1917; Wrecked 29th March 1917, to A.R.S. No.1 A.D., same day.

A813 From A.R.S. No.1 A.D., 30th March 1917; On 8th April 1917, shot down near Mont St Eloi at 19.00hrs while returning from bombing raid on Pont-à-Vendin. (2/Lt E V A Bell, pilot, and 2/Lt A H S McCallum, observer made PoW).

A815 From A.R.S. No.1 A.D., 8 April 1917; On 1st May 1917, while returning from bombing raid on Izel-lès-Équerchin, encountered nine enemy aircraft and, at 18.00hrs was shot down in flames over Rouvrouy by Obltn. Kurt Wolff of *Jasta* 11, his 29th victory. (Lt Gerald Sidney French, pilot, wounded and made PoW; Lt Geoffrey Parker Harding, MC, made PoW, but later escaped).

A837 During photo escort and line patrol shot down in flames at 09.35hrs on 25th April 1917 between Willerval and Bailleul by Ltn K Schaefer of *Jasta* 11. Pilot, 2/Lt C V Darnell, and observer, 2/Air Mech G Pawley, both killed in action.

A842 On 3rd May 1917, while returning from raid on Izel-lès-Équerchin, the aircraft caught fire and crashed near Fiefs, 10 miles west of the airfield. 2/Lt B King, pilot, and Trumpeter J Lawrence, observer, both killed.

Built by Boulton & Paul Ltd, Norwich, Norfolk.

A5439 From A.R.S. No.1 A.D., 12 November 1916; Shared in shooting down an LVG C with 7025, 7693 and 7809 over Courriéres at 11.15hrs on 4th March 1917 (Lt A E Boultbee, pilot, and Sgt J Brown, observer). On 17th March 1917 this aircraft was shot down south-east of Oppy by Manfred Freiheer von Richthofen of *Jasta* 11.

A E Boultbee, pilot, and 2/Air Mech F King, observer, both killed. (Manfred von Richthofen's 27th victory. In von Richthofen's biography *The Red Knight of the Air* (John Hamilton, London, 1934) it is stated on page 129 that his 27th victory was scored on 12th March 1917. However, the circumstances of the combat described make it most likely that he shot down A5439 on 17th March 1917.)

A5451 From A.R.S. No.1 A.D., 10th December 1916; Wrecked, 28th December 1916, and to A.R.S. No.1 A.D., the same day.

A5478 Based at Auchel and flown as bomber; otherwise nothing known.

A5484 From A.R.S. No.1 A.D., 13th February 1917; During an operational patrol by six F.E.2bs on 16th March 1917, sixteen German scouts were encountered, the crew of this aircraft claiming one of the enemy shot down out of control from 10,000ft over Neuvireuil (Lt J Whittaker, pilot, and 2/Air Mech F King, observer). On 17th March 1917, between 11.00 and 11.30hrs, Lt C H C Chapman, pilot, and Sgt J H Booth, observer, shot down an Albatros DIII out of control between Oppy and Beaumont. Wrecked, 26th April 1917; To A.R.S. No.1 A.D., 29th April 1917.

A5487 From A.R.S. No.1 A.D., 9th April 1917. Fate unknown.

A5502 From A.R.S. No.1 A.D., 19th April 1917 to at least 24th April 1917. Fate unknown.

A5505 From A.R.S. No.1 A.D., 19th April 1917 to at least 1st May 1917. Fate unknown.

A5510 From A.R.S. No.1 A.D., 29th April 1917 to at least 1st May 1917. Fate unknown.

A5512 From A.R.S. No.1 A.D., 27th April 1917 to at least 1st May 1917. Fate unknown.

A5515 From A.R.S. No.1 A.D., 26th April 1917 to at least 1st May 1917. Fate unknown.

A5522 On strength by 1st May 1917. Fate unknown.

Unidentified Aircraft on No.25 Squadron. A number of actions were recorded in Squadron documents in which the identities of the aircraft were not mentioned.

23rd November 1916. Lt A P Maurice, pilot, wounded in arm during offensive patrol; his observer was unhurt.

1st March 1917. While escorting reconnaissance aircraft, 2/Lt G R F Waner, observer, received wounds from which he died the following day; his pilot was unhurt.

16th March 1917. Sgt C Buchannan, observer, was wounded in combat; his pilot was unhurt.

17th March 1917. 2/Lt I W Parnell, pilot, was wounded in combat; his observer was unhurt.

In March 1917 No.25 Squadron, while based at Auchel in France, began to take delivery of F.E.2ds, but these were regarded as no more than interim equipment pending the delivery of Airco D.H.4s in June that year. The last of the F.E.2bs were disposed of in May 1917.

Royal Aircraft Factory F.E.2c *(One only)*

6371 Delivered from A.R.S. No.1 A.D., 19th June 1916; crashed, 19th July 1916.

Royal Aircraft Factory F.E.2d

Built at the Royal Aircraft Factory, Farnborough.

A4 Crashed while returning from a forced landing, 7th May 1917; Pte J Dillon killed.

A32 While on reconnaissance in the area of Douai-St Armand-Orchies on 28th May 1917 was claimed shot down by Ltn Werner Voss of *Jasta* 5; 2/Lt E H Stevens, pilot, died of wounds while a PoW; L/Cpl C Sturrock, observer, wounded, made PoW.

A1957 On strength by 1st June 1917. Missing from raid on Chateau de Sart, 7th June 1917. Pilot, 2/Lt G H Pollard, made PoW, seriously wounded; observer, Lt F S Ferriman, killed in action.

A5152 Flown by Lt C. Dunlop on bombing raids, April 1917. Gunner Lt Weir shot down an enemy scout on 26th April 1917 during reconnaissance over Drocourt. Still on strength 1st June 1917.

Built by Boulton & Paul Ltd, Norwich, Norfolk.

A6360 On strength by 1st June 1917. During the Battle of Messines on 8th June 1917, damaged in action with four Albatros DIIIs west of Haubourdin; one of these was shot down out of control at 07.35hrs. Pilot, Sgt R Mann, wounded in thigh; observer, 2/Air Mech J Harris, unhurt. Still with squadron 22nd July 1917.

A6363 Aircraft on operations with Squadron, 8th June 1917.

A6365 On strength by 1st June 1917. On 6th June 1917 at 12.05hrs, shared with A6401 and A6500 in forcing down out of control an Albatros DIII over Sallaumines (Sgt J H R Green, pilot and Pte H Else, observer). Aircraft suffered engine failure during take-off on photographic sortie, 7th July 1917; pilot, Capt M G B Copeman, injured, observer assumed unhurt.

A6369 From A.R.S. No.1 A.D., 19th April 1917. Still on strength, 11th July 1917.

A6370 On strength by 1st June 1917. During afternoon line patrol on 11th July 1917 was in combat with three Albatros DVs, one of which was shot down behind enemy lines at Oppy Wood at 15.30hrs. Own aircraft then attacked by Oblt Adolf Ritter von Tutschek of *Jasta* 12 and force landed at Monchy Fosse Farm in Allied territory. 2/Lt F H St C Sargent, pilot, wounded; Lt J Kirk, observer, unhurt.

A6371 From A.R.S. No.1 A.D., 2nd April 1917; Forced down behind German lines while on photographic sortie to Mericourt-Gravelle, 3rd April 1917, by Ltn K Schaefer of *Jasta* 11. Pilot, Lt L Dodson, wounded and made PoW; observer, 2/Lt H S Richards, died of wounds.

A6372 From A.R.S. No.1 A.D., 4th April 1917; During bombing raid on Henin Lietard shot down by Obltn Hans Klein of *Jasta* 4 near Vimy on 13th April 1916 at 19.30hrs. Capt L L Richardson MC, pilot, and 2/Lt D C Wollen, observer, both killed in action.

A6373 From A.R.S. No.1 A.D., 4th April 1917; Often flown by Lt C Dunlop on photo-escort sorties, April 1917. Shot down Albatros, which crashed at Thelus on 21st April 1917 (2/Lt R G Malcom, pilot, and 2/Lt J B Weir, observer).

A6378 While on reconnaissance on 28th May 1917, was shot down by Ltn Kurt Schneider of *Jasta* 5. Pilot, Capt A De Selincourt, and observer, Lt H Cotton, both wounded and made PoW.

A6381 On strength by 21st May 1917; Crashed, 6th June 1917.

A6382 From A.R.S. No.1 A.D., 31st March 1917; during photographic sortie to Mericourt-Gravelle, driven down by Rittmeister Manfred Freiherr von Richthofen of *Jasta* 11 at 16.30hrs on 3rd April 1917 near Lens (his 34th victory). 2/Lt D P MacDonald, pilot, made PoW; 2/Lt John Ingram Mullanniffe O'Bieme, observer, killed.

A6383 From A.R.S. No.1 A.D., 31st March 1917; On 13th April 1917 at 19.30hrs shot down an Albatros DIII (shared with F.E.2b 7003). Lt R G Malcom, pilot, and 2/Lt J B Weir, observer. On 21st April 1917 forced down an Albatros DIII out of control between Rouvray and Oppy at 18.55hrs; A6383 was damaged by enemy fire, force landed and overturned in Allied territory (Capt J H Leith, pilot, and Lt G M A Hobart-Hampden, observer, unhurt); To No.20 Sqn, 7th June 1917.

A6385 On 13th April 1917 at 19.30hrs, shot down an Albatros DIII over Henin-Lietard. Lt R G Malcom, pilot, and Cpl L Emsden, observer.

A6386 From A.R.S. No.1 A.D., 4th April 1917; Often flown by Lt C Dunlop on photo-escort sorties. Wrecked 21st April 1917; To A.R.S. No.1 A.D., 22nd April 1917.

A6401 On strength by 1st June 1917. Albatros DIII forced down out of control Sallaumines, shared with A6365 & A6500, 12.05hrs 6th June 1917 (Capt C Dunlop & 2/Lt F Cornish); Still on strength 11th July 1917.

A6403 From A.R.S. No.1 A.D., 29th May 1917; disposed of to No.20 Sqn., 6th June 1917.

A6404 On strength by 1st June 1917. Flown in bombing raids by Capt Roulstone and Lt D Taylor-Fox.

A6407 Flown in bombing raids by Capt Roulstone and Lt D Taylor-Fox.

A6410 Missing after reconnaissance in area of Douai-St Armand-Orchies on 28th May 1917. Shot down by Vizefeldwebel Otto Konnecke of *Jasta* 5. Pilot, Lt T N Southom, made PoW, and observer, Lt V Smith, wounded and made PoW.

A6416 On strength by 1st June 1917 until at least 11th July 1917.

A6417 On strength by 1st June 1917; On 7th June 1917, between 07.00 and 07.05hrs, shot down two Albatros out of control (one smoking) west of Lille. (Lt Conrad Tolendal Lally, pilot, and 2/Lt L F Williams, observer). Wrecked 13th June 1917; To A.R.S. No.1 A.D., 16th June 1917.

A6419 From A.R.S. No.1 A.D., 24th April 1917; On 24th June 1917 at 16.45hrs, shot down an Albatros out of control south-west of Lille, but was then hit in the engine and made a forced landing near Choques in Allied territory. Sgt A N Stretton, pilot, and 1/Air Mech W Trezise, observer, both unhurt.

A6427 From A.R.S. No.1 A.D., 25th April 1917; disposed of to No.20 Sqn, 6th June 1917.

A6432 On strength by 1st June 1917. Fate unknown.

A6447 On 21st May 1917, while on line patrol between Hulluch and Gavrelle, was forced down over enemy territory in combat with four German aircraft. Pilot, 2/Lt J H Blackall, and observer, 2/Lt B C Moody, both wounded and made PoW. Claimed shot down by Ltn Emst Mohnicke of *Jasta* 11.

A6500 From A.R.S. No.1 A.D., 3rd June 1917; Albatros DIII forced down out of control Sallaumines, shared with A6365 & A6401, 12.05hrs 6th June 1917 (Lt D Maclaurin, pilot, and 2/Lt EC Middleton, observer).

Built by the Royal Aircraft Factory, Farnborough.

A8950 From A.R.S. No.1 A.D., 29th April 1917. Nothing known after 1st May 1917.

Unidentified No. 25 Squadron Aircraft.

3rd July 1917. Crashed after engine failure during line patrol. Observer, 2/Air Mech C B Thomas seriously injured, pilot unhurt.

Royal Aircraft Factory B.E.2e

At least three of these aircraft were delivered to No.25 Squadron, Nos 2542 and 7247, and were flown operationally, although they were used principally to fly local orientation familiarity sorties in May and June 1917.

2542 Built by Wolseley Motors. Aircraft broke up in loop and fell from 2,000ft on 12th June 1917; 2/Lt T R C Birkin killed.

7247 Built by British & Colonial. Received from A.R.S. No.1 A.D., 7th June 1917, used to at least 1st July 1917

A3166 Built by Wolseley Motors. Received from A.R.S. No.1 A.D., 2nd June 1917; returned there 5th July 1917

Airco D.H.4

No.25 Squadron received a total of 21 Airco D.H.4s during June and July 1917 while still based at Auchel, and by the end of September had 27 such aircraft on charge. The Squadron continued to fly the D.H.4 until the end of the War.

Built by The Aircraft Manufacturing Co Ltd, (Airco), Hendon, London NW.

A2144 From A.R.S. No.2 A.D., 4th September 1917; On 15th September 1917, suffered landing accident when port wing struck ground (2/Lt L G Bristowe unhurt). To A.R.S. No.2 A.D., 17th September 1917; Rejoined sqn from No.1 A.I., 4th February 1918; Overshot and crashed while landing on 26th March 1918 (2/Lt A E Hulme, pilot, and Cpl T Ramadaden, observer, unhurt). To Repair Park No.2 A.S.D., 1st April 1918 and rebuilt as F6169.

A2145 From A.R.S. No.1 A.D., 15th October 1917; On 4th December 1917, stalled and crashed during practice landing (Lt N Braithwaite, pilot flying solo, unhurt).

A2155	From A.R.S. No.2 A.D., 31st July 1917; Flown on operations principally by 2/Lt Simpson, August-September 1917. Crashed while landing, 16th September 1917. To A.R.S. No.2 A.D., 17th September 1917.
A2159	From A.R.S. No.1 A.D., 7th August 1917; Shot down (probably by Ltn Emst Udet of *Jasta* 37) and broke up in the air near Wingles while on a bombing raid on 14th August 1917. Pilot, 2/Lt P L McGavin, and observer, 2/Lt N Field, both killed in action.
A2161	From A.R.S. No.1 A.D., 27th July 1917; Force landed following engine failure and turned over on 19th August 1917. 2/Lt F W Watson, pilot, and 2/Lt L E Bradshaw, observer, both unhurt. To A.R.S. No.2 A.D., 21st August 1917.
A2170/L	From A.R.S. No.1 A.D., 1st October 1917; Missing from bombing sortie over Somain during Battle of Cambrai on 23rd November 1917. Pilot, 2/Lt R Main, and observer, 1/Air Mech G P Leach, both made PoW.
A2171	From A.R.S. No.1 A.D., 9th August 1917; Flown on operations principally by Capt Pearce, August-September 1917. On 18th March 1918, it failed to return from a reconnaissance sortie; the pilot, Lt James Haywood Wensley, and observer, 2/Lt Arthur William Matson, were notified as PoW.
A2174	From No.2 A.I., 29th June 1918; Suffered engine failure and crashed near airfield at Villers-Brettoneux (Lt. L L K Straw, pilot, and 2/Lt E F Boyce, observer, unhurt. Aircraft later re-built as F6236.
A7402	From A.R.S. No.2 A.D., 31st August 1917; Overshot airfield on landing and crashed, 19th November 1917. 2/Lt N Braithwaite, pilot, and 2/Lt R Nobbs, observer, both unhurt. To Repair Park No.1 A.S.D., 20th November 1917.
A7405	From A.R.S. No.1 A.D., 26th July 1917; While on bombing sortie was attacked by twelve Albatros DIIIs near La Bassée on 4th September 1917; Lt D G E Jardine, pilot, and, 2/Lt G Bliss, observer, shared in the destruction of a DIII at 18.50hrs. On 1st October 1917, shot down at 14.00hrs near Burbure while flying a contact patrol; the pilot, 2/Lt C O Rayner, and the observer, 2/Lt J L Hughes, were killed. Remains to A.R.S. No.2 A.D., 2nd October 1917.
A7426	From A.R.S. No.2 A.D., 31st July 1917; While flying a line patrol on 12th August 1917 the engine lost power and the aircraft overshot in forced landing at 20.00hrs. 2/Lt D McLaurin, pilot, and Lt J H Lark, observer, both unhurt. Aircraft repaired. On 12th October 1917 Sgt A L Clear, pilot, and 2/Lt F W Talbot, observer, failed to return from raid on Beythem and were made PoWs. Talbot escaped from captivity but was interned in Holland on 9th April 1918.
A7442/B	From A.R.S. No.1 A.D., 7th August 1917; On 24th October 1917, during a practice flight the aircraft stalled on landing and crashed; 2/Lt J A Baker, pilot, and Lt J H Kirk, observer, unhurt. Aircraft despatched to No. 1 Repair Park No.1 A.S.D.
A7452	From No.1 A.I., 28th November 1917; On 16th February 1918, after running out of fuel, was damaged in forced landing at Thieville. 2/Lt C Ross, pilot, and 2/Lt J CO'R King, observer, unhurt. To Repair Park No.2 A.S.D., 27th February 1918.
A7463	From A.R.S. No.1 A.D., 26th July 1917; On 28th July 1917. After overshooting the airfield on landing, pilot attempted to go round again but struck a tree and the aircraft overturned. 2/Lt H A Hope, pilot, killed, and 2/Air Mech H Else injured. Remains to A.R.S. No.2 A.D., 29th July 1917.
A7464	From A.R.S. No.1 A.D., 7th August 1917; Flown on several bombing raids by Capt A Roulstone and Lt D Taylor-Fox. Force landed at Clairmarais on 28th November 1917, crew unhurt. To Repair Park No.1 A.S.D., 29th November 1917.
A7470	From A.R.S. No.1 A.D., 2nd October 1917; On 11th October 1917 damaged in forced landing owing to radiator leak; Lt J E Pugh, pilot, and 2/Lt W J Walsh, observer, both unhurt. To A.R.S. No.1 A.D., 16th October 1917; Retd sqn from No.1 A.I., 12th December 1917; On 23rd January 1918, pilot became lost in bad visibility and attempted forced landing, struck trees near Recques and crashed. Lt E Gordon, pilot, severely bruised, and Lt C M Sinclair severely shaken. Remains to Repair Park No.1 A.S.D., 28th January 1918.
A7477	From A.R.S. No.1 A.D., 24th June 1917; Lt C T Lally shot down an Albatros DV on 5th August 1917; observer not known. On 5th September 1917 aircraft damaged in cross-wind landing; 2/Lt G S Wood, pilot, and 2/Lt D D Humphreys, observer, unhurt. To A.R.S. No.2 A.D., 7th September 1917.

A7479 From A.R.S. No.1 A.D., 19th June 1917; Shot down in combat during photo reconnaissance sortie on 27th July 1917 near Foufflin; 2/Lt W L Lovell, pilot, and 2/Lt W W Fitzgerald, observer, both killed. Remains to A.R.S. No.2 A.D., 28th July 1917.

A7480 From A.R.S. No.1 A.D., 31st August 1917; During a patrol on 4th September 1917 was in combat with ten Albatros DIIIs of *Jasta* 30 and was shot down out of control. 2/Lt C J Pullen, pilot, and 2/Lt E D S Robinson, observer, were both killed. Aircraft claimed destroyed by Oblt H Bethge of *Jasta* 30, but this was not one of his victims.

A7482 From A.R.S. No.1 A.D., and marked 'NUS' 24th June 1917; Capt Alexander Roulstone shot down an Albatros DV out of control on 20th July 1917. Damaged during landing in strong wind on 8th October 1917; 2/Lt E S Pfeiffer, pilot, and Pte R Ireland, observer, unhurt. To A.R.S. No.2 A.D., 10th October 1917.

A7486 From A.R.S. No.1 A.D., 17th June 1917; Aircraft damaged during practice landing when wing tip struck the ground on overshooting, 7th August 1917. 2/Lt P L McGavin, pilot, and 2/Air Mech F Millington, observer, unhurt. To A.R.S. No.2 A.D., 8th August 1917.

A7487 From A.R.S. No.1 A.D., 23rd August 1917; While on bombing sortie at 18.50hrs on 4th September 1917 was attacked by twelve Albatros DIIIs near La Bassée. Pilot, Lt C A Pike, claimed one enemy aircraft shot down in flames, but his observer, 2/Lt A T Williams died of wounds sustained. On 27th October 1917, Lt J A McCudden, pilot, with Air Mech J Harris, observer, shot down an enemy aircraft (details of action not known). On 3rd January 1918, after landing at Filescamp to refuel, crashed after engine cut on take-off, Lt J H Wensley, pilot, and Lt A W Matson, observer, unhurt. To Repair Park No.1 A.S.D., 12th January 1918.

A7489 From A.R.S. No.1 A.D., 4th July 1917; On 19th August 1917, pilot undershot during practice landing and landing gear struck raised ground on approach (2/Lt L A Hacklett slightly injured; Lt V P Barbat unhurt). To A.R.S. No.2 A.D., 20 August 1917.

A7503 From A.R.S. No.1 A.D., 24th June 1917; Struck object on forced landing following engine failure, 2nd July 1917; Lt A Roulstone, pilot, and Lt N Field, observer, unhurt. Missing, 21st October 1917, after photographic sortie near Poelcappelle. Pilot, 2/Lt D McLaurin, and observer, 2/Lt O M Hills, MC, made PoWs.

A7505 From A.R.S. No.1 A.D., 4th July 1917; At 13.00hrs on 7th July 1917 Capt J Fitz-Morris, MC, with Lt D L Burgess, observer, shot down an Albatros DV over Dorignies out of control, the first claim by the pilot of a No.25 Sqn, D.H.4. In the same aircraft he also shot down another Albatros DV on 22nd July 1917. On 27th January 1918 2/Lt R M Tate overshot the airfield while landing and, in making too sharp a turn, broke the undercarriage. He and his observer, Lt H A Lloyd, were unhurt. To Repair Park No.1 A.S.D., 30th January 1918.

A7507 From No.1 A.I., 5th December 1917; On 2nd January 1918 was damaged when pilot approached to land without adequate speed and stalled; 2/Lt B L Lindley, pilot, unhurt. To Repair Park No.1 A.S.D., 6th January 1918; Returned to the squadron from No.2 A.I., 6th June 1918; On 7th July 1918, while standing on the airfield, was damaged when the bombs on a No.27 Squadron's D.H.4 (B9338, which had crashed) exploded. A7507 was re-built as F6214.

A7526 From Repair Park No.2 A.S.D., 13th March 1918; While attacking enemy trenches near Bapaume on 26th March 1918, the aircraft's engine and radiator were hit by ground machine gun fire, made forced landing in No Man's Land between Warfussée and Abancourt; the pilot, 2/Lt C J Fitzgibbon (who had been wounded), and his observer, 2/Lt R W Hobbs, MC, salvaged the guns and instruments and then set fire to the aircraft before escaping back to Allied territory on foot.

A7527 From A.R.S. No.1 A.D., 28th July 1917; After completing a line patrol on 21st August 1917 the pilot became lost and force landed near Hesdin; the aircraft overturned, but 2/Lt G S Wood, pilot, and 1/Air Mech J Harris, observer, were unhurt. To A.R.S. No.2 A.D., 23rd August 1917, and returned to Squadron and coded 'P' 10th October 1917. On 4th January 1918 the engine cut on take-off and the aircraft crashed (2/Lt J S Macaulay, pilot, and 2/Lt A E Thornhill, observer, both injured). To Repair Park No.1 A.S.D., 10th January 1918.

A7535/H, B From A.R.S. No.1 A.D., 24th October 1917; Left for Bray 11.25hrs, shell hit u/c axle which broke in two, crashed on landing 13.15hrs 27th March 1918 (2/Lt BL Lindley, pilot, and Sgt A Remington, observer both unhurt); To Repair Park No.2 A.S.D., 1st April 1918.

A7536 From A.R.S. No.1 A.D., 9th August 1917; On practice flight, landed too slowly, stalled and overturned 18th October 1917 (2/Lt FV Bird, pilot, unhurt and 2/Lt G Dixon, observer, cuts); To A.R.S. No.1 A.D., 18th October 1917.

A7543 From A.R.S. No.1 A.D., 27th July 1917; Force landed Compiègne 8th November 1917, then returning attempted to land Le Crotoy, dived in from 100ft, wrecked 9th November 1917 (2/Lt SB Cragg, pilot, killed and 2/Lt G Dixon, observer, injured); To Repair Park No.1 A.S.D., 12th November 1917.

A7547 From A.R.S. No.1 A.D., 27th July 1917; Flown by Lt A Roulstone in raid on Carvin on 22nd August 1917; attacked by 15 Albatros DIIIs, of which his observer, Lt D Taylor-Fox, shot down one. On 6th December 1917 the pilot became lost and attempted a forced landing but overshot into a ditch; Lt J Anderson, pilot, and 2/Lt A E Thornhill, observer, unhurt.; To Repair Park No.1 A.S.D., for extensive repairs, 9th December 1917, but was returned to Squadron 21st April 1918. On 14th August 1918 the pilot overshot on landing and was slightly damaged; Lt H C Bryant, pilot, and 2/Lt Skidmore, observer, unhurt. SOC Repair Park No.2 A.S.D., 15th August 1918.

A7561 From No.1 A.I., 25th January 1918; On 5th February 1918, during practice flight, engine failed and, during a forced landing, the aircraft ran into a ditch and overturned; 2/Lt J Loupinsky, pilot, and 2/Lt C A Sundy, observer, unhurt. To Repair Park No.1 A.S.D.

A7562 From A.R.S. No.1 A.D., 9th August 1917; After engine failure during practice flight on 22nd August 1917, aircraft crashed during forced landing when it hit corn sheaves; Lt C J Pullen, pilot, and 2/Lt D D Humphreys, observer, unhurt. To A.R.S. No.2 A.D., 30th August 1917.

A7563 From No.2 A.I., 10th March 1918; Aircraft reported missing after reconnaissance sortie in the Valenciennes-Busigny area on 21st April 1918. Pilot, 2/Lt C J Fitzgibbon, and observer, 2/Lt W Rudman, MC, both killed.

A7565 From No.1 A.I., 3rd January 1918; On 9th March 1918 engine suffered a burst cylinder and aircraft force landed near Bailleul; 2/Lt A W P Cumming, pilot, and Sgt J R Wright, observer, unhurt. To Repair Park No.1 A.S.D.; Returned to the Squadron from No.2 A.I., 20th May 1918. On 21st May 1918 the aircraft collided with No.27 Squadron's D.H.4 B2083 on take-off, Lt R P Bufton, pilot, and Sgt W C Elliott, observer, unhurt. SOC Repair Park No.2 A.S.D., 22nd May 1918.

A7569 From A.R.S. No.1 A.D., 7th August 1917; On the 20th August 1917 the undercarriage collapsed during a landing at Auchel; 2/Lt M A Hancock, pilot, and 2/Lt O M Hills, observer, unhurt. To A.R.S. No.2 A.D., 21st August 1917.

A7573 From No.2 A.I., 9th March 1918; On 11th March 1918 aircraft stalled on landing approach and crashed; 2/Lt C J Fitzgibbon, pilot, and 2/Lt C A Sundy, observer, unhurt.

A7595 From A.R.S. No.1 A.D., 19th October 1917; On 13th November 1917 aircraft force landed in fog at La Capelle on the Calais road and crashed. 2/Lt J A Baker, pilot injured, and Lt W A Miller, observer, seriously injured. To Repair Park No.1 A.S.D., 17th November 1917.

A7599 From A.R.S. No.1 A.D., 31st August 1917; During practice flight on 19th October 1917 aircraft stalled on approach to landing and crashed. 2/Lt F V Bird, pilot flying solo, unhurt. Aircraft badly damaged, to A.R.S. No.1 A.D., 19th October 1917 for extensive repair; Returned to Squadron from No.1 A.I., on 27th February 1918. It collided with A7823 while being taxied into hangar on 26th March 1918. To Repair Park No.2 A.S.D., 1st April 1918.

A7600 From No.1 A.I., 10th December 1917; While flying a photo reconnaissance sortie on 13th January 1918 was in combat with a Fokker DrI triplane and four Albatros DIIIs north of Cambrai, but returned safely. Capt A G Whitehead, pilot, unhurt, and Lt J H Haughan, observer, wounded and also suffered from frostbite. Aircraft failed to return from photo reconnaissance sortie on 29th January 1918; shot down by Leutnant Fritz Rumey of *Jasta* 5, his 8th victory. Capt A G Whitehead, pilot, and Lt W J Borthistle, observer, killed.

A7602 From A.R.S. No.1 A.D., 5th September 1917; Damaged in heavy landing on test flight 9th June 1918 (Lt R G Dobeson, pilot, & 1/Air Mechanic F E Warren, observer, both unhurt); SOC Repair Park No.2 A.S.D., 18th June 1918.

A7605 From No.1 A.I., 20th November 1917; Force landed after the fuel tank had been hit in combat during a reconnaissance sortie on 6th December 1917, but hit overhead wires and crashed. Capt C T Lally, MC, pilot, severely shaken, and Lt J E Cole, observer, wounded. SOC Repair Park No.1 A.S.D., 7th February 1918.

A7609 From A.R.S. No.1 A.D., 2nd September 1917; While flying at 17,000ft over the Roulers-Ypres area on 25th January 1918, was attacked by a formation of twelve enemy aircraft, of which one was shot down by the observer, Hinson (rank and initials not known). The pilot, Lt C A Pike, managed to disengage and returned safely. The aircraft was later fitted with an additional fuel tank. Capt J E Pugh shot down an enemy aircraft on 27th March 1918. Withdrawn after report dated 4th April 1918 stated that the aircraft was no longer fit for first line service. To No.2 A.I., 19th April 1918.

A7626/N From No.2 A.I., 3rd December 1917; Lieut W H G Milanese shot down a Fokker DrI triplane out of control on 8th June 1918. On 8th July 1918 the aircraft suffered an undercarriage collapse while landing (Capt J F Gordon, pilot, and Cpl H Emerson, observer, unhurt). Following this failure a technical report stated that this aircraft had already been rebuilt twice, the fuselage had been overstrained and that the wooden structure was saturated with oil. It was withdrawn from the Squadron and later rebuilt at Repair Park No.2 A.S.D., as F6215.

A7637 From No.2 A.I., 8th June 1918; On 4th August 1918 Lieut J H Latchford, pilot, and 2/Lieut H Pullen, observer, shot down a Pfalz DIII out of control near Douai while on a bombing sortie on 4th August 1918. During a photographic sortie on 14th October 1918, aircraft was hit by ground fire and force landed in Allied territory; pilot, Lt L L K Straw, and observer, 2/Lt J Skidmore, both unhurt.

A7657 From No.1 A.I., 1st March 1918; FL in ploughed field, overturned 15th May 1918 (Lt T R Hatton, pilot, and Cpl H Edwards, observer): Rebuilt as F6127.

A7660 From No.1 A.I., 28th January 1918; Crashed on take-off on 29th January 1918. Lt G M Shaw, pilot, and 1/Air Mech L Jones, observer, unhurt. Aircraft to No.1 Repair Park No.1 A.S.D., 31st January 1918.

A7664 Delivered new from No.1 A.I., to Boisdinghem, 27th February 1918. During a dawn bombing sortie on 27th March 1918, aircraft was shot down east of Albert while under attack by *Jasta* 36. Both pilot, 2/Lt C G Pentecost, and observer, Lt A Rentoul, were killed. Both Ltn H Bongartz and A Hübner of *Jasta* 36 claimed the victory.

A7670 From No.2 A.I., 7th March 1918; On 28th June 1918 this aircraft failed to return from a photo reconnaissance sortie over Landrecies (Lt J Webster, pilot, and 2/Lt G M Gray both made PoW).

A7672 From A.R.S. No.1 A.D., 2nd October 1917; Damaged landing gear and airframe during heavy landing on 24th October 1917. 2/Lt R P Pohlmann, pilot, and 2/Air Mech C N Harvey, observer, both unhurt. To A.R.S. No.1 A.D., 24th October 1917; Returned sqn from No.1 A.I., 6th February 1918; On 26th February 1918 crashed during forced landing, probably caused by running out of fuel. 2/Lt E W Guest, pilot, died from injuries received; Lt H G Ashton, observer, injured. To Repair Park No.1 A.S.D., 28th February 1918.

A7680 From A.R.S. No.1 A.D., 15th October 1917; While on a bombing sortie to Deynze railway station on 5th February 1918, formation was attacked by fifteen enemy aircraft of *Jasta* 36. Aircraft forced down in enemy territory and both pilot, 2/Lt E O Cudmore, and observer, 1/Air Mech L J W Bain, were made PoW. Aircraft claimed shot down by Ltn H Bongartz of *Jasta* 36.

A7683 From No.1 A.I., 28th November 1917; On 28th December 1917, pilot became lost and force landed at Laigle; on the 31st he took off, but crashed near Rouen. 2/Lt A W P Cumming, pilot, and Sgt F Hopper, observer, unhurt. Wreckage of aircraft recovered by rail. To Repair Park No.2 A.S.D., 10th January 1918.

A7697 From A.R.S. No.1 A.D., 27th October 1917; Aircraft failed to return from photo reconnaissance sortie over Laon on 26th February, 1918. Claimed shot down by Leutnant Fritz Rumey of *Jasta* 5, his 9th victory. Lt G M Shaw, pilot, wounded, and Lt C H S Ackers, observer, unhurt, were made PoW.

A7713 From A.R.S. No.1 A.D., 27th October 1917; While on a photo reconnaissance sortie on 6th March 1918, was in combat with six enemy aircraft over Le Cateau. On return flight it was hit by ground fire but managed to force land in Allied territory; 2/Lt C Ross, pilot, and Lt H E Pohlmann, observer, unhurt. To No.2 A.S.D.

A7716 From No.1 A.I., 6th February 1918; Aircraft stalled and crashed during landing approach after practice flight on 1st April 1918. 2/Lt L L K Straw, pilot (flying solo) unhurt. To Repair Park No.1 A.S.D., 9th April 1918 and rebuilt as F5826.

A7723 From Repair Park No.1 A.S.D., 12th November 1917; Damaged landing 26th November 1917; To Repair Park No.1 A.S.D., 26th November 1917.

A7725 From Repair Park No.1 A.S.D., 15th November 1917; On 30th November 1917 pilot made forced landing, but aircraft struck the parapet of an old trench and was badly damaged. 2/Lt H G Milnes, pilot, and Capt J H Graham, observer, both unhurt but shaken. To Repair Park No.1 A.S.D., 2nd December 1917.

A7733 From No.1 A.I., 28th December 1917; While on air test, aircraft was seen to crash into the sea on 27th February 1918, but no enemy aircraft was seen. It was later salvaged and found to have been shot down. Lt M W Dickens, pilot, and Sgt F J Swain, observer, both listed as killed in action.

A7775 From No.2 A.I., 29th March 1918; Damaged in heavy landing on 9th June 1918. Lt A E Hulme, pilot, and 1/Air Mech W Gray, observer, unhurt. SOC Repair Park No.2 A.S.D., 19th June 1918.

A7776 From No.1 A.S.D., 5th December 1917; Aircraft stalled and crashed on approach to landing at Ruisseauville, 3rd May 1918. Lt T R Hatton, pilot, and Cpl T Ramsden, observer, unhurt. To Repair Park No.2 A.S.D., and rebuilt as F6075.

A7785 From No.1 A.I., 29th November 1917; On 28th December 1917 the engine seized ten minutes after take-off, pilot force landed but crashed. 2/Lt J Anderson, pilot, unhurt; 2/Air Mech R Ireland, observer, injured. To Repair Park No.1 A.S.D., 2 January 1918.

A7788 From No.2 A.I., 11th July 1918; Aircraft failed to return from photo reconnaissance sortie on 16th September 1918. Capt R L Whalley, pilot, and 2/Lt E B Andrews, observer, both later confirmed killed in action. Circumstances not known.

A7805 From No.2 A.I., 24th July 1918; Aircraft damaged, 1st November 1918 (circumstances not known). 2/Lt F Meenan, pilot, and 2/Lt P E Olley, observer, unhurt. To Repair Park No.2 A.S.D. the same day.

A7820 From No.2 A.I., 26th May 1918; During a photo reconnaissance sortie on 17th September 1918, was damaged in combat with enemy aircraft and made forced landing in Allied territory; observer, Lt A G Grant, wounded in action. Pilot, Lt R G Dobeson, unhurt. Rebuilt as H6882.

A7822 From No.2 A.I., 11th July 1918; Aircraft force landed and crashed in poor visibility on 29th October 1918. Lt R P Bufton, pilot, and 2/Lt H W H Argyle, observer, both unhurt. To Repair Park No.2 A.S.D., 29th October 1918.

A7823 From No.1 A.I., 2nd February 1918; On 26th February 1918 at Boisdinghem, aircraft swung on take-off and crashed into hangar, killing two Air Mechanics and injuring one, also A7599 damaged. 2/Lt A W P Cumming, pilot, and 2/Lt J E Pulling, observer, unhurt. To Repair Park No.2 A.S.D., 1st April 1918.

A7825 From No.1 A.I., 20th March 1918; Aircraft stalled and crashed on landing approach on 27th March 1918. 2/Lt C E H Allen, pilot, Sgt J R Wright, observer, both unhurt. To Repair Park No.2 A.S.D., 1st April 1918.

A7834 From No.1 A.I., 14th September 1918; Joined Squadron on 14th September 1918 at Ruisseauville; disposed of, 19th May 1919.

A7835 From No.2 A.I., 10th January 1918; While on photo reconnaissance sortie on 6th March 1918, was damaged, possibly by ground fire, over Le Cateau and force landed in Allied territory. 2/Lt R M Tate, pilot, wounded, and Sgt A H Muff, observer, unhurt. SOC Repair Park No.2 A.S.D., 19th March 1918.

A7838 From No.1 A.I., 30th January 1918; Aircraft crashed in Allied territory on 24th March 1918 (circumstances not known, but believed no injuries to crew); wreckage from Repair Park No.2 A.S.D., to Repair Park No.1 A.S.D., by rail 2nd April 1918, rebuilt as F5825.

A7865 From No.1 A.I., 3rd January 1918; During bombing sortie on 5th February 1918, was in combat with enemy aircraft and was shot down in flames west of Deynze (claimed by Ltn Heinrich Bongartz, commanding *Jasta* 36, Royal Prussian, his 29th or 30th victory). 2/Lt R P Pohlmann, pilot, and 2/Air Mech R Ireland, observer, both killed.

A7873/M From No.1 A.I., 6th January 1918; During bombing raid on Melle railway sidings on 3rd February 1918, was attacked and shot down near Mariakerke at 10.40hrs by Ltn Otto Loffier of *Jasta* 2 'Boelcke', his 2nd of 15 victories. Lt E G Green, MC, pilot, and Lt P C Campbell-Martin, observer, made PoWs. Aircraft captured intact.

A7877 From No.2 A.I., 11th July 1918; Excessive vibration, forced landed, crashed 30th July 1918 (Capt J F Gordon, pilot, and Lt G M Lawson, MC, observer, both unhurt); To Repair Park No.2 A.S.D.

A7882 From No.1 A.I., 21st February 1918; Made forced landing on 26th February when engine seized owing to leaking radiator. 2/Lt C Ross, pilot, and Lt H E Pohlmann, observer, unhurt. Aircraft repaired and returned to Sqn., 30th May 1918. On 2nd June 1918, during a dawn bombing raid on Cambrai, was shot down by Ltn Aloys Freiherr von Brandenstein of *Jasta* 49 (his 2nd of nine victories) over west Grand-Sec-Bois area, but landed intact; crew seen to set fire to their aircraft before capture. Lt John Robert Zieman, pilot, and, 2/Lt Harold Tannenbaum, observer made PoW.

A7890 From No.2 A.I., 13th September 1918; disposed of to No.6 A.I., 13th May 1919.

A7891 From No.2 A.I., 5th August 1918; Failed to return from reconnaissance sortie to Douai on 15th August 1918; aircraft crashed behind enemy lines. Lt T J Arthur, pilot, and Lt A G Lawe, observer, both unhurt and made PoW.

A7895 From No.1 A.I., 12th February 1918; Aircraft overturned on 6th March 1918 when making forced landing on rough ground. 2/Lt F F Keen, pilot, and 2/Lt B D Bennett, observer, both unhurt. To Repair Park No.2 A.S.D.

A7913 From No.2 A.I., 10th March 1918; On 27th March 1918 Capt J E Pugh, pilot, and 2/Lt W L Dixon, observer, forced down a Siemens Schuckert DIII. Pfalz DIII forced down out of control and another down in flames Thourout 08.20hrs 8th May 1918 (Lt JE Pugh MC & 2/Lt WL Dixon); Aircraft failed to return from photographic sortie to Bruges on 29th June 1918; Lt B L Lindley MC, pilot, killed; 2/Lt David Boe, observer, made PoW.

A7916 From No.2 A.I., 25th May 1918; Aircraft overshot aerodrome and badly damaged in heavy landing on 16th June 1918. Lt J Webster, pilot, and Sgt E Edwards, observer, both unhurt. To Repair Park No.1 A.S.D., and rebuilt as F5833.

A7967 From No.2 A.I., 2 July 1918; Aircraft overturned during heavy landing on 20th July 1918 and was badly damaged. Lt A E Hulme, pilot, and Sgt W B Gray, observer, both unhurt. Aircraft struck off charge at Repair Park No.2 A.S.D., on 27th July as not worth repairing.

A7968 From No.2 A.I., 31st March 1918; Aircraft damaged in heavy landing on 28th May 1918 (Lt A E Hulme, pilot, and Cpl T Ramsden, observer, both unhurt. Aircraft rebuilt as F5829.

A8016 From No.2 A.I., 21st April 1918; Overshot and crashed while landing on 22nd July 1918. Lt H C Bryant, pilot, and 2/Lt E F Boyce, observer, both unhurt. Aircraft badly damaged and rebuilt later as F6222.

A8028 From No.2 A.I., 31st March 1918. Crashed on landing and badly damaged, 30th June 1918. Lt C E H Allen, pilot, and 2/Lt H G Wepener, observer, unhurt. Aircraft to Repair Park No.2 A.S.D., rebuilt as F6207.

A8031 From No.2 A.I., 26th July 1918; Aircraft failed to return from reconnaissance sortie over Mons on 17th September 1918. Lt D H Hazell, pilot, and 2/Lt D B Robertson, observer, both killed in action (circumstances not known).

A8051 From No.2 A.I., 30th August 1918; During photographic sortie on 25th September 1918 pilot, Capt S Jones, pilot, landed to assist his observer, 2/Lt J Pullar, who had been wounded in combat, to hospital. He asked two orderlies to put ballast in rear cockpit. The engine was left ticking over and the throttle was accidentally opened. The aircraft ran on for fifty yards before overturning. Capt S Jones was unhurt.

A8052 From No.2 A.I., 25th August 1918; Failed to return from reconnaissance sortie over Maubeuge on 3rd October 1918; pilot, Sgt F P Clarke, and observer, Lt E W A G Middlecote, both killed in action.

A8054 From No.2 A.S.D., 31st March 1918; Failed to return from photo reconnaissance of Bruges, on 1st July 1918. Pilot, G E Dobeson, and observer, 2/Lt J E Pilling, both killed in action, claimed shot down by Vizefeldwebel Franz Piechulek of *Jasta* 56.

A8055 From No.2 A.I., 31st July 1918; To No.6 A.I., 13th May 1919.

A8057 From No.2 A.I., 5th September 1918; Listed missing in action following reconnaissance sortie on 4th October 1918; pilot, Lt L Young, killed in action; observer, Sgt H E Whitehead, died of wounds the same day (as PoW?).

A8058 From No.2 A.I., 27th March 1918; During a forced landing on 20th April 1918, occasioned by bad weather, aircraft ran into a bomb or shell crater near the front line. 2/Lt F F Keen, pilot, slightly injured; 2/Lt W Rudman, MC, observer, unhurt. Aircraft wreckage recovered, to Repair Park No.1 A.S.D., 22nd April 1918.

A8075 From No.2 A.I., 27th March 1918; Aircraft was severely damaged in heavy landing, 7th June 1918. Lt J Loupinsky, pilot, and Sgt J R Wright, observer, unhurt. Aircraft struck off charge at Repair Park No.2 A.S.D., 19th June 1918.

A8077 From No.1 A.I., 5th March 1918; Aircraft ran into shell crater on 11th March 1918 while making a forced landing at a disused aerodrome. 2/Lt A W P Cumming, pilot, and 2/Lt V G Stanton, observer, unhurt. To Repair Park No.2 A.S.D.

A8078 From No.2 A.I., 25th March 1918; 2/Lt S Jones destroyed an unidentified enemy aircraft on 29th March 1918. On 21st April 1918, during a bombing raid, was in combat with ten enemy aircraft; the pilot, 2/Lt J D Dingwall was hit and killed, but the wounded observer, Lt C M Sinclair, managed to fly the aircraft back to Allied territory and effect a successful forced landing at Serny and survived. Aircraft struck off charge at Repair Park No.1 A.S.D., on 25th April 1918.

A8087 Aircraft delivered From No.2 A.I., 18th September 1918.

Built by F W Berwick, Ltd, Park Royal, London NW10.

B2113 While on bombing sortie on 16th June 1918, was engaged by enemy aircraft and damaged. Capt J Anderson, pilot, and Lt J H Holland, observer, both wounded, evidently returned safely. Ltn J Veltjens of *Jasta* 15 claimed it as a victory.

Built by Westland Aircraft Works, Yeovil, Somerset.

B3964 From A.R.S. No.1 A.D., 19th October 1917; After returning from a bombing raid on 2nd December 1917, it landed heavily and overturned. Lt F V Bird, pilot, and 2/Air Mech L J W Bain, observer, unhurt. Repair Park No.1 A.S.D., 3rd December 1917.

Built by The Aircraft Manufacturing Co., Ltd., Hendon, London NW.

B7911 From No.2 A.I., 13th September 1918; Aircraft crashed and severely damaged on landing after test flight, 18th October 1917. Lt J G Farquhar, pilot, and 2/Lt I McEachran, observer, unhurt. Later rebuilt as H6887.

B7933 Aircraft delivered from No.6 A.I., 15th March 1919; disposed of to No.6 S.S., 13th May 1919.

B7938 Aircraft delivered from No.6 A.I., 21st March 1919; disposed of to No.6 S.S., 13th May 1919.

D8372 From No.2 A.I., 12th March 1918; While on a dawn patrol on 27th March 1918 was hit by ground fire which shot away the elevator controls. Pilot force landed south-east of Asq, but aircraft overturned. 2/Lt F F Keen, pilot, and Cpl T Ramsden, observer, both unhurt.

D8375 From No.2 A.I., 27th March 1918; While stationary on the airfield at Villers-Brettoneux on 21st April 1918, was taxied into by D9240 (returning from raid). There were no casualties. To Repair Park No.1 A.S.D., 23rd April 1918.

D8378 From No.2 A.I., 6th July 1918; During a reconnaissance sortie on 16th September 1918, was in combat with enemy aircraft over Mont St Eloi; aircraft returned with damage. Lt C Brown, pilot, unhurt, but Lt E W Griffin, observer, killed in action. Aircraft later rebuilt as H6885.

D8380 From No.2 A.I., 27th March 1918; Shot down in air combat during photographic sortie to Tournai on 16th July 1918, possibly by Vizefeldwebel Franz Piechulek of *Jasta* 56. Pilot, Capt E Waterlow, and observer, Lt J M Mackie, DCM, MM, both killed in action.

D8381 From No.2 A.I., 30th June 1918; To Repair Park No.2 A.S.D., 15th September 1918.

D8383 From No.2 A.I., 2nd July 1918; Aircraft delivered to No.25 Sqn., 2nd July 1918, but reported to be unable to climb; disposed of 15th August 1918; To Repair Park No.1 A.S.D., rebuilt as H7124.

D8389 From No.2 A.I., 10th June 1918; Damaged in a heavy landing, 28th July 1918. 2/Lt F Meehan, pilot, flying solo, unhurt. (Was flying with ballast in lieu of observer); To Repair Park No.2 A.S.D., 30th July 1918.

D8395 From No.2 A.I., 7th June 1918; Overshot airfield on landing, 6th July 1918, and crashed into rifle butts. Lt C E H Allen, pilot, and Lt J M Mackie, DCM, MM, observer, both unhurt. Struck off charge at Repair Park No.2 A.S.D., 11th July 1918.

D8410 From No.2 A.I., 2nd May 1918; Aircraft stalled close to the ground and crashed, 2nd July 1918. Capt R L Whalley, pilot, and 2/Lt H H Watson, observer, both unhurt. Aircraft Struck off charge at Repair Park No.2 A.S.D., 8th July 1918.

D8413 Aircraft suffered damage during the delivery from No.2 A.I., on 9th April 1918; Returned No.2 A.I., 11th April 1918.

D8414 From No.2 A.I., 10th June 1918; On 22nd August 1918 engine's fuel pump failed and during subsequent forced landing aircraft ran into a shell crater and was struck off charge. Sgt F P Clarke, pilot, and 2/Lt J Harrington, observer, unhurt. SOC Repair Park No.2 A.S.D., 10th September 1918.

D8426 From No.2 A.I., 29th July 1918; Returned to England 18th January 1919.

D8427 From No.2 A.I., 20th July 1918; Aircraft crashed 18th September 1918 (circumstances and crew names not known). Rebuilt as H6859.

D9235 From No.2 A.I., 28th May 1918; Aircraft overshot on landing and ran into sunken road, 7th June 1918; Lt L A Hacklett, pilot, and Sgt W C Elliott, observer, unhurt; repaired by 16th August 1918. During practice flight at 17.15hrs on 3rd September 1918 was attacked by five enemy aircraft over Dixmude; observer mortally wounded and due to damage received, pilot force landed at Capelle. 2/Lt E F Boyce, observer, killed in action; Lt S Crosfield, pilot, unhurt.

D9237 From No.2 A.I., 28th March 1918; Swung on take-off, 31st March 1918, and crashed when port wing skid struck the ground; 2/Lt C E H Allen, pilot, and 2/Lt W Rudman, MC, observer, both unhurt. To Repair Park No.1 A.S.D.

D9239 From No.2 A.I., 15th April 1918; On 20th May 1918, while on a bombing sortie and flying at 15,000ft, the aircraft was hit by ground anti-aircraft gunfire and crashed in flames at Aulnoye, killing the pilot, Lt A H Herring, and his observer, 2/Lt R S Lasker.

D9240 From No.2 A.I., 10th April 1918; On return from a bombing raid on 21st April 1918, collided with D8375 after landing; 2/Lt S Jones, pilot, and Cpl H Edwards, observer, unhurt. To Repair Park No.1 A.S.D., 23rd April 1918.

D9242 From No.2 A.I., 22nd April 1918; Aircraft overshot on landing at Ruisseauville, 7th May 1918, and collided with D.H.4 (B2139) of No.27 Squadron at. Lt J Loupinsky, pilot, and Sgt J R Wright, observer, both unhurt. Aircraft to Repair Park No.2 A.S.D., rebuilt as F6136.

D9247 From No.2 A.I., 21st April 1918; Crashed on landing at Ruisseauville, 20th May 1918. Lt A E Hulme, pilot, and 2/Lt D Boe, observer, both unhurt. Aircraft to Repair Park No.2 A.S.D., rebuilt as F6104.

D9251 From No.2 A.I., 2nd May 1918; Aircraft hit in the fuel tank by ground fire during a bombing sortie on 21st May 1918, and then attacked by enemy aircraft; and forced landed behind Allied lines. Lt L L K Straw, pilot, and 2/Lt H H Watson, observer, unhurt. To Repair Park No.2 A.S.D.

D9252 From No.2 A.I., 16th May 1918; Stalled in turn while low flying, 30th May 1918. Capt R L Whalley, pilot, and Sgt C A F Johnson, observer, both unhurt. Aircraft to Repair Park No.2 A.S.D., rebuilt as F6133.

D9255 From No.2 A.I., 28th September 1918; Report on aircraft, dated 18th October 1918, states that aircraft is unsuitable as it will not climb; To No.2 A.S.D., for UK that day.

D9259 From No.2 A.I., 25th Sqn, 8th May 1918; Report on the aircraft, dated 11th June 1918, states that the aircraft's performance is only adequate up to 7,000ft and 'is useless for our work'. Struck off charge and was later rebuilt as F5832.

D9266 From No.2 A.I., 21st May 1918; While on bombing sortie on 7th June 1918, hit by ground fire south-west of Valenciennes and last seen descending under control. Lt L A Hacklett, pilot, and Sgt W C Elliott, observer both unhurt and made PoW.

D9270 From No.2 A.S.D., early 1919; disposed of to No.6 S.S., 13th May 1919.

D9271 From No.2 A.I., 17th June 1918; Lieut L Young with 2/Lieut H Pullen, observer, shot down a Pfalz DIII over Lille on 4th August 1918. In combat with thirty enemy aircraft during a photographic sortie on 7th September 1918, the aircraft was damaged and its observer, 2/Lt J Harrington was wounded; the pilot, 2/Lt C H Saffery, was unhurt and flew home safely.

D9272 From No.2 A.I., 3rd June 1918; Aircraft struck tree while landing and crashed, 9th June 1918. Lt L V F Atkinson, pilot, injured, and 2/Lt H H Watson, observer, unhurt. To Repair Park No.2 A.S.D.

D9274 From No.2 A.I., 12th June 1918; Pilot overshot while landing and, in trying to take-off again, the undercarriage fouled high corn and the aircraft crashed. Lt R de Bruyn, pilot, unhurt, and Lt M F St Clair Fowles, observer, injured. SOC Repair Park No.2 A.S.D., 11th July 1918.

D9279 From No.2 A.I., 7th July 1918; Missing from photographic sortie in the Renaix area on 10th July 1918. Pilot, Lt J Loupinsky, wounded in action and made PoW; observer, Sgt J R Wright, unhurt, made PoW.

E4627 From No.2 A.I., 20th May 1918; During practice flight on 24th September 1918 the engine throttle fractured and the aircraft crashed. 2/Lt J E Mann, pilot (flying solo) unhurt.

Built by Glendower Aircraft Co Ltd, London

F2641 From No.6 A.I., 5th May 1919; disposed of to No.6 S.S., 13th May 1919.

Built by Palladium Autocars. Ltd, London

F5699 From No.2 A.I., 7th July 1918; Pilot became lost in poor visibility, 31st July 1918, and landed on dummy aerodrome, but crashed in deep ridge. Lt C Brown, pilot, and 2/Lt H Roberts, observer, both unhurt. Aircraft rebuilt as F6234.

F5701 From 6th A.I., 22nd March 1919; disposed of to 6th SS 13th May 1919.

F5738 Delivered from No.2 A.I., 8th November 1918; Subsequent history not known.

F5739 From No.2 A.I., October 1918; Damaged in air combat during reconnaissance sortie over Maubeuge on 30th October 1918; Lt D S Crumb, pilot, and Lt T A Chilcott, observer, returned unhurt. To Repair Park No.2 A.S.D., same day.

Rebuilds in France

F5826 From No.2 A.I., 1st August 1918; Propeller struck ground during take-off and aircraft crashed, 1st October 1918. 2/Lt A L Wilcox, pilot flying solo, unhurt. Aircraft rebuilt as H6873.

F5830 From No.1 A.S.D., October 1918; While on reconnaissance sortie on 7th October 1918, aircraft force landed on Hangard road; 2/Lt F W Seed, pilot, unhurt, and 2/Lt H C Shires, observer, injured.

F5832 From No.2 A.I., 2nd July 1918; Forced down in Allied territory on 22nd July 1918 during photographic sortie to Landrecies after engine hit in air combat. Lt S Jones, pilot, and Lt M F St Clair Fowles, observer, both unhurt. Aircraft repaired on the Squadron. On 4th August 1918 aircraft undershot on landing and undercarriage ripped off by corn on the edge of aerodrome. Lt S Jones, pilot, and 2/Lt J E Hermon, observer, unhurt. Aircraft struck off charge at Repair Park No.2 A.S.D., 11th August 1918.

F6076 Aircraft sideslipped too low and crashed, 21st December 1918; Lt C Addenbrooke, pilot, and 2/Lt H J Raiment, observer, unhurt.

F6099 Delivered from No.2 A.I., 18th September 1918; subsequent history not known.

F6103 From No.2 A.I., 15th August 1918; Force landed and crashed owing to bad weather conditions, 8th September 1918. Lt C Brown, pilot, and Lt E W Griffin, observer, both unhurt. SOC at Repair Park No.2 A.S.D., 30th September 1918.

F6120 From No.2 A.I., 18th September 1918; disposed of, 19th May 1919.

F6127 From No.2 A.I., 14th August 1918; Suffered engine failure during practice flight and crashed, 28th August 1918. 2/Lt R L Henning, pilot flying solo, injured. Aircraft struck off charge at Repair Park No.2 A.S.D., 2nd October 1918.

F6232 Delivered from Repair Park No.2 A.S.D., 6th October 1918; disposed of to No.6 A.I., 13th May 1919.

Replacement aircraft from The Aircraft Manufacturing Co Ltd, (Airco), Hendon, London NW.

F7598 From No.2 A.I., 28th September 1918; Aircraft stalled during take-off and fouled telephone wires, 21st January 1919. Lt C Addenbrooke, pilot, and Sgt J Bourne, observer, both unhurt. Aircraft remained on Squadron until 19th May 1919.

Rebuilds in France

H7120 Delivered from Repair Park No.1 A.S.D., 7th October, 1918; disposed of 19th May 1919.

H7121 Delivered from No.2 A.I., 8th November 1918; Stalled and crashed while turning too low while approaching to land, 9th May 1919. 2/Lt J G Barclay, pilot flying solo, killed. Aircraft disposed of to No.6 S.S., 13th May 1919.

(Aircraft Not Identified)

30th January 1918 In action (pilot unhurt, and 2/Air Mech C N Harvey killed).

5th February 1918 In action (pilot unhurt, and Sgt Hupper wounded).

26th March 1918 In action (pilot unhurt, and 2/Lt J Mitchell died of wounds, 3rd April 1918).

28th March 1918 In action (pilot unhurt, and Sgt A H Muff wounded).

8th June 1918 Reconnaissance (pilot unhurt, 2/Lt W H Dixon died of wounds, 23rd June 1918).

16th June 1918 Photo sortie (pilot unhurt, Sgt C A F Johnson wounded).

12th August 1918 In combat (pilot unhurt, and Sgt T Lirnley wounded).

12th August 1918 In combat (pilot unhurt, and Sgt W B Gray wounded).

Airco D.H.9a

At the time of the Armistice, No.25 Squadron had begun to take delivery of Airco D.H.9as ('Nine-Acks') and move forward into Germany. The first D.H.9as were received at Ruisseauville before the Squadron moved to La Brayelle, where it was based at the time of the Armistice.

Built by Whitehead Aircraft Ltd, Richmond, Surrey.

E706 From No.2 A.I., 11th November 1918.

Built by The Aircraft Manufacturing Co Ltd, (Airco), Hendon, London NW.

E8412 On delivery from 5th A.I., crashed on landing 20th October 1918 (Lt R de Bruyn & 2/Lt W L A Wilkinson unhurt).

E8428 From No.2 A.I., 3rd November 1918; Ran into an obstruction on landing 23rd November 1918 (2/Lt F Ollenbittle, pilot, and 2/Lt F H H White, observer, unhurt).

E8509 From No.2 A.I., 7th November 1918.

E8557 From No.2 A.I., 27th November 1918.

E8598 Left UK for No.25 Sqn, 16th February 1920; Arrived A.D. Aboukir, 25th February 1920.

E8768 Wrecked 27th May 1919; To No.6 S.S., 6th June 1919.

E8771 From No.1 A.S.D., 21st May 1919.

Built by Mann Egerton & Co Ltd, Norwich.

E9705 Aircraft failed to return from photographic sortie on 4th November 1918; pilot, Lt L L K Straw, and observer, 2/Lt P Cartwright, both killed in action.

Built by Vulcan Motor & Engineering Co (1906) Ltd, Southport

E9930 From No.6 A.I., 10th June 1919.

Built by Westland Aircraft Works, Yeovil.

F957 From 5th A.I., 10th 1918; Photo mission, Albatros C destroyed west of Maubeuge, then forced landed due to engine failure 4th November 1918 (Lt J H Latchford, pilot, and Lt H L H Tate, observer, both unhurt); To Repair Park No.2 A.S.D., 4th November 1918.

F993 From No.6 A.I., 13th February 1919. Fate unknown.

F1045 Crashed into by a French machine at Maubeuge aerodrome 9th February 1919; To No.6 A.I., 9th Feb 1919.

F1068 Built by Westland Aircraft. Shot down by Ltn Otto Konnecke of *Jasta* 5 on 1st November 1918, his 34th victory. Pilot, 2/Lt R G Dobeson, and observer, 2/Lt F G Mills, both made PoWs. First loss in action of a D.H.9a of No.25 Sqn.

Built by The Aircraft Manufacturing Co Ltd, (Airco), Hendon, London NW.

H4300 From No.6 A.I., 10th June 1919.

Built by Mann Egerton & Co Ltd, Norwich

J586 From No.1 A.I., 21st May 1919; Wrecked 3rd June 1919; To No.6 S.S., 6th June 1919.

The Squadron returned to England, bringing its remaining D.H.9as to South Carlton (three miles north of Lincoln) where it remained as a cadre; it then moved to Scopwick (later renamed Digby, between Lincoln and Sleaford) where it was disbanded on 31st January 1920, being re-formed the following day at Hawkinge, Kent. To begin with the Squadron received a number of Avro 504Ks, retaining some of these for up to four years.

Avro 504K

E3798 On Squadron, August 1921 to September 1921.

F8734 On Squadron, July 1922 to December 1922.

F8794 On Squadron, 1924.

F9718 On Squadron, from 21st October 1921.

F9719 On Squadron, from October 1921.

F9727 On Squadron, August 1921 to October 1921.

H2978 On arrival at Manston turned sharply after flying across aerodrome at 200ft, dived in, wrecked, 10th Jan 1922. Flt Lt E B Mason injured.

Bristol F.2B Fighter

F4864 On Squadron by May 1929.

J6623 Squadron Commander's personal aircraft 1921 to 1922.

Sopwith 7F.1 Snipe

No.25 Squadron's first peacetime operational equipment was the Sopwith Snipe. Although most of the aircraft had been manufactured a year or more earlier, few had flown more than a dozen hours when they arrived at Hawkinge. A total of 22 Snipe were taken to San Stefano in 1922.

E6061 With Squadron at San Stefano, 1922.

E6156 Turned over and spun in inverted off half roll at 1,500ft near Folkestone during practice landings, completely wrecked, 24th June 1921. Flg Off H M Struben killed.

E6243 On Squadron, March 1921 to August 1921.

E6266 Delivered to Squadron by March 1921. Engine failure at 150ft on take-off from Hawkinge, turned back, stalled while trying to avoid other aircraft and hangars, crashed and overturned, 12th July 1921. Flg Off J Bradbury unhurt.

E6307 Two-seat dual control trainer. On Squadron, August 1921 to October 1921.

E6493 Two-seat dual control trainer. On Squadron from September 1921 to October 1921.

E6600 Two-seat dual control trainer. Spun in off sharp turn at 2,000ft, near Folkestone, Kent, wrecked 24th July 1922. Flg Off H E Walker, MC, AFC, seriously injured and AC1 F Kershaw killed.

E6623 Delivered to Squadron, December 1922. Wheels sank in mud while landing at San Stefano and overturned, 15th December 1922.

E6632 On Squadron, November 1922 to 1923.

E6651 On Squadron, March 1924 to October 1924.

E6944 On Squadron by April 1924.

E6961 Erected by 29th October 1922 to at least January 1923.

E6970 Erected by 29th October 1922 to at least January 1923.

E7411 Crashed when both wing spars failed on turn, 27th October 1924 WOC.

E7423 Suffered engine failure in sharp turn at 800ft after take-off, forced landed in snow-covered ploughed field and overturned, near Hawkinge, 18th January 1922. Flg Off D M I Macarthur unhurt.

E7429 While based at San Stefano, suffered engine failure, and force landed at Haidi Pasha, Ismid Peninsula 25th January 1923; aircraft burnt by pilot.

E7439 Delivered to Squadron by September 1921.

E7456 Erected by 29th October 1922. Suffered engine failure on take-off at San Stefano; wing struck telegraph pole, 19th February 1923.

E7501 Delivered to Squadron, May 1921. Suffered engine failure, 2nd September 1921; pilot attempted to force land at Hawkinge but undershot; aircraft written off.

E7504 On Squadron, July 1921 to September 1921.

E7509 On Squadron, April 1921 to November 1921.

E7528 On Squadron, April 1922 to October 1922.

E7543 On Squadron by May 1921 to November 1921.

E7558 Delivered to Squadron, April 1922. Suffered engine failure at 1,500ft over Sandgate, forced landed in sea just off beach near Folkestone, Kent 18th September 1922. Flg Off S G Williams slightly injured.

E7560 On Squadron, April 1921 to July 1921.

E7563 On Squadron, 1922.

E7565 Erected by 29th October 1922 to at least January 1923 (at San Stefano).

E7598 On Squadron, March 1924.

E7601 Delivered to Squadron, November 1922. Flt Lt G H H Scutt MC killed.

E7665 On Squadron, 1922.

E8237 Long-range version of Snipe (Type 7F.1A); Erected by 29th October 1922 to January 1923 at San Stefano.

E8239 Long-range version of Snipe (Type 7F.1A); on Squadron at San Stefano by December 1922 to January 1923.

E8598 Left UK for No.25 Sqn 16th February 1920; Arrived A.D. Aboukir 25th February 1920.

F2398 On Squadron, April 1924.

F2425 On Squadron, 1922.

F2426 Erected by 29th October 1922 to January 1923 (at San Stefano).

F2437 Engine failed while flying near ground in bad weather, forced landed near Hawkinge, completely wrecked, 19th September 1922. Flg Off B A Davy slightly injured.

F2463 Delivered to Squadron, August 1921.

F2464 Erected by 29th October 1922 to January 1923 (at San Stefano).

F2485 On Squadron, November 1922 to January 1923 (at San Stefano).

Gloster Grebe II

As winner of the most flying competitions during 1923 and 1924, No.25 (Fighter) Squadron was nominated to be the first to equip with the Gloster Grebe II and therefore carried out the Service trials on the first production aircraft in September 1924.

J7283 First production aircraft. Service trials, Hawkinge, September 1924.

J7284 Served on Squadron in 1924; and again from September 1925 to August 1926, and in 1928.

J7285 Delivered new to Squadron, October 1924.

J7286 Delivered new to Squadron, October 1924.

J7287 Served on Squadron from October 1924 to September 1926.

J7288 Served on Squadron from October 1924 to April 1926.

J7289 Served on Squadron from October 1924 to May 1925.

J7290 Served on Squadron from October 1924 to November 1925 and from September 1928 to June 1929.

J7291 Delivered new to Squadron, October 1924.

J7292 Served on Squadron from May 1925 to May 1929.

J7293 Served on Squadron from October 1924 to December 1925.

J7294 Served on Squadron from October 1924 to December 1926.

J7358 Served on Squadron during 1927 and from 24th February 1928.

J7360 Served on Squadron from November 1927 to March 1928.

J7361 Served on Squadron from June 1927 to February 1928.

J7363 Served on Squadron from December 1925 to January 1927 and from March 1927 to May 1927.

J7365 On Squadron, January 1926.

J7368 On Squadron, January 1926.

J7370 Served on Squadron from October 1926 to March 1927 and from October 1928.

J7372 Delivered to Squadron, September 1927. Collided with J7392 in mock dogfight over Capel, near Folkestone, and crashed at Crete Road East, two miles from Hawkinge, 17th February 1928. Flg Off L A Walsh parachuted safely, being unhurt. Aircraft struck off charge.

J7374 Served on Squadron from January 1925 to December 1927.

J7379 Served on Squadron from November 1927 to October 1928.

J7384 Served on Squadron from June 1926 to October 1928.

J7385 On Squadron, July 1926.

J7392 Delivered to Squadron, October 1926. Collided with J7372 in mock dogfight over Capel, near Folkestone, 17th February 1928; Plt Off E J Watson killed. Aircraft struck off charge.

J7400 Delivered to Squadron, 25th January 1927.

J7402 Delivered to Squadron, October 1926. Hit on the ground by J7581 which was landing, Hawkinge, 13th June 1927. Flg Off R J A Ford unhurt. Aircraft repaired.

J7403 Served on Squadron, September 1925.

J7406 Served on Squadron, September 1925 to March 1926.

J7407 Served on Squadron, September 1925 to December 1925.

J7409 Served on Squadron, September 1925 to September 1926; crashed and overturned (date unknown).

J7410 Delivered new to Squadron, October 1924; wing flutter in dive, lost control and crashed on approach, Hawkinge, 6th January 1925. Flg Off R Scott-Taylor slightly injured.

J7411 Delivered new to Squadron, October 1924; Lost control recovering from dive with engine off, attempted to land at high speed but overturned, 27th October 1924; Flg Off A E T Bruce slightly injured. Developed violent oscillation while diving at 160mph with two other aircraft, crashed from low height attempting to land at Hawkinge, completely wrecked 6th January 1925. Plt Off R Scott-Taylor slightly injured.

J7412 Delivered new to Squadron, October 1924; Diving after camera gun practice, flew into garden wall of a house on brow of hill, completely wrecked, 17th November 1924. Flg Off L E Maynard seriously injured. Suffered air collision in poor visibility, and abandoned near Hawkinge, 17th February 1928.

J7413 Two-seat dual control trainer (but not Mk.IIIDC); delivered 3rd July 1928.

J7417 Served on Squadron from August 1928 to July 1929.

The following Grebe Mk.IIs incorporated anti-flutter mods.

J7569 Delivered to Squadron, August 1928.

J7572 Delivered to Squadron, October 1925. Force landed on Port Meadow, Oxford, 4th August 1926, but engine caught fire on take-off and aircraft overturned in dyke.

J7576 Served on Squadron from August 1925 to June 1927.

J7578 Served on Squadron from September 1926 to January 1927.

J7580 Served on Squadron from December 1925 to c.March 1927.

J7581 Served on Squadron from June 1927 to June 1928. Ran onto tarmac on landing at Hawkinge and hit J7402, 13th June 1927. Flg Off L A Walsh unhurt. Aircraft repaired.

J7583 Served on Squadron, December 1927.

J7586 Served on Squadron from 30th September 1926 to September 1927.

J7587 Served on Squadron from January 1926 to September 1927.

J7588 Served on Squadron from December 1925 to April 1926.

J7589 Served on Squadron from November 1926 to February 1927 and from December 1927 to February 1928.

J7591 Served on Squadron, May 1927.

J7602 Served on Squadron from November 1925 to October 1926.

J7603 Served on Squadron from September 1925 to September 1926.

Gloster Grebe Mk.IIIDC (two-seat trainers)

J7520 Served on Squadron from July 1925 to April 1926, and from August 1928.

J7530 Served on Squadron from August 1925 to April 1926.

J7532 Served on Squadron, September 1925.

J7534 Served on Squadron from July 1926 to March 1927.

J7536 Served on Squadron from September 1927 to December 1927.

J7538 Served on Squadron, September 1926.

Unidentified Grebe accident:
9th December 1926. Collided with another aircraft, dived into ground and burnt out at Terlingham Manor Farm, near Hawkinge. Flt Off J H C Purvis killed.

Armstrong Whitworth Siskin IIIA

Having established itself as the R.A.F.'s leading exponent with the Gloster Grebe, No.25 Squadron was required to fly the aircraft longer than any other squadron, and therefore was never equipped with the Grebe's much-improved development, the Gamecock. Conversion by the Squadron to the Armstrong Whitworth Siskin began in December 1928 and occupied almost five months. The aircraft was disliked.

Armstrong Whitworth-built in 1924.

J7176 Served on Squadron from December 1931 to March 1932. (This aircraft had been built in 1924 as a Siskin Mk.III, had flown tropical trials at Hinaidi, Iraq, in 1925; served in India with No.5 Squadron in 1927-28, returning to the U.K. in 1929 to serve with No.19 Squadron in 1930. After being disposed of by No.25 Squadron it was issued to the RAF College, Cranwell, but crashed one mile from the College after catching fire in the air on 20th February 1933.)

J7358 Served on No.25 Squadron during 1927-28 for air experience.

J7360 Served on No.25 Squadron during 1927-28 for air experience.

Armstrong Whitworth-built in 1927-28.

J8629 Delivered to Squadron, August 1930, after reconditioning. Collided with J8632 while taking off at Hawkinge, 22nd October 1931, and written off. Sgt R H H Ross unhurt.

J8631 Delivered to Squadron, August 1930, after reconditioning.

J8632 Delivered to Squadron, April 1932, after reconditioning. Struck by J8629 during take-off at Hawkinge, 22nd October 1931, and written off. Flg Off B W Knox unhurt.

J8846 Delivered to Squadron, March 1932; disposed of, April 1932.

J8852 Served on Squadron from December 1931 to March 1932.

Blackburn-built in 1927-28.

J8878 Delivered to Squadron, 31st October 1930. Collided with stationary Fury I K2053 after landing at Hawkinge, 10th March 1932, and written off. Flg Off K B B Cross unhurt.

J8881 Delivered to Squadron, March 1931. Spun from 700 feet and crashed on side of hill near Folkestone, 27th October 1931. Siamese officer Lt Aat Sucaritkul killed.

J8885 Delivered to Squadron, c.May 1931. Force landed on golf links but struck embankment, Lampeter, Cardigan, 10th September 1930; written off.

J8889 Served on Squadron, December 1931 to February 1932.

J8958 Delivered to Squadron in 1929; crashed at Hawkinge, 17th February 1931.

Bristol-built in 1928-29.

J9305 Delivered new to Squadron, December 1928; disposed of, April 1929.

J9306 Delivered new to Squadron, December 1928; disposed of, March 1929.

J9307 Delivered new to Squadron, 29th December 1928; suffered propeller accident at Hawkinge, 12th November 1930, and disposed of.

J9308 Delivered new to Squadron, December 1928; crashed, April 1930; repaired and disposed of.

J9310 Delivered new to Squadron, c.February 1929; disposed of, February 1931.

J9311 Delivered new to Squadron, April 1929; disposed of (returned to makers), April 1929.

J9312 Delivered new to Squadron, April 1929; crashed at Hawkinge in crosswind landing, May 1929. Repaired and disposed of to No.56 Squadron.

J9313 Delivered to Squadron (ex-training unit), November 1930. Overshot while landing at Hawkinge and hit trees, 20th January 1932; written off. Flt Lt Radana Woa Sakol (Siamese) unhurt.

J9319 Probably the new aircraft in which the pilot was overcome by CO^2 poisoning while on delivery from Filton to the Squadron at Hawkinge. Crashed Godstone, Surrey. Sgt J W Pearce killed.

J9324 Delivered new to Squadron, May 1929; disposed of, December 1931.

J9325 Delivered new to Squadron, May 1929. Stalled in steep low level turn and crashed during army co-operation exercise with 167th Infantry Brigade, near Falmer, Sussex, 8th August 1930. Sgt O H McNair killed.

J9326 Delivered new to Squadron, May 1929; disposed of to No.3 Flying Training School, February 1931.

J9327 Delivered new to Squadron, May 1929; disposed of to No.5 Flying Training School, October 1931.

J9328 Delivered new to Squadron, June 1929; disposed of, February 1930.

J9329 Delivered new to Squadron, June 1929; disposed of, December 1929.

Gloster-built in 1929.

J9346 Delivered new to Squadron, April 1929; disposed of to R.A.E., 11th March 1930.

J9348 Delivered new to Squadron, January 1930. Force landed during formation sortie; hit hay-rake during subsequent take-off and overturned, South Ockendon, Essex, 8th December 1930.

J9349 Delivered new to Squadron, May 1929; disposed of, March 1932.

J9350 Delivered new to Squadron, May 1929; disposed of, February 1932.

J9352 Delivered to Squadron (after reconditioning by Vickers), January 1931; disposed of, January 1932.

Vickers-built in 1929-30.

J9356 Delivered to Squadron (after repairs), 1930.

J9358 Delivered to Squadron (ex-No.17 Sqn,), 1930; passed to No.43 Sqn., May 1930.

J9369 Delivered to Squadron (ex-C.F.S.), February 1932; disposed of, March 1932.

J9377 Delivered to Squadron (ex-No.32 Sqn,), January 1931; while stationary, taxied into by Fury 1 K2059 at Hawkinge, 21st March 1932; repaired and disposed of, April 1932.

J9874 Delivered new to Squadron, 14th January 1930.

Armstrong Whitworth Siskin Mk.IIIDC

Armstrong Whitworth-built in 1928. Two-seat dual control trainer.

J9192 Delivered to Squadron, April 1932, after reconditioning. Stalled and cartwheeled while landing at Hawkinge, 3rd November 1932. Lt A Vega Gracia (Spanish?) unhurt.

J9198 Delivered to Squadron, February 1933 (ex-No.111 Sqn). Disposed of, August 1933.

J9218 Delivered new to Squadron, September 1929; disposed of, 1932.

J9227 Delivered new to Squadron, November 1930; disposed of, April 1932.

Hawker Fury Mk.I

By the time No.25 (Fighter) Squadron began disposing of its tiresome Siskins early in 1932, it was public knowledge that they were to be replaced by Sydney Camm's beautiful Hawker Fury. On account of continuing success in the Fighting Area Trophy competitions, despite not having been equipped with Gloster Gamecocks in the late 1930s, it had been announced as early as April 1930 that No.25 Squadron was to be one of three Squadrons to be equipped with Hawker Furies. However, on account of severe limitations in the Defence Budget, it was not until February 1932 that the new fighters began to arrive at Hawkinge.

K1930 (5th production aircraft). Delivered to Squadron, April 1931, for experience on type; 70 hrs flown by No.25 Squadron. Passed to No.43 Sqn., May 1931. Returned to Sqn., 1st July 1936. Disposed of to No.43 Sqn., 29th July 1936.

K1945 (20th production aircraft). Delivered to Squadron, April 1931, for experience on type; 56 hrs flown by No.25 Squadron. Passed to No.43 Sqn., May 1931.

K2041 Delivered to Squadron ex-No.1 Sqn. as replacement; disposed of, January 1937.

K2048 Delivered to Squadron ex-No.1 Sqn. as replacement; disposed of, January 1937.

K2050 Delivered to Squadron ex-No.1 Sqn. disposed of to No.43 Sqn.

K2051 Delivered to Squadron ex-No.43 Sqn; 28th July 1936; disposed of to No.1 Sqn. 11th December 1936.

K2052 Delivered new to Squadron, 10th February 1932. First of new equipment. Disposed of to No.1 Sqn., 11th December 1936.

K2053 Delivered new to Squadron, 20th February 1932; disposed of 8th January 1935.

K2054 Delivered new to Squadron, 20th February 1932. Written off, 28th July 1932.

K2055 Delivered new to Squadron, 24th February 1932; disposed of to No.1 Sqn,11th December 1936.

K2056 Delivered new to Squadron, 24th February 1932. Written off, 8th May 1934.

K2057 Delivered new to Squadron, 24th February 1932. Collided in formation with K2055 and crashed near Hawkinge written off, 17th September 1932. Flg Off F P R Dunworth parachuted safely.

K2059 Delivered new to Squadron, 24th February 1932. Stalled on approach at North Weald and crashed, written off, 30th March 1936. Flg Off M Dawnay slightly injured.

K2060 Delivered new to Squadron, 24th February 1932; disposed of to No.1 Sqn.

K2062 Delivered new to Squadron, 10th February 1932; disposed of to No.1 Sqn., 27th January 1937.

K2066 Delivered to replace K2054 ex-No.1 Sqn; disposed of to No.87 Sqn, 15th March 1937.

K2067 Delivered to replace K2057 ex-No.1 Sqn; disposed of to No.3 Flying Training School.

K2068 Delivered new to Squadron, 25th February 1932; written off, 9th March 1933.

K2069 Delivered ex-No.1 Squadron as replacement. Disposed of 15th March 1937.

K2070 Delivered new to Squadron, 25th February 1932; disposed of to No.43 Sqn., 11th December 1936.

K2071 Delivered new to Squadron, 25th February 1932; disposed of 27th July 1935.

K2072 Delivered new to Squadron, 25th February 1932; disposed of 10th August 1932.

K2073 Delivered new to Squadron, April 1932. Crashed at Thorney Island, 25th September 1933.

K2076 Ex-No.43 Squadron as replacement, 24th July 1936; disposed of to No.1 Sqn., 11th December 1936.

K2077 Delivered new to Squadron, 5th April 1932; disposed of to A & AEE, 12th March 1934.

K2078 Delivered to Squadron, 12th January 1933; disposed of 15th April 1937.

K2079 Delivered to Squadron, 31st March 1933. Crashed near Canterbury and written off in forced landing in fog, 3rd September 1936. Flg Off F G Frow unhurt.

K2877 Delivered new to Squadron, 3rd November 1932; disposed of 4th January 1934.

K2878 Delivered to Squadron, 29th November 1933; disposed of to No.1 Sqn., 21st December 1936.

K2882 Delivered to Squadron, 3rd February 1934; disposed of to No.43 Sqn., 11th December 1936.

K2883 Delivered to Squadron, 3rd February 1934; disposed of to No.43 Sqn., 11th December 1936.

K5677 Delivered new to Squadron, December 1935; disposed of to RAF College, Cranwell, 23rd October 1936.

Hawker Fury Mk.II

K7263 Delivered new to Squadron, 2nd October 1936; disposed of to No.41 Sqn., October 1937.

K7264 Delivered new to Squadron, 2nd October 1936; disposed of to No.41 Sqn., October 1937.

K7265 Delivered new to Squadron, 2nd October 1936; disposed of to No.41 Sqn., October 1937.

K7266 Delivered new to Squadron, 2nd October 1936; disposed of to No.41 Sqn., October 1937.

K7267 Delivered new to Squadron, 2nd October 1936. Engine cut, forced landed, hit trees, 26th April 1937. Sgt E W J Monk unhurt.

K7268 Delivered new to Squadron, 2nd October 1936; disposed of to No.41 Sqn., October 1937.

K7269 Delivered new to Squadron, 2nd October 1936; disposed of to No.41 Sqn., October 1937.

K7270 Delivered new to Squadron, 2nd October 1936; disposed of to No.41 Sqn., October 1937.

K7271 Delivered new to Squadron, 2nd October 1936; disposed of to No.41 Sqn., October 1937.

K7272 Delivered new to Squadron, 2nd October 1936; disposed of to No.41 Sqn., October 1937.

K7273 Delivered new to Squadron, 2nd October 1936; disposed of to No.41 Sqn., October 1937.

K7274 Delivered new to Squadron, 2nd October 1936; disposed of to No.41 Sqn., October 1937.

K7275 Delivered new to Squadron, 2nd October 1936; disposed of to No.41 Sqn., October 1937.

K7276 Delivered new to Squadron, 2nd October 1936; disposed of to No.41 Sqn., October 1937.

K7277 Delivered new to Squadron, 3rd November 1936; disposed of to No.41 Sqn., October 1937.

K7278 Delivered new to Squadron, 3rd November 1936; disposed of to No.41 Sqn., October 1937.

K7279 Delivered new to Squadron, 3rd November 1936. Crashed, Burmarsh, near Dymchurch, 3rd August 1937. Plt Off K L Keith injured.

K7280 Delivered new to Squadron, 3rd November 1936; disposed of to No.41 Sqn., October 1937.

K7281 Delivered new to Squadron, 3rd November 1936; disposed of to No.41 Sqn., October 1937.

K7282 Delivered new to Squadron, 3rd November 1936; disposed of to No.41 Sqn., October 1937.

K7283 Delivered new to Squadron, 3rd November 1936; disposed of to No.41 Sqn., October 1937.

Hawker Demon I

In the autumn of 1937 observer/gunners began arriving on No.25 Squadron in preparation for conversion to two-seat Demon fighters, it being intended that the Squadron would become a night fighter squadron. The Demons began arriving in October, in most instances being transferred from No.41 Squadron in exchange for No.25's Fury IIs, that unit simultaneously becoming a single-seat fighter squadron.

K2853 Delivered to Squadron, ex-No.41 Sqn., 26th October 1937. Became ground instructional machine, 1109M, 2nd August 1938.

K2905 Delivered to Squadron, ex-No.41 Sqn., October 1937. Disposed of to A & AEE, January 1938.

K2906 Delivered to Squadron, ex-No.64 Sqn., October 1937. Disposed of to No.607 Sqn., February 1938.

K3770 Delivered to Squadron, ex-No.29 Sqn., October 1937. Struck off charge, 25th May 1938.

K3791 Delivered to Squadron, ex-No.41 Sqn., October 1937. Disposed of to No.64 Sqn., February 1938.

K3798 Delivered to Squadron, ex-No.41 Sqn., October 1937. Struck off charge, 21st October 1938.

K3976 Delivered to Squadron, ex-No.29 Sqn., October 1937. Struck off charge, June 1938.

K3979 Delivered to Squadron, ex-No.29 Sqn., October 1937. Disposed of to No.601 Sqn., March 1938.

K3982 Delivered to Squadron, ex-No.29 Sqn., October 1937. Disposed of to No.601 Sqn., March 1938.

K3983 Delivered to Squadron, ex-No.41 Sqn., October 1937. Collided with K4538 and crashed, Tilmanstone Colliery, near Dover, 5th November 1937. Plt Off J G Cave, pilot safely chuted, AC1 J Dale died of injuries.

K4525 Delivered to Squadron, ex-No.41 Sqn., October 1937. Disposed of, March 1938.

K4526 Delivered to Squadron, ex-No.41 Sqn., October 1937. Struck off charge, 1st July 1938.

K4529 Delivered to Squadron, ex-No.604 Sqn., November 1937. Disposed of, 1938.

K4532 Delivered to Squadron, ex-No.41 Sqn., October 1937; returned to No.41 Sqn., c.March 1938.

K4538 Delivered to Squadron, ex-No.41 Sqn., October 1937. Damaged in collision with K3983, force landed in small field, 5th November 1937. Sgt P R Smith, pilot, and Cpl H Stoten unhurt. Became ground instructional machine, *1038M*, January 1938.

K4539 Delivered to Squadron, ex-No.41 Sqn., November 1937. Disposed of to No.1 Air Armament School, 1938.

K4540 Delivered to Squadron, ex-No.41 Sqn., November 1937. Disposed of to No.601 Sqn., March 1938.

K4542 Delivered to Squadron, ex-No.41 Sqn., October 1937. Disposed of to No.607 Sqn., March 1938.

K4543 Delivered to Squadron, ex-No.41 Sqn., October 1937. Disposed of to No.64 Sqn., February 1938.

K4544 Delivered to Squadron, ex-No.41 Sqn., October 1937. Became ground instructional machine, *1067M*, March 1938.

K8205 Boulton Paul-built. Delivered new to Squadron, December 1937. Disposed of to No.608 Sqn., June 1938.

K8206 Boulton Paul-built. Delivered new to Squadron, December 1937. Disposed of to No.608 Sqn., June 1938.

K8208 Boulton Paul-built. Delivered new to Squadron, January 1938. Disposed of to No.608 Sqn., June 1938.

K8211 Boulton Paul-built. Delivered new to Squadron, January 1938. Disposed of to No.608 Sqn., June 1938.

K8212 Boulton Paul-built. Delivered new to Squadron, January 1938. Disposed of to No.608 Sqn., June 1938.

K8213 Boulton Paul-built. Delivered new to Squadron, January 1938. Disposed of to No.608 Sqn., June 1938.

Gloster Gladiator Mk.II

With the successful conversion of the Blenheim Mark I to the night fighter rôle, No.25 Squadron was notified in mid-1938 that it was to become one of the first night fighter Squadrons to be thus equipped. However, the airmen observers who had flown in the Demons were required to re-muster and receive navigation training for operations in the Blenheims. In the meantime No.25 Squadron was re-equipped with Gladiators, primarily to provide experience for the pilots in night-landing a high-performance fighter aircraft equipped with flaps. Most of the aircraft delivered to No.25 were received from No.56 Squadron which was one of the first to convert on to the new Hawker Hurricane fighters.

K6147 Delivered to Squadron, ex-No.56 Sqn.,28th June 1938; disposed of to No.607 Sqn., 30th December 1938.

K6149 Delivered to Squadron, ex-No.56 Sqn., 23rd June 1938; disposed of to No.607 Sqn.5th January 1939.

K7961 Delivered to Squadron, ex-No.56 Sqn., 23rd July 1938; disposed of to No.65 Sqn., 23rd February 1939.

K7982 Delivered to Squadron, ex-No.56 Sqn., 22nd June 1938; disposed of to No.607 Sqn., 10th January 1939.

K7983 Delivered to Squadron, ex-No.65 Sqn., 28th June 1938; disposed of to No.607 Sqn., 30th December 1938.

K7988 Delivered to Squadron, ex-No.56 Sqn., 21st June 1938; disposed of to No.607 Sqn., 12th January 1939.

K7989 Delivered to Squadron, ex-No.56 Sqn., 22nd June 1938; disposed of to No.607 Sqn., 12th January 1939.

K7992 Delivered to Squadron, ex-No.56 Sqn., 29th June 1938; disposed of to No.607 Sqn., 5th January 1939.

K7995 Delivered to Squadron, ex-No.56 Sqn., 25th June 1938; disposed of to No.607 Sqn., 5th January 1939.

K7996 Delivered to Squadron, ex-No.56 Sqn., 25th June 1938; disposed of to No.607 Sqn., 10th January 1939.

K7997 Delivered to Squadron, ex-No.56 Sqn., 28th June 1938; disposed of to No.607 Sqn., 13th February 1939.

K7998 Delivered to Squadron, ex-No.56 Sqn., 28th June 1938; Ran out of fuel on ferry flight, hit tree in forced landing, Great Corby, Cumberland, 3rd January 1939. Plt Off A G Evans unhurt.

K7999 Delivered to Squadron, ex-No.65 Sqn., 28th June 1938; disposed of to No.607 Squadron, 5th January 1939.

K8000 Delivered to Squadron, ex-No.56 Sqn., 22nd June 1938; disposed of to No.607 Sqn., 2nd January 1939.

K8020 Delivered to Squadron, ex-No.56 Sqn., 24th June 1938; disposed of to No.607 Sqn., 30th December 1938.

K8030 Delivered to Squadron, ex-No.56 Sqn., 21stJune 1938; disposed of to No.607 Sqn., 30th December 1938.

Bristol Blenheim Mk.I and IF

Apart from a single aircraft (equipped as a bomber) loaned to the Squadron for air experience in the autumn of 1938, the first Blenheim fighters to arrive on No.25 Squadron were received during the winter of 1938-39. The majority of these were not initially fully-armed, being fitted with the four-gun tray after arrival on the Squadron. Prior to the outbreak of war, they were usually flown with two-man crews, but thereafter they were flown with both a navigator and a gunner.

Bristol-built

K7058/RX-K Delivered on extended loan from School of Army Co-operation, c. December 1938.

K7090 Delivered ex-No.248 Sqn., 22nd February 1940. Disposed of to No.55 O.T.U., 21st November 1940.

K7113 Bomber-equipped. Delivered ex-No.90 Sqn., c.September 1938, on loan for air experience. Later received on Squadron, 20th March 1940. Disposed of to No.68 Sqn., 4th March 1941.

K7125 Bomber-equipped. Delivered ex-No. 114 Sqn., 1939. Disposed of to No.5 Bombing & Gunnery School, 1939. Later received on Squadron, 18th August 1940. Disposed of, 23rd October 1940.

K7142/ ZK-T Delivered on extended loan from No.44 (Bomber) Squadron, c.May 1939.

L1109 Bomber, converted to fighter. Received ex-No.82 Sqn., 17th June 1940. Disposed of to No.219 Sqn., 18th June 1940.

L1169 Bomber, converted to fighter. Received 18th June 1940. Disposed of, 25th June 1940.

L1172 Fighter, received 13th September 1940. Disposed of, 17th June 1940.

L1200/ ZK-H Bomber, converted to fighter. Received ex-No.44 Sqn., c.September 1939. Disposed of to No.114 Sqn,.

L1207 Bomber, converted to fighter. Received 13th June 1940. Disposed of to No.68 Sqn., 4th March 1941.

L1212 Received ex-No.248 Sqn, 1st March 1940. After take-off from North Weald, stalled and a wing hit the ground in turn, 27th March 1940. Plt Off P D W Brierley killed.

L1233 Fighter, received ex-No248 Sqn., 21st March 1940. Disposed of, 3rd May 1940.

L1235 Bomber, converted to fighter. Received 16th February 1940. Control lost in bad weather during black-out tests over Peterborough, dived into the ground at Elton, Northamptonshire, burnt out. Flt Lt J M M Hughes, pilot, and Sgt J R Friend, air gunner, both killed, 7th December 1940.

L1241 Bomber, converted to fighter. Received ex-No.18 Sqn., 19th February 1938. Overshot and hit bank while landing at Hawkinge, 1st August 1939. Plt Off Rofe unhurt.

L1257/ZK-I. Bomber, converted to fighter. Received ex-34 Sqn, c-August 1939. Disposed of to No.92 Sqn., c.Dec 1939.

L1290 Bomber, converted to fighter. Received 12th June 1940. Disposed of 25th June 1940.

L1291 Bomber, converted to fighter. Received ex-No.248 Sqn., 12th March 1940. Disposed of to No.54 O.T.U., 16th January 1941.

L1312 Bomber, converted to fighter. Received 20th October 1941. Disposed of to No.12 (P)AFU, 15th Feb 1943.

L1406/ZK-E Delivered new to Squadron, 31st January 1939. Overshot night landing and overturned at Martlesham Heath, 12th August 1940, and written off. Plt Off N H Corry unhurt.

L1408/ZK-J Delivered new to Squadron, 19th December 1938. Collided with Blenheim L6722 of No.29 Sqn., during A.I. tests over Bristol Channel, 31st July 1940. Sgt J B Thompson killed.

L1409 Delivered new to Squadron, 19th December 1938. Shot down by Hurricanes near North Weald, 3rd September 1940.

L1418 Delivered new to Squadron, 5th December 1938. Damaged beyond repair, 14th August 1940.

L1420 Delivered new to Squadron, 5th December 1938. Skidded during night landing in icy conditions, hit earth mound, at Northolt, 24th November 1939. Sgt R C Haine unhurt.

L1422 Delivered new to Squadron, 30th November 1938. Disposed of to No.604 Sqn., 1st December 1939.

L1423 Delivered new to Squadron, 19th December 1938. Swung on take-off at North Weald and undercarriage raised to stop, 9th July 1939. Flt Lt C H Bull unhurt.

L1424 Ex-trials aircraft with gun tray, delivered to Squadron, 18th January 1939; passed to R.A.E., 2nd Feb 1939.

L1426 Delivered new to Squadron, 5th December 1938. Engine cut after take-off for air test, belly landed, Northolt, 17th December 1939. Flt Sgt Monk and crew unhurt.

L1433/RX-R Delivered new to Squadron, 10th December 1938, later ZK-R. Disposed of to No.68 Sqn., January 1941.

L1436/RX-M Delivered new to Squadron, 10th December 1938. Belly-landed in error at Sutton Bridge, 16th August 1939, and disposed of to M.U. Plt Off A J S Pattinson unhurt.

L1437/ ZK-P Delivered new to Squadron, 10th December 1938. Disposed of to No.54 O.T.U., 16th January 1941.

L1438 Bomber-converted to fighter. Received 22nd August 1940. Disposed of to No.54 O.T.U., 23rd March 1941.

L1439 Delivered new to Squadron, 10th December 1938. Pilot lost control in cloud at night, crashed near Dartford, Kent, 18th May 1939. Sgt J C Lingard parachuted safely, AC F R Jones killed.

L1440 Delivered new to Squadron, 10th December 1938. Disposed of, 21st September 1940.

L1472 Received ex-No.64 Sqn., 25th April 1940. Disposed of to No.29 Sqn., 22nd May 1940.

L1510 Delivered new to Squadron, 30th January 1939. Undercarriage collapsed in heavy landing at Hawkinge, 13th July 1939.

L1511 Delivered new to Squadron, 30th January 1939. Disposed of to No.248 Sqn., 21st October 1939.

L1512 Delivered new to Squadron, 1st February 1939. Shot down by Hurricanes over North Weald, 3rd September 1940. Plt Off D W Hogg, pilot, killed. Sgt E Powell baled out safely.

L1523 Received 4th September 1940. Disposed of to No.600 Sqn., 17th December 1940.

Avro-built

L6602 Received ex-No.604 Sqn., 3rd August 1940. Struck off charge, 13th March 1941.

L6676/ZK-A Delivered new to Squadron, 26th May 1939. Disposed of, 15th January 1941.

L6677 Delivered new to Squadron, 26th May 1939. Disposed of to No.54 O.T.U., 4th February 1941.

L6678 Delivered new to Squadron, 31st May 1939. Engine cut, stalled on approach, wing hit ground, Filton, 16th September 1939. Plt Off B J Rofe and crew unhurt.

L6679/RZ-L Delivered new to Squadron, 31st May 1939, later ZK-L. Iced up in cloud, broke up during dive and crashed at Ingatestone, Essex, 16th November 1940. Sgt L T Winter, pilot, Sgt A J Theasby, radio operator and Sgt A L Romanis, W.Op/Air gunner, all killed.

L6686 Delivered new to Squadron, 12th June 1939. Disposed of to No.23 Sqn. 15th September 1939.

L6726 Received 22nd August 1940. Flap failed during landing approach to Wittering, 14th June 1941, and dived into the ground at Barnack. Sgt H A H Gigney killed.

L6727 Received 18th August 1940. Struck off charge, 12th January 1942.

L6736 Delivered new to Squadron, 28th August 1939. Disposed of, 31st July 1940.

L6787 Delivered new to Squadron, January 1940. Disposed of, 8th February 1940.

Rootes-built

L8656 Delivered new to Squadron, 13th December 1939. Disposed of, 24th September 1940.

L8657 Delivered new to Squadron, 15th December 1939. Disposed of to No.54 O.T.U., 16th January 1941.

L8659 Received ex-No.29 Sqn., 10th October 1939. Damaged by bombs at Wittering, 15th March 1941.

L8660 Delivered new to Squadron, 18th December 1939 (as replacement for L1510). Disposed of, 18th March 1941.

Bristol Blenheim IVF (most or all A.I., equipped)

About a month before the outbreak of war No.25 (Fighter) Squadron took delivery of a small number of Bristol-built Blenheim Mark IVFs, these aircraft forming a special Flight, based at Northolt and North Weald and operating forward from Martlesham Heath. The aircraft were equipped with rudimentary airborne radar, variously referred to as A.I., Mark I, or possibly a bread-board version of A.I., Mark III. These were the first aircraft in the world to be equipped with airborne interception radar, and at least three of the Squadron's pilots who were involved in the trials with these aircraft were later posted to the Fighter Interception Unit which took over the aircraft and trials in November 1939. Because of the high security classification attached to these trials, it has not yet proved possible to identify with any certainty the aircraft; the following five Blenheim IVFs appear to have been the only examples recorded as serving with No.25 Squadron.

L4906 Aircraft taken over from R.A.E 14th July 1940 (may have been flown by No.25 Squadron while on R.A.E. charge). Overshot on landing at Hendon and hit gun emplacement, 21st September 1940; written off. Flt Lt J F R Jones, gunner, injured.

N6193 Previously flown by No.107 Sqn, as bomber but delivered to No.25 Squadron 30th Aug 1939 as a Mk IVF.

N6194 Previously flown by No.107 Sqn, as bomber but delivered to No.25 Squadron 30th August 1939 as a Mark IVF. Disposed of to No.248 Sqn 18th February 1940 as standard Mark IVF. (Almost certainly equipped with A.I. radar while with No.25 Squadron.)

N6233 Delivered new to No.25 Squadron 30th August 1939, Taken on charge by A & AEE at Martlesham Heath in September, but returned to No.25 Squadron later that month and remained with the Squadron until 9th March 1940 when it was disposed of to No.248 Squadron. (Probably equipped with A.I. radar while with No.25 Squadron.)

N6239 Received from No.110 Sqn 30th August 1939, with only 4 hours previously flown; disposed of to No.248 Squadron 2nd February 1940. (Probably equipped with A.I. Mk.III radar while with No.25 Squadron.)

Westland Whirlwind

L6845 Second prototype. Delivered c.9th May 1940 from the A & AEE, Boscombe Down, for Service trials at North Weald including night operation; flown by a total of nine pilots by day, and five by night. One pilot undertook limited gun firing at night. A highly critical report was forwarded to the newly-formed Ministry of Aircraft Production, the main criticisms being the difficulties experienced in landing the aircraft at night, and muzzle flash when the guns were fired at night, this destroying the pilot's night vision. Aircraft returned to A & AEE, May 1940.

Airspeed Oxford II

R6080 Delivered to Squadron, 24th May 1942. Struck off charge owing to age and exposure, 15th July 1943.

V3506 Delivered to Squadron, 16th May 1942. Disposed of, 26th November 1942.

Bristol Beaufighter Mk.I

Despite being the first radar-equipped night fighter in the world to gain a combat victory (an aircraft of the Fighter Interception Unit flown by a No.25 Squadron pilot), the Blenheim was generally unsatisfactory as a fighter either by day or night owing to severe performance deficiencies. In the summer of 1940, however, the Bristol Beaufighter, the result of a private venture, was approaching full production, and during the Battle of Britain the Fighter Interception Unit became the first unit to fly the aircraft operationally. No.25 (Fighter) Squadron became the first front-line squadron to receive

Beaufighters, and the first to fly them on operational patrols. (It was also the first squadron to lose a Beaufighter on an operational sortie.) The Beaufighter was the first purpose-designed twin-engine night fighter to enter RAF squadron service, and at the time of its entry into service was the most heavily-armed fighter in the world, and in speed performance was second only to the Spitfire.

R2056 First production aircraft. Delivered to Squadron, 1st September 1940, ex-Air Fighting Development Unit; passed to No.604 Squadron, 28th February 1941, but returned to No.25 Squadron charge 29th July 1941. Crashed in forced landing after air collision near Wittering, 1st April 1942. Series III aircraft with experimental landing lights.

R2057 Second production aircraft. Delivered to Squadron, 3rd September 1940, ex-Air Fighting Development Unit; disposed of to the A & AEE, Boscombe Down, 25th March 1941.

R2059 Fourth production aircraft. Delivered to Squadron, 1st September 1940, at RAF North Weald. No wing guns. Disposed of, 24th September 1940.

Bristol Beaufighter Mk.IF

R2067 12th production aircraft. Delivered new to Squadron, 8th September 1940. Missing on night operations, 15th September 1940. Flg Off H M S Lambert, Flg Off M J Miley and LAC J P Wyatt all killed.

R2068 Delivered new to Squadron, 8th September 1940. Soon after take-off, crashed in sea off Tangmere, 21st November 1940. Plt Off E W J Monk and Sgt E Powell both killed.

R2069 Delivered new to Squadron, 8th September 1940. Disposed of, 24th August 1941.

R2077 Received ex-No.604 Sqn., 28th February 1941. Disposed of to No. 141 Sqn., 8th July 1941.

R2080 Delivered new to Squadron, 8th September 1940. Damaged by bombs, Wittering, 15th March 1941.

R2081 Delivered new to Squadron, 13th September 1940. Plt Off J L B Norris, pilot, and Plt Off J R F Guyton, nav/rad, probably destroyed a Dornier Do 217 off Flamborough Head, Yorkshire, 19th September 1942.

R2082 Delivered new to Squadron, 20th September 1940. Plt Off D W Thompson, pilot, and Plt Off L D Britain, radar operator, destroyed a Heinkel He 111H over south Lincolnshire, 25th June 1941. Disposed of to No.51 OTU, 3rd August 1941.

R2091 Delivered new to Squadron, 2nd October 1940. Disposed of to No.604 Sqn., 8th December 1940.

R2092 Delivered new to Squadron, 17th September 1940. Disposed of to No.604 Sqn., 8th December 1940.

R2098 Delivered new to Squadron, 1st October 1940. Disposed of to No.604 Sqn., 29th October 1940.

R2101 Delivered new to Squadron, 13th November 1940. Disposed of to No.604 Sqn., 8th December 1940.

R2122 Delivered new to Squadron, 5th November 1940. Sgt S Bennett, pilot, and Sgt F W Curtis, observer, shot down a Junkers Ju 88 near Cottesmore, Rutland, 9th April 1941. Overshot in night landing, engine cut, belly landed in field, 5th May 1941. Plt Off J E King injured. Disposed of, 21st May 1941.

R2129 Delivered new to Squadron, 13th November 1940. Disposed of, 5th February 1941.

R2137 Received ex-No.604 Sqn., 5th August 1942. Disposed of, 23rd December 1942.

R2145 Delivered new to Squadron, 28th November 1940. Sgt K B Holloway, pilot, and Sgt R G Crossman, radar operator, destroyed a Heinkel He 111 over the Wash, 5th June 1941. Crashed at Coltishall, 3rd August 1941.

R2146 Received ex-No.219 Sqn, 12th August 1942. Disposed of, 2nd September 1942.

R2149 Delivered new to Squadron, 4th December 1940. Disposed of, 29th January 1941.

R2151 Received ex No.23 Sqn., 22nd March 1941. Disposed of to No.219 Sqn., 26th December 1941.

R2156 Delivered new to Squadron, 9th December 1940. Flt Lt C D S Smith, pilot, and Sgt C A Johnson, observer, damaged a Dornier Do 17 near Stowmarket, Suffolk, 16th January 1941. Wg Cdr D F W Atcherley, pilot, and Flt Lt J H Hunter-Tod, radar operator, probably destroyed a Ju 88 near Market Deeping, Lincolnshire, 4th

May 1941, and also damaged another unidentified enemy aircraft, 5th May 1941. On 17th May 1941, Sgt K B Holloway, pilot, and Sgt R G Crossman, radar operator, destroyed a Heinkel He 111H near West Runton, Norfolk, but crashed on landing at Wittering. SOC.

R2157 Delivered new to Squadron, December 1940. Sgt H A H Gigney, pilot, and Sgt G Charnock, radar operator, destroyed a Heinkel He 111 near Louth, 5th June 1941. Plt Off D W Thompson, pilot, and Plt Off L D Britain, radar operator, near King's Lynn, Norfolk, 14th June 1941. Missing from night patrol, 6/7th August 1941, probably attacked by another Beaufighter. Flt Lt T H Worth, pilot, and Sgt F P Nekludow both killed.

R2181 Delivered new to Squadron, 15th January 1941. Plt Off D W Thompson, pilot, and Plt Off L D Britain, radar operator, destroyed a Dornier Do 17Z near Boston, Lincolnshire, 8th May 1941, and damaged a Heinkel He 111H(?) on 9th May 1941. Engine failure on night patrol, overshot and crashed while landing at Wittering, 17th May 1941, written off. Flg Off B G Hooper and crew unhurt.

R2191 Delivered new to Squadron, 15th January 1941. Disposed of to No.600 Sqn., 27th May 1941.

R2194 Delivered new to Squadron, 15th January 1941. Struck off charge, 16th November 1942.

R2197 Delivered new to Squadron, 15th January 1941. Sgt S V Holloway, pilot, and Sgt R R C Pound, radar operator, damaged a Junkers Ju 88 near Watton, 6th May 1941. Crashed on overshoot from landing at Wittering, 28th March 1942. Pilot, Sgt K Fuller of No.153 Sqn, injured.

R2198 Delivered new to Squadron, 26th Dec 1940. Sgt S V Holloway, pilot, and Sgt R R C Pound, radar operator, damaged a Junkers Ju 88 near Grantham, 9th May 1941. Disposed of to No.252 Sqn., 27th March 1941.

R2205 Delivered new to Squadron, 28th February 1941. Abandoned off Hornsea, East Yorkshire, 8th September 1942. Flt Sgt K Gill, pilot, and Sgt R W Catlin both killed.

R2206 Delivered new to Squadron, 23rd February 1941. Crashed on overshoot from night landing at Wittering, 22nd March 1941. Plt Off J E King unhurt.

R2209 Delivered new to Squadron, 25th February 1941. Plt Off M J Herrick, pilot, and Sgt J Lewis, radar operator, damaged a Junkers Ju 88, south of Hull, 8th May 1941. Undershot and hit wall on landing approach to Wittering, burnt out, 18th May 1941. Plt Off J H Chase and crew unhurt.

R2247 Delivered new to Squadron, 28th February 1941. Sgt A M Hill, pilot, and Sgt E J Hollis, radar operator, damaged a Ju 88 near Holt, Norfolk. Disposed of to No.256 Sqn., 5th May 1942.

R2251 Delivered new to Squadron, 25th February 1941. Wg Cdr D F W Atcherley, pilot, and Flt Lt J H Hunter-Tod, radar operator, destroyed a Junkers Ju 88(?) near Sheringham, Norfolk, 17th June 1941. The same crew destroyed a Junkers Ju 88 over Norfolk, 5th July 1941. Disposed of, 25th May 1942.

R2254 Delivered new to Squadron, 25th February 1941. Shot down in error by Beaufighter X7941 five miles NE of Bridlington, Yorks, 23rd July 1942. Plt Off G G Pizey lost; Sgt Walsh picked up after four days in the sea.

R2255 Delivered new to Squadron, 25th February 1941. Destroyed in air raid on Wittering, 15th March 1941.

R2257 Delivered new to Squadron, 25th March 1941. Disposed of to No.604 Sqn., 29th July 1941.

R2263 Delivered new to Squadron, 19th March 1941. Undercarriage leg jammed up, damaged beyond repair on landing at Wittering, 10th May 1941. Flt Lt G T B Clayton unhurt.

Bristol Beaufighter Mk.IIF

R2277 Received ex-No.604 Sqn., 24th May 1941, for operational trials evaluation with Squadron; Flg Off M J Herrick, New Zealand, pilot, and Plt Off L Yeomans, radar operation, destroyed a Junkers Ju 88 near Market Deeping, Lincolnshire, 22nd June 1941. Disposed of to No.600 Sqn., 26th June 1941.

Bristol Beaufighter Mk.IF

Built by Fairey at Heaton Chapel.

T4629 Delivered new to Squadron, 3rd April 1941. Sqn Ldr H P Pleasance, pilot, and Sgt Benjamin Bent, damaged an unidentified enemy aircraft near Aldeburgh, Suffolk, but crashed while landing at Wittering, 3rd April

1941; crew unhurt. Stalled on pulling out of a diving turn from 500 feet at Wittering and crashed, 8th July 1941. Plt Off D W Thompson, pilot, and Flt Sgt R G Crossman, W.Op/Air gunner both killed.

T4634 Delivered new to Squadron, 11th April 1941. Sqn Ldr H P Pleasance, pilot, and Sgt B Bent, destroyed a Dornier Do 17Z near Skegness, Lincolnshire, 8th May 1941, and another 15 miles north of Holt, Norfolk, 9th May 1941. The same crew damaged a Heinkel He 111H north-west of Wells, Norfolk on 12th May 1941, and destroyed a Junkers Ju 88 near Swaffham, Norfolk, 14th June 1941. To No.132 O.T.U., 16th November 1942.

T4636 Delivered new to Squadron, 27th April 1941. Plt Off A J Picknett, pilot, and Plt Off G F Sellick, radar operator, destroyed a Heinkel He 177 south-east of Boston, 10th May 1941. To No.51 O.T.U., 7th May 1943.

V8326 Delivered to Squadron, 24th June 1942. Wg Cdr H P Pleasance, pilot, and Flt Lt L D Britain, nav/rad, destroyed a Dornier Do 217 east of Hornsea, East Yorkshire, 9th August 1942. The same crew destroyed a Dornier Do 217 east of Mablethorpe, Lincolnshire, 23rd August 1942. Disposed of 13th January 1943.

V8329 Delivered to Squadron, 24th June 1942. Sqn Ldr C J Alington, pilot, and Flg Off D B Keith, nav/rad, destroyed a Dornier Do 217, east of Sutton Bridge, Lincolnshire, 23rd August 1942. The same crew destroyed a Dornier Do 217, seven miles north of Sheringham, Norfolk, 25th Sept 1942. Disposed of, 23rd Dec 1942.

V8379 Delivered to Squadron, 11th September 1942. Disposed of to No.51 O.T.U, 8th January 1943.

Bristol-built at Weston-super-Mare

X7541 Delivered new to Squadron, 25th March 1941. Spun into ground at Burghley Park while approaching to land at Wittering, 3rd April 1941. Sgt H I Maxwell, pilot, and Flt Sgt D F Roberts, wireless operator, both killed.

X7546 Delivered new to Squadron, 8th May 1941. Series II Beaufighter with modified cabin heating. Crashed while landing at Leconfield, 2nd October 1941. Disposed of, 12th October 1941.

X7549 Delivered new to Squadron, 21st May 1941. Disposed of, 28th November 1942.

X7551 Received ex-No.68 Sqn., 29th January 1941. Disposed of to Fighter Interception Unit, 16th December 1942.

X7560 Delivered new to Squadron, 18th June 1941. Disposed of to No.51 O.T.U., 16th June 1943.

X7566 Received ex-No. 141 Sqn, 26th July 1942. Disposed of, 30th November 1942.

X7567 Delivered new to Squadron, 10th July 1941. Disposed of, 9th December 1942.

X7569 Delivered new to Squadron, 9th August 1941. Flt Sgt H L Middlemast, pilot, and Flt Sgt D McCracken, nav/rad, damaged a Junkers Ju 88 nine miles west of Selby, Yorkshire, 12th August 1942. Engine failure, struck houses on landing approach to Church Fenton, 8th October 1942. Flt Sgt H L Middlemast killed, and Flt Sgt D McCracken injured.

X7570 Delivered new to Squadron, 10th July 1941. Struck trees during take-off at Wittering, 25th August 1941. Wg Cdr D F W Atcherley injured.

X7578 Delivered new to Squadron, 30th January 1942. Disposed of to No.51 O.T.U., 30th November 1942.

X7580 Delivered new to Squadron, 16th August 1941. Stalled and crashed on take-off at Wittering, 9th December 1941. Plt Off R E Holder, RCAF, pilot, and Flg Off G G Waddington, air gunner, both killed.

X7582 Delivered new to Squadron, 21st August 1941. Crashed on take-off at Kirton-in-Lindsey, 25th August 1941.

X7587 Delivered new to Squadron, 26th August 1941. Disposed of, 4th August 1942.

X7589 Received ex-No. 141 Squadron, 18th October 1942. Disposed of to Fighter Interception Unit, 23rd Dec 1942.

X7617 Delivered new to Squadron, 29th August 1941. Disposed of, 3rd August 1942.

X7619 Delivered new to Squadron, 29th August 1941. Disposed of to No.219 Sqn., 26th December 1941.

X7620 Delivered new to Squadron, 4th September 1941. Crashed while approaching to land at Wittering, 12th October 1941. Sgt P H C Windett killed. Flg Off R G Setchell, pilot, survived.

X7621 Delivered new to Squadron, 3rd September 1941. Sqn Ldr H P Pleasance, pilot, and Plt Off L D Britain, radar operator, probably destroyed a Junkers Ju 88 near Wells, Norfolk, 1st October 1941. Disposed of, 21st October 1941.

X7623 Delivered new to Squadron, 23rd September 1941. Crashed on take-off at Ballyhalbert, burnt out, 16th April 1942. Sgt D Sakinner, pilot, injured, and Plt Off A C Griffith, nav/rad, unhurt.

X7625 Delivered new to Squadron, 12th September 1941. Crashed off Irish coast during night training flight, 11th February 1942. Sgt A W Lavender, pilot, and Sgt N Ranganatha both killed.

X7626 Delivered new to Squadron, 23rd September 1941. Disposed of, 15th December 1942.

X7643 Delivered new to Squadron, 22nd September 1941. Flg Off J Singleton, pilot and Plt Off C J Bradshaw, nav/rad, damaged a Dornier Do 217 over south Lincolnshire, 23rd August 1942. Disposed of to No.604 Sqn., 8th November 1942.

X7680 Delivered new to Squadron, 14th February 1942. Disposed of, 9th August 1942.

X7698 Received ex-No.219 Sqn., 17th August 1942. Engine cut, lost height, attempted to land at Pocklington but crashed three miles south of aerodrome on approach, burnt out, 7th November 1942. Sgt M H Griffith, pilot, killed, and Sgt G H Wheatland, nav/rad, seriously injured.

X7705 Delivered new to Squadron, August 1941. Flt Lt J L Shaw, pilot, and W/Off C Guthrie, nav/rad, damaged a Heinkel He 111H over the sea off Flamborough Head, 6th September 1942. Disposed of to No.51 O.T.U., 30th January 1942.

X7706 Delivered new to Squadron, 31st January 1942. Disposed of to No.51 O.T.U., 20th June 1943.

X7711 Delivered new to Squadron, 28th March 1942. Flg Off A J Picknett, pilot, and Plt Off H D Rodgers, radar operator, destroyed a Dornier Do 217 off south Yorkshire coast, 30th May 1942. Disposed of, 4th Aug 1942.

X7714 Delivered new, 12rg February 1942. Disposed of to No.604 Sqn., December 1942.

X7773 Received ex-No.219 Sqn., 21st July 1942. Damaged by enemy action, 23rd July 1942. Disposed of to Fighter Interception Unit, 6th November 1942.

X7814 Delivered new to Squadron,15th August 1942. Sgt J H Staples, pilot, and Sgt J S D Gravell, nav/rad, probably destroyed a Dornier Do 217 over the sea off Flamborough Head, Yorkshire, 19th September 1942. Plt Off R Peake, pilot, and Sgt T R Parry, nav/rad, destroyed a Dornier Do 217 north-east of Flamborough Head Yorkshire, 24th September 1942. Disposed of to Fighter Interception Unit, 9th December 1942.

X7824 Delivered new to Squadron, 20th August 1942. Shot down one Heinkel He 111, flown by Flt Lt J Singleton, pilot and Plt Off Christopher J Bradshaw, nav/rad, 2nd September 1942 east of Filey, Yorkshire. The same crew damaged a Dornier Do 217 near Hunstanton, Norfolk, 17th September 1942. Disposed of to No.51 O.T.U., 20th August 1943.

X7876 Delivered new to Squadron, 25th March 1942. Flt Lt J F Inkster, pilot, and Flg Off L Yeomans, radar operator, damaged an unidentified enemy aircraft near Whitby, Yorkshire, 5th June 1942. Disposed of to No.51 O.T.U., January 1943.

Douglas Havoc Mk.1

For a brief period during the summer of 1941 a few American Douglas Havoc night fighters - some fitted with Helmore Turbinlites - were taken on charge by No.25 Squadron for operational evaluation trials flown from Wittering. The aircraft were disliked by all who flew then, being underpowered and generally sluggish on the controls. The nosewheel undercarriage was unfamiliar to the pilots and the aircraft was found to be tricky to land at night on the short runways at satellite airfields. It was not adopted for use by the Squadron.

Z2184 Received from the A & AEE, fitted with Turbinlite, 8th July 1941, but passed to the Aircraft Gun Mounting Establishment after 24 hours.

AX910 Received from the Aircraft Gun Mounting Establishment (via the Air Fighting Development Unit), July 1941. Disposed of to No.1453 Turbinlite Flight at Wittering, 23rd September 1941.

BB899 Received from the Air Fighting Development Unit, 8th July 1941. Disposed of to No.1453 Turbinlite Flight, 23rd September 1941. (Not fitted with Turbinlite)

BD120 Received from the Air Fighting Development Unit, 8th July 1941. Disposed of to No.1453 Turbinlite Flight, 23rd September 1941. (Fitted with Turbinlite)

BJ469 Received from the Aircraft Gun Mounting Establishment (via the Air Fighting Development Unit), 19th July 1941. Disposed of to No.1453 Turbinlite Flight at Wittering, 24th September 1941. (Fitted with Turbinlite)

Miles Magister 1

L8062 Delivered to Squadron, 23rd April 1941. Disposed of April 1945.

L8277 Received from Station Flight North Weald, 18th September 1940; Struck off charge (due to deterioration), 5th January 1942.

P6466 Delivered to Squadron, 23rd April 1941. Disposed of to No.604 Sqn, 27th November 1941.

Avro Tutor

K6109 Received from No.245 Sqn., 26th April 1941. Disposed of to No.19 M.U., 7th July 1942.

de Havilland Mosquito NF Mk.II

No.25 Squadron was about the sixth of seventeen squadrons to be equipped with Mosquito night fighters, taking delivery of twenty new aircraft between October 1942 and January 1943 while based at Church Fenton in Yorkshire. The aircraft was a marked improvement over the Beaufighter IF, although there was a number of bad accidents early in the training period, mostly during take-off and landing. The A.I. Mark IV was the same as that fitted in the Beaufighters.

DD617 Replacement received ex-No.456 (Australian) Sqn., 1943. Became ground instructional aircraft, *4360M*, 30th November 1943.

DD629 Replacement received ex-No.151 Sqn., 15th September 1943. Disposed of to No.169 Sqn., 13th Jan 1944.

DD631 Delivered new to Squadron, 1st June 1943. Disposed of to No.169 Sqn., January 1944.

DD637 Replacement received ex-No.264 Sqn., 1943. Dived into ground at Sigglesthome, Yorkshire, 12th August 1943; Pchor J N Nowak, Polish Air Force, pilot, and Wt Off C G Kendall, observer, both killed.

DD725 Replacement received ex-No.85 Sqn., 9th September 1943. Disposed of to No. 141 Sqn., 19th October 1943.

DD733 Delivered new to Squadron, 21st October 1942. Suffered accident during landing, 4th February 1943, and disposed of to M.U.

DD738 Replacement received ex-No.85 Sqn. Flt Lt E R F Cooke, pilot, Flt Sgt F M Ellacott, radar operator. destroyed a Junkers Ju 88, four miles south-west of Westland, 24th July 1943. Collided with HJ713 near Market Weighton and crashed at Shipton Thorpe, Yorkshire, 2nd October 1943. Sgt H A Hay, pilot, and Sgt J C Scammell, observer, both killed.

DD746 Delivered new to Squadron, 21st October 1942. Damaged in action and disposed of to M.U., 4th Feb 1943.

DD747 Delivered new to Squadron, 7th November 1942. Broke up in the air and crashed at Airmyn, Yorkshire, 8th April 1943. Flt Sgt T E Procureur, pilot, and Sgt G H Wheatland, observer, both killed.

DD748 Delivered new to Squadron, 21st October 1942. Crashed in the sea at dusk ten miles east of Flamborough Head, Yorkshire, 29th July 1943. Lt E R F Cooke, pilot, and Flg Off F H Ellacott, observer, both killed.

DD750 Delivered new to Squadron, 22nd October 1942. While awaiting turn to land, flew into hill on turn at night at White Craig, Silsden, near Keighley, Yorkshire, 22nd March 1943. Sgt J H Staples, pilot, and Sgt R E Andrews, nav/W.Op, both killed.

DD752 Delivered new to Squadron, 21st October 1942. Flt Lt Joseph Singleton, pilot, and Flt Lt C J Bradshaw, nav/rad, damaged a Dornier Do 217 over Holland, 16th January 1943. Disposed of to No.54 O.T.U., Jan 1944.

DD754 Delivered new to Squadron, 22nd October 1942. Banked and spun into marshy ground near Filey, Yorkshire, 12th December 1943. Sqn Ldr C Robertson, pilot, and Flg Off E Bartholomew, navigator, both killed.

DD756 Delivered new to Squadron, 24th October 1942. Disposed of to No.239 Sqn., January 1944.

DD757 Delivered new to Squadron, 21st October 1942. Became ground instructional aircraft, *4242M*, October 1943.

DD758 Delivered new to Squadron, 9th September 1943. Aircraft unsatisfactory, returned to M.U 17th Sept 1943.

DD759 Delivered new to Squadron, October 1942. Damaged in action, 17th May 1943, repaired and disposed of to No.141 Sqn., October 1943.

DD782 Delivered new to Squadron, 7th November 1942. Crashed while approaching to land at Church Fenton on one engine, 30th November 1942; Plt Off R Peake, pilot, and Sgt T R Parry, navigator, both killed.

DZ256 Delivered new to Squadron, December 1942. Disposed of to No.410 (Canadian) Sqn., 1943.

DZ258 Delivered new to Squadron, 17th December 1942. Undershot while landing at Church Fenton, 21st January 1943, and crashed at Ryther. Flt Sgt B Travers, pilot, and Sgt Patterson, navigator, both injured.

DZ264 Delivered new to Squadron, 30th December 1943. Stalled and crashed while approaching to land on single engine at Church Fenton, 28th May 1943. Sqn Ldr D Evans killed.

DZ655 Delivered new to Squadron, 26th January 1943. Disposed of to No.239 Sqn., 3rd February 1944.

DZ685 Delivered new to Squadron, January 1943. Shot down by FW 190 while on patrol over the Bay of Biscay, 13th June 1943. Flg Off J E Wootton, pilot, and Plt Off J M Dymock both killed.

DZ688 Delivered new to Squadron, January 1943. Missing from patrol over the Bay of Biscay, 13th June 1943. Flg Off J Cheney, pilot, and Flg Off J K Mycock both killed.

DZ689 Delivered new to Squadron, January 1943. Missing from bomber support sortie, 20th/21st October 1943. Flg Off D C Burrow, PoW.

DZ759 Delivered new to Squadron, March 1943. After air-to-sea firing, crashed in forced landing at Bempton, near Bridlington, Yorkshire, after constant speed unit went fully fine, 21st October 1943. Pilot Wg Cdr C M Wight-Boycott and navigator both unhurt.

HJ644 Mk.IIF Intruder. Delivered new to Squadron, 15th September 1943. Disposed of, 3rd February 1944.

HJ645 Mk.IIF Intruder. Delivered new to Squadron, 2nd October 1943. Disposed of, 6th March 1944.

HJ653 Mk.IIF Intruder. Delivered new to Squadron, 15th September 1943. Aircraft flew into ground, bounced, ballooned, turned over on Acklington airfield, 7th January 1944. Flt Sgt D P Forryan slightly injured and observer safe.

HJ654 Mk.IIF Intruder. Delivered new to Squadron, 15th September 1943. Disposed of, 2nd February 1944.

HJ713 Mk.IIF Intruder. Delivered new to Squadron, 9th September 1943. Collided over Market Weighton with DD738, 2nd October 1943, and crashed at Holme Lane, Shipton Thorpe, Yorkshire; Plt Off T P Quinn, pilot, and Flt Sgt S A Carter, observer, both killed.

HJ912 Delivered new to Squadron, 7th November 1942. Squadron modification, mounting one single dorsal Vickers machine gun. Disposed of, 13th January 1944.

HJ914 Mk.IIF Intruder. Delivered new to Squadron, 17th November 1942. Disposed of, 5th May 1944.

HJ918 Mk.IIF Intruder. Delivered new to Squadron, 22nd December 1942. Broke up in cloud and crashed two miles east of Church Fenton, 5th February 1943. Sqn Ldr W F Carnaby, pilot, and Flt Off J H L Kemp, observer, both killed.

HJ920 Mk.IIF Intruder. Delivered new to Squadron, 23rd November 1942. Severely damaged in belly landing at Acklington after undercarriage failed to lower, 20th January 1944, and disposed of to M.U.

HJ921 Mk.IIF Intruder. Delivered new to Squadron, 15th November 1942. Stalled and spun off steep turn and crashed among houses at Weardale Road, Sherwood, Nottingham, 13th July 1943; Plt Off J Grundy killed.

HJ922 Mk.IIF Intruder. Delivered new to Squadron, 17th November 1942. Severely damaged in taxying accident, 5th February 1943, and disposed of to M.U.

de Havilland Mosquito T Mk.III Trainers

HJ862 Squadron dual conversion aircraft. Delivered, 21st October 1942. Disposed of 15th September 1943.

HJ878 Squadron dual conversion aircraft. Delivered, 23rd November 1942. Crashed while on loan to No.410 (Canadian) Squadron at Coleby Grange, 1st June 1943.

de Havilland Mosquito FB Mk.VI

Beginning on 16th February 1943 No.25 (Fighter) Squadron began flying intruder sorties and, in addition to defensive patrols, also flew bomber support operations over Germany. At first these were flown only by Mosquito IIFs, but in August that year the Squadron received a number of Mark VI fighter-bombers.

HJ743 Delivered new to Squadron, 24th August 1943. Disposed of to M.U., 21st September 1943.

HJ756 Delivered new to Squadron, 24th August 1943. Disposed of to M.U., 21st September 1943.

HJ757 Delivered new to Squadron, 24th August 1943. Disposed of to M.U., 21st September 1943.

HX826 Delivered new to Squadron, 10th August 1943. Missing on operations, 17th August 1943. Sqn Ldr F N Brinsden, pilot, and Flg Off P G F Sewell both PoW.

HX827 Delivered new to Squadron, 10th August 1943. Damaged in action, 17th August 1943, disposed of to M.U.

HX828 Delivered new to Squadron, 24th August 1943. Disposed of to M.U., 21st September 1943.

HX853 Delivered new to Squadron, 24th August 1943. Disposed of to M.U., 21st September 1943.

HX866 Delivered new to Squadron, 22nd August 1943. Disposed of to M.U., 21st September 1943.

PZ200 Delivered to Squadron, 3rd January 1945. Disposed of, 9th February 1945.

de Havilland Mosquito NF Mk.XVII

HK237/G (High-security aircraft) Delivered new to Squadron, 22nd December 1943. Plt Off K V Panter, pilot, and W/Off A W Mogg, nav/rad, destroyed a Messerschmitt Me 410 off Dutch coast on 19th April 1944. Disposed of, 17th June 1944.

HK239 Delivered as replacement aircraft, 22nd May 1944. Flt Lt J F R Jones, pilot, and Flg Off R Skinner, nav/rad, destroyed a Heinkel He 111* over the sea off the Norfolk coast, 5th Oct 1944. Disposed of, 22nd Oct 1944.

HK243/G (High-security aircraft) Delivered new to Squadron, 22nd December 1943. Disposed of, 19th February 1944.

HK244 Delivered new to Squadron, 21st January 1944. Disposed of, 25th September 1944.

HK250 Delivered as replacement aircraft, 24th August 1944. Disposed of, 24th October 1944.

HK255/G (High-security aircraft) Delivered new to Squadron, 6th January 1944. Flt Lt Joseph Singleton, pilot, and Flg Off William Geoffrey Haslam, nav/rad, destroyed a Dornier Do 217 over the sea off Lowestoft, Suffolk, 20th February 1944. Flt Lt A S H Baillie, pilot, and Flg Off J M Simpson, nav/rad, destroyed a Heinkel He 177 over Yoxford, Suffolk, 23rd February 1944. Flt Lt Joseph Singleton, pilot, and Flg Of William Geoffrey Haslam, nav/rad, destroyed a Junkers Ju 188 over the sea off Southwold, Suffolk, 14th March 1944. The same crew destroyed three Junkers Ju 188s over the sea off the Lincolnshire coast, 19th March 1944; aircraft damaged in landing, crew slightly injured.

HK256 — Delivered to Squadron, 26th May 1944. Missing from patrol, 7th October 1944. Failed to return from patrol, possibly hit the sea while attacking He 111 carrying flying bomb. Flg Off J S Henderson, pilot, and Flg Off R A Nicholls, nav/rad, both killed.

HK257/G — (High-security aircraft) Delivered new to Squadron, 22nd December 1943. Suffered damage in taxying accident, 25th March 1944, but repaired. Wg Cdr C M Wight-Boycott, pilot, and Flt Lt D M Reid, nav/rad, destroyed a Messerschmitt Me 410 over the sea north-west of Cromer, Norfolk, 29th May 1944. Flt Lt Alfred Emest Marshall, pilot, and Flg Off C A Allen, nav/rad, destroyed a Heinkel He 111* over the sea 40 miles east of Southwold, Suffolk.

HK265/G — (High-security aircraft) Delivered new to Squadron, 30th December 1943. Damaged in action and pilot baled out at Coltishall rather than make flapless, one-wheel landing, 26th September 1944. Disposed of to M.U.

HK278 — Delivered new to Squadron, 20th January 1944. Flt Lt Douglas Haig Greaves, pilot, and Flg Off F M Robbins, nav/rad, destroyed a Do 217 off the Lincolnshire coast, 19th March 1944. Disposed of, 21st October 1944.

HK280 — Delivered new to Squadron, 15th February 1944. Disposed of to M.U., 20th October 1944.

HK283 — Delivered new to Squadron, 6th January 1944. Damaged in action, 20th March 1944, and disposed of to M.U.

HK285/G — (High-security aircraft) Delivered new to Squadron, 27th December 1943. Flt Lt J R Brockbank, pilot, and Plt Off D McCausland, nav/rad, destroyed two Junkers Ju 188s over Braintree, 19th October 1944. Disposed of, 5th November 1944.

HK288 — Delivered new to Squadron, 21st January 1944. Flt Lt R M Carr, pilot, and Flt Lt Saunderson, nav/rad, destroyed a Junkers Ju 88, and probably destroyed another, over the North Sea, 19th April 1944. Night intruder to Deelen, crashed at Eupen, 13th June 1944. Flt Lt A S H Baillie, pilot, and Flg Off J M Simpson, nav/rad, both killed.

HK293 — Delivered new to Squadron, 29th Jan 1944. Flt Lt V H Linthune, pilot, and Flg Off A B Cumbers, nav/rad, destroyed a Junkers Ju 188 off the Suffolk coast, 25th March 1944. Disposed of to M.U., 12th July 1944.

HK298 — Delivered new to Squadron, 2nd March 1944. Disposed of to M.U., 31st July 1944.

HK300 — Delivered new to Squadron, 23rd January 1944. Lost attacking a V-1, 24th September 1944. Flg Off H S Cook, pilot, and Flt Lt J S Limbert, nav/rad both killed.

HK301 — Delivered new to Squadron, 24th January 1944. Disposed of to No.125 Squadron, 16th October 1944.

HK304 — Delivered new to Squadron, 23rd January 1944. Plt Off B Travers, pilot, and Plt Off A H C W Patterson, nav/rad, probably destroyed a Do 217 off the coast at Great Yarmouth, Norfolk, 19th April 1944. The same crew destroyed a Messerschmitt Bf 109G(?) (location not known), 28th August 1944. Disposed of to M.U., 4th November 1944.

HK305 — Delivered new to Squadron, 23rd January 1944. Aircraft crashed into sea after drogue firing off Wareham, Norfolk, 26th September 1944. Flt Sgt E A Walker, pilot, and Wt Off W H Watts, nav/rad, both killed.

HK308 — Delivered as replacement aircraft, 7th June 1944. Disposed of to M.U., 27th August 1944.

HK322/G — (High-security aircraft). Delivered new to Squadron, 21st January 1944. Flt Lt R L E Davies, pilot, and Flg Off Benjamin Bent, nav/rad, destroyed two Junkers Ju 188s off the Suffolk coast, 22nd March 1944. The same crew destroyed a Messerschmitt Bf 110 west of Schiermonnikoog, Holland, 6th June 1944. Disposed of to M.U., 16th July 1944.

HK354 — Delivered new to Squadron, 28th January 1944. Flt Sgt D J Carter, pilot, and Sgt W J Hutchings, nav/rad, destroyed a Junkers Ju 188 off the Suffolk coast, 20th April 1944. Flt Lt Douglas Haig Greaves, pilot, and Flg Off F M Robbins, nav/rad, destroyed a Messerschmitt Me 410 off the Norfolk coast at Great Yarmouth, 8th June 1944. Missing from bomber support operations, 9th June 1944. Flg Off K W Gray and Flg Off D A Harwood both killed.

HK357 — Delivered new to Squadron, 23rd January 1944. Wg Cdr C M Wight-Boycott, pilot, and Flt Lt D M Reid, nav/rad, destroyed a Junkers Ju 188 north-west of Orfordness, Suffolk, 23rd June 1944. Wg Cdr L J C Mitchell, pilot, and Flt Lt D L Cox, nav/rad, probably destroyed a Heinkel He 111* off the Norfolk coast, 25th September 1944. The same crew destroyed two Heinkel He 111s* over the sea 40-50 miles east of Great Yarmouth, Norfolk, 29th September 1944. Disposed of to M.U., 25th October 1944.

HK362 Delivered as replacement aircraft, 2nd October 1944. Disposed of to No.125 Squadron 25th October 1944.

* Probably a V-1 flying bomb launch aircraft.

de Havilland Mosquito NF Mk.XXX

MM810/ZK-Y Delivered new to Squadron, 23rd September 1944. Disposed of, 10th September 1946.

MT470 Delivered new to Squadron, 26th September 1944. Lost power during air test, crashed into tree during forced landing at Brookhall Farm, near Borley, Essex, 6th March 1945; Flt Lt E G Sheppard, pilot, and Flt Sgt F G Ward, nav/rad, killed.

MT471/ZK-C Delivered new to Squadron, 23rd September 1944. Disposed of, 30th April 1946.

MT472 Delivered new to Squadron, 23rd September 1944. While recovering from a dive during an air test, both wings broke off over Castle Camps, 27th November 1944; Flt Lt A E Marshall, pilot, and Flg Off C A Allen, nav/rad, both killed.

MT474 Delivered new to Squadron, 23rd September 1944. Engine lost power, belly landed in a field near Saffron Walden, Essex, 29th June 1945. Plt Off R B Harper, pilot, and Flt Sgt R E Jefferies, navigator, both unhurt.

MT481 Delivered new to Squadron, 28th September 1944. Aircraft damaged in taxying accident and disposed of, 28th March 1945.

MT483/ZK-S Delivered new to Squadron, 3rd January 1945. Disposed of to No.29 Sqn., 3rd May 1945.

MT487/ZK-L Delivered new to Squadron, 18th October 1944. Disposed of, 20th February 1946.

MT489 Delivered new to Squadron, 1st October 1944. Aircraft struck tree during take-off, crashed and caught fire at Bendish Hall, Radwinter, Essex, 9th February 1945; crashed caught fire. Flt Lt M Corrie, pilot, killed.

MT490 Delivered new to Squadron, 3rd January 1945. Disposed of to No.29 Sqn., 3rd May 1945.

MT492 Delivered new to Squadron, 25th October 1944. Flt Lt Douglas Haig Greaves, pilot, and Flg Off Robbins, nav/rad, destroyed a Heinkel He 111 (probably a V-1 flying bomb launch aircraft), over the sea 70 miles east of Lowestoft, Suffolk, 11th November 1944. CSU trouble, belly landed at Gatwick, 27th September 1946. Flt Lt H Smith unhurt.

MT494 Delivered new to Squadron, 27th October 1944. Collided with MV529 during practice interception and crashed at Camps Hill, Cambridgeshire, 23rd September 1945. Sqn Ldr J Arnsby, pilot and Flt Lt D M Reid, nav/rad, both killed.

MT498 Delivered new to Squadron, 25th October 1944. Disposed of to Central Fighter Establishment, 25th Oct 1945.

MV521 Delivered new to Squadron, 25th October 1944. Flt Lt J M Lomas, pilot, and Flt Lt N B Fleet, nav/rad, destroyed a Heinkel He 111 (probably a V-1 flying bomb launch aircraft) over the sea 35 miles east of Clacton-on-Sea, Essex, 9th Nov 1944. The same crew destroyed a Heinkel He 219 night fighter ten miles east of Bonn, Germany, while on bomber support operations, 1st February 1945. Disposed of, 1st March 1945.

MV524/ZK-T Delivery details not known. Disposed of to No.85 Squadron, 13th June 1946.

MV526 Delivered new to Squadron, 4th November 1944. Aircraft damaged by AA fire off Southwold while being guided through defences with fuel shortage by ground radar; crew abandoned aircraft, which crashed at Garboldisham, Norfolk, 14th November 1944. Wg Cdr L J Mitchell, pilot, and Flt Lt D L Cox, navigator, both parachuted safely.

MV528/ZK-F Delivered new to Squadron, 13th October 1944. Aircraft overshot on night landing at Boxted and hit a fence, 7th February 1946, and written off. Wt Off J Boal, pilot, and Flt Sgt Craine, navigator, both unhurt.

MV529 Delivered new to Squadron, 27th October 1944. Collided with MT494 during practice interception, dived into the ground and caught fire, Camps Hill, Cambridgeshire, 23rd January 1945. Flt Lt D L Ward, pilot, and Flt Lt E D Eyles, navigator, both killed.

MV530 Delivered new to Squadron, 12th January 1945. Gee calibration, shot down by American anti-aircraft fire over Germany, belly landed on fire near Ingolstadt, burnt out, 7th May 1945. Flt Lt J F R Jones, pilot, unhurt, and Flg Off R Skinner, navigator, wounded.

MV535 Delivery details not known. Disposed of, 11th October 1946.

MV537 Delivered new to Squadron, 29th Oct 1944. Disposed of to Night Fighter Development Wing, 8th May 1945.

NT245/ZK-D Disposed of, 4th October 1946.

NT265 Delivered new to Squadron, 1st December 1944. Disposed of, 29th May 1946.

NT360 Delivered new to Squadron, 3rd February 1945. Disposed of, 21st October 1946.

NT367 Delivered new to Squadron, 9th February 1945. Overshot after single-engined forced landing at South Cerney and went into a ditch, caught fire, 11th March 1945. Wg Cdr R A W Grove, pilot, and Flt Sgt K L Allen, navigator both unhurt.

NT373 Delivered as replacement aircraft, 25th July 1946. Disposed of, 25th November 1946.

NT378/ZK-G Delivered new to Squadron, 9th February 1945. Disposed of, 21st October 1946.

NT391 Received from No.29 Squadron, 22nd August 1946. Disposed of, 5th February 1947.

NT393 Pilot lost control when engine cut during low flying and crashed at Bulpham, five miles south of Brentwood, Essex, 28th May 1946. Flt Sgt H K Sellers, pilot, and Flt Sgt Riley, navigator both injured.

NT425/ZK-H Delivered new to Squadron, 14th February 1945. Disposed of, 30th September 1946.

NT433 Delivered as replacement aircraft, 29th August 1945. Disposed of, 11th March 1946.

NT479 Delivered new to Squadron, 7th March 1945. Disposed of, 20th March 1947.

NT481 Delivered new to Squadron, 20th March 1945. Aircraft force landed, 19th April 1945 (not due to enemy action), and struck off charge.

NT503 Delivered new to Squadron, 13th March 1945. Undercarriage leg collapsed on landing at Lubeck, damaged beyond repair, 3rd May 1946. Flt Lt C I Ledwidge, pilot, unhurt.

NT508/ZK-L Disposed of, 29th October 1946.

NT510 Delivered new to Squadron, 25th March 1945. Disposed of, 13th November 1946.

NT541/ZK-P Delivered new to Squadron, 20th April 1945. Disposed of, 24th October 1946

NT548 Delivered new to Squadron, 10th April 1945. Disposed of, 31st October 1946.

NT562 Delivered new to Squadron, 17th April 1945. Disposed of, 29th October 1946.

Avro Anson I (GEE Trainers)

EG353 Delivered to Squadron, 20th December 1944. Struck off charge, 26th January 1945.

EG544 Delivered to Squadron, 20th December 1944. Struck off charge, 20th January 1945.

MG676 Delivered to Squadron, 20th December 1944. Struck off charge, 26th January 1945.

MG970 Delivered to Squadron, 20th December 1944. Struck off charge, 20th January 1945.

de Havilland Mosquito NF.36

On being designated as a permanent peacetime home defence night fighter squadron, No.25 moved to West Malling in No.11 Group, Fighter Command, for the night defence of London, being re-equipped with Mosquito NF.Mk.36s. Like the NF.30s, these were fitted with the American A.I. Mk.X centimetric radar. They continued to be flown until September 1951.

RK959/ZK-X Delivered to Squadron, 30th November 1950. Disposed of, 20th November 1951.

RK977 Delivered to Squadron, 30th April 1951. Disposed of to No.85 Squadron, 31st August 1951.

RK980/ZK-E Delivered to Squadron, 31st December 1950. Disposed of, 30th November 1951.

RK989/ZK-B Delivered to Squadron, 11th November 1948. Disposed of, 8th June 1950.

RK992 Delivered to Squadron, 30th November 1950. Disposed of to No.228 O.C.U., 31st October 1951

RL117/ZK-B Delivered to Squadron, by 10th October 1946. Collided in formation with VT612 of No.85 Squadron (which landed safely) and spun down, crashing near West Malling 13th September 1948. Flt Lt E N Hart, pilot, and Flg Off R L Palmer, navigator, both killed.

RL120/ZK-A Delivered to Squadron, 10th October 1946. Disposed of, 6th August 1948.

RL123/ZK-F Delivered to Squadron, 10th October 1946. Disposed of, 29th June 1950.

RL125/ZK-G Delivered to Squadron, 12th August 1948. Disposed of, 26th October 1949.

RL136/ZK-N Delivered to Squadron, 30th November 1950. Disposed of, 30th November 1951.

RL138/ZK-G Delivered to Squadron, 30th November 1950. Disposed of, 31st August 1951.

RL176/ZK-D Delivered to Squadron, 6th December 1946. Disposed of, 18th May 1950.

RL179/ZK-F Delivered to Squadron, 10th May 1950. Disposed of to No.85 Squadron, 31st October 1951.

RL181/ZK-C Delivered to Squadron, 25th October 1946. Disposed of, 25th May 1950.

RL204/ZK-Y Delivered to Squadron, 22nd July 1947. During single-engine circuits, crashed four miles WNW of West Malling, 7th June 1949. Flg Off R J Wilkie, pilot, killed.

RL212/ZK-H Delivered to Squadron, 9th November 1949. Disposed of, 11th May 1950.

RL214/ZK-J Delivered to Squadron, 9th November 1949. Disposed of, 15th June 1950.

RL242/ZK-S Delivered ex-No.23 Squadron, 1st May 1951. Disposed of, 31st August 1951.

RL243/ZK-G Delivered to Squadron, 30th April 1951. Disposed of, 15th September 1951.

de Havilland Vampire NF Mk.10

In 1951 No.25 (Fighter) Squadron, still based at West Malling, was selected to become the world's first jet night fighter squadron (if certain wartime Luftwaffe units, formed for the last-ditch defence of Berlin in 1945 and equipped with Messerschmitt Me 262s, are discounted). Armstrong Whitworth was at that time preparing the two-seat Meteor NF Mk.11 for the RAF, while de Havilland had received an export order from Egypt for a two-seat night fighter version of the Vampire. However, the Air Ministry refused to allow the export of American A.I. Mark X radar, and it was decided instead to deliver these Vampires to Fighter Command, the aircraft demonstrating a considerable performance superiority over the Mosquito night fighters. Accordingly, No.25 Squadron received its first Vampire night fighter in July 1951, having received a small number of FB Mk.5s earlier that year for the initial conversion of the squadron's pilots.

WM668 Delivered ex-MU, 4th April 1952. Disposed of, 8th April 1954.

WM669/L Delivered ex-MU, 4th April 1952. Crashed into sea six miles off Dungeness during low-level practice interception, 18th Dec 1952; Flt Lt C C W Smith, pilot, and Flg Off James McNicol Adams, nav/rad, both killed.

WM670/B Received ex-No.23 Squadron, 12th December 1953. Disposed of, 5th March 1954.

WM673 Delivered ex-MU, 21st April 1952. Collided with naval Oxford training aircraft (2 killed) over River Medway, returned to West Malling and forced landed on airfield, 12th June 1952. Sgt G Fry and Sgt E F Hall both unhurt. SOC 9th July 1952.

WM705 Received ex-No.23 Squadron, 22nd December 1953. Disposed of, 8th April 1954.

WM713 Delivered ex-MU, 8th August 1952. Disposed of, 5th March 1954.

WM729/E Received ex-No.151 Squadron, 16th August 1953. Disposed of, 5th March 1954.

WM733 Received ex-No.23 Squadron, 29th December 1953. Disposed of, 29th March 1954.

WP233/A Delivered ex-MU, 26th July 1951. Disposed of, 22nd March 1954.

WP234/B Delivered ex-MU, 26th July 1951. Disposed of, 7th May 1954.

WP235/D Delivered ex-MU, 27th July 1951. Disposed of, 23rd March 1954.

WP237 Delivered ex-MU, 26th July 1951. Crashed on take-off at West Malling, 16th August 1951. Flt Lt R A K Winton, pilot, and Sgt T G Petrie, navigator, both killed.

WP238/M Delivered ex-MU, 3rd July 1951. Disposed of, 5th March 1954.

WP239/P Received ex-CFE, 19.12.51. Disposed of, 5th March 1954.

WP242/N Delivered to Squadron, 3rd August 1951. Disposed of, 5th March 1954.

WP245/F,O,J Delivered to Squadron, 10th August 1951. Disposed of, 5th March 1954.

WP246/D Delivered ex-MU, 20th September 1951. Disposed of, 16th February 1954.

WP252/B Received ex-No.151 Squadron, 4th March 1952. Pilot abandoned aircraft in spin over the sea ten miles south-east of South Foreland, 19th October 1953; Flg Off J A Didmon-White, pilot, killed.

de Havilland Vampire FB Mk.5

VV528 Received ex-Fighter Command Communication Squadron, 31st January 1951. Disposed of to No.23 Squadron, 5th July 1951.

VV685 Received ex-No.54 Squadron, 31st January 1951. Disposed of to No.23 Squadron, 28th May 1951.

WZ581 Delivered new to Squadron, 5th June 1953. Disposed of, 1st March 1954.

Gloster/Armstrong Whitworth Meteor NF Mk.12

It soon became obvious that, despite a slight increase in power of the Goblin 3 over the engines in the single-seat Vampires, the Vampire two-seaters (with a heavy radar set in the nose) were much badly under-powered, particularly when carrying underwing tanks. Yet it was not until March 1954 that No.25 Squadron received its first Meteor NF Mk. 12s, and NF Mk.14s the following month. These proved adequate to provide night defence against bombers whose performance was no better than the RAF's Lincolns and Washingtons, but with the arrival in service of the Canberra and Valiant jet bombers the Meteor was quite inadequate, possessing insufficient altitude and speed performance.

WS612/E Delivered ex-MU, 27th March 1954. Disposed of to No.153 Squadron, 1st March 1955. Returned to No.25 Squadron 31st July 1958. Disposed of, 20th January 1959.

WS613/A Delivered ex-MU, 5th March 1954. Disposed of to No.153 Squadron, 1st March 1955. Returned to No.25 Squadron 31st July 1958. Struck off charge 6th August 1958.

WS622/R Delivered ex-MU, 27th March 1954. Disposed of to No.153 Squadron, 1st March 1955. Returned to No.25 Squadron 31st July 1958. Disposed of, 30th January 1959.

WS637/L Delivered ex-MU, 5th March 1956. Disposed of, 11th July 1958.

WS665/L Received ex-No.153 Squadron, 31st July 1958. Disposed of, 20th January 1959.

WS680/T Delivered ex-MU, 6th April 1954. Disposed of, 10th July 1958.

WS685/D Received ex-No.153 Squadron, 31st July 1958. Disposed of, 20th January 1959.

WS686/E Received ex-No.153 Squadron, 31st July 1958. Struck off charge, 13th August 1958.

WS693/M Received ex-No.153 Squadron, 31st July 1958. Disposed of, 10th April 1959.

WS694/O Delivered ex-MU, 15th March 1954. Disposed of to No.153 Squadron, 1st March 1955.

WS695/Q Delivered ex-MU, 23rd March 1954. Disposed of to No.85 Squadron, 2nd July 1958.

WS696/F Delivered ex-MU, 11th April 1954. Disposed of, 10th July 1958.

WS697/N Delivered ex-MU, 12th March 1954. Disposed of to No.72 Squadron, 26th April 1958.

WS699/C Delivered ex-MU, 15th March 1954. Disposed of to No.153 Squadron, 1st March 1955. Returned to No.25 Squadron 31st July 1958. Disposed of, 17th September 1958.

WS716/B Delivered ex-MU, 1st April 1954. Disposed of, 10th July 1958.

WS717/F Delivered ex-MU, 4th March 1954. Disposed of to No.153 Squadron, 1st March 1955. Returned to No.25 Squadron 31st July 1958. Disposed of, 10th April 1959.

WS719/D Delivered ex-MU, 18th March 1954. Disposed of, 10th July 1958.

WS720/G Received ex-No.153 Squadron, 31st July 1958. Disposed of, 10th April 1959.

WS721 Delivered ex-MU, 8th March 1954. Disposed of to No.228 Operational Conversion Unit, 11th October 1954.

Gloster/Armstrong Whitworth Meteor NF Mk.14

WS723/T Received ex-No.153 Squadron, 31st July 1958. Disposed of to No.228 Operational Conversion Unit, 19th March 1959.

WS725/G Delivered ex-MU, 28th March 1954. Disposed of, 10th July 1958.

WS726/H Delivered ex-MU, 29th March 1954. Disposed of, 10th July 1958. Later preserved as 'Gate Guardian'.

WS728/P Delivered ex-MU, 29th March 1954. Disposed of to No.72 Squadron, 15th July 1958.

WS729/A Delivered ex-MU, 31st July 1958. Disposed of, 20th January 1959.

WS732/L Delivered ex-MU, 6th April 1954. Tyre burst on take-off at West Malling, overshot and caught fire, 30th December 1955. Flg Off A R Lewis, pilot, unhurt.

WS733/S Delivered ex-MU, 29th March 1954. Disposed of to No.64 Squadron, 13th December 1956.

WS736/P Received ex-No.153 Squadron, 31st July 1958. Disposed of to No.228 Operational Conversion Unit, 3rd April 1959.

WS738/B Received ex-No.153 Squadron, 31st July 1958. Disposed of, 12th January 1959.

WS739/X Delivered ex-MU, 30th March 1954. Disposed of, 10th July 1958. Later preserved as 'Gate Guardian'.

WS748/N Delivered ex-MU, 25th April 1954. Disposed of to No.85 Squadron, 4th July 1958.

WS750/W Delivered ex-MU, 25th April 1954. Disposed of, 10th July 1958.

WS752/Q,D Received ex-No.153 Squadron, 31st July 1958. Disposed of to No.228 Operational Conversion Unit, 25th March 1959.

WS753/J Delivered ex-MU, 25th May 1954. During a high level cross-country sortie, aircraft suffered cockpit canopy structural failure, flew into high ground four miles east of Oxford, 4th February 1957. Sqn Ldr A E Hall, pilot, and Flg Off A G Levett, nav/rad, both killed.

WS757/C Received ex-No.153 Squadron, 31st July 1958. Disposed of, 23rd January 1959.

WS776/K Received ex-MU, 16th June 1954; to No.85 Sqn., 31st July 1958; to No.92 Sqn., 25th November 1958; to No.60 Sqn., June 1959; to No.228 OCU (Leeming), 26th July 1960; to No.33 MU, Lyneham, 25th January 1961. Became ground instructional aircraft *7716M* and then Gate Guardian at RAF Station, North Luffenham, remaining there in the 1990s, retaining No.25 Squadron markings and original letter K on fin.

WS781/J Received ex Station Flight West Malling, 29th March 1957. Disposed of to No.85 Squadron, 2nd July 1958.

WS791/J Received ex-No.33 Squadron, 30th July 1958. Disposed of, 21st January 1959.

Gloster Meteor T Mk.7 (Squadron training aircraft)

VW422/Z Delivered ex-MU, 12th December 1955. Disposed of, 10th July 1958.

VZ638/Z Received ex-No.500 Squadron, 1st April 1951. Disposed of to No.54 Squadron, 15th July 1953. (Later restored and carried civilian markings *G-JETM)*.

WF816 Received ex-No.141 Squadron, 4th February 1954. Disposed of to No.41 Squadron, 17th November 1956.

WH224/Z Received ex-No.151 Squadron, 30th November 1961. Disposed of to No.43 Squadron, 10th August 1962. Returned to No.25 Squadron, 30th October 1962. Disposed of to No.23 Squadron, 20th May 1963.

Gloster Meteor F Mk.8

WH404 Received ex-No.153 Squadron, 31st July 1958. Disposed of, 18th November 1960.

WH423 Received ex-No.12 Group Communication Flight, 7th August 1956. Disposed of, 10th July 1958.

WF443/A Received 11th July 1955. Disposed of, 14th February 1956.

Gloster Javelin F(AW) Mk.7

Both the Vampire and Meteor night fighters were never intended as anything more than temporary equipment for Fighter Command in the United Kingdom, and both de Havilland and Gloster began development of much larger, transonic all-weather fighters before the end of the 1940s. The D.H.110 and Gloster Javelin each ran into problems, principally concerned with control at transonic speeds (the phenomena of pitch-up and control reversal not then being fully understood). No.25 Squadron was not to be equipped with the early versions of the delta-wing Javelin, retaining its Meteor NF Mk.14s until March 1959, having in the meantime moved from West Malling, first to Tangmere and then in July 1959 to Waterbeach. The first Javelin FAW Mk.7s were delivered in March 1959, and were joined by FAW Mk.9s (with reheat) in October that year, the former being flown until January 1961, the later until November 1962.

XH897/M Delivered new to Squadron, 12th March 1959. Disposed of, 12th April 1960.

XH898/N Delivered new to Squadron, 20th April 1959. Disposed of, 10th December 1959.

XH899/P Delivered new to Squadron, 1st April 1959. Disposed of, 19th December 1960.

XH905/A Delivered new to Squadron, 12th December 1958. Disposed of, 4th January 1960.

XH906/B Delivered new to Squadron, 5th December 1958. Disposed of, 4th January 1960

XH907/C Delivered new to Squadron, 30th December 1958. Disposed of, 2nd March 1960.

XH908/D Delivered new to Squadron, 2nd January 1959. Disposed of, 11th January 1961.

XH909/E Delivered new to Squadron, 30th December 1958. Disposed of, 10th December 1959.

XH910/F Delivered new to Squadron, 3rd March 1959. Disposed of, 19th August 1960.

XH911/G Delivered new to Squadron, 4th February 1959. Disposed of, 4th January 1960.

XH912/H Delivered new to Squadron, 25th February 1959. Disposed of, 12th April 1960

XH955/K Delivered new to Squadron, 3rd April 1959. Disposed of to No.23 Squadron, 29th January 1960.

XH956/L Delivered new to Squadron, 29th February 1959. Disposed of to No.23 Squadron, 20th January 1960.

XH957/J Delivered new to Squadron, 25th March 1959. Disposed of, 4th January 1960.

XH959/Q Delivered new to Squadron, 5th April 1959. Disposed of, 11th January 1961.

XH961/R Delivered new to Squadron, 24th April 1959. Disposed of, 19th December 1960.

Note: A Javelin FAW Mk.7, belonging to No.25 Squadron suffered a ground explosion in the starter bay which ripped the under-fuselage open from below the cockpit to the tail; the aircraft was declared Cat 5 (Spares only). Aircraft identity and date not known.

Gloster Javelin F(AW) Mk.9

XH760/B Delivered new to Squadron after conversion to Mk.9, 3rd December 1962. Disposed of to No.11 Squadron, 3rd September 1965.

XH767/A Delivered new to Squadron after conversion to Mk.9, 4th December 1959. Disposed of to No.11 Squadron, 12th December 1962.

XH768/E Delivered new to Squadron after conversion to Mk.9, 8th December 1959. Disposed of to No.11 Squadron, 3rd December 1962.

XH769/N Delivered new to Squadron after conversion to Mk.9, 8th December 1959. Disposed of to No.11 Squadron, 3rd December 1962.

XH770/K Delivered new to Squadron after conversion to Mk.9, 3rd February 1960. Disposed of to No.11 Squadron, 12th December 1962.

XH771/F Delivered new to Squadron after conversion to Mk.9, 5th July 1960. Disposed of to No.11 Squadron, 12th December 1962.

XH772/G Delivered new to Squadron after conversion to Mk.9, February 1960. Disposed of to No.11 Squadron, 11th December 1962.

XH776/P Delivered new to Squadron after conversion to Mk.9, 29th November 1960. Disposed of to No.11 Squadron, 3rd December 1962.

XH880/JHW:J Delivered new to Squadron after conversion to Mk.9, 2nd February 1960. Disposed of to No.11 Squadron, 3rd December 1962.

XH881/M Delivered new to Squadron after conversion to Mk.9, 1st April 1960. Disposed of to No.11 Squadron, 3rd December 1962.

XH882/L Delivered new to Squadron after conversion to Mk.9, 4th March 1960. Disposed of to No.11 Squadron, 3rd December 1962.

XH883/ H:JHW:T Delivered new to Squadron after conversion to Mk.9, 17th March 1960. Disposed of to No.11 Squadron, 3rd December 1962.

XH884/C Delivered new to Squadron after conversion to Mk.9, 2nd March 1960. Disposed of to No.11 Squadron, 4th January 1963.

XH898/D Converted from Mk.7 and returned to Squadron, 24th October 1960. Mechanical fault caused two Firestreak SRAAMs to be jettisoned near Waterbeach, 12th October 1961; no damage to aircraft. Disposed of to No.11 Squadron, 12th December 1962.

XH906/Q Converted from Mk.7 and returned to Squadron,.2nd December 1960. During practice night interceptions, collided with Canberra WD995 of No.32 Squadron, 2.5 miles north of Akrotiri, Cyprus, 26th October 1961; Flt Lt R H Lloyd, pilot, survived, and Flt Lt J H Morris, nav/rad, killed.

XH909/R Converted from Mk.7 and returned to Squadron, 2nd December 1960. Disposed of to No.11 Squadron, 12th December 1962.

Gloster Javelin T Mk.3

The Squadron continued to fly Javelin 9s until 30th November 1962, having moved from Waterbeach to Leuchars on 23rd October the previous year, and it was at this station that No.25 disbanded on the day that the last Javelin was flown away. It was re-formed the following day at North Coates in Lincolnshire as a Bloodhound Mk.1 surface-to-air missile unit, moving to Bruggen in West Germany in 1970 with detachments at Laarbruch and Wildenrath. The Squadron was disbanded while equipped with Bloodhound Mk.2s in 1989.

XH443/Z Delivered new to Squadron, 21st July 1959. Disposed of, 1st January 1960.

Panavia Tornado F Mk.3

In 1989 No.25 (Fighter) Squadron was reformed once more as a manned interceptor fighter squadron, being the fifth to be equipped with the Panavia Tornado F Mk.3, and based at Leeming, Yorkshire. By this time most of the early teething troubles that had been experienced with the Foxhunter radar had been overcome and the Squadron became fully operational before the end of that year. In addition to the following aircraft, several more have been loaned from time to time by other squadrons.

ZE154 Received 14th September 1989. Disposed of, 1990.

ZE156/FI Received 15th October 1989. Disposed of, 1990.

ZE158/FK Received January 1990. Disposed of, 1990.

ZE161/FLG Received by April 1991. Disposed of, 2000.

ZE162/FK Received by May 1991. Still on strength, 2001.

ZE165/FO Received by April 1993. Disposed of, 1998.

ZE167 Received by May 1991. Painted in 75th Anniversary livery scheme (2nd version, 1991-92). Disposed of, 1992.

ZE168/FN Received by January 1998. Still on strength, 2001.

ZE199/FL Received by May 1991. Disposed of, 2000.

ZE203/FI Received October 1989. Still on strength, 2001.

ZE206/FH Received by August 1994. Still on strength, 2001.

ZE210/FB Received by April 1991. Disposed of, 1996.

ZE251/FB Received by April 1999. Disposed of, 2000.

ZE257/FZ Received from No.43 Squadron 10th November 1998. Disposed of, 2000.

ZE290/FE Received by January 1990. Battle of Britain 50th Anniversary Flypast, 15th September 1990. Disposed of, 1991.

ZE339/FO Received by January 1993. Special markings for 1992 display season. Disposed of, 1994.

ZE729 Received 4th July 1989. Disposed of to No.23 Squadron, August 1989.

ZE731 Received September 1989. Disposed of, 1990.

ZE733/FH Received September 1989. Battle of Britain 50th Anniversary Flypast, 15th September 1990. Disposed of, 1991.

ZE735/FE Received 4th July 1989. Battle of Britain 50th Anniversary Flypast, 15th September, 1990. Disposed of, 1990.

ZE737/FF Received by April 1991. Still on strength, 2001.

ZE759/FC Received 4th July 1989. Disposed of, March 1991.

ZE786/FM Received by January 1991. Disposed of to Coningsby, April 1991.

ZE788/FH Received by April 1991. Disposed of, 1993.

ZE789/FI Received 7.90. To Leuchars, April 1991.

ZE791/FF, FP Received by October 1989. Battle of Britain 50th Anniversary Flypast, 15th September 1990; Akrotiri, Cyprus, detachment, 1991. Disposed of, 1995.

ZE794/FD Received 4th July 1989. Disposed of, April 1991.

ZE808/FA Received May 1991. Still on strength, 2001.

ZE837/FL Received July 1990. Dual control trainer F.3T. Battle of Britain 50th Anniversary Flypast, 15th September 1990; Disposed of, 1990.

ZE838/FA Received July 1989. Became Solo Aerobatic Demonstrator (1990), in 75th Anniversary livery scheme (1st version, not approved). Disposed of, March 1991.

ZE839/FJ Received by 9.90. To Leuchars, March 1991.

ZE858/FB First Tornado delivered to No.25 Sqn., July 1989 (temporarily 'FK-?'; Battle of Britain 50th Anniversary Flypast, 15th September 1990). Disposed of to Leuchars, April 1991.

ZE888/FV Received September 1994. Disposed of, 1995.

ZE907/FM Received by November 1994. Still on strength, 2001.

ZE908/FC Received by April 1991. Disposed of, 1995.

ZE936 Received September 1989. Fate unknown.

ZE941/FE Received April 1993. Disposed of, 2000.

ZE961/FD Received by April 1991. Still on strength, 2001.

ZE962/FJ Received by June 1991. Still on strength, 2001.

ZE963/FT Received July 1994. Disposed of, 1996.

ZE967/FE,FJ,FU Received by April 1991. Still on strength, 2001.

APPENDIX 6

CHRONOLOGY OF SQUADRON DEPLOYMENT

(EXCLUDING ARMAMENT PRACTICE CAMPS, GOODWILL AND EXCHANGE VISITS)

Location	***Date of Movement***	***Remarks***
Montrose, Angus	Formed 25th September 1915	Formed from No.6 Reserve Squadron.
Thetford, Norfolk	31st December 1915	Advanced detachment arr. mid-October.
St Omer, France	20th February 1916	Some Sqn HQ staff remained at Thetford.
Auchel, France	1st April 1916	Whole Squadron assembled. (F.E.2b)
Boisdinghem, France	11th October1917	(D.H.4)
Villers-Brettoneux, France	6th March 1918	(D.H.4)
Beauvois, France	24th March 1918	(D.H.4)
Ruisseauville, France	29th March 1918	German offensive (D.H.4)
La Brayelle, France	27th October 1918	Final Allied advance.
Mauberge, France	29th November 1918	
Bickendorf, Germany	26th May 1919	With occupation forces; (some D.H.9as)
Merheim, Germany	7th July 1919	Much reduced personnel.
South Carlton, Lincs.	6th September 1919	Warned for cadre status.
Scopwick, Lincs.	10th-18th December 1919	Cadre plans cancelled.
Hawkinge, Kent	1st January 1920	Personnel gradually increased.
Left for Turkey	28th September 1922	Chanak crisis.
Arr. San Stefano, Turkey	11th October 1922	(Snipes)
Left San Stefano, Turkey	22nd September 1923	(Snipes)
Arr Hawkinge, Kent	3rd October 1923	Permanent peacetime station, for most of the inter-War years was the sole Squadron stationed here.
Northolt, Middlesex	12th September 1938	War station; Munich crisis.
Hawkinge, Kent	10th October 1938	Warned for night fighters.
Northolt, Middlesex	22nd August 1939	War station; Blenheim night fighters.
Filton, Glos	15th September 1939	Aircraft fitted with IFF.
Northolt, Middlesex	4th October 1939	First regular night operations.
Martlesham Heath Detachment	c. October 1939	AI Radar Flt's 2-month detachment.
North Weald, Essex	16th January 1940	(Blenheim night fighters)
Martlesham Heath, Suffolk	19th June 1940	Early Battle of Britain period.
North Weald, Essex	1st September 1940	(First Beaufighters and AI Blenheims)
Debden, Essex	8th October 1940	Increasing operations with Beaufighters.
Wittering, Northants	27th November 1940	Regular night ops. (Beaufighter NF)
Ballyhalbert, Co Down, NI	24th January 1942	Night patrols over Irish Sea.
Church Fenton, Yorkshire	16th May 1942	First Mosquito NF (from October 1942)
Perranporth, Cornwall	June 1943	One Flight detached for Biscay patrols.
Acklington, Northumberland	19th December 1943	Some Mosquito VI night intruders.

Coltishall, Norfolk	5th February 1943	Night defence; anti-V-1 patrols.
Predannack, Cornwall	June 1943	Detachment of one Flight for patrols over the Bay of Biscay. (Mosquito NF.IIs)
Castle Camps, Cambridge	27th October 1944	(Mosquito FB.VI, NF.XVII and NF.XXX)
Boxted, Essex	January 1946	Reduced establishment (NF.XXX and NF.36)
West Malling, Kent	September 1946	Mosquito NF.36, later Vampire NF.10.
Tangmere, Sussex	30th September 1957	(Meteor NF.14)
Waterbeach, Cambridge	1st July 1958	Meteors replaced by Javelin FAW.7s.
Leuchars, Fife	23rd October 1961	(Javelin FAW.9)
North Coates, Lincs	1st October 1963	(Bloodhound Mk.1 SAM)
Laarbruch, Germany Bruggen, Germany Wildenrath, Germany	22nd April 1970	(Bloodhound Mk.2); 'A' Flight and HQ at Bruggen; 'B' Flight at Wildenrath; 'C' Flight at Laarbruch.
Wattisham	November 1981	Bloodhound Mk.2; 'C' Flight only.*
Wyton	1981	Bloodhound Mk.2; 'B' Flight and HQ.
Barkston Heath, Lincs	1981	Bloodhound Mk.2; 'A' Flight only.
Leeming, Yorkshire	July 1989	(Tornado F3)

* Became 'E' Flight of No.85 Squadron from November 1981 until April 1983 when it reverted to 'C' Flight, No.25 (Fighter) Squadron.

APPENDIX 7

Random Biographical Notes

No.25 (Fighter) Squadron Personnel

ALLEN, Lieut Charles Edward Hamilton, RFC (later Air Vice-Marshal, CB, DFC, BA, RAF). Born 3-1-99. Joined RFC in 1917 and was posted to No.25 Squadron at Boisdinghem, France, in February 1918, and fought over Western Front (D.H.4s and D.H.9as). Remained with Squadron until December 1919 having been granted a permanent commission in the RAF. (Posted as flying instructor at CFS in 1920 and subsequently served on No.27 Squadron in India and later on No.142 Squadron Staff appointments during Second World War, and Air Ministry from 1952-54. Retired as Air Vice-Marshal in 1954, appointed CB).

ALLEN, Fg Off R D. Served on Squadron between 1950 and 1952, and during 1957-58. (Mosquitos, Vampires and Javelins) *Member of Association.*

ARNOTT, Flt Lt R D, (later Air Cdre, CBE). Pilot. Served on Squadron from 1960 to 1962. (Javelins) *Past President of Association.*

ATCHERLEY, Sqn Ldr David Francis William (later Air Vice-Marshal, CB, CBE, DSO, DFC AND BAR). Pilot, RAF. Commanded No.25 (Fighter) Squadron at Wittering from January to August 1941. One of the most illustrious pair of twin brothers ever to have served in the RAF, of whose lives the best account appears in the book *Pride of Unicorns* by John Pudney (Oldbourne, London, 1960). Personal recollections of this extraordinary officer abound in letters from ex-Squadron members who served under him at Wittering in 1941. 'There was no nonsense with David who, by his behaviour and total commitment to the Service he loved, was an officer and a gentleman in every conceivable interpretation of those terms. He was, quite simply, revered and admired both by his peers and those on the ground. We would do anything for him, and he would do anything for us. It was a privilege and an unforgettable experience to have served alongside this man.' And from John Wray, 'If you haven't served with an Atcherley, and I have served with both, you haven't lived, neither are you familiar with their unusual thought processes.' He must be the only fighter pilot ever to have continued flying in combat wearing a plaster jacket soon after breaking his neck and, while doing so, destroyed an enemy bomber at night. David received a BAR to his DFC from HM King George VI at an investiture at Wittering, still wearing the plaster cast. To state that he was entirely fearless would be to suggest that he was either foolhardy or lacked imagination. His exploits and achievements suffice to contradict this. After leaving No.25 Squadron, about which period he is on record as having stated as being among the happiest and most rewarding of his Service career, he continued up the promotion ladder of the RAF, and continued to fly whenever he could. (Unlike his twin, he never suffered the loss of seniority as the outcome of some indiscretion, and despite being commissioned at Cranwell on the same day, was two months the senior at the time of his death.) He died while still serving. As an Air Vice-Marshal, he was appointed AOC, No.205 Group in Egypt, arriving there in a photo reconnaissance Meteor which he flew from Abingdon in January 1952. Several months later, on 8th June, he undertook a solo photo reconnaissance sortie from Fayid to Nicosia, Cyprus, but disappeared while *en route* and, despite a huge search by aircraft of four air forces, no trace of David or his aircraft was ever found.

AUSTIN, Sqn Ldr C E. Served on Squadron from 1938 to 1941. (Demons, Gladiators, Blenheims and Beaufighters). *Member of Association.*

BADDELEY, Sgt Douglas Hiram, RAF, 814205. Air gunner. Joined Squadron at North Weald early in October 1940. Posted away after Squadron received Beaufighters. Killed in action at the age of 25 on 26th June 1942. Buried in Kiel War Cemetery, Germany. Battle of Britain Clasp.

BAKER, Lieut Brian Edmund, RFC (later Air Marshal Sir Edmund, KBE, CB, DSO, MC, AFC, RAF). Pilot and founder member of No.25 Squadron at Montrose, 1915. Later served with No.48 Squadron; was credited with shooting down ten enemy aircraft. Later appointed Chief Flying Instructor, RAF Leuchars, 1932-34; served in HMS *Eagle*, 1934, and HMS *Courageous*, 1936. Commanded RAF Station, Gosport, 1937-38, and RAF Station, Leuchars, 1938; appointed Air Officer Commanding, RAF East Africa, 1945, and then Senior Air Staff Officer, RAF Middle East, 1945; Retired 10th May 1950.

BARNARD, W/Off Eric Charles, RAuxAF, 178934. Navigator Radar. Charles Barnard originally served with No.601 Squadron, AAP, before the War and flew in Blenheims with No.600 Squadron during the Battle of Britain as an AC2 Air Gunner without flying pay. (On 8th September 1940 he and the other members of his crew baled out when his aircraft ran out of fuel.) He subsequently served on No.125 Squadron as a Sergeant (later F/Sgt) and joined No.25 Squadron at Acklington on 18th January 1944 as a W/Off Navigator Radar flying in Mosquito night fighters. Only three months later he was commissioned Plt Off and posted to No.85 Squadron. He was released from the Service as a Flight Lieutenant on 24th July 1946.

BARNES, Sergeant William Alfred, RFC. Observer on No.25 Sqn at Auchel, France (F.E.2bs). It is known that, with 2/Lieut W D Matheson as pilot, he was one of those who shared in the destruction of an LVG reconnaissance aircraft on 4th March 1917. On 13th April ('Bloody April'), while flying with 2/Lieut Allan Harold Bates (pilot), they were shot down and killed by Manfred von Richthofen in the Noyelle-Godault area; this was von Richthofen's 43rd combat victory.

BATES, 2/Lieut Allan Harold Bates, RFC. Pilot on No.25 Squadron at Auchel in 1917. While flying with Sergeant William Alfred Barnes (observer) on 13th April, their B.E.2c was attacked by Manfred von Richthofen (of *Jasta* 11) and shot down in the Noyelle-Godault area, and both were killed.

BEAMISH, Flt Lt Francis Victor (later Wg Cdr, DSO AND BAR, DFC, AFC), RAF, 16089. Pilot. Irish. One of the legendary figures of the Service, Victor Beamish was one of the original Cranwell cadets, born on 27-9-03, graduating as Pilot Officer in July 1921. After service as an army co-operation pilot with Nos.14, 31 and 60 Squadrons, he came to No.25 Squadron at Hawkinge as a flight commander in 1931 flying Siskins. Bypassing his CO, he wrote to the Air Ministry stating that the Siskin 'was quite the worst machine it had ever been his misfortune to have to fly and would resign from the Service unless the Squadron was re-equipped with Hawker Furies without delay'. (Although this letter earned an abrasive rebuke, Beamish was appointed Personal Assistant to the AOC-in-C, ADGB at Uxbridge in January 1932 (a month before the Squadron started receiving Furies). A year later he contracted tuberculosis and had to resign his commission. In January 1937 he was reinstated in the General Duties branch of the Service and given command of No.64 Squadron (being awarded the AFC, 1-1-38, for establishing the Met Flight at Aldergrove). He commanded No.504 Sqn, AAF, from 13th September 1939 and was appointed station commander as a Wing Commander of North Weald from 7th June 1940. During the Battle of Britain he flew Hurricanes whenever he could join up with a squadron. (Note. He was still station commander at North Weald when No.25 Squadron was stationed there between 1st September and 8th October 1940; John Brisley has relevant anecdotes of this period.) During the Battle he was credited with six enemy aircraft destroyed and seven probably destroyed. Even after being posted to HQ No.11 Group, he continued to visit his stations and fly with the squadrons, this despite suffering the effects of TB. He will be remembered as the pilot of a Spitfire who first spotted the German ships, *Scharnhorst*, *Gneisenau* and *Prinz Eugen* as they escaped up the Channel after breaking out from Brest on the morning of 12th February 1942. He was ultimately shot down into the English Channel on 28th March 1942, when his score stood at 8 destroyed and 11 probably destroyed. His body was never recovered and he is remembered on the Runnymede Memorial, Panel 64.

BENT, LAC (later Sgt and Flt Lt.) Benjamin, RAF, 52078. Born 22nd August 1919. Joined RAF on 8th November 1937 and completed wireless operator's course (ground duties). Volunteered for flying duties in June 1940. Joined No.25 Squadron at Martlesham Heath on 6th August 1940 and began flying duties a few days after as an LAC with flying Badge. Promoted Sergeant on 27th September in category of Wireless Operator (Air). While flying in Beaufighters with the Squadron in 1941 Bent participated in the destruction of an enemy aircraft on 5th May, a Heinkel He 111 on the 8th, a Dornier Do.17 on the 9th, a Heinkel He 111 damaged on the 14th and a Junkers Ju 88 destroyed on 14th June. He then served as an instructor with No.54 OTU before returning to No.25 Squadron as a Navigator/Radar Operator on 8th September 1942, remaining until July 1944. During this period he was commissioned from Warrant Officer in April 1943 and assisted in the destruction of two Junkers Ju 188s on 21st March 1944 (his pilot being Flt Lt R L Davies) and a Messerschmitt Bf 110 over the Frisian Islands in the early hours of D-Day, 6th June 1944. He was awarded the DFC on 26th May 1944 and on leaving the Squadron became Light Fighter Liaison Officer with a USAAP P-61 Black Widow squadron. Bent was released from the RAF on 2nd February 1947 as a Flight Lieutenant, but rejoined the Service in 1950, afterwards being granted a Permanent Commission in the Fighter Control Branch. He retired from the RAF at his own request on 5th December 1970. Battle of Britain Clasp. *Member of Association.*

BERWICK, Sgt Robert Charles (later Flt Lt), RAF, 745915. Wop/AG. Early service detail not known. Served with No.25 Squadron during the Battle of Britain and qualified for Battle of Britain Clasp. Early in 1941 he was posted to No.78 Squadron at Disforth to fly Whitleys, but was killed in action on 19th June 1941; he is buried in Reichswald Forest War Cemetery, Germany.

BLACKETT, 2/Lieut Basil John. Observer on No.25 Squadron at Auchel, France in 1917. Flying with Lieut Conrad Tolendal Lally (pilot), he forced down an Albatros DV near Quesnoy on 3rd September 1917, and on 5th September (again flying with Dally as pilot) forced down another Albatros DV.

BLACKWOOD, Plt Off (later Wg Cdr, Czech Military Cross), RAF, 32181. Pilot. Eton-educated George Blackwood joined the RAF in 1933 on a short service commission and received pilot training with No.2 FTS at Digby. He joined No.25 Squadron at Hawkinge on 26th August 1933 and flew a Fury in the tied-together air drill demonstration at the 1934 Hendon Display. In September 1934 he was temporarily seconded as Personal Assistant to the AOC Coastal Area, Lee-on-Solent, but returned to the Squadron as a Flying Officer on 1st July 1935. (He was posted to No.600 Squadron, AAF, at Hendon in 1936 as flying instructor and assistant adjutant. During the Battle of Britain he commanded No.310 (Czech) Squadron, and destroyed a Dornier Do.17 on 26th August 1940, but was himself shot down; he baled out unhurt. He was awarded the Czech Military Cross (24-12-40). He was released from the RAF early in 1945 as a Wing Commander.)

BLENKHARN, Sgt Frank, RAF, 1002007. Radar Operator. Born 28th April 1920. Joined the RAF in May 1940, and posted to No.25 Squadron at Martlesham Heath in September, qualifying for Battle of Britain Clasp. On 7th December 1940 Blenkharn was a crewmember of a Blenheim checking the blackout over Peterborough when it was in collision with another aircraft; both the other crewmembers were killed, as were the six trainee pilots in the other aircraft. Blenkharn survived but never flew again. He was transferred to Flying Control and was posted to Dum Dum, India, being released from the Service early in 1947.

BOULTBEE, Lieut Arthur Elsdale, RFC. Served on No.25 Sqn as pilot at Auchel, France. Flying an F.E.2b he shared in the destruction of an LVG reconnaissance aircraft over Courrières on 4th March 1917. On 17th March, while flying with 2nd Air Mechanic Frederick King (observer), their F.E.2b was attacked and shot down by Manfred von Richthofen in a Halberstadt DII near Oppy (his 27th victory). Both the British airmen were killed.

BOWIE, Flt Lt (later Sqn Ldr) Roy. Pilot. After serving with No.54 Sqn on Vampire day fighters, was posted to No.25 Squadron at West Malling. (Vampire NF), 1952-1953. *Member of Association.*

BRINSDEN, Sqn Ldr (later Wg Cdr) Francis Noel, RAF. 40338. Pilot. New Zealander. Born in Auckland, New Zealand, 27-3-19, Brinsden came to England with a short service commission in 1937. He served in Spitfires with No.19 Squadron during the Battle of Britain, being credited with destroying a Junkers Ju 87 over Dunkirk on 26th May 1940. He served as a flight commander on No.485 (New Zealand) Squadron. newly formed in 1941, and joined No.25 Squadron at Church Fenton in the spring of 1943. While with the Squadron on 17th August that year Brinsden was flying a Mosquito NF II on a bomber support sortie during a night raid on Peenemünde and. while carrying out a low-level attack on the German base at Sylt, he was caught by searchlights and lost his night vision. Turning out to sea he struck the water and buckled both propellers. being forced to ditch a short distance from the shore. He and his navigator managed to get free of the aircraft and clambered aboard their dinghy, raising the sail and being blown away from the land. When dawn broke, however. the wind changed and at midday they were blown back to the shore and into the arms of German troops who had been watching them for hours. Brinsden was incarcerated in Stalag Luft III and was released from captivity on 9th May 1945, after which he commanded No.3 Missing Research and Enquiry Unit. tracing Allied aircrew members. He was granted a Permanent Commission in June 1947 and continued to serve until his retirement on 31st December 1966 as a Wing Commander. He returned to the Antipodes to live in Western Australia.

BRISLEY, LAC (later F/Sgt) John L. Served on No.25 Squadron at Hawkinge from 1933 to 1935 (Hawker Furies) and from 1938 to 1944 (Demons, Gladiators, Blenheims, Beaufighters and Mosquitos). Probably the longest serving member of the Squadron (10 years). *Member of Association.*

BROUGHTON, Wg Cdr (later Air Cdre) John, FBIM. Pilot. Born 18-2-34. Commanded No.25 Squadron from 1973 to 1975. (Bloodhound SAMs). Retired from RAF. 1-1-89, as Air Cdre. *Member of Association.*

BROWN, Plt Off Archibald Wilkinson, RAF, 78744. Air Gunner. Brown was commissioned in April 1940 and joined No.25 Squadron shortly after while at North Weald. On the night of 14th September he was flying over London with Plt Off M J Herrick in a Blenheim when they intercepted and shot down a Heinkel He 111 which crashed at Newmans End, near Sheering, Essex. (Brown was released from the RAF in 1945 as a Flight Lieutenant.) KGW.

BROWN, Flt Lt J E, RAF. Navigator (Display). Aged 29, Jim Brown joined the RAF in 1983 having been educated at Central Grammar School in Birmingham. After training, his first operational tour was on the Tornado GR Mk.1 with No.16 Squadron at RAF Laarbruch in Germany. Jim completed the Tornado F.3 operational conversion course in 1988 and joined No.25 (Fighter) Squadron at Leeming on its reformation in 1989. He became the RAF's 1991 Tornado F.3 Display Navigator, flying with Flight Lieutenant Archie Neill. *Member of Squadron Association.*

BULL, Fg Off Cecil Halford, RAF, 37594. Pilot. Bull joined the RAF in January 1936 and was trained at No.3 FTS, Grantham. He served as a staff pilot with No.1 Anti-Aircraft Co-operation Unit in 1937 before joining No.25. He was captain of one of the Squadron's Blenheims that flew the RAF's first attack of the War on German territory – the raid on Borkum of 28th November 1939. He was still with No.25 Squadron during the early stages of the Battle of Britain only to be killed in a shooting accident on 8th August 1940 whilst on leave. He had flown operational sorties during the Battle of Britain, thereby qualifying for the Clasp posthumously.

BURGESS, Lieut David Luther, RFC. Observer on No.25 Squadron at Auchel, France, 1917 (D.H.4s). Known to have shot down an Albatros DV near Lille on 11th July 1917, an Albatros DV on 5th August, an Albatros DIII near Dourgies on 14th August and an Albatros DV on 15th August, also near Dourgies; his pilot was usually Capt J F Morris, MC.

CAMERON-COX, Flt Lt (later Wg Cdr) J, MBIM. Pilot. Served on Squadron from 1948-51 as flight commander (Mosquitos) and commanded Squadron as Sqn Ldr, 1954-55 (Meteor NF). Retired from RAF as Wg Cdr, 15-7-68. *Member of Association.*

CANDY, Plt Off Robert John, RAF, 79229. Air Gunner. Joined No.25 Squadron at Martlesham Heath in June 1940 and flew operational sorties with the Squadron in July, thereby qualifying for the Battle of Britain Clasp. (He was posted to Iceland at the end of that month with No.98 Squadron, flying in Fairey Battles. He later served on No.264 and No.12 Squadrons and was released from the RAF as a Flight Lieutenant in 1945.)

CARNABY, Flt Lt William Fleming, RAF, 90157. Pilot. A former Defiant pilot who had flown with No.264 Squadron during the Battle of Britain, Carnaby later joined No.85 Squadron on Hurricanes. He joined No.25 Squadron, probably in 1942, to fly Beaufighters but was killed in a flying accident in a Mosquito on 5th February 1943. Aged 29, he is buried in Newmarket Cemetery, Suffolk.

CASSIDY, Fg Off Ernest, RAF, 40507. Pilot. Cassidy was born on 25th October 1916. He joined the RAF on a short service commission in December 1937, attending No.7 FTS, Peterborough, for his flying training. He joined No.25 Squadron on 17th September 1938, and flew Blenheims with the Squadron during the Battle of Britain until posted to No.249 Squadron on 21st October 1940. (He subsequently flew Hurricanes based on Malta in 1941, destroying one Italian and one German aircraft. He was awarded the DFC on 2nd January 1942 and was granted a permanent commission after the War. He was awarded the AFC on 5th June 1952 and retired from the RAF on 1st June 1958, retaining the rank of Wg Cdr.)

CAVE, Fg Off (later Sqn Ldr) John Geoffrey, RAF, 39271. Educated in Canada, Cave came to England in 1936 to join the RAF, receiving his flying training with No.8 FTS at Montrose. He joined No.25 Squadron at Hawkinge on 7th August 1937 flying Demons, Gladiators and Blenheims until posted to No.600 Squadron early in 1940. He transferred to the Aircraft Control branch towards the end of the War and was serving as a Squadron Leader when he died early in 1962.

CHAMBERLAIN, Plt Off (later Air Vice-Marshal) George Philip, CB, OBE, RAF. 8013. Pilot. Born 18-8-05. Graduated from RAF College, Cranwell, July 1925. Joined No.25 Squadron at Hawkinge on 25th July 1925 flying Gloster Grebes. (He served on No.5 (Army Co-operation) Squadron at Risalpur, India, flying Bristol Fighters from April 1927 until August 1930 when he returned home. He served on No.17 Sqn at Kenley as a flight commander from 1934 to 1936 flying Bulldogs.) As a Wg Cdr in March 1940 he was asked by Dowding to establish the Fighter Interception Unit at Tangmere, flying Blenheims, and to introduce AI radar into service. He asked that those pilots of No.25 Squadron, who had undertaken the early AI trials in 1939, be posted as the FIU's initial pilots, one of whom was Ker-Ramsay (*qv*). After serving tours with Coastal and Transport Command, at the Air Ministry and with the RAAF, Chamberlain retired from the Service on 1st July 1955. He was appointed to the OBE on 24th September 1941 for his work with the FIU and made CB on 13th June 1946. He qualified for the Battle of Britain Clasp. *Late Member of the Association.*

CHICK, Sqn Ldr John F H, Pilot. Flight Commander, 'B' Flight; Javelin 7s and 9s, Waterbeach, 1959-61. Born 9th January 1929. Graduated, RAF College, Cranwell, 13th December

1950. Promoted Wg Cdr, 1st July 1970. Retired as Gp Capt, 9th January 1984.

CHRISTIAN, W/Off B W. Joined No.25 Squadron at Church Fenton in 1943 and served on it until 1946 when stationed at Boxted. (Mosquitos). *Member of Association.*

CLAYTON, Flt Lt S. Joined No.25 Squadron on reforming at Leeming in 1989 until 1991. (Tornados). *Member of Association.*

CLOUSTON, Fg Gnd Arthur Edmund (later Air Cdre, CB, DSO, DFC, AFC AND BAR), RAF, 29162. New Zealander. Born 7-4-08 Clouston was born at Motueka, New Zealand and learned to fly in the late 1920s. He sailed for England in 1930 and joined the RAF, being trained at No.3 FTS. He joined No.25 Squadron as a Plt Off at Hawkinge on 7th April 1931, first flying Siskins and later Fury Is. His short service commission ended in October that year but he was accepted for experimental flying at Farnborough for which he was awarded the AFC (1-1-38). Gained international acclaim for a number of record-breaking long distance flights in the mid-1930s. Was at Farnborough during the early War months. Despite frustration by orders not to take off against enemy raiders in the vicinity of Farnborough, Clouston took off against a Heinkel He 111 – which he lost – and was promptly grounded by his CO on his return.

Shortly afterwards some of the fighters at Farnborough were armed for local defence and Clouston was usually the first to take off. During the Battle of Britain Clouston shot down a Heinkel He 111 and set off after its escorting Messerschmitt Bf 110, a chase that took him across the Channel. After severely damaging the enemy aircraft, he returned to Farnborough only to be grounded once more for taking his aircraft so far from base. Thereafter he successfully applied for a transfer to operational flying and during the remainder of the War received a BAR to his AFC (1-1-42), the DFC (1-10-43) and the DSO (14-4-44). After the War he was appointed Commandant of the Empire Test Pilots' School and retired as an Air Cdre on 7th April 1960, having been appointed CB. His autobiography *The Dangerous Skies* (Cassell, 1954) is widely regarded as a classic.

COKER, Fg Off Frank L. Served on Squadron from 1941 to 1943 at Wittering, Ballyhalbert and Church Fenton. (Beaufighters and Mosquitos). *Member of Association.*

COOK, Sqn Ldr Kenneth H, DFC. Pilot. Born 9-4-23. Served as Sqn Ldr on Squadron at Waterbeach from 1958 to 1959, and appointed Sqn Cdr, 1959. (Meteor NF and Javelin 7s). Retired from RAF, 13-1-68, as Wg Cdr. *Member of Association.*

COPEMAN, Capt M C B, RFC, Pilot. Served on No.25 Squadron during 1916, and on 15th July that year, with Sgt L S Court as observer/gunner shot down a Fokker EIII monoplane scout near Fromelles.

CORNWELL, Flt Lt Norman H. Born 12-9-24. Engineering Branch. Served as Flt Lt on Squadron from 1968 to 1973 at North Coates and Bruggen. (Bloodhound SAMs). *Member of Association.*

CORRY, Plt Off Noel Henry (later Sqn Ldr), RAF, 80544. Pilot. After completing his flying training at No.11 FTS and No.5 OTU, Corry joined No.25 Squadron at Martlesham Heath on 26th June 1940, flying Blenheims. He flew during the Battle of Britain and remained with the Squadron until 29th January 1941 when he was posted to the Special Duties Flight, No.72 Group. (He subsequently served as a flying instructor and then joined No.12 Squadron flying Lancasters, eventually completing 24 ops. He was awarded the DFC on 8th December 1944 and was released from the RAF as a Squadron Leader on 27th November 1945).

COURT, Sgt Leslie Simpson, Observer/gunner. Joined No.25 Squadron as an Air Mechanic in 1916 and became 2/Lieut L L Richardson's observer, being promoted Corporal; he was credited with shooting down three Fokker EIII monoplane scouts during June and July 1916, and later, flying with other pilots, shot down three other German aircraft. On 5th August 1916 he, now a Sergeant, and his pilot were shot down behind the lines by the well-known German crew, Dossenbach and Schilling, whom Court also shot down before crashing. Court was awarded the French Medaille Militaire. He survived the War.

CROSS, Plt Off Kenneth Brian Boyd (later Air Chief Marshal Sir Kenneth, KCB, CBE, DSO, DFC. Forever, and universally known in the RAF as 'Bing', Plt Off Cross joined No.25 Squadron at Hawkinge in April 1931 'for the happiest years of his life'. At that time the Squadron still flew Siskins, somewhat unpopular for their tricky landing characteristics. Flight Commanders at that time were Flt Lts W.E. Swan ('A' Flight), Victor Beamish ('B') and Anthony Caron Evans-Evans ('C'). The latter was said to be one of the RAF's high-qualified signals officers, and was logically the Squadron's Signals Officer as well. Other pilots on the Squadron at that time were Fg Offs Harry St George Burke (ex-Cambridge University Air Squadron), Brian Wright Knox (ex-Cranwell), Peter Heath (ex-Cranwell), Miles Herbert Garnon-Williams, Arthur Edmund Clouston, Eric Alfred Douglas-Jones, Neil ('Michael') Daunt and Felix Patrick Edward Dunworth. Many of these pilots were to attract considerable esteem in the course of their lives – Victor Beamish, A E Clouston and Michael Daunt to mention but three.

Shortly after Cross's arrival on the Squadron, No.25 Squadron left Hawkinge for its annual armament camp at Sutton Bridge, situated on the Wash. Under the watchful eye of its CO, Sqn Ldr H M 'Daddy' Probyn, who fully understood the importance of these 'camps', the Squadron acquitted itself well in 1931-32, coming second out of the RAF's thirteen home-based fighter squadrons. Cross is on record as having been highly critical of the apparent absence of discipline displayed by No.23 Squadron (who 'shared' Sutton Bridge with No.25), and was not surprised to see No.23 'way down the list' in the results. Among the pilots on No.23 at that time was one Douglas Bader – who was severely injured in a flying accident soon afterwards while performing aerobatics.

In due course Cross began to distinguish himself on the Squadron, being selected to join No.25's formation aerobatic team, and at the 1933 Hendon Air Display – by which time Hawker Furies had replaced the 'old' Siskins. Indeed it was Cross's idea that it should be possible to barrel-roll three flights of Furies in line abreast formation, an item first included in No.25 Squadron's aerobatic routine – and the first time an RAF squadron had done so. It should be mentioned here that Cross was still aged 22.

In the 1934 Hendon Display, No.25 was again selected to give the aerobatic display, and again Cross was one of the pilots. He was also nearing the last year of his Short Service Commission. However, with the international situation deteriorating, a new extension of Service was introduced, Cross gaining a five year extension. With a flying categorisation as

'Exceptional', he was posted from Hawkinge to the Central Flying School, then at Wittering. Thereafter his climb through numerous appointments (not least his miraculous survival as CO of No.46 (Hurricane) Squadron when the carrier HMS *Glorious* was sunk by German battleships following the Norwegian campaign of 1940), make for fascinating study. He finally retired from the Service on 24th February 1967 in the rank of Air Chief Marshal.

CROSSMAN, Sgt Richard George, RAF, 746701. Wop/AG. Crossman joined No.25 Squadron at Debden early in October 1940 and flew operational sorties during the Battle of Britain. He was still serving on this Squadron on 8th July 1941 when, as a Flight Sergeant, he was killed. He is buried in Watford Cemetery.

CULMER, Sgt James Douglas (later Flt Lt), RAF, 177211. Air Gunner. Born on 15th March 1913, Culmer was with No.25 Squadron at Martlesham Heath in June 1940 and flew operational sorties during the Battle of Britain. He was awarded the DFM on 24th December 1940 for services in action during the early weeks of the night Blitz, and remained with the Squadron until 1942. (He was commissioned Pilot Officer on 24th August 1944, and remained in the Service after the War, retiring as a Flight Lieutenant in the Aircraft Control Branch on 15th March 1963.)

CUNNINGHAM, LAC Frank R. Engine Fitter. Served on Squadron from 1951 to 1953 at West Malling. (Vampire NF). *Member of Association.*

CUNNINGHAM, Sqn Ldr M R S, MBE. Commanded No.25 Squadron at North Coates (Bloodhound SAMs), 1965-1967. *Member of Association.*

DAUNT, Fg Off Neill ('Michael'), RAF. Pilot. Joined Squadron c.1930 (Siskins and Furies) at Hawkinge. (Transferred to RAFO and became production test pilot with Gloster Aircraft Co, 1937. Test flew Gladiators, Henleys, Hurricanes and Typhoons. Became company Chief Test Pilot in October 1942 after death of P E G Sayer in Typhoon. Was first to fly the prototype Gloster Meteor on 5th March 1943. Died 1993.)

DAVIES, Flt Lt R L, RAF. Pilot. Was serving on No.25 Squadron in 1943-1944 with Fg Off B Bent (*qv*) as his navigator radar operator. Shot down two Junkers Fu 188s in one night, 21st/22nd March 1944.

DEY, Wg Cdr Andy. No.25 Squadron Commander at Leeming, 1998-2000. Tornados. *Member of Association.*

DICKSON, Sqn Ldr William Forster (later Marshal of the Royal Air Force Sir William, GCB, KBE, DSO, AFC, Chief of the Air Staff). Born 24-9-98. Served in RNAS during First World War. Received permanent commission in RAF in 1918 and later served as Fg Off on No.56 Sqn. Posted to command RAF Hawkinge and No.25 Squadron as Sqn Ldr from 1935 to 1936 (Hawker Fury Is). Subsequently commanded Desert Air Force, 1944-45; C-in-C, MEAF, 1948-50; Chief of the Air Staff, 1953-1955.

DUNLOP, Lieut Colin, RFC. Pilot. Had been commissioned 2/Lieut in the 2/1st Lovat Scouts before volunteering for transfer to the RFC early in 1916. He received pilot training at Thetford in Norfolk and joined No.25 Squadron at Auchel, France, in mid-October 1916 to fly F.E.2bs. On the 21st, two days after arriving on the Squadron, he was flying a patrol over the front line when he was attacked by a German scout, which his gunner, Lieut Weir, shot down in flames. On 17th November four of the Squadron aircraft were bombing Provin airfield when they were attacked by eight German scouts. Two of the F.E.2bs were shot down (though their crews were unhurt) and two of the enemy were probably shot down. On the 23rd Dunlop was the pilot of one of four F.E.2bs which, while bombing Brebières, were attacked by about 20 German aircraft. Four of the enemy aircraft were shot down in flames (one by Dunlop and Weir) and two gunners were slightly wounded; all No.25 Squadron aircraft returned safely. Dunlop and Weir shot down single enemy aircraft on 9th February and 4th March 1917. On 26th April, during a reconnaissance sortie over Drocourt, two No.25 Squadron F.E.2ds (one flown by Dunlop and Weir), escorted by six Sopwith Triplanes, were attacked by twelve German Fokker scouts. Three of the enemy were shot down (one by Dunlop and Weir), but Dunlop's engine was hit and burned out. He managed to force land safely near Arras. He was posted away to No.26 Training Squadron at Turnhouse on 1st July 1917, having been awarded the MC. (Dunlop's logbook is held by the RAF Museum, and fourteen of the Squadron's observer/gunners are mentioned by name.)

DURHAM, Wg Cdr E, RAF. Commanded No.25 Squadron, May 1977–Dec 1978, at Bruggen and Wildenrath (Bloodhound SAMs), and was later Station Commander, RAF West Raynham. Retired as a Group Captain in the 1980s.

EMSDEN, Sgt Leonard, RFC. Observer on No.25 Squadron, 1917. Flying with 2/Lieut R G Malcolm (pilot), shared in the destruction of an LVG over Courrières on 4th March 1917; flying with Lieut H E Davis (pilot) shot down an Albatros DIII in flames on 17th March; flying with Capt J L Leith shot down out of control another Albatros DIII near Arras on 17th March; flying with Lieut B King (pilot) destroyed a Halberstadt scout near Vimy Ridge on 6th April 1917; flying with 2/Lieut R.G. Malcolm (pilot) destroyed an Albatros DIII on 13th April; on 1st May, flying with Capt J L Leith (pilot) destroyed an Albatros DIII over Izel, and forced down another Albatros DIII near Lens (crew captured); on a second sortie on 1st May 1917, Sgt Emsden and Capt J L Leith destroyed an Albatros DIII over Bois de Bernard.

EVANS, Sqn Ldr David, RAF. 42491. Pilot. Joined the RAF on short service commission in June 1939, and served as a Pilot Officer with Nos.615 and 607 Squadrons during the Battle of Britain. He joined No.25 Squadron late in 1942 or early 1943 to fly Mosquito night fighters. He was killed flying a Mosquito as a Squadron Leader on 28th May 1943 (circumstances not known), and is buried in St Andrew's churchyard, Bebington, Cheshire.

FIELDEN, Fg Off Edward Hedley. Pilot. RAF, later RAFO. (Later AVM Sir Edward, KCVO, CB, DFC, AFC). Born, 1903. Served on No.25 Squadron, 1924-1925 on Snipes and Grebes with Short Service Commission. Then joined Duxford Station Flight (the original Met Fright), 1926-29. During the Second World War commanded No.161 (Special Duties) Sqn at Tempsford (landing agents in France), 1942, and commanded Tempsford, 1942-44. Commanded the King's Flight during Royal Tour of South Africa, 1947, and was Captain of the Queen's Flight from 1953 until 1962. Died 8th November 1976.

FORRYAN, F/Sgt Donald P. Pilot. Served on Squadron from 1943 to 1944 at Church Fenton, Acklington and Coltishall. (Mosquitos). *Member of Association.*

FOSTER, At Lt Kenneth E. Served as Adjutant on Squadron from 1958 to 1962 at Waterbeach and Leuchars (Javelins). *Member of Association.*

FOX, Lieut Donald William Taylor, RFC. Observer/Air Gunner. (Later RAFVR in Second World War). Was commissioned 2/Lieut in the Royal Irish Rifles before volunteering for transfer to the RFC. Came to No.25 Squadron in July 1917 and almost immediately began flying with 2/Lieut Simpson, Capt Roulstone and Capt Pearce who were collecting D.H.4s from No.1 Air Depot as the Squadron was then converting to this light bomber. He became Capt Roulstone's regular gunner and shot down one of 15 Albatros scouts which attacked No.25 Squadron during a raid on Carvin on 22nd August. No Squadron aircraft was lost. During the next few months Fox, flying with Roulstone, took part in bombing raids on Courrières, Sallaumines, Carvin, Quiery-la-Motte, Estevelles, Bauvin, Lauwin, Don and Hantay. However, while flying a reconnaissance sortie at 20,000 feet on 15th October 1917 (open cockpit, no heating) he suffered severe frostbite to both hands and was in hospital until the following February when he was posted to No.39 Squadron. In the Second World War he joined the RAFVR for special administrative duties.

FRIEND, Sgt Jack Richard. 904234, RAF. Air Gunner. Jack Friend from Norwich, Norfolk, joined No.25 Squadron at North Weald early in October 1940. He flew operational sorties during the Battle of Britain and so qualified for the Clasp. He was a member of the crew of a Blenheim checking the Peterborough blackout on the night of 7th December 1940; the aircraft was in collision with a trainer and only one crew member survived (Sgt Frank Blenkharn, *qv.*). Friend, who was 26 at the time of his death, is buried in All Saints' churchyard, Wittering.

GLOSSOP, W/Off George T, RAF. Served on Squadron from 1943 to 1945 at Church Fenton, Acklington, Coltishall and Castle Camps. (Mosquitos). *Member of Association.*

GRATTAN-BELLEW, Capt W A, MC, RFC. Second son of Sir Henry Grattan-Bellew, 3rd Bt, (younger brother of 4th Bt) and late of 5th Dragoon Guards, Capt Grattan-Bellew accompanied No.25 Squadron to France as a flight commander with 21 hours' flying experience. On 18th June 1916 (the same day that McCubbin shot down Max Immelmann), Grattan-Bellew was leader of three F.E.2bs which were attacked by seven Fokker D.IIIs. One of the F.E.2bs was shot down but Grattan-Bellew and the other surviving pilot each destroyed a Fokker before making their escape. About five days later Grattan-Bellew, flying alone, was attacked by eight Fokkers (including two Eindekkers). In a running fight he shot down two Fokkers and possibly forced a third down and managed to escape by descending to 20 feet over the trenches. For these two actions Grattan-Bellew was awarded the MC. He was posted to command No.29 Squadron, then flying D.H.2s at Abeele, an appointment he held until March 1917.

GRAY, Fg Off Kenneth William, RAF. 127525. Pilot. Gray, from Basford, Newcastle-under-Lyme, had served as a sergeant pilot with No.85 Squadron during the Battle of Britain. He was commissioned in June 1942 and came to No.25 Squadron shortly afterwards to fly Mosquitos. He was killed, probably in action, on 9th June 1944 while with the Squadron, but has no known grave. He is remembered on the Runnymede Memorial, Panel 206.

GREAVES, Sqn Ldr Douglas Haig, RAF. Served on Squadron as pilot from 1941 to 1943 at Wittering, Ballyhalbert and Church Fenton (Beaufighter and Mosquitos), and again from 1944 to 1946 at Coltishall and Castle Camps (Mosquitos). *Member of Association.*

GREIG, Capt Oscar, RFC, served on No.25 Squadron as a pilot and flight commander in 1916-1917 at Auchel on F.E.2bs. While flying with Lieutenant John Eric MacLennan as observer on 24th January 1917, they were attacked and shot down by Manfred von Richthofen in an Albatros DIII and crash-landed behind the German lines west of Vimy. Both the British officers were wounded and taken prisoner.

HAINE, Plt Off (later Gp Capt, OBE, DFC, FBIM) Richard Cummins. RAF Pilot. Born, 1-10-16. Haine learned to fly while still at school. He joined the RAF as an NCO pilot in 1935 and the following year attended No.11 FTS Shawbury. He came to No.25 Squadron at Hawkinge at the age of 20 and was considered sufficiently proficient to join the Squadron's aerobatic team for the 1937 Hendon display, flying Fury IIs. He subsequently flew Demons, Gladiators and Blenheims with the Squadron and was still with it at the outbreak of War. He flew the first defensive night patrol of the War on the night of 4th September 1939, and was captain of one of No.25 Squadron's Blenheims which, with six others from No.601 Squadron, attacked the German seaplane base at Borkum on 28th December 1939 – the first fighter attack on Germany of the War. He was commissioned on 1st April 1940 and posted away to No.600 Squadron at Manston. He was later a flight commander on No.68 Squadron and commanded No.488 (New Zealand) Squadron. In September 1945 he was appointed station commander at Kai Tak, Hong Kong. He retired from the Service on 1st October 1970 (after being appointed OBE, 1-1-62).

HALLINGS-POTT, Sqn Ldr John Robert, DSO, RAF. Pilot and commanded No.25 Squadron from January 1939 until May 1940. He led No.25 and No.601 Squadrons in the first air attack on German territory in the Second World War, with the raid on the German seaplane base at Borkum of 28th November 1939, for which he was awarded the DSO. He retired as an Air Vice-Marshal, CBE, DSO, AFC, on 13th July 1957.

HARCOURT-SMITH, Flt Lt Gilbert, RAF. Pilot. Was posted to the Squadron on 20th September 1927 having previously flown 783 hours, mostly on transport aircraft (Vimys, Vernons and Virginias). He attended armament practice camp between 10th and 28th September 1928, having been appointed a flight commander. He was a member of the Grebe formation Air Drill and aerobatic teams and participated in the AOC Inspection aerobatic display on 2nd May 1929. It was said that 'if the Squadron gave an outstanding aerobatic display at Hendon that year it would be first to be equipped with a new fighter'. During the course of practising the display routine, Harcourt-Smith reached his 1,000 flying hours. He participated in the Hendon Display on 13th July and two days later flew to Sutton Bridge for the annual armament camp. He was posted to flying boats at Calshot, and afterwards served with Nos.201 and 205 Squadrons. On leaving No.25 Squadron, his flying was assessed as 'Above the Average'. He retired from the Service as an Air-Vice Marshal, CB, CBE, MVO, on 1st November 1955. (Logbooks examined at RAF Museum).

HARRY, Sgt Peter D, RAF. Served on Squadron from 1973 to 1976 at Bruggen (Bloodhound SAMs) *Member of Association.*

HASLAM, Flt Lt W Geoffrey, OBE, DFC, RAF. Navigator Radar. Served on Squadron from 1943 to 1944 at Church Fenton, Acklington and Coltishall. Was Squadron Leader Joe Singleton's Nav Rad on the occasion (March 1944) when, flying from Coltishall, they destroyed three Junkers Ju 188s in a single night defence sortie. (Mosquitos) *Member of Association.*

HEMMING, Major Hank, RCAF. Pilot on No.25 Sqn (Exchange Posting), Javelins at Waterbeach, 1958-1960.

HERRICK, Plt Off (later Flt Lt) Michael James, DFC AND BAR, RAF. 33566. Pilot. New Zealander. Born in Hastings, New Zealand on 5-5-21. He applied for and was granted a cadetship at the RAF College, Cranwell, and sailed for England on 9th March 1939 and was granted a permanent commission on 7th March 1940, joining No.25 Squadron ten days later. On the night of 4th September, while flying a Blenheim with Sgt J S Pugh as his gunner, he destroyed two Heinkel He 111s, the second breaking up after a burst fired from less than thirty yards. He destroyed a third on the night of 13th September and was awarded the DFC (24-9-40). He may have destroyed an enemy aircraft in December and, after converting to Beaufighters, damaged a Junkers Ju 88 on 9th May 1941, and destroyed another on 22nd June. He left No.25 Squadron in October 1941 and returned to New Zealand. He commanded No.15 Squadron, RNZAF, flying P-40s from Fiji and destroying several Japanese aircraft. He later returned to the UK and was awarded a BAR to his DFC (10-2-44). He joined No.302 (Polish) Squadron, flying Mosquitos, but was shot down during an attack on Aalborg airfield on 16th June 1944. He and his navigator baled out too low over the sea and were lost. Herrick's body was recovered and is buried in the Military Cemetery at Friedrichshafen.

HILL, Sgt (later Flt Lt) Arnold Maurice, DFC, RAF. 121333. Air Gunner. Arnold Hill was with No.25 Squadron in June 1940 and continued to serve with the squadron until 1942. During the Battle of Britain he flew in Blenheims (qualifying for the Clasp) and remained after the Squadron converted to Beaufighters. He was commissioned Pilot Officer on 1st May 1942 and was awarded the DFC (2-2-43) by which time he had shot down two enemy aircraft at night. He qualified as a Specialist Armament Officer and was released from the Service as a Flight Lieutenant in 1945. KGW. *Member of Association.*

HOGG, Plt Off Douglas William, RAF. 77977. Pilot. At the age of 23, Hogg joined No.25 Squadron during the Battle of Britain on 1st September 1940 at Martlesham Heath. He was killed three days later when his aircraft was shot down over North Weald by an RAF Hurricane. His gunner, Sgt Edwin Powell (*qv*), baled out unhurt. The Blenheim crashed near Greensted Green, and Plt Off Hogg is buried in Eastwood Cemetery, Glasgow.

HOLLIS, Sgt (later W/Off) Ernest James, DFC, RAF. 970073. Aircrew. Sgt Hollis joined No.25 Squadron on 30th September 1940 and flew in Blenheims during the Battle of Britain. He remained with the Squadron until 1st July 1942 having converted to Beaufighters and was promoted Warrant Officer on that day. He was posted to No.141 Squadron later and was awarded the DFC (12-12-44). He was released from the RAF in 1945 and died on 27th January 1975.

HOLLOWAY, Sgt (later Sqn Ldr, OBE) Sydney Victor, RAF. 121329. Pilot Sgt Holloway joined the RAFVR in March 1938 aged 20 and received his flying training with No.3 FTS, South Cerney, converted to Blenheims with No.5 OTU, Aston Down. He joined No.25 Squadron at Martlesham Heath on 6th July 1940 and flew throughout the Battle of Britain. His first combat victory was scored (after the Battle) on 15th November when he destroyed a Heinkel He 111 at night After flying Beaufighters for more than a year, he left the Squadron in May 1942 on being commissioned. After a year as a flying instructor he was posted to No.85 Squadron with whom he destroyed a Ju 88 on 8th October 1943 while flying a Mosquito. After the War he remained in the Service in ground appointments and was appointed an OBE for work done during the Berlin Airlift. He retired from the Service on 2nd March 1968 as a Squadron Leader was is included in the Retired List of 1990.

HOLT, Major Felton Vesey, DSO, RFC (later Air Vice-Marshal, DSO, CMG, RAF). It is well known that No.25 (Fighter) Squadron was formed at Montrose on 25th September 1915, comprised largely of the instructors formerly on No.6 (Reserve) Squadron. But what of No.25 Squadron's first Commanding Officer? He was surely one whose career took him at lightning speed up the ladder of promotion and, but for a tragic accident, might well have commanded Fighter or Bomber Command – at least during the Second World War.

Felton Vesey Holt was the third son of Sir Vesey Holt, KBE, born on 23rd February 1886. All four brothers were to enjoy distinguished careers; Martin Drummond Vesey, the eldest, followed his father into banking; however, despite not being a 'military' man, he was a member of the British Olympic Fencing Team (Epée) in 1908, 1912, 1920 and 1924, as well as being the Epée Champion of England; he was still living during the 1950s. The second son, Reginald Vesey Holt, joined the Royal Navy, and at the end of the Second World War was a Vice-Admiral, CB, DSO, MVO. The youngest son, Alwyn Vesey, was commissioned into the 1st Battalion, The Black Watch, was wounded early in the Kaiser's War, then seconded to the RFC in which he rose to Lieut-Col (Wing Commander), DSO, Officer of *Legion d'Honneur*, and Mentioned in Despatches three times.

Felton Vesey Holt entered Eton College in 1898, and left in 1903, entering the RMA Sandhurst in 1905. He was commissioned into the Oxfordshire and Buckinghamshire Light Infantry the following year. He became 'interested' in flying and took a course in flying (at his own expense) with the Bristol Flying Club at Brooklands on Boxkites and was granted the RAeC Aviator's Certificate No.312 on 1st October 1912. He applied for and obtained a secondment to the RFC as a Lieutenant in 1913, joining No.4 Squadron in 1914, to fly B.E.2s.

He accompanied the Squadron to France on the outbreak of War, being then employed in flying *ad hoc* reconnaissance patrols. On 22nd January 1915, while flying alone, he spotted a formation of German aircraft beginning a bombing raid on the port of Dunkirk, and immediately flew in to attack, armed only with a cavalry rifle; as he attacked an aircraft (which crashed, its crew being captured) he was joined by two other No.4 Squadron B.E.2s. and the enemy aircraft hurriedly withdrew. For his single-handed attack on the twelve aircraft, he was awarded an immediate DSO, and was Mentioned in Despatches. This is generally recognised as having been the first confirmed air combat victory between aeroplanes in history – no other air force in the world having authoritatively disputed the fact.

Holt was recalled home in April and, after a spell of leave, he was posted to Montrose, Angus, where he took command of No.6 (Reserve) Squadron, then engaged in pilot training on a variety of aircraft. Montrose was however prone to long spells of bad weather and, without any form of weather forecasting, the flying syllabus suffered frequent delays, often lasting weeks on end. Recognising that, for the time being at any rate, such was the backlog of partly trained student pilots, the War Department decided to end the current programme and ordered Holt to examine the possibility of forming an operational Squadron, composed of No.6 (Reserve) Squadron's flying instructors, all of whom had completed the CFS course. Holt suggested also including those students who had almost completed their training, and during August undertook a much more strenuous flying regime, authorising flying in doubtful weather, even if only for fifteen to twenty minutes per flight, simply to give all pilots the experience of flying in very restricted visibility. Within three weeks all the pilots on the current course had reached the necessary standard for conversion to advanced training standards. Moreover, all his pilots, instructors and students alike, had acquired plenty of poor weather flying.

He reported the progress to the War Department and on 25th September Holt was given authority to form No.25 Squadron at Montrose and take the necessary steps to create the ground personnel infrastructure of a fully operational fighter squadron, with the intention of equipping it with D.H.2 single-seat fighters.

The Squadron moved south to Thetford, Norfolk, late in December, but by then production of the D.H.2 had fallen behind so much that only No.24 Squadron was equipped immediately with that aircraft, and No.25 Squadron received F.E.2b two-seaters in January 1916, and, after giving the entire Squadron leave, Holt took No.25 Squadron across the Channel to St Omer, pending its move to the Western Front.

So impressed was the Air Department with the speedy and efficient preparation of No.25 Squadron that Holt was summarily ordered home to begin the training of two further fighter Squadrons. Because of the increase in German airship attacks on Britain at this time, these Squadrons remained in England while Holt began evolving regular night flying patrols, as well as laying the foundations of night interception tactics – for which he was Mentioned in Despatches three times, before being promoted Brevet Major in the Field, and promoted Lieut-Col (Temporary) and given command of No.3 Wing in France, during 1917. The more famous early night fighter pilots, Capts G W Murlis-Green and C J Quintin Brand, later acknowledged that all the successful night fighting operational tactics were based entirely on Holt's pioneering night flying procedures.

Early in 1918 Holt was promoted Acting Brigadier-General (at the age of 31), the youngest in the new RAF's first Air Force list, and was afterwards posted to the Air Ministry with the substantive rank of Gp Capt. In 1919 he was made CMG. In 1923 he was appointed Commandant of the Central Flying School as an Air Commodore, remaining until late in 1925, during which period CFS Course Nos.6-12 (approximately) attended the School. In 1927 he was appointed SASO at HQ Air Defence of Great Britain as an Air Vice-Marshal, formalising the first Night Fighter Defence system, based on Nos.3 and 17 Squadrons at Upavon for night defence of the Industrial Midlands.

Felton Vesey Holt still held this appointment on 23rd February 1931 (his 45th birthday) when he was killed 'in a flying accident' at Tangmere. It is known that No.1 Squadron was giving a public display of formation Siskin flying that day when two Siskins collided and crashed (as No.1 Squadron didn't possess a two-seat Siskin, Felton would not have been flying), and it is tentatively assumed that the Siskins' wreckage fell among the spectators, and that Felton was among those killed.

At the date of his death, Holt was under notice for promotion to Air Marshal and a position (not divulged in traceable records) on the Air Staff. There is no doubt but that his Commands and experience had marked him down for the highest appointments in the RAF, possibly Commander-in-Chief, Fighter or Bomber Command – or even higher. He was several years senior to, and had been the principal mentor of such officers as Portal, Leigh-Mallory, Harris and others who were to achieve Air Rank and top appointments during the Second World War.

Felton had married in 1926, and a son and a daughter had been born before the date of his death. However, these dates are not consistent with any 'Vesey Holt' being among those who subsequently entered Eton or the Royal Air Force, although it seems that several nephews (sons of his brothers) went to Eton, and the 'Vesey Holt' progeny (as well as the Eton College Archivist) have provided most of the material on which this brief biography is based. Two officers, who knew Felton 'fairly well' in the middle and late 1920s, both remarked on his short stature (about 5ft 6in tall), his astonishing energy, constant optimism and *bonhomie*. Yet he was modest, and always anxious to afford credit to others. He was clearly devoted to his family, and admired his parents beyond all. His seven-times Mentions in Despatches are evidence of the esteem held for him by his superior officers.

HOOPER, Plt Off (later Flt Lt) Beresford Gwynne, RAF. 40707. Pilot. Hooper joined the RAF on a short service commission in March 1938 and after attending No.11 FTS at Shawbury was posted to No.25 Squadron at Hawkinge in December that year. He flew Gladiators and Blenheims, and was one of the first Squadron pilots to convert to the Beaufighter early in September 1940. On the 15th of that month his Beaufighter, R2067, crashed on the approach to Biggin Hill, the cause never being established. Hooper survived but the second crewmember was killed. He transferred to the Admin branch late in 1942 and in 1945 moved to the Fighter Control branch in 1945 as a flight lieutenant. He retired from the Service in the early 1950s.

HOUGHTON, Flt Lt (later Wg Cdr) Roy, MBE, RAF. Served on Squadron during 1957 and 1958 (Meteor NF) at Tangmere, and from 1961 to 1963 (Javelins) at Waterbeach and Leuchars. *Member of Association.*

HOWE, Plt Off (later Fg Off) Bernard, RAF. 33427. Pilot. From Wadebridge in Cornwall, Bernard Howe was a Cranwell cadet who graduated in April 1939 and joined No.25 Squadron in September that year, flying Blenheims during the Battle of Britain. (According to his contemporaries at Cranwell, he had always expressed his determination 'to go to No.25 Squadron' having, as a schoolboy, watched the Squadron's displays at Hendon.) He was promoted Flying Officer at the end of the Battle of Britain and was posted early in 1941 to No.263 Squadron to fly Whirlwinds. He was killed on 20 April 1941, aged 22, and is buried in All Saints' churchyard at Wittering.

HOY, Wg Cdr W, DFC, AFC, RAF. Born, 23-12-18, Hoy was commissioned on 8th October 1939 and commanded No.25

Squadron from April to December 1945 at Castle Camps (Mosquito NF.30s and 36s). He retired from the Service as a Wing Commander on 5th April 1966. *Member of Association.*

HOYLE, Cpl A, RAF. Served on Squadron as Airframe Fitter from 1940 to 1942 at Martlesham Heath, North Weald, Debden, Wittering and Ballyhalbert (Blenheims and Beaufighters). *Member of Association.*

HUGHES, Flt Lt W D, RAF. Served on Squadron from 1953 to 1957 at West Malling (Vampire and Meteor NF). *Member of Association.*

HUNTER-TOD, Fg Off John Hunter (later Air Marshal Sir Hunter, KBE, CB. This officer was intimately involved with the early operational use of airborne intercept radar, and was commissioned into the RAF direct from Cambridge in 1940 with a Master's degree. He flew with No.23 Squadron during the Battle of Britain (thereby qualifying for the Clasp), and began to formulate operational procedures while operating night fighter radar. He moved to Wittering early in 1941, at the time No.25 Squadron was based there, and although not strictly a member of the Squadron, became Wg Cdr David Atcherley's (the Squadron's CO) 'unofficial nav-rad', sharing many of that officer's combat and other experiences in Beaufighters at that that time, including the major accident while landing at Wittering, from which he emerged little hurt. His official status at Wittering was 'Navigator, Station Flight, RAF Wittering, variously for operational purposes attached to No.25 Squadron'. He continued to serve in Fighter Command until posted to the Middle East. He was promoted Gp Capt in 1957 and became Director, Guided Weapons (Air), Ministry of Aviation, in 1962 and, as an Air Commodore, Air Officer Engineering, RAF Germany, in 1965. He was appointed Head of the Engineering Branch and Director General of Engineering, RAF, in 1970. He retired from the Service as an Air Marshal on 30th April 1973.

HUTCHINGS, Fg Off Henry L J, RAF. Served on Squadron from 1952 to 1954 at West Malling (Vampire NF). *Member of Association.*

HUTCHINGS, Flt Lt J P, RAF. Served on Squadron ('A' Flight, from 1989 to 1991 at Leeming. (Tornados). *Member of Association.*

JAMES, Flt Lt (later Sqn Ldr) H G, AFC AND BAR, DFM, RAF. 173932. Pilot. Born on 3-10-21, and joining the RAF at the age of 18 (by misrepresenting his age), James served as a sergeant pilot of Bombay transports with No.216 Squadron in the Western Desert during the early part of the War. At the age of 21, he was pilot of a Bombay briefed to carry Lt-Gen W H E Gott forward to assume command of the British Eighth Army when the aircraft was attacked by a number of Messerschmitt Bf 109s; the aircraft was forced down in the desert, James being the only survivor; he was discovered still alive in the cockpit of the burnt-out transport several days later. He was commissioned (12-2-44) and, with No.24 Squadron), became personal pilot to the C-in-C Transport Command, carrying numerous VIPs from the UK on visits overseas. James joined No.25 Squadron in 1951 as a Flight Lieutenant, and was appointed a flight commander flying Vampire night fighters from West Malling (by which time he had already flown 5,000 hours). He left the Squadron in 1954 and subsequently received an exchange posting to the USAF to fly F-89 Scorpions in Alaska, after which he returned to the UK as a Squadron Leader to fly Javelins. He retired from the Service on 31st July 1965. *Committee Member of Association.*

JOHNSON, LAC John E, RAF. Served on No.25 Squadron from 1941 to 1944 at Wittering, Ballyhalbert, Church Fenton, Aclington and Coltishall (Beaufighters and Mosquitos). *Member of Association.*

JOHNSON, Sqn Ldr Michael C, RAF. Served on No.25 Squadron at Leeming from 1989 to 1992, 'A' Flight. (Tornados). *Member of Association.*

KER-RAMSAY, Flt Lt (later Sqn Ldr, MBE), Robert Gerald, RAF. 37321. Pilot. Ker-Ramsay joined the RAF in 1935 on a short service commission, received flying training with No.5 FTS at Sealand and was posted to No.17 Squadron. He became a flying instructor with No.8 FTS in 1938, but is believed to have been with the A & AEE at Martlesham Heath shortly before the War, joining No.25 Squadron's experimental radar flight before the end of 1939. It is evident that he became one of the most adept pilots of the AI Mark III-equipped Blenheims, and when the Fighter Interception Unit was formed the CO at Shoreham (G.P. Chamberlain, ex-No.25 Squadron, *qv*) specifically asked that Ker-Ramsay should be posted in. Ker-Ramsay, who had already qualified for the Battle of Britain Clasp, joined the FIU on 13th July 1940 and took part in numerous night sorties aimed at evolving AI-assisted tactics. On the night of 13th September, however, during a long stern chase, his Blenheim (Z5721) was shot down off the French coast near Calais. The crew baled out safely and all three were made POWs. While in Stalag Luft III, Ker-Ramsay played a major part in the various tunnel-escape plans, including the tunnels Tom, Dick and Harry. He organised and controlled the exit in the mass break-out of March 1944. The tunnel was discovered before he himself managed to escape. He was made an MBE (28-6-46) for his services as a POW, and retired from the Service as a Squadron Leader in 1948. (He had been promoted Wg Cdr on 1st June 1942 while in Stalag Luft III.) (His name does not appear in the Retired List of April 1962.)

KERRISON, Flt Lt H R, RAF. Served on No.25 Squadron, from 1942 to 1944 at Church Fenton, Acklington and Coltishall (Beaufighters and Mosquitos). *Member of Association.*

KERRISON, Cpl M P, WAAF, Served on No.25 Squadron from 1943 to 1944 at Church Fenton, Acklington and Coltishall (Mosquitos). *Member of Association.*

KING, Flt Lt John, RAF. Served on No.25 Squadron c.1951-53. West Malling; Vampire NF.10s. Navigator Radar. John King had served with Bomber Command during the Second World War, being shot down over enemy territory. The only survivor of his crew, he was taken prisoner and incarcerated in Stalag Luft III (being mentioned in Brickhill's book *Escape or Die*). He became involved in 'The Great Escape' from that POW camp, but was still in the tunnel when the escape was discovered. After the War he left the Service and returned to his peacetime profession as a school teacher. Dissatisfied with the pacifist environment that he found in post-War Britain, he returned to the RAF and joined No.25 Squadron as a navigator-radar in about 1951. In the course of a Lightstrike exercise at West Malling in 1953, he accepted an invitation to fly in the flare-dropping Lancaster (supplied by Coastal Command). On the way to the exercise area in the Thames Estuary, one of the Lancaster's flares ignited and the pilot opted to return to West Malling. However, not only was the pilot unable to jettison the blazing flare but the remaining flares caught fire and, blinded by the smoke and glare, the pilot attempted to crash land beside the runway but over-ran into an orchard. Not being regular crew members, the four passengers from No.25 Squadron had to take up makeshift crash stations, but all were killed. (The Lancaster's crew survived). John was an extremely popular member of the Squadron, well remembered for his charm and modesty, and respected for his wartime experiences and his outstanding professionalism.

KNIGHT, Flt Sgt Thomas, RAF. Served on Squadron at Wittering, Ballyhalbert and Church Fenton from 1941 to 1942. (Beaufighters). *Member of Association.*

LALLY, Lieut. Conrad Tolendal, RFC (Canadian), served as a pilot with No.25 Squadron at Auchel, France, in 1917 on B.E.2ds. While flying with 2/Lieut L F Williams (observer) shot down an Albatros DIII out of control near Lille on 7th June, and on the same sortie destroyed another Albatros west of Lille five minutes later. Having converted to the D.H.4, and flying with 2/Lieut L F Williams (observer), he shot down an Albatros DV over Perenchies on 5th August. On 3rd September, (with 2/Lieut B J Blackett as observer), forced down an Albatros DV out of control during a bombing sortie. Two days later, again with Blackett, he forced down another Albatros DV, this time near Douai.

LEGGETT, Sqn Ldr (later Wg Cdr) Richard W, RAF. Pilot. Commanded No.25 Squadron at West Malling from 1950 to 1952. Retired from RAF, 1- 4-68, as Wg Cdr. (Mosquito NF.36s and Vampire NF.10s). *Member of Association.*

LEITH, 2/Lieut J L, RFC. Served on No.25 Sqn as a pilot at Auchel, France (F.E.2b). While flying with Sgt L S Court (observer) on 22nd October 1916, shot down a single-seat scout near Seclin. On 9th November, with Sgt L S Court (observer), shot down out of control an Albatros D(?) Promoted Captain and flying with Sgt Leonard Emsden (observer), shot down an Albatros DIII near Arras on 17th March 1917; on 1st May, again with Sergeant Emsden, shot down an Albatros DIII on a dawn patrol near Lens, and the same evening, on an escort sortie, shot down an Albatros DIII in flames over the Bois de Bernard.

LEZEMORE, Flt Lt R B. Served on No.25 Sqn at Hawkinge (Furies), 1933-1937. *Member of Association.*

LIDDELL, Plt Off Alvar Q, RAFVR. Squadron Intelligence Officer for much of the Second World War. Subsequently became one of the best-known BBC news readers between 1945 and c.1955. Died c. 1965?

LINDLEY, LAC Wilfred E, RAF. Served on No.25 Squadron from 1940 to 1944 at North Weald, Debden, Wittering, Ballyhalbert, Church Fenton, Acklington and Coltishall. (Blenheims, Beaufighters and Mosquitos). *Member of Association.*

LOXTON, Sqn Ldr (later Wg Cdr, AFC) Wilfred William, RAF. 36032. Born, 20-1-09, Loxton entered the RAF as a boy apprentice at the age of 16. On leaving Halton, he applied for pilot training, was accepted and learned to fly at Sealand. He joined No.32 Squadron at Kenley in 1931, was commissioned and posted to No.43 Squadron at Tangmere in 1935. He flew with No.822 (Fleet Spotter Reconnaissance) Squadron at Tangmere (and aboard HMS *Furious*) from 1936 until 1939 when he was posted as a flying instructor to No.5 FTS. He commanded No.25 Squadron at North Weald from 1st June until 24th September 1940 during the Battle of Britain (Clasp). Loxton was posted to Canada in December 1940 for flying training duties and returned to Britain in 1943, being awarded the AFC (1-1-45). He retired from the RAF on 31-5-57 after 32 years' service, and was still included in the Retired List of 1990.

LUCKING, At Lt (later Sqn Ldr, AFC) John W, RAF. Born 16th March 1932. Served with No.25 Squadron between 1959 and 1962 at Waterbeach and Leuchars (Javelins). Retired from Service as Sqn Ldr, AFC, 16-3-89.

LUSK, Fg Off (later Flt Lt) Harold Stewart, RNZAF. Pilot. Born in Auckland, New Zealand, on 7-8-18, Lusk came to England and went up to Oxford in 1937, joining the University Air Squadron and entering the RAF on a short service commission. He served as a pilot on Blenheims with No.25 Squadron in 1940 (and qualified for the Battle of Britain Clasp). In August 1941 he transferred to the Flying Control Branch and later returned to New Zealand with the RNZAF. On arriving home he transferred to the New Zealand Reserve. He was appointed a QC on 23rd October 1973.

McCUBBIN, 2/Lieut G R, RFC. McCubbin was a pilot of No.25 Squadron, flying from Auchel, France, shortly before the Battle of the Somme. In the late evening of 18th June 1916, flying with Cpl W A Waller, he attacked a Fokker E.III over the front lines and shot it down, Waller making excellent use of his wide arc of fire in the nose of the F.E. It transpired that the enemy pilot was Max Immelmann, the much-haunted German fighter ace of the early War period. The Germans have always claimed that Immelmann shot off his own propeller (thereby destroying the engine) and was not shot down. However, this has been discounted on the evidence of McCubbin's account of the fight and the fact that Immelmann had made a much publicised statement that he would never be shot down; nor have any substantiated eye-witness accounts ever supported the German claim, whereas observers state that Immelmann's Fokker appeared to break up under the onslaught of Waller's machine gun, the German aircraft not at that moment being in a position to be firing its gun.

McILWRATH, Flt Lt (later Sqn Ldr) J, RAF. 181685. Navigator Radar. Served as Nav Rad Leader on No.25 Squadron between c. 1951-1954 at West Malling. (Vampire NF) and c.1957-1960 (Meteor NF and Javelin FAW).

McRAE, Fg Off B A, RAF. Served with No.25 Squadron from 1944 to 1945 at Castle Camps. (Mosquitos). *Member of Squadron Association.*

McROBB, Sqn Ldr Keith D, AFC, RAF. Served on No.25 Squadron from 1959 to 1962 at Waterbeach and Leuchars (Javelins); retired from Service, 8-11-87. *Member of Association.*

MARSHALL, Flt Lt Alfred Ernest, DFC, DFM, RAF. 47124. Pilot. Marshall, of Hitchin, Hertfordshire, had served with No.73 Squadron in the Battle of France and Battle of Britain, flying Hurricanes. He accompanied that Squadron to the Middle East soon after the Battle of Britain, reaching Egypt by way of Takoradi and the trans-Africa ferry route. He later joined No.250 Squadron, also in the Middle East. By the time he returned to Britain in the late summer of 1942 he had destroyed eight German and Italian aircraft, had been awarded the DFM (6-6-41), was commissioned Pilot Officer on 11-8-41, and was awarded the DFC (6-10-42). On arrival in the UK, he was posted to No.51 OTU at Cranfield as a flying instructor, and joined No.25 Squadron, flying Mosquitos from Coltishall, in July 1944 as a Flight Lieutenant. On 27th November that year he was killed, aged 29, in a flying accident in Mosquito NF.XVII MT472, and was buried in Hitchin Cemetery, his home town.

MARTIN, Wg Cdr A Michael, RAF. Navigator. Commanded the Squadron from 1989 to 1992 at Leeming (Tornados). Retired from the RAF to enter the Avionics Industry. *Founder Member of Association, being elected its President in 1999.*

MATHEWS, Sqn Ldr Kenneth, RAF. 82954. Pilot. Mathews flew Blenheims with No.23 Squadron during the latter half of the Battle of Britain, and was promoted Flight Lieutenant on 21st July 1942. In September that year he was posted to command No.534 (Turbinlite) Squadron at Tangmere, joining No.25 Squadron at Church Fenton in January 1943 as a Squadron Leader aged 27. Flying Mosquito IIF Intruder, DZ689, Mathews failed to return from a bomber support sortie over Germany on 20th October 1943, and is now known to be buried in Sneek General Cemetery, Holland.

MEADOWS, LAC Robert E, RAF. Served on No.25 Squadron from 1941 to 1944 at Wittering, Ballyhalbert, Church Fenton, Acklington and Coltishall (Beaufighters and Mosquitos). *Member of Association.*

MEDWORTH, Sgt (later Flt Lt) John Charles Oswald, RAF, 146294. Navigator Radar. Medworth joined No.25 Squadron at North Weald in September 1940 for flying duties in Blenheims, and later Beaufighters. He was commissioned Pilot Officer on 25th April 1943, and released from the RAF in 1946 as a Flight Lieutenant.

MELSOM, Flt Sgt J Served on No.25 Sqn at North Coates, 1967-1969 (Bloodhound SAMs). *Member of Association.*

MILEY, Plt Off (later Fg Off) Miles John. RAF. 33345. Pilot. Miley joined the Service in September 1936 with a cadetship at the Royal Air Force College, Cranwell, from which he graduated in 1938 and came to No.25 Squadron at Hawkinge on 30th July that year. He was flying Blenheims with the Squadron as a Flying Officer at the beginning of the Battle of Britain and was one of the first pilots to convert to the Beaufighter. He was pilot of Beaufighter R2067 on the night of 15th September which crashed near Biggin Hill, it being assumed that the aircraft had been in collision with one of the Squadron's Blenheims (see also Fg Off H.M.S. Lambert). Aged 22 at the time of his death, Miley lies buried in St Andrew's churchyard, North Weald Bassett, Essex.

MITCHELL, Sqn Ldr (later Wg Cdr, DFC), Henry Maynard. DFC, RAuxAF. Pilot. Born on 16th April 1914 and educated at Harrow and Birmingham University, Henry Mitchell joined the Auxiliary Air Force, learning to fly with No.605 (County of Warwick) Squadron on Hawker Harts and Hinds. He was called to full-time service in August 1939 and served during the Norwegian campaign of 1940. He was promoted Squadron Leader on 1st September 1940 and assumed command of No.25 Squadron from Sqn Ldr W W Loxton (*qv*) at North Weald on the 25th of that month. He was awarded the DFC (22-10-40) and was posted away the following January. (He subsequently formed and commanded No.125 Squadron at Colerne with Defiants, and later served in the Middle East. He was released from the RAF in 1946 as a Wing Commander).

MOIR, Flt Lt Iain W, RAF. Served with No.25 Squadron from 1953 to 1956 (Vampire and Meteor NF) at West Malling and Tangmere. *Member of Association.*

MONK, Plt Off Ernest William John, RAF. 44403. Pilot. Monk came to No.25 Squadron at Martlesham Heath on 12th August 1940 on commissioning. He flew with the Squadron throughout the remainder of the Battle of Britain. but was killed when his aircraft crashed into the sea shortly after take-off on 21st November 1940. Neither his body or that of his air gunner, Sgt E Powell, was recovered and Monk is remembered on the Runnymede Memorial, Panel 9.

MOORE, Flt Lt Kenneth, RAF. Served on No.25 Squadron at Leeming (Tornados), 1993-1996. *Member of Association.*

MORGAN, Flt Lt V J, RAF. Served on No.25 Squadron from 1950 to 1952 at West Malling (Mosquito NF.36s and Vampire NF.10s). Retired from the RAF as Wg Cdr, 5-7-82. *Member of Association.*

MORRIS, Capt J F, MC, RFC. Pilot and Flight Commander on No.25 Squadron at Auchel, France, 1917 (D.H.4s). (All the following sorties were flown with Lieut D L Burgess as observer.) On 7th July on a bombing sortie, shot down an Albatros west of Lille. On 11th July, on a bombing sortie, shot down an Albatros DV out of control west of Douai. On 22nd July, on a bombing sortie, shot down an Albatros DV in flames. On 5th August, on a bombing raid, shot down an Albatros DIII. On 14th August, while on patrol, shot down two Albatros DIIIs. On 15th August, while on a bombing/reconnaissance sortie, shot down an Albatros DV over La Bassée.

MORRISON, Flt Lt Donald, RAF. Served with No.25 Squadron, 'A' Flight, at Leeming from 1989 to 1992. (Tornados). *Member of Association.*

MOSSMAN, Flt Lt G Keith, RAF. Served with No.25 Squadron from 1960 to 1962 at Waterbeach and Leuchars (Javelins). Retired from Service as Gp Capt, CBE, 1-2-78. *Member of Association.*

NEILL, Flt Lt (later Sqn Ldr) Archie, RAF. Archie Neill was educated at Ross High School in East Lothian and Edinburgh University, joining the RAF in 1983. After training, he became a Qualified Flying Instructor on the BAe Hawk at Valley, gaining over 1,100 hours on type. In 1989 he undertook his operational conversion on to the Tornado F3 and joined No.25 (Fighter) Squadron on reformation at Leeming in 1989 to serve a three-year tour with 'B' Flight. In 1991 he was appointed the RAF's Tornado F3 Display pilot, flying with Flight Lieutenant Jim Brown. *Member of Association.*

NESBITT-DUFORT, Fg Off John (later Wg Cdr, DSO). Trained on Siskins at Grantham (Spittalgate), he joined No.25 Squadron at Hawkinge with a Short Service Commission late in 1931, joining 'A' Flight under Flt Lt Swann, but then moving shortly afterwards to 'C' Flight under Flt Lt C R Hancock. After about a year he was posted to Leuchars for a spell with the Fleet Air Arm before returning to No.25 Squadron in 1933, by which time the Siskins had been discarded in favour of the Hawker Fury. Having flown Nimrods with the Fleet Air Arm, he was soon at home in the Fury and, in due course became a member of the Squadron's aerobatic team, attending the Hendon displays in 1934, 1935 and 1936. Nesbitt-Dufort was then transferred to the RAF Reserve of Officers.

At the outbreak of war and after a visit to the Central Flying School, he became a flying instructor with No.2 SFTS at Brize Norton before joining No.23 Squadron on Blenheims for a short spell on intruder operations. He was then recruited to join No.1419 (Special Duties) Flight at Stradishall for clandestine operations over France, flying agents and equipment to the Resistance forces in Whitleys, Lysanders and Hudsons, often landing in isolated fields to pick up agents and return them to Britain. On one occasion his Lysander was damaged and, after landing in France, was unable to return and he had to be concealed from the Germans by the French Resistance until another Lysander could land and return him to England. After the War he went into commercial flying, and wrote his autobiography *(Black Lysander* – see Bibliography), in which he recalls that his two periods, which he spent with No.25 Squadron, were 'the happiest days of my life'.

PASCOE, P W, (Rank not known) Served on No.25 Squadron from 1959 to 1960 at Leuchars (Javelins) and from 1965 to 1969 at North Coates (Bloodhound SAMs). *Member of Association.*

PATTINSON, Plt Off Aberconway John Sefton, RAF. 40563. Pilot. Chelsea-born Pattinson joined the RAF on a short service commission in December 1937, and after completing his flying training with No.5 FTS at Sealand joined No.25 Squadron at Hawkinge on 17th September 1938 to fly Gladiators and, later, Blenheims. Early in 1940 he was posted to No.23 Squadron and on 5th September to No.92 Squadron to fly Spitfires. On 12th October he was shot down and killed by a Messerschmitt Bf 109 over Hawkinge, his aircraft falling at Postling Wents. At the time of his death he was 21 and he is buried in Parkestone Cemetery, Poole, Dorset.

PICKLES, Fg Off Ronald, RAF. Served on No.25 Squadron from 1943 to 1946 at Coltishall, Castle Camps and Boxted. (Mosquitos). *Member of Association.*

PICKNETT, Flt Lt (later Wg Cdr, DFC) Alan I, RAF. 77615. Pilot. Served on No.25 Squadron from 1941 to 1943 at Wittering, Ballyhalbert and Church Fenton (Beaufighters and Mosquitos). Retired from Service as Wg Cdr, DFC, 28-1-68. *Member of Association.*

PLEASANCE, Sqn Ldr (later Gp Capt, OBE, DFC AND BAR) Harold Percival, RAF. Born 12-4-14, 'Flash' Pleasance was commissioned in the RAF on 11th May 1936 and was posted to command No.25 Squadron at Wittering in August 1941, then on Beaufighters. He later took the Squadron to Ballyhalbert and, in May 1942, to Church Fenton. He was posted away in September that year. By the end of the War he was a Group Captain, and retired in this rank on 1st December 1960. *Member of Association.*

POWELL, Sgt Edwin, RAF. 548940. Air Gunner. Sgt Powell joined No.25 Squadron at Martlesham Heath in September 1940. He flew defensive patrols during the remainder of the Battle of Britain, but was killed when his Beaufighter (being flown by Plt Off E.W. Monk, *qv*) crashed into the sea soon after take-off on 21st November 1940. His body was not recovered and he is remembered on the Runnymede Memorial, Panel 18.

PRESCOTT, Sqn Ldr John C, RAF. Served of No.25 Squadron at Leeming (Tornados). Two tours (1989-1992 and 1995-1996). *Member of Association.*

PUGH, Capt John Edward Pugh, RFC. Pilot and Flight Commander on No.25 Squadron, at Beauvois and Ruisseauville, France, during 1918 (D.H.4s). While on a bombing sortie, with 2/Lieut O S Hinson as observer, forced down an enemy scout out of control near La Jardinet on 13th January. On 27th March, with Sgt A H Muff as observer on a bombing sortie, forced down a Siemens Schuckert DIII at Foucaucourt. On 8th May, with 2/Lieut W Dixon as observer on a bombing escort sortie, destroyed a Pfalz and forced another down out of control near Thorout. On 5th June, while probably on a bombing sortie with Lieut S C Eschmann as observer, shot down a Rumpler C near Albert.

PUGH, Sgt (later Flt Lt, DFC) John Stewart, RAF. 120329. Air Gunner. Sgt Pugh joined No.25 Squadron in August 1940 from No.23 Squadron. He teamed up with the New Zealander, Plt Off M J Herrick (*qv*), in Blenheims, and was flying with him on the night of 4th September when they shot down two Heinkel He 111s (the second one breaking up after Pugh had fired from a range of less than 30 yards). These two men destroyed a third He 111 on the night of 15th September. After the Squadron had become fully converted on to Beaufighters, Pugh, as an air gunner, applied for transfer to bombers and was commissioned Pilot Officer on 13th March 1942. He served on Lancasters with No.149 Squadron at Methwold, being awarded the DFC (21-9-45). After the War he transferred to the Physical Fitness branch in the RAF Reserve of Officers and evidently retired as a Flight Lieutenant in 1954 or shortly after.

PULLEN, 2/Lieut H, RFC. Served as an observer with No.25 Squadron during 1918 at Ruisseauville, France, on D.H.4s. Pullen opened his score on 29th March by shooting down an unidentified German aircraft, his pilot on this occasion being 2/Lieut S Jones. His second victory was gained on 8th June when his pilot was Lieut W H G Milnes on a bombing sortie when an attacking Fokker DrI triplane was shot down between Lille and Tournai. On 24th June with Lieut L Young as pilot, again on a bombing sortie, they destroyed a Pfalz DIII near Lille. On 4th August the same crew destroyed another Pfalz DIII over Lille. In a bombing raid on 22nd August, Pullen and his pilot, Lieutenant J H Latchford, shot down a third Pfalz.

PYE, Sgt John Walter, RNZAF. 66503. (English-born New Zealander). Air gunner. Born on 15-11-17 at Aldbourne, Wiltshire, of New Zealand parents, Sgt Pye spent almost all his life in New Zealand (other than the War years). He was holidaying in England on the outbreak of war and was unable to return home, so joined the RAF on 11th September 1939. He came to No.25 Squadron in May 1940 as an Aircraftman (AC2) Air Gunner at North Weald, earning 4d per day flying pay. He was promoted Sergeant on the 27th. He flew in Blenheims until September but, with the arrival of the Beaufighter he remustered as Radio Observer, being retained in the operation of radar on the Squadron. He continued to fly in Beaufighters until May 1941 when he was commissioned Pilot Officer and posted to No.1453 (Turbinlite) Flight flying alongside No.25 Squadron at Wittering. In September 1942 Pye underwent training as a Specialist Armament Officer and as a Flight Lieutenant he was posted as Wing Armament Officer at Tangmere on 31st January 1944, responsible for four Typhoon squadrons. He was repatriated to New Zealand in May 1945 and joined the RNZAF Reserve in 1946.

RICHARDSON, 2/Lieut L L, MC, RFC. Pilot on No.25 Squadron during 1916-1917 at Auchel, France (F.E.2bs). While on an escort sortie with Sgt L S Court as observer, shot down a Fokker EIII monoplane in combat over Lens. On 20th July 1916 the same pilot and observer shot down another Fokker EIII, also in the Lens area. On 13th April 1917 Richardson's

F.E.2b was shot down by Ltn Karl Emil Schäfer of *Jasta* 11 behind the German lines. The pilot and his observer, 2/Lieut D C Woollen, were taken prisoner. By this date Richardson had achieved ten air combat victories.

ROBERTS, Sgt David Francis, RAF. 965482. WOp/Air Gunner. Joined No.25 Squadron in August 1940 at Martlesham Heath flying in Blenheims during the Battle of Britain. Underwent on-squadron training in use of AI radar and converted to Beaufighters, remaining with No.25 until he was killed on 3rd April 1941 when X7541 spun in while approaching to land at Wittering. He lies buried in All Saint's churchyard, Wittering. At the time of his death he was aged 32.

ROBERTS, Sqn Ldr Paul J, RAF. Served on No.25 Squadron at Leeming (Tornados). Two tours (1989-1992 and 1997-2000). *Member of Association.*

ROCKMINSKI, F/Sgt S (later Flt Lt S ROCKMINSTER), RAF. Pilot. *Né* Polish. Served on No.25 Squadron at West Malling from 1951 to 1954 (Vampire NF). *Member of Association.*

RODDAN, Fg Off S J, RAF. Served on No.25 Squadron from 1941 to 1944 at Wittering, Ballyhalbert, Church Fenton, Acklington and Coltishall (Beaufighters and Mosquitos). *Member of Association.*

ROFE, Fg Off (later Flt Lt) Bernard John, RAF. 40751. Pilot. From Douglas, Isle of Man, Bernard Rofe entered the RAF on a short service commission in March 1938, receiving his flying training with No.2 FTS at Brize Norton. He joined No.25 Squadron at Hawkinge on 17th December 1938. He flew Blenheims on operations during the Battle of Britain and on the night of 4th September 1940, while in a stern chase on an enemy bomber, the ground defences opened fire and severely damage his Blenheims tail (only a day after the Squadron had lost two Blenheims, shot down by RAF fighters). In another attack on a German bomber on 18th September, Rofe's Blenheim was badly damaged by the enemy's return fire. He left the Squadron in 1941 and was killed, aged 21, on 12th January 1942, and is buried in Sherwood Cemetery, Charlottetown, Canada.

ROSS, Sqn Ldr R M H, RAF. Jock Ross was born on 24th March 1907 and served with No.25 Squadron at Hawkinge from 1930 to 1932 at the time it was equipped with Siskins. He was commissioned on 30th July 1940 and retired as a Squadron Leader on 24th March 1956, his 49th birthday. *Member of Association.*

ROULSTONE, Capt Alexander, RFC. Pilot and Flight Commander on No.25 Squadron at Auchel, France (F.E.2bs). Flying with 2/Lieut E G Green (observer) on 6th April 1917 on an escort sortie, shot down an Albatros DIII in flames near Givenchy. On 24th April, again with Green as observer, destroyed an Albatros DIII over Billy-Montigny. On 21st May, during a reconnaissance sortie with Lieut H Cotton as observer, forced down an Albatros DIII out of control west of Lille. On 20th July, while providing cover for reconnaissance aircraft, with 2/Lieut L F Williams as observer, shot down an Albatros out of control. On 22nd July, with 2/Lt Donald William Taylor Fox as observer, shot down an Albatros DV in flames.

SANDERSON, Sqn Ldr Steve P, RAF. Served on No.25 Squadron at Leeming (Tornados) 1989-1991. *Member of Association.*

SCLANDERS, Plt Off Kirkpatrick MacLure, RAF. 37301. Canadian. Pilot. Sclanders was born at Saskatoon, Sasketchewan, and learned to fly at the age of 15. He did not gain a pilot's license until he was 17 but on one occasion as a Boy Scout, while sitting in an aircraft at an air show, he 'accidentally' started the engine. He then took off and gave a display of aerobatics. He came to England in 1935 and joined the RAF on a short service commission in September. After training with No.3 FTS at Grantham he joined No.25 Squadron at Hawkinge on 5th August 1936, flying Hawker Fury IIs. However, owing to ill health, he returned to Canada in September 1937, resigning his commission. Later he tried unsuccessfully to join the RCAF, so he volunteered to fight in the Russo-Finnish war of 1939-40, but this ended before he arrived in Finland, so he went to France to join the *Armée de l'Air*. He escaped from the South of France in a boat loaded with Polish refugees in June 1940, and eventually reached England where he re-joined the RAF as a pilot officer, being posted to No.242 Squadron on 26th August 1940 flying Hurricanes. Sclanders was shot down and killed in combat with Messerschmitt Bf 110s over Thameshaven on 9th September. He was 24 and lies buried in St Luke's churchyard, Whyteleafe, Surrey.

SHENTON, Flt Lt Paul J, RAF. Joined No.25 Squadron ('B' Flight) on its being reformed with Tornados at Leeming in 1989, and remained unti11992 when posted to No.5 Squadron, also with Tornado F.3s. *Member of Association.*

SIMMONS, Flt Lt A J, RAF. Joined No.25 Squadron ('A' Flight') on its being reformed with Tornado F.3s at Leeming in 1989, remaining until 1992. *Member of Association.*

SINGLETON, Plt Off (later Wg Cdr, DSO, DFC, AFC), RAF. Pilot. Born, 12-3-16, Joe Singleton was commissioned in the RAF on 17th May 1941, his first squadron posting being to No.25 in 1941, then at Acklington flying Beaufighters. He remained until June 1943 when, as a Flt Lt, he was posted away to retrain on Mosquitos. He returned to the Squadron once more in December the same year when at Acklington. It was in March 1944, while flying with Geoff Haslam (*qv*), that Singleton destroyed three Junkers Ju 188s in a single night sortie while flying in the vicinity of the Humber estuary. He was posted away later that year, only to return in 1947 as a substantive Squadron Leader to command the Squadron at West Malling (Mosquito NF.36s). He retired from the RAF on 22nd May 1958 as a Wing Commander. Died 1998. *Late Member of Association.*

SMITH, Flt Lt (later Sqn Ldr) Christopher Dermont Salmond, DFC, RAF. 33287. Pilot. From Overy Staithe, Norfolk, Smith entered the RAF with a cadetship at the Royal Air Force College, Cranwell, in September 1934. He joined No.220 (GR) Sqn flying Ansons at Bircham Newton in November 1936, and was posted to the A & AEE, Martlesham Heath on 1st June 1938 where, nicknamed 'Blood-Orange', he took command of a special flight working on ground and airborne radar; it was not until 1939 that this, the Experimental Co-operation Unit, received aircraft in which an airborne radar set might be installed, namely the Blenheim. Breadboard radar sets were fitted in two aircraft at Martlesham Heath in mid-1939, and it was decided to incorporate this part of the ECU into a detached flight of No.25 Squadron so as to introduce operational tactics into the operation of the two radar sets (then referred to as the Mark I and II). Still a flying officer, Smith therefore was included on the 'ration strength' of No.25 Squadron from September 1939 although he was not formally posted to the Squadron at North Weald until 20th September 1940, by which time he had engaged in operational sorties, employing the bread-board radar sets to stalk enemy aircraft as early as October 1939, for which he was awarded the DFC (7-5-40). He remained on No.25 Squadron until November 1941 when as a Squadron Leader he was appointed to command No.79 Squadron at Fairwood Common, then preparing to move to India with Hurricanes. Smith was killed on 22nd December in unknown circumstances. He has no known grave and is remembered on the Runnymede Memorial, Panel 28.

SMITH, Sgt Philip Richard, RAF. 45352. Pilot. Sgt Smith was on No.25 Squadron early in July 1940 and flew Blenheims throughout the Battle of Britain. He was commissioned Pilot Officer on 18th December that year and posted away. He was killed as a Flight Lieutenant serving with No.278 (Air-Sea Rescue) Squadron on 4th April 1943, and may have been lost at sea; he has no known grave and is remembered on the Runnymede Memorial, Panel 121.

SMYTHE, Fg Off (later Flt Lt) Geoffrey, RAF. Navigator/Radar. Served on Squadron from 1946 to 1947 (Mosquito NF.36s) and again from 1951 to 1954 (Vampire NF.10s), both at West Malling. Was F K Mason's Nav Rad in the latter tour. *Member of Association.*

SNAPE, W/Off (later Fg Off) William George, RAF. 50692. Air Gunner. Snape was serving on No.25 Squadron at the outbreak of war in September 1939 flying in Blenheims. He was promoted Warrant Officer on 12th January 1940 and continued flying with the Squadron throughout the Battle of Britain. He assumed charge of the radar section with the arrival of Beaufighters (the first such section on an RAF fighter squadron fully staffed by Service personnel) and eventually transferred to the Technical Branch (Signals), commissioned Pilot Officer, in July 1942. Snape was released from the RAF as a Flying Officer in 1946. He died on 22nd August 1955.

STEVENS, Cpl C J, RAF. Served on No.25 Squadron from 1941 to 1946 at Wittering, Ballyhalbert, Church Fenton, Acklington, Coltishall, Castle Camps and Boxted (Beaufighters and Mosquitos). *Member of Association.*

STEINKE, Master Pilot Ludwik. *Né* Polish Pilot on No.25 Squadron, two tours – 1949-1951 and 1954. Mosquito, Vampire and Meteor night fighters; winner of Squadron gunnery trophy, and Fighter Command Gunnery Competition, beating all the day fighter entrants, 1949. *Member of Squadron Association.*

STEWART, Sgt Dennis A, Served on No.25 Squadron at North Coates from 1964 to 1967 (Bloodhound SAMs). *Member of Association.*

SULLY, Flt Lt Dave S, RAF, BSc. Served on No.25 Sqn at Leeming (Tornados), 1995-1998. *Member of Association.*

SVENSSON, Sqn Ldr I A G, RAF. Served on No.25 Squadron from 1953 (Vampire NF) until 1955 (Meteor NF) at West Mailing. *Member of Association.*

SWORD-DANIELS, Plt Off (later Sqn Ldr) Albert Thomas, RAF. 77127. Air Gunner. Posted to Squadron on 2nd March 1940 at North Weald as Blenheim gunner, and became squadron gunnery leader. He flew throughout the Battle of Britain and qualified for the Clasp. Scarcely anything is known of his subsequent service other than that he was released from the RAF as a Squadron Leader in 1947.

TEDDER, Capt Arthur, RFC (later Marshal of the Royal Air Force The Lord Tedder, GCB, DCL, LLD, BA, 1st Baron of Glenguin). Surely the most distinguished officer ever to serve on No.25 Squadron, Arthur Tedder had joined the Dorset Regiment on 2nd September 1913, but transferred to the Royal Flying Corps, having missed his Regiment's transfer to France owing to a knee injury. He was posted to No.25 Squadron as a Flying Officer on 16th June 1916 having completed a flying course at the Civil Flying School, joining the Squadron at Auchel, then equipped with F.E.2bs. On 9th August he was promoted Temporary Captain and appointed a flight commander on No.25. Greater details of his period on the Squadron appear in the text of this work, and the following can only be an outline of his subsequent career. Promoted Temporary Major on 1st January 1917, he took command of No.70 Squadron in France, and six months later he assumed command of No.67 Training Squadron. Promoted Acting Lieut-Col in June 1918, he was posted to the Middle East to command No.38 Training Wing. He commanded No.274 Squadron as a substantive Major, and three months later was offered a Permanent Commission in the Royal Air Force as a Squadron Leader. Thereafter his appointments were as follows: OC No.207 Squadron, from November 1921; Naval Staff College, from September 1923; promoted Wg Cdr, January 1924; OC, No.2 FTS at Digby from November 1924; Directorate of Training, Air Ministry, from January 1927; student, Imperial Defence College, January 1928; promoted Gp Capt, January 1931; OC Air Armament School, Eastchurch, January 1932, April 1934; promoted Air Cdre, July 1934; Air Officer Commanding HQ Far East, November 1936; promoted Air Vice-Marshal, July 1937; Director General of Research and Development, Air Ministry, July 1938; appointed Air Marshal (Acting), November 1940 as Deputy Air Officer Commanding-in-Chief, RAF Middle East; promoted Air Chief Marshal, Air Officer Commanding-in-Chief, RAF Middle East; promoted Air Chief Marshal (Temporary), July 1942; appointed Commander-in-Chief, Mediterranean Allied Air Forces, February 1943, and in January 1944 appointed Air Commander-in-Chief and Deputy Supreme Allied Commander, Allied Expeditionary Force. On 1st January 1945 he was promoted Marshal of the Royal Air Force, and on 1st January 1946 became Chief of the Air Staff. He relinquished his Service Appointments on the 31st December 1949.

TENNET, Stanley (Rank not known). Served on No.25 Squadron from 1968 to 1972 (Bloodhound SAMs) at North Coates and in Germany. *Member of Association.*

THEASBY, Sgt Alec John, RAF. 1161473. Radar Operator. After a short course in radar, Theasby joined No.25 Squadron in October 1940 and flew several operational sorties in both Blenheims and Beaufighters during the Battle of Britain. He was one of the First 'specialist' radar operators to serve on a fighter squadron. He was killed on 16th November 1940 when the Blenheim L6679 in which he was flying on a night patrol crashed and burned at Ingatestone, Essex; the cause of the crash was never established. Theasby, who was 23, was buried in Norton Cemetery, Yorkshire.

THIRUMALAI, Chief Tech Douglas L, RAF. Served on No.25 Squadron from 1956 to 1958 at West Malling and Tangmere (Meteor NF). *Member of Association.*

THIRUMALAI, Cpl Tech N S, RAF. Served on No.25 Squadron from 1954 to 1958 at West Malting and Tangmere (Meteor NF). *Member of Association.*

THOMPSON, Sgt Joseph Beckett, RAF. 566058. Pilot. Thompson was one of the pilots who flew in No.25 Squadron's radar flight with C D S Smith, being posted in late in 1939. One of the first Blenheim Is to be equipped with AI Mk.III was L1408 and this aircraft was returned to the M.U. (believed to be No.5 at Kemble) for a check on the radar. On 31st July 1940 Thompson was flying the air test over the Bristol Channel when a collision occurred with a Blenheim of No.29 Squadron (flying as 'target'). Thompson and two M.U. crewmembers were killed. He was buried in the Church of Ireland churchyard in his home town of Magheragall, Co Antrim. At the time of his death, Thompson was 24 and had qualified for the Battle of Britain Clasp.

THOMPSON, F/Sgt Robert, RAF. Served on No.25 Squadron from 1928 to 1929 (Grebes and Siskins at Hawkinge) and from 1934 to 1937 (Hawker Fury Is and IIs, still at Hawkinge). *Member of Association.*

TOMLINSON, Cpl J M, RAF. Served on No.25 Squadron from 1941 to 1946 at Wittering, Ballyhalbert, Church Fenton, Acklington, Coltishall, Castle Camps and Boxted (Beaufighters and Mosquitos). *Member of Association.*

TRAVERS, Fg Off B, RAF. Served on No.25 Squadron from 1941 to 1943 (Mosquito IIs) at Wittering, Ballyhalbert and Church Fenton, and from 1943 to 1945 (Mosquito IIs, VIs, XVIIs and 30s) at Acklington, Coltishall and Castle Camps. *Member of Association.*

TURNBULL, Sgt (later Fg Off, DFC) Robert Nesbit, RAF. 171858. Air Gunner, later Radio Observer, then Navigator Radar. Sgt Turnbull joined No.25 Squadron at North Weald late in September 1939 flying in Blenheims, and qualified for the Battle of Britain Clasp. As the Beaufighter was flown increasingly, Turnbull was retrained on the Squadron as a Radio Observer, but was posted away early in 1941 to gain formal training as a Navigator Radar and did not return to No.25. In 1942 he joined No.89 Squadron in the Middle East and participated in the destruction of six German aircraft over North Africa. He was promoted Warrant Officer and as such he was awarded the DFC (25-5-43). Commissioned in 1944, he was released from the Service in 1945 as a Fg Off, and died on 18th September 1980.

VARLEY, Mrs Alma. Formerly LACW, Intelligence Section, RAF Station, Church Fenton, 1943. *Honorary Member of No.25 Squadron Association.*

WAKEMAN, Sqn Ldr M A, RAF. Pilot on No.25 Sqn at Leeming (Tornados). 1995-1997. *Member of Squadron Association.*

WALKER, Fg Off (later Sqn Ldr) John Harold Gilbert, RAF. 40036. Pilot. Walker, from Nottingham, entered the RAF on a short service commission in June 1937. Posted for flying training with No.3 FTS, South Cerney, he joined the staff of the School of Naval Co-operation at Ford on 26th March 1938. Shortly after the outbreak of war he was posted to No.25 Squadron and converted to twins on the Squadron. He flew throughout the Battle of Britain, but was posted away in 1941 as a Flight Lieutenant to join the newly formed No.118 Squadron with Spitfires. He was killed, aged 23, as a Squadron Leader in an accident on 9th May 1942 and is buried in St Leonard's churchyard, Wollaton, Nottingham.

WALLIS, W/Off Leonard S, RAF. Served on No.25 Squadron at Hawkinge from 1931 to 1933 (Siskins and Hawker Fury Is). *Member of Association.*

WALTON, Wg Cdr J H, AFC. Nav Rad. Javelins, Waterbeach, 1960-61. Squadron Commander. Born 14th March 1923. Commissioned 5th August 1943. Gp Capt, July 1967. Retd, 5th April 1972.

WANSTALL, Flt Lt David E, RAF. Served on No.25 Squadron at West Mailing from 1947 to 1950 (Mosquito NF.36s) and again from 1959 to 1961 at Waterbeach (Javelins). Retired as Flt Lt on 30-1-83. *Member of Association.*

WEST, LAC H W, RAF. Served on No.25 Squadron from 1940 to 1944 at North Weald, Debden, Wittering, Ballyhalbert, Church Fenton, Acklington and Coltishall (Blenheims, Beaufighters and Mosquitos). *Member of Association.*

WHITTINGHAM, R A, RAF. Served on No.25 Squadron from 1941 to 1943 at Wittering, Ballyhalbert and Church Fenton (Beaufighters and Mosquitos). Now lives in Kenya. *Member of Association.*

WIGHT-BOYCOTT, Wg Cdr (later Air Cdre, CBE, DSO AND BAR) C. Michael, DSO. RAF, Pilot. Commanded No.25 Squadron from 15th October 1943 to August 1944 at Church Fenton, Acklington and Coltishall. Flying with Flt Lt E A Saunders as his Nav Rad, Wight-Boycott shot down two flying bombs on 17th and 24th July 1944, and a Junkers Ju 188 on 26th September (flying with Flt Lt Sandy Reid) after having handed over the Squadron to Wg Cdr L J C Mitchell. He retired from the RAF as an Air Cdre, CBE, DSO AND BAR, on 1-7-64. *Member of Association.*

WILLIAMS, 2/Lieut L F, RFC. Served as an observer on No.25 Squadron at Auchel, France in 1917 on F.E.2Bs and D.H.4s. His first victory was achieved in an F.E.2b on 7th June when, with the Canadian Lieut, Conrad Lally, they destroyed an Albatros DIII near Lille. Later the same day, the same crew destroyed a second Albatros DIII again near Lille. On 20th July, while flying with Capt A Roulstone, Williams shot down an Albatros DV while giving cover to Corps reconnaissance aircraft. Williams' finally confirmed victory was gained on 5th August when, flying once more with Lieut Lally, this time in a D.H.4, they shot down an Albatros DV over Perenchies.

WILLIAMS, Flt Lt Peter, RAF. Served on No.25 Squadron from 1954 to 1956 at West Malling (Meteor NF) and again from 1957 to 1958 at Tangmere and Waterbeach (Meteor NF). *Committee Member of Squadron Association.*

WILLSHER, Sgt Frank. Served on No.25 Sqn at West Malling and Tangmere (Meteor night fighters), 1954-1958. *Member of Association.*

WOODS, Sqn Ldr Guy P, RAF. Served with No.25 Squadron from 1958 to 1961 at Waterbeach (Javelins) *Founder Member and First Honorary Secretary of Association.*

WOOLLEN, 2/Lieut D C, RFC. Served as observer with No.25 Squadron in 1917 (F.E.2bs). On 13th April ('Bloody April') he and his flight commander, Capt L L Richardson, MC, were shot down by Ltn. Karl Emil Schäfer of *Jasta* 11. Both Richardson and Woollen were taken prisoner. This was Schäfer's 17th victory.

WRAY, Sqn Ldr (later Gp Capt, CBE, DFC) John B, RAF. Pilot. Joined No.25 Squadron in c.May 1941 as Flight Commander, 'A' Flight, at Wittering, under David Atcherley. John Wray kept valuable diaries during his service with the Squadron, constant reference to which has been of great value in researching events during the Second World War. He remained on the Squadron until August 1942 when he was posted 'on rest' to Acklington to train radar operators. This did not appeal to him and a quiet word in the ear of Basil Embry (SASO, 12 Group) got the posting changed to day fighters. John Wray retired from the RAF on 21st August 1967 as a Gp Capt, CBE, DFC. *Member of Association.*

APPENDIX 8

No.25 (Fighter) Squadron Association

DURING THE PERIOD 1963 – 1989 in which No.25 (Fighter) Squadron was 'grounded' as a Bloodhound surface-to-air missile squadron, despite being officered predominantly by former (and later) General Duties flying personnel, its day-to-day work was technically orientated, and the NCO and other ranks were exclusively technical. Yet despite its non-flying rôle, the Squadron was well aware of its long and distinguished history and traditions. Nevertheless it was deemed impractical to form a Squadron Association, owing primarily to the high security associated with the SAM defences – and its deployment to Germany for much of the period. However, in the same month, September 1989, in which No 25 returned to the interceptor fighter rôle, equipped with Tornados at Leeming, the first steps were taken to begin forming a Squadron Association, initially under the aegis of its new CO, Wg Cdr Mick Martin, who enlisted the help of a number of ex-Squadron members, including Air Cdre Bob Arnott – who would become the Association's first President.

The object of the Association is to assemble as many ex-members of the Squadron, irrespective of rank, gender, and flying or non-flying service, to renew old friendships forged during their time on the Squadron, to keep in touch once more through periodic reunions and, once a year to have an opportunity to meet and mingle with the Squadron's personnel of today. How successful those early founding members were may be seen by the membership figures, which in ten years has trebled from about 60 to around 200, and continues to increase slowly but steadily (with a growing number of Tornado aircrews who have since been posted elsewhere – for they, no less than the numerous Second World War veterans, are now 'past Squadron personnel').

The membership may not appear to be as large as some other Associations, but it should be remembered that a fighter squadron establishment has never been more than perhaps 200 personnel at anyone time, while a bomber squadron was frequently double this or more, especially a heavy bomber squadron of the Second World War.

Such Associations, apart from the strictly social aspects, may seem nebulous, perhaps even superfluous. Yet, in these days of high professionalism in our Armed Services, which tend to inflict something akin to social isolation – even a monastic lifestyle – the fact that not only do some of No.25 Squadron Association members attend reunions from across the seas, albeit having passed four-score years in age, but it can do no harm at all to Squadron pride to know that there is an avid interest in and concern for those who continue to forge new traditions and reach undreamed-of levels of expertise.

In a somewhat different vein, yet with a powerful historical connotation, the Association played a minor rôle in the adoption of the Squadron by the town of Folkestone. It happened that a member of the Association had an old friend, Dick Windrow, who held an appointment connected with the town's plans to invite surviving Battle of Britain veterans to be the town's honoured guests at the 1990 Air Display on the 50th Anniversary of that great Battle. The 25 Squadron Association member was able to provide the names and addresses of these guests, and they were duly fêted during the carnival week, which ended with a superb flying display. As a result Mr Windrow and the Association member discussed various means by which Folkestone might perpetuate a link with the RAF, and it was suggested that the town might consider 'adopting' No.25 (Fighter) Squadron as having been stationed for so many years at the former airfield at nearby Hawkinge, and had itself participated in the Battle of Britain. The town council expressed enthusiasm for the proposal, and it was put to Wg Cdr Martin at Leeming, it being planned that both he and the Chairman of Folkestone Council should submit the suggestion simultaneously to RAF Strike Command – the ultimate authority.

The proposal was accepted and, during the following year, members of No 25 Squadron were invited to attend a formal ceremony in the Council Chambers at which the Instrument of Association between town and Squadron would be presented, as well as a flying display by the Squadron's Tornado display crew; the Squadron Standard was paraded and a memorable Guest Night was hosted by No.25 Squadron's officers at a sea front hotel, which was attended by all principal members of the Town Council, the Lord Lieutenant of Kent, the Chief Constable and other dignitaries, all being accompanied by their ladies.

Folkestone has perpetuated the annual 'Battle of Britain' air display, and it has been customary for the climax of the show to be provided by a 'four ship' formation aerobatic display from No.25 (Fighter) Squadron. During the 1992 Folkestone festival, members of No.25 Squadron Association were invited to hold their autumn reunion at the same sea front hotel in which the participants in the flying display were staying!

CORRESPONDENCE ACKNOWLEDGEMENTS

I believe that I have received letters from members of No.25 Squadron with recollections of life on every station on which the Squadron served since the First World War; and that period has been covered by letters from the families of Squadron members, quoting from letters home and diaries.

Leading Aircraftman John Aspinall – Flt Mech (Engines) on No.25 Squadron (March 1940 – late 1941)

Sgt Walter ('Wally') Barnard – Compass Adjuster on No.25 Squadron (1946)

SAC William Ernest Beer – Airframe Mechanic on No.25 Squadron (1954 – 1958)

The late Air Cdre Walter Karl Beisiegel – Plt Off on No.25 Squadron (1928 – 1930)

Flt Lt Benny Bent, DFC – Nav-Rad on No.25 Squadron. (Two tours, 1940 – 1942 and 1942 – 1944)

Sqn Ldr Roy Bowie – Pilot on No.25 Squadron (1952 – 1953)

Leading Aircraftman Harry Bullock – on No.25 Squadron (1944)

Flt Lt Chris Bulteel – on No.25 Squadron (1999)

Wing Commander John Cameron Cox – Two tours on No.25 Squadron (1948 – 51 and 1954 – 55)

The late Air Vice-Marshal George P Chamberlain, CB, OBE – on No.25 Squadron (1924 – 1926)

Flt Lt Raymond Stephen Clifton – Squadron Orderly Room with No.25 Squadron (1943)

Flt Sgt Walter Fairclough Craine – Nav-Rad on No.25 Squadron (c.1945 – 1946)

LAC Frank Reuben Cunningham – Engine Fitter on No.25 Squadron (1951 – 1953)

Sqn Ldr M R S Cunningham (Russ), MBE – Commanded No.25 Squadron (1965 – 1967)

The late (Fg Off) Neill ('Michael') Daunt, RAFO – Pilot on No.25 Squadron (1930 – 1934)

Wg Cdr Andy Dey – Commanding No.25 Squadron (1997 – 2000)

The late Marshal of the Royal Air Force Sir William Dickson GCB, KBE, DSO, AFC – Commanding No.25 Squadron (1935 – 1936)

Cpl Derek Fallis – on No.25 Squadron (1939 – 1941)

LAC – WO John Henry Reuben Flood – Fitter on No.25 Squadron (1939 – 1941)

F/Sgt Don Forryan – Pilot on No.25 Squadron (1943 – 1944)

Flt Lt Kenneth E Foster – Adjutant on No.25 Squadron (1958 – 1962)

LAC Geoff Gibson – Signals Section, No.25 Squadron (Wittering, 1941)

W/Off George T Glossop – Pilot on No.25 Squadron (1943 – 1945)

Wg Cdr Phil Goodman, MBE – Commanding No.25 Squadron (1995 – 1998)

Sqn Ldr Douglas Haig Greaves – Pilot on No.25 Squadron (1944 – 1946)

Sgt Peter Harry – on No.25 Squadron (1973 – 1976)

Flt Lt W Geoffrey Haslam, OBE, DFC – Nav-Rad on No.25 Squadron (1943 – 1944)

Flt Lt George Hogarth – Pilot on No.25 Squadron (1942 – 1944)

Sqn Ldr (later Wg Cdr) Steve Howard – Pilot on No.25 Squadron (1993 – 1996)

Cpl Alfred Hoyle – Airframe Fitter on No.25 Squadron (1940 – 1942)

Sqn Ldr H G James, AFC AND BAR, DFM* § – Pilot and Flt Cdr on No.25 Squadron (1951 – 1954)

Flt Lt Peter John Jones – Nav-Rad on No.25 Squadron (1955 – 1958)

Master Pilot Robert Edward Kelly – Pilot on No.25 Squadron (1960 – 1962)

Flt Lt K Kerrison – Pilot on No.25 Squadron (1942 – 1944)

F/Sgt Tommy Knight – Radar Section on No.25 Squadron (1941 – 1942)

Sqn Ldr Richard William Leggett – Commanding No.25 Squadron (1950 – 1952)

SAC Rick Leigh – Fitter, 'A' Flight, No.25 Squadron (1954 – 1957)

Bill McLardy – Nav-Rad on No.25 Squadron (1954 – 1958)

Flt Lt Kevin Magee – on No.25 Squadron, Leeming, (1992 – 1996)

Mager, Roy – on No.25 Squadron (1934 – 1936)

Sqn Ldr Archie Neill, § – Flt Cdr on No.25 Squadron (1989 – 1993)

The late Wg Cdr John Nesbitt-Dufort, DSO – Two tours with No.25 Squadron (1929 – 1932 and 1934 – 1935)

Cpl Frank Page – on No.25 Squadron (1943).

Flt Lt Peter William Pascoe, AFC * – Navigator.
Two tours with No.25 Squadron (1959 – 1960 and 1965 – 1967)

LAC, later Fg Off, A W Patterson, MBE – Navigator.
Two tours with No.25 Squadron (1942 – 1943 and 1943 – 1945)

Gp Capt Harold Percival Pleasance, OBE, DFC AND BAR § – Pilot and Commanding Officer, No.25 Squadron (1941 – 1942)

Wg Cdr Alan J Picknett, DFC – Pilot on No.25 Squadron (1941 – 1943)

The late Air Cdre Harold Melsome Probyn, CB, CBE, DSO – Commanding No.25 Squadron (1929 – 1932)

Fg Off S J ('Sam') Roddan – Radio/Radar Officer on No.25 Squadron (1941 – 1944)

The late Sqn Ldr R M H ('Jock') Ross – Sgt Pilot on No.25 Squadron (1930 – 1932)

Sqn Ldr W W (Bill) Sharp – Pilot on No.25 Squadron (1928 – 1930)

The late Wing Commander Joseph Singleton, DSO, DFC, AFC – Pilot and Commanding Officer.
Three tours with No.25 Squadron (1941 – June 1943; Dec 1943 – 1944; 1947 – 1948.

Flight Lieutenant Geoff Smythe – Nav-Rad, two tours on No.25 Squadron
(1946 – 1947 and 1951 – 1954 – the Author's navigator during the latter tour)

Master Pilot Ludwik Steinke (Gunnery Officer) – Pilot.
Two tours with No.25 Squadron (1949 – 1951 and 1954)

Cpl C J Stevens – on No.25 Squadron (1941 – 1946)

Flt Lt Dave Sully

ChiefTech Douglas Louis Thirumalai # – Engine Mechanic on No.25 Squadron (1956 – 1958)

Cpl Tech Norton Seshikanth Thirumalai – Air Radar Fitter on No.25 Squadron (1954 – 1958)

LAC Robert Thompson – Engine Fitter on No.25 Squadron (two tours, 1927 – 1929 and 1934 – 1937)

Travers, Fg Off Barney – Pilot on No.25 Squadron (two tours, 1941 – 43 and 1943 – 1945)

LAC Henry West – Flight Mechanic (Engines), No.25 Squadron (1940 – 1944)

Whittingham, Dick – on No.25 Squadron (1941 – 1943)

Air Cdre M Wight-Boycott – Commanding No.25 Squadron (1943 – 1944)

AC1 D G ('Bill') Williams – Aircraft Fitter on No.25 Squadron (1939 – 1940)

Flt Lt Peter Williams – on No.25 Squadron (two tours, 1954 – 1956 and 1957 – 1958)

Flt Lt Anthony Norman Wilson – Pilot on No.25 Squadron (1943 – 1944)

Squadron Leader Guy Phillip Woods – Nav-Rad on No.25 Squadron 1958 – 1959

Group Captain John Basil Wray, CBE, DFC – OC 'A' Flight, No.25 Squadron (1941 – 1943)

Cpl Archie Yates, SAC ADO – on No.25 Squadron (1970 – 1973)

Young, Rob – on No.25 Squadron (1969 – 1970)

Flt Lt Z Zmitrowicz, 'Zed-Zed' – Pilot on No.25 Squadron (1950 – 1954)

§ Commanding No.25 Squadron, January 1941 – March 1941 and August 1941 – September 1942

* Queen's Commendation for Valuable Services in the Air.

AOC's Commendation

The Late Major Felton Vesey Holt, DSO, RFC
(later Air Vice-Marshal, CMG, DSO, RAF)

I am particularly indebted to the following for their unstinted assistance afforded me by the family members of, the above founding Commanding Officer of No.25 (Fighter) Squadron, in particular to

Mrs Rosemary Knox, Felton's daughter,
Oliver Vesey Holt, Felton's son,
Mrs C R Vesey Holt,

and to

Mrs P Hatfield, College Archivist, Eton College Library,
Mrs Christine Vickers, Secretary, Eton College Photographic Archive,
Eton College Association,
Sqn Ldr John Norton, Archivist, the Central Flying School, Royal Air Force,
Hazel Crozier, Research and Archive Dept, Royal Air Force Museum, Hendon,
Norris McWhirter, CBE,
Lt.-Col W.A. Weightman, The Green Howards Regiment,
Mr Stuart Leslie, Scarborough.

Obituary

It is with great sadness that the Author learned of the death of Steve Stevens after this book had been delivered. Steve had contributed much information about No.25 (Fighter) Squadron's wartime service. The Publisher and Author offer their sincere sympathy to Marjorie, whose name and photograph are also included in this book.

Appreciation

Members of Air-Britain have been particularly kind and of the utmost assistance in helping with the Appendices, and I must acknowledge the work of my old friend Ray Sturtivant, both for all the advice he has given me and for martialling the skills and specialist knowledge accumulated by Air-Britain's members.
Without them, this book could not possibly have been written.

BIBLIOGRAPHY

R Dallas Brett, *The History of British Aviation, 1908-1914.* Hamilton, London, 1933.

Ralph Barker, *The Royal Flying Corps in France; from Bloody April 1917 to Final Victory.* Constable, London, 1995. ISBN 0 0947 6550 2

Air Chief Marshal Sir Philip Joubert, KCB, CMG, DSO, *Fun and Games.* Hutchinson & Co (Publishers) Ltd, London, 1964.

Air Chief Marshal Sir Kenneth ("Bing") Cross, KCB, CBE, DSO, DFC, and Professor Vincent Orange, *Straight and Level.* Grub Street, London, 1993. ISBN 0 9488 1772 0.

Air Commodore A E Clouston, DSO, DFC, AFC AND BAR, *The Dangerous Skies.* Cassell & Co, London, 1954.

Roderick Owen, *Tedder.* Collins, London, 1952.

Marshal of the Royal Air Force Baron Tedder of Glenguin, GCB, *With Prejudice; the War Memoirs of Lord Tedder.* Cassell, 1966.

Wing Commander John Nesbitt-Dufort, DSO, C DE G, *Black Lysander.* Jarrolds, Norwich, 1973. ISBN 0 0911 5670 x

Basil Collier, *Dowding, Leader of the Few.*

John Laffin, *Swifter than Eagles: a Biography of Sir John Salmond, GCB, CMG, CVO, DSO.* Blackwood, London, 1964.

Lewis, G H, *Wings over the Somme.* Bridge Books, 1994.

Floyd Gibbons, *The Red Knight of Germany: Baron von Richthofen.* Cassell, London, 1927.

Air Marshal Sir Gerald Gibbs, KBE, CIE, MC, *Survivor's Story.* (Autobiography of Author) Hutchinson, London, 1956.

Air Commodore Henry A Probert, MBE, *High Commanders of the Royal Air Force.* HMSO, London, 1991. ISBN 0 1177 2635 4

Revell, A, *British Fighter Units on the Western Front, 1914-1916.* Osprey, London, 1978

J M Bruce, *British Aeroplanes 1914-1918.* Putnam, London. 1957.

Roy S Humphreys, *Hawkinge, 1912-1961; An in-depth history of the former Royal Air Force Station.* Meresborough, Rainham, Kent, 1981. ISBN 0 9481 9352 2

Henshaw, Trevor, *The Sky Their Battlefield:* Air Fighting and the Complete list of Allied Air Casualties from Enemy Action in the First War. Grub Street, London, 1995. ISBN 0 8986 9730 2

Franks, N L R, Guest, R and Shores, C, *Above the Trenches.* Grub Street, London, 1990. ISBN 0 9488 1719 4

Franks, N L R, Bailey, F W and Guest, R, *Above the Lines.* Grub Street, London, 1993. ISBN 0 9488 1773 9

Franks, N L R, Guest, R and Alegi G, *Above the War Fronts.* Grub Street, London, 1997. ISBN 1 8986 9756 6

Immelmann, Franz, *Immelmann, The Eagle of Lille* (translation by C W Sykes). Hamilton, London, c.1936. (No ISBN)

Unpublished Sources In the Public Record Office:

Operational Record Books (No.25 Squadron, with Appendices), under AIR 27.

AIR1/843, 204/5/368 to 377 – RFC Aircraft and Personnel Casualty Reports, Mar-Dec 1916 (for example).

AIR1/846, 204/5/378 to 397 – Ditto, Jan-Dec 1917 (for example) and

AIR1/852, 204/5/398 to 515 – Ditto, Jan-Dec 1918 (for example).

Correspondence *(see also Acknowledgements):*

The late Nigel (Michael) Daunt

The late Philip Lucas, GM

The late Wg Cdr Joseph Singleton, DSO, DFC, AFC

The late Air Vice-Marshal George Chamberlain, CB, OBE

Index To Persons

C

D

E

F

G

H

N

O

P

Q

R

S

T

U

V

W

Y

Z

AIR-BRITAIN – THE INTERNATIONAL ASSOCIATION OF AVIATION HISTORIANS – FOUNDED 1948

Since 1948, Air-Britain has recorded aviation events as they have happened, because today's events are tomorrow's history. In addition, considerable research into the past has been undertaken to provide historians with the background to aviation history. Nearly 18,000 members have contributed to our aims and efforts in that time and many have become accepted authorities in their own fields.

Every month, *AIR-BRITAIN NEWS* covers the current civil and military scene. Quarterly, each member receives *AIR-BRITAIN DIGEST* which is a fully-illustrated quality journal containing articles on various subjects, both past and present.

For those interested in military aviation history, there is the quarterly *AEROMILITARIA* which is designed to delve more deeply into the background of, mainly, British and Commonwealth military aviation than is possible in commercial publications. This publication is responsible for the production of the present volume and other monographs on military subjects. Also published quarterly is *ARCHIVE*, produced in a similar format but covering civil aviation history in depth on a world-wide basis. Both magazines are well-illustrated by photographs and drawings.

In addition to these regular publications, there are monographs covering type histories, both military and civil, airline fleets, Royal Air Force registers, squadron histories, civil registers of a large number of countries and various other topics. Although our publications are available to non-members, prices are appreciably lower for Air-Britain members, who have priority over non-members when availability is limited. Normally, the accumulated price discounts for which members qualify when buying monographs far exceed the annual subscription rates.

A large team of aviation experts is available to answer members' queries on most aspects of aviation. If you have made a study of any particular subject, you may be able to expand your knowledge by joining those with similar interests. Also available to members are libraries of colour slides and photographs which supply slides and prints at prices considerably lower than those charged by commercial firms.

There are local branches of the Association in Blackpool, Bournemouth & District, Heston, London, Luton, Manchester, Merseyside, Midlands, North-East England, Rugby, Scotland, Severnside, Solent, South-West Essex, Stansted and West Cornwall. Also overseas in France and the Netherlands.

If you would like to receive samples of Air-Britain magazines, please write to the following address enclosing 50p and stating your particular interests. If you would like only a brochure, please send a stamped self-addressed envelope to the same address (preferably 230mm by 160mm or over) - Air-Britain Membership Enquiries (Mil), 1 Rose Cottages, 179 Penn Road, Hazlemere, High Wycombe, Bucks., HP15 7NE.

Our website may be found at www.air-britain.com.

MILITARY AVIATION PUBLICATIONS

(prices are for members / non-members and are post-free)

Royal Air Force Aircraft series:

J1–J9999	(£8.00 / £10.00)	K1000–K9999	(see The K-File)	L1000–N9999	(£12.00 / £15.00)
P1000–R9999	(£11.00 / £14.00)	T1000–V9999	(£12.00 / £15.00)	W1000–Z9999	(£13.00 / £16.50)
AA100–AZ999	(£13.00 / 16.50)	BA100–BZ999	(£6.00 / £7.50)	DA100–DZ999	(£5.00 / £6.00)
EA100–EZ999	(£5.00 / £6.00)	FA100–FZ999	(£5.00 / £6.00)	HA100–HZ999	(£6.00 / £7.50)
JA100–JZ999	(£6.00 / £7.50)	KA100–KZ999	(£6.00 / £7.50)	LA100–LZ999	(£7.00 / £8.50)
MA199–MZ999	(£8.00 / £10.00)	NA100–NZ999	(£8.00 / £10.00)	PA100–RZ999	(£10.00 / £12.50)
		XA100–XZ999	(£9.00 / £11.00)		

Type Histories:

The Battle File	(£20.00 / £25.00)	The Beaufort File	(£11.00 / £13.50)	The Camel File	(£13.00 / £16.00)
The Defiant File	(£12.50 / £16.00)	The D.H.4 / D.H.9 File	(£24.00 / £30.00)	The Hampden File	(£12.00 / £14.50)
The Harvard File	(£8.00 / £9.50)	The Hornet File	(£10.00 / £12.00)	The Hoverfly File	(£16.50 / £19.50)
The Martinsyde File	(£24.00 / £30.00)	The Norman Thompson File	(£13.50 / £17.00)	The Oxford, Consul & Envoy File	(printing)
The Scimitar File	(£26.00 / £32.00)	The S.E.5 File	(£16.00 / £20.00)	The Sopwith Pup File	(in preparation)

Individual R.A.F. Squadron Histories:

With Courage and Faith – The History of No.18 Squadron (£5.00 / £7.50)
United in Effort – The Story of No.53 Squadron (£15.00 / £19.00)
Always Prepared – The History of No.207 Squadron (£22.00 / £27.50)
Flat Out – the History of No.30 Squadron (printing)
Scorpions Sting – The Story of No.84 Squadron (£12.00 / £16.50)
The Hornet Strikes – The Story of No.213 Squadron (£20.00 / £25.00)
Rise from the East – The History of No.247 Squadron (£13.00 / £16.50)

Naval Aviation titles:

The Squadrons of The Fleet Air Arm (£24.00 / £30.00)
Royal Navy Aircraft Serials and Units 1911 – 1919 (£12.00 / £12.00)
Fleet Air Arm Aircraft 1939 –1945 (new edition in preparation)
Royal Navy Shipboard Aircraft Developments 1912 – 1931 (£10.00)
Fleet Air Arm Aircraft, Units and Ships 1920 – 1939 (£26.00 / £32.50)
Fleet Air Arm Fixed Wing Aircraft since 1946 (in preparation)
Royal Navy Instructional Airframes (£14.00 / £17.50)

Other titles:

The K-File (the RAF of the 1930s) (£23.00 / £30.00)
Aviation in Cornwall (£14.00 / £17.50)
Aerial Refuelling at Farnborough 1924 – 1937 (£11.00 / £14.00)
The British Aircraft Specifications File (£20.00 / £25.00)
The British Air Commission and Lend-Lease (£28.00 / £29.00)
Broken Wings – Post-War RAF accidents (£21.00 / £26.00)

The above are available from Air-Britain (Historians) Ltd, 41 Penshurst Rd, Leigh, Tonbridge, Kent TN11 8HL or by e-mail to mike@sales.demon.co.uk. Payment in Sterling only.
Visa, Mastercard, Delta/Visa accepted with card number and expiry date, also Switch (with Issue Number).